后浪 大学堂 073　　Pearson

AMERICAN WAYS

AN INTRODUCTION TO AMERICAN CULTURE
FOURTH EDITION

美国文化背景

第4版　　汉英对照

[美] 玛丽安娜·卡尼·戴特斯曼　乔安·克兰德尔　爱德华·N. 卡尼——著　张 菁——译

北京联合出版公司
Beijing United Publishing Co.,Ltd.

图书在版编目（CIP）数据

美国文化背景：汉英对照/（美）玛丽安娜·卡尼·戴特斯曼,（美）乔安·克兰德尔,（美）爱德华·N.卡尼著；张菁译. -- 4版. -- 北京：北京联合出版公司，2019.11

ISBN 978-7-5596-3241-8

Ⅰ.①美… Ⅱ.①玛…②乔…③爱…④张… Ⅲ.①英语—教材②美国—概况—汉、英 Ⅳ.① H319.4：K

中国版本图书馆CIP数据核字(2019)第092063号

Authorized Adaptation from the English language edition, entitled AMERICAN WAYS: AN INTRODUCTION TO AMERICAN CULTURE, 4th Edition by DATESMAN, MARYANNE; CRANDALL, JOANN; KEARNY, EDWARD N., published by Pearson Education, Inc, Copyright © 2014 by Pearson Education, Inc.

All rights reserved. No part of this book may be reproduced or transmitted in any form or by any means, electronic or mechanical, including photocopying, recording or by any information storage retrieval system, without permission from Pearson Education, Inc.

ENGLISH language adapted edition 美国文化背景 第4版（汉英对照）published by POST WAVE PUBLISHING CONSULTING (BEIJING) CO., LTD., Copyright © 2019.

仅限于中华人民共和国境内（不包括中国香港、澳门特别行政区和中国台湾地区）销售发行。
本书封底贴有Pearson Education（培生教育出版集团）激光防伪标签。无标签者不得销售。

美国文化背景 第4版（汉英对照）

著　者：[美]玛丽安娜·卡尼·戴特斯曼　乔安·克兰德尔　爱德华·N.卡尼
译　者：张　菁
选题策划：后浪出版公司
出版统筹：吴兴元
特约编辑：杨宇珊
责任编辑：李　伟
营销推广：ONEBOOK
装帧制造：墨白空间
封面设计：陈文德

北京联合出版公司出版
（北京市西城区德外大街83号楼9层　100088）
北京盛通印刷股份有限公司印刷　新华书店经销
字数800千字　889毫米×1194毫米　1/16　30.5印张
2019年11月第1版　2019年11月第1次印刷
ISBN 978-7-5596-3241-8
定价：118.00元

后浪出版咨询(北京)有限责任公司常年法律顾问：北京大成律师事务所　周天晖 copyright@hinabook.com
未经许可，不得以任何方式复制或抄袭本书部分或全部内容
版权所有，侵权必究
本书若有质量问题，请与本公司图书销售中心联系调换。电话：010-64010019

CONTENTS

To the Teacher iii

    About the Fourth Edition vii

    The Book at a Glance xi

    About the Authors xiii

1   Introduction: Understanding the Culture of the United States 1

2   Traditional American Values and Beliefs 27

3   The American Religious Heritage 51

4   The Frontier Heritage 77

5   The Heritage of Abundance 99

6   The World of American Business 123

7   Government and Politics in the United States 149

8   Ethnic and Racial Diversity in the United States 177

9   Education in the United States 201

10   How Americans Spend Their Leisure Time 229

11   The American Family 255

12   American Values at the Crossroads 281

    Academic Word List 306

    Bibliography 309

    Credits 324

参考译文

第一章	引言：理解美国文化	327
第二章	美国传统价值观与信仰	333
第三章	美国的宗教传统	339
第四章	边疆传统	346
第五章	富足传统	352
第六章	美国商业世界	360
第七章	美国的政府和政治	368
第八章	美国的民族与种族多样性	378
第九章	美国的教育	385
第十章	美国人如何休闲	394
第十一章	美国家庭	402
第十二章	十字路口的美国价值观	410

指导手册及参考答案 ·· 417

TO THE TEACHER

What is "culture"? There are many definitions. Some would define it as the art, literature, and music of a people, their architecture, history, religion, and traditions. Others might focus more on the customs and specific behavior of a people. We have chosen to use a sociological definition of culture as the way of life of a group of people, developed over time, and passed down from generation to generation. This broad definition includes every aspect of human life and interaction. However, it would be impossible to cover every facet of American culture in a single book. We have, therefore, taken a values approach to our discussion, focusing on the traditional mainstream values that have attracted people to the United States for more than two hundred years. After explaining how these traditional values developed, we will trace how they influence various aspects of American life.

Why a book on American culture? There are many reasons. Those of us who have worked with foreign students in American universities or who have taught English to students both here and overseas repeatedly encounter questions about life in the United States. These students are frequently confused or even mystified about American values, attitudes, and cultural patterns. Even those students who have mastered enough English to take courses in an American university often find that they do not understand the cultural rules well enough to be successful as students. Many of these rules can be understood only within the broader context of American cultural patterns.

It is not only students who need the kind of information presented in this book. Foreign businesspeople, visiting scholars or government officials, and even tourists find their time in the United States more satisfying when they understand the values that underlie American behavior patterns and institutions. Newly-arrived immigrants and refugees adapt more easily to their new home when given a systematic introduction to their new country and its inhabitants.

For all of these reasons, *American Ways* is suitable for a wide audience. It has been used as a text in a number of programs for foreign students, including intensive English programs, short summer courses in the United States for foreign high school and college students, both quarter and semester courses at American universities, government programs for foreign visitors, and classes for immigrants. It has also been used in many different settings outside the United States, both as a text for students and as a reference guide—for U.S. Peace Corps volunteers, for example, and others who are teaching American culture.

What do we really learn when we study other cultures? First and foremost, we learn about our own. Until we are confronted by a different way of doing things, we assume that everyone does things the same way that we do, and thus our own culture—our values, attitudes, behavior—is largely hidden from our view. When we spend time analyzing another culture, however, we begin to see our own more clearly and to understand some of the subtleties that motivate our behavior and our opinions. By reading *American Ways*, students can begin to understand themselves and their own cultures better. To enhance this understanding, each chapter in the book is followed by a series of exercises. Some of these exercises are specifically designed to encourage students to think about their own values or patterns of behavior and to compare them with what they are learning about or experiencing in American settings. We have also included a number of exercises to encourage students to interact with and talk with Americans. In these exercises we have provided a set of carefully structured questions that students can ask Americans. The answers they receive will help students form a composite picture of American beliefs and practices as they relate to education, business, government, sports, recreation, and so on.

Some of the chapter exercises provide students with an opportunity to explore more fully an idea that has been presented or to discuss ideas with other students. You may wish to assign different exercises to different students or to small groups of students, and then ask them to share their findings and opinions with the class. If possible, small groups should include students from different countries so that, in addition to learning about American culture and their own, they are also learning about other cultures.

Perhaps this is the real goal of a course about culture: to help us become more sensitive to cultural differences and more accepting of them. However, there will always be aspects of another culture that we may not like, no matter how much we understand it. The objective of this book is not to persuade others to approve of life in the United States, but rather to help them understand it more fully.

致教师

何为"文化"？文化的定义有很多。有人将其定义为一个民族的艺术、文学、音乐，以及他们的建筑、历史、宗教和传统；有人可能更关注一个民族的习俗及其特有的行为方式。我们采用了文化的社会学定义——一个群体长期形成并世代相传的生活方式。这个定义很宽泛，涵盖了人类生活和交往的各个方面。然而仅靠一本书是不可能将美国文化面面俱到地呈现的。因此，我们选择从价值观入手，重点讨论两百多年来吸引着人们来到美国的传统主流价值观。在阐述了传统价值观如何形成发展之后，我们还将追溯这些价值观是如何影响美国生活的方方面面的。

为何要编写这样一部关于美国文化的书？原因有很多。我们之中有人在美国大学与外国学生共事，也有人在美国和其他国家教学生学习英语，经常会被问及有关美国生活的问题。学生们常常对美国的价值观、态度和文化模式感到疑惑甚至困惑。即便是那些英语水平足以应对美国大学课程的学生也时常发现，想要取得学业的成功，自己对于美国文化规则的理解还有欠缺。很多规则只有在更为广阔的美国文化模式的背景下才能更好地理解。

本书所介绍的信息并非只有学生才需要，外国商务人士、访问学者、政府官员，甚至旅游者，如果他们能理解美国行为模式和制度背后的价值观，他们的美国生活也会更为如鱼得水。而对于初来乍到的移民和难民来说，能得到有关这个全新的国度及其居民的系统性介绍，会使他们更容易适应新的家园。

基于上述原因，《美国文化背景》适合的读者群体非常广泛。本书已在一些针对外国学生的课程中被作为教材使用，包括英语强化课程、针对外国高中生和大学生在美的暑期短期课程、美国大学的季度及学期课程、面向外国参访者的政府项目以及为移民开设的课程。本书在美国境外也被广泛使用，既可以被用作学生的教材，也可以作为美国和平队志愿者及其他教授美国文化人士的参考指导。

我们在学习别国文化时，真正学到的是什么呢？首先也是最重要的是，了解我们自己的文化。在接触到一种不同于自身的行为方式之前，我们总是理所当然地认为每个人的处事方式都与我们相同，因而对于我们自己的文化——我们的价值观、态度与行为——往往无法识见其真面目。然而，当我们花时间去分析另一种文化时，便会开始对自己的文化有更清晰的认识，并开始理解一些激发我们行为与见解的微妙细节。通过阅读《美国文化背景》，学生可以开始更好地理解自身及自身的文化。为了强化理解，本书每个章节都附有一系列练习。其中一些练习是为鼓励学生思考自身的价值观和行为方式，并与在美国环境中所学习和经历的进行比较。还有一些练习，鼓励学生与美国人接触和交谈，在这些练习中我们提供了一系列精心设置的问题让学生们可以向美国人提问，涉及教育、商业、政府、体育、娱乐等众多领域，而学生们获得的回答可以帮助他们形成关于美国人的信念与习俗的综合印象。

  一些章节练习也让学生有机会去深入探索书中的某个观点，或是与同学一起讨论各种想法。您可以给不同的学生或小组布置不同的作业，并让他们与全班同学分享各自的发现和看法。尽可能让每个小组都包含来自不同国家的学生，从而使学生在学习美国文化与自己的文化的同时，还能了解其他文化。

  或许这才是一门关于文化的课程真正的目标：让我们对文化差异更加敏感，也更加包容。不过，无论我们对另一种文化的理解有多么深入，这种文化里总会有一些方面是我们不喜欢的。本书的目的并非要说服他人认同美国的生活方式，而是帮助人们更全面地理解它。

ABOUT THE FOURTH EDITION

In revising the content of this book, we concentrated on updating events that have occurred since the third edition was published in 2005. The issues surrounding multiculturalism continue to be of great importance, as the cultural diversity of the United States continues to increase. Indeed, estimates are that by the mid-2000s, the United States will be majority minority. That is, the majority of Americans will be from minority groups. The traditional group of white Americans of European descent will be in the minority. Already this is the situation in the largest school systems in the country. And since the last edition of this book, the country has elected and re-elected its first African-American president, Barack Obama. His first cabinet (the heads of executive branches of the government and principal government agencies) was one of the most diverse in history, and he appointed three women to serve on the U.S. Supreme Court, one of whom is the first Hispanic Supreme Court Justice. This expanding diversity makes it increasingly difficult to describe the American culture, and it is uncertain whether the traditional mainstream culture will continue to be the dominant culture in the future.

In the fourth edition of this book, the basic conceptual framework of traditional values remains the same. However, it is not clear how future generations will interpret or change them. Chapter 12 has been largely rewritten to focus more clearly on what is happening to traditional American values and on the challenges the United States faces (some of which are global in nature). These challenges include economic decline and rising national debt, the growing gap between the wealthiest individuals and the rest of the population, and needed reform of immigration policy. Perhaps the greatest challenge is the growing polarization between the two American political parties—the Democrats and Republicans—that has led to a Congress in which little gets done. Gun violence and national security continue to be a concern, as attacks on American schools and the 2013 bombings at the Boston Marathon demonstrate.

Originally, we envisioned this book primarily for use in English language courses designed to prepare students to study in American universities. We believe students in those courses need experience presenting information and voicing their personal opinions to others; they should be encouraged to make both oral and written reports and participate in debates and formal discussions. We have written many exercises that suggest appropriate topics and activities. The fourth edition provides more explicit development of reading skills (skimming, scanning, predicting, and understanding main ideas and details) and an expanded writing section (identifying and organizing academic information into main ideas and supporting details, often preceded by discussion, research, and completion of graphic organizers). New to this edition is explicit focus on critical thinking: on assessing information, comparing alternative points of view, identifying potential problems and solutions, and being a questioning reader. There is also more attention to vocabulary in this edition, including exercises on collocation and a focus on the most important academic words (from the Academic Word List*). The book continues to offer activities such as Ask Americans, but with this addition, students will also be able to listen online to a diverse group of Americans as they answer these questions. Throughout, you will also notice the new photos, new poll data, and the exhaustive bibliography of sources that we have used in developing this edition. More than 200 new sources were consulted for the fourth edition. Of particular note is the extensive use of Pew Research Center data, and we urge teachers to have students explore this valuable continuous source of new information available online. Additionally, answers to the exercises, more teaching tips, and graphic organizers can be found in the Teacher's Manual.

We have been delighted to hear from many teachers about creative ways they have used *American Ways*—not only in courses that introduce American culture, but also in courses focusing on cross-cultural communication, listening/speaking, reading/writing, academic preparation, and even literature. Teachers have used the values framework to design courses where students could explore ways in which the values appear in American literature, American films, or current events, for example, focusing on materials the teacher developed from other sources and presented in addition to the text.

关于第四版

修订本书内容时，我们重点增加了2005年第三版出版以后发生的新事件。随着美国文化多样性的不断发展，围绕多元文化主义的问题依然相当重要。事实上，据估计，到21世纪中叶，美国将成为少数族裔占主体的国家。也就是说，届时大多数的美国人将会是来自少数族裔群体，而传统的欧洲裔美国白人群体则将成为少数。本书上一版出版之后，巴拉克·奥巴马当选并连任了美国总统，成为第一位非洲裔美国总统。他的首届内阁（政府行政部门及主要政府机构的领导人）也是历史上最多样化的内阁之一。他任命了三名女性为美国最高法院法官，其中一名也是首位西班牙裔最高法院大法官。多样性的日益发展也使描述美国文化变得愈发困难，我们很难断言，传统的主流文化在未来是否仍然会是主导文化。

本书第四版中，传统价值观的基本概念框架保持不变。至于后世会如何解读或改变它们，我们不得而知。第十二章做了大幅重写，更加清楚地关注美国传统价值观的现状以及美国所面临的挑战（其中有一些挑战本质上是全球性的）。这些挑战包括经济衰退、国债增长、贫富差距的扩大，以及亟待改革的移民政策等。也许，最大的挑战来自美国两大政党——民主党和共和党，其日益严重的两极分化导致了国会的罕有作为。此外，美国校园枪击案以及2013年波士顿马拉松赛爆炸案都表明，枪支暴力和国家安全依然是值得关注的问题。

我们编著此书的初衷是用于学生预备赴美攻读大学的英语课程。我们认为参加这些课程的学生需要体验如何展示信息以及表达个人观点；应当鼓励他们多进行书面和口头报告，参加辩论和正式讨论。我们编写了许多练习，为学生提供适当的话题和活动。第四版提供了更为明确的阅读技能培养内容（包括略读、寻读、预测和理解主要观点和细节等），以及一个拓展写作部分（确定并将学术信息按照主要观点与支持论据组织起来，通常之前会有讨论、研究以及组织结构图等练习）。第四版中新增了对批判性思维的明确关注：评估信息、比较不同的观点、确定潜在问题和解决方法，以及做质疑型的读者。这一版也更注重词汇，包括搭配练习和最重要的学术词汇聚焦（来自学术词汇表*）。本书保留了诸如"提问美国人"之类的活动，但除此之外，学生还可以上网去倾听具有不同背景的美国人是如何回答这些问题的。翻阅本书，你还会注意到，我们在编写新版时采用了新的照片、新的民调数据，以及详尽的参考文献资料。第四版参考了二百多份新资料。特别值得一提的是，本书大量采用皮尤研究中心的数据，我们也强烈建议教师让学生去探索这个可以持续提供新信息的宝贵的在线资源。此外，教师手册中提供了练习答案、补充教学指导以及结构图表等。

我们很高兴收到了许多教师创造性地使用《美国文化背景》的反馈——不仅用于美国文化导论课程，也在一些跨文化交际、听力/口语、阅读/写作、学术预备课程，甚至文学课程中使用。教师利用价值体系框架来设计课程，让学生可以从中探究价值观在美国文学、美国电影或时事中的体现方式，例如，集中探讨教师为课文补充编写的其他来源的材料。

THE BOOK AT A GLANCE

Purpose

- To increase students' awareness and understanding of the cultural values of the United States, their own country, and, we hope, other countries
- To provide interesting cross-cultural activities for small group and class discussions, and topics for oral presentations, research, and writing projects
- To develop students' critical thinking and use of academic English

Level

High intermediate to advanced. The vocabulary level is in the range of 3,000 to 4,000 words, with emphasis on the Academic Word List.* (See page 306.) Grammatical structures are not controlled, although an effort has been made to avoid overly complex patterns.

Content

Information about traditional basic American values, where they came from, and how these values affect various institutions and aspects of life in the United States, for example, religion, business, government, race relations, education, recreation, and the family.

Types of Exercises

Pre-reading activities (previewing content and vocabulary), comprehension questions on both main ideas and details, topics for discussion and debate, critical thinking, extensive vocabulary development (with a focus on the Academic Word List and collocations), values clarification, questions for Americans, suggestions for research and oral reports, ideas for pair work and group projects, proverbs, people watching and experiments, understanding polls and the media, Internet activities, writing topics and activities to develop academic writing skills, and suggested books and movies.

Use of Text

- To orient students to American culture
- To foster cross-cultural communication
- To promote reading, writing, and discussion
- To encourage conversation
- To serve as a conceptual framework and accompany other cultural materials focusing on literature, the media, current events, and so on.

---

*For details on the development and evaluation of the AWL, see Coxhead, Averil (2000) A New Academic Word List. TESOL Quarterly, 34(2): 213–238.

For more information about the AWL and how to use it, visit the Internet site http://www.victoria.ac.nz/lals/resources/academicwordlist/

本书概览

目的

- 增进学生对美国、自己的国家以及（我们希望）其他国家的文化价值观的认识和理解；
- 为小组和课堂讨论提供有趣的跨文化活动，以及口头表达、研究及写作计划的话题；
- 培养学生的批判性思维和学术英语的运用能力。

水平

中高级至高级，词汇量为三千到四千词，重点为学术词汇表中的词汇（见306页）。语法结构没有限制，但已尽量避免使用过于复杂的句式。

内容

美国的传统基本价值观、它们从何而来，以及这些价值观对美国的各种制度和生活，例如宗教、商业、政府、种族关系、教育、娱乐以及家庭等方方面面的影响。

练习类型

读前活动（预览内容和词汇）、关于主旨和细节的理解问题、讨论及辩论话题、批判性思考、词汇拓展（侧重于学术词汇表中的词汇以及固定搭配）、价值澄清、提问美国人、研究和口头报告建议、双人活动和小组项目设计、谚语、人物观察和实验、理解民调和媒体、网络活动、写作话题和培养学术写作技能的活动，以及推荐书籍和影片。

课文用途

- 引导学生理解美国文化；
- 营造跨文化交际环境；
- 促进阅读、写作和讨论；
- 鼓励交流；
- 作为概念框架，配合其他侧重文学、媒体、时事等的文化资料。

* 要了解学术词汇表的发展和评估细节，请参看 Coxhead, Averil (2000), *A New Academic Word List*. TESOL Quarterly, 34(2): 213 – 238.

要了解学术词汇表及其使用方法的更多信息，请访问网址 http://www.victoria.ac.nz/lals/resources/academicwordlist/

ABOUT THE AUTHORS

Maryanne Kearny Datesman is the author of several ESL reading texts. She has taught ESL and administered programs at Western Kentucky University and American University. She has also taught at Georgetown University. In Kentucky, she established and administered a private language school and directed programs for refugees. She was co-founder of Kentucky TESOL and is a former president of WATESOL.

JoAnn (Jodi) Crandall is a professor emerita of education at the University of Maryland Baltimore County. At UMBC, she co-directed the master's program in ESOL/Bilingual Education and directed the interdisciplinary Ph.D. program in Language, Literacy, and Culture. She is a former president of TESOL and AAAL (American Association for Applied Linguistics) and a frequent speaker at national and international conferences.

Edward N. Kearny is professor emeritus of government at Western Kentucky University. He earned his Ph.D. in government from American University in 1968. He also holds a bachelor's degree in economics and a master's degree in psychology, and he has written a number of books and articles on American politics.

Acknowledgments

Our great appreciation goes to George Datesman for many hours of research, editing, help with the logistics of matching exercises with new content, and moral support, and to Lisa Kearny for help with research and contributing creative ideas for exercises and activities that would be fun to do. We also want to thank our editors at Pearson, Debbie Sistino and Joan Poole, for their considerable efforts and contributions.

We would also like to thank Averil Coxhead at the School of Language Studies, Massey University, Palmerston North, New Zealand, for allowing us the use of the Academic Word List. We wish to acknowledge the comments and encouragement we have received from many colleagues who have used this book in a wide range of settings all over the world. We would also like to thank the students we have worked with over the years for sharing their insights and perceptions of the United States with us and, in the process, helping us to better understand our own American culture.

M. K. D.

J. A. C.

E. N. K.

作者简介

玛丽安娜·卡尼·戴特斯曼撰写过多篇关于英语作为第二语言（ESL）的阅读文章。她曾在西肯塔基大学和美国大学教授英语并管理课程。她也曾在乔治敦大学执教。在肯塔基，她曾创立并掌管一所私立语言学校，并负责为难民开设的课程。她是肯塔基对外英语教学（TESOL）协会的创始人之一，也是华盛顿地区对外英语教师协会（WATESOL）的前主席。

乔安·克兰德尔是马里兰大学巴尔的摩县分校的教育学荣誉退休教授。在该校，她是对外英语（ESOL）/双语教育硕士项目的负责人之一，还是语言文学与文化跨学科博士项目的负责人。她是TESOL及美国应用语言学协会（AAAL）的前任主席，并经常在国内和国际会议上发言。

爱德华·N.卡尼是西肯塔基大学政治学荣誉退休教授。他于1968年获得美国大学政治学博士学位，同时还拥有经济学学士学位和心理学硕士学位。他撰写了大量关于美国政治的书籍和文章。

致谢

我们对乔治·戴特斯曼深表感谢。他不仅为研究、编辑、统筹安排新内容的匹配练习付出了大量时间，还给予我们以精神支持。我们也要感谢莉萨·卡尼，她为研究提供了帮助，并为增添练习和活动的趣味性贡献了富有创意的想法。我们还要感谢为本书付出努力与贡献的培生教育集团的编辑，戴比·西斯蒂诺和琼·普尔。

我们同时还想感谢新西兰北帕默斯顿市梅西大学语言研究学院的埃夫丽尔·考克斯黑德允许我们使用学术词汇表。全世界有很多同行在各种不同的背景中使用了本书，并给予我们很多建议和鼓励，在此也向他们致谢。我们还要感谢多年来与我们合作过的学生，他们同我们分享了对美国的见解和认识，并在此过程中使我们自己对美国文化有了更好的理解。

玛丽安娜·卡尼·戴特斯曼

乔安·克兰德尔

爱德华·N.卡尼

CHAPTER 1

INTRODUCTION: UNDERSTANDING THE CULTURE OF THE UNITED STATES

Culture hides much more than it reveals, and strangely enough what it hides, it hides most effectively from its own participants. Years of study have convinced me that the real job is not to understand foreign culture but to understand our own.

Edward T. Hall (1914–2009)

How can you define the culture of a diverse country like the United States, and what does it mean to be an American?

BEFORE YOU READ

Preview Vocabulary

A. Every chapter of ***American Ways*** contains many words from the Academic Word List (AWL).* Notice the AWL words in italics as you work with a partner to discuss the following questions.

1. If a country has great *ethnic diversity,* would you expect to find many people who speak different languages and have different customs?
2. Could planning a visit to another country *motivate* someone to learn a foreign language?
3. Should *immigrants* be required to learn the language of their new country before they become citizens?
4. How could you learn about the customs and *traditions* for a holiday in another country?
5. If there are more people in the United States who speak English than Spanish, which is the *dominant* language in the United States?
6. Is the climate of a country a *significant factor* in the daily lives of the people? Why?

B. There are five AWL words in the quotation by Edward T. Hall at the beginning of the chapter. Read the quotation and find the words with the following meanings. Write each word next to its meaning.

_____ 1. made someone think that something is true

_____ 2. shows something that was hidden

_____ 3. ideas, beliefs, and customs

_____ 4. work

_____ 5. people who are taking part in an activity

---

*See page 306 for an explanation of the AWL and how to use it. Some of these words are key to understanding the chapter reading.

Preview Content

A. Before you read the chapter, think about what you know about the "culture" of a country. Work with a partner and answer the questions.

1. What is the culture of a country? If someone asked you to describe your country's culture, which of these would you mention?

beliefs	government
cities	history
climate	holidays
customs	houses
dance	literature
food	music
geography	

    Anything else? _____

2. Do you agree with the quotation by Edward T. Hall? Do people really not understand their own culture? What aspects of a country's culture are the hardest to understand?

B. Look at the pictures, charts, and graphs in this chapter, and read the headings. Then predict three topics you think this chapter will discuss.

1. _____

2. _____

3. _____

LIFE IN THE UNITED STATES

1. People are naturally curious about each other, and when we meet people from different countries, we want to know many things:
   - What is life like in their country?
   - What kind of houses do they live in?
   - What kind of food do they eat?
   - What are their customs?

2. If we visit another country, we can observe the people and how they live, and we can answer some of these questions. But the most interesting questions are often the hardest to answer:
   - What do the people believe in?
   - What do they value most?
   - What motivates them?
   - Why do they behave the way they do?

3. In trying to answer these questions about Americans, we must remember two things: (1) the immense size of the United States and (2) its great ethnic diversity. It is difficult to comprehend the size of the country until you try to travel from one city to another. If you got in a car in New York and drove to Los Angeles, stopping only to get gas, eat, and sleep, it would take you four or five days. It takes two full days to drive from New York to Florida. On a typical winter day, it might be raining in Washington, D.C., and snowing in New York and Chicago, while in Los Angeles and Miami it is warm enough to swim. It is not difficult to imagine how different daily life might be in such different climates, or how lifestyles could vary in cities and towns so far apart.

4. The other significant factor influencing American life—ethnic diversity—is probably even more important. Aside from the Native Americans who were living on the North American continent when the first European settlers arrived, all Americans came from other countries—or their ancestors did. (Incidentally,[1] some Native Americans are still members of separate and distinct Indian nations, each with its own language, culture, traditions, and even government.) In the 1500s, Spain established settlements in Florida, California, and the Southwest, and France claimed large territories in the center of the North American continent. But from the 1600s to the birth of the United States in 1776, most immigrants to the colonies that would form the United States were from northern Europe, and the majority were from England. It was these people who shaped the values and traditions that became the dominant, traditional culture of the United States.

A Nation of Immigrants

5. In 1815, the population of the United States was 8.4 million. Over the next 100 years, the country took in about 35 million immigrants, with the greatest numbers coming in the late 1800s and the early 1900s. Many of these new immigrants were not from northern Europe. In 1882, 40,000 Chinese arrived, and between 1900 and 1907 there were more than 30,000 Japanese immigrants. But by far the largest numbers of the new immigrants were from central, eastern, and southern Europe. The new immigrants brought different languages and different cultures to the United States, but gradually most of them assimilated[2] to the dominant American culture they found here.

6. In 1908, a year when a million new immigrants arrived in the United States, Israel Zangwill wrote in a play,

---

[1] incidentally: by the way

[2] assimilated: became part of a county or group and were accepted by other people in it

America is God's Crucible,³ the great Melting-Pot where all the races of Europe are melting and re-forming... Germans and Frenchmen, Irishmen and Englishmen, Jews and Russians—into the Crucible with you all! God is making the American!

7   Since Zangwill first used the term *melting pot* to describe the United States, the concept has been debated. In Chapter 8 we consider this issue in more detail, and trace the history of African Americans as well. Two things are certain: The dominant American culture has survived, and it has more or less successfully absorbed vast numbers of immigrants at various points in its history. It has also been changed over time by all the immigrant groups who have settled here.

8   If we look at the immigration patterns of the 1900s, we see that the greatest numbers came at the beginning and at the end of the century. During the first two decades of the twentieth century, there were as many as one million new immigrants per year, so that by the 1910 census, almost 15 percent of all Americans had been born in another country. In 1921, however, the country began to limit immigration, and the *Immigration Act* of 1924 virtually closed the door. The total number of immigrants admitted per year dropped from as many as one million to only 150,000. A quota system was established that specified the number of immigrants that could come from each country. It heavily favored immigrants from northern and western Europe and severely limited everyone else. This system remained in effect until 1965, with several exceptions allowing groups of refugees from countries such as Hungary, Cuba, Vietnam, and Cambodia into the United States.

9   Immigration laws began to change in 1965 and the yearly totals began to rise again—from about 300,000 per year in the 1960s to more than one million per year in the 1990s. By the end of the century, the United States was admitting more immigrants than all the other industrialized countries combined. In addition to legal immigration, estimates were that illegal immigration was adding more than half a million more people per year. Changes in the laws that were intended to help family reunifications⁴ resulted in large numbers of non-Europeans arriving, thus creating another group of new immigrants. By the late 1900s, 90 percent of all immigrants were coming from Latin America, the Caribbean, and Asia.

10 In the twenty-first century, the numbers of new immigrants have begun to approach the percentages of the early twentieth century. Between 1990 and 2010, the number of foreign-born living in the United States almost doubled from 20 million to 40 million, with about one-third arriving since 2000. These new immigrants accounted for about one-third of the total growth in population and have had an enormous impact on our country. By the year 2010, about 13 percent of all Americans were foreign born. Twelve states and the nation's capital had even higher percentages of foreign-born residents:

- California, 27 percent
- New York and New Jersey, each over 21 percent
- Florida and Nevada, each over 19 percent

---

³ *crucible: a container in which substances are heated to a very high level*

⁴ *reunifications: the joining of the parts of something together again*

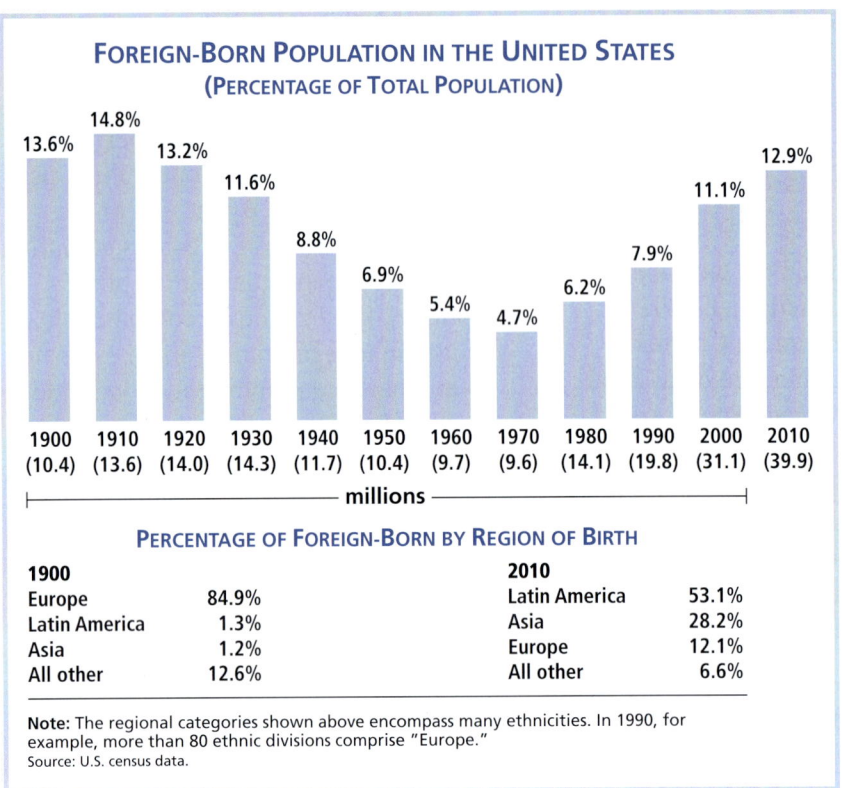

- Hawaii and Texas, each over 16 percent
- Arizona, Illinois, Massachusetts, Connecticut, Maryland, and the District of Columbia, each over 13 percent

11 The twenty-first-century immigration patterns are continuing to change the color and the ethnic mix of the American population. First, the percentage of white Americans of European descent[5] continues to decrease. Few Europeans are immigrating to the United States now, and many of those who came in the early 1900s have died. Their descendants have married Americans with ancestors from other countries, and many of these second- and third-generation immigrants no longer think of themselves as Irish or German or English.

12 Second, in the early 2000s, more than half of all new immigrants were from Latin America, resulting in large concentrations of Spanish speakers around the country, particularly in California, Florida, Texas, Arizona, and other southwestern states. Hispanics now represent the largest minority in the United States (16%), larger than the number of African Americans (13%). With their growth in numbers has come a growth in political and economic influence. Presidential candidates now consider how to win Hispanic votes, and there are more than 6,000 elected Hispanic leaders nationwide. There has been a rise in Hispanic-owned businesses and Spanish-language media. Perhaps the largest impact is in the schools, where more than 20% of the children are Hispanic.

13 The numbers of Hispanic-Americans will probably continue to grow because many of them are young adults or children. However, the number of new Hispanic immigrants has declined. In

---

[5] *descent: family origins, especially in relation to the country where one's family came from*

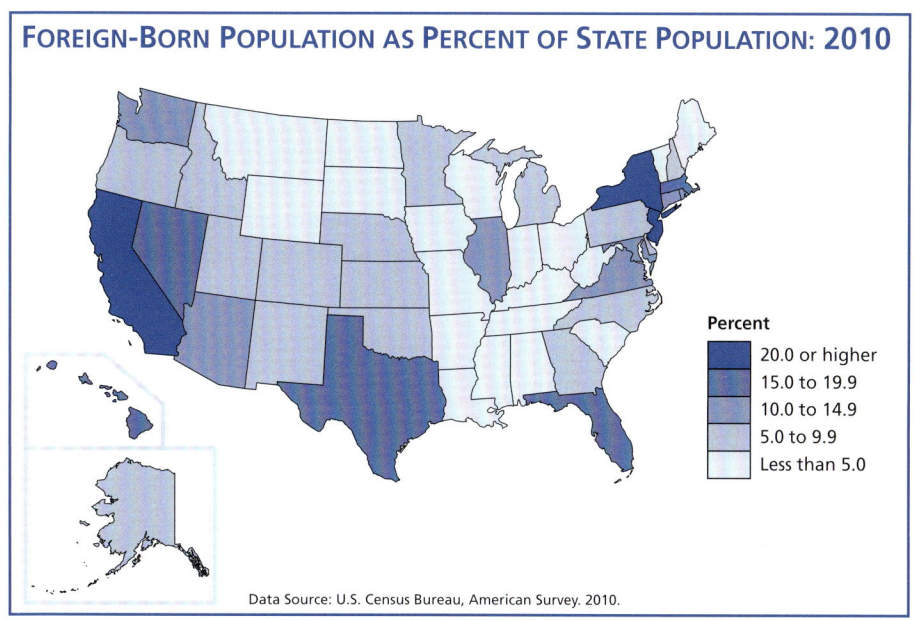

2000, they made up more than 50% of all new immigrants, but the number fell to about 30% in 2010. Because of the poor economy, a number of immigrant residents returned to their home countries in Latin America. Due to tighter border restrictions, the number of illegal immigrants fell, and the total population of Hispanics living in the United States may have actually declined.

14 The immigrants from Asian countries are also contributing to the new American mix. According to the 2010 census, for the first time there were more Asian immigrants than Hispanic. Today, more than 35 percent of all first-generation immigrants are from Asia, and they now make up about 6 percent of the total population of the United States. If this trend continues, Asian immigrants will have an increasing impact on the American culture. As the minority non-white population of the United States continues to grow, the white majority grows smaller. In 2011, for the first time, there were more minority babies born than white majority babies. The white majority will probably fall below 50 percent sometime between 2040 and 2050. Already, several states and many of the nation's largest cities are "majority minority." This means more than half of the population are members of minority groups.

Cultural Pluralism in the United States

15 One of the critical questions facing the United States today is what role new immigrants will play in their new country. To what degree will they choose to take on the traditional American values and culture? How much will they try to maintain their own language and cultural traditions? Will they create an entirely new culture based on some combination of their values and those of the traditional American culture?

16 Historically, although the children of immigrants may have grown up bilingual and bicultural, for a number of reasons many did not pass on their language and culture. Thus, many grandchildren of immigrants do not speak the language of the old country and are simply American by culture. However, in parts of the country with established communities

that share a common language or culture, bilingualism[6] and biculturalism continue. This is particularly true in communities where new immigrants are still arriving. In California, for example, the test for a driver's license is given in more than thirty different languages. In general, cultural pluralism[7] is more accepted in the United States today than it was in the first half of the twentieth century, and some school systems have bilingual programs and multicultural curricula.

17 The census of 2010 recognized the increase in the diversity of the American population. There were many racial and ethnic categories to choose from, and it was possible to select more than one category.*

18 On the one hand, many Americans try to

CENSUS 2010 SUMMARY: DIVERSITY OF THE AMERICAN POPULATION		
SUBJECT	NUMBER	PERCENT
RACE		
Total population	308,745,538	100.0
One race	299,736,465	97.1
White	223,553,265	72.4
Black or African American	38,929,319	12.6
American Indian and Alaska Native	2,932,248	0.9
American Indian, specified	1,985,245	0.6
Alaska Native, specified	100,522	0.0
Both American Indian and Alaska Native, specified	869	0.0
American Indian or Alaska Native, not specified	845,612	0.3
Asian	14,674,252	4.8
Native Hawaiian and Other Pacific Islander	540,013	0.2
Some Other Race	19,107,368	6.2
Two or More Races	9,009,073	2.9
Two races with Some Other Race	2,464,690	0.8
Two races without Some Other Race	5,800,628	1.9
Three or more races with Some Other Race	176,026	0.1
Three or more races without Some Other Race	567,729	0.2
HISPANIC OR LATINO		
Total population	308,745,538	100.0
Hispanic or Latino (of any race)	50,477,594	16.3
Mexican	31,798,258	10.3
Puerto Rican	4,623,716	1.5
Cuban	1,785,547	0.6
Other Hispanic or Latino	12,270,073	4.0
Not Hispanic or Latino	258,267,944	83.7
RACE AND HISPANIC OR LATINO		
Total population	308,745,538	100.0
One race	299,736,465	97.1
Hispanic or Latino	47,435,002	15.4
Not Hispanic or Latino	252,301,463	81.7
Two or More Races	9,009,073	2.9
Hispanic or Latino	3,042,592	1.0
Not Hispanic or Latino	5,966,481	1.9

[6] *bilingualism: the ability to speak two languages equally well*

[7] *cultural pluralism: the principle that people of different races, religions, and political beliefs can live together peacefully in the same society*

For the 2010 census, people were allowed to check as many ethnic and racial categories as they wished. This chart is the U.S. government's presentation of the very complicated census information that resulted. The chart reflects the difficulties in determining ethnic and racial identities of Americans. For further information, visit the government website www.census.gov.

maintain their ethnic heritage and their cultural traditions. On the other hand, the number of interracial marriages is increasing, and the majority of young people believe it does not matter which race or ethnic group they marry into. Evidence of this racial acceptance was the 2008 election of Barack Obama, the first African-American president. President Obama is actually bi-racial, the son of a white mother and a black father, a native of Kenya. His ethnic heritage[8] includes an Irish great, great, great grandfather who immigrated to the United States in 1850. More and more children are born of mixed race or ethnicity. By the middle of the century, the nation will probably no longer have a white majority; some say the color of most Americans will be beige, or light brown, as a result of the mixing of races and ethnic groups.

19 In the United States, most people are very sensitive to the language used to describe racial and ethnic groups, and they try to be politically correct, or "P.C." For example, some black Americans prefer the term African-American instead of black to identify with their African heritage. The terms Native American and American Indian are used interchangeably by those native to the North American continent, while some self-identify by tribe (Navajo, Hopi, and so forth). Some Spanish speakers prefer to be called Latinos (referring to Latin America) instead of Hispanics (referring to Spain), while others prefer to be identified by their country of origin (Cuban-American or Cuban, Mexican-American, Chicano, or Mexican, etc.). Since the census uses

President Barack Obama and his family

[8] *heritage: that which belongs to you because of your birth*

a variety of terms, we will also use the terms white, Native American or American Indian, black or African-American, and Hispanic or Latino.

20 In spite of all this diversity, there is still a tie that binds Americans together. That tie is a sense of national identity—of being an American. Incidentally, when citizens of the United States refer to themselves as Americans, they have no intention of excluding people from Canada or Latin American countries as residents of the American continents. There is no term such as United Statesians in the English language, so people call themselves Americans. Thus, what is really a language problem has sometimes caused misunderstandings. Although citizens of Latin American countries may call the people in the United States North Americans, to many people in the United States this makes no sense either, because the term North American refers to Canadians and Mexicans as well as citizens of the United States. (NAFTA—the North American Free Trade Agreement, for example, is a trade agreement among Canada, the United States, and Mexico.) The word *American*, then, is used in this text as the nationality of the people who live in the United States of America.

Making Generalizations About American Beliefs

21 What, then, can we say about Americans? What holds them together and makes them feel American? Is it possible to make generalizations about what they believe? It is, but we must be cautious about generalizations. As we talk about basic American beliefs, we must remember that not all Americans hold these beliefs, nor do all Americans believe these things to the same degree. The ways in which some Americans practice their beliefs may also differ, resulting in a great variety of lifestyles. What we attempt to do is to define and explain the traditional, dominant cultural values that have for so many years attracted immigrants to the United States.

22 It is important to know that today there is much talk about American values and what they really are. Much of the debate is over *moral*, or religious values. In this book we are not discussing moral values. Instead, we are describing *cultural* values—the cultural engine of the country. These cultural values have defined the United States and caused people from all over the world to embrace the way of life here and eventually to identify themselves as "Americans." Indeed, by the third generation here, most immigrants have lost the language and culture of their grandparents and they think of themselves as just plain "Americans."

23 Throughout this book we will be drawing on the wisdom of a famous observer of the American scene, Alexis de Tocqueville. Tocqueville came to the United States as a young Frenchman in 1831 to study the American form of democracy and what

Immigrants being sworn in as new American citizens

it might mean to the rest of the world. After a visit of only nine months, he wrote a remarkable book called *Democracy in America,* which is a classic study of the American way of life. Tocqueville had unusual powers of observation. He described not only the democratic system of government and how it operated, but also its effect on how Americans think, feel, and act. Many scholars believe that he had a deeper understanding of traditional American beliefs and values than anyone else who has written about the United States. What is so remarkable is that many of these traits of the American character, which he observed nearly 200 years ago, are still visible and meaningful today.

24 Another reason why Tocqueville's observations of the American character are important is the time when he visited the United States. He came in the 1830s, before America was industrialized. This was the era of the small farmer, the small businessman, and the settling of the western frontier. It was the period of history when the traditional values of the new country were being established. In just a generation, some forty years since the adoption of the U.S. Constitution, the new form of government had already produced a society of people with unique values. The character traits Tocqueville describes are the same ones that many Americans still take pride in today. He, however, was a neutral observer and saw both the good and the bad sides of these qualities.

25 This is a book about those traditional basic American beliefs, values, and character traits. It is not a book of cold facts about American behavior or institutions,[9] but rather it is about the motivating forces behind the people and their institutions. It is about how these traditional basic beliefs and values affect important aspects of American life: religion, business, work and play, politics, the family, and education.

26 We invite you to participate in this book. We will describe what many Americans think and believe, but you will have an opportunity to test these descriptions by making your own observations. As you read about these traditional basic values, think of them as working hypotheses[10] which you can test on Americans, on people of other nations, and on people of your nationality. Compare them with your own values and beliefs and with what is most important in your life. Through this process, you should emerge with a better understanding not only of Americans, but also of your own culture and yourself. It is by studying others that we learn about ourselves.

---

[9] *institutions: large organizations, especially ones dedicated to public service*

[10] *hypotheses: ideas that are suggested as an explanation for something but that have not yet been proven to be true*

AFTER YOU READ

Understand Main Ideas

Academic English organizes information into main (or most important) ideas and supporting details. That is, there are usually three or four major points presented, and the rest of the information serves to explain or support these main ideas:

- *First main idea*
    - *Supporting details*
- *Second main idea*
    - *Supporting details*
- *Third main idea*
    - *Supporting details*

When reading academic English or listening to a lecture, it is important to recognize the main points. The introduction focuses your attention on the topic. Then the main points are presented, and the conclusion reminds you of one or more central ideas. Noticing the headings in a text will help you figure out the main points the writer is presenting.

Check the predictions that you made on page 3. Did the chapter include any of the information you predicted? Then work with a partner and answer these questions about the main ideas.

1. What are two important factors that affect life in the United States?
2. What is the heading for the section that discusses the history of immigration in the United States?
3. What is cultural pluralism?
4. What is the main idea of the section headed *Making Generalizations About American Beliefs*?
5. What relationship is there between the quotation at the beginning of the chapter, the introduction (first two paragraphs), and the conclusion (paragraphs 25 and 26) of the reading?

Understand Details

Write **T** if the statement is true and **F** if it is false according to the information in the chapter.

_____ 1. One factor affecting lifestyles in the United States is the variety of climates.

_____ 2. American Indians all speak the same language.

_____ 3. The dominant American culture was established by immigrants who came from southern Europe.

_____ 4. For the first time, in the 2010 census, there were more Asian than Hispanic immigrants.

_____ 5. Zangwill believed that immigrants would lose their native cultures and become something different when they came to the United States.

_____ 6. Immigrants change American culture and are changed by it.

_____ 7. U.S. immigration policy has stayed the same for the last 100 years.

_____ 8. The English language has no adjective for *United States* and therefore uses the term *American* to refer to its people.

_____ 9. It is not possible to make generalizations about what Americans believe because they are so different.

_____ 10. Many of the characteristics of Americans that Alexis de Tocqueville observed in the 1830s are still true today.

Talk About It

Work in small groups and choose one or more of the following questions to discuss.

1. How would you compare the size and ethnic diversity of your country with that of the United States? What are some of the challenges that size (large or small) and diversity (great or limited) present to a country?

2. Should a country have immigration quotas based on country of origin? Should immigrants become citizens? Should countries allow "guest workers" (people who work there temporarily) to come? Should they allow them to become citizens?

3. How would you describe the average person in your country and what he or she believes?

4. Do you think people all over the world are basically the same or basically very different?

SKILL BUILDING

Improve Your Reading Skills: Scanning

In order to become a good reader in English, your reading speed and techniques should vary according to your purpose. For example, you may look down a page (or over several pages) to find a particular piece of information—a number, a date, a place, or the time a movie begins. This type of reading for a specific fact is called scanning.

Read the questions below. Scan the reading to find the specific information you need to answer each question.

1. Which states have the largest numbers of immigrants?

_____

2. In what year did Alexis de Tocqueville come to visit the United States?

   _____

3. In 1910, what percentage of the U.S. population was foreign born?

   _____

4. What was the total U.S. population according to the 2010 census?

   _____

5. In what year did Israel Zangwill write a play in which he used the term *melting pot*?

   _____

6. What is Obama's family tie to Ireland?

   _____

Develop Your Critical Thinking Skills

Analyzing Polls

Conducting opinion polls is very popular in the United States. A newspaper, a magazine, a TV station, or a professional polling organization asks a representative group of Americans several questions to determine their opinions about topics such as politics, religion, or social issues. The pollsters usually choose men and women of different ages, occupations, and races in the same proportion that these groups are found in the population. Sometimes, however, a random sample is taken which selects people by chance.

There are three well-known polling organizations that measure public opinion on a variety of topics: Louis Harris and Associates, Gallup International Research Institutes, and the Pew Research Center. Pew also studies aspects of American life. For example, the Pew Hispanic Center recently published a report on Hispanics in the United States and how they identify themselves. As mentioned in the chapter, the terms Hispanic and Latino are generally used in the media interchangeably. In this poll, Pew found that only 24% of all Hispanics self-identify as Hispanic or Latino. When they do use these terms, 33% of them choose "Hispanic" and 14% prefer "Latino."

Read the poll and answer the questions that follow.

WHEN LABELS DON'T FIT: HISPANICS AND THEIR VIEWS OF IDENTITY

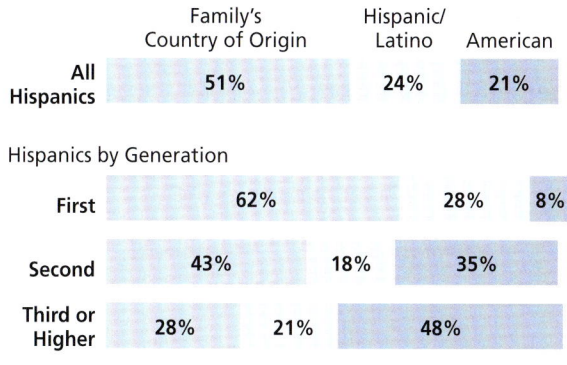

Source: Pew Research

1. What does the phrase "country of origin" mean? What percent of all Hispanics identify themselves by their country of origin? Give some examples of these countries of origin.
2. What does "generation" mean? What do the terms "first, second, or third generation" Hispanic mean? Why did the researchers divide the group this way?
3. Who are more likely to identify with the family's country of origin—new immigrants or those who were born in the United States?
4. What percent refer to themselves as just "American?" Who are more likely to self-identify as American than by any other term—new immigrants or those born in the United States?
5. What change happens to the identity of the grandchildren of Hispanic immigrants? Why do you think this happens?

Build Your Vocabulary

Use Context Clues

There are several types of context clues that will help you guess the meaning of words you do not know. By looking at the words around an unfamiliar word, you may be able to figure out its meaning. See the four kinds of context clues below. In the examples, the vocabulary words are boldfaced. The context clues are in italics.

1. The word may be defined in the sentence. Sometimes the definition is set off by commas or dashes. Other times it is not.

EXAMPLE: There is still a tie that binds Americans together. That tie is a sense of national **identity**—*of being an American.*

EXAMPLE: A **quota** system was established that *specified the number of immigrants that could come from each country.*

2. There may be a synonym used in the same sentence.

EXAMPLE: Native Americans belong to *separate* and **distinct** Indian nations, each with its own language, culture, and even government.

3. There may be a comparison or contrast with a word (or a phrase) more familiar to you.

EXAMPLE: As the **minority** non-white population of the United States continues to grow, the white *majority* grows smaller.

4. The sentence may give an example that helps you figure out the meaning.

EXAMPLE: Tocqueville, however, was a **neutral observer** and *saw both the good and bad sides of these qualities.*

A. Use the context clues to figure out the meaning of the boldfaced words in the sentences above. Then write the correct word next to its definition.

_____ 1. a limit on the number allowed

_____ 2. a group of people whose race is different from that of most people in a country

_____ 3. someone who makes decisions based on facts, not personal feelings

_____ 4. the qualities that a group of people have that make them different from other people

_____ 5. clearly different or separate

Now fill in the blanks with some of the boldfaced words above to complete the paragraph.

What qualities give people a national _____? Do they have to have
                                              1

characteristics that are _____ from those of other countries? The
                             2

people who are part of a _____ group may feel they have a set of
                              3

characteristics that differ from those of the majority in their country.

B. Test your knowledge of these AWL words by matching them with their definitions.

   _d_   1. aspect   a. large organization, especially one dedicated to public service

_____ 2. category   b. to start something that will continue

_____ 3. concept   c. to be different

_____ 4. debate   d. one part of an idea that has many parts

_____ 5. establish   e. to continue in spite of difficulties

_____ 6. estimate   f. group of things that all have the same qualities

_____ 7. hypothesis   g. to judge by calculating and guessing

_____ 8. incidentally   h. one of a kind

_____ 9. institution   i. an idea

_____ 10. survive   j. an explanation that is not yet proven

_____ 11. unique   k. a discussion of different opinions

_____ 12. vary   l. by the way

Understand Prefixes

Recognizing the meaning of a prefix, a group of letters added to the beginning of a word (or its root), will also help you guess the meaning of a new word. For example, the prefix mis- means "wrong," so misunderstand means "not understand correctly."

Each of the boldfaced words in the sentences below has a prefix. Identify the prefix and write its meaning. Use a dictionary, if necessary.

EXAMPLE: Before the 1960s, the majority of immigrants to the United States were Europeans, but changes in immigration laws resulted in large numbers of **non-Europeans**.

   Prefix: __non__   Meaning: __not__

1. Estimates were that, in addition to legal immigration, **illegal** immigration was adding more than half a million more people per year.

   Prefix: _____   Meaning: _____

2. In some parts of the country with established communities that share a common language or culture, bilingualism and **biculturalism** continue. Cultural pluralism is more accepted now than it was in the first half of the twentieth century, and many school systems have developed bilingual programs and **multicultural** curricula.

   Prefix: _____   Meaning: _____
   Prefix: _____   Meaning: _____

3. People may migrate to another location in order to find work. While many people **immigrate** to the United States each year, very few Americans choose to **emigrate** to another country to live.

   Prefix: _____   Meaning: _____
   Prefix: _____   Meaning: _____

4. In the census of 2010, there were nineteen racial categories to choose from. The number of **interracial** marriages is increasing...and the majority of young people believe it does not matter which race they marry.

   Prefix: _____   Meaning: _____

Word Partners

*Certain words and phrases tend to go together in English, for example, "ethnic diversity" or "traditional values." This is called **collocation**. Learning these word partners will increase your ability to use new words correctly and help you express yourself as native speakers do.*

First read the sentences below. Then find the collocations to complete these sentences by matching the adjectives on the left with their noun partners on the right. Use the collocations to complete the sentences.

<u> c </u> 1. established   a. immigrants

_____ 2. significant   b. culture

_____ 3. neutral   c. communities

_____ 4. industrialized d. pluralism

_____ 5. legal   e. hypotheses

_____ 6. dominant   f. countries

_____ 7. cultural   g. factor

_____ 8. working   h. observer

1. In parts of the country with <u>established communities</u> that share a common language, bilingualism continues.

2. Tocqueville was a _____ who saw both the good and bad sides of the American character traits.

3. Ethnic diversity is a _____ affecting American life.

4. Think of the traditional values in this book as _____ that you can test against your own observations.

5. The United States now takes in more _____ each year than all other _____ combined.

6. When several cultures exist together successfully in a society, there is _____.

7. The _____ in the United States is becoming less white in the twenty-first century.

EXPAND YOUR KNOWLEDGE

Ask Americans

Interview several Americans of different ages (if possible) and ask them to complete the following statements. If there are no Americans to interview, you can ask other international students or your classmates about their view of Americans.

1. Americans are _____.

2. They like _____.

3. They don't really like _____.

4. They act _____.

5. Most Americans believe in _____.

6. The United States is a country where _____.

7. The average American is _____.

8. Americans today are worried about _____.

9. The most important thing in life to most Americans is _____.

Ask Yourself

Using the statements above as examples, complete the following statements about people from your own country.

1. People from my country are _____.

2. People from my country believe in _____.

3. My country is a place where _____.

4. The average person from my country is _____.

5. People from my country are worried about _____.

6. The most important thing in life to most people from my country is

   _____.

Think, Pair, Share

Think about the following questions and write down your answers. Then discuss your answers with a partner and share your answers with another pair of students.

1. How would you define *culture*? Look at several dictionaries to find definitions and read the first paragraph of the introduction to this book.
2. What do you think are the most important aspects of your native culture?

People Watching

Different countries have different rules for personal space, that is, when people touch, how close they stand when they are speaking to one another, how close they sit, how they behave on elevators, etc. The rules for personal space sometimes differ according to how well people know each other. People are usually not consciously aware of these rules, but they may become very uncomfortable if the rules are broken and their space is entered without permission. You can discover the rules by observing people interacting and also by testing or breaking the rules to see how other people respond.

Conduct two experiments about personal space. Follow these steps.

1. Read the rules for personal space below.
2. Make your own observations of people. Write your observations in a journal. It may be helpful to work in pairs: One person tests the rules while the other observes and records what happens.
3. Experiment with the rules. Write the responses you receive.
4. If you are not in the United States, and if you do not have an opportunity to observe Americans, you may still learn from these experiments by watching people in your own country or by observing Americans in movies or TV shows.

People in line try to avoid touching each other.

First Rule: When they are in a crowd, Americans have a bubble of space around their bodies which is about an inch thick. This bubble of space must not be broken by a stranger. If American strangers touch each other accidentally, they mutter an apology such as "Pardon me," "Excuse me," "Oh, I'm sorry," or just "Sorry."

Observation: Watch people in a crowd, standing in line, waiting in a group, or passing on a street or in a hallway. Who is touching whom? What does their relationship appear to be? What happens when people touch accidentally? How does the person touched respond? What does the one who has broken the other's bubble do? Record gestures, facial expressions, emotional responses, and words exchanged.

Experiment: See how close you can stand to someone in a crowd without touching him or her. Try breaking someone's bubble of space with a very light touch of your elbow or arm. What is the person's response? (Warning: This may provoke an angry response!)

Second Rule: When standing in elevators, Americans usually face the door, speak quietly, and try to avoid touching one another. If a stranger enters an elevator where there is only one other person, he or she will stand on the opposite side of the elevator. As more people get on the elevator, they occupy the corners first and then try to disperse themselves evenly throughout the available space.

Observation: Observe people in elevators. Which direction are they facing? If you are alone in an elevator and someone comes in, where does that person stand? As more people enter the elevator, where do they stand? Do the people talk to one another? How loudly do they speak? Do strangers touch? What happens in a crowded elevator when someone in the back has to get off?

Experiment: Get on an elevator where there is only one person and stand next to that individual. What is the person's reaction? In an elevator where there are a number of people, turn and face the group with your back to the door. How do the people react? Have a conversation with someone in a crowded elevator and don't lower your voice. How do you think people feel about this? Note their facial expressions.

People in an elevator avoid eye contact.

Use the Internet

Although polls are usually scientific, polling organizations also conduct informal polls online. These informal polls only reflect the views of the people who happen to visit their website and answer the poll questions. Some poll sites have interactive pages or allow you to participate in online polls. Visit these websites and compare the topics they are polling now:

www.harrisinteractive.com

www.gallup.com

www.pewresearch.org

WRITE ABOUT IT

Choose one of the following topics. Then write a short composition about it.

1. Write a short essay describing three places in your country that you would want to take someone visiting from another country. Use a graphic organizer to organize your thoughts before you write. Make notes about the names of the places, their locations, any special features, and your reasons for choosing the places.

First Place	Second Place	Third Place

2. Write a report about your country. Read the following information on regions and population growth in the United States to get ideas for your report.

The United States can be divided into different regions with different characteristics. There are a number of ways to divide and name the different regions; the map below shows the regions the U.S. Census Bureau uses. Each region contains different divisions. Notice the Mountain Division of the West Region. This is where the Rocky Mountains are located.

CENSUS REGIONS AND DIVISIONS OF THE UNITED STATES

Data Source: U.S. Census Bureau.

Compare this area with the second U.S. Census map. This map shows the population density of the United States. Notice the areas that are the most highly populated in the country. Notice that the area where the mountains are has a low population density.

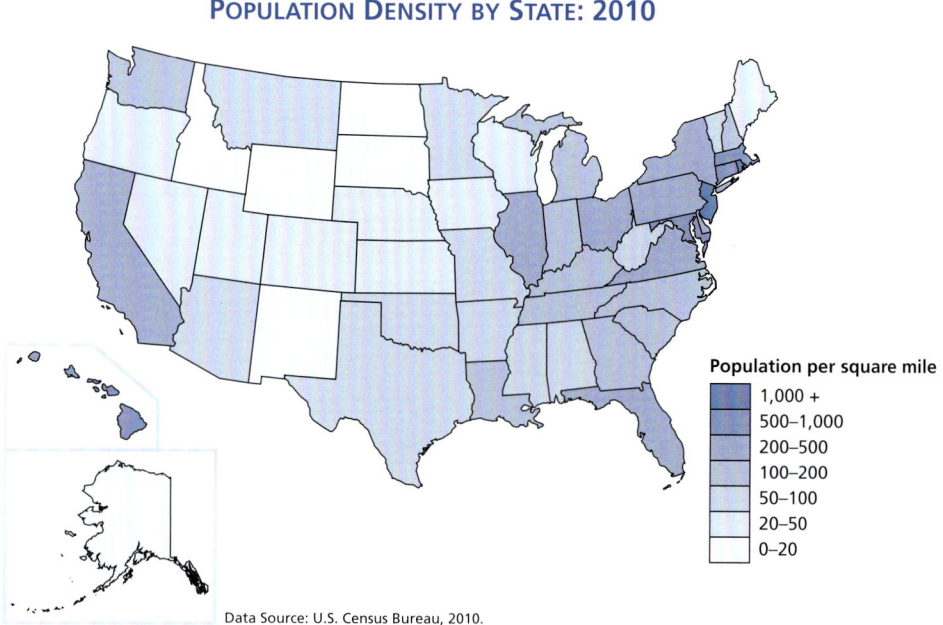

In 1981, Jack Garreau wrote a book entitled *The Nine Nations of North America* describing nine diverse regions of the North American continent. The book he wrote is no longer in print, but his map is of lasting interest. (It is discussed on Wikipedia and available as a Google image.) Garreau believed that the North American continent is made up of nine regions so different that each might be thought of as a separate nation. Each "nation" has a different culture, economy, political concern, and set of values:

The Empty Quarter	The Islands
Ecotopia	MexAmerica
New England	The Breadbasket
The Foundry	Quebec
Dixie	

Locate Garreau's nine "nations" on the U.S. Census map of regions and divisions. The Mountain Division has very low population density, so Garreau calls it "The Empty Quarter." "Ecotopia" is the area along the west coast from Alaska to Los Angeles, an area where people are particularly concerned about environmental issues. "New England" includes the northeastern coastal strip of Canada. "The Foundry" is the original industrial/manufacturing area from the Middle Atlantic through the East North Central Great Lakes region. "Dixie" is the old South that tried to leave the United States during the Civil War, including the South Atlantic (except for Kentucky, Maryland, and Delaware) and East South Central Divisions, and the eastern part of Texas. "The Islands" include south Florida, Puerto Rico, and the other islands of the Caribbean. "MexAmerica" includes southern California and the other states that border Mexico. "The Breadbasket" is made up of the West North Central Great Plains states and stretches from up in Canada to northern Texas. It is where much of the nation's food is grown. Quebec is the home of most French Canadians.

Write a report about the regions of your country. Where are the most populated areas? What are the major geographic regions? As you prepare your report, include some information on geographical features, natural resources, major cities, and special characteristics of each region. Use a graphic organizer to organize your ideas.

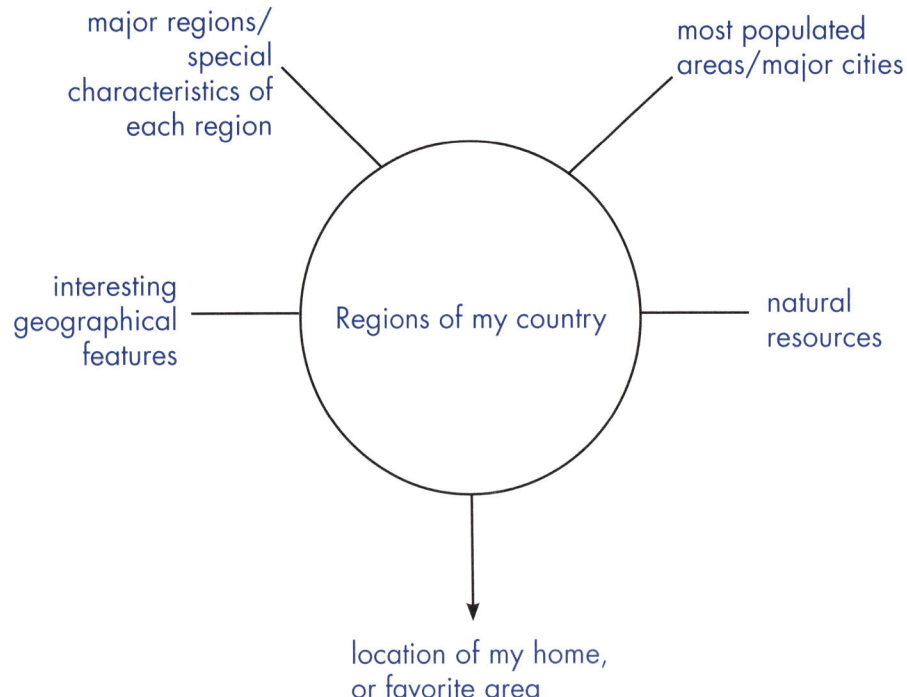

EXPLORE ON YOUR OWN

Books to Read

Sherwood Anderson, *Winesburg, Ohio*—Published in 1919, this literary masterpiece explores the hidden passions of ordinary lives in a small American town.

Richard Paul Evans, *The Road to Grace*—An advertising executive walks across the country from Seattle, Washington, to Key West, Florida.

John F. Kennedy, *A Nation of Immigrants*—President Kennedy, himself the grandson of Irish immigrants, discusses how old immigrant traditions mix with the new experiences of immigrants starting life over in America.

Barack Obama, *Dreams of My Father*—In this "Story of Race and Inheritance," President Obama reflects on his life from his birth in Hawaii to a father from Kenya and a mother from Kansas, to his enrollment in Harvard Law School.

Marco Rubio, *An American Son*—This book is a memoir by the Cuban-American U.S. Senator from Florida.

Movies to See

La Bamba—Ritchie Valens, a young 1950s rock and roll singer, rose to fame from poverty and brought the Latin American influence to his hit songs.

Last of the Mohicans—This film tells the story of Native Americans' life in 1757 and how they interacted with the British.

Sweet Land—A young woman comes to Minnesota from Norway to marry a man she has never met and faces many difficulties.

The Terminal—An eastern European immigrant who is not permitted to enter the United States decides to take up temporary residence at a JFK airport terminal.

Under the Same Moon—A young Mexican boy travels to the United States to find his mother after his grandmother passes away.

CHAPTER 2

TRADITIONAL AMERICAN VALUES AND BELIEFS

We hold these truths to be self-evident, that all men are created equal, that they are endowed by their Creator with certain inalienable rights, that among these are Life, Liberty and the pursuit of Happiness.

The Declaration of Independence (1776)

Why do so many people want to come and live in the United States? What is so attractive about the American way of life and the values of the society?

BEFORE YOU READ

Preview Vocabulary

A. Here are some key AWL words in this chapter. Look at their definitions. Put a check next to the words you already know.

_____ 1. **individual** one person, considered separately from the group

_____ 2. **achieve** to succeed in getting the result you want

_____ 3. **benefit** something that gives advantages or improves life in some way

_____ 4. **reliant** being dependent on someone

_____ 5. **constitution** a set of basic laws and principles that a democratic country is governed by

_____ 6. **ethical** relating to principles of what is right and wrong

_____ 7. **resources** a country's land, minerals, or natural energy that can be used to increase its wealth

_____ 8. **status** social or professional rank or position in relation to others

_____ 9. **welfare** money paid by the government to people who are very poor, sick, not working, etc.

_____ 10. **foundation** a basic idea or principle

B. Work with a partner. Complete each question with a word from the preceding list. Then answer the questions.

1. Why would the _____ of a country forbid titles of nobility? (titles such as "princess" or "sir")

2. If there are no titles of nobility, how does a society recognize people with high social _____.

3. Which do you think is more important to Americans, the well-being of the group or the _____?

4. What do immigrants have to do to _____ success in their new country?

5. What are some of the natural _____ found on the North American continent?

6. What _____ does a person get from being self-_____?

7. When would it not be _____ to compete with someone?

8. What country provided the language and the _____ for the political and economic systems of the United States?

9. What situations might cause a person to need _____?

C. Read the quotation from the *Declaration of Independence* at the beginning of the chapter, and find the words with the following meanings. Write each word next to its meaning.

_____ 1. the act of trying to achieve something in a determined way

_____ 2. easily noticed or understood; obvious

_____ 3. that cannot be taken away from you

_____ 4. given a good quality

Preview Content

A. Before you read, preview the chapter by looking at the illustrations and reading the headings and captions under the pictures. Work with a partner and discuss these questions.

1. What is the main idea of the quotation at the beginning of the chapter?
2. What are some reasons people want to come live in the United States? Use this graphic organizer to write down your ideas. Are any of these ideas similar? If so, draw lines connecting them.

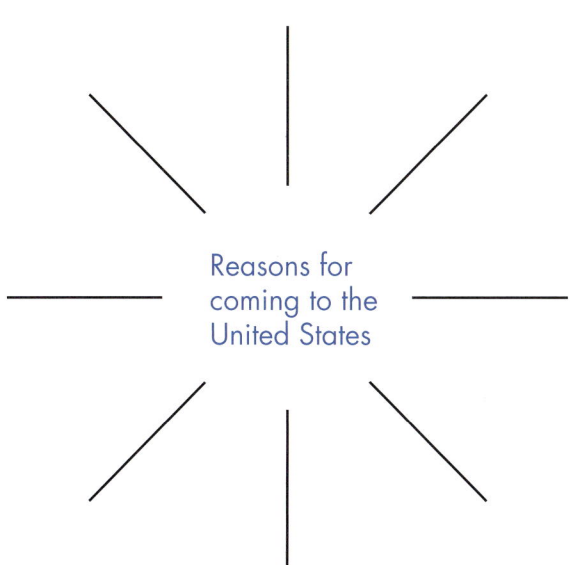

3. What is the "American Dream"? (Hint: Give a one-sentence summary of the ideas you wrote for question #2.)

4. What do you think Americans believe is the best thing about their country?

B. Think about what values and beliefs could be important to Americans. Work with a partner and make three predictions about what you will read. Write your predictions here.

1. _____

_____

2. _____

_____

3. _____

_____

THE CONTEXT OF TRADITIONAL AMERICAN VALUES: RACIAL, ETHNIC, RELIGIOUS, AND CULTURAL DIVERSITY

1. From the beginning of the history of the United States there has been diversity— Native Americans throughout the North American continent, Spanish settlers in the Southwest and in Florida, French missionaries and fur traders along the Mississippi River, black slaves brought from African countries, Dutch settlers in New York, Germans in Pennsylvania, and of course the British colonists, whose culture eventually provided the language and the foundation for the political and economic systems that developed in the United States.

2. Most early Americans recognized this diversity, or pluralism, as a fact of life. The large variety of ethnic, cultural, and religious groups meant that accepting diversity was the only practical choice, even if some people were not enthusiastic about it, or were even threatened by it. However, in time, many Americans came to see strength in their country's diversity. Today, there is widespread recognition of the value of cultural pluralism, particularly among young people.

3. When we examine the system of basic values that emerged in the late 1700s and began to define the American character, we must remember this context of cultural pluralism. How could a nation of such enormous diversity produce a recognizable national identity?

4. John Zogby, an American pollster who surveys public opinion, says that what holds the United States together is that "we all share a common set of values that make us American... We are defined by the rights we have... Our rights are our history, why the first European settlers came here and why millions more have come here since."

NEW WORLD COLONIES IN 1750

Source: http://web.uccs.edu/~history/index/151maps.html.

5 Historically, the United States has been viewed as "the land of opportunity," attracting immigrants from all over the world. The opportunities they believed they would find in America and the experiences that most people actually had when they arrived nurtured a unique set of values. We will examine six basic values that have become traditional American values. Three represent traditional reasons why immigrants have been drawn to America: the chance for individual freedom, equality of opportunity, and material wealth. In order to achieve these benefits, however, there were prices to be paid: self-reliance, competition, and hard work. In time, these prices themselves became part of the traditional value system. This system of values, then, consists of three pairs of benefits and the price people paid to have these benefits:
- individual freedom and self-reliance,
- equality of opportunity and competition,
- material wealth and hard work.

6 These three pairs of values have determined the unique culture of the United States and its people. Another way of thinking about these basic values involves rights and responsibilities. Americans believe that people have the right to individual freedom, equality of opportunity, and the promise of material success, but these all require substantial responsibility: self-reliance, a willingness to compete, and hard work. After examining the historical origin of each of these pairs, we will discuss the current state of these values in the United States.

Individual Freedom and Self-Reliance

7 The earliest settlers came to the North American continent to establish colonies that were free from the controls that existed in European societies. They wanted to escape the controls placed on many aspects of their lives by kings and governments, priests and churches, noblemen and aristocrats.[1] To a great extent, they succeeded. In 1776, the British colonial settlers declared their independence from England and established a new nation, the United States of America. In so doing, they defied[2] the king of England and declared that the power to govern would lie in the hands of the people. They were now free from the power of the kings. In 1787, when they wrote the Constitution for their new nation, they separated church and state so that there would never be a government-supported church. This greatly limited the power of the church. Also, in writing the Constitution they expressly forbade titles of nobility to ensure that an aristocratic society would not develop. There would be no ruling class of noblemen in the new nation.

8 The historic decisions made by those first settlers have had a profound[3] effect on the shaping of the American character. By limiting the power of the government and the churches and eliminating a formal aristocracy, the early settlers created a climate of freedom where the emphasis was on the individual. The United States came to be associated in their minds with the concept of *individual freedom*. This is probably the most basic of all the American values. Scholars and outside observers often call this value *individualism*, but many Americans use the word *freedom*. It is one of the most respected and popular words in the United States today.

9 By *freedom*, Americans mean the desire and the right of all individuals to control

---

[1] *aristocrats: people who belong to the highest social class*

[2] *defied: refused to obey someone or do what was expected*

[3] *profound: important and having a strong influence or effect*

their own destiny without outside interference from the government, a ruling noble class, the church, or any other organized authority. The desire to be free of controls was a basic value of the new nation in 1776, and it has continued to attract immigrants to this country.

10 There is, however, a cost for this benefit of individual freedom: *self-reliance.* Individuals must learn to rely on themselves or risk losing freedom. They must take responsibility for themselves. Traditionally, this has meant achieving both financial and emotional independence from their parents as early as possible, usually by age eighteen or twenty-one. Self-reliance means that Americans believe they should take care of themselves, solve their own problems, and "stand on their own two feet." Tocqueville observed the Americans' belief in self-reliance in the 1830s:

> *They owe nothing to any man, they expect nothing from any man; they acquire the habit of always considering themselves as standing alone, and they are apt to[4] imagine that their whole destiny is in their own hands.*

11 This strong belief in self-reliance continues today as a traditional American value. It is perhaps one of the most difficult aspects of the American character to understand, but it is profoundly important. Most Americans believe that they must be self-reliant in order to keep their freedom. If they rely too much on the support of their families or the government or any organization, they may lose some of their freedom to do what they want. Even if they are not truly self-reliant, most Americans believe they must at least appear to be so. In order to be in the mainstream of American life—to have power and/or respect—individuals must be seen as self-reliant.

12 For example, if adult children return home to live with their parents because of economic conditions or a failed marriage, most members of the family expect this to be a short-term arrangement, until the children can find a job and be self-reliant. Although receiving financial support from charity,[5] family, or the government is possible, it is usually expected to be for a short time, and it is generally not admired. Eventually, most Americans would say, people have a responsibility for taking care of themselves.

Equality of Opportunity and Competition

13 The second important reason why immigrants have traditionally been drawn to the United States is the belief that everyone has a chance to succeed here. Generations of immigrants have come to the United States with this expectation.

Immigrants on Ellis Island around 1900

[4] *are apt to: have a natural tendency to do something*

[5] *charity: an organization that gives money, goods, or help to people who are poor, sick, etc.*

They have felt that, because individuals are free from excessive political, religious, and social controls, they have a better chance for personal success. Of particular importance is the lack of a hereditary[6] aristocracy.

14. Because titles of nobility were forbidden in the Constitution, no formal class system developed in the United States. In the early years of American history, many immigrants chose to leave older European societies because they believed that they had a better chance to succeed in America. In "the old country," the country from which they came, their place in life was determined largely by the social class into which they were born. They knew that in America they would not have to live among noble families who possessed great power and wealth inherited and accumulated over hundreds of years.

15. The hopes and dreams of many of these early immigrants were fulfilled in their new country. The lower social class into which many were born did not prevent them from trying to rise to a higher social position. Many found that they did indeed have a better chance to succeed in the United States than in the old country. Because millions of these immigrants succeeded, Americans came to believe in *equality of opportunity*. When Tocqueville visited the United States in the 1830s, he was impressed by the great uniformity of conditions of life in the new nation. He wrote:

    The more I advanced in the study of American society, the more I perceived that...equality of condition is the fundamental fact from which all others seem to be derived.

16. It is important to understand what most Americans mean when they say they believe in equality of opportunity. They do not mean that everyone is—or should be—equal. However, they do mean that each individual should have an equal chance for success. Americans see much of life as a race for success. For them, equality means that everyone should have an equal chance to enter the race and win. In other words, equality of opportunity may be thought of as an ethical rule. It helps ensure that the race for success is a fair one and that a person does not win just because he or she was born into a wealthy family, or lose because of race or religion. This American concept of "fair play" is an important aspect of the belief in equality of opportunity.

17. President Abraham Lincoln expressed this belief in the 1860s when he said:

    We...wish to allow the humblest man an equal chance to get rich with everybody else. When one starts poor, as most do in the race of life, free society is such that he knows he can better his condition; he knows that there is no fixed condition of labor for his whole life.

18. However, the price to be paid for this equality of opportunity is *competition*. If much of life is seen as a race, then a person must run the race in order to succeed; a person has the responsibility to compete with others, even though we know not everyone will be successful. If every person has an equal chance to succeed in the United States, then many would say that it is every person's duty to try.

19. The pressures of competition in the life of an American begin in childhood and continue until retirement from work. Learning to compete successfully is part of growing up in the United States, and competition is encouraged by strong programs of competitive sports provided by the public schools and community groups. Competitive sports are now popular with both men and women.

---

[6] *hereditary: can be passed from an older to a younger person in the same family*

Shaking hands may be a polite acknowledgment of your competitor as well as a greeting.

20 The pressure to compete causes Americans to be energetic, but it also places a constant emotional strain on them. When they retire, they are at last free from the pressures of competition. But then a new problem arises. Some may feel useless and unwanted in a society that gives so much prestige[7] to those who compete well. This may be one reason older people in the United States sometimes do not have as much honor and respect as they have in other less-competitive societies. In fact, generally speaking, any group of people who do not compete successfully—for whatever reason—do not fit into the mainstream of American life as well as those who do compete and succeed.

Material Wealth and Hard Work

21 The third reason why immigrants have traditionally come to the United States is to have a better life—that is, to raise their standard of living. For the vast majority of the immigrants who came here, this was probably the most compelling reason for leaving their homeland. Because of its incredibly abundant natural resources, the United States appeared to be a land of plenty where millions could come to seek their fortunes. Of course, most immigrants did not "get rich overnight," and many of them suffered terribly, but the majority of them were eventually able to improve upon their former standard of living. Even if they were not able to achieve the economic success they wanted, they could be fairly certain that their children would have the opportunity for a better life. The phrase "going from rags to riches" became a slogan[8] for the "American Dream." Because of the vast riches of the North American continent, the dream came true for many of the immigrants. They achieved material success and many became very attached to material things. *Material wealth* became a value to the American people.

22 Placing a high value on material possessions is called *materialism*, but this is a word that most Americans find offensive. To say that a person is materialistic is an insult. To an American, this means that this person values material possessions above all else. Americans do not like to be called materialistic because they feel that this unfairly accuses them of loving only material things and of having no religious values. In fact, most Americans do have other values and ideals. Nevertheless, acquiring and maintaining a large number of material possessions is still of great importance to most Americans. Why is this so?

23 One reason is that material wealth has traditionally been a widely accepted measure of social status in the United States. Because Americans rejected the European system of hereditary aristocracy and titles of nobility, they had to find a substitute for judging social status. The quality and quantity of an individual's material possessions became an accepted measure of success and social status. Moreover, as we shall see in the religion chapter, the Puritan work ethic associated material success with godliness.

[7] prestige: *the respect and importance that a person, organization, or profession has*

[8] slogan: *a short, easily-remembered phrase used in advertising or politics*

24 Americans have paid a price, however, for their material wealth: *hard work*. The North American continent was rich in natural resources when the first settlers arrived, but all these resources were undeveloped. Only by hard work could these natural resources be converted into material possessions, allowing a more comfortable standard of living. Hard work has been both necessary and rewarding for most Americans throughout their history. Because of this, they came to see material possessions as the natural reward for their hard work. In some ways, material possessions were seen not only as tangible[9] evidence of people's work, but also of their abilities. In the late 1700s, James Madison, the father of the American Constitution, stated that the difference in material possessions reflected a difference in personal abilities.

25 Most Americans still believe in the value of hard work. Most believe that people should hold jobs and not live off welfare payments from the government. There have been many efforts to reform the welfare system so that people would not become dependent on welfare and stop looking for jobs to support themselves. However, a larger question is how much hard work will really improve a person's standard of living and level of material wealth. Is it still possible to work hard and get rich in America?

26 As the United States has shifted from an industry-based economy to one that is service- or information-based, there has been a decline in high-paying jobs for factory workers. It is now much more difficult for the average worker to go from rags to riches in the United States, and many wonder what has happened to the traditional American Dream. As the United States competes in a global economy, many workers are losing their old jobs and finding that they and their family members must now work longer hours for less money and fewer benefits. When the economy weakens, everyone suffers, and there are greater numbers of the working poor—those who work hard but have low-paying jobs that do not provide a decent standard of living and may not provide health insurance and retirement benefits, and many have to rely on some outside assistance from the government or other sources.

American Values and the State of the American Dream

27 In recent years, as the economy has declined, many observers have asked if the American Dream is really dead. For the most part, the American Dream has not meant that the average American can really go from rags to riches. It has traditionally meant that by working hard, parents can enable their children to have a better life when they grow up. Every generation could be a little more prosperous and successful than their parents. While the distance between the very rich one percent and the rest of the population has dramatically increased over the last years, the overwhelming majority of Americans still believe in the ideal of the American Dream—that is, if they work hard, they and their children can have a better life. The ideal of upward mobility still exists in America. However, we must distinguish between idealism and reality in understanding the relationship between what Americans believe and how they live. Some who find that they are working longer hours for less money still hope that the American Dream will exist again, if not for them, then for their children.

28 American values such as equality of opportunity and self-reliance are ideals that may not necessarily describe the reality of American life. Equality of

---

[9] *tangible: concrete, able to be touched*

opportunity, for example, is an ideal that is not always put into practice. In reality, some people have a better chance for success than others. Those who are born into rich families have more opportunities than those who are born into poorer families. Inheriting money does give a person a decided advantage. Race and gender may still be factors affecting success, although there are laws designed to promote equality of opportunity for all individuals. And, of course, new immigrants continue to face challenges unique to their situation.

29   The fact that American ideals are only partly carried out in real life does not diminish their importance. Most Americans still believe in them and are strongly affected by them in their everyday lives. It is easier to understand what Americans are thinking and feeling if we can understand what these traditional American cultural values are and how they have influenced almost every facet[10] of life in the United States.

30   It is important to remember two things about these values. First, they are cultural values; they are the cultural engine that drives the United States and continues to power a nation where people from all over the world come and become "American." Secondly, putting these six values together into a system creates something new. As Aristotle said, the whole is greater than the sum of its parts. The relationship among these values—the rights and the responsibilities—creates the fabric[11] of the American society. It is this fabric that defines the American Dream— the belief that if people take responsibility for their lives and work hard, they will have the individual freedom to pursue their personal goals and a good opportunity to compete for success. These values are so tightly woven together that if any one of them is pulled out or even disturbed, the entire fabric is affected and may come apart.

31   Finally, these six cultural values— individual freedom, self-reliance, equality of opportunity, competition, material wealth, and hard work—do not tell the whole story of the American character. Rather, they form the basic structure or framework of the American culture. They enable a nation of enormous diversity to create and maintain a national identity.

32   In the next three chapters we will examine three historical factors that reinforced and helped to shape these values: the religious heritage, the frontier heritage, and the heritage of abundance. The remaining chapters will explore how these values appear in aspects of American culture: business, government, ethnic and racial diversity, education, leisure time, and the family. The final chapter will discuss the challenges facing the United States and their potential impact on the future of the country and its values.

To some, owning a beautiful house means they have achieved the American Dream.

---

[10] *facet: one of several parts of someone's character, a situation, etc.*

[11] *fabric: basic structure and way of life*

AFTER YOU READ

Understand Main Ideas

1. Check the predictions you made on page 30. How many of these six values did you predict—individual freedom, self-reliance, equality of opportunity, competition, material wealth, and hard work?

2. In Chapter 1, we looked at the relationship between the introduction and the conclusion, and at how the headings signaled the main ideas. Now look at the structure of Chapter 2. Reread paragraph 6 of the introduction section on page 32. What does this paragraph tell you about the structure of the reading? Notice that the six values are written as headings in the chapter. The outline below shows the structure of Chapter 2: the introduction (A), the three sections containing the six traditional values (B, C, D), and the conclusion (E). The numbers under each heading show the main ideas of each section. Work with a partner to complete the outline. (Part of it is done for you.)

   A. Introduction: The Context of Traditional American Values: Racial, Ethnic, Religious, and Cultural Diversity

   　1. The United States has great diversity, but it also has a national identity.

   　2. What holds the United States together is a common set of _____.

   B. Individual Freedom and Self-Reliance

   　1. The early settlers came to the North American continent for individual freedom—the most basic of all the American values.

   　2. The price for individual freedom is _____.

   C. _____

   　1. Immigrants have always come for equality of opportunity—the belief that everyone should have an equal chance to _____.

   　2. _____

   D. _____

   　1. Immigrants have traditionally come for material wealth—the chance for a higher standard of _____.

   　2. _____

E. Conclusion: _____.

   1. Many Americans believe that with hard work their dreams of success can

   _____.

   2. Even though many of the traditional values are ideals that may not describe the reality of American life, they still influence

   _____.

Understand Details

Choose the best answer to complete the sentences based on the chapter.

_____ 1. Early settlers came to the North American continent and established colonies mainly because they wanted to be free from
   a. the power of kings, priests, and noblemen.
   b. the influence of their families.
   c. the problems of poverty and hunger.

_____ 2. There are no titles of nobility in the United States today because
   a. no one likes aristocrats.
   b. the church does not allow it.
   c. they are forbidden by the Constitution.

_____ 3. The price that Americans pay for their individual freedom is
   a. self-reliance.
   b. competition.
   c. hard work.

_____ 4. The American belief in self-reliance means that
   a. receiving money from charity, family, or the government is never allowed.
   b. if a person is very dependent on others, he or she will be respected by others.
   c. people must take care of themselves and be independent, or risk losing their personal freedom.

_____ 5. The American belief in equality of opportunity means that
   a. all Americans are rich.
   b. Americans believe that everyone should be equal.
   c. everyone should have an equal chance to succeed.

_____ 6. In the United States, learning to compete successfully is
   a. part of growing up.
   b. not seen as healthy by most people.
   c. not necessary, because Americans believe in equality.

_____ 7. Traditionally, immigrants have been able to raise their standard of living by coming to the United States because
   a. Americans value money more than anything else.
   b. there were such abundant natural resources.
   c. the rich have shared their wealth with the poor.

_____ 8. Americans see their material possessions as
   a. having nothing to do with social status.
   b. the natural reward for their hard work.
   c. showing no evidence of a person's abilities.

_____ 9. A belief in the value of hard work
   a. developed because it was necessary to work hard to convert natural resources into material goods.
   b. developed because the immigrants who came here had a natural love of hard work.
   c. has never been a part of the American value system because people have so much.

_____ 10. In reality, such American ideals as equality of opportunity and self-reliance
   a. do not exist because there is no equality in the United States.
   b. are always put into practice in the United States and truly describe American life.
   c. are only partly carried out in real life, but are still important because people believe in them.

Talk About It

Work in small groups and choose one or more questions to discuss.
1. Americans believe strongly in self-reliance and the freedom and independence of the individual. What are the advantages and disadvantages of being very independent? Which is more important to you, pleasing your family or having the freedom to do what you want?
2. If Americans had to pick one aspect of their country that they are most proud of, over 90 percent would choose freedom. What aspect of your country are people most proud of? How does that quality affect life there?
3. Is it healthy for a person to want to compete? Which is more important in a society—competition or cooperation? Which do you value more? Why?

SKILL BUILDING

Improve Your Reading Skills: Scanning

Read the questions below. Scan the chapter to find the specific information you need to answer each question.
1. What three types of freedoms were the early settlers seeking?
2. What happened in 1776?
3. In what year was the *Constitution of the United States* written?
4. What do Americans mean by the word *freedom*?

5. Why didn't a hereditary aristocracy develop in the United States?
6. Who was James Madison and what did he say in the late 1700s?
7. Who said, "We... wish to allow the humblest man an equal chance to get rich with everybody else"?

Develop Your Critical Thinking Skills

Using poll data to support research conclusions.

The Center for the Study of the American Dream at Xavier University conducts an annual survey of the state of the American Dream. In their 2011 survey, they found that the American Dream is still alive in spite of economic bad news and international uncertainty. Here are the results of the survey.

_____ 1. While people are worried about the economy and America's place in the world, they are still confident about their personal ability to achieve their personal American Dream.

_____ 2. Currently, the most popular definitions of the American Dream are "a good life for my family," "financial security," "opportunity," and "freedom."

_____ 3. Most Americans believe that immigration is important for keeping the American Dream alive.

_____ 4. But people have lost faith in American institutions that have protected the American Dream, including politics, business, government, and the media.

_____ 5. People also believe that the United States is losing economic power and influence in the world, and the world is looking to other countries as the standard for success.

The results of the survey are based on polls that the Center conducted. Read the following poll data and match them to the results above. Write the letter of the poll in the blank next to the result that it supports.

a. 54 percent believe that "One of America's greatest strengths is that it has always been a beacon of opportunity to the rest of the world. People still yearn to come here for a better life."

b. 63 percent believe that China's role in the world economy is more powerful than that of the U.S.

c. 83 percent have less trust in politics in general, 79 percent have less trust in big business and major corporations, 78 percent have less trust in government, and 72 percent have less trust in the media.

d. 45 percent choose "a good life for my family" as their first or second choice of how they would define the American Dream, while 34 percent choose "financial security," 32 percent choose "freedom," and 29 percent choose "opportunity."

e. 63 percent are extremely or fairly confident of reaching their American Dream in their lifetime, and 75 percent say they have already attained some measure of it.

Visit the website of the Center for the Study of the American Dream
http://www.xavier.edu/americandream to learn more about their work.

Build Your Vocabulary

More AWL Words

Test your knowledge of these AWL words by matching them with their definitions.

_____ 1. accumulate   a. to become smaller or less important

_____ 2. authority   b. of central and underlying importance

_____ 3. convert   c. the physical and mental strength that makes you able to be active

_____ 4. diminish   d. to gradually get more and more money, possessions, or knowledge over a period of time

_____ 5. eliminate   e. to move from one place or position to another

_____ 6. energy   f. the power you have because of your official position

_____ 7. ethic   g. to get rid of something completely

_____ 8. financial   h. to change from one form, system, or purpose to a different one

_____ 9. fundamental   i. a general idea or set of moral beliefs that influences people's behavior and attitudes

_____ 10. global   j. relating to the whole world

_____ 11. promote   k. relating to money

_____ 12. shift   l. to help something or someone advance and be successful

Use Context Clues

Review the four kinds of context clues on pages 15 and 16 in Chapter 1. Use context clues in these sentences to choose the best meaning for the boldfaced words.

_____ 1. In 1776, the British colonial settlers declared their independence from England and established a new nation, the United States of America. In so doing, they **defied** the king of England and declared that the power to govern would lie in the hands of the people.
    a. They killed the king and members of his court.
    b. They openly resisted the king's power to govern them.

_____ 2. By *freedom,* Americans mean the desire and the right of all individuals to control their own **destiny** without outside interference from the government, a ruling class, the church, or any other organized authority.
   a. They wanted to control their own future lives.
   b. They wanted to control their Constitution.

_____ 3. To say that a person is **materialistic** is an insult. To an American, this means that this person values material possessions above all else.
   a. The person loves things.
   b. The person fears being poor.

_____ 4. John Kenneth White observes that in spite of all the changes in the nation's population, economy, and culture, the behaviors and values of Americans have remained remarkably **constant**.
   a. The behaviors and values have stayed the same.
   b. The behaviors and values have changed.

_____ 5. Because of its incredibly **abundant** natural resources, the United States appeared to be a land of plenty where millions could come to seek their fortunes.
   a. There were many natural resources.
   b. There were very few natural resources.

Word Partners

There are many verb + noun object collocations, or word partners, in English.

EXAMPLE: achieve independence

Americans expect their adult children to achieve independence and support themselves.

A. Read these word partners. Then complete the sentences that follow with the correct verb + noun object collocation.

face challenges
seek their fortunes
provide a decent standard of living
surveys public opinion
control their own destiny

1. John Zogby is an American pollster who
   _____.

2. By *freedom,* Americans mean the desire and the right to
   _____.

3. Millions came to the United States to
   _____.

Traditional American Values and Beliefs ★ 43

4. The working poor have low-paying jobs that do not

   _____.

5. Of course, new immigrants continue to

   _____.

Multiple Word Partners

Some English words can collocate, or partner, with only a few words; others have a great many collocations. For example, the verb *survey* has relatively few collocations with nouns:
   survey (public) opinion
   survey a group of people (teachers, voters)
   survey a piece of land or property

When *face* is used as a verb, it has many collocations. It usually means confronting someone or something that is difficult or unpleasant:
   face the facts, reality, the truth, the consequences
   face the problem head-on, face the music
   face an opponent, a rival, another sports team
   face a challenge

The verb *seek* also has many collocations. It often means to look for something you need or to ask someone for advice:
   seek shelter, sanctuary, comfort, help, advice, counseling
   seek your fortune, a better life, an opportunity
   seek a solution to a problem or seek a compromise
   seek the truth, seek justice, seek an answer
   seek employment, seek re-election

Choose two collocations each for *survey*, *face*, and *seek*, and then use them in your own sentences.

Word Forms

Many words have verb and noun forms.

Verb Form	Noun Form
achieve	achievement
conceptualize	concept
emphasize	emphasis
reject	rejection
rely	reliance

Choose the correct verb or noun forms from the chart above and write them in the following sentences. (Change the verb tenses, if necessary.)

Self-_____ is an important American value. Most Americans _____ the importance of eventually becoming independent and standing on their own two feet. They teach this _____ to their children as they are growing up, expecting them to _____

American children often earn spending money by selling lemonade.

financial and emotional independence by the time they are in their early twenties. Americans do not _____ their adult children; they still love them and believe this is the best preparation for life in the American culture.

EXPAND YOUR KNOWLEDGE

Ask Yourself

Do you agree or disagree with each of the following statements? Put a check under the number that indicates how you feel.

+2 = Strongly agree
+1 = Agree
 0 = No opinion
−1 = Disagree
−2 = Strongly disagree

	+2	+1	0	−1	−2
1. The welfare of the individual is more important than the welfare of the group.	___	___	___	___	___
2. Our destiny is in our own hands.	___	___	___	___	___
3. People should take care of themselves, solve their own problems, and stand on their own two feet.	___	___	___	___	___
4. If I could have a better life in another country, I would go and live there.	___	___	___	___	___

Traditional American Values and Beliefs ★ 45

5. Earning a lot of money is more important than having an interesting job. _____ _____ _____ _____ _____

6. The government should take care of the poor and homeless. _____ _____ _____ _____ _____

7. Life is basically a competitive race for success. _____ _____ _____ _____ _____

8. Money and material possessions are the best indicators of high social status. _____ _____ _____ _____ _____

9. People who work hard deserve to have a higher standard of living than others. _____ _____ _____ _____ _____

10. If I work hard, I am sure I can be a success and get what I want in life. _____ _____ _____ _____ _____

Ask Americans

Interview several Americans of different ages and ask them about their basic beliefs. If this is not possible, try to interview people from several different countries. Ask each one the following questions and record their answers.

1. Some people say that people achieve success by their own hard work; others say that luck and help from other people are more important. Which do you think is more important?
2. Do you agree or disagree with this statement: If you work hard in this country, eventually you will get ahead.
3. Do you think that the economic inequality in the United States today is a major problem, a minor problem, or not a problem at all?

Conduct a Poll

Read the results of the poll that follows, and then conduct a poll among your classmates asking the same questions. Compare your results with the answers that Americans gave.

How much do you think that each of the following is a cause of inequality in the U.S. today? A great deal, somewhat, not very much, not at all, or not at all sure.

CAUSES OF INEQUALITY

	Great deal/ Somewhat (NET)	A great deal	Somewhat	Not very much/ Not at all (NET)	Not very much	Not at all	Not at all sure
	%	%	%	%	%	%	%
The loss of manufacturing jobs to China, India, and other low cost countries	81	55	26	11	6	5	9
The influence of big business on government policies	78	55	23	13	7	5	9
The tax system	77	49	28	15	9	5	9
The influence of very rich people on government policy	76	56	21	16	10	6	8
The failure of the public school systems to educate many people	73	40	33	18	13	5	9
Globalization of the world economy	68	27	40	20	14	7	12

Note: Percentages may not add up to 100% due to rounding

People Watching

Rule: Americans usually stand about two and a half feet apart and at a slight angle (not facing each other directly) for ordinary conversation. They may touch when greeting each other by shaking hands (during a formal introduction) or by placing a hand briefly on the other's arm or shoulder (friends only). Some people kiss on the cheek or hug when greeting a friend. Note that the hug usually is not a full-body hug; only the shoulder and upper part of the bodies touch.

Observation: Observe people who are standing and talking. How far apart are they? Do they touch as they speak? What do you think their relationship is? Observe people greeting each other. What do they do? What is their relationship? Observe formal introductions. Do the people shake hands? Do women usually shake hands? If a man and a woman are introduced, who extends a hand first?

Experiment: Ask someone on the street for directions. When you are standing two or three feet apart and the other person seems comfortable with the distance, take a step closer. What is the person's reaction? Try standing more than two to three feet from the other person. What does the other person do? Try facing the person directly as you talk instead of standing at an angle. What happens?

Use the Internet

Many Americans interested in tracing their family history can learn when family members immigrated to the United States. Immigrants who came from Europe between 1892 and 1924 first landed on Ellis Island (in the New York harbor). There they went through Immigration. Off the coast of California is Angel Island, known as the Ellis Island of the West. From 1910 until 1940, many Asian immigrants entered the United States by first going to this island. The Statue of Liberty-Ellis Island Foundation has a museum and a website to help people do family research. The Angel Island Conservancy has just begun the process of creating a historical site on Angel Island.

Work with a partner. Visit the website http://www.ellisisland.org and click on *Ellis Island*, then *Immigrant Experience*.

You then have two choices: (1) *Family Histories* will tell you stories about individuals from different countries, or (2) *The Peopling of America* will give you a timeline that traces the history of immigration to the United States. Choose one of these, read the information, and discuss it with your partner.

Work with a partner. Visit the website http://angelisland.org/history.

How does this website compare with the Ellis Island site? How do you think it could be developed?

WRITE ABOUT IT

Choose one of the following topics. Then write a short compostion about it.

A. Write an essay about the responsibilities people in a community have to each other.

Organize your thoughts before you write. Here are a few tips.

- *Write a short plan, or outline, of your main ideas: an introduction, two or three main ideas, and a conclusion.*
- *Begin your essay by defining what you mean by the word <u>community</u>.*
- *Be sure to introduce each of your main points, using words such as <u>first</u>, <u>second</u>, <u>third</u>.*
- *Try to tie your conclusion to the introduction.*

B. Write a report about using census data to plan for the future.

How can census data help predict what the future population will be? To get some ideas for your report, read about a prediction of the future population of the United States made over 100 years ago.

In 1907, N. D. North, the Director of the Census, made a prediction about what the population of the United States would be in the year 2000. He explained this in an article in The Youth's Companion, a popular periodical of the day. According to the census of the year 1900, the population of the United States was 76,212,168. North predicted that it would grow to 311,000,000 in the year 2000, an increase of 235,000,000.

In the article, North discussed what such a large increase might mean. How would the nation feed such a larger number of people? How would the economy be affected? What would the population density look like? North observed that the only way to really measure the impact of such an enormous population would be in connection with the land area. He noted that the census of 1900 computed population density at 25.6 persons to a square mile. In the year 2000, if his prediction were accurate, the density would be 105 persons per square mile.

North's prediction was surprisingly accurate. The census of 2010 showed a population of 308,745,538. In making his prediction, North tried to consider such factors as immigration, the birth rate, the percentage of women of child-bearing age, and the percentage of children under the age of 18. He also mentioned that people were living longer than they had before.

Traditional American Values and Beliefs ★ 49

For your report, consider the changes in population in another country. It can be your own. If you can find a recent census and a past census, use these in your discussion. If there is no census, then think about your own city or country and discuss what you see as the changes in population and the reasons for these changes. How do you think the population will change in the future and why? Include in your report a graph or illustration such as the ones above. Use a graphic organizer like the one below to help you organize your information.

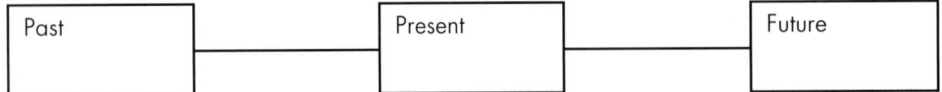

EXPLORE ON YOUR OWN

Books to Read

Sandra Cisneros, *The House on Mango Street*—Esperanza Cordero, a girl coming of age in the Hispanic quarter of Chicago, uses poems and stories to reveal her life in a difficult environment.

Ralph Waldo Emerson, *Self-Reliance*—This is a classic essay on the American value of self-reliance and Emerson's philosophy of moral idealism.

Richard Rodriguez, *Hunger of Memory: The Education of Richard Rodriguez*—A Mexican American describes his academic success, his assimilation to middle-class America, and his loss of connection to his cultural roots.

Amy Tan, *The Kitchen God's Wife*—A Chinese immigrant mother tells her daughter about growing up in China and her life there before coming to the United States.

John Kenneth White, *The Values Divide: American Politics and Culture in Transition*—White discusses the split between conservative Republicans and liberal Democrats and the American "culture wars" of the 2000s.

Movies to See

Coming to America—An African prince goes to Queens, New York, to find a wife whom he can respect for her intelligence and independence.

The Immigrants—An immigrant endures a challenging sea voyage and gets into trouble as soon as he arrives in America.

In America—An Irish immigrant family adjusts to life in the United States.

The Joy Luck Club—This film shows the life histories of four Asian women and their relationships with their daughters who were born in the United States.

The Pursuit of Happyness—Based on a true story, this movie tells about a homeless salesman and his son trying to start a new life.

CHAPTER 3

THE AMERICAN RELIGIOUS HERITAGE

The care of every man's soul belongs to himself.

Thomas Jefferson (1743–1826)

How has religion shaped American values and what is the role of religion in the lives of Americans today?

BEFORE YOU READ

Preview Vocabulary

A. Read the following sentences from the chapter and notice the words in italics. Use context clues to help you figure out the meanings. Then choose which definition is best for the italicized word. These key AWL words will help you understand the chapter reading.

_____ 1. Although the overwhelming majority of Americans are Christians, all religions make important *contributions* to the American culture.
   a. things you give or do in order to help make something successful
   b. official statements made by religious leaders to inspire people

_____ 2. In place of the power and authority of priests, Protestants *substituted* what they called the priesthood of all believers.
   a. used something new or different
   b. fought against the idea of

_____ 3. The idea of mixing materialism (love of things) and religion may seem *contradictory*. Religion is considered to be concerned with spiritual matters, not material possessions.
   a. different or opposite
   b. similar or almost the same

_____ 4. Many businesses encourage their employees to do *volunteer* work, such as helping clean up parks, helping a child who is having difficulty in school, or working in an animal shelter.
   a. without being paid
   b. necessary or required

_____ 5. Perhaps the most *dramatic* example of the idea of self-improvement is the experience of being "born again."
   a. uncertain or undecided
   b. exciting and impressive

_____ 6. America's religious heritage seems to have encouraged certain basic values that members of many diverse faiths find easy to accept. This has helped to unite many different religious groups in the United States without requiring any to *abandon* their faiths.
   a. to leave behind or give up
   b. to try to convince others to join

B. In this chapter, there are words dealing with religion, such as *priest, soul,* and *church*. Other words have to do with wealth, such as *money, financial,* and *sum*. Look at the words below and classify them into one of two groups. Write **R** next to words dealing with *religion* and **W** next to words dealing with *wealth*.

_____ 1. bless   _____ 9. prosperity

_____ 2. faith   _____ 10. Protestant denomination

_____ 3. forgiveness   _____ 11. riches

_____ 4. fortune

_____ 5. holy

_____ 6. material success

_____ 7. missionary

_____ 8. pray

_____ 12. save and invest

_____ 13. sin

_____ 14. soul

_____ 15. spiritual

_____ 16. evangelical

Preview Content

A. Think about these questions. Discuss them with your classmates.

1. Read the quotation by Thomas Jefferson at the beginning of the chapter. What do you think he meant? How could this belief affect religion in the United States?

2. What do you know about religion in the United States? Do you think that the United States has the same religions as your country? Fill in the Venn diagram with the names of religions found only in your country, only in the United States, or in both countries.

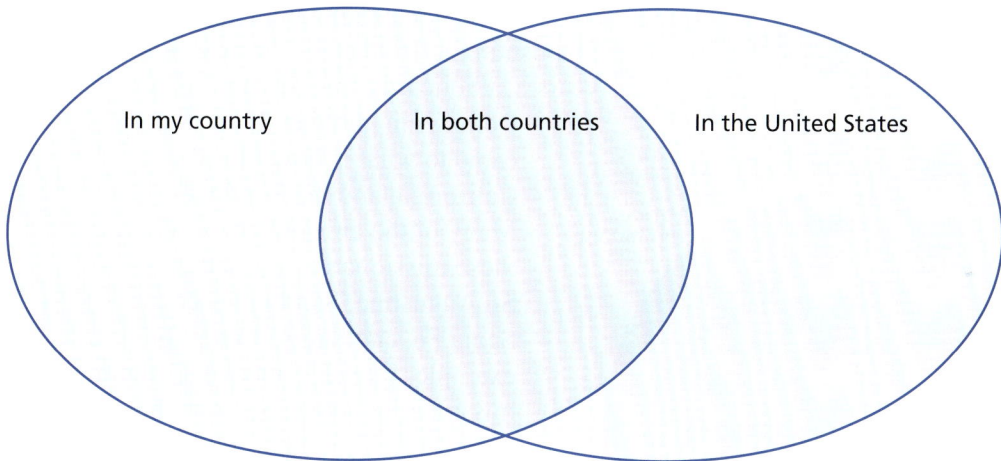

B. Before you read the chapter, look at the headings of each section. Which sections do you think will have the answers to these questions? Write the heading of the section in the space below each question.

1. How many Americans say they believe in God?

   _____

2. What are the most popular religions in the United States?

   _____

3. Do Americans have an official national religion?

   _____

4. How has religion shaped American values?

   _____

THE RELIGIOUS HERITAGE OF THE UNITED STATES: STRENGTHENING AMERICAN CULTURAL VALUES

1 The United States is and has always been a religious nation, by a number of measures. Ninety percent of Americans still say they believe in God, or a higher power/universal spirit, although their beliefs and practices are quite diverse. The majority of Americans are Christian, but all the major religions of the world are practiced in the United States. In some parts of the country, large numbers of people belong to churches and many attend worship services more than once a week. Other areas are more secular, with fewer people who are active in churches. Increasingly, young people do not belong to any church or other religious group, but most still say they believe in God. Many refer to themselves as being "spiritual," not "religious."

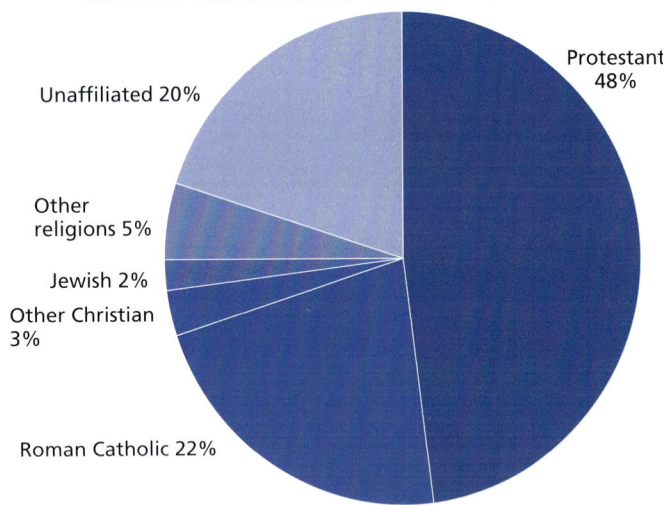

RELIGIOUS PREFERENCES IN THE UNITED STATES

2 The landscape of religion in America is complicated and constantly changing, but it has always been a very important aspect of the culture. In Chapter 2 we introduced six basic cultural values—individual freedom, self-reliance, equality of opportunity, competition, material wealth, and hard work. These values developed in and were strengthened by the nation's religious heritage. Several of these values—individual freedom, self-reliance, material wealth, and hard work—were particularly affected. In this chapter, we will first examine how the historical context shaped the nation's religious heritage and helped produce and reinforce these cultural values. Then we will look at how these values affect the religious landscape today.

3 From the beginning, religion played an important role in the history of the United States. The Catholic faith was first brought to the North American continent by the Spanish in the 1500s. For the next 300 years, Catholic missionaries and settlers from Spain and then Latin America came to what is now Florida, California, and the Southwest. Many of the cities were named by these missionaries and settlers—St. Augustine, San Francisco, Santa Fe, and San Antonio, for example. French Canadian Catholic missionaries also came with the explorers and traders from Quebec, down the Mississippi River to New Orleans. In the 1600s, European settlers began establishing colonies along the east coast of North America. Although there were some Catholics, the vast majority of the European settlers were Protestants, most from England. As the new nation formed, it was the Protestant branch of the Christian faith that had the strongest effect on the development of the religious climate in the United States.

The Development of Protestantism

4   The Protestant branch of the Christian faith broke away from the Roman Catholic Church in Europe in the sixteenth century because of important differences in religious beliefs. (The Eastern Orthodox branch of the Christian faith had separated from the Roman Catholic Church in 1054.) At the time of the Protestant Reformation, the Roman Catholic Church was the center of religious life in western European countries; the Catholic pope and the priests played the role of parent to the people in spiritual matters. They told people what was right and wrong, and they granted them forgiveness for sins[1] against God and the Christian faith.

5   The Protestants, on the other hand, insisted that all individuals must stand alone before God. If people sinned, they should seek their forgiveness directly from God rather than from a priest speaking in God's name. In place of the power and authority of priests, Protestants substituted what they called the "priesthood of all believers." This meant that every individual was solely responsible for his or her own relationship with God.

6   After the Protestants broke away from the Catholic Church, they found that they could not agree among themselves about many beliefs. Therefore, the Protestants began to form separate churches, called *denominations*. (The traditional Protestant denominations in the United States are Baptist, Methodist, Lutheran, Presbyterian, Episcopal, and United Church of Christ). There was much bitterness among some of the religious groups in the 1600s, and many Protestant denominations experienced religious persecution.[2] A number of people were even killed

Americans at worship in a Christian church

because of their beliefs. The result of this persecution was that many Protestants were ready to leave their native countries in order to have freedom to practice their particular religious beliefs. Consequently, among the early settlers who came to America in the 1600s, there were many Protestants seeking religious freedom.

7   In the previous chapter we noted that this desire for religious freedom was one of the strongest reasons why many colonial settlers came to America. Generally speaking, the lack of any established national religion in America appealed

---

[1] *sins: things someone does that are against religious laws*
[2] *persecution: cruel or unfair treatment, especially because of religious or political beliefs*

strongly to European Protestants, whether or not they were being persecuted. A large number of Protestant denominations were established in America. At first, some denominations hoped to force their views and beliefs on others, but the colonies were simply too large for any one denomination to gain control over the others. The idea of separation of church and state became accepted.

8   When the Constitution was adopted in 1789, the government was forbidden to establish a national church; no denomination was to be favored over the others. The government and the church had to remain separate, and freedom of religion was guaranteed by the first amendment. Under these conditions, a great variety of different Protestant denominations developed and grew, with each denomination having a "live and let live" attitude toward the others. Diversity was accepted and strengthened. Today, the various Protestant denominations have completely separate church organizations, and although there are many similarities, there are also significant differences in their religious teachings and beliefs.

Self-Reliance and the Protestant Heritage of Self-Improvement

9   Protestantism has been a powerful force in shaping the values and beliefs of Americans. One of the most important values associated with American Protestantism is the value of self-improvement, an outgrowth of self-reliance. Christianity often emphasizes the natural sinfulness of human nature. However, unlike Catholics, Protestants do not go to priests for forgiveness of their sins; individuals are left alone before God to improve themselves and ask for God's guidance, forgiveness, and grace. For this reason, Protestantism has traditionally encouraged a strong and restless desire for self-improvement.

10 Perhaps the most dramatic example of the idea of self-improvement is the experience of being "born again." Individuals who have had this experience say that opening their hearts to God and Jesus Christ changed their lives so completely that it was like being born again. Many evangelicals, or religious conservatives, believe this is an important experience to have.

11 The need for self-improvement has reached far beyond self-improvement in the purely moral or religious sense. Today it can be seen in countless books that offer advice to people on how to stop smoking, lose weight, or have better relationships. Books of this type often offer advice on how to be happier and more successful in life. They are referred to as "self-help" books, and many are best sellers. They are the natural products of a culture in which people believe that "God helps those who help themselves."

Material Success, Hard Work, and Self-Discipline

12 The achievement of material success is probably the most widely respected form of self-improvement in the United States. Many scholars believe that the nation's Protestant heritage is also largely responsible for bringing this about. The idea of mixing materialism and religion may seem contradictory; religion is considered to be concerned with spiritual matters, not material possessions. How can the two mix?

13 Some of the early European Protestant leaders believed that people who were blessed by God might be recognized in the world by their material success. Other church leaders, particularly in the United States, made an even stronger connection between gaining material wealth and being blessed by God. In 1900, for example,

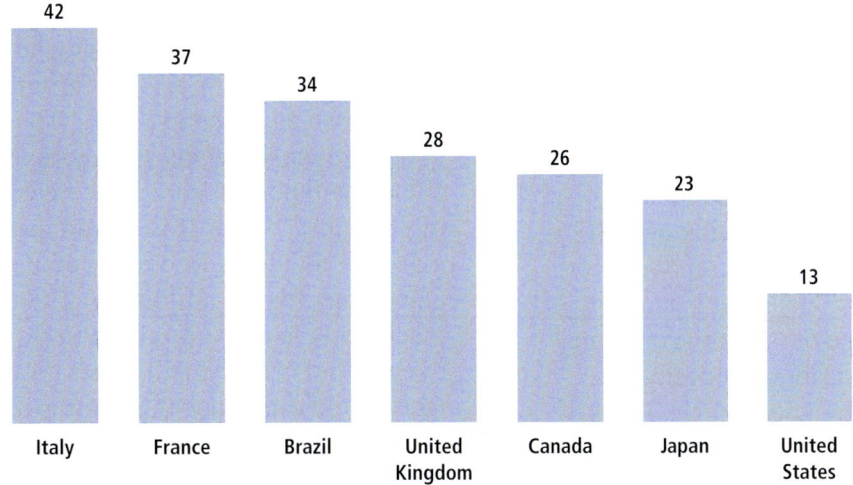

Source: World Tourism Organization (WTO). Information Please® Database, © 2007 Pearson Education, Inc. All rights reserved.

Bishop William Lawrence proclaimed,[4] "Godliness is in league with[5] riches... Material prosperity is helping to make the national character sweeter, more joyous, more unselfish, more Christlike."

14 American religious leaders, however, never encouraged the idea of gaining wealth without hard work and self-discipline. Many scholars believe that the emphasis on these two values made an important contribution to the industrial growth of the United States. Protestant leaders viewed the work of all people as holy, not just that of priests. They also believed that the capacity for self-discipline was a holy characteristic blessed by God. Self-discipline was often defined as the willingness to save and invest one's money rather than spend it on immediate pleasures. John Wesley, the leader of the Methodist faith, told his followers, "Earn all you can, give all you can, save all you can." Encouraging people to save may also have helped create a good climate for the industrial growth of the United States, which depended on hard work and a willingness to save and invest money.

15 The belief in hard work and self-discipline in pursuit of material gain and other goals is often referred to as "the Protestant work ethic" or "the Puritan work ethic." It is important to understand that this work ethic has had an influence far beyond the Protestant church. Many religious groups in the United States share this work ethic, and even Americans who have no attachment to a particular church are influenced by the work ethic in their daily lives. Interestingly, the United States is the only industrialized country that does not have a legal requirement for workers to have a certain number of paid vacation days. Americans take an average of only two weeks of vacation time a year, while workers in other countries take as many as four, five, or even more weeks. Also, many Americans who could retire at age 65 or 66 continue to work for more years.

[4] *proclaimed: said publically or officially that something is true*
[5] *in league with: working together secretly*

Many Americans are proud to be called "workaholics," people who work long hours, often seven days a week.

Volunteerism and Humanitarianism

16 The idea of self-improvement includes more than achieving material gain through hard work and self-discipline. It also includes the idea of improving oneself by helping others. Individuals, in other words, make themselves into better persons by contributing some of their time or money to charitable, educational, or religious causes that are designed to help others. The philosophy is sometimes called *volunteerism* or *humanitarianism*.

17 Historically, some extremely wealthy Americans have made generous contributions to help others. In the early 1900s, for example, Andrew Carnegie, a famous American businessman, gave away more than $300 million to help support schools and universities and to build public libraries in thousands of communities in the United States. John D. Rockefeller, another famous businessman, in explaining why he gave a large sum from his private fortune to establish a university, said, "The good Lord gave me my money, so how could I withhold it from the University of Chicago?" Julius Rosenwald, part-owner of the Sears Roebuck company, helped pay for the building of 5,000 black schools in the rural South. In the twenty-first century, Bill Gates, Warren Buffet, and other wealthy Americans have established charitable foundations and have donated huge sums of money. Traditionally, many average Americans have also agreed that they should devote part of their time and wealth to religious or humanitarian causes. Their motivation may be part idealism and part self-improvement, a desire to be acceptable in the eyes of God and also in the eyes of other Americans.

Volunteers clean up trash.

18 The spirit of charitable giving and volunteerism continues in America today. Some religious faiths believe that it is the responsibility of their members to contribute 10 percent of what they earn to their church and other charities. Incidentally, individuals may get tax deductions for giving money to charity. This spirit of giving can be seen outside religious contexts as well. Many businesses encourage their employees to do volunteer work, such as helping clean up parks, helping a child who is having difficulty in school, or working in an animal shelter in their spare time. Parents often try to teach their children that they have a responsibility to help others. A recent *Parents* magazine had a cover story advising parents how to "raise a child who gives back." The article said that children should be taught the value of volunteering, including giving money to charity. "Volunteering boosts kids' self-esteem and teaches them to be grateful," the article promised, a good illustration of the American mixture of idealism and self-improvement.

September 11, 2001, and the National Religion

19 All Americans and many people around the world can remember exactly what they were doing at the moment they heard that terrorists had attacked the World Trade Center and the Pentagon on September 11, 2001. People in New York City and Washington, D.C., were especially devastated. Everyone knew someone who was touched by the tragedy. Immediately, there was an outpouring of love, charity, and patriotism around the country. So many people volunteered to help that officials had to limit the numbers. Millions of dollars were raised for the families of the victims, and Americans felt a huge surge of pride and love for their country. Eighty percent of them displayed the American flag—in the windows of their houses, on their cars, even on their clothing. Crowds spontaneously sang "God Bless America," a patriotic song that is more popular (and much easier to sing) than the national anthem, along with "America the Beautiful" and "My Country' Tis of Thee."

Firefighters stand at a memorial to those killed at the World Trade Center.

20 This mixture of religion and patriotism is an example of what some scholars have called the "national religion" of the United States. The roots of the national religion go back to colonial times. In the countries from which the American colonists emigrated, the dominant values of the nation were often supported by an organized national church. Although Americans made certain that no organized national church would exist in their young country, they have, over the years, developed a number of informal practices that combine national patriotism with religion. The

main function of this national religion is to provide support for the dominant values of the nation and comfort in times of grief. Thus, it does in an informal and less organized way what nationally organized churches did for European nations in earlier times.

21 Some observers of American society believe that the various practices that are called the national religion can have harmful effects, however. Sometimes these practices can help to create a climate in which disagreement with current national practices is discouraged or not tolerated. There have been times when citizens have disagreed with their government's decision to wage war, for example, and other Americans accused them of being unpatriotic. This happened during the war in Vietnam, when protesters were told, "America—love it, or leave it." A similar division of opinion occurred over the U.S. decision to invade Iraq in 2003.

The Religious Landscape Today: Polarization Vs. Pluralism

22 The religious landscape in the United States is complicated and changing. In *American Grace: How Religion Divides and Unites Us*, Robert D. Putnam and David E. Campbell discuss two forces at work in the United States today: religious polarization and pluralism. There is growing polarization between evangelicals, or religious conservatives, and secular liberals. Increasingly, Americans find themselves at one end of the spectrum or another, while the number of moderates in the middle decreases. Evangelicals believe in strictly following the teachings of the Bible (as they and the church leaders interpret it) and regularly attending worship services. They are socially (and often politically) more conservative than religious moderates or liberals. They may be against abortion and gay marriage, for example, and they may believe in creationism instead of evolution. The debate between religious conservatives and liberals can grow quite heated. Some commentators have even described this split as "culture wars." However, Putnam and Campbell say there is another force at work:

> *America peacefully combines a high degree of religious devotion with tremendous religious diversity—including growing ranks of the nonreligious.... How can religious pluralism coexist with religious polarization? The answer lies in the fact that, in America, religion is highly fluid....Religions compete, adapt and evolve as individual Americans freely move from one congregation to another, and even from one religion to another.*

Firefighters hang a giant American flag over the side of the American Express tower.

23 What American value has allowed religious pluralism to coexist with religious polarization? The fundamental American belief in individual freedom and the right of individuals to practice their own religion is at the center of religious experience in the United States. The great diversity of ethnic backgrounds has produced a climate of religious pluralism, and most of the religions of the world are now practiced here. Although the overwhelming majority of Americans are Christians, other religions and people from other cultures make important contributions to the religious landscape. There are now about as many Muslims living in the United States as there are Jews. People of Hispanic origin now make up nearly one-half of the Catholic Church here. In addition to Buddhism and Hinduism, Asian immigrants have brought with them other traditional religions of East Asia—Daoism, Confucianism, and Shintoism. And the Native American religions are still practiced and studied today, particularly for their teachings about living in harmony with nature.

24 The Census of American Religious Congregations has been tracking 236 different religions in the United States, from Albanian Orthodox to Zoroastrian, every ten years. They report in the latest census that Muslims (Islam) and Mormons (Church of the Latter-day Saints) are two of the fastest growing religious groups in the country. Between 2000 and 2010, the number of Muslims grew by 66 percent and the number of Mormons grew by 44 percent, while the number of Protestants fell by 5 percent to below 50 percent of the population for the first time. (There are also estimates of about one million Buddhists and Hindus.) Remembering that the total population of the United States is now over 310 million, here are America's top 10 religions:

1.	Catholic	58.9 million
2.	Baptist	27.2 million
3.	Methodist	12.2 million
4.	Non-denominational Evangelical Protestant	12.2 million
5.	Lutheran	7.2 million
6.	Latter-day Saints (Mormons)	6.4 million
7.	Pentecostal	5.8 million
8.	Presbyterian Reformed	5.0 million
9.	Islam (Muslims)	2.6 million
10.	Judaism (Jews)	2.3 million*

Source: The Association of Religion Data Archives

American Muslims at prayer

25 One of the most dramatic developments in recent years is the rapid rise in the number of people who say they have no religious affiliation. Almost 20 percent of adults and one third of those under 30 do not consider themselves to be a part of any particular church or faith. They are referred to as the unaffiliated, or the "nones" (since they choose "none" when asked about their religious affiliation), and now number 49 million. Interestingly, 68 percent of them say that they believe in God, but they

have no desire to be part of organized religion. Often they refer to themselves as being "spiritual, but not religious." They are more liberal and more secular than Americans who are affiliated with some religious group.

26 Another important development is the decline in the membership of traditional mainline Protestant churches. In the list of top ten faiths above, only four are traditional Protestant denominations (Baptist, Methodist, Lutheran, and Presbyterian). Mainline churches tend to be moderate and more liberal than the evangelicals and religious conservatives, with the exception of the Baptist Church. Most Baptists are evangelicals. (Pentecostals are evangelicals, too, but they are not generally considered as traditional mainline Protestants.)

27 There has also been a rise in the number of *non-denominational* evangelical Protestants. These churches are not affiliated with a traditional Protestant denomination and are often community churches organized by dynamic religious leaders. Some of them are "megachurches." Rick Warren's Saddleback Church in Orange County, California, which was founded in 1980, now has 100,000 members and an average weekend attendance of over 20,000. Megachurches have contemporary worship services and often focus on helping people live "happy, fulfilled Christian lives," a modern message of self-improvement. They are an example of how some American churches have evolved and adapted to meet changing needs, particularly of young people.

Religious Diversity in the United States: A Spiritual Kaleidoscope[6]

28 This chapter began with the assertion that the United States has been and still is a religious country, but that the religious landscape is complicated and changing. The historical "live and let live" tolerance of early Protestant faiths has led to a modern acceptance of diverse religions by most Americans. Although there are some who are intolerant and would disagree, the majority of Americans believe that there are many paths to God and their particular religion is not the only valid faith. The traditional lines drawn between members of different religions have broken down so that Americans frequently marry people of different faiths. This is especially true of younger Americans. More and more people work with, live near, and are friends with people of different cultures and faiths. This has created a spiritual kaleidoscope, where people move between faiths, sometimes creating their own collection of beliefs drawn from a number of different religious traditions.

29 The belief that the individual, not the organized church, should be the center of religious life has encouraged a tolerance and acceptance of all faiths by most Americans. Most also believe that religious freedom must be protected—that everyone has the right to practice his or her own religion without interference by the government or anyone else. America's religious heritage seems to have encouraged certain basic values that members of many diverse faiths find easy to accept. This has helped to unite many different religious groups in the United States without requiring any to abandon their faiths. Cultural and religious pluralism has also created a context of tolerance that further strengthens the American reality of many different religions living peacefully within a single nation.

[6] *kaleidoscope: colors or patterns that change quickly*

AFTER YOU READ

Look at the predictions you made on page 53 before reading the chapter. Did you find the information in the sections you predicted? Answer these questions:

1. How many Americans say they believe in God?

2. What are the most popular religions in the United States?

3. Do Americans have an official national religion?

4. How has religion shaped American values?

Understand Main Ideas

In Chapters 1 and 2, we discussed the importance of organizing and presenting main ideas for clear writing and formal speaking in English. Academic writing in English looks like a series of capital letter Ts:

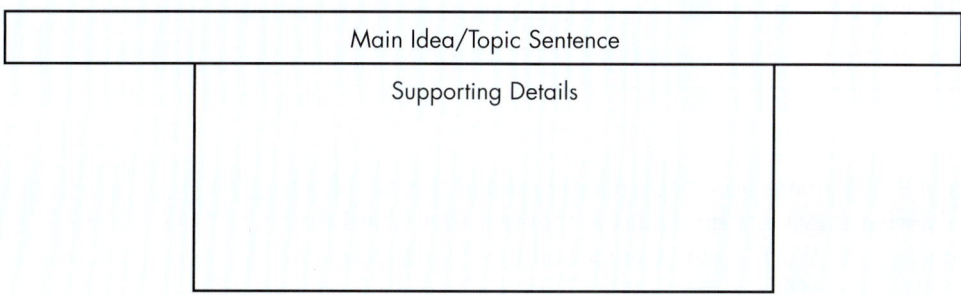

Usually, each paragraph has a topic sentence that states the main idea of the paragraph. Often, this is the first sentence. The rest of the paragraph contains supporting details that develop or explain the main idea. There are many types of supporting details:

- *definitions*
- *facts or opinions*
- *statistics*
- *examples or illustrations*
- *descriptions*
- *quotations*

The first paragraph of this reading begins with a topic sentence supported by facts, statistics, and examples. (See page 54.) Look back at the reading and find the paragraphs that begin with the following topic sentences. Then find the details that support the main ideas stated in the topic sentence.

1. Topic sentence: Some of the early European Protestant leaders believed that people who were blessed by God might be recognized in the world by their material success. (page 56)

   Supporting detail: (quotation) _____

   _____

   _____

2. Topic sentence: American religious leaders, however, never encouraged the idea of gaining wealth without hard work and self-discipline. (page 57)

   Supporting detail: (definition) _____

   _____

   _____

3. Topic sentence: Historically, some extremely wealthy Americans have made generous contributions to help others. (page 58)

   Supporting details: (example and quotation) _____

   _____

   _____

4. Topic sentences: All Americans and many people around the world can remember exactly what they were doing at the moment they heard that terrorists had attacked the World Trade Center and the Pentagon on September 11, 2001. (page 59)

   Supporting details: (descriptions) _____

   _____

   _____

5. Topic sentence: The belief that the individual, not the organized church, should be the center of religious life has encouraged a tolerance and acceptance of all faiths by most Americans. (page 62)

   Supporting details: (example and facts) _____

   _____

   _____

Understand Details

Write **T** if the statement is true and **F** if it is false according to the information in the chapter.

_____ 1. Although there is cultural pluralism in the United States, there is no religious pluralism.

_____ 2. Protestant denominations (such as Methodist, Baptist, and Presbyterian) are part of the Roman Catholic Church.

_____ 3. No single church has become the center of religious life in the United States because the emphasis is on the individual, not a particular church.

_____ 4. Most of the settlers who came to colonial America to escape religious persecution in Europe were Catholics.

_____ 5. The Constitution of the United States separates church and state and forbids the government from ever establishing a national church.

_____ 6. Protestantism encourages a strong desire for self-improvement.

_____ 7. Some American Protestant leaders have said that people who are rich have been blessed by God.

_____ 8. The Protestant work ethic is the belief that people should share their time and their wealth to help others.

_____ 9. Evangelicals are Christians who are religiously and socially liberal.

_____ 10. The national religion of the United States is a mixture of religion and patriotism.

Talk About It

Work in small groups and choose one or more of these questions to discuss.

1. Do the majority of the people in your country belong to one particular church or religious faith? Is there a government-supported church or official religion? What are the advantages and disadvantages of having a government recognize one official religion for a country?

2. The United States does not have a national legal requirement for workers to have a certain number of paid vacation days. Does your country have such a legal requirement? Explain.

3. What is humanitarianism? Do you think that people should volunteer their time to help the poor?

4. What do you think being _religious_ means?

SKILL BUILDING

Improve Your Reading Skills: Compare and Contrast Information

In this chapter, the term "evangelical" is used to describe Americans who belong to several different religious groups. Some polls estimate that about 26 percent of Americans are evangelical. What is an evangelical, then? Reread paragraphs 10, 22, and 26 that mention evangelicals, and compare and contrast the information found there with the two definitions below. How are the definitions the same and how are they different? How do the definitions compare and contrast with information in the chapter? Summarize your findings.

The National Association of Evangelicals website www.nae.net states that evangelicals are a diverse group found in many churches, denominations, and nations. Many evangelicals rarely use the term to describe themselves. They focus instead on core theological convictions summarized by historian David Bebbington:

Conversionism: the belief that lives need to be transformed through a "born-again" experience and a life-long process of following Jesus

Activism: the expression and demonstration of the gospel in missionary and social reform efforts

Biblicism: a high regard for and obedience to the Bible as the ultimate authority

Crucicentrism: a stress on the sacrifice of Jesus Christ on the cross (crucifixion) as making possible the redemption of humanity

Wikipedia stated that evangelicals have four beliefs:

The need for personal conversion, or being "born again"

A high regard for biblical authority

An emphasis on teachings that proclaim the saving death and resurrection of the Son of God, Jesus Christ

Active expression and sharing of the gospel

Develop Your Critical Thinking Skills

Create a questionnaire with a rating scale.

In American Grace: How Religion Divides and Unites Us, Putnam and Campbell describe their measure of "religiososity," or what it means to be "religious." They used six questions, which they say can apply to any religion:

How frequently do you attend religious services?
How frequently do you pray outside of religious services?
How important is religion in your daily life?
How important is your religion to your sense of who you are?
Are you a strong believer in your religion?
How strong is your belief in God?

Choose answers for each question and give points for each answer. For example:

How frequently do you attend religious services?
every day — 5 pts.
more than once a week — 4 pts.
every week — 3 pts.
every month — 2 pts.
several times a year — 1 pt.
never — 0 pts.

Look at the polls that follow to get ideas for answers. When you have scores for each question, add the points to create your scale of what it means to be "religious."

UNAFFILIATED, BUT NOT UNIFORMLY SECULAR

	U.S. General Public %	Unaffiliated %	Affiliated %
How important is religion in your life?			
Very important	58	14	67
Somewhat	22	19	24
Not too/not at all	18	65	8
Don't know/refused	1	1	—
	100	100	100
Believe in God or universal spirit?			
Yes, absolutely certain	69	30	77
Yes, but less certain	23	38	20
No	7	27	2
Other/don't know	2	5	1
	100	100	100
Frequency of prayer			
Daily	58	21	66
Weekly/monthly	21	20	22
Seldom/never	19	59	11
Don't know	2	1	1
	100	100	100
Think of self as . . .			
Religious person	65	18	75
Spiritual but not religious	18	37	15
Neither spiritual nor religious	15	42	8
Don't know	2	2	1
	100	100	100

Source: Pew Research Center survey, June 28–July 9, 2012. Q50, Q53–54, Q52, Q97a–b.
Figures may not add to 100% due to rounding.

PROFILE OF THE "SPIRITUAL BUT NOT RELIGIOUS"

Who are the "spiritual but not religious," and how do they compare with those who reject both labels, as well as those who do consider themselves religious?

RELIGIOUS PROFILE

	Among those who identify as . . .		
	Spiritual not religious	Religious	Neither
	%	%	%
Religion			
Protestant	39	60	21
Catholic	18	25	17
Unaffiliated	32	5	52
Other	9	8	8
Don't know	2	2	3
	100	100	100
Worship attendance			
Weekly or more	19	52	6
Monthly/yearly	34	35	30
Seldom/never	47	13	64
Don't know	0	1	–
	100	100	100
Importance of religion			
Very important	31	78	7
Somewhat important	32	20	23
Not too/not at all important	36	2	69
Don't know	1	–	1
	100	100	100
Frequency of prayer			
Daily or more	44	73	11
Weekly/monthly	25	20	22
Seldom/never	31	5	66
Don't know	1	2	2
	100	100	100
Do you believe in God?			
Yes, believe in God	92	99	60
Absolutely certain	55	84	20
Fairly certain	25	13	26
Not too/not at all certain	10	1	13
Don't know how certain	1	1	2
Do not believe in God	7	1	33
Other/Don't know	2	1	6
	100	100	100
N	729	2,077	610

Source: Pew Research Center survey, June 28–July 9, 2012. Combined Q97a–b, RELIG, ATTEND, Q50, Q52, Q53–54. Based on those who think of themselves as a religious person, as a spiritual but not a religious person, and neither a religious nor a spiritual person. Figures may not add to 100% due to rounding.

Build Your Vocabulary

Use Prefixes

Some words use prefixes to create negative or opposite meanings:

connect—disconnect   patriotic—unpatriotic   significant—insignificant

Make the following words negative by adding the correct prefix. Check your answer in a dictionary.

| dis- | un- | in- |

1. tolerance   ____tolerance

2. affiliated   ____affiliated

3. respectful   ____respectful

4. selfish   ____selfish

5. agreement   ____agreement

6. motivated   ____motivated

Use the six words with their new prefixes in sentences.

Some prefixes add to the meaning of a word. For example, self-identify means to identify yourself as having some particular identity. Someone may self-identify as spiritual, evangelical, or non-religious.

Write a brief definition for each of these words:

1. Self-improvement _____

2. Self-discipline _____

3. Self-reliance _____

Use Suffixes

Some words add suffixes, or endings, to add to the meaning of a word. For example, the suffix –ism means a set of ideas or beliefs, or the action or process of doing something. Humanitarianism means the belief in being humanitarian—concerned with improving bad living conditions and preventing unfair treatment of people.

Write a brief definition for each of these words:

1. Volunteerism _____

2. Activism _____

3. Hinduism _____

4. Catholicism _____

5. Atheism _____

6. Agnosticism _____

7. Secularism _____

8. Mormonism _____

9. Judaism _____

10. Protestantism _____

Recognize Word Forms

Many adverbs end in –ly. Usually, these words are the adverb forms of words that function as adjectives.

Use the following adverbs to fill in the blanks in the sentences from the chapter. (Some have more than one possible answer.)

| consequently | immediately | solely | traditionally |
| historically | particularly | spontaneously | |

1. In Protestantism, every individual is _____ responsible for his or her own soul.

2. There was freedom of religion in the new nation. _____ there were many Protestants who came seeking religious freedom.

3. _____, some wealthy Americans, such as Andrew Carnegie in the 1900s, have made generous contributions to help others.

4. Crowds _____ sang "God Bless America" in the weeks after 9/11.

5. The Native American religions are studied today, _____ for their teachings about living in harmony with nature.

6. _____ after 9/11, there was an outpouring of love, charity, and patriotism around the country.

7. Protestantism has _____ encouraged a strong and restless desire for self-improvement.

Collocations

This chapter has many adjective + noun collocations.

Circle the one word in each of the following groups that will not form a collocation with the boldfaced word.

EXAMPLE: European / colonial / (national) / early / British **settlers**

(You can say European settlers, colonial settlers, early settlers, or British settlers, but not national settlers.)

1. **spiritual**   values / beliefs / practices / banks / experiences
2. **religious**   freedom / diversity / grief / persecution / climate
3. **overwhelming**   grief / examples / fear / frustration / sadness

More AWL Words

Test your knowledge of these AWL words by matching them with their definitions.

_____ 1. capacity   a. a set of beliefs about how people should live

_____ 2. adapt   b. put things in a place where people can see them

_____ 3. consequently   c. an amount of money

_____ 4. display   d. ability to do or produce something

_____ 5. function   e. relating to the most basic parts of something

_____ 6. fundamental   f. as a result

_____ 7. liberal   g. gradually change to fit a new situation

_____ 8. devote   h. give time or money to help

_____ 9. philosophy   i. the usual purpose of something

_____ 10. sum   j. supporting changes in social systems that give people more equality

EXPAND YOUR KNOWLEDGE

Ask Americans

Americans have a saying, "Never discuss religion and politics." These are not "safe" topics because they may touch on personal beliefs. Most Americans, however, will be willing to talk to you if you make it clear that this is an assignment for a class you are taking. You could begin by saying: "I wonder if you could help me with an assignment I have. I'm taking a course at _____ (school) and I am supposed to interview Americans about their religious beliefs. Would you be willing to answer some questions? I won't use your name. (Show them the list of questions.) Please tell me if there are any questions you don't feel comfortable answering."

Interview several Americans and ask them questions about their religion. Choose questions from the questionnaire and rating scale you created on pages 66–67. If you cannot ask Americans, interview international students or your classmates. Compare your findings with your classmates' findings and with the poll results on page 67.

Proverbs and Sayings

There are a number of proverbs and sayings about right and wrong. For example, the golden rule, "Do unto others as you would have them do unto you," means that you should treat people the way you want them to treat you. What proverbs do you know that deal with right and wrong?

Ask Americans to explain these sayings to you. Do they know any more sayings about money? Collect as many sayings as you can and share them with your classmates.

1. A penny saved is a penny earned.
2. Early to bed and early to rise makes a man healthy, wealthy, and wise.
3. Save something for a rainy day.
4. Eat, drink, and be merry, for tomorrow you die.
5. Idle hands are the devil's workshop.

Observe the Media

Working with a partner, look at the titles of some popular American self-help books. What aspects of life do they promise to improve? What conclusions about American values can you draw from these titles?

Collect other book titles by visiting an American bookstore, checking best-seller lists or websites, and looking at ads for books in magazines and newspapers. Share your findings with the class.

Use the Internet

Work with a partner. Search the Internet and visit these websites. Discuss your findings.

1. The Committee for the Study of Religion at Harvard University sponsors a website—http://www.pluralism.org/. The website lists information about their studies of religious diversity in the United States. Go to their website and learn about their mission and what they do. How do they define pluralism? What religions do they list, and how are they practiced? Where are the religious centers for Islam, Buddhism, and Hinduism?

2. Americans volunteer in many ways: at churches, in libraries or museums, in hospitals, in animal shelters, or in schools. Former President Jimmy Carter volunteers with Habitat for Humanity. The goal of this organization is to build houses for poor people. Visit their website www.habitat.org and learn about what they do. If you are in the United States, you can find a Habitat for Humanity project near where you are.

3. The following people are highly regarded by some Americans for their religious work. Do you know who these people are and why they are important? Choose one person, do research about him or her on the Internet, and then tell a classmate about your findings.

   - Martin Luther King, Jr.
   - Desmond Tutu
   - Mother Teresa
   - Muhammad

WRITE ABOUT IT

The Gallup polling organization has published a book titled God Is Alive and Well: The Future of Religion in America based on more than one million interviews, 320,000 of which were conducted in 2012. Here is the "bottom line" of what they found:

America remains a generally religious nation, with more than two-thirds of the nation's residents classified as very or moderately religious. These overall national averages, however, conceal dramatic regional differences in religiosity across the 50 states and the District of Columbia. Residents of Southern states are generally the most religious, underscoring the validity of the "Bible Belt" sobriquet [name] often used to describe this region. Coupled with the Southern states in the high-religiosity category is Utah, the majority of whose residents are Mormon—the most religious group in America today. On the other hand, residents of New England and a number of far Western states tend to be the least religious.

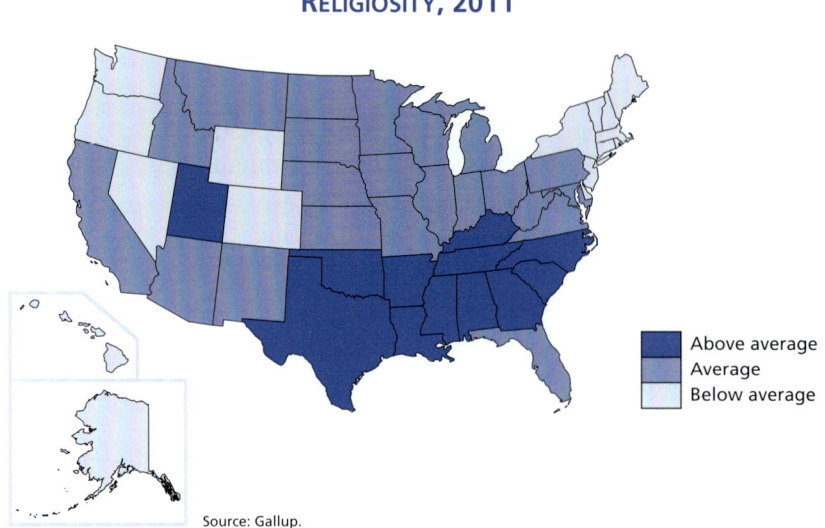

Write a report describing the religions in your country. Are there any regions where people are more religious than those of another region? If you can find one or more maps to show the distribution of religions there, include them in your report. Check on the Pew Research site and look at "The Global Religious Landscape: A Report on the Size and Distribution of the World's Major Religious Groups as of 2010." You may be able to find information about the distribution of the religions in your country there.
http://www.pewforum.org/maps

MAJORITY RELIGION, BY COUNTRY

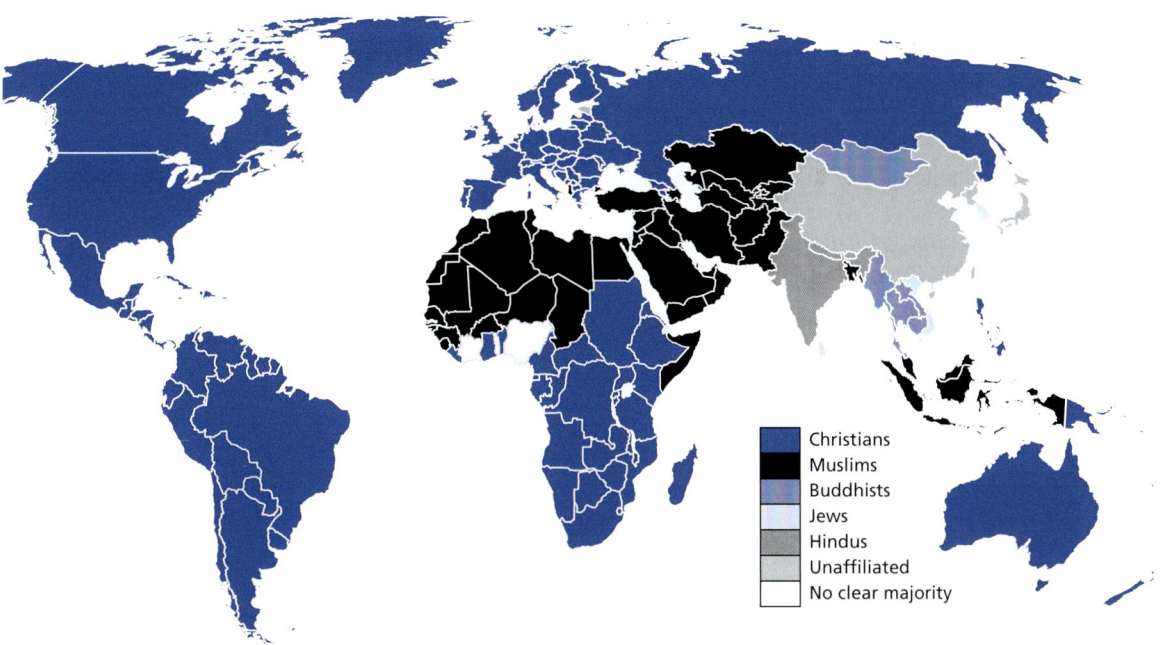

Review the Understand Main Ideas exercise on page 63. Use the graphic organizer for each paragraph of your composition. Write a clear topic sentence for the beginning of each paragraph and then list the supporting details below. Review the types of supporting details to get ideas of what kinds of information to use. You should have one "T" organizer for the introduction, several for your main ideas, and one for your conclusion. Try to make your conclusion refer back to your introduction. After you fill out the "T" organizers, write your composition.

Main Idea
Supporting Details

The American Religious Heritage

EXPLORE ON YOUR OWN

Books to Read

Ross Douthat, *Bad Religion: How We Became a Nation of Heretics*—The author believes that the United States, which does not have a national church, is losing the Christian center that has helped hold the diverse nation together.

Diana L. Eck, *A New Religious America: How a "Christian Country" Has Become the World's Most Religiously Diverse Nation*—Eck explains how the immigration of Muslims, Buddhists, Hindus, Sikhs, and other religious groups has brought religious pluralism to the United States.

Nathaniel Hawthorne, *The Scarlet Letter*—Set in early colonial times in New England, this classic story reveals the impact of an act of passion in a Puritan society.

Frank Newport, Editor, *God Is Alive and Well: The Future of Religion in America*—Newport discusses religion in America based on more than a million Gallup interviews.

Robert D. Putnam and David E. Campbell, *American Grace: How Religion Divides and Unites Us*—Putnam and Campbell discuss how personal religious ties bring a diversity of religions together in a pluralist society.

Movies to See

Doubt—The conservative principal of a Catholic school, a nun, accuses a popular, liberal priest of molesting a student.

Elmer Gantry—Elmer Gantry, a salesman, teams up with Sister Sharon Falconer, an evangelist, to sell religion in America in the 1920s.

Pay It Forward—A social studies teacher assigns his students the task of doing a favor for another person when someone else has done something for them, paying the favor forward.

Saved—In this comedy, teenagers in a religious school have difficulty deciding what is really the right thing to do.

A Simple Plan—Two brothers find a bag of stolen money and must decide what to do with it.

CHAPTER 4

THE FRONTIER HERITAGE

This ever-retreating frontier of free land is the key to American development.
Frederick Jackson Turner (1861–1932)

Why are Americans still so fascinated with life on the old western frontier, and how did the frontier shape American values?

BEFORE YOU READ

Preview Vocabulary

A. Work with a partner to answer the questions. Make sure you understand the meaning of the AWL words in italics.

1. If "spiritual" has to do with your soul, and "mental" has to do with your mind, what does *physical* have to do with?
2. If people are discussing a *controversial* topic, such as religion or politics, would you expect there to be a lot of agreement or disagreement?
3. If we say that the settlement of the western frontier had an *impact* on American culture, do we mean that it had some influence or that it was not very important?
4. If you wanted to *reinforce* your cowboy *image*, what would you wear?
5. Would someone who had a "can-do" attitude be an *optimist* or a *pessimist*?
6. Is gun control an *issue* in the United States, or do all Americans believe that everyone should have complete access to guns? What percentage of American households do you think have guns?

B. Read this paragraph from the chapter. Then use context clues and write the correct word next to its definition.

How Americans reacted to the terrorist attacks of September 11, 2001, reveals another legacy of the frontier: Americans' willingness to take the law into their own hands to protect themselves and their families. This tendency usually appears when Americans believe the police cannot adequately protect them. For example, when the passengers fought with the terrorists on the 9/11 flight that crashed in Pennsylvania, they were hailed as heroes.

_____ 1. well enough for a particular purpose

_____ 2. described someone as being very good

_____ 3. shows something that was hidden

_____ 4. acted in response

_____ 5. a situation that exists as a result of things that happened at an earlier time

Preview Content

A. Read the quotation at the beginning of the chapter. Discuss these questions with your classmates.

1. What is a frontier?
2. Why do you think Turner says that the frontier is the "key" to understanding the development of America?
3. Which of these can be a frontier?

   _____ the border between two countries

   _____ an unsettled region

   _____ space exploration

   _____ deep-ocean exploration

   _____ understanding how the mind works

   _____ new or experimental medical treatments

4. What American movies about the Old West have you seen?

B. Before you read the chapter, look at the headings of each section. Examine the photos and other illustrations. Predict three values that were reinforced by the frontier experience. Write your predictions here.

1. _____
2. _____
3. _____

THE IMPACT OF THE AMERICAN FRONTIER

1. Although the American civilization took over and replaced the frontier more than a century ago, the heritage of the frontier is still evident in the United States today. Many people are still fascinated by the frontier because it has been particularly important in shaping American values. When Ronald Reagan was president in the 1980s, he liked to recall the image of life on the frontier. He was often photographed on his western ranch—chopping wood or riding his horse, and wearing his cowboy hat. More recently, in the 2000s, President George W. Bush reinforced this cowboy image by inviting members of the press to photograph him on his Texas ranch, wearing his cowboy boots and hat.

2. For many years, the frontier experience was romanticized[1] in popular movies and television shows that featured cowboy heroes fighting Indian villains. Little attention was given to the tragic story of what really happened to the Native Americans, also known as the American Indians. Today, most Americans are more aware of the darker side of the settling of the continent, when thousands of American Indians were killed and their lands were taken. When the buffalo were hunted and killed off by the white settlers, the Indians' major source of food and clothing was lost, and much of their culture was destroyed. Today, there is a renewed interest in Indian cultures, and the Smithsonian has a museum in Washington, D.C. that is dedicated to Indian culture.

3. The frontier experience began when the first colonists settled on the east coast of the continent in the 1600s. It ended about 1890 when the last western lands were settled. The American frontier consisted of the relatively unsettled regions of the United States, usually found in the western part of the country. Here, both land and life were more rugged and primitive than in the more settled eastern part. As one frontier area was settled, people began moving farther west into the next unsettled area, sweeping aside the Native Americans as they went. By settling one frontier area after another, Americans moved across an entire continent that was 2,700 miles wide. They came to believe that it was their destiny to control all the land, and eventually they did. The Native Americans were given small portions of land, called *reservations*, to control, but the United States government broke many promises and created much misery for the Indian nations.

4. While most Americans have a more balanced view of the settling of the West, many Americans still see aspects of the frontier, its people, and their beliefs as inspiring examples of traditional American values in their original and purest form. How did the frontier movement, which lasted more than two centuries, help to shape these basic American values?

5. To be sure, the frontier provided many inspiring examples of hard work as forests were turned into towns, and towns into large cities. The competitive race for success was rarely more colorful or adventurous than on the western frontier. The rush for gold in California, for silver in Montana, and for fertile land in all the western territories provided endless stories of high adventure. When it was announced that almost 2 million acres of good land in Oklahoma would be opened for settlement in April 1889, thousands of settlers gathered on the border waiting for the exact time to be announced. When it

---

[1] romanticized: talked or thought about things in a way that made them seem more attractive than they really were

The 1889 rush to claim land in Oklahoma

was, they literally[2] raced into the territory in wagons and on horseback to claim the best land they could find for themselves.

6   Although daily life on the frontier was usually less dramatic than the frontier adventure stories would lead one to believe, even the ordinary daily life of frontier men and women exemplified[3] national values in a form which seemed purer to many Americans than the life of those living in the more settled, more cultivated eastern United States.

7   Individual freedom, self-reliance, and equality of opportunity have perhaps been the values most closely associated with the frontier heritage of America. Throughout their history, Americans have tended to view the frontier settler as the model of the free individual. This is probably because there was less control over the individual on the frontier than anywhere else in the United States. There were few laws and few established social or political institutions to confine people living on the frontier. In the United States, where freedom from outside social controls has traditionally been valued, the frontier has been idealized, and it still serves as a basis for a nostalgic[4] view of the early United States, a simpler time that was lost when the country became urbanized and

---

[2] *literally: according to the most basic or original meaning of a word or expression*

[3] *exemplified: was a very typical example of something*

[4] *nostalgic: feeling or expressing a slight sadness when remembering happy events or experiences from the past*

more complex. Many people living in the West today still hold these beliefs about freedom from government controls.

Self-Reliance and the Rugged Individualist

8 Closely associated with the frontier ideal of the free individual is the ideal of self-reliance. If the people living on the frontier were free of many of society's rules, they were also denied many of society's comforts and conveniences. They had to be self-reliant. Men and women often constructed their own houses, hunted, tended their own gardens, and made their own clothing and household items.

9 The self-reliant frontiersman has been idealized by Americans who have made him the classic American male hero: *the rugged individualist*. This hero is a man who has been made physically tough and rugged by the conditions of frontier life. He is skilled with guns and other weapons. He needs no help from others and often appears in stories as alone, unmarried, and without children. Standing alone, he can meet all the dangers that life on the frontier brings and he is strong enough to extend his protection beyond himself to others.

10 There are two types of heroic rugged individualists. Each is drawn from a different stage of life on the frontier. In the early frontier, which existed before the Civil War of the 1860s, the main struggle was man against the wilderness. Daniel Boone is probably the best-known hero of this era. Boone explored the wilderness country of Kentucky in the 1760s and 1770s. On one trip, he stayed in the wilderness for two years, successfully matching his strength and skills against the dangers of untamed nature and hostile Native Americans. In 1778, Boone was captured by Native Americans who were so impressed with his physical strength and skills that they made him a member of their tribe. Later, he succeeded in making a daring escape. Boone's heroic strength is seen primarily in his ability to master the harsh challenges of the wilderness. Although he had to fight against Indians from time to time, he is admired mainly as a survivor and conqueror of the wilderness, not as a fighter.

11 The second type of heroic rugged individualist is drawn from the last phase of the western frontier, which lasted from the 1860s until the 1890s. By this time, the wilderness was largely conquered. The struggle now was no longer man against nature, but man against man. Cattlemen and cowboys* fought against farmers, outlaws, Native Americans, and each other for control of the remaining western lands. The traditions of law and order were not yet well established, and physical violence was frequent. The frontier became known as "the Wild West."

12 It is not surprising, then, that the hero drawn from this period is primarily a fighter. He is admired for his ability to beat other men in fistfights,[5] or to win in a gunfight. The principal source of his heroism is his physical prowess[6] and he is strong enough to defeat two or three ordinary men at one time. This rugged individualist is typically a defender of good against evil.

13 This hero of the Wild West is based on memories of a number of gunfighters and lawmen of the time, men such as Jesse

---

*Cattlemen were men who raised large herds of cattle as a business and needed large areas of land on which their cattle could graze before being sent to market. Cowboys usually worked for the cattlemen. They would spend most of the day on horseback rounding up the cattle or taking them on long drives to market.

[5] *fistfights:* fights using bare hands with the fingers curled in toward the palm

[6] *prowess:* great skill at doing something

James and Wyatt Earp. The Wild West hero had more impact on the American idea of heroism than Daniel Boone, the hero of the earlier wilderness frontier. It is the Wild West hero who has inspired countless western movies; until the 1960s, 25 percent of all American movies made were westerns.

American Macho Heroes

14 Through movies and television programs, this Wild West hero has helped shape the American idea of "macho," or male, strength. For the most part, almost all American male heroes on television and in movies have traditionally had the common ability to demonstrate their strength through physical violence. Once the western macho hero had been created, the model for this hero was used in other settings—for soldiers in battle, and tough detectives and policemen fighting crime. From the cowboy heroes to the Terminator, Captain America, and Jenko, these heroes can fight with their fists, guns, and other weapons. Although there are movie and TV heroes who are respected more for their intelligence and sensitivity than their physical prowess, these classic macho male heroes still dominate much of American entertainment and video games. There are now also female versions of this macho image, including Katniss Everdeen, who competes in *the Hunger Games* armed with just a bow and arrow.

15 The image of the rugged individualist has been criticized for overlooking many factors that played a central part in the development of the frontier. First, the rugged individualist image overstates the importance of complete self-reliance and understates the importance of cooperation in building a new nation out of the wilderness. Second, because the image has been traditionally masculine, it has overlooked the importance of pioneer women and their strength, hard work, resourcefulness, and civilizing influence on the untamed frontier.

16 Finally, the rugged individualist image is criticized because of its emphasis on violence and the use of guns to solve problems. On the frontier, men did use guns to hunt and protect themselves and their families, but western movies romanticized and glorified gunfights in the Old West. The good guys and the bad guys "shot it out" in classic westerns such as *High Noon*. Incidentally, the classic old western movies always featured the "good guys" wearing white hats, while the "bad guys" wore black hats. Gradually, however, the western hero was largely replaced in the movies by the soldier or the crime fighter—guns still blazing—and the violence in movies, and later on TV and in video games, increased.

17 Some Americans worry about the impact of these entertainment heroes on the lives and imaginations of young people. At the very least, many young people have become desensitized[7] to the sight of violence and killings. In the twenty-first century, guns became a critical issue when there were shootings in several public schools and universities. It is all too easy for teenagers to get guns, and they are much more at risk of being killed by guns than adults are. The problem is particularly bad in the inner cities, where a number of young gang members carry guns. However, several of the most shocking incidents occurred in normally peaceful suburban communities, and now many schools require students to pass through metal detectors as they enter school buildings. Other recent mass shootings in public places included the wounding of Congresswoman Gabrielle Giffords in

---

[7] desensitized: made emotionally insensitive

2011, and the killing of people in a movie theater and children in an elementary school in 2012.

18 Americans have a long history of owning guns, and many people strongly believe having a gun in their house is an important right. In fact, the right to bear arms is even guaranteed by the Second Amendment of the Constitution, although there is debate about what the founding fathers meant by this:

> A well-regulated militia, being necessary to the security of a free state, the right of the people to keep and bear arms, shall not be infringed.

Today, there are well over 200 million privately held guns in the United States, enough for every adult to own one, and most estimates range from 270 to over 300 million. These are guns held by private citizens and do not include those possessed by the military or the police. Most firearms (rifles, shotguns, and hand guns) are owned by Americans who enjoy hunting, target practice, or gun collecting, and these individuals usually own more than one gun. Some firearms are owned by people who want their own gun for protection of their homes and families. For example, after the terrorist attacks of September 11, 2001, the sale of guns rose. Estimates are that anywhere from 25 percent to 45 percent of U.S. households now have at least one gun.

19 How Americans reacted to the terrorist attacks of September 11, 2001, reveals another legacy of the frontier: Americans' willingness to take the law into their own hands to protect themselves and their families. This tendency usually appears when Americans believe the police cannot adequately protect them. For example, when the passengers fought with the terrorists on the 9/11 flight that crashed in Pennsylvania, they were hailed as heroes.

20 The issue of gun control is very controversial in the United States, and people on both sides of the issue have strong opinions. Many Americans favor stricter government controls on the sale of guns, and they would not consider having a gun in their home. Others who oppose gun control feel strongly enough about the issue that they have created powerful political pressure groups, such as the National Rifle Association (NRA), which has worked to prevent most gun control legislation from passing. They argue that limiting gun sales will keep law-abiding citizens, not criminals, from owning guns. On the other side are gun-control organizations such as the Brady Campaign to Prevent Gun Violence named after Jim Brady, who was shot and became paralyzed when a man tried to kill President Ronald Reagan, and a new organization founded by Gabrielle Giffords

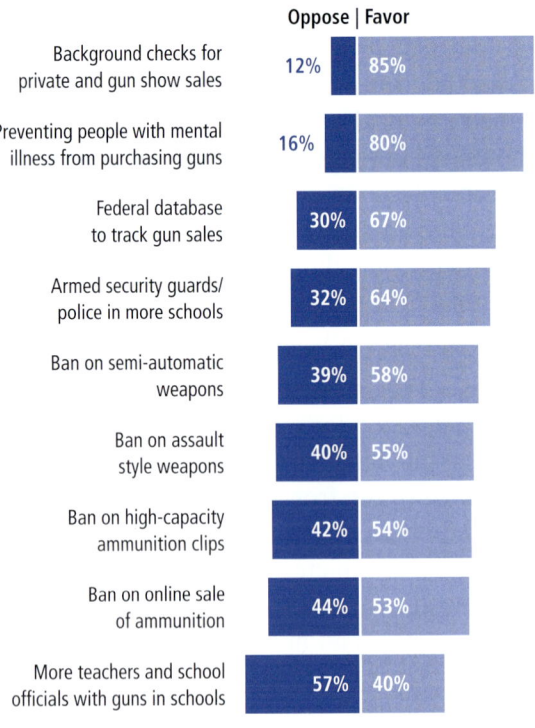

BROAD PUBLIC SUPPORT FOR MANY GUN POLICY PROPOSALS

	Oppose	Favor
Background checks for private and gun show sales	12%	85%
Preventing people with mental illness from purchasing guns	16%	80%
Federal database to track gun sales	30%	67%
Armed security guards/police in more schools	32%	64%
Ban on semi-automatic weapons	39%	58%
Ban on assault style weapons	40%	55%
Ban on high-capacity ammunition clips	42%	54%
Ban on online sale of ammunition	44%	53%
More teachers and school officials with guns in schools	57%	40%

Source: Pew Research Center Jan. 14, 2013.

and her husband Mark Kelly, Americans for Responsible Solutions. These groups are especially concerned about the sale of handguns and automatic assault rifles. They argue that American homes, particularly where there are children, are safer without guns. Interestingly, public opinion about gun control has remained about the same for over a decade, with Americans equally divided for and against it. After each mass shooting, the sale of guns rises, while those who oppose firearms (particularly automatic weapons) call for stronger gun control.

Inventiveness and the Can-Do Spirit

21   While the frontier idealized the rugged individual as the great American hero, it also respected the inventive individual. The need for self-reliance on the frontier encouraged a spirit of inventiveness. Frontier men and women not only had to provide most of their daily life essentials, but they were also constantly facing new problems and situations that demanded new solutions. Under these circumstances, they soon learned to experiment with new ways of doing things.

22   Observers from other countries were very impressed by the frontiersman's ability to invent useful new farm tools. They were equally impressed by the pioneer woman's ability to make clothing, candles, soap, and many other items needed for the daily life of her family. Lord Bryce, a famous English observer of American life, believed that the inventive skills of American pioneers enabled them to succeed at tasks beyond the abilities of most ordinary men and women in other countries. Although Americans in the more settled eastern regions of the United States created many of the most important inventions in the new nation, the western frontier had the effect of spreading the spirit of inventiveness throughout the population and helping it to become a national character trait.

23   The willingness to experiment and invent led to another American trait, a "can-do" spirit, or a sense of optimism that every

A nineteenth-century frontier family in front of their sod house

problem has a solution. Americans like to believe that a difficult problem can be solved immediately—an impossible one may take a little longer. They take pride in meeting challenges and overcoming difficult obstacles.[8] This can-do spirit has traditionally given Americans a sense of optimism about themselves and their country. Many have said that if the United States can land a man on the moon, no problem on earth is impossible. In the 1830s, Alexis de Tocqueville said that no other country in the world "more confidently seizes the future" than the United States. Traditionally, when times are hard, political leaders have reminded Americans of their frontier heritage and the tough determination of their pioneer ancestors; the can-do spirit is still a source of pride and inspiration.

Equality of Opportunity

24 The frontier is an expression of individual freedom and self-reliance in its purest (and most extreme) forms, and it is also a pure expression of the ideal of equality of opportunity. On the western frontier, there was more of a tendency for people to treat each other as social equals than there was in the more settled eastern regions of the country. On the frontier, the highest importance was placed on what people could do in their own lifetimes. Hardly any notice was taken of their ancestors. Frontier people were fond of saying, "What's above the ground is more important than what's beneath the ground."

25 Because so little attention was paid to a person's family background, the frontier offered a new beginning for many Americans who were seeking opportunities to advance themselves. One English visitor to the United States in the early 1800s observed that if Americans experienced disappointment or failure in business, in politics, or even in love, they moved west to make a new beginning. The frontier offered millions of Americans a source of hope for a fresh start in the competitive race for success and for a better life. On the frontier, there was a continuing need for new farmers, skilled laborers, merchants, lawyers, and political leaders.

26 There were fewer differences in wealth between rich and poor on the frontier than in the more settled regions of the nation. People lived, dressed, and acted more alike on the frontier than in other parts of the United States. The feeling of equality was shared by hired helpers who refused to be called "servants" or to be treated as such. One European visitor observed, "The clumsy gait[9] and bent body of our peasant is hardly ever seen here....Everyone walks erect[10] and easy." Wealthy travelers to the frontier were warned not to show off their wealth or to act superior to others if they wished to be treated politely.

27 The American frontier may not be *the key* to American development, as Frederick Jackson Turner said, but it is certainly one major factor. The frontier provided the space and conditions that helped to strengthen the American ideals of individual freedom, self-reliance, and equality of opportunity. On the frontier, these ideals were enlarged and made workable. Frontier ideas and customs were continuously passed along to the more settled parts of the United States as newer frontier regions took the place of older ones during a westward march of settlers which lasted more than two centuries. In this way, many of the frontier values became national values.

---

[8] *obstacles: things that make it difficult for someone to succeed*

[9] *clumsy gait: walking in an awkward way*

[10] *erect: in an upright position*

AFTER YOU READ

Understand Main Ideas

A. Check the predictions you made on page 79 before you read the chapter. Work with a partner. Answer these questions about the main ideas.

1. What are the three values that are traditionally associated with the frontier heritage?
2. What two new values are introduced in this chapter?
3. What are the two types of rugged individualists?
4. Describe someone with a can-do spirit.
5. What personal characteristics did the frontier settlers share?

B. In academic writing, paragraphs often begin with a topic sentence that contains the main idea. Read and highlight the first sentence of each paragraph of the reading. Then choose one main idea from each of the five main sections that you think is the most important. Write these ideas below. Compare your list with a partner's.

1. _____
2. _____
3. _____
4. _____
5. _____

Understand Details

Write **T** if the statement is true and **F** if it is false according to the information in the chapter.

_____ 1. The frontier experience began in about 1890 and is still continuing in the American West today.

_____ 2. One reason why many Americans are still fascinated by the frontier period is that it represents a time when the traditional basic American values were expressed in their purest form.

_____ 3. The settling of the frontier did little to affect the lives of the American Indians.

_____ 4. Daniel Boone is an example of the earliest type of rugged individualist hero, a man who fights against the wilderness.

_____ 5. The primary qualities of the American macho hero are intelligence, sensitivity, and caring for others.

_____ 6. It is difficult for the average American to buy a gun, so very few people own them.

_____ 7. Members of the NRA (and many gun owners) believe the right to own a gun is guaranteed in the United States Constitution.

_____ 8. The can-do spirit came from the willingness of the pioneers to work together on a cooperative project for the good of all.

_____ 9. On the frontier, family name and ancestry were more important than what a person could do.

_____ 10. On the frontier, the rich and the poor rarely mixed, and social class was more important than in the more settled regions.

Talk About It

Work in small groups and choose one or more of the following questions to discuss.

1. What effect do you think seeing violence on TV or in movies has on children? What happens when people become desensitized to violence?
2. What qualities should a true hero have? Who are some of your own personal heroes? Why do you admire and respect these people?
3. Would you have a gun in your own home? Why or why not?
4. If you were going to live in the wilderness for a week, what ten things would you take with you? Why?
5. Some Americans are nostalgic for the Old West, and there may be a period of your country's history that is romanticized in a similar way. If you could travel back in time to anywhere in the world, what place and what period in history would you like to visit? Why?

SKILL BUILDING

Improve Your Reading Skills: Scanning

Scanning is looking for a specific piece of information. Scan the chapter to find these dates. Write what happened next to the date to complete the timeline. Some are done for you.

1600s: _Settlers established colonies on the East Coast_

1760s and 1770s: _____

1778: _Boone was captured by Native Americans_

1860s: _____

April 1889: _____

1890 _____

Until 1960s: *25 percent of all American movies made were Westerns*

1980s: _____

2001: _____

Develop Critical Thinking Skills

Evaluating Pros and Cons: *Some consider space to be the final frontier, but spending money on space exploration has become controversial. Should we continue to support the international space station? Should we go to the moon again or plan to visit Mars? What are the benefits that have come from space exploration? What scientific discoveries have been made? Should we continue to send astronauts into space, or should we concentrate on unmanned missions? Think about the pros and cons of space exploration and fill out the chart below. You may wish to do some research on the Internet to get ideas.*

Pros of Space Exploration	Cons of Space Exploration

Build Your Vocabulary

Use Context Clues

Review the four kinds of context clues on pages 15–16 of Chapter 1. Use context clues to choose the correct words to fill in the blanks.

| desensitized | fascinated | nostalgic | romanticize |
| exemplified | fists | obstacles | |

1. In many action movies, the heroes are expected to be able to fight with their

   _____.

2. Some people prefer to _____ life on the frontier; they do not

   want to look at its negative aspects.

3. If you are reading a book that is so interesting that you can't put it down, you

   are _____ by the book.

The Frontier Heritage ★ 89

4. Frontier people were good examples of the American national values; these people _____ these values.

5. In order to succeed, people living on the frontier had to overcome many difficulties and _____, such as clearing the land for farming.

6. Americans like to remember the days on the frontier; they feel _____ about the Old West.

7. Some Americans worry that their children are becoming _____ to the violence and killing on television. It doesn't seem to bother their children.

More AWL Words

Test your knowledge of these AWL words in the chapter by matching the words with their definitions.

_____ 1. area   a. someone who is still alive after almost being killed

_____ 2. automatic   b. to keep someone in a place that they cannot leave

_____ 3. aware   c. something that tests strength, skill, or ability

_____ 4. challenge   d. someone paid to discover information

_____ 5. classic   e. easily noticed or understood; obvious

_____ 6. confine   f. the act of working with someone to achieve something

_____ 7. consist   g. realizing that a problem exists

_____ 8. construct   h. to build something large

_____ 9. cooperation   i. designed to operate by itself

_____ 10. deny   j. a fairly large area of a state

_____ 11. detective   k. a single thing in a set, group, or list

_____ 12. evident   l. to be made of a number of things

_____ 13. feature   m. to say that something is not true

_____ 14. item   n. considered important, with a value that lasts for a long time

_____ 15. phase   o. one of the stages of a process

_____ 16. region   p. something you notice because it seems interesting

_____ 17. survivor   q. a particular part of a country or city

Word Partners

Match the word partners to form collocations. Then use the correct collocations in the paragraph.

_____ 1. unsettled   a. fathers

_____ 2. law-abiding   b. spirit

_____ 3. can-do   c. individualism

_____ 4. founding   d. citizens

_____ 5. physical   e. region

_____ 6. rugged   f. prowess

Many Americans believe that when the _____(1)_____ wrote the Constitution, they meant to ensure the right of the people to own guns. They would argue that _____(2)_____ should be allowed to keep guns in their homes. The frontier strengthened the tradition of owning guns because it was an _____(3)_____, and settlers needed guns for hunting and protection. They had to be tough, and part of the frontier legacy is the _____(4)_____ and _____(5)_____ of Western movie heroes. Frontier settlers were also known for their inventiveness and their _____(6)_____.

Proverbs and Sayings

Ask Americans, if possible, to explain these proverbs and sayings about succeeding on your own or being tough. What similar proverbs and sayings are there in your culture?

1. Pull yourself up by the bootstraps.
2. If at first you don't succeed, try and try again.
3. Actions speak louder than words.
4. Life is what you make it.
5. Every problem has a solution.
6. When the going gets tough, the tough get going.

Ask Yourself

Do you agree or disagree with each of the following statements? Put a check under the number that indicates how you feel.

+2 = Strongly agree
+1 = Agree
 0 = No opinion
−1 = Disagree
−2 = Strongly disagree

	+2	+1	0	−1	−2
1. I love action movies that have a lot of gunfights.	___	___	___	___	___
2. A real man should be able to defend himself well and even win in a fistfight.	___	___	___	___	___
3. Intelligence and sensitivity in a man are more important than physical strength.	___	___	___	___	___
4. Watching fights in movies and on TV shows probably doesn't hurt children.	___	___	___	___	___
5. Having a gun in your home is a good way to protect yourself against robbers.	___	___	___	___	___
6. I believe people should not own guns and there should be strict laws controlling the sale of them.	___	___	___	___	___
7. Every problem has a solution.	___	___	___	___	___
8. What you do is more important than who your ancestors were.	___	___	___	___	___

Your teacher will place the numbers +2, +1, 0, −1, −2 around the room with the zero in the middle. As the teacher reads the above statements, walk to the number that reflects your opinion. Explain your choice.

Ask Americans

Read the statements from the previous exercise to several Americans. If this is not possible, try to interview people from several different countries. Ask them if they agree or disagree with each statement. Write their opinions in your notebook.

Think, Pair, Share

Think about this question, and write your answer. Then share it with a partner and with another pair of students.

In 2003, Arnold Schwarzenegger was elected Governor of California in a special election. During his campaign, he frequently referred to his movie role as "the Terminator" and talked about how he was going to clean up the state government. He was re-elected in 2006 and served as governor until 2011. Some people nicknamed him "the Governator." Based on the information in this chapter, why do you think this image appealed to Californian voters?

People Watching

Americans are very conscious of space and have a strong sense of territory—that is, the idea that a particular space belongs to them. Children may have a special place to play with their toys; Mom may have her own desk; Dad may have a workshop. Observe Americans at home, in a public place, or in a social situation to see how they use space. (Watch TV shows, if you are not in the United States.) If someone has been sitting in a particular chair and gets up, does the person tend to come back to the same chair? When someone asks, "Is that seat taken?" what does that person mean?

Conduct the following experiment and record the results in your journal.

Rule: When an American sits down at a table where a stranger is sitting alone, the American will choose a seat across from the other person or at least one chair away. The space is divided in half between them, and personal belongings must be kept on each person's respective side of an imaginary boundary line.

Observation: Observe people sitting in a public place where there are tables, such as a cafeteria or library. What happens when a stranger sits down at a table where a person is sitting alone? If someone sits down next to a stranger, what happens? How do the people acknowledge each other's presence? Does the person who was sitting there first move his or her belongings?

Experiment: Choose a table where a stranger is sitting alone and sit down in the next chair. What happens? Sit across from someone at a table and put some personal belongings (such as books) on the table in front of you. Push them toward the other person so that they are more than halfway across the table. What is the person's reaction?

Observe the Media

Work in small groups and choose one of the following activities to do together.

1. Cowboys and the Old West are frequently used in advertisements for blue jeans, SUVs, trucks, cars, and other American products. What image do they have? Why does this image help sell this or that product? Collect examples of ads in magazines or newspapers that use cowboys or western themes. Make a collage and share it with your classmates. Explain what the message is to the people who may buy these products.

2. Watch American TV shows or movies that have male heroes. Compare the heroes of several shows. How do they compare with the description of *American macho* presented in this chapter? What personality traits do they have? Compare the heroes of several shows. Reread the section on page 83 for help with descriptions.

Use the Internet

Choose one of these topics and do research on the Internet.

1. The rush to the West to find gold or silver created a number of very wealthy towns with hotels, opera houses, and beautiful houses. Today, many of these cities are "ghost towns." Some towns have no people living in them;
in others only a few people remain. Choose one of these ghost towns and find information about it. Answer the questions, and then write a summary of what you learned about the town.

Restored Western ghost town in Cody, Wyoming

Bodie or Calico, California	Pinos Altos, New Mexico
Gold Hill or Silver City, Utah	Goldfield, Nevada
Shakespeare Ghost Town, New Mexico	

- Why did people come to the town?
- What can be seen there today?
- What did you find most interesting about the town?

2. From May 1804 until September 1806, Meriwether Lewis and William Clark traveled from St. Louis, Missouri, to the Oregon coast, and back again. Work with a partner to find out more about this historic trip. Do an online search for "Lewis and Clark Expedition." Answer these questions.

- Who was the U.S. President who ordered the expedition?
- What territory had the United States purchased from France in 1803?
- What was the purpose of the expedition?
- Who was Sacajawea?
- What route did Lewis and Clark follow?
- What important discoveries did they make?

WRITE ABOUT IT

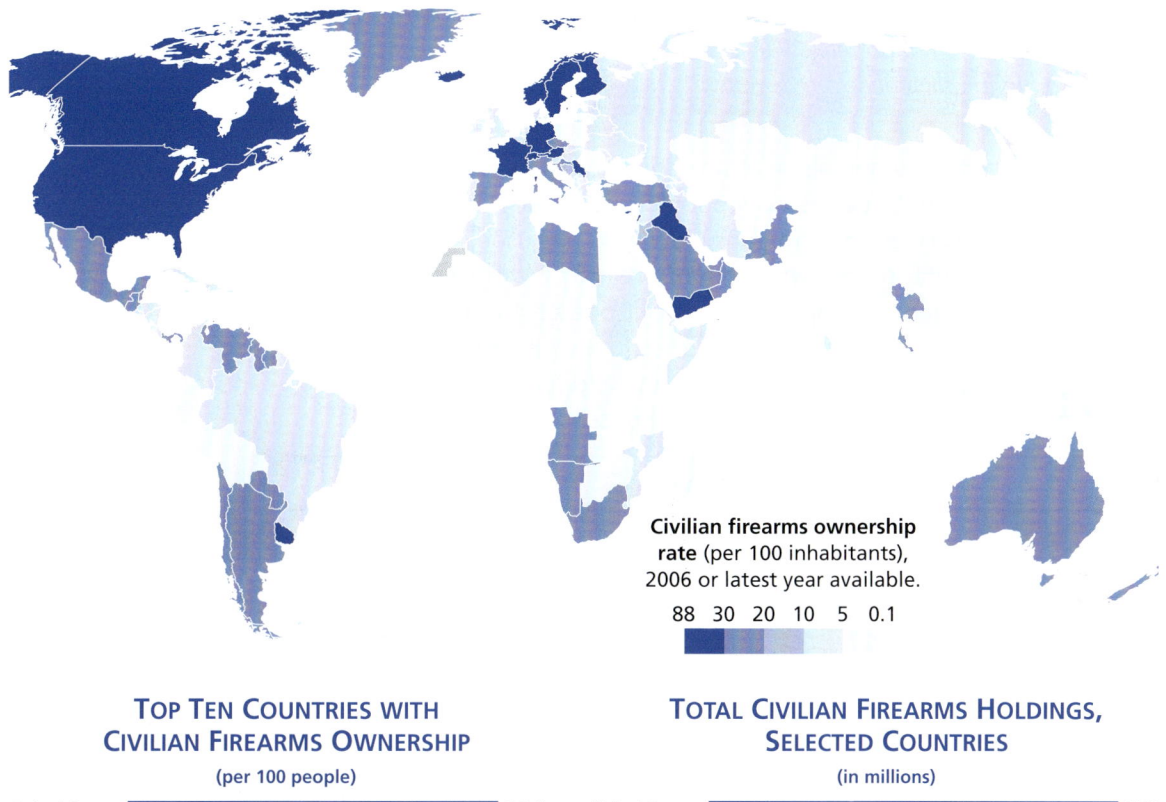

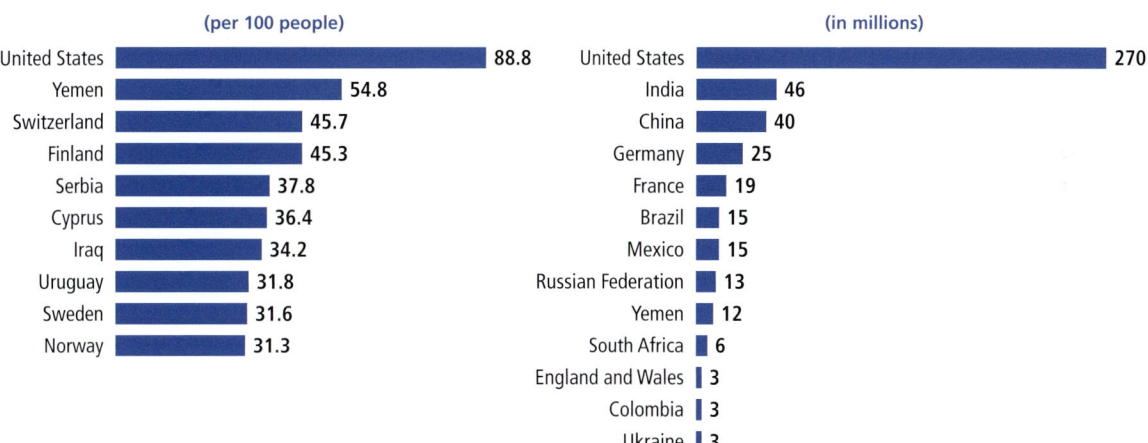

Civilian Firearms Ownership: A United Nations Map of the World

This map shows the rate of civilian (or private) gun ownership in countries around the world. It indicates how many firearms are owned per 100 inhabitants in each country, not counting the military or police. The first bar graph below the map lists the top ten countries with the highest per capita (per 100 people) rate, and the other bar graph shows the total number of guns owned in selected countries. How does the United States rank by each measure? Notice that Switzerland, Finland, Sweden, and Norway are also on the top ten list. Why does the second bar graph compare the number of guns in the United States with India and China? Why is gun ownership so high in the United States?

This chapter has explored the profound influence of the historical frontier period on the values and beliefs of Americans. It includes an explanation of how the gun culture of the United States evolved on the frontier and continues today. Reread the parts of the chapter that talk about how Americans feel about guns, paragraphs 9, 12–14, 16–18, and 20. What do these paragraphs tell you about why the rate of gun ownership is so high in the country today?

Write a report about gun ownership in your country. Include information about the laws concerning owning firearms, how people feel about guns, whether there are as many handguns as rifles and shotguns, how guns are used, and any historical information that helps explain the ownership of firearms in your country. Use a graphic organizer to plan your composition. Fill out one of these "T"s for each paragraph. Write a clear topic sentence to express the main idea, and then list the supporting details. Remember to start with an introduction and end with a conclusion that refers back to the introduction, if possible.

Main Idea
Supporting Details

EXPLORE ON YOUR OWN

Books to Read

Stephen E. Ambrose, *Undaunted Courage: Meriwether Lewis, Thomas Jefferson and the Opening of the American West*—This book is a best-selling account of the expedition by Lewis and Clark through the American West in the early 1800s, as they traveled from St. Louis, Missouri, to the Pacific Ocean.

Dee Brown, *Bury My Heart at Wounded Knee: An Indian History of the American West*—In this best-selling book, Brown presents a documented historical account of the systematic destruction of the American Indian during the last half of the 1800s.

Willa Cather, *O Pioneers!*—A classic novel written in 1913 about the physical hardships of the frontier and the enormous changes it brought to the United States.

Larry McMurtry, *Lonesome Dove*—A best-selling novel about life, love, and adventure on the American frontier.

O. E. Rölvaag, *Giants in the Earth: A Saga of the Prairie*—This is the classic story of a Norwegian pioneer family's struggles as they try to make a new life on the American frontier.

Movies to See

Bowling for Columbine—In this controversial documentary, filmmaker Michael Moore explores the roots of America's fascination with guns and violence.

Dances with Wolves—A soldier sent to a remote western Civil War outpost makes friends with wolves and Indians, eventually falling in love with a white woman raised by the Indians.

Far and Away—A young Irishman who loses his home after his father's death decides to go to America to begin a new life and eventually goes to live on the frontier.

High Noon—In this classic movie, a sheriff who must face a returning deadly enemy finds that his own town refuses to help him.

True Grit—A young girl hires Rooster Cogburn, a Deputy U.S. Marshal, to hunt for the murderer of her father.

Native American dancing with rings—Hopi hoop dance

CHAPTER 5

THE HERITAGE OF ABUNDANCE

For millions of people throughout this world, during the past three centuries, America has symbolized plenty, wealth, and abundance of goods.

David Potter (1910–1971)

How did the abundance of natural resources affect the development of American values and how is abundance being redefined today?

BEFORE YOU READ

Preview Vocabulary

A. Read the following sentences from the chapter and notice the words in italics. These key AWL words will help you understand the chapter. Use context clues to help you figure out the meanings. Then choose which definition is best for the italicized word.

_____ 1. In the aristocratic European nations the settlers left behind, the material wealth and comforts of the ruling classes were *guaranteed* by their birth.
   a. certain to happen
   b. unlikely to happen

_____ 2. Unlike many countries where the love of material things was seen as a vice, a mark of weak moral character, in the United States it was seen as a virtue, a positive *incentive* to work hard, and a reward for successful efforts.
   a. encouragement
   b. discouragement

_____ 3. It was not until the twentieth century that Americans began to think of themselves more as *consumers* than producers.
   a. someone who buys and uses products and services
   b. someone who makes things to sell

_____ 4. Advertising *techniques* were so successful that over time they began to be used to change Americans' attitudes, behavior, and beliefs.
   a. new products and inventions
   b. special ways of doing something

_____ 5. *Technological* devices that can engage us 24 hours a day have increased the pace of life in the United States, and they have changed the way we receive and exchange information.
   a. based on modern knowledge about science and computers
   b. expensive, old pieces of equipment

_____ 6. Big Data is an extraordinary knowledge *revolution* that is sweeping, almost invisibly, through business, academia, government, health care, and everyday life.
   a. a complete change in ways of thinking, methods of working
   b. a very expensive action that people do not like

_____ 7. In order to be valuable and useful, Big Data has to be managed. One way is to rely on *experts* to analyze large amounts of data and then tell us what is important.
   a. people who have special knowledge or skills
   b. people who enjoy using the Internet

_____ 8. Diamandis, Kotler, and others detail the ways that Americans can join with individuals around the world to find *innovative* solutions for providing clean water, enough food, and adequate shelter to everyone.
   a. methods that have been used successfully for many years
   b. new, different, and better methods

_____ 9. Americans viewed the material wealth and abundance of the United States as an ever-*expanding* pie that would continue to grow so that all people could get a bigger piece of a bigger pie.
  a. becoming larger
  b. becoming smaller

B. Read the quotation by David Potter at the beginning of the chapter. Find the words with the following meanings. Write each word next to its meaning.

_____ 1. periods of 100 years

_____ 2. represented an idea or quality

_____ 3. products

_____ 4. enough, or more than enough

_____ 5. a large quantity of something

Preview Content

A. Think about the David Potter quotation and discuss the questions with your classmates.

1. Do you agree with David Potter? Why or why not? What is the source of American abundance?
2. What are the advantages and disadvantages of having abundance? List the positive and negative aspects in the chart.

American Abundance	
Plus +	Minus –

3. Think about your daily activities. What do you throw away every day?
4. How do you use the Internet? How many communication devices do you have?

B. Read the headings in the chapter and look at the illustrations. Write three topics that you predict will be covered in this chapter.

1. _____

2. _____

3. _____

A HISTORY OF ABUNDANCE

1. Although the population of the United States accounts for only about 5 percent of the total population of the world, Americans use up more than 20 percent of the world's energy per year, generating about four and a half pounds of trash and garbage per person each day.

WHAT HAPPENS TO STUFF WE THROW AWAY?

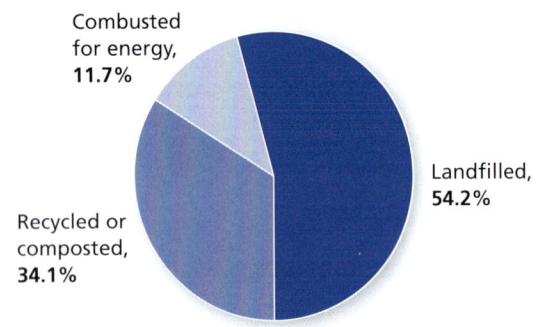

Combusted for energy, **11.7%**
Landfilled, **54.2%**
Recycled or composted, **34.1%**

Based on the 2010 Municipal Solid Waste Characterization Report

Only a country that has great abundance could afford to throw so much away. America has sometimes been criticized as a "throw-away" country, a land where there is so much abundance that people are sometimes viewed as wasteful. Scholars like David Potter, an American historian, believe that the abundant material wealth of the United States has been a major factor in the development of the American character.

2. This abundance is the gift of nature. In what is now the continental United States, there are more than 3 million square miles of land. When the European settlers first arrived in the seventeenth and eighteenth centuries, much of this land was rich, fertile farmland, with an abundance of trees and animals. There were relatively few Native Americans living on this land, and they had neither the weapons nor the organization necessary to keep the European settlers out. Never again can human beings discover such a large area of rich, unfarmed land, with such a small population and such great undeveloped natural resources.

3. But it would be a mistake to say that the abundant natural resources of North America were the only reason why the United States became a wealthy nation. The beliefs, determination, and hard work of the early settlers were equally important.

4. In the aristocratic European nations the settlers left behind, the material wealth and comforts of the ruling classes were guaranteed by their birth. Therefore, as Tocqueville said, the wealthy took these things for granted and assumed they would always have their wealth and social status. The poor people in those aristocratic nations also did not concern themselves with wealth, since they knew that they had little hope of becoming wealthy or changing their status.

5. In the early years of the United States, however, wealth and social position were not permanently determined at birth. The idea of equality of opportunity in America made the level of material wealth of both the rich and the poor much less certain. At any time, the rich might lose some of their wealth and the poor might increase theirs. Therefore, all classes in American society thought about protecting their material possessions and looked for ways to acquire more. Tocqueville believed that this was not so much a matter of greed; rather, it was a matter of their insecurity. People might be naturally insecure if their material wealth, and that of their children, could change so rapidly either upward or downward during a lifetime, or even a single generation. Tocqueville concluded that it was extremely important both to rich Americans and poor Americans to increase their personal wealth and material comforts. Therefore, the entire population

joined in the task of increasing the nation's material abundance as quickly as possible.

6   Tocqueville visited the United States fifty years after the nation had won its independence from England. He was impressed with the great progress made in such a short time. Although the country was still in an early stage of development, and there was not much money available for investment, the United States had already made great progress in both trading and manufacturing. It had already become the world's second leading sea power and had constructed the longest railroads in the world. Tocqueville worried, however, about the effect of all this material success. In such a society, materialism could be made into a moral value in itself rather than a means to an end.

7   Tocqueville's concern, to a large extent, became a reality. In the process of creating a land of abundance, Americans began to judge themselves by materialistic standards. Unlike many countries where the love of material things was seen as a vice or a mark of weak moral character, in the United States it was seen as a virtue, a positive incentive to work hard, and a reward for successful efforts.

8   Traditionally, the people of the United States have been proud of their nation's ability to produce material wealth so that they could maintain a high standard of living. This helps to explain why Americans use materialistic standards not only to judge themselves as individuals, but also to judge themselves as a nation. And the opportunity to share in the good life has attracted immigrants to the United States for generations.

From Producers to Consumers

9   The emphasis on producing wealth and maintaining a high standard of living developed over a period of time. In the 1700s and 1800s, most Americans thought of themselves more as producers than consumers. As farmers they produced food and many of their own household goods, and later as factory workers they produced manufactured goods. It was not until the twentieth century that Americans began to think of themselves more as consumers than as producers. This image change is probably due to the coming of mass advertising, made possible by the beginning of radio broadcasts in the 1920s and the spread of television programming in the 1950s. In the 1920s, businesses agreed to pay for, or sponsor, radio programs that would run short commercials advertising their products. Companies were able to reach large numbers of Americans at one time to convince them to buy their products; the emphasis was now on consuming.

10 The development of mass advertising continued with television, and by the end of the 1960s, scholars had begun to study the effect of mass advertising on American society. Historian David Potter observed that mass advertising in the United States had become so important in size and influence that it should be viewed as an institution, such as the school or the church. One effect of advertising was that sponsors had some control over the content of television programs. If businesses did not like the content, they could withdraw their sponsorship. A second effect was that advertising techniques were so successful that over time they began to be used to change Americans' attitudes, behavior, and beliefs. For example, the government ran ads to urge teenagers not to use drugs; charities had ads to ask for donations; and politicians paid to advertise their campaigns. In the 2012 presidential election, candidates spent a total of more than $900 million on TV ads alone, with most of the money spent in states where the race was competitive.

11 Advertising money follows the consumer as well as the voter. Today, almost all homes in the United States have at least one television set (the average household has more than two), and the family TV is in use about eight hours a day. Some

estimates are that the average American sees about 50,000 commercials a year. When popular events such as the Super Bowl are on, mass advertising may reach 50 million or more viewers during a single program. In addition to radio and television, there are ads in magazines and newspapers, and marketers try to reach people outside their homes with ads everywhere. By 2007, many Americans felt mass advertising was out of control. A *New York Times* article, "Anywhere the Eye Can See, It's Likely to See an Ad," talked about the (then) new video screens in New York taxicabs and public elevators, and the new, ever-changing digital billboards. New York City's Times Square is the best-known and most spectacular example of American outdoor advertising, with its huge digital billboards that have ads showing 24 hours a day.

Times Square, New York—the city that never sleeps

12 And then came the Internet. By 2008, more than 75 percent of homes in the United States had a computer, and over the next few years, Americans abandoned their desktops for laptops, tablets, and smartphones. Over 80 percent of adults 18 and older now use the Internet, and the numbers continue to grow. This use of digital media has had a profound effect on advertising: it has changed the emphasis from mass advertising to target marketing. That is, advertisers are now creating ads for individual users on the Internet, using digital information about their use of digital media. Perhaps mass advertising has reached the point when most consumers simply ignore most of the ads, and businesses have learned that they can reach consumers better by appealing to their individual buying habits and other aspects of their lives. Some aspects that target marketers consider are geographic location and climate, gender, age, income, and education, as well as people's values, attitudes, and lifestyles.

What American Consumers Like

13 People in the advertising business, and others who study American society, are interested in the question: *What does the American consumer like?* Max Lerner, a well-known scholar who has studied American society, has said that American consumers are particularly fond of three things: comfort, cleanliness, and novelty.

14 Lerner believes that the American love of comfort perhaps goes back to the frontier experience, where life was tough and there were very few comforts. This experience may have created a strong desire in the pioneers and their children for goods that would make life more comfortable. Today, the Americans' love of comfort is seen in the way they furnish their homes, design their cars, and travel. How Americans choose a new mattress for their bed is an

example of the American love of comfort. Many Americans will go to a store where beds are set up and lie down on several mattresses to see which is the most comfortable.

Bath time for the family dog

15 Cleanliness is also highly valued by Americans. Perhaps their Puritan heritage has played some role in their desire for cleanliness. The Puritans, a strict Protestant church group whose members were among the first settlers of America, stressed the need to cleanse[1] the body of dirt and of all evil tendencies, which for them included sexual desire. The saying "Cleanliness is next to godliness" reflects the belief of most Americans that it is important to keep not only their bodies, but also their clothes, their houses, their cars, and even their pets clean and smelling good. Indeed, many Americans are offended by anyone who does not follow their accepted standards of cleanliness.

16 Marketing to American consumers requires an awareness of their desire for cleanliness. In his book, *The Power of Habit: Why We Do What We Do in Life and Business*, Charles Duhigg tells of Proctor & Gamble's (P&G) experience marketing Febreze, a spray that makes things smell good. Febreze actually destroys the molecules of odors, and P&G was sure it would be a great seller. Their ads focused on how their product could eliminate, not just cover up, bad smells—even pet smells. To their shock, the product didn't sell. After analyzing the behavior of potential customers, they discovered that people didn't want to be reminded that their houses smelled bad and therefore needed Febreze. P&G changed their ad campaign completely. Instead of marketing it as a cleaning product, they presented it as a reward for when the cleaning was finished: "Who wants to admit their house stinks? ... On the other hand, lots of people crave a nice smell after they've spent thirty minutes cleaning....Within a year, customers had spent more then $230 million on the product." Sometime later, P&G began reminding customers that Febreze also gets rid of odors.

17 Along with cleanliness and comfort, Americans love having things that are new and different. Perhaps this love of novelty is reinforced by their pride in their inventiveness. Americans have always been interested in inventing new products and improving old ones. Advertisements encourage people to get rid of old products and try new ones, whether the old ones still work or not. And if they cannot afford to buy something now, advertisers encourage

[1] *cleanse: to make something completely clean*

consumers to charge it on a credit card—"Buy now, pay later."

18 In addition to the three qualities that Lerner mentions, there is a fourth quality that American consumers like very much—convenience. In the late 1900s, there was a dramatic increase in such labor-saving devices as automatic washing machines, clothes dryers, dishwashers, food processors, microwave ovens, garbage disposals, and power lawn mowers. Today, all of these, and many more, are found in a typical suburban home. The American desire for convenience also created the concept of *fast-food* restaurants such as McDonald's and KFC, which are now found in every city and almost every small town in the United States, and are now exported all over the world. For those who prefer to prepare their food at home, American grocery stores are full of convenience foods that are packaged and ready to cook, or are even precooked.

19 Like microwaves and dishwashers, fast-food restaurants and convenience foods save the American consumer time that would otherwise be spent fixing meals or cleaning up. These conveniences, however, do not cause Americans to be less busy. Women now make up more than one-half of the American workforce, and the majority of mothers with children under the age of eighteen work outside the home. With both parents employed, children eat a lot of take-out food, a significant contributor to childhood obesity.[2] These conveniences reflect not so much a leisurely lifestyle as a busy one in which even minutes of time are too valuable to be wasted. Alexis de Tocqueville was one of the first to see in this a curious paradox[3] in the American character. He observed that Americans were so busy working to acquire comforts and conveniences that they were unable to relax and to enjoy leisure time when they had it. Today, as in Tocqueville's time, many Americans have what one medical doctor has called "the hurry sickness."

An Abundance of Technology

20 Technological devices that can engage us 24 hours a day have increased the pace of life in the United States, and they have changed the way we receive and exchange information. For example, computers and other digital devices have changed our television viewing habits. By 2003, the majority of American homes had either cable or satellite TV. Consequently, in addition to the broadcast networks—ABC, CBS, NBC, and Fox—most Americans can now choose from hundreds of TV channels. There is everything from 24-hour news to movies, children's programs, reality shows, sports, and games, and there are many specialty channels that focus on cooking, home improvement, music, travel, history, drama, comedy, public affairs, entertainment news, and lifestyles. There are also public TV networks offering educational and cultural programs, supported by contributions from viewers, donations from private companies and foundations, and government grants.

21 The result of all these choices is that the TV viewing audience has become more fragmented, with a smaller percentage watching any given program. This means that mass advertisers must also use other ways to reach the buying public. Some companies pay for product placement in TV shows and movies—the hero drinking a Coke, for example, and many companies are doing target marketing. Most large companies do extensive market research

---

[2] *obesity: the condition of being too heavy in a way that is dangerous to your health*

[3] *paradox: a situation that seems strange because it involves two ideas or qualities that are opposite or very different*

to find individuals who are most likely to buy their products. They then focus on delivering their ads to these individuals, often using the Internet and other direct-marketing techniques.

22. Advertising money is going to the Internet also because more and more Americans are online instead of watching TV at all. Increasingly, Americans are using their computer, smartphone, tablet, or other digital device—instead of television—to get their news and entertainment. This is especially true of the Millennials, young people who came of age at the start of the new millennium, the year 2000. Because they are such a desirable market group, advertising money is especially targeting them on the Internet. Traditional sources of news such as TV, newspapers, and news magazines have lost advertising revenue with serious consequences. Many big city papers have gone out of business because there are not enough readers to attract the advertisers needed to pay publishing costs. Some news magazines have gone to online publishing only. The problem is that much of the advertising money in papers and news magazines traditionally went to support the covering of news events. News reporters worked on stories for months to gather and analyze details of complicated and important stories. With a loss of advertising revenue, news organizations have had to downsize, employing fewer staff reporters. As a result, in American media it is sometimes difficult to get in-depth coverage and analysis of news in the United States and around the world.

23. The Internet and the 24-hour cable news networks have created a desire for instant reporting and explanation of news events, sometimes leading to factual mistakes or the wrong interpretation of what is happening. Sometimes the news can be superficial and even silly. A great deal of time and attention is paid to the lives of celebrities, for example, resulting in a mixture of news and entertainment sometimes called "newsertainment" or "infotainment." However, the Internet can also be a source of valuable news reports by eyewitnesses of events around the world, although it may be difficult to verify the accuracy of videos taken on iPhones. Another aspect of the Internet is that individuals can customize, or personalize, the news they receive about current events, and they can set up their own news sites or blogs. Increasingly social media such as Facebook, Twitter, Tumblr, Pinterest, and others are informing and shaping the opinions of their users, as more and more Americans spend more and more time online.

The majority of American families have access to the Internet.

An Abundance of Knowledge: Big Data

24 The first time most Americans heard the term *Big Data* was probably during the 2012 presidential election. President Obama's campaign had purchased huge quantities of digital information on prospective voters. This Big Data, collected from many sources and then carefully analyzed, allowed the Obama team to run the presidential campaign in a whole new way, with such a deep understanding of their potential voters that they could win them over vote by vote. In doing this, the campaign "overturned the long dominance of TV advertising in U.S. politics and created something new in the world: a national campaign run like a local ward election, where the interests of individual voters were known and addressed," according to *MIT Technology Review*.

25 Rick Smolan and Jennifer Erwitt have written a large "coffee table" book called *The Human Face of Big Data*. Smolan and Erwitt say that some people define Big Data as more information than can fit on a personal computer. Others say that it is more than just the quantity of the information—it is also the tools that allow us to see patterns and make use of the knowledge. "Big Data is an extraordinary knowledge revolution that is sweeping, almost invisibly, through business, academia, government, health care, and everyday life," the authors state. Here are some startling facts they reveal about this revolution:

> *The average person today processes more data in a single day than a person in the 1500s did in an entire lifetime.*

> *According to BabyCenter.com, today one in three children born in the United States already have [sic] an online presence (usually in the form of a sonogram[4]) before they are born. That number grows to 92 percent by the time they are two....with a third of all children's photos and information posted online within weeks of their birth.*

> *Each of us now leaves a trail of digital exhaust,[5] an infinite stream of phone records, texts, browser histories, GPS data, and other information that will live on forever.*

26 This supply of Big Data about us raises important personal questions. What happens to all this information? What will it mean to have a complete digital record of our lives from before birth to death? How will this information about us be stored? Who owns our personal information, and who decides how it can be used? Some of these questions are already being debated. For example, who owns the photos we post or store on the Internet? There are also questions about how the government and law enforcement agencies can use our personal information. What can governments do with it? What about the police? And, of course, there is already a concern about criminals and terrorists having access to knowledge about us. Identity theft[6] on the Internet is a big problem, and there are worries that terrorists could get control of important national infrastructure, such as defense[7] networks or power systems.

27 Big Data also raises larger questions about how humanity uses all this new information. Until the coming

---

[4] sonogram: *an image of an unborn baby inside its mother's body*

[5] exhaust: *a gas or stream that is produced when a machine is working*

[6] identity theft: *a crime in which someone steals personal information about another person, such as a bank account number, and uses this information to deceive other people and get money or goods*

[7] defense: *the act of protecting something or someone from attack or destruction*

of computers, the human race often suffered from a lack of knowledge; now many believe we have too much of it. Every 18 months computing power doubles, and the amount of knowledge we have is increasing exponentially. (1+1=2+2=4+4=8+8=16, and so on.) This incredible[8] limitless[9] supply of information is a double-edge sword—it cuts both ways. That is, it has both positive and negative effects. On the positive side, it enables us to solve important problems and can bring many benefits to humanity. On the negative side, it can overwhelm us and may even cause us to make poor decisions. Brain research reveals that when we try to process too much information, the decision-making part of our brain actually shuts down. We then focus on the last piece of information and forget important facts that came before. Research shows that we then make bad decisions that are more affected by our emotions. What we should do is stop, do something else, and let our subconscious[10] mind sort through the data for us. Our subconscious mind evaluates the data, sees connections, and makes creative use of the knowledge. When we return to the task, our brains can then see what is important and enable us to make good decisions.

28 In order to be valuable and useful, Big Data has to be managed. One way is to rely on experts to analyze large amounts of data and then tell us what is important. The problem is that there is so much data that it overwhelms even the experts. We no longer just load information into a computer and tell it what to do. Now computers talk to each other and generate their own new information. This has created new ways of processing data some call "crowdscience,"[11] or "citizenscience." In *Reinventing Discovery: The New Era of Networked Science*, Michael Nielsen explains how scientists can collaborate online to solve complex problems. And they can multiply their efforts by engaging the general public to sort through masses of information. For example, Galaxy[12] Zoo enables people to classify galaxies on their smartphones, enlarging what Nielsen calls the collective intelligence. In fact, a citizen scientist discovered a whole new classification of galaxies.

Redefining American Abundance

29 The United States has always come from a culture of abundance, not scarcity. Bono, the rock star/activist, observed that Americans avoided the "curse of natural resources" that some developing nations now face. Americans learned how to develop the enormous natural resources on their continent and use them "not just to build a modern society but also to feed and supply the world." Now Americans are redefining their abundance as a powerful supply of ideas that can help bring solutions to the problems of the world. In *Abundance: The Future Is Better Than You Think*, Peter H. Diamandis and Steven Kotler say that scarcity of resources is a matter of perspective and accessibility. It you have a tree full of oranges and you pick all the fruit that you can reach, you have run out of your source of oranges. But if someone invents a ladder, you have access to a new supply.

---

[8] *incredible: difficult to believe*

[9] *limitless: without a limit or end*

[10] *subconscious: the part of your mind that has thoughts and feelings that you do not always realize that you have*

[11] *crowdscience—a group of people work together to solve a scientific problem or do scientific research. The group may be a few people, or it may involve thousands.*

[12] *galaxy—any of the large groups of stars that make up the universe*

30 A good example of this is the development of the controversial technology of "fracking." This allows drilling companies to get oil and natural gas from underground supplies in the United States that had not been previously accessible. The supplies of gas and oil are so vast that in 2012, the International Energy Agency projected that by 2020 the United States would become the world's leading oil producer. However, environmental groups are afraid of what this technique will do to the water supply and the ecology of the areas where this is being done.

31 Diamandis, Kotler, and others detail the ways that Americans can join with individuals around the world to find innovative solutions for providing clean water, enough food, and adequate shelter to everyone. Diamandis and Kotler refer to the populations of the world who lack basic necessities as "the rising billion." With the spread of mobile phones around the world, anyone anywhere will have the opportunity to join in creating a world of shared abundance. They define abundance:

> Abundance is not about providing everyone on this planet with a life of luxury[13]—rather it's about providing all with a life of possibility. To be able to live such a life requires having the basics covered and then some....Today most poverty-stricken Americans have a television, telephone, electricity, running water, and indoor plumbing.

32 Definitions of poverty and abundance may be relative, as Diamandis and Kotler suggest. But there is probably universal agreement about the basics that everyone needs: clean water, enough food, and adequate shelter. The sharing of Big Data and networking technology gives us the tools to meet these basic needs and bring "a life of abundant possibility" to all. This will not happen automatically. There are many obstacles to overcome—pollution of the environment, scarcities of food and clean water, and bad decisions by government leaders or even human greed—but the good news is that there are individuals around the world who are dedicated to making it happen.

33 We began by explaining where the American ideal of abundance came from historically, and how it has affected the development of the United States. In contrast to most nations, Americans have traditionally believed that the wealth of their country was like an ever-expanding pie. Instead of the rich getting a larger piece and the poor getting a smaller one, the pie would continue to expand to provide large pieces for everyone. Most important, there would always be enough pie for all. The belief in the continuing heritage of abundance made Americans an optimistic people with confidence that human problems could be solved. It greatly reduced the conflict between the rich and poor that has torn many other nations apart. Perhaps most important, the belief in an always growing abundance gave strong support to such basic national values as freedom, self-reliance, equality of opportunity, competition, and hard work. It seemed to Americans that their high standard of living was a reward for practicing these values.

34 Today, some Americans worry that their economic pie may not continue to expand. But individuals like Diamandis and Kotler say that the revolution in Big Data and new tools to use and share the knowledge are the new face of American abundance. We will simply make more pies.

---

[13] *luxury: very great comfort and pleasure, such as you get from expensive food, beautiful things, etc.*

AFTER YOU READ

Understand Main Ideas

Check the predictions you made on page 101 before reading the chapter. Write your predictions that were correct:

_____

_____

_____

Work with a partner and answer these questions about the main ideas of each section of the chapter. Skim the sections for the main ideas if you do not remember them.

1. *A History of Abundance:* What three values were strengthened by the abundant natural resources of the United States?
2. *From Producers to Consumers:* What caused Americans to change from thinking of themselves mainly as producers to thinking of themselves mainly as consumers?
3. *What American Consumers Like:* What four things do American consumers like?
4. *An Abundance of Technology:* What changes have new technologies brought in American TV-viewing habits and in the way Americans access entertainment and information?
5. *An Abundance of Knowledge: Big Data:* What is Big Data and why is it important? What two kinds of questions does it raise?
6. *Redefining American Abundance:* What is the new definition of American abundance, and how can it benefit the rest of the world?

Understand Details

Write the letter of the best answer according to the information in the chapter.

_____ 1. Which of the following statements is not true?
   a. The European settlers found a North American continent that was rich in undeveloped resources.
   b. The values of the American people inspired them to develop a wilderness continent into a wealthy nation.
   c. The American government discouraged them from developing the natural resources.

_____ 2. Tocqueville believed that in a nation such as the United States, where wealth and social position are not determined by birth,
   a. the rich are not worried about keeping their wealth.
   b. everyone is worried about either acquiring wealth or holding on to it if they have it.
   c. people worry about money so much because they are basically very greedy.

_____ 3. Americans probably think of themselves more as consumers than producers because
   a. few people are still farmers.
   b. they are influenced by mass advertising.
   c. they are concerned about competing on the international market.

_____ 4. Advertisers are now creating ads for individual users on the Internet, using digital information about their use of digital media. This means that
   a. advertisers create personal ads for you by following what you do on the Internet.
   b. advertisers use media experts to design digital ads.
   c. advertisers use mass media technology to reach as many people as possible.

_____ 5. The spread of cable and satellite TV has meant that
   a. more Americans watch the networks ABC, NBC, CBS, and Fox than other channels.
   b. there is a virtually unlimited variety of television programs available.
   c. the number of people watching one program at the same time has increased dramatically.

_____ 6. Another aspect of the Internet is that individuals can customize, or personalize, the news they receive about current events, and they can set up their own news sites or blogs. This means that
   a. the Internet offers no real way for people to share news and their opinions about news.
   b. most people are interested in general news and there are few individual differences.
   c. people can choose to receive only news that interests them personally.

_____ 7. Which of these is implied, but not stated directly, in the *What American Consumers Like* section of the chapter?
   a. Fast food is as healthy as home-cooked food.
   b. Most of the cooking is done by women.
   c. Men use credit cards more than women.

_____ 8. Based on information in the *What American Consumers Like* section, which one of these statements is true?
   a. Americans like new products and want to improve old ones.
   b. When buying a chair, most Americans would be more concerned about its beauty than its comfort.
   c. At first, Febreze did not sell well because Americans are not concerned about how their houses smell.

_____ 9. The view that a country's economy is an ever-expanding pie
   a. is held by most nations in the world today.
   b. is a belief held by Americans and reinforced by their experiences.
   c. is a belief that a country's food supply will continually expand.

_____ 10. Fracking is a new technique that allows drilling companies to get oil and natural gas from underground supplies in the United States that had not been accessible. This means that
   a. oil and gas supplies have always been easy to reach in the U. S.
   b. oil and gas companies are not permitted to use the fracking technique.
   c. the fracking technique gives companies the opportunity to reach oil and gas they could not get to before.

Talk About It

Work in small groups and choose one of these questions to discuss.

1. Which do you think is more important for economic growth: a good supply of natural resources or the values of the people in the society? Give examples.
2. What are the basic necessities of life? Do we have a responsibility to make sure everyone has them?
3. What do you think of fast-food restaurants? Are convenience foods (canned goods, frozen food, pre-cooked dinners, etc.) popular in your country?
4. What personal information do you put on the Internet? Who owns your personal information? Who should be able to use it and how?

SKILL BUILDING

Improve Your Reading Skills: Highlighting

For successful academic reading, use strategies for identifying and remembering the main points. One strategy is to highlight the first sentence in each paragraph as you read. The first sentence is often the topic sentence and states the topic, or main idea, of the paragraph.

Practice this strategy. Highlight the first sentence of each paragraph in the *What American Consumers Like* section of the chapter. In your notebook, copy the seven sentences to make a one-paragraph summary of the section.

Develop Your Critical Thinking Skills

Reread the quotation from Diamandis and Kotler: "Abundance is not about providing everyone on this planet with a life of luxury—rather it's about providing all with a life of possibility. To be able to live such a life requires having the basics covered and then some..."

Evaluate this definition of abundance. In what ways do you agree or disagree with it? Be prepared to participate in a classroom discussion about this issue.

Build Your Vocabulary

Opposites

Match the words with opposite meanings. Then fill in the sentence blanks with the correct words.

_____ 1. abundance   a. expand

_____ 2. consumer   b. wealth

_____ 3. downsize   c. downward

_____ 4. mass   d. vice

_____ 5. positive   e. scarcity

_____ 6. poverty   f. private

_____ 7. public   g. poor

_____ 8. rich   h. producer

_____ 9. upward   i. targeted

_____ 10. virtue   j. negative

1. Unlike many countries where the love of material things was seen as a _____, a mark of weak moral character, in the United States it was seen as a _____, an incentive to work hard, and a reward for successful efforts.

2. Tocqueville thought that Americans might be insecure if their material wealth could change so rapidly either _____ or _____ during a lifetime.

3. Mass advertising reinforces the American's self-image as a _____.

4. The United States comes from a culture of abundance, not _____.

5. _____ television has no commercials, and programs are paid for by donations and government grants.

114 ★ Chapter 5

6. Today most _____-stricken Americans have a television, telephone, electricity, running water, and indoor plumbing.

7. With a loss of advertising revenue, news organizations have had to _____, employing fewer staff reporters.

Technology Words

There are a number of words and phrases in the chapter that deal with technology. Some of these words apply to television; others relate to the Internet, and some relate to both. In the Venn diagram that follows, write the words that apply to these three categories. Write the words that only apply to television in one circle, the words that only apply to the Internet in the other circle, and the words that apply to both in the area that overlaps. Look on the Internet for any words you do not know.

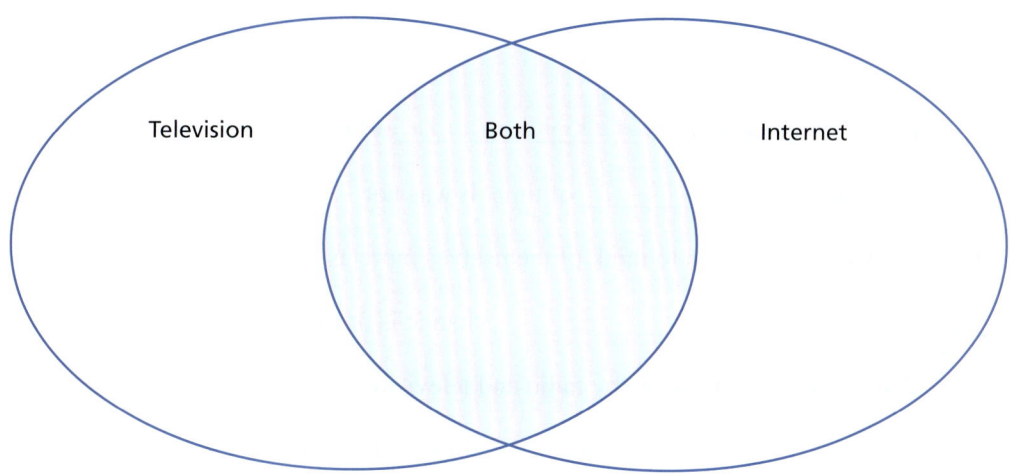

Advertisements	Facebook	Sponsor
Blog	Mass marketing	Targeted marketing
Cable	Movies	Tumblr
Channel	Network	Twitter
Commercials	News	Video
Data	Online	Viewer
Digital	Pinterest	Website
Entertainment	Satellite	World Wide Web

More AWL Words

Test your knowledge of these AWL words by filling in the blanks in these sentences from the chapter.

concluded	generation	institution	task
consumers	image	maintaining	technique
emphasis	insecure	period	

People might be naturally _____1_____ if their material wealth, and that of their children, could change so rapidly either upward or downward during a lifetime, or even a single _____2_____. Tocqueville _____3_____ that it was extremely important both to rich Americans and poor Americans to increase their personal wealth and material comforts. Therefore, the entire population joined in the _____4_____ of increasing the nation's material abundance as quickly as possible.

The _____5_____ on producing wealth and _____6_____ a high standard of living developed over a _____7_____ of time. It was not until the twentieth century that Americans began to think of themselves more as _____8_____ than producers. This _____9_____ change is probably due to the coming of mass advertising, made possible by radio and television. Television used the same _____10_____ that radio had developed. Historian David Potter observed that mass advertising in the United States became so important in size and influence that it should be viewed as an _____11_____ such as the school or the church.

EXPAND YOUR KNOWLEDGE

Conduct an Experiment

In the chapter, there is information about how advertisers target people they want to have as customers. Newspaper editor Arthur Brisbane says that there are several things an ad must accomplish to be successful:

"A good advertisement must do five things and do them all. If it fails in one, it fails in all. It must make people see it, read (listen/watch) it, understand it, believe it, want it."

Choose one (or more) of these activities to count the ways advertising is part of your life. Write your findings in your notebook. Then report your findings to the rest of the class.

1. Count the number of TV commercials you see in one hour.
2. Count the number of billboards or other outdoor advertising messages you see in a day.
3. Count the number of advertisements you see on the Internet in one hour.
4. Count the number of advertising messages you see on people's clothing in one day.

People Watching

1. Observe what Americans throw away. Visit a fast-food restaurant and count the containers that are thrown away from one person's meal. How much food is wasted? How does this compare with people eating in fast-food restaurants in your country?

2. Visit a supermarket and note the kinds of convenience or packaged foods available. Be sure to check all the departments. Here are some examples of what you may find: salad in a bag, fruit already cut up and ready to eat, rice and pasta boxed dinners, ready-to-cook meat and poultry dishes, and frozen dinners. Notice what Americans are buying at the grocery store. How does this compare with grocery shoppers in your country? Notice the different varieties of the same type of products. How many kinds of milk do you count? How many kinds of bread? How many kinds of rice? Record your observations in your journal.

A family enjoys eating at a fast-food restaurant.

Think, Pair, Share

Think about current environmental problems and possible solutions. For these words and phrases, write **P** for the environmental problems, and **S** for the solutions.

_____ endangered species   _____ conserving energy

_____ trash and garbage   _____ protecting wildlife

_____ recycling   _____ air pollution

_____ wastefulness   _____ global warming

What other environmental problems and solutions can you think of? Write your answers below and share them with your partner.

_____

_____

_____

Ask Americans / Create a Poll

All countries must now consider their energy needs and how to meet them in the future. The United States is no exception. This chart is based on a poll that asked Americans about their government's policy for addressing the nation's energy supply.

Create your own poll by writing questions for each item, and then ask Americans to answer your questions. Compare your results with this poll.

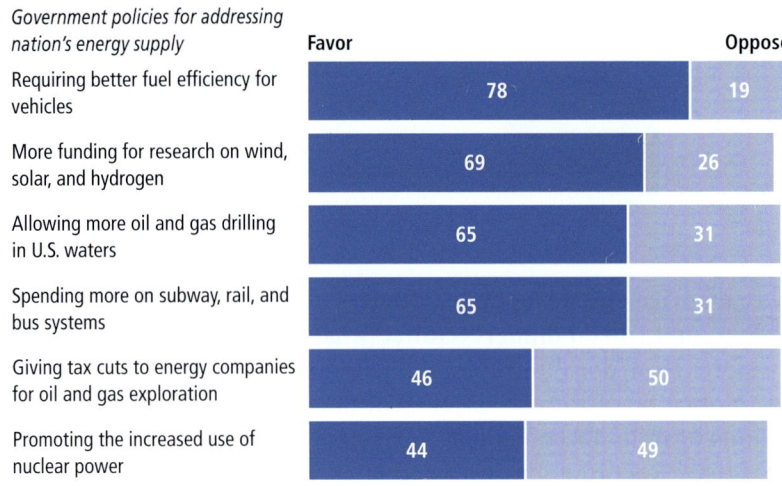

PUBLIC CONTINUES TO SUPPORT BROAD RANGE OF ENERGY POLICIES

Government policies for addressing nation's energy supply	Favor	Oppose
Requiring better fuel efficiency for vehicles	78	19
More funding for research on wind, solar, and hydrogen	69	26
Allowing more oil and gas drilling in U.S. waters	65	31
Spending more on subway, rail, and bus systems	65	31
Giving tax cuts to energy companies for oil and gas exploration	46	50
Promoting the increased use of nuclear power	44	49

Source: Pew Research Center Mar. 7–11, 2012. Q43.

Small-Group Project

An interesting example of Big Data is the phenomenon of YouTube. It started in 2007 and by 2012 there were 60 hours of video uploaded every minute and more than 4 billion page views per day, with the numbers continuing to rise at a faster and faster pace. An article in Time magazine proclaimed, "There's never been an object like YouTube in human history." Modern life generates huge quantities of video, and most of it is created by amateurs, not professionals. Before YouTube, there was no central place for videos to be gathered and stored. One of Google's main challenges is to keep the site from crashing because of all these videos. Another challenge is how to organize the videos so that people can find what they want to see. YouTube is using a type of crowdsourcing by having its users do the organizing of the videos themselves. This process is evolving.

Work in a small group to look at how YouTube organizes videos. Visit YouTube and look for a type of video that you want to see. What words do you use to describe this type of video? How does YouTube organize videos? Is it easy to find the videos you want on YouTube? How would you organize YouTube videos to make the site easier to use?

Use the Internet

Choose one of the topics below and do research on the Internet:

1. Learn more about what Diamandis and Kotler have to say about abundance: "We think it's critically important for you to have access to this ongoing evidence for abundance. Therefore, we've created five different ways for you to stay plugged in, interact with the authors, and join an ongoing conversation about radical advances in energy, food, water, health, education, technophilanthropy, DIY [Do It Yourself] innovation, and all the rest." Visit their websites to learn more: http://www.AbundanceHub.com

2. In spite of all the abundance in the United States, you may be surprised to learn that hunger is still a problem. Many Americans do not make enough money to provide adequate food for their families. Also, because of poverty, many Americans do not have access to fresh fruits and vegetables in their neighborhoods, and so they eat a lot of cheap fast food. Childhood obesity
is a problem, as well as hunger. Learn about a documentary film that was made about the problem. Search on the Internet for the film "A Place at the Table." Find more information at websites such as www.takepart.com or www.magpictures.com/aplaceatthetable/

3. If you are interested in the protection of endangered species, visit websites such as www.worldwildlife.org or the U.S. government site www.fws.gov/endangered/

WRITE ABOUT IT

In this chapter, there was a discussion of advertising and what Americans like to buy. What happens to all the "stuff" that people buy? What happens to the old electronic products (phones, computers, etc.) when people buy new ones? The Environmental Protection Agency (EPA) is the government agency that is in charge of what happens to Americans' trash and garbage.

How Americans Dispose of Trash and Garbage

Information from the EPA website

http://www.epa.gov/epawaste/nonhaz/municipal/index.htm

Municipal Solid Waste (MSW)—more commonly known as trash or garbage—consists of everyday items we use and then throw away, such as product packaging, grass clippings, furniture, clothing, bottles, food scraps, newspapers, appliances, paint, and batteries. This comes from our homes, schools, hospitals, and businesses.

Each year EPA produces a report on MSW generation, recycling, and disposal. In 2010, Americans generated about 250 million tons of trash and recycled and composted over 85 million tons of this material, equivalent to a 34.1 percent recycling rate. On average, we recycled and composted 1.51 pounds of our individual waste generation of 4.43 pounds per person per day.

EPA encourages practices that reduce the amount of waste needing to be disposed of, such as waste prevention, recycling, and composting.

- *Source reduction,* or waste prevention, is designing products to reduce the amount of waste that will later need to be thrown away and also to make the resulting waste less toxic.
- *Recycling* is the recovery of useful materials, such as paper, glass, plastic, and metals, from the trash to use to make new products, reducing the amount of new raw materials needed.
- *Composting* involves collecting organic waste, such as food scraps and yard trimmings, and storing it under conditions designed to help it break down naturally. This resulting compost can then be used as a natural fertilizer.

Recycling and composting prevented 85.1 million tons of material from being disposed of [in] 2010, up from 15 million tons in 1980. This prevented the release of approximately 186 million metric tons of carbon dioxide equivalent into the air in 2010—equivalent to taking 36 million cars off the road for a year. Learn more about how common wastes and materials, including food and yard wastes, paper, metals, and electronics, contribute to MSW generation and how they can be recycled.

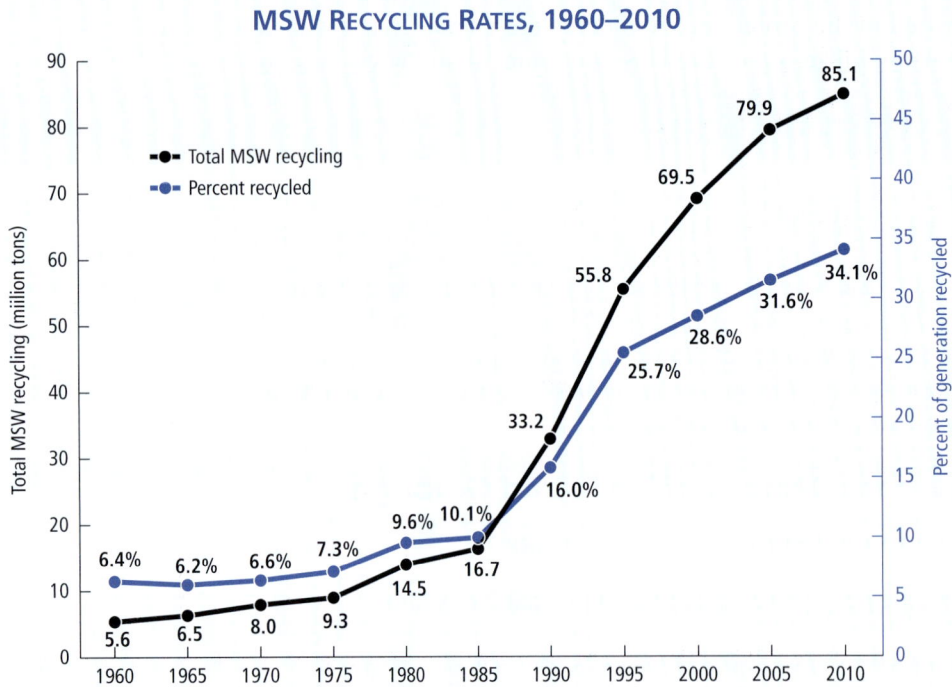

MSW Recycling Rates, 1960–2010

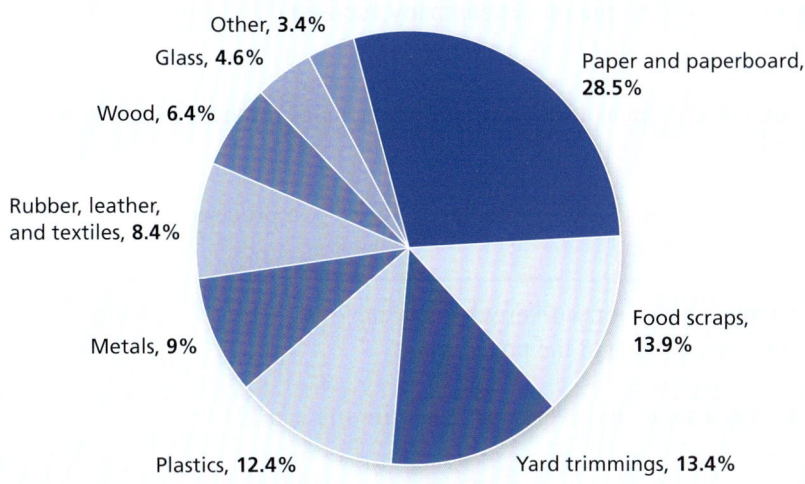

The EPA is trying to teach Americans to reduce, reuse, and recycle. It is clear that Americans are doing better at recycling. Write a report about how your country deals with trash and garbage. Do research on the Internet and share your own personal experiences.

EXPLORE ON YOUR OWN

Books to Read

Rachel Carson, Silent Spring—This best-selling book published in 1962 was one of the first to warn of environmental problems and the dangers of chemical pollution.

Peter H. Diamandis and Steven Kotler: *Abundance: The Future is Better Than You Think*—This book details ways that technology, innovators, technophilanthropists, and ordinary people are finding solutions to some of the world's worst problems.

Al Gore, *Earth in the Balance: Ecology and the Human Spirit*—In this best seller, the former vice president calls on Americans to rethink their relationship with the environment or face terrible consequences.

Eric Schlosser, *Fast Food Nation: The Dark Side of the All-American Meal*—A disturbing look at the fast-food industry in the United States and how it affects American food production, health, and popular culture.

Rick Smolan and Jennifer Erwitt, *The Human Face of Big Data*—A large, "coffee table" picture book that illustrates how huge quantities of information are affecting our lives.

Movies to See

Erin Brockovitch—An unemployed single mother becomes a legal assistant and almost single-handedly brings down a California power company accused of polluting a city's water supply.

An Inconvenient Truth—Al Gore presents an award-winning documentary movie about the effects of global warming.

Promised Land—The film presents one town's experience with fracking, a process for getting natural gas from deep underground.

Silkwood—Karen Silkwood is a nuclear reactor worker who may have been murdered to prevent her exposing wrongdoing at the power plant.

The Truman Show—An insurance salesman discovers that his entire life is a TV show.

CHAPTER 6

THE WORLD OF AMERICAN BUSINESS

The business of America is business.

President Calvin Coolidge (1872–1933)

What effect does business have on American values? Do Americans see business owners and leaders as heroes or as villains?

BEFORE YOU READ

Preview Vocabulary

A. Here are some key AWL words in Chapter 6. Look at their definitions. Put a check next to the words you already know.

_____ 1. **ultimate**   the best or most perfect example of something

_____ 2. **aid**   help or advice given to someone who needs it

_____ 3. **alternative**   something you can choose instead of something else

_____ 4. **cycles**   events that happen again and again

_____ 5. **overseas**   happening abroad

_____ 6. **policy**   an official way of doing something

_____ 7. **priorities**   things that are most important and need your attention before anything else

_____ 8. **submitting**   agreeing to obey

_____ 9. **theoretically**   supposed to be true

B. Work with a partner. Read these sentences from the chapter. Fill in the blanks with words from the preceding list.

1. _____, if one business tries to take unfair advantage of its customers, it will lose to a competing business which treats its customers more fairly.

2. Gaining success and status through competition is often seen as the American _____ to systems where social rank is based on family background.

3. Entrepreneurs often began as common people themselves; without the _____ of inherited social title or inherited money, they became "self-made" millionaires.

4. A final characteristic of entrepreneurs that appeals to most Americans is their strong dislike of _____ to higher authority.

5. The site keeps track of everyone's contribution online, and all who participate in the process get a percent of the profits from the sales; such websites offer the _____ form of collaboration.

6. Some American businesses that had moved their operations _____ are now returning, and manufacturing is coming back.

7. Americans' respect for their business institutions rises and falls in _____, going back to the Industrial Revolution of the 1800s.

8. Traditionally, Republicans have been in favor of a laissez-faire, or hands-off _____, and Democrats have favored more regulations and safeguards.

9. *MetLife*'s most recent study of the American Dream shows a significant shift in _____.

Preview Content

A. Read the questions and discuss them with your classmates.

1. Read the quotation by President Calvin Coolidge at the beginning of the chapter. What do you think the quotation means? Do you agree? Why is business so important to Americans?
2. What does it mean to "go from rags to riches"?
3. What is an entrepreneur?
4. What are the advantages and disadvantages of starting and running your own business? Write some ideas in a pro-and-con chart.

B. Preview the chapter by reading the headings and looking at the illustrations. Predict what the chapter is about. Put a check by the ideas you predict will be discussed in the chapter.

____ the natural resources of the United States

____ what Alexis de Tocqueville said about business in the 1830s

____ the role of entrepreneurs in American business

____ how to start your own business

____ what Americans think they can do to get rich

____ what Americans think of corporate CEOs

____ what products the United States exports to other countries

____ differences in wealth or social class

____ how the American Dream has changed

____ changes American business faces

THE CHARACTERISTICS OF AMERICAN BUSINESS

1 It is essential to become familiar with two words in order to understand the meaning of *business* to Americans: They are *private* and *profit*. Businesses are directly or indirectly owned and operated by private individuals (or groups of individuals) in order to make a profit. In contrast to these privately owned, for-profit businesses, there are also (1) public, government-owned-and-operated institutions, and (2) nonprofit organizations, such as churches, charities, and educational institutions. These organizations and institutions should not be confused with businesses. However, in recent years a new type of business called "for purpose" or "for benefit" has appeared, a form of for-profit charity. We will discuss these new benefit corporations later in the chapter.

How Business Competition Reinforces Other Values

2 The statement by President Coolidge in the 1920s, "The business of America is business," still points to an important truth today—that business institutions are at the heart of the American way of life. One reason for this is that Americans view business as being more firmly based on the ideal of competition than most other institutions in society. Since competition is seen as the major source of progress and prosperity by most Americans, competitive business institutions have traditionally been respected. Competition is seen not only as a value itself; it is also the means by which other basic American values such as individual freedom, self-reliance, equality of opportunity, and hard work are protected.

3 Competition protects the freedom of the individual by ensuring that there is no monopoly of power. In contrast to one all-powerful government, many businesses compete against each other for profits. Theoretically, if one business tries to take unfair advantage of its customers, it will lose to a competing business that treats its customers more fairly. Where many businesses compete for the customers, they cannot afford to give them inferior products or poor service.

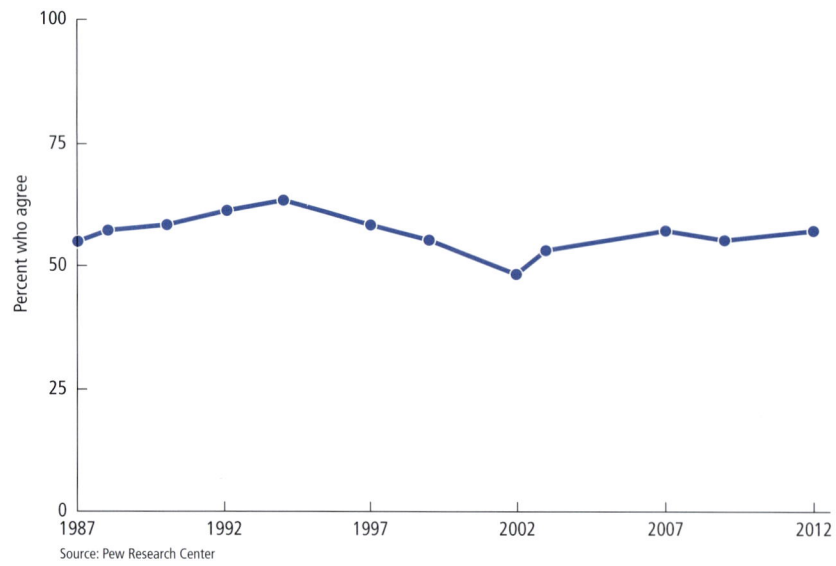

GOVERNMENT REGULATION OF BUSINESS USUALLY DOES MORE HARM THAN GOOD

Source: Pew Research Center

4   A contrast is often made between business, which is competitive, and government, which is a monopoly. Because business is competitive, many Americans believe that it may be even more supportive of freedom than government, even though government leaders are elected by the people and business leaders are not. Many Americans believe that competition is vitally important to preserving freedom. So closely is competitive business associated with freedom in the minds of most Americans that the term *free enterprise*, rather than the term *capitalism*, is most often used to describe the American business system.

5   Competition in business is also believed to strengthen the ideal of equality of opportunity. Americans compare business competition to a race open to all, where success and status go to the swiftest[1] person, regardless of social class. Gaining success and status through competition is often seen as the American alternative to systems where social rank is based on family background. Business is therefore viewed as an expression of the idea of equality of opportunity rather than the aristocratic idea of inherited privilege.

6   Business competition is also seen by most Americans as encouraging the value of hard work. If two businesspeople are competing against each other, the one who works harder is likely to win. The one who spends less time and effort is likely to lose. Because businesspeople must continually compete against each other, they must develop the habit of hard work in order not to fail.

7   Americans are aware that business institutions often do not live up to the ideals of competition and the support of freedom, self-reliance, equality of opportunity, and hard work. Americans sometimes distrust the motives of businesspeople, believing that they are capable of putting profit before product safety or a cleaner environment. Therefore, most Americans believe businesses need some government regulation, although they may disagree on how much. Even with these flaws,[2] however, most Americans believe that business comes closer than other institutions to encouraging competition and other basic values in daily practice.

The Dream of Getting Rich

8   There is a second reason why business institutions have traditionally received respect in the United States. One aspect of the great American Dream is to rise from poverty or modest wealth to great wealth. In the United States, this has usually been accomplished through successful business careers. Most of the great private fortunes in the nation have been built by people who were successful in business, many of whom started life with very little. Indeed, today about 35 percent of the Forbes 400 (the 400 wealthiest Americans) were raised poor or middle class. Careers in business still offer the best opportunity for the ambitious individual to become wealthy, although many of the wealthiest Americans have inherited fortunes from their family.

9   Alexis de Tocqueville observed the great attractiveness of business careers for Americans as early as the 1830s. He wrote that Americans strongly preferred business to farming because business offered the opportunity to get rich more quickly. Even those who were farmers were possessed with a strong business spirit. They often ran small businesses to add to the money they made from

[1] *swiftest: quickest and fastest*
[2] *flaws: mistakes, marks, or defects*

Longwood Mansion, Natchez, Mississippi, is an example of the opulent lifestyle many Americans hope to have.

farming. Tocqueville also noticed that American farmers were often more interested in buying and selling land for a profit than in farming it. Thus, even in Tocqueville's day, when most Americans were still farmers, the seeds of a business civilization had already been planted.

10 Not only is business seen as the easiest way for individuals to become rich, it is also seen as generally benefiting the entire nation. Through competition, more people gain wealth and the nation prospers. By contrast, a government-run system of production and distribution of goods is seen as inferior. It is distrusted because of the monopoly of power held by the government, which eliminates competition. Most Americans would probably prefer to limit government's control over businesses and let the free enterprise system, or the free market, work on its own. However, there is a great debate about the role of the government vs. business in providing services such as health care and retirement benefits. The United States is one of the few industrialized countries in the world that does not have universal health care guaranteed and managed by the government. Health care in the United States has been tied to employment since the 1940s, although the government's role has been increasing in the 2000s. *The Affordable Care Act* (passed in 2009 and implemented 2010-2015) has the goal of enabling all Americans to have access to affordable health insurance. However, this plan (known as Obama Care) has been controversial from the start, with opposition from many business leaders and conservative politicians.

11 As for retirement, since the 1980s most businesses have switched from offering pensions to retired workers to offering

them 401K retirement accounts for saving and investment. This has allowed employees access to their retirement funds while still working, and it has resulted in many workers spending this money and not saving enough for their retirement. This is a growing problem in the United States. In the future, as these workers face retirement without adequate savings, the government retirement benefits may also be reduced. Both individuals and companies now contribute money into the government Social Security System (and Medicare, the government health care system for retirees), but there is serious concern that as the aging population grows, there will not be enough money to fund these benefits. We will examine this problem more in the next chapter on government.

The Entrepreneur as Business Hero

12 Because of the many beliefs that connect business to the wealth and the traditional values of the United States, people who are successful in business have sometimes become heroes to the American people. Entrepreneurs provide examples of traditional American values in their purest form for a number of reasons. The first reason is that they succeed in building something great out of nothing. The people who, more than 100 years ago, built up the nation's great industries, such as steel, railroads, and oil refining, were usually entrepreneurs. They started with very little money or power and ended up as the heads of huge companies that earned enormous fortunes.

13 The fact that these early entrepreneurs built great industries out of very little made them seem to millions of Americans like the heroes of the early frontier days, who went into the vast wilderness of the United States and turned forests into farms, villages, and small cities. The entrepreneur, like the earlier hero of the frontier, was seen as a rugged individualist who reinforced the values of freedom, self-reliance, and hard work. The nineteenth-century entrepreneurs often began as common people themselves; without the aid of inherited social title or inherited money, they became "self-made" millionaires. They were thus perfect examples of the American idea of equality of opportunity in action.

14 The strong influence of the success stories of the early entrepreneurs can be found in the great popularity of the novels of Horatio Alger, which were published in late-nineteenth and early-twentieth-century America. About 17 million copies of these books were sold to the American public. The central theme of Alger's novels is that in the United States a poor city boy or a poor farm boy can become a wealthy and successful businessman if he works hard and relies on himself rather than others. This is because the United States is a land of equality of opportunity where everyone has a chance to succeed.

15 In Alger's first published novel, *Ragged Dick*, a poor city boy who shines shoes for a living becomes Richard Hunter, a successful and wealthy businessman. The hero rises "from rags to riches" and fulfills the American Dream. Dick succeeds only partly because he lives in a land of equality of opportunity. His success is also due to the fact that he practices the American virtues of self-reliance and hard work. According to Alger, Dick "knew that he had only himself to depend upon, and he determined to make the most of himself...which is the secret of success in nine cases out of ten." Dick was also a hardworking shoe-shine boy, "energetic and on the alert for business." This quality marked him for success, explained Alger, because in all professions, "energy and industry are rewarded."

16 Although few Americans today read Horatio Alger's stories, they continue to be inspired by the idea of earning wealth and success as entrepreneurs who "make it on their own." A final characteristic of entrepreneurs that appeals to most Americans is their strong dislike of submitting to higher authority. Throughout their history, Americans have admired entrepreneurs who conduct their business and their lives without taking orders from anyone above them. Americans have great respect for those who can say, "I am my own boss." Many American workers still dream of one day having their own business and being their own boss.

The Corporate CEO/CFO

17 In contrast to business entrepreneurs who are seen as creating something new, there are the leaders of existing large business corporations—the CEO (Chief Executive Officer) and the CFO (Chief Financial Officer) who manage the businesses. The great entrepreneurs of the late nineteenth century built huge business organizations that needed new generations of business leaders to run them in the twentieth century. These leaders, sometimes referred to as "organizational men or women," now run large American corporations. They are powerful and often acquire great personal wealth, but they do not usually have the hero image of entrepreneurs because they are managing businesses that someone else started. Although most Americans admire the earning power of entrepreneurs and would probably not want to put a limit on their income, they are less generous in their view of CEOs. Indeed, many highly paid CEOs have come under severe attack for their multi-million-dollar-a-year salaries and their self-serving management decisions.

18 In her book *Pigs at the Trough: How Corporate Greed and Political Corruption Are Undermining America*, Arianna Huffington details how certain CEOs took huge sums of money from the corporations they were managing and spent it on themselves. She describes how John Rigas, the CEO of Adelphia, a large cable company, borrowed $3.1 billion from the company when it was in financial trouble and spent it outrageously:

He spent $13 million to build a golf course in his backyard, $150 million to buy the Buffalo Sabres hockey team, $65 million to fund a venture capital[3] group run by his son-in-law, thousands to maintain his three private jets, and $700,000 for a country-club membership.

19 It is not just the greed of some corporate leaders; it is the effect their decisions have had on the employees of their companies, their stockholders, and the society at large. The early 2000s saw a number of other corporate scandals, when CEOs and other corporate officers received huge sums of money from companies that were failing. One of the worst examples was the Enron Corporation, which left thousands of employees out of work and destroyed their retirement savings. What angered Americans was not only the outrageous greed of the corporate executives, but also their lies to the stockholders, their criminal mismanagement of the business, and their cruel treatment of their own employees.

20 For most of the twentieth century, there were many good-paying manufacturing jobs. Many of these factory jobs did not require a college degree, and large numbers of average Americans could earn enough money to have a comfortable middle class existence. However, the realities of the global economy caused some American businesses to make significant changes. In order to make products that were cheap enough to compete in the global market, many companies moved their factories overseas. Companies could no longer afford to pay Americans those high wages. Second, some companies downsized to become more competitive. Old, giant corporations such as IBM laid off thousands of workers, downsizing to become more efficient, as well as more competitive. Third, some companies reduced the number of full-time employees and replaced them with part-time workers so they did not have to pay health insurance or retirement benefits. Finally, some companies started outsourcing[4] work to other countries. Telephone customer support is a good example of outsourcing. Today, when an American calls about a problem with a product or to inquire about the status of an order, the person answering the call may be in India or the Philippines, rather than the United States.

21 In the twenty-first century, in addition to watching CEOs send their good-paying jobs overseas, Americans were hit by an economic recession. Most of the wealth held by the middle class was in the homes they owned. The value of their homes had increased dramatically in the late 1990s and the 2000s creating a "housing bubble."[5] When the bubble burst, middle class homeowners were devastated. Suddenly their homes were worth half of what they had been, and at the same time, many people lost their jobs. To make matters worse, American financial institutions went into a crisis. The banking system was in danger of collapsing[6] and the government had to loan them money so they would not fail. The government also gave loans to two American automobile companies, Chrysler and General Motors, to keep them from collapsing. The decision was made that some companies were simply "too big to fail."

---

[3] *venture capital: money that is lent to people so that they can start a new business*

[4] *outsourcing: hiring employees in another country instead of using workers where the business is located*

[5] *bubble: a successful or happy time, especially in business*

[6] *collapsing: suddenly failing to work*

The Middle Class vs. the One Percent

22 By 2010, many middle-class Americans were really angry. Their incomes had remained the same (adjusted for inflation) for 25 years. They were discouraged about finding a good job and paying the mortgage[7] on their home. Many people took money out of their retirement accounts to survive. And they learned that what they had left in their investment retirement accounts had declined along with the stock market fall of 2008. *The Huffington Post* reported that their Real Misery Index was the highest it had ever been. The Misery Index combines data on unemployment, credit card debt, and inflation of essentials such as gas, food, medical costs, and housing. In some locations, large numbers of homes went into foreclosure because the owners could no longer afford the mortgage payments, and the banks took back the houses.

23 But not all Americans were miserable. The gap between the very rich and the rest of the population had been growing since the late 1980s. Now it was clear that the very rich one percent had gotten even richer during the economic crisis. Some corporate CEOs had made fortunes downsizing companies and buying others that were in financial trouble. Banks and other financial institutions were selling financial products that few people understood. It seemed to some that the business institutions that had brought America jobs and new products and services were now just making money off of money. And people suddenly realized that because of the tax structure, investment income was taxed at a lower rate than earned income. Warren Buffet, one of the richest Americans, said that his secretary paid a higher tax rate than he did. This became an issue in the 2012 presidential election because Mitt Romney, the Republican candidate, had made a fortune with his corporation that downsized American companies. Also, most of his income came from investments that were taxed at the lower rate, and much of his money was in off-shore bank accounts, outside the United States.

24 Then the economy started to improve. As the stock market recovered and rose higher and higher, so did the anger of the working class Americans. In the fall of 2011, some people started a movement called Occupy Wall Street, demanding that the rich pay "their fair share" of taxes. They camped out in the park near the Wall Street stock exchange in New York City, and the demonstrations spread to other cities. Eventually cold weather and other factors put a stop to most demonstrations, but the

More and more business on the New York Stock Exchange is done electronically.

---

[7] mortgage: money borrowed from a bank to buy a house and paid back over a number of years

anger continued.

25 It was not just the working class Americans who were disturbed. News commentators began asking if the American Dream was dead, and books about how to save or restore the American Dream appeared. Huffington sounded the alarm in her book *Third World America: How Our Politicians Are Abandoning the Middle Class and Betraying the American Dream.* Huffington, herself an immigrant from Greece, said she wrote the book as a warning about what could happen. In 1980, when she came to the United States to find "a better life," that was the phrase everyone associated with America—a better life. "Upward mobility has always been at the center of the American Dream—a promise that if you work hard and play by the rules, you'll do well, and your children will have the chance to do even better." But in the last few years, Huffington said she saw that the middle class was "getting the short end of the stick." Washington had rushed to the rescue of Wall Street but had forgotten about Main Street. Our political system is broken, she observed, and our economic system "has been reduced to recurring episodes of Corporations Gone Wild."

26 Americans' respect for their business institutions rises and falls in cycles, going back to the Industrial Revolution of the 1800s. At times, business leaders are seen as greedy and corrupt villains; at other times, they are hailed as heroes. This is not the first time that Americans have questioned the motives of business leaders. In the late 1800s, for example, some business leaders were known as "robber barons" because of their corrupt practices and their disregard for others. This caused the government to pass laws to regulate business practices. Now, when there are business scandals, the government responds with more rules and regulations. Traditionally, Republicans have been in favor of a laissez-faire, or hands-off policy, and Democrats have favored more regulation and safeguards. The one factor that does not change is the strong belief in the value and importance of the American Dream.

Redefining the American Dream

27 Why does the American Dream of a better life persist in a bad economy or in the midst of other troubles? And why does it seem to encourage and inspire many Americans instead of discouraging and depressing them? Huffington says that, when writing her book *Third World America,* she was again and again struck by the resilience,[8] creativity, and acts of compassion[9] that she discovered taking place all over America.

28 First, many Americans truly are resilient. Perhaps part of this trait comes from their frontier heritage, where people believed they could pull themselves up by their bootstraps in times of trouble. The strong belief in self-reliance and individual freedom has led many Americans to redefine the American Dream for themselves. MetLife, a large American company that provides insurance, annuities, and employee benefits, has been doing an annual study of the American Dream for more than five years. Their most recent study shows a significant shift in priorities. It reveals the rise of what they call the "Do-It-Yourself" (DIY) American Dream and a portrayal of Americans as "resilient and adaptive." Faced with economic hardship, Americans now say that having close relationships with their friends and family is more important than acquiring additional material possessions.

---

[8] *resilience: the ability to quickly become strong, healthy, or happy after a difficult situation*

[9] *compassion: sympathy for people who are suffering and a desire to help them*

They are more content with what they already have, and they are seeking a better balance between their work and their personal lives. The study concludes that for most Americans now, "Achieving a sense of personal fulfillment is more important toward realizing the American Dream than accumulating material wealth."

29 Second, creativity is highly valued in American society. Gary Shapiro, president and CEO of the Consumer Electronics Association (which is responsible for the world's largest annual technology trade show), believes that innovation in business is critical. In *The Comeback: How Innovation Will Restore the American Dream*, Shapiro says that throughout history, our great innovators have been the real drivers of American economic success. American innovation is what creates new jobs and even whole new industries that never existed before. "Most importantly," Shapiro concludes, "innovation moves us forward as a nation, pushing us to succeed and strive for a better tomorrow. In short, innovation is the American Dream."

30 Richard Florida, author of *The Rise of the Creative Class*, believes that the role of innovation and creativity is rising in the United States today, and not just in the field of technology. Based on his analysis of census data, Florida estimates that nearly one-third of the American workforce now belong to "the creative class." They either create new ideas, technology, or content in fields such as science, education, design, the arts, and entertainment, or they engage in solving complex problems, in fields such as business, law, finance, and health care. These creative workers tend to cluster on the east and west coasts, in high-tech centers, and near major research universities and institutions. They have a strong, positive impact on the economic future of these areas.

31 Third, the compassionate nature of Americans and their search for meaning are a part of the redefinition of the American Dream. In *Abundance: The Future Is Better than You Think*, Peter Diamandis and Steven Kotler talk about the DIY (Do-It-Yourself) innovator. They say that the marriage of self-reliance and technology has helped shape the DIY innovator into a force for spreading abundance and a force for good. DIY innovators now have the technical tools to turn their visions of a better world into real businesses that can solve real problems. For example, Chris Anderson, the editor in chief of *Wired* magazine leads a nonprofit online community called DIY Drones. Using crowdscience techniques, his group of DIY innovators learned to build drones[10] for about $300.00 apiece, instead of the military's price of $35,000 to $250,000. Now they are looking at using drones to carry supplies into places where monsoons wash out roads, or areas with no roads at all. Another company, part of what Diamandis and Kotler call the Maker Movement, has a network of drones and recharging stations housed in shipping containers and spread throughout Africa. Smartphones are used to place orders in villages that are in remote locations, and then drones deliver the orders. Drones such as the Quad Copter can carry everything from medicine to replacement parts for farm machinery at a cost less than six cents per kilogram-kilometre.

32 Ebay's first president Jeff Skoll, Facebook founder Mark Zuckerberg, and Pay Pal founder Elon Musk are part of a new group of billionaires that Diamandis and Kotler call the *technophilanthropists*. They have made their fortunes in new fields of

---

[10] *drone: an airplane or piece of equipment that does not have a person inside it, but is operated by radio*

technology and now they are changing the face of philanthropy in the United States. Traditionally, philanthropists have started giving their money to charity toward the end of their lives. However, many of these technophilanthropists were billionaires before the age of 30, and they turned to philanthropy right afterward. Skoll says that they are full of the energy and confidence "that come from building global businesses at such a young age. They want to tackle audacious goals like nuclear proliferation[11] or pandemics[12] or water." They think big and believe that they can find solutions to "impossible" problems such as providing clean, safe drinking water to everyone on the planet. Because of their young age, they think they can really make a difference in their lifetime, solving enormous social problems.

33 A number of the technophilanthropists are DIY social entrepreneurs. Diamandis and Kotler say these are individuals who "combine the pragmatic, results-oriented methods of a business entrepreneur with the goals of a social reformer." Some social entrepreneurs start benefit corporations where profits are spent bringing about social change. These benefit corporations are established to solve particular social problems; they raise profits but use the money for projects often done by nonprofit organizations. The Center for Association Leadership says that the newly emerging benefit corporations are blurring the traditional line between for-profit corporations and nonprofit organizations. Benefit corporations must commit to providing social or environmental benefits, "while still showing a healthy bottom line." They are "devoted to what is known in the business community as the triple bottom line: people, planet, and profit," and they must publicly report on their social and environmental performance. They are also a potential source of financial support for nonprofit organizations, and their profit structure allows benefit corporations to continue their work without constantly having to look for outside funding.

34 Jeff Skoll, the first president of eBay, says social entrepreneurs are intensely enthusiastic people who are anxious to reach their goals. They go beyond what charities usually do to bring about change. He describes social entrepreneurs this way:

> *By nature, entrepreneurs aren't satisfied until they do change the world, and let nothing get in their way. Charities may give people food. But social entrepreneurs don't just teach people to grow food—they're not happy until they've taught a farmer how to grow food, make money, pour the profits back into the business, hire ten other people, and in the process, transform the entire industry.*

The Future of American Business

35 In good economic times and bad, a number of Americans still try to start their own business. Many of these hopeful entrepreneurs have regular jobs, and they run their business venture on the side, in their spare time. The government encourages small business start-ups through the Small Business Administration (SBA), because they are the creators of most new jobs in the United States and employ more than half of all American workers. The SBA defines a small business as one that employs fewer than 500 people, but the vast majority of them (over three-quarters) have no employees at all— only the self-employed owner. About half of all small businesses are home-based, and the Internet plays an important role.

---

[11] *nuclear proliferation: the spread of nuclear weapons*

[12] *pandemic: an illness or disease that affects the population of a very large area*

Surprisingly, more than 99 percent of all American firms *with* employees are small businesses, with half of them employing 10–99 people. In the United States, there are over 23,000,000 small businesses and only about 18,500 large firms employing more than 500 workers.

36 The Internet has given individuals the tools to collaborate on almost everything, and many Americans who have business ideas find support there. Sites such as www.quirky.com will even help you develop an idea for a new invention. You submit an idea, and they ask their online crowd of people to vote on whether they think it's an invention worth bringing to life. If your idea is chosen, you participate in a crowdsourcing process of designing, engineering, financing, manufacturing, and then distributing your product. The quirky site keeps track of everyone's contribution online, and all who participate in the process get a percentage of the profits from the sales, even a fraction of a percent. Such websites offer the ultimate form of collaboration.

37 The Internet provides the global connections that allow businesses, large and small, to interact with potential customers everywhere, at any time.

The United States remains one of the largest markets in the world, and it will undoubtedly continue to be a major player in the global economy. The World Bank ranks the United States fourth in the world for ease of doing business, behind Singapore, Hong Kong, and New Zealand. And the diverse multicultural American workforce will continue to be an asset in coming years.

38 Some American businesses that had moved their operations overseas are now returning, and manufacturing is coming back. However, much of the new manufacturing uses robotics[13] and requires fewer workers, and the workers must have higher-level skills. American education systems and business communities are trying to collaborate to help provide workers with the new skills necessary for future employment. Significant changes will be necessary.

39 Although the institution of American business has certainly undergone enormous changes in recent decades, it has remained one of the most important institutions in the United States. In many ways, the business of America is still business.

---

[13] *robotics: the study of how robots (machines that do the work of a person) are made and used*

AFTER YOU READ

Understand Main Ideas

Check the predictions you made on page 125 before reading the chapter. How many of your predictions were correct? Look at the headings in the chapter and work with a partner to complete the outline of the main ideas.

A. The Characteristics of American Business: private, for-profit

B. How Business Competition Reinforces Other Values

    1. Competition protects individual _____freedom_____

    2. Competition strengthens _____

    3. Business competition encourages _____

C. The Dream of Getting Rich

    1. Careers in business offer _____

    2. Americans distrust _____

D. The Entrepreneur as Business Hero

    1. Entrepreneurs are respected because _____

    2. The early entrepreneurs may be compared to _____

    3. Americans were influenced by Horatio Alger's _____

    4. Americans also respect entrepreneurs' dislike of _____

E. The Corporate CEO/CFO

    1. CEOs do not create new businesses, they _____

    2. Americans have lost respect for CEOs because _____

F. The Middle Class vs. the One Percent

    1. Middle class Americans became discouraged about _____

    2. They were angry because _____

    3. Books were written about _____

G. Redefining the American Dream

    1. Americans are _____

    2. There is a high value placed on _____

3. They are compassionate and are searching for _____

   4. The technophilanthropists are _____

H. _____

   1. Many Americans still choose to _____

   2. The Internet _____

Understand Details

Write **T** if the statement is true and **F** if it is false according to the information in the chapter.

_____ 1. Most American businesses are directly or indirectly owned by the government.

_____ 2. Most Americans believe that business supports ideals and values that are important to the country.

_____ 3. Americans believe that competition among businesses is good for the economy but it does little to protect the freedom of the individual.

_____ 4. To succeed in American business, Americans believe that family background and social position are more important than anything, including hard work.

_____ 5. Most Americans believe that success in business offers the best chance to fulfill the dream of being wealthy.

_____ 6. A CEO may be admired since he or she started a successful business from practically nothing.

_____ 7. Some American companies moved their factories overseas because they could not afford to pay the high wages expected in the United States.

_____ 8. Most American companies pay their workers good retirement pensions, so people do not have to worry about having enough money when they stop working.

_____ 9. There are many more large corporations in the United States than small businesses.

_____ 10. Even in bad economic times, many Americans still try to start their own small businesses.

Talk About It

Work in small groups and choose one or more of these questions to discuss.

1. What qualities should a good businessperson have in order to be successful? Are these the same personal qualities that you would like your own boss to have?
2. How do you find out about job openings in your country? How important are family and personal connections?
3. Who do you admire more: people who start their own business from nothing, or those who save a big corporation that is in trouble? Why?

SKILL BUILDING

Improve Your Reading Skills: Scanning

Scan the chapter to look for these names. Then identify each person with a short phrase.

EXAMPLE: Alexis de Tocqueville *observed Americans' attraction to business in the 1830s.*

1. Calvin Coolidge _____
2. Arianna Huffington _____
3. Mark Zuckerberg _____
4. Warren Buffet _____
5. Gary Shapiro _____
6. Jeff Skoll _____
7. Chris Anderson _____
8. Horatio Alger _____
9. Richard Florida _____
10. Mitt Romney _____

Develop Your Critical Thinking Skills

Analyze a Reading

Read the following article from the website of the Small Business Administration (SBA) and analyze what it says. Write answers to these questions:

1. Who do you think the intended readers are, and why?
2. The article has a heading that reads "Small business is BIG!" What information is given that supports that claim?
3. What do you think are the most important and convincing facts in this article?

SMALL BUSINESS, BIG IMPACT!

One thing is for sure, as a small business owner you are not alone! There are millions of small businesses across the United States traveling the same road as you each and every day. Although your business operates in its own unique fashion, the cumulative impact of the small business sector is enormous.

SMALL BUSINESS IS BIG!

- The 23 million small businesses in America account for 54 percent of all U.S. sales.
- Small businesses provide 55 percent of all jobs and 66 percent of all net new jobs since the 1970s.
- The 600,000 plus franchised small businesses in the U.S. account for 40 percent of all retail sales and provide jobs for some eight million people.
- The small business sector in America occupies 30–50 percent of all commercial space, an estimated 20–34 billion square feet.

Furthermore, the small business sector is growing rapidly. While corporate America has been "downsizing," the rate of small business "start-ups" has grown, and the rate for small business failures has declined.

- The number of small businesses in the United States has increased 49 percent since 1982.

Since 1990, as big business eliminated four million jobs, small businesses added eight million new jobs.

Build Your Vocabulary

Same or Different

Read these sentences, which contain AWL words in bold. Look at the list of words after each sentence. Write the letter of the one word that has a different or opposite meaning from the boldfaced word.

_____ 1. A government-run system of production and **distribution** of goods is seen as inferior.
    a. sharing   b. giving   c. supplying   d. collecting

_____ 2. The people who, more than 100 years ago, built up the nation's great industries, such as steel, railroads, and oil **refining**, were usually entrepreneurs.
    a. purifying   b. selling   c. cleaning   d. improving

_____ 3. The strong influence of the success stories of the early entrepreneurs can be found in the great popularity of the novels of Horatio Alger, which were **published** in late-nineteenth and early-twentieth-century America.
    a. produced   b. printed   c. hidden   d. created

_____ 4. Jeff Skoll, the first president of eBay, says social entrepreneurs are **intensely** enthusiastic people who are anxious to reach their goals.
   a. strongly   b. seriously   c. mildly   d. deeply

_____ 5. Even in a bad economy, the American Dream makes people feel encouraged and inspired, not discouraged and **depressed**.
   a. happy   b. unhappy   c. sad   d. miserable

More AWL Words

Test your knowledge of these AWL words in the chapter by matching the following words with their definitions.

_____ 1. acquire   a. to support an idea

_____ 2. aware   b. a difference between things that are compared

_____ 3. benefit   c. an official rule or order

_____ 4. capable   d. understanding what is happening

_____ 5. contrast   e. main idea in a piece of writing

_____ 6. creative   f. having the skills needed to do something

_____ 7. decline   g. something that supplies information

_____ 8. energy   h. social or professional position

_____ 9. enormous   i. something that improves your life

_____ 10. financial   j. relating to money

_____ 11. global   k. physical and mental strength

_____ 12. guarantee   l. to buy or obtain something

_____ 13. regulation   m. a group of people who play a game or sport together

_____ 14. reinforce   n. producing or using new ideas

_____ 15. source   o. a formal written promise that something will be done or will happen

_____ 16. status   p. extremely large

_____ 17. team   q. affecting the whole world

_____ 18. theme   r. to decrease in quantity or importance

Idioms and Popular Phrases

The chapter contains several idioms and popular phrases that add color to the language. Look at the explanations below, and then read the sentences taken from the chapter. Find the phrase in italics for each of these meanings and write the letter of the sentence next to the correct meaning.

__a__ 1. do what is right and expected

____ 2. warn that something bad will happen

____ 3. get the worst deal

____ 4. take care of yourself and help yourself, be self-reliant

____ 5. keep a record

____ 6. work toward completing or achieving something

____ 7. change completely

____ 8. profit after expenses, after all the numbers are added/subtracted

   a. "Upward mobility has always been at the center of the American Dream—a promise that if you work hard and *play by the rules,* you'll do well, and your children will have the chance to do even better."
   b. But in the last few years, Huffington said she saw that the middle class was *"getting the short end of the stick."*
   c. Perhaps part of this trait comes from their frontier heritage, where people believed they could *pull themselves up by their bootstraps* in times of trouble.
   d. Huffington *sounded the alarm* in her book about how American politicians are abandoning the middle class and betraying the American Dream.
   e. The quirky site *keeps track of* everyone's contribution online, and all who participate in the process get a percent of the profits from the sales, even a fraction of a percent.
   f. They want to *tackle* audacious *goals* like nuclear proliferation or pandemics or water.
   g. They're not happy until they've taught a farmer how to grow food, make money, pour the profits back into the business, hire ten other people, and in the process, *transform* the entire industry.
   h. Benefit corporations must commit to providing social or environmental benefits, "while still showing a healthy *bottom line.*"

EXPAND YOUR KNOWLEDGE

Ask Yourself / Ask Americans

Do you agree or disagree with each of the following statements? Put a check under the number that indicates how you feel.

+2 = Strongly agree

+1 = Agree

 0 = No opinion

−1 = Disagree

−2 = Strongly disagree

	+2	+1	0	−1	−2
1. I admire a person who is his or her own boss more than someone who must answer to others.	___	___	___	___	___
2. I would like to own my own business.	___	___	___	___	___
3. I think we should work to live, not live to work.	___	___	___	___	___
4. A teacher has more prestige than a businessperson.	___	___	___	___	___
5. Companies should offer loyal employees lifetime employment.	___	___	___	___	___
6. Corporate CEOs deserve as much money as they can get.	___	___	___	___	___
7. The place where I live is more important to me than where I work.	___	___	___	___	___
8. I would take a job I liked for less pay over a job I didn't like for more pay.	___	___	___	___	___
9. I would work on an assembly line in a factory if the pay were good.	___	___	___	___	___
10. All things considered, a government-run system is better for a country and its people than capitalism.	___	___	___	___	___

Ask several Americans to respond to these statements, if possible. If there are no Americans available, ask people from other countries.

People Watching

Who works in the United States? What ages? Men, women, teenagers, the elderly? What kind of jobs do they do? To answer these questions, if you are in the United States, look around you in various businesses open to the public: restaurants, banks, stores, drugstores, supermarkets, clubs, dry cleaners, doctors' offices, theaters, and so on. If you are near a university, check to see who is working in the library and the cafeteria. (If you are not in the United States, you may gather information from Americans you know, or you can observe people in your country.)

Observe people working in at least ten different places and record your results in this chart.

Kind of Job	Gender of Worker	Age of Worker	Other Observations
1.			
2.			
3.			
4.			
5.			
6.			
7.			
8.			
9.			
10.			

Proverbs and Sayings

Americans have a strong "sense of time." They think of it as a resource—something to be used, saved, spent, shared, etc. How they talk about time is an indication of how they feel about it.

Add to the list of time expressions below by asking Americans for suggestions, by listening to conversations, and by watching TV.

1. A stitch in time saves nine.
2. Time is money.
3. Time and tide wait for no man.
4. I don't have time for that today.
5. Can you give me a few minutes of your time?
6. We lost a lot of time on that.

Small-Group Discussion

Read the following explanation about how different cultures structure time, and then discuss the questions with members of your small group. When you have finished, report your group's findings to the rest of the class.

Edward T. Hall has described two basic types of cultures, with regard to the ways those cultures deal with time. He calls these "monochronic" and "polychronic" cultures. In monochronic cultures, people do one thing at a time. In polychronic cultures, people do many things at a time. For example, in a monochronic culture, when someone has a business appointment, that person expects to have the complete attention of the other party until the appointment has ended. On the other hand, in a polychronic culture, a person who has a business appointment expects there to be many others waiting and being dealt with at one time, sometimes both in person and on the phone.

1. How are activities scheduled in your country?
2. Is your culture monochronic or polychronic?
3. Which best describes the United States?
4. Which would best describe the following situations?
    a. You arrive at the airport an hour before your flight to find that there are large crowds pushing their way to the counter. Whoever pushes hardest gets to the front and gets waited on. The ticket agent behind the counter serves several people at once, focusing attention on the one who has made himself or herself most noticed.
    b. The doctor has told you that he will meet you at the hospital at 10:00 A.M. to take care of a minor problem. You have difficulty finding transportation, but finally arrive at 10:45. The doctor is seeing another patient and sends word that he will not be able to see you now until he can "squeeze you in" around his other appointments. You will probably have to wait until late afternoon.
5. What other monochronic or polychronic situations can you think of?

Use the Internet

Work with a partner and do research on the Internet. Look for information about one of these super-rich business leaders.

Bill Gates

Ted Turner

Oprah Winfrey

Michael Bloomberg

Jeff Bezos

Sergey Brin

Laurene Powell Jobs

Melissa Mayer

Small-Group Project

Work in a group to create a small business.
- Decide on a name and describe what business the company will conduct.
- Choose a slogan for your business.
- List what the qualifications of the employees will be and what benefits the company will offer.

- Make up an advertisement for the business and, if possible, videotape it.
- Present your company to the rest of the class.

WRITE ABOUT IT

Choose one of the following topics. Then write a short composition about it.

1. Compare the way American businesses operate with the way businesses operate in your country. For example, compare a typical transaction at a shop. How do the activities differ? Consider these points:

    a. When the employees work

    b. Who the employees are and how long they have worked there

    c. Whether the shopkeeper waits on one person or several people at a time

    d. If the customer bargains or there is a set price

    e. If the employees know the customers

    f. What the relationship is between the employees and their employer

2. Most businesses in America require those applying for a job to submit a résumé, a summary of their work experience, education, and qualifications. Write a résumé for a job that you would like to have. Describe the position you want, and then write a résumé to convince an employer to hire you. As you write, consider the following advice from Jerrold G. Simon, EdD, a psychologist and career development specialist at Harvard Business School, who advises people to "sell themselves" in their résumé:

    The most qualified people don't always get the job. It goes to the person who presents himself more persuasively in person and on paper. So don't just list where you were and what you did. This is your chance to tell how well you did. Were you the best salesman? Did you cut operating costs? Give numbers, statistics, percentages, and increases in sales or profits.

EXPLORE ON YOUR OWN

Books to Read

Horatio Alger, *Ragged Dick; Or, Street Life in New York with the Boot Blacks*—Horatio Alger wrote this classic story of "rags to riches" about a young boy who works hard and eventually becomes a middle-class gentleman.

F. Scott Fitzgerald, *The Great Gatsby*—In this classic American novel about a self-made man, Jay Gatsby's pursuit of wealth causes his fall.

Chrystia Freeland, *Plutocrats: The Rise of the New Global Super-Rich and the Fall of Everyone Else*—Freeland looks at the economic elites who threaten the democratic, politically open society of the United States and the American Dream.

Arianna Huffington, *Third World America: How Our Politicians Are Abandoning the Middle Class and Betraying the American Dream*—Huffington, herself an immigrant from Greece, warns about what could happen if the government does not protect the middle class.

Gary Shapiro, *The Comeback: How Innovation Will Restore the American Dream*—Shapiro says that throughout history, our great innovators have been the real drivers of American economic success.

Movies to See

9 to 5—In this popular comedy, three women who are tired of being treated badly by their boss decide to capture him and make changes at their workplace.

Class Action—A lawyer who is suing an auto company over a safety defect faces his daughter, who is the attorney representing the company.

Trading Places—A rich stockbroker and a street-smart beggar find themselves trading places as part of a bet by two old millionaires.

Up in the Air—A businessman makes his living traveling around the country firing people for different companies.

Wall Street—A young and impatient stockbroker is willing to do anything to get to the top, including trading on illegal inside information.

GOVERNMENT AND POLITICS IN THE UNITED STATES

A wise and frugal Government shall restrain men from injuring one another, [and] shall leave them otherwise free to regulate their own pursuits of industry and improvements.

Thomas Jefferson (1743–1826)

What role do Americans think their government should play in their lives? How do American values affect how the United States government functions?

BEFORE YOU READ

Preview Vocabulary

A. Read the following sentences from the chapter and notice the words in italics. These key AWL words will help you understand the chapter reading. Use context clues to help you figure out the meanings. Then choose which definition is best for the italicized word.

____ 1. The way in which the national government is organized in the U.S. Constitution provides an excellent *illustration* of the American suspicion of governmental power.
   a. example that shows the truth very clearly
   b. argument against an idea

____ 2. The judicial branch both *interprets* the law and determines whether the law is constitutional—that is, whether the law is permitted under the U.S. Constitution.
   a. explains
   b. rejects

____ 3. The Senate has certain powers over foreign treaties and *military* actions.
   a. relating to law
   b. relating to war

____ 4. This requires the president to have "the advice and *consent* of the Senate" before taking certain action on the international front.
   a. permission to do something
   b. a careful plan for action

____ 5. The *Bill of Rights* guarantees the right of a fair criminal *procedure* for those accused of breaking laws.
   a. punishment
   b. method

____ 6. After a *series* of legal challenges, the U.S. Supreme Court decided about a month after the election that the Florida state legislature had a right to stop recounting the ballots and certify the electoral votes.
   a. events that are related and have a particular result
   b. events that break the law and have consequences

____ 7. The Great *Depression* of the 1930s greatly weakened the businessperson's position as the American ideal of the free individual, and big business lost respect.
   a. a time when there was not much business activity and many people had no jobs
   b. a time when there was much corruption and greed among business leaders

_____ 8. The widespread unemployment and other economic hardships of the Depression gave rise to the *assumption* that individuals could not be expected to rely solely on themselves in providing for their economic security.
   a. promise that something will happen in the future
   b. belief (that you think is true although you have no proof)

_____ 9. There is an *ideological* divide over the role and size of the national government—Republicans have traditionally believed that big government is not only inefficient, it also endangers individual rights and freedoms, while Democrats have called for more government regulation of financial institutions and corporate polluters and higher taxes on upper income Americans to fund social programs.
   a. based on a particular set of beliefs or ideas
   b. based on historical differences

_____ 10. Still, it is individuals, their rights, their interests, and their ambitions, not those of the nation as a whole, that are the *focus* of attention.
   a. the most important part
   b. the most difficult part

B. There are four AWL words in the quotation by Thomas Jefferson at the beginning of the chapter. Read the quotation and find the words with the following meanings. Write each word next to its meaning.

_____ 1. acts of trying to get something

_____ 2. prevent someone from doing something

_____ 3. to control an activity by rules

_____ 4. hurting

Preview Content

A. Before you read, preview the chapter by looking at the illustrations and reading the headings and the captions under the pictures. Work with a partner and answer these questions.

1. Do you agree with the quotation by Thomas Jefferson? Paraphrase (rewrite) the quotation in your own words.
2. In the United States, who has more power, the president or Congress? Why do you think so?
3. What are the two major political parties in the United States? What is the main difference in their beliefs?

B. Make a graphic organizer about government. Write the word *government* in the center of a piece of paper. Then draw lines out from the center, as you did on page 29. Write all the things you think a government should do for its people.

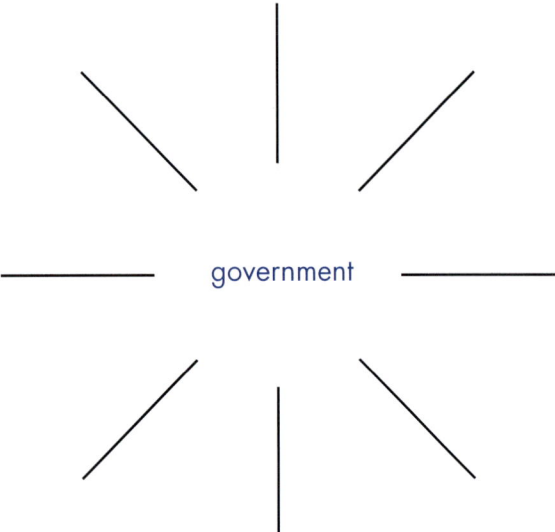

C. Predict five topics that will be discussed in this chapter. Write your predictions here.

1. _____
2. _____
3. _____
4. _____
5. _____

A SUSPICION OF STRONG GOVERNMENT

1 The ideal of the free individual has had a profound effect on the way Americans view their government. Traditionally, there has been a deep suspicion that government is the natural enemy of freedom, even if it is elected by the people. The bigger and stronger the government becomes, the more dangerous many Americans believe it is to their individual freedom.*

The Signing of the *Declaration of Independence*, a painting by John Trumbull

2 This suspicion of strong government goes back to the men who led the American Revolution in 1776. These men believed the government of Great Britain wanted to discourage the freedom and economic opportunities of the American colonists by excessive taxes and other measures that would ultimately benefit the British aristocracy and monarchy. Thomas Paine, the famous revolutionary writer, expressed the view of other American revolutionists when he said, "...Government even in its best state is but a necessary evil; in its worst state, an intolerable[1] one..."

The Organization of the American Government

3 The way in which the national government is organized in the U.S. Constitution provides an excellent illustration of the American suspicion of governmental power. The provisions of the Constitution are more concerned with keeping the government from doing evil than with enabling it to do good. The national government, for example, is divided into three separate branches. This division of governmental power is based on the belief that if any one part or branch of government has all, or even most of the power, it will become a threat to the freedom of individual citizens.

4 The legislative or lawmaking branch of the government is called the *Congress*. Congress has two houses—the Senate, with two senators from each state regardless of the size of its population, and the *House of Representatives,* consisting of a total of 435 representatives divided among the fifty states by population. (In the House, states with large populations have more representatives than states with small populations, while in the Senate, each state has equal representation.) The

---

*It is important to note that all 50 states have state governments, and within the states there are local governments at the city and/or county level, all of which have their own laws, police, and court systems. According to the Constitution, states have all powers not given to the national (or federal) government. If there is a conflict between a state law and a national law, the national law prevails.

[1] intolerable: too difficult, bad, or annoying to accept or deal with

Government and Politics in the United States ★ 153

president, or chief executive, heads the executive branch, which has responsibility to carry out the laws. The *Supreme Court* and lower national courts make up the judicial branch. The judicial branch settles disputes about the exact meaning of the law through court cases. It both interprets the law and determines whether the law is *constitutional*—that is, whether the law is permitted under the U.S. Constitution.

5 If any one of the three branches starts to abuse[2] its power, the other two may join together to stop it, through a system of *checks* and *balances.* The Constitution is most careful in balancing the powers of the legislative and executive branches of the government because these two (Congress and the president) are the most powerful of the three branches. In almost every important area of governmental activity, such as the power to make laws, to declare war, or to conclude treaties with foreign countries, the Constitution gives each of these two branches enough power to prevent the other from acting on its own.

6 Observers from other countries are often confused by the American system. The national government may seem to speak with two conflicting voices, that of the president and that of Congress. For example, a treaty with a foreign government signed by the president dies if the Senate refuses to *ratify* it—that is, if the Senate doesn't vote to accept it. The Senate has certain powers over foreign treaties and, with the House, military actions. This requires the president to have "the advice and consent of the Senate" before taking certain actions on the international front. The Senate also must approve all the members of the president's cabinet, such as the Secretary of State and the Secretary of Defense.

7 On the other hand, the president may prevent a bill passed by Congress from becoming law. When both houses of Congress have agreed on a piece of legislation or a resolution, it is sent to the president. The president has ten days to act, not counting Sundays. At that point, there are four possibilities:

1. The president agrees with the bill, signs it, and it becomes law.

2. The president disagrees with the bill, vetoes it, and sends it back to the Congress with his or her reasons for refusing to sign it. If two-thirds of both the House and the Senate vote to override the president's veto, the bill becomes law.

3. The president may take no action and after ten days (not counting Sundays), the bill becomes law without his signature.

4. If the Congress adjourns[3] before the ten-day period is over, and the president has neither signed nor vetoed the bill, it is defeated. This is called a *pocket veto.* Presidents sometimes do this with bills they do not like but do not want to go on record as having vetoed.

8 Although the American system of divided governmental power strikes many observers as inefficient and even disorganized, most Americans still strongly believe in it for two reasons: (1) It has been able to meet the challenges of the past, and (2) it gives strong protection to individual freedoms.

9 In addition to dividing government powers into three branches, the Constitution includes a *Bill of Rights* that is designed to protect specific individual rights and freedoms from government interference. Some of the guarantees in the *Bill of*

[2] *abuse: to deliberately use power or authority for the wrong purpose*

[3] *adjourns: stops meeting for a short time*

Rights concern the freedom of expression. The government may not interfere with an individual's freedom of speech or freedom of religious worship, or the right to assemble (get together). The *Bill of Rights* also guarantees the right of a fair criminal procedure for those accused of breaking laws. These rights are sometimes called "due process." They include provisions that someone accused of a crime must be charged with the crime and is presumed innocent until proven guilty. The accused has the right to an attorney, and there must be a trial declaring someone guilty before punishment is given. Thus, the *Bill of Rights* is another statement of the American belief in the importance of individual freedom.

The Election of the President and the Congress

10   The president and both houses of Congress have almost complete political independence from each other because they are all chosen in separate elections. For example, the election of the Congress does not determine who will be elected president, and the presidential election does not determine who will be elected to either house of Congress. This system is quite different from the way a parliamentary system of government chooses a prime minister. Another difference is that there are only two important political parties in the United States: the Democrats, who are traditionally liberal or progressive, and the Republicans, who are more conservative. In parliamentary systems, there may be a number of significant political parties that must agree to form a government, while in the United States this is not the case. The president, the representatives, and the senators are all chosen by the American citizens in elections.

11   Because the elections of the president and members of the two houses of Congress are separate from each other, it is quite possible in the American system to have the leader of one political party win the presidency while the other major political party wins a majority of the seats in Congress. Thus, the Republicans may control one house, while the Democrats may control the other. During the late 1900s, while most of the presidents were Republican, the Democrats often controlled one or both of the houses of Congress. In 1994, the reverse happened: While Bill Clinton, a Democrat, was president, the Republicans won control of both the House of Representatives and the Senate. Then in the early 2000s, for a time, the Republican Party controlled the presidency (George W. Bush) and both houses of Congress. The presidency of Barack Obama (a Democrat) has again seen divided government; after the first two years, in both of his terms the House was controlled by the Republicans, and the Senate was controlled by Democrats.

12   In order to understand what is happening in Washington, it is important to know not only the party of the president, but also which parties control the House and the Senate. Because both the House of Representatives and the Senate must agree on all legislation before it goes to the president, legislation may pass one house but be blocked in the other. Furthermore, the party in control of the House or Senate has the potential of changing every two years. Members of the House of Representatives are elected for two-year terms, while senators serve six-year terms. The Senate terms are staggered[4] so that only one-third of the senators run for re-election each time the House elections are held, every two years.

---

[4] *staggered: arranged so that their terms of office (time serving as a senator or representative) do not all begin and end at the same time*

13 Presidential elections are held every four years, on the first Tuesday in November. When the Constitution was written, the founding fathers had a disagreement about how the president should be elected. Some did not want the members of Congress to choose the president, and others were afraid to leave the choice entirely to the voters. The result was a compromise—the electoral college, a system for indirectly electing the president. The system persists today. In presidential elections, people are actually voting for representatives called *electors*, and it is these electors who officially choose the president. With the electoral college system, the winner of the plurality[5] (the highest number) of each state's popular votes gets all of that state's electoral votes, in most cases. (There are several exceptions.) The number of each state's electoral votes is equal to the total number of their representatives in the House and the Senate. Though the number of electoral votes varies according to each state's population, it is still possible for a person to be elected president without getting the highest number of the popular, or individual, votes.

14 Although Americans were aware of the electoral college system, the average voter did not give it much thought until the election of 2000. There had been only three previous instances of presidents ever losing the popular vote but winning the electoral vote, and it seemed a remote possibility. The last time it had happened was in 1888, when Benjamin Harrison won the presidency, even though Grover Cleveland had the majority of popular votes. All through the 1900s, the presidents who were elected had won at least a plurality, (the highest number of the popular votes), in addition to winning the electoral votes. However, in the election of 2000, Al Gore, the Democratic candidate, won more popular votes than George W. Bush, the Republican candidate, but Bush won the most electoral votes and became president. (In the 2004 election between George W. Bush and John Kerry, the electoral college was not an issue, because Bush won both the popular vote and the electoral vote.)

15 The result of the election of 2000 sent shock waves through the American political system. One reason was that the vote was incredibly close, and several states had to count their votes a second time. The state with the most controversial results was Florida, where the governor of the state was Jeb Bush, George W. Bush's brother. Although Gore had won the popular vote nationwide, whoever won the twenty-five Florida electoral votes would win the election. The recounts of the votes in Florida showed Bush winning by fewer than 1,000 votes out of almost six million votes cast. After a series of legal challenges, the U.S. Supreme Court decided about a month after the election that the Florida state legislature had the right to stop recounting the ballots and certify the electoral votes. The Supreme Court ruled that a state has the ultimate right to determine how its electors are chosen.

The Ideal of the Free Individual

16 In the late 1700s, most Americans expected the new national government created by the Constitution to leave them alone to pursue their individual goals. They believed the central purpose of government was to create the conditions most favorable to the development of the free individual.

17 Before the Civil War of the 1860s, the American ideal of the free individual was the frontier settler and the small farmer. President Thomas Jefferson expressed this

---

[5] *plurality: the number of votes received by the winning person in an election where there are three or more people trying to be elected*

ideal when he said, "Those who labor in the earth are the chosen people of God, if ever he had a chosen people...." Jefferson glorified farmers for being free individuals who relied on no one but themselves for their daily needs. Being dependent on none but themselves, farmers, he believed, were the most honest of citizens. Throughout his life Jefferson favored a small, weak form of government, which he believed would encourage the development of a nation of free, self-reliant farmer citizens.

18 From the end of the Civil War until the Great Depression of the 1930s, the successful businessperson replaced the farmer and the frontier settler as the ideal expression of the free individual. The prevailing view of Americans was that government should not interfere in business. If it were to do so, it would threaten the development of free individuals whose competitive spirit, self-reliance, and hard work were developing the United States into a land of greater and greater material prosperity.

19 Government, therefore, remained small and inactive in relation to the great size of the nation and the amount of power held by business corporations. Some government regulations were in place during this period, but these had only a small impact on business practices. From the 1870s until the 1930s, business organizations and ideas dominated American government and politics. During much of this time, the Republican Party was in power, and it strongly supported these policies.

The Development of Big Government

20 Traditionally, Republicans have favored letting businesses compete with little or no government regulation: Let the free enterprise system regulate itself in the marketplace. On the other hand, Democrats have traditionally favored using government to regulate businesses, protect consumers and workers, and also to solve social problems. Not surprisingly, it was a Democratic president who presided over the creation of "big government."

21 The Great Depression of the 1930s greatly weakened the businessperson's position as the American ideal of the free individual, and big business lost respect. The Depression also created the need for emergency government action to help the needy on a scale never before seen in the United States in peacetime. As a result, the idea that government should be small and inactive was largely abandoned. Moreover, the ideal of the free individual underwent some very important changes.

22 The widespread unemployment and other economic hardships of the Depression gave rise to the new assumption[6] that individuals could not be expected to rely solely on themselves in providing for their economic security. This new assumption, in turn, led to a large and active role for the national government in helping individuals meet their daily needs. The Democratic Party, led by President Franklin Roosevelt, brought about a number of changes in the 1930s, which he referred to as a "New Deal" for Americans.

23 Even with the return of prosperity after the Depression and World War II (1941–1945), the growth of government's role in helping to provide economic security for individuals did not end. It continued in the prosperous postwar years, and it was greatly expanded during the presidency of another Democrat, Lyndon Johnson, in the 1960s. Roosevelt's New Deal grew into what some saw as a permanent "welfare state" that provided payments for retired persons, government checks

[6] *assumption: something you think is true although you have no proof*

for the unemployed, support for families with dependent children and no father to provide income, health care for the poor and the elderly, and other government benefits. Johnson called the new welfare programs "The Great Society."

The Controversy over Entitlements

24 The development of big government, and the establishment of government social programs, is not without controversy. On the one hand, some Americans fear that economic security provided by the government will weaken self-reliance, an ideal that is closely associated in the minds of Americans with individual freedom. At worst, it presents a danger to individual freedom by making an increasing number of Americans dependent on the government instead of on themselves. In this way, the strong traditions of individualism and self-reliance have made Americans less accepting of social programs than the citizens of other democracies such as those in Western Europe, which have more extensive social programs than those of the United States.

25 A Pew Research study reveals the contrast between European and American attitudes:

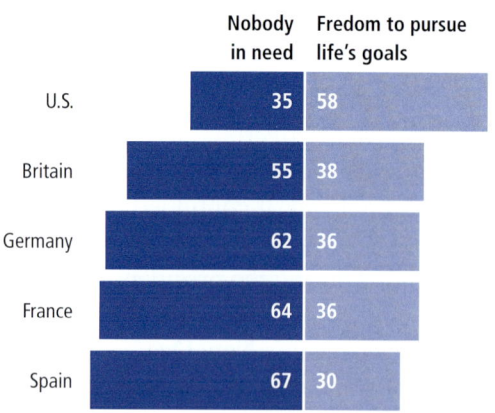

WHICH IS MORE IMPORTANT

	Nobody in need	Freedom to pursue life's goals
U.S.	35	58
Britain	55	38
Germany	62	36
France	64	36
Spain	67	30

American opinions continue to differ considerably from those of Western Europeans when it comes to views of individualism and the role of the state.

Nearly six-in-ten (58%) Americans believe it is more important for everyone to be free to pursue their life's goals without interference from the state, while just 36% say it is more important for the state to play an active role in society so as to guarantee that nobody is in need.

26 Americans generally are not in favor of European-style socialism that guarantees benefits for all who are needy. Indeed, some consider socialism a potentially dangerous, foreign economic system. Some conservatives have accused President Obama of being a socialist for some of his liberal stands. On the other hand, most Americans believe that their national government should provide some kind of "safety net" to take care of people in certain circumstances such as temporary loss of employment, damages from a natural disaster such as a hurricane, and of course retirement. It is interesting that the term for these benefits has changed. We used to make a distinction between welfare benefits and entitlements. Programs such as unemployment benefits, food stamps, and Medicaid (health care for the poor), were known as "welfare." Social Security and Medicare (health care for the retired) were seen as "entitlements," because working Americans and their employers pay into these systems. Therefore, when workers retire, they consider that they have paid for these benefits and they are entitled to them. Now the term welfare is almost never used, and all these government benefits are referred to as entitlements.

27 While most Americans would believe that the national government should provide them with some support, if they should need it, they may disagree about how much support and for how long. Democrats generally favor more generous support from the government than Republicans do. Republicans believe in a smaller role for the government and a greater emphasis on individual responsibility. During the 2012 election,

Republican presidential candidate Mitt Romney was overheard saying that 47 percent of Americans were dependent on government support and saw themselves as victims who could not take care of themselves:

> There are 47 percent of the people who will vote for the president no matter what...who are dependent upon government, who believe that they are victims....These are people who pay no income tax...and so my job is not to worry about those people. I'll never convince them that they should take personal responsibility and care for their lives.

28 In fact, about half of all American households have someone who receives some aid from the federal government. However, this number includes people who are retired and are receiving Social Security and Medicare benefits, now about 14 percent of the population, plus another 2 percent who are receiving other Social Security benefits. Most Americans believe that they have earned the right to having Social Security and Medicare when they retire, but the problem is that these benefits now take about one-third of the federal budget.

29 As the population ages, there are fewer younger workers and their employers paying Social Security taxes into the system, and more retired workers taking money out. Americans are living longer in retirement, and their medical expenses are rising. Because older Americans are more likely than young people to vote, politicians pay particular attention to their needs. They want the older Americans' votes. However, as budget deficits[7] grow, the reality is that some adjustments to all entitlements are likely to be needed, including Social Security and Medicare.

The Role of Special Interest Groups

30 Over time, practically all social and economic classes of Americans have seen the need to take advantage of, or to protect themselves from, the actions of government, especially the national government. To accomplish this, Americans with similar interests have formed special interest groups to more effectively influence the actions of government. These special interest groups are often called "lobbying[8] groups" or "pressure groups." Although lobbying groups have existed throughout the nation's history, they have grown significantly in both numbers and power since the late 1900s.

31 The National Rifle Association (mentioned in Chapter 4) is an example of a powerful and effective lobby. Its members are mostly people who own guns for hunting, target practice, and personal protection. The NRA, however, receives a great deal of money from business corporations that manufacture guns. Because of the attitudes and interests of its members, the NRA strongly opposes almost all government restrictions on the sale of all handguns, rifles, shotguns, and even semi-automatic and assault weapons. Even though most of the general public favors some gun control measures, the NRA has always been able to block the passage of most gun-control legislation. (See poll on page 167.)

---

[7] *deficit: the difference between the amount of money that a government spends and the amount that it takes in from taxes and other activities*

[8] *lobbying: trying to influence the government or someone with political power so that they make laws favorable to you*

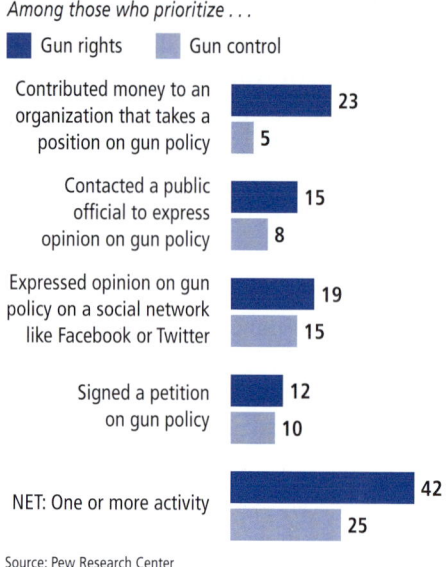

GUN RIGHTS PROPONENTS MORE POLITICALLY ACTIVE

32 Those who are concerned about the right to own guns are more likely to be politically active. The public sees both parties as being supportive of their views on gun control/gun rights—conservative Republicans are more concerned about their right to own guns, and liberal Democrats are more likely to favor stricter gun control laws.

33 Although few interest groups have been as successful as the NRA, most well-organized interest groups have achieved a large measure of success. By organizing into groups which put pressure on government officials, people can gain more rewards and avoid more government restrictions than if they tried to do it as individuals.

34 With this principle in mind, business interest groups have multiplied in recent decades so that most major trades, businesses, and even professions have their lobbyists in Washington. There are influential lobbies representing labor unions, farm groups, teachers, doctors, lawyers, and specific industries such as oil and natural gas, pharmaceuticals, and biotechnology. Interest groups representing ethnic groups such as African Americans, Native Americans, Mexican Americans, and Jewish Americans have also expanded. There are also interest groups representing a variety of ideals or causes that want government support. These include groups pressing for a clean environment and those promoting greater protection for consumers. As one congressman exclaimed, "Everybody in America has a lobby!"

35 The political tendency of recent decades is for the size of the government to bring about an increase in the number and size of interest groups, and for the greater demands made on the government by interest groups to increase the size of the government. Groups such as the AARP (American Association of Retired Persons) not only demand new government programs, regulations, and benefits for their members, they also strongly resist any attempts to reduce existing programs that

Interest groups represent a variety of populations in the United States.

160 ★ Chapter 7

they believe protect their interests, such as Social Security and Medicare. The result of this continuing cycle can be referred to as "interest group government." No single interest dominates government and politics as business groups did before the Great Depression. Instead, government and politics are based on reaching compromises with a large number of groups and pleasing as many as possible.

The New Individualism: Interest-Group Government

36 Interest-group government can be seen as expressing a new form of American individualism. Unlike the old frontier or business individualism, individuals do not claim to succeed on their own, but rather by forming groups to influence the government. Still, it is individuals, their rights, their interests, and their ambitions, not those of the nation as a whole, that are the focus of their attention. The interest group is no more than a tool to achieve the goals of the individual by influencing the government.

37 Although many Americans have benefited in some way from government-sponsored programs, some experts believe that interest-group government is harmful to the United States. The effect on politicians is enormous. First, interest groups often focus on one issue that is more important to their members than all others. For example, some people feel very strongly that abortion should not be legal in the United States. They may choose to vote for candidates primarily because of their stand on the abortion issue. Generally, because their members feel so strongly, lobby groups are able to promise that their members will vote for a candidate if he or she promises to support their issue once elected. The NRA gives members of Congress grades for their voting record on gun control, and it has been particularly effective in re-electing or defeating senators and representatives.

38 Second, members of special interest groups contribute large sums of money to election campaigns. Because candidates must rely mostly on private, not public, funding, they are often forced to depend on special interest groups for their campaign funds. Candidates at all levels of government—national, state, and local— must spend enormous amounts of their time raising funds for their re-election. For example, because members of the House of Representatives are elected every two years, they engage in continual fundraising. Senators and presidential candidates are also pressured. The situation has become so bad that many people are agreeing with the statement, "We have the best government that money can buy!" There have been efforts to reform the system, but the Supreme Court's *Citizens United* decision in 2010 ruled that corporations, individuals, and labor unions could make unlimited contributions to political campaigns through Super PACs (Political Action Committees). In the presidential election of 2012, Super PACs spent over $524 million, according to the Federal Election Commission.

The Political Landscape in the 2000s: Red States vs. Blue States

39 In reporting the results of presidential elections, TV news reports show the map of the United States with red states (awarding the state's electoral votes to the Republican candidate), and blue states (giving the electoral votes to the Democratic candidate). These colors have come to symbolize the deep divisions in America. In Obama's first national speech at the Democratic Convention in 2004, he offered his vision of a country where we are not red states or blue states—we are one people—the United States of America. But the divisions persist.

40 In *Barack Obama and the New America: The 2012 Election and the Changing Face of Politics*, Alan Abramowitz says the American voters are strongly divided

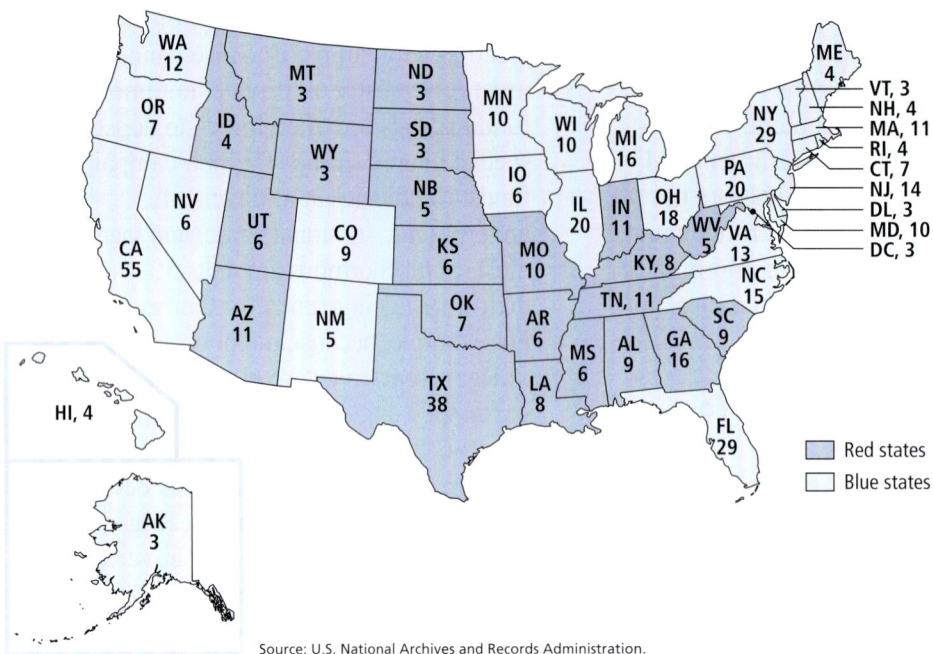

Source: U.S. National Archives and Records Administration.

along party lines. In an unusually partisan election, over 90 percent of the Democrats voted for Obama, and over 90 percent of the Republicans voted for Romney. Even the Independents, now about one-third of the electorate, were split 50/50 Obama/Romney. Also, more than 90 percent of voters chose their House or Senate representatives according to their party. Abramowitz says that this unusual degree of party loyalty reflects the deep divisions in American society:

> A close examination of the voting patterns in 2012 demonstrates the existence of three major divisions between Democrats and Republicans—a racial divide between a Democratic Party increasingly dependent on votes from non-whites and an overwhelmingly white Republican Party, an ideological divide over the role and size of government, and a cultural divide over values, morality, and lifestyle.

41   *First, the racial divide.* Barack Obama's winning the presidency in 2008 was truly a historical event. For the first time ever, the United States had an African-American president. The Democrats had traditionally had more support from non-white Americans than the Republicans, but this election brought people of all races together behind a candidate that promised "hope and change"—an America where the ultimate American Dream could come true. Some believed that it was a fluke,[9] something that happens only by chance or luck. But Obama captured the imagination of millions of Americans. Young voters were energized for the first time since the anti-war movements of the 1960s and early 1970s, and also for the first time, social media played an important role. Obama built a grass-roots organization where his campaigners came to know potential voters personally, and many Americans felt like they were part of history. Well over a million people stood outside in the freezing weather on the Washington, D.C., Mall in January, 2009, to watch Obama's inauguration on huge TV screens.

42   Obama's re-election in 2012 proved that his winning in 2008 was not a fluke.

---

[9] *fluke: something that only happens because of chance or luck*

Obama lost a number of white voters, but his coalition of non-white voters held. By 2012, 28 percent of the voting public were non-white: African Americans, Hispanics, Asian Americans, and other non-whites. Republicans were greatly surprised by Obama's victory and realized that it reflected a new reality in the United States: In spirit, the country has already become the multi-racial, multicultural country the demographers predicted for 2050. We do not have to wait thirty or forty years to see the political effects of being a majority-minority country—the demographic shift is already affecting elections. The Republican Party is in search of a new direction. Because the Republican Party hopes to attract new voters, it will have to appeal to Hispanics, African Americans, Asian Americans, and other non-white voters. The color of the electoral map is also changing, as Democratic Hispanic populations in states such as New Mexico, Colorado, and Nevada are starting to turn these red states blue.

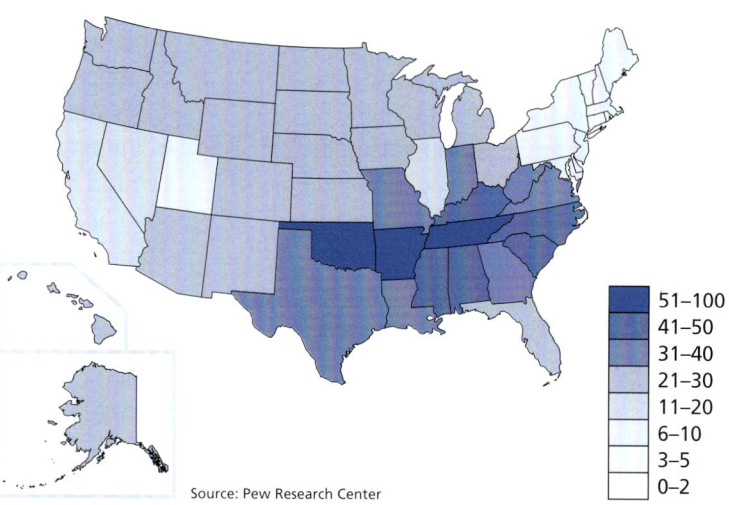

PERCENTAGE OF EACH STATE'S POPULATION THAT AFFILIATES WITH EVANGELICAL PROTESTANT TRADITION

Source: Pew Research Center

51–100
41–50
31–40
21–30
11–20
6–10
3–5
0–2

43 *Second, the ideological divide over the role and size of the national government.* Republicans have traditionally believed that big government is not only inefficient, it also endangers individual rights and freedoms. In 2012, the Tea Party* pushed the Republican Party more to the very conservative right, insisting that government spending is the cause of all economic problems and demanding severe budget cuts. Romney campaigned on a plan to reduce huge budget deficits through significant cuts in social programs; the elimination of many health, safety, and environmental regulations; and the repeal of the Obama health care law, while cutting taxes on upper income households and corporations. Obama and the Democrats called for more government regulation of financial institutions and corporate polluters, higher taxes on upper income Americans to fund social programs, and full implementation of the new health care law.

44 *Third, the cultural divide over values, morality, and lifestyles.* Republicans have increasingly built an alliance with religious conservatives of all faiths, particularly evangelical Christians. Republicans have become associated with traditional values and lifestyles, such as limiting access to abortions and opposition to gay marriage and other rights for homosexuals. They have also been against some birth control methods, including the "morning after" pill. In the meantime, the Democratic Party has moved further left on these issues. Obama allowed gays to serve openly in the military, and he called for gays' right to marry and other minority rights in his second inaugural address.

The Tea Party is a very conservative grass-roots movement originally organized by people who were worried about growing government debt (the amount of money owed). The name refers to the Boston Tea Party when American colonists threw tea into the Boston Harbor to protest the British tax on tea.

Government and Politics in the United States ★ 163

45 The country as a whole has become more liberal on these social issues, with a majority now favoring gay marriage and the right to abortion in early months of a pregnancy. Most young people are more liberal and less religious than their parents, so the demographics favor the Democrats in the future. Other lifestyle differences include the legalization of marijuana and the passage of laws recognizing gay marriage in a number of states. A look at the red state/blue state map shows the Democratic strength in the liberal Northeast and West coast states and the big cities, while Republicans find their supporters in the more conservative South and in rural areas.

Finding the Way Forward

46 Both the Republicans and the Democrats truly believe that they have the roadmap that will lead the United States to a safe and prosperous future. Republicans believe the country's economic difficulties are due to a spending problem, while Democrats believe it is an income problem. Republicans believe that dependence on entitlements seriously weakens individual freedom and responsibility. They believe that Americans are living beyond their means, borrowing money they need to run a larger and larger government, and creating a terrible financial burden for their children and grandchildren.

47 Democrats are concerned about the widening gap between those who are very, very wealthy and those who are very, very poor. They believe that the government can protect individual freedom by passing laws that ensure equal access to health care and jobs for all Americans, and by showing the way forward with government programs that will engage private businesses in cooperative projects to rebuild needed infrastructure, roads and bridges, and create partnerships between schools and businesses to provide the educated workforce of the future.

48 In *Our Divided Political Heart: The Battle for the American Idea in an Age of Discontent*, E.J. Dionne, Jr. urges Americans to look back at their history to understand who they are as a people. They must recognize that from the beginning, Americans have lived with a tension between two core values: their love of individualism and their respect for community. These two values work together to give the nation balance, and both values interact with the important value of equality.

49 Obama has spoken about this need for balance between the individualism of private business and the community of common government:

> *From our first days as a nation, we have put our faith in free markets and free enterprise as the engine of America's wealth and prosperity. More than citizens of any other country, we are rugged individualists, a self-reliant people with a healthy skepticism of too much government.*

> *But there has always been another thread running throughout our history—a belief that we are all connected; and that there are some things we can only do together, as a nation... The America I know is generous and compassionate; a land of opportunity and optimism. We take responsibility for ourselves and each other; for the country we want and the future we share.*

50 Obama is expressing a belief in the role traditional American values play in the nation and its government. The twenty-first century will continue to offer challenges to the United States citizens and its government leaders. Hopefully, the six basic cultural values—individual freedom, self-reliance, equality of opportunity, competition, material wealth, and hard work will continue to guide and direct the United States and its people in the future.

AFTER YOU READ

Understand Main Ideas

Check the predictions you made on page 152 before reading the chapter. Next to each of your predictions, write the number of the paragraph where you found the information you predicted.

Work with a partner and answer these questions about main ideas from each section of the chapter. Skim the sections for the main ideas if you do not remember them.

1. *A Suspicion of Strong Government:* Why are Americans suspicious of a strong government?
2. *The Organization of the American Government:* What are the four possible things that can happen once Congress sends a bill to the president?
3. *The Election of the President and the Congress:* What is the Electoral College? How does it work?
4. *The Ideal of the Free Individual:* What effect did the two ideals of the free individual have on the development of the government before the Great Depression of the 1930s? Why?
5. *The Development of Big Government:* What major effect did the Great Depression have on the government?
6. *The Controversy over Entitlements:* What are entitlements and why are they controversial?
7. *The Role of Special Interest Groups:* What are special interest groups? Why are they formed and whom do they represent?
8. *The New Individualism: Interest-Group Government:* How do special interest groups affect how the government operates?
9. *The Political Landscape in the 2000s: Red States vs. Blue States:* What are the traditional beliefs of the Republican and the Democratic parties? What are three important differences?
10. *Finding the Way Forward:* What do the two political parties believe should happen in the future? What is the balance needed between their two ideologies?

Understand Details

Write the letter of the best answer according to the information in the chapter.

_____ 1. Americans do not want to have a strong national government because
   a. they are afraid of their political leaders.
   b. they are afraid it will put limits on their individual freedom.
   c. they are much more concerned with national glory.

_____ 2. The *Constitution of the United States*
   a. gives by far the most power to Congress.
   b. gives by far the most power to the president.
   c. tries to give each branch enough power to balance the others.

_____ 3. The president of the United States
   a. has the power to make official treaties with foreign governments without the approval of Congress.
   b. can veto a law that has been passed by Congress.
   c. is elected if his political party wins most of the seats in Congress.

_____ 4. The *Bill of Rights*
   a. explains the rights of Congress and the rights of the president.
   b. guarantees citizens of the United States specific individual rights and freedoms.
   c. is part of the *Declaration of Independence.*

_____ 5. The American ideal of the free individual
   a. was exemplified by the farmers and the frontier settlers in the late 1700s and early 1800s.
   b. was exemplified by the businessman before the Civil War of the 1860s.
   c. caused the national government to grow in size and strength during the late 1800s.

_____ 6. The number of electoral votes a candidate receives
   a. is determined by who wins the total popular vote nationwide.
   b. is determined by the electoral votes of the states the candidate wins.
   c. is equal to the number of seats each state has in the House of Representatives.

_____ 7. Which of these statements is true about the 2000 presidential election?
   a. George W. Bush became president in 2000 because he won a plurality of votes nationwide.
   b. The Supreme Court played a major role in the 2000 election.
   c. Jeb Bush played an important role in the election because he was governor of California.

_____ 8. Stronger gun-control laws are favored by
   a. the National Rifle Association.
   b. most of the American people.
   c. very few Americans.

_____ 9. Which statement about lobby groups is not true?
   a. They have become less powerful in recent years.
   b. They try to influence the government and public opinion.
   c. They have caused the government to get larger.

_____ 10. Which statement about the traditional beliefs of the political parties is false?
   a. The Democrats believe that government should play a major role in solving society's problems.
   b. The Republicans believe that business and the free market can solve society's problems.
   c. The Republicans and the Democrats basically agree about the role of government and they have the same political beliefs.

Talk About It

Work in small groups and choose one or more of these questions to discuss.

1. How is the government of your country organized? Which system do you think works better, one that has separate elections for the different branches and divides the power, or a parliamentary system? Why?

2. What personal qualities do you think political leaders should have? What kind of leader do you admire?

3. How do lobby groups affect the operation of a government? Who do you think is more trustworthy—business or government leaders?

4. Look at the following poll about gun control policy proposals in the United States. Why do you think it is so difficult for Americans to agree on what gun control policy should be? What are the limits on gun ownership in your country? Compare the policies in your country with what is proposed in the United States.

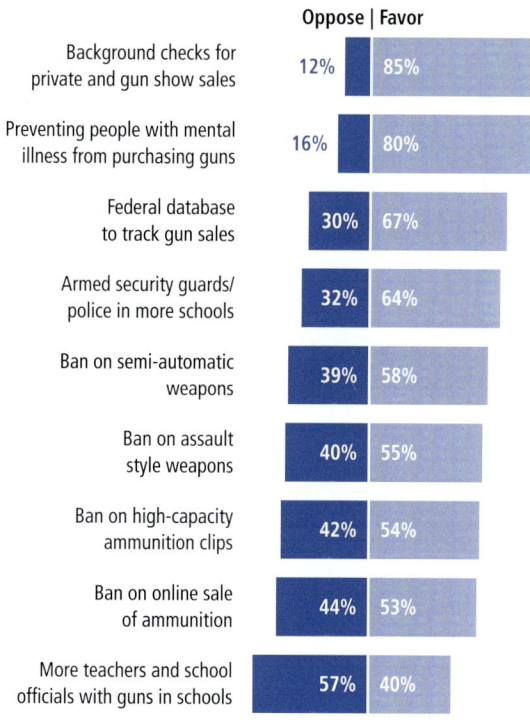

BROAD PUBLIC SUPPORT FOR MANY GUN POLICY PROPOSALS

Oppose | Favor

Proposal	Oppose	Favor
Background checks for private and gun show sales	12%	85%
Preventing people with mental illness from purchasing guns	16%	80%
Federal database to track gun sales	30%	67%
Armed security guards/police in more schools	32%	64%
Ban on semi-automatic weapons	39%	58%
Ban on assault style weapons	40%	55%
Ban on high-capacity ammunition clips	42%	54%
Ban on online sale of ammunition	44%	53%
More teachers and school officials with guns in schools	57%	40%

Source: Pew Research Center Jan. 9–13, 2013.

SKILL BUILDING

Improve Your Reading Skills: Note Taking

Fill in this graphic organizer with information about how the U.S. government is organized. Take notes about each branch and fill in the boxes with your notes. First, write the names of the three branches of government. Then write who the people are in each branch. Finally, write what the responsibilities are for each branch. When you have finished, share your notes with a partner.

BRANCHES OF GOVERNMENT

Branch	People	Responsibilities
<u>Executive</u>	_____ <u>Cabinet</u> _____	_____ _____ _____ _____
_____	<u>Congress</u> _____ <u>Senate and</u> _____ _____ 100 _____ 435 _____	<u>Enact laws</u> _____ _____ _____ _____
_____	<u>Supreme Court</u> _____ <u>9 Justices</u> _____	_____ _____ _____ _____ *Note: There are many possible responses for responsibilities.*

Develop Your Critical Thinking Skills

One of the sections in this chapter is The Controversy over Entitlements. *Reread that section and think about why there is a controversy over entitlements in the United States. Then consider this: The Pew Research Center asked Americans if they had ever received any of six different government benefits or services. They found that 27% had received unemployment benefits, 26% had received Social Security, 22% had received Medicare, and 8% had received welfare benefits. Pew then studied different demographic groups and reported on how many benefits each group had received. The results are in the chart that follows.*

TOTAL NUMBER OF BENEFITS RECEIVED BY SELECTED DEMOGRAPHIC GROUPS

% in each group who received each number of government benefits in their lifetimes

	No Benefits	One Benefit	Two Benefits	Three or More
All	45	23	17	15
Men	51	23	15	12
Women	39	22	19	19
White	44	23	19	14
Black	36	20	17	27
Hispanic	50	27	12	11
Republican	48	21	19	12
Democrat	40	23	17	20
Independent	47	24	17	11
Family income				
<$30,000	30	21	21	29
$30–49,999	44	21	21	15
$50–99,999	57	26	11	6
$100,000+	61	25	10	4
Community type				
Rural	38	22	20	20
Suburban	47	23	16	14
Urban	46	23	17	14

Note: Based on total sample, N = 2,511. Whites and blacks include only non-Hispanics. Hispanics are of any race. "Don't know/Refused" responses not shown.

Work with a partner to use information from these different sources—the chapter section and the poll—to make generalizations about who is most likely to receive government benefits in the United States. Be sure your generalizations include all the demographic categories: sex, race, political party, family income, and community type. Take notes, and then share your findings with another pair of students. Include answers to these questions:

- Who is more likely to receive more than one benefit: a man or a woman?
- Who is more likely to receive benefits: someone living in a city or someone living in a rural area?
- What impact do you think age has on who is likely to receive benefits?
- What impact does income have on who is likely to receive benefits?
- What is the relationship between the positions that the Republican Party and the Democratic Party have on entitlements and the people who are actually receiving them?

Build Your Vocabulary

More AWL Words

Test your knowledge of these AWL words by matching the words and definitions.

_____ 1. area   a. in a noticeable or important way
_____ 2. challenge   b. a particular subject or range of activities
_____ 3. conclude   c. existing or happening in many places or situations
_____ 4. core   d. basic structures or systems a country needs
_____ 5. considerably   e. a length of time with a beginning and an end
_____ 6. grades   f. something that tests strength, skill, or ability
_____ 7. impact   g. particular
_____ 8. infrastructure h. the most important or central part
_____ 9. period   i. to continue doing something, even though it is difficult
_____ 10. persist   j. happening before
_____ 11. previous   k. the effect or influence that an event has on something
_____ 12. specific   l. marks (numbers or letters) that show how well you have done
_____ 13. widespread   m. to complete successfully

Fill in the blanks with the correct words to complete these sentences:

1. E.J. Dionne, Jr., urges Americans to look back at their history to understand who they are as a people. They must recognize that from the beginning, Americans have lived with a tension between two _____ values: their love of individualism and their respect for community.

2. The NRA gives members of Congress _____ for their voting record on gun control, and it has been particularly effective in re-electing or defeating senators and representatives.

3. Republicans believe that the government can protect individual freedom by passing laws that ensure equal access to health care and jobs for all Americans, and by showing the way forward with government programs that will engage private businesses in cooperative projects to rebuild needed _____ roads and bridges, and create partnerships between schools and businesses to provide the educated workforce of the future.

4. Some government regulations were in place during this period, but these had only a small _____ on business practices.

5. In almost every important _____ of governmental activity, such as the power to make laws, to declare war, or to _____ treaties with foreign countries, the Constitution gives each of these two branches enough power to prevent the other from acting on its own.

Which Word Doesn't Belong?

This chapter contains a number of words that have to do with government and politics. Look at each group of words, and decide which one does not belong with the boldfaced word. Circle the words that do not belong. Then, on a separate piece of paper, use each one in a sentence.

EXAMPLE: **parties:** Republican, Democrat, (NRA)

1. **executive branch:** president, cabinet, bureaucracy, Congress, policy, veto
2. **legislative branch:** Congress, Supreme Court, Senate, House of Representatives, bill
3. **judicial branch:** national courts, Supreme Court, judges, vice president

4. **elections:** candidate, vote, veto, plurality, electoral college, convention
5. **politics:** party, campaign, lobby, fund-raisers, strategy, Bill of Rights

Collocations

This chapter contains many verb + noun object collocations. Read the sentences below. Fill in the blanks with the missing nouns to complete the collocations.

| ballots | bill | disputes | law | term | treaty |

1. The Supreme Court both *interprets* a _____ and determines whether it is constitutional.

2. The president may *veto* a _____ he doesn't like and send it back to Congress.

3. The Senate has to *ratify* a _____ that the president has signed.

4. If an election is very close, a candidate may request that the officials *recount* the _____.

5. The president *serves* a _____ of four years.

6. The judicial branch *settles* _____ about the exact meaning of the law through court cases.

EXPAND YOUR KNOWLEDGE

Group Project

Work in a small group to create the profile of a perfect candidate for public office.
- First decide what office your candidate is running for.
- Then describe what the person would look like (female or male, age, appearance) and what qualifications he or she would have.
- Think about how you would run the campaign.
- What kinds of advertisements would you create? What activities and appearances would you have?
- Make a poster for your candidate, perhaps with a collage of pictures that illustrate the issues your candidate is supporting in the campaign. Look on the Internet or in newspapers and magazines for ideas.
- When you have finished, present your candidate to the rest of the class.

Ask Yourself / Ask Americans

Who do you trust? Look at the list below, and put a check next to the people you would trust. Put two checks next to your top three choices. Share your list with a group of classmates. Then compare your opinions with the poll results that follow.

Advertising practitioners	Journalists
Bankers	Lawyers
Business executives	Medical doctors
Car salespeople	Members of Congress
Chiropractors	Nurses
Clergy	Pharmacists
College teachers	Police officers
Dentists	Psychiatrists
Engineers	Senators
HMO Managers	State governors
Insurance salespeople	Stockbrokers

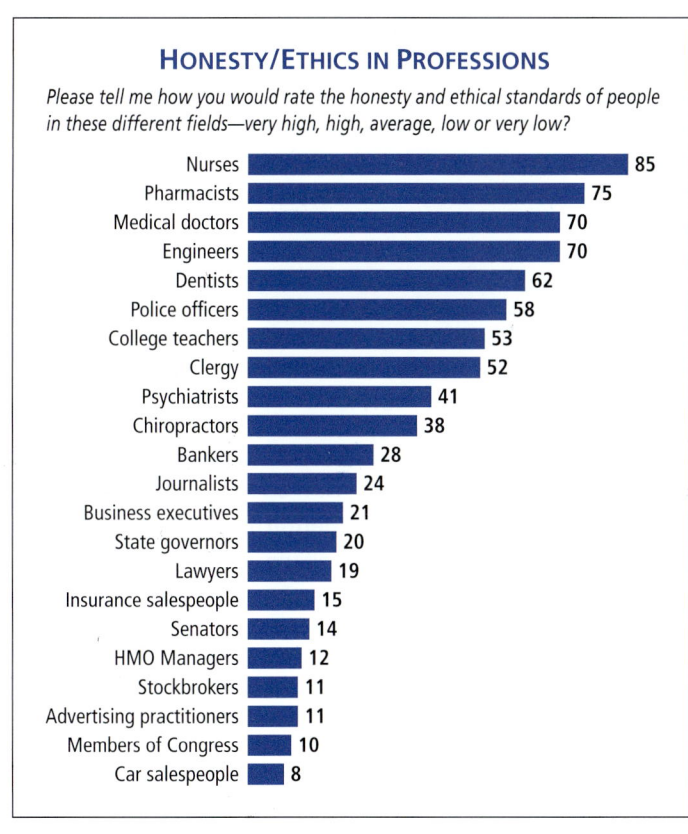

HONESTY/ETHICS IN PROFESSIONS

Please tell me how you would rate the honesty and ethical standards of people in these different fields—very high, high, average, low or very low?

- Nurses 85
- Pharmacists 75
- Medical doctors 70
- Engineers 70
- Dentists 62
- Police officers 58
- College teachers 53
- Clergy 52
- Psychiatrists 41
- Chiropractors 38
- Bankers 28
- Journalists 24
- Business executives 21
- State governors 20
- Lawyers 19
- Insurance salespeople 15
- Senators 14
- HMO Managers 12
- Stockbrokers 11
- Advertising practitioners 11
- Members of Congress 10
- Car salespeople 8

Use the Internet

Work with a partner to find information about how governments spend their money.

Reread paragraphs 28 and 29 of the chapter. In the United States, a large percentage of the budget is for mandatory programs (those that must be paid). Mandatory expenditures include the interest on the public debt and entitlement programs such as Medicare (medical benefits for the elderly) and Medicaid (medical benefits for the poor). The rest of the budget is discretionary spending (the government has a choice about how to spend this money). This includes defense and all other expenditures. The graph below shows the percentages of federal spending in 2010 by the American government. Note that the interest on the federal debt is almost 6 percent.

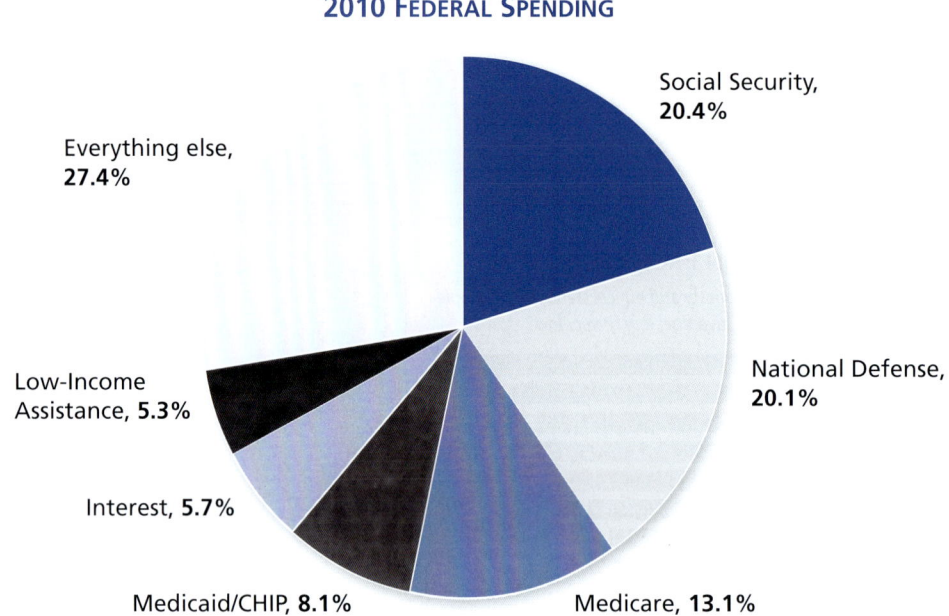

2010 FEDERAL SPENDING

- Social Security, **20.4%**
- Everything else, **27.4%**
- National Defense, **20.1%**
- Low-Income Assistance, **5.3%**
- Interest, **5.7%**
- Medicaid/CHIP, **8.1%**
- Medicare, **13.1%**

Use the Internet to look for information about the budget of your country, or choose another country. What has the largest percentage of expenditures? What percentage is spent on defense? How much is spent on social welfare, such as health care and education? What can you tell about the priorities of a people by looking at the budget of their country?

People Watching

As mentioned in Chapter 3, Americans sometimes say that it is dangerous to talk about two topics: religion and politics. It is also often difficult to know what you should say to people when you first meet them. The questions you might ask others from your country may not be appropriate or acceptable in another society or culture.

Ask a number of Americans of different ages, of both sexes, and of different ethnic or racial backgrounds, if possible, to look at the following questions. Ask them whether these are polite, acceptable questions that they would ask someone themselves. Record each person's reaction to each question. If they say certain questions are unacceptable, ask them why. How would it make someone feel if you asked one of these questions? Are there some circumstances when it would be all right to ask a question and other circumstances when it would not be all right? Which questions are acceptable in your country and which are not? Compare your findings with those of your classmates.

1. What is your name?
2. What do you do for a living?
3. Where are you from? or Where do you live?
4. Do you like your job?
5. How much do you make?
6. Are you a Republican or a Democrat? Why?
7. Are you married? Why, or why not?
8. Do you have children? Why, or why not?
9. How old are you?
10. What is your religion?

WRITE ABOUT IT

Choose one of the following topics. Then write a short compostion about it.

1. Write a letter to the president of the United States about an issue that interests or concerns you. You might write about health care, global warming, or oil drilling in the Arctic wilderness. Use persuasive techniques:

    a. Begin with a fact or statistic that is an attention-getter.

    b. Order your arguments so that you end with your strongest point.

    c. Anticipate the other side of the argument and deal with those points.

    d. End on a strong, positive note.

2. In 1960, President John F. Kennedy appointed his brother Robert Kennedy to be attorney general of the United States. In 1992, President Bill Clinton announced that he wanted to appoint his wife Hillary to an important government position, perhaps a cabinet-level post. Polls showed, however, that two-thirds of the American public disapproved of Hillary Clinton's having a major post, and Clinton was forced to reconsider. Why do you think Americans accepted the appointment of a president's brother but not his wife? What do you think about any president appointing a spouse or family member to government office? Write a "letter to the editor" (of a newspaper) expressing your opinion.

EXPLORE ON YOUR OWN

Books to Read

E.J. Dionne, Jr., *Our Divided Political Heart: The Battle for the American Idea in an Age of Discontent*—Dionne explores the effects of an extreme form of individualism that endangers the constructive role of government and community.

Nancy Gibbs and Michael Duffy, *The Presidents' Club: Inside the World's Most Exclusive Fraternity*—Two journalists examine the relationships between sitting presidents and their predecessors.

Barack Obama, *The Audacity of Hope: Thoughts on Reclaiming the American Dream*—Writing before his election, Obama calls for a new kind of politics based on shared values that bring us together.

Larry J. Sabato, Editor, *Barack Obama and the New America: The 2012 Election and the Changing Face of Politics*—A series of articles examines what happened in the election and what it means for the country.

Robert Penn Warren, *All the King's Men*—This classic American novel is about the rise and fall of a fictional southern politician who resembles Huey P. Long, a governor of Louisiana.

Movies to See

All the President's Men—Tells how reporters Woodward and Bernstein uncovered the details of the Watergate scandal that led to President Nixon's resignation.

The American President—A romantic comedy about a widowed U.S. president who falls in love with a lobbyist.

The Candidate—A candidate for the U.S. Senate from California has no hope of winning, so he is able to run his campaign any way he chooses.

The Ides of March—In the final days of a presidential primary, there is a scandal that threatens the campaign.

Milk—This movie is based on the true story of the gay rights activist and politician Harvey Milk, the first openly gay person to be elected to public office in California.

CHAPTER 8

ETHNIC AND RACIAL DIVERSITY IN THE UNITED STATES

So in this continent, the energy of Irish, Germans, Swedes, Poles and all the European tribes, of the Africans, and of the Polynesians—will construct a new race, a new religion, a new state.

Ralph Waldo Emerson (1803–1882)

In the United States, how do immigrants from different countries and people of different ethnicities get along together?

BEFORE YOU READ

Preview Vocabulary

A. Work with a partner to answer the questions. Make sure you understand the meaning of the AWL words in italics.

1. If a country tries to *accommodate* new immigrants, is it trying to help them succeed or trying to prevent them from entering the country?
2. If there is *discrimination* against a minority group, how might the people be treated differently?
3. Is a *federal* government program one at the state level or at the national level?
4. If you are *inclined* to do something, are you likely or unlikely to do it?
5. Is *instruction* usually given by a teacher or by a student?
6. When public *facilities* were segregated in the South, did blacks and whites go to different schools and sit in separate areas of restaurants and movie theaters?
7. Do most people live in *residential* or commercial (business) areas?
8. If an ethnic minority wants to *retain* its culture, are families more likely to continue speaking their native language at home or to speak English?
9. If a law has a *bias,* does it treat everyone equally?
10. How many generations back can you *trace* your ancestry?

B. The following words refer to positive or negative situations or conditions. Write a plus sign (+) next to the positive and write a minus sign (−) next to the negative connotation.

_____ accommodation   _____ enrich

_____ inspire   _____ prejudice

_____ civil rights   _____ inequality

_____ integrated   _____ resources

_____ degrade   _____ inferior

_____ poverty   _____ segregation

_____ despair   _____ slavery

_____ discrimination

Preview Content

Before you read, think about what you know about the racial and ethnic diversity of the United States. Discuss the questions with your classmates.

1. Read the quotation by Emerson at the beginning of the chapter. How did people from so many different countries create the American culture in the United States?
2. Skim the first paragraph of the reading. What does *assimilation* mean? What group had the strongest influence on shaping the dominant American culture? Why do you think so?
3. Why do you think some immigrants from some countries might have more success in the United States than others have?
4. What do you know about the history of African Americans in the United States?

In 1899, a Native American speaks to a history class at Hampton Institute, a historically black college in Virginia.

MELTING POT OR SALAD BOWL

1. The population of the United States includes a number of different ethnic groups coming from many races, nationalities, and religions. The process by which these many groups have been made a part of a common cultural life with commonly shared values is called *assimilation*. Scholars disagree as to the extent to which assimilation has occurred in the United States. As we mentioned in Chapter 1, some have described the United States as a "melting pot" where various racial and ethnic groups have been combined into one culture. Others are inclined to see the United States as a "salad bowl" where the various groups have remained somewhat distinct and different from one another, creating a richly diverse country.

2. The truth probably lies somewhere between these two views. Since 1776, an enormous amount of racial and ethnic assimilation has taken place in the United States, yet some groups continue to feel a strong sense of separateness from the culture as a whole. Many of these groups are really *bilingual and/or bicultural*. That is, they consider themselves Americans, but they may also wish to retain the language and sometimes the cultural traditions of their original culture.

3. People of Hispanic origin were on the North American continent before settlers arrived from other European countries in the early 1600s. In Florida and the Southwest, Spanish and Latin American settlements were established centuries before the thirteen colonies joined together to form the United States in the late 1700s. Because of their long history and the continued influx of newcomers into the established communities, many Hispanics, or Latinos, have taken a special pride in maintaining their cultural traditions and the use of the Spanish language.

4. Generally speaking, over the years whites from different national and religious backgrounds have been gradually assimilated into the larger American culture, with some exceptions. For example, American Jews are one group who have traditionally retained a strong sense of group identity within the larger culture. This may be a result of the long history of persecution in the Christian countries in Europe, the weaker forms of discrimination and anti-Jewish feeling that have sometimes existed in the United States, and their own strong feeling of ethnic pride. Yet along with their own group identity, most American Jews have a strong sense of being a part of the larger American culture.

The Establishment of the Dominant Culture

5. The first census of the new nation, conducted in 1790, counted about 4 million people, most of whom were white. Of the white citizens, more than eight out of ten traced their ancestry back to England. African Americans made up a surprising 20 percent of the population, an all-time high. There were close to 700,000 slaves and about 60,000 "free Negroes." Only a few Native Americans who paid taxes were included in the census numbers, so there is no accurate count of the total Native American population.

6. It was the white population that had the greater numbers, the money, and the political power in the new nation, and therefore this majority soon defined what the dominant culture would be. At the time of the American Revolution, the white population was largely English

in origin, Protestant, and middle-class. Such Americans are sometimes referred to as "WASPs" (white Anglo-Saxon Protestants); however, many people now consider this an insulting term. Their characteristics became the standard for judging other groups. Those having a different religion (such as the Irish Catholics), or those speaking a different language (such as the Germans, Dutch, and Swedes), were in the minority and would be disadvantaged unless they became assimilated. In the late 1700s, this assimilation occurred without great difficulty for most immigrants. According to historians Allan Nevins and Henry Steele Commager, "English, Irish, German, ...Dutch, Swedish—mingled[1] and intermarried with little thought of any difference."

7 The dominant American culture that grew out of the nation's early history, then, was English-speaking, western European, Protestant, and middle-class in character. It was this dominant culture that established what became the traditional values described by Tocqueville in the early 1830s. Immigrants with these characteristics were welcome, in part because Americans believed that these newcomers would probably give strong support to the basic values of the dominant culture, such as freedom, equality of opportunity, and the desire to work hard for a higher material standard of living.

The Assimilation of Non-Protestant and Non-Western Europeans

8 As is the case in many cultures, the degree to which a minority group was seen as different from the characteristics of the dominant majority determined the extent of that group's acceptance. Although immigrants who were like the earlier settlers were accepted, those with significantly different characteristics tended to be viewed as a threat to traditional American values and way of life.

9 This was particularly true of the immigrants who arrived by the millions during the late nineteenth and early twentieth centuries. Most of them came from poverty-stricken nations of southern and eastern Europe. They spoke languages other than English, and large numbers of them were Catholics or Jews.

10 Americans at the time were very fearful of this new flood of immigrants. They were afraid that these people were so accustomed to lives of poverty and dependence that they would not understand such traditional American values as freedom, self-reliance, and competition. There were so many new immigrants that they might even change the basic values of the nation in undesirable ways.

11 Americans tried to meet what they saw as a threat to their values by offering English instruction for the new immigrants and citizenship classes to teach them basic American beliefs. The immigrants, however, often felt that their American teachers disapproved of the traditions of their homeland. Moreover, learning about American values gave them little help in meeting their most important needs, such as employment, food, and a place to live.

12 Far more helpful to the new immigrants were the "political bosses" of the larger cities of the northeastern United States, where most of the immigrants first arrived. Those bosses saw to many of the practical needs of the immigrants and were more accepting of the different homeland traditions. In exchange for their help, the bosses expected the immigrants to keep them in power by voting for them in elections.

---

[1] mingled: met and talked with a lot of different people socially

Immigrant boys study in night school because they work during the day.

13 Many Americans strongly disapproved of the political bosses. This was partly because the bosses were frequently corrupt;[2] that is, they often stole money from the city governments they controlled and engaged in other illegal practices. Perhaps more important to disapproving Americans, however, was the fact that the bosses seemed to be destroying such basic American values as self-reliance and competition.

14 The bosses, it seemed, were teaching the immigrants to be dependent on them rather than to rely on themselves. Moreover, the bosses were "buying" the votes of the immigrants in order to give themselves a monopoly of political power in many larger cities. This practice destroyed competition for political office, which Americans viewed as an important tradition in politics just as it was in other facets of American life.

15 Despite these criticisms, many scholars believe that the political bosses performed an important function in the late nineteenth and early twentieth centuries. They helped to assimilate large numbers of new immigrants into the larger American culture by finding them jobs and housing, in return for their political support. Later the bosses also helped the sons and daughters of these immigrants find employment, but the second generation usually had the advantage of growing up speaking English.

16 The fact that the United States had a rapidly expanding economy at the turn of the century made it

[2] *corrupt: dishonest*

possible for these new immigrants, often with the help of the bosses, to better their standard of living in the United States. As a result of these new opportunities and new rewards, immigrants came to accept most of the values of the larger American culture and were in turn accepted by the great majority of Americans. For white ethnic groups, therefore, it has generally been true that their feeling of being a part of the larger culture—that is, *American*—has usually been stronger than their feeling of belonging to a separate ethnic group—Irish, Italian, Polish, etc.

The African-American Experience

17 The process of assimilation in the United States has been much more successful for white ethnic groups than for non-white ethnic groups. Of the non-white ethnic groups, Americans of African descent have had the greatest difficulty in becoming assimilated into the larger culture. African Americans were brought to the United States against their will to be sold as slaves. Except for the American Indian tribes who inhabited the United States before the first white settlers arrived, other ethnic groups came to America voluntarily—most as immigrants who wanted to better their living conditions.

18 The enslavement of African Americans in the United States was a complete contradiction of such traditional basic American values as freedom and equality of opportunity. It divided the United States into two increasingly different sections: the southern states, in which black slavery became the basis of the economy, and the northern states, which chose to make slavery against the law.

19 A minority of whites in the North insisted that slavery and freedom could not exist together in a free country and demanded that slavery be abolished,[3] even if this meant war with the South. A much larger number of northern whites believed that freedom and equality of opportunity needed to be protected for white people only, but they were afraid that black slavery would eventually take away their economic freedom. If, for example, the slave system of the South were allowed to spread into the frontier regions of the West, poor and middle-income whites could no longer look to the western frontier as a land of equality and opportunity where people could better their position in life. Rather, whites would have to compete with unpaid slave labor, a situation that they believed would degrade their work and lower their social status.

20 Abraham Lincoln was able to become president of the United States by appealing to both the white idealists who saw slavery as an injustice to African Americans and to the larger numbers of northern whites who saw slavery as a threat to themselves. Lincoln's argument was that if black slavery continued to spread westward, white freedom and equality would be threatened. Lincoln also believed that basic ideals such as freedom and equality of opportunity had to apply to all people, black and white, or they would not last as basic American values.

21 When Lincoln won the presidency in 1860, the southern states left the Union and tried to form a new nation of their own based on slavery. A Civil War (1861–1865) between the North and South resulted, which turned out to be the bloodiest and most destructive of all the nation's wars. When the North was finally victorious, black slavery ended in the United States.

22 Back in the 1830s, Tocqueville predicted

---

[3] *abolish: officially end a law or system*

Martin Luther King, Jr., addresses followers at a civil rights protest.

trouble between blacks and whites in the United States:

> These two races are fastened to each other without intermingling; and they are unable to separate entirely or to combine. Although the law may abolish slavery, God alone can obliterate[4] the traces of its existence.

23 Although slavery was abolished in the 1860s, its legacy[5] continued and African Americans were not readily assimilated into the larger American culture. Most remained in the South, where they were not allowed to vote and were legally segregated from whites. Black children were not allowed to attend white public schools, for example, and many received an inferior education that did not give them an equal opportunity to compete in the white-dominated society. Many former slaves and their families became caught in a cycle of poverty that continued for generations. Although conditions were much worse in the segregated South, blacks continued to be the victims[6] of strong racial prejudice in the North as well.

The Civil Rights Movement of the 1950s and 1960s

24 This state of affairs remained unchanged until after World War II. Over one million African Americans had served in segregated units during the war. After the war was over, black leaders began to lead a civil rights movement for equality with whites. In 1948, President Harry Truman ordered that the military be fully integrated. Then in 1954, the United States Supreme Court declared that racially segregated public schools did not provide equal educational opportunities for black Americans and were therefore illegal.

---

[4] *obliterate: to destroy something so that almost nothing remains*

[5] *legacy: a situation that exists as a result of things that happened at an earlier time*

[6] *victims: people who suffer bad treatment even though they have done nothing to deserve it*

Incidentally, Thurgood Marshall, Chief Counsel for the National Association for the Advancement of Colored People (NAACP) argued the case before the court, and in 1967 he became the first African-American Supreme Court Justice.

25 Black leaders throughout the United States were greatly encouraged by the 1954 decision to desegregate the schools. They decided to try to end racial segregation in all areas of American life. The most important of these leaders was Martin Luther King Jr., a black Protestant minister with a great gift for inspiring[7] people. From the late 1950s until his assassination[8] by a white gunman in 1968, King led thousands of people in nonviolent marches and demonstrations against segregation and other forms of racial discrimination. King's goal was to bring about greater assimilation of black people into the larger American culture. His ideals were largely developed from basic American values. He wanted greater equality of opportunity and "freedom now" for his people. He did not wish to separate his people from American society, but rather to gain for them a larger part in it.

26 Some black leaders, such as Malcolm X, urged a rejection of basic American values and complete separation of blacks from the white culture. Malcolm X believed that American values were nothing more than "white men's values" used to keep blacks in an inferior position. He believed that blacks needed to separate themselves from whites, by force if necessary, and build their own society based on values that they would create for themselves. Because he saw Christianity as a "white" religion, Malcolm turned to a faith based on Islam, and he became a leader of the "black Muslim" faith (founded in 1930). The great majority of American blacks, however, shared Martin Luther King's Protestant religious beliefs and his goal of assimilation rather than separation. Most African Americans continued to look to King as their leader.

27 Largely as a result of King's activities, two major civil rights[9] laws were passed during the 1960s, which brought about great changes in the South. One law made it illegal to segregate public facilities. The other law made it illegal to deny black people the right to vote in elections.

28 The civil rights laws of the 1960s helped to bring about a significant degree of assimilation of blacks into the larger American culture. Most important, the laws eventually helped to reduce the amount of white prejudice toward black people in all parts of the country. A federal program called affirmative action required employers to actively seek black workers and universities to recruit black students. As a result of the civil rights laws and affirmative action, the number of African Americans attending the nation's colleges and universities, holding elective public office, and earning higher incomes increased dramatically in the late 1960s and 1970s. Today, African Americans are sports and entertainment heroes, university professors, medical doctors, lawyers, entrepreneurs, and reporters. There is now a sizable black middle class, and there are a number of wealthy African Americans.

29 African Americans are active politically and voted in large numbers in the elections of 2008 and 2012. They are now mayors of major cities and members of Congress; they hold offices in all levels of government—local, state, and national.

---

[7] *inspiring: encouraging people to achieve something great*

[8] *assassination: the murder of an important person*

[9] *civil rights: rights that every person should have, such as the right to vote or to be treated fairly by the law, whatever his or her sex, race, or religion*

In 2008, Barack Obama became the first black American president, truly a dream come true for many who had worked in the civil rights movement. Congressman John Lewis, himself a black civil rights leader, reflected on what Obama's election meant to him personally:

> When we were organizing voter-registration drives, going on the Freedom Rides, sitting in, coming here to Washington for the first time, getting arrested, going to jail, being beaten, I never thought—I never dreamed—of the possibility that an African American would one day be elected President of the United States. My mother lived to see me elected to the Congress, but I wish my mother and father both were around. They would be so happy and so proud, and they would be so gratified. And they would be saying that the struggle, and what we did and tried to do, was worth it.

Diversity in the Twenty-first Century

30 The civil rights movement benefited not only African Americans, but all minorities in the United States—American Indians, Hispanics, Asians, and others. Racial discrimination in employment and housing was forbidden by law. The civil rights laws also advanced the rights of women, and these laws have reinforced the ideal of equality of opportunity for all Americans. Recently, sexual orientation entered the picture. President Obama called for equality for gays in his second Inaugural Address and for laws that permit them to marry. Public opinion polls showed that a majority of Americans agreed with him. The Congress that took office that year was the most diverse ever, although it was not as diverse as the nation as a whole. Among its 535 members, it included 98 women, 43 African Americans, 31 Latinos, 12 Asian-Americans or Pacific Islanders, seven openly gay or bisexuals, two Muslims, one Buddhist, and one Hindu.

31 Although African Americans represent about 13 percent of the population, they are still grossly underrepresented in Congress, and the same is true of Hispanics. The median income of a married black or Hispanic man working full-time is still significantly less than that of a married white man. Segregation and discrimination are against the law, but residential patterns create largely segregated neighborhood schools, particularly in many urban areas. Whites are more likely than blacks and Hispanics to live in the suburbs, where the neighborhood schools are usually in better condition and offer a better education. Many blacks and other ethnic minorities

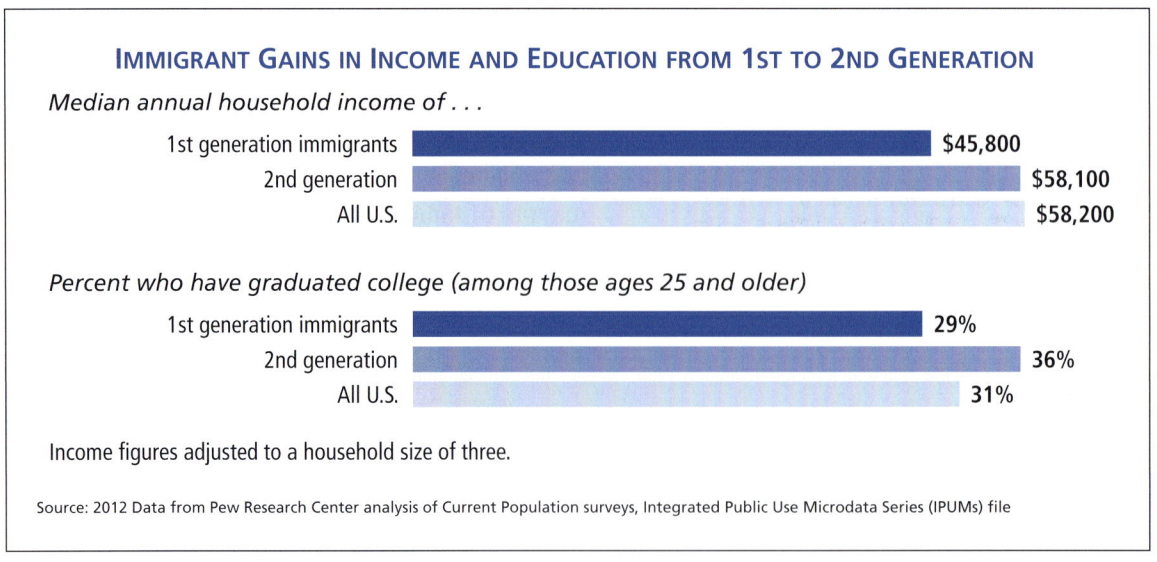

IMMIGRANT GAINS IN INCOME AND EDUCATION FROM 1ST TO 2ND GENERATION

Median annual household income of . . .

- 1st generation immigrants: $45,800
- 2nd generation: $58,100
- All U.S.: $58,200

Percent who have graduated college (among those ages 25 and older)

- 1st generation immigrants: 29%
- 2nd generation: 36%
- All U.S.: 31%

Income figures adjusted to a household size of three.

Source: 2012 Data from Pew Research Center analysis of Current Population surveys, Integrated Public Use Microdata Series (IPUMs) file

in the inner city are trapped in cycles of poverty, unemployment, violence, and despair. Blacks are the most frequent victims of violent crime, and as many as one in five young males may have a criminal record. A larger percent of black and Hispanic children than white children live in poverty and may have only one parent at home.

32 On the other hand, Americans continue to believe strongly in the ideal of equality of opportunity and to search for ways to give everyone an equal chance at success. The American Dream still attracts immigrants and inspires people of all races and ethnic backgrounds. In reality, some immigrant groups have more success than others. As one would expect, history shows that immigrants who come with financial resources, a good educational background, and the necessary work skills are likely to do the best. For example, immigrants from the Middle East tend to have a higher socioeconomic level than the average white American. So do Asians, as a group. Those who come without financial resources and a strong educational background do not do as well. However, studies show that the second generation does significantly better than the first. The adult children of immigrants have a higher standard of living:

> A new analysis of the 20 million adult U.S.-born children of immigrants finds they are substantially better off than immigrants themselves; they have higher incomes, more are college graduates and homeowners, and fewer live in poverty. Among Latinos and Asian Americans, the second generation are more likely than immigrants to speak English, have friends outside their racial and ethnic group, and think of themselves as "a typical American."

33 Sonia Sotomayor, the first Hispanic Supreme Court Justice, is an inspiring example of the success some Hispanic Americans have achieved. In her book, *My Beloved World,* she describes being born into and growing up in a world that was "a tiny microcosm of Hispanic New York City." Her grandparents, aunts, uncles, and cousins lived in a few square blocks of the South Bronx:

> My playmates were my cousins. We spoke Spanish at home, and many in my family spoke virtually no English. My parents had both come to New York from Puerto Rico* in 1944, my mother in the Women's Army Corps, my father with his family in search of work as part of a huge migration from the island, driven by economic hardship.

34 Sotomayor's father died when she was a child and her family had a difficult time financially. They lived in low-income housing and both she and her brother worked part-time jobs during the school year and full-time in the summer to help with the family's finances. She knew little of the world outside her neighborhood as a child, and *the Perry Mason* TV show inspired her to want to become an attorney. Sotomayor was an excellent student, but she was surprised by the number of great universities that offered her admission and even full scholarships. She says for the next several years, she "lived the day-to-day reality of affirmative action." As a Hispanic minority woman, she benefited from the affirmative action law that was just beginning to cause universities to recruit minority students. Out of many offers, she chose Princeton, and then went to Yale for her law degree.

35 Today, immigrants with all kinds of backgrounds and skill levels find their way to the United States. Some of them are highly educated, and they may find employment in fields such as technology, medicine, and science. Others may come

---

People who live in Puerto Rico are citizens of the United States.

from poor rural or urban areas and have a limited education. Many of these are young people who risk their lives to come without documentation to do agricultural or construction work. Others find work taking care of children or cleaning homes or buildings. Often, they are paid less than a documented worker would be. However, what they are able to earn in dollars and send back to their countries can support many family members there. Many of these individuals do not want to become U.S. citizens; their only wish is to be able to work here. Americans are trying to find ways to accommodate these workers, while still protecting the interests of U.S. citizens.

A Universal Nation

36 It is important to remember that the dominant culture and its value system established by the early settlers had its roots in white, Protestant, western Europe. In the late 1800s and early 1900s, millions of immigrants came from eastern and southern Europe, bringing cultural traditions perceived by the dominant culture as quite different. By the 1920s, Americans had decided that it was time to close the borders to mass immigration, and the number of new immigrants slowed to a trickle.[10] In spite of the worries of those in the dominant culture, the new immigrants did assimilate to life in the United States. They greatly enriched the cultural diversity of the nation, and they ultimately did not cause major changes to its system of government, its free enterprise system, or its traditional values.

37 In 1965, the United States made important changes in its immigration laws, allowing many more immigrants to come and entirely eliminating the older laws' bias in favor of white European immigrants. As a result, the United States now takes in large numbers of new immigrants who are non-white and non-European. The majority are from Asia and Latin America. In addition to the large numbers of legal immigrants, for the first time the United States has significant numbers of immigrants without legal documentation. Many worry about what the impact will be on American society. Can the American economy offer these new immigrants the same opportunities that others have had? What will be the effect on the traditional value system that has defined the United States for over 200 years?

38 Many Americans see wonderful benefits for their country. Ben Wattenberg, a respected expert on American culture, believes that the new immigration will be of great help to the nation. According to Wattenberg, something very important is happening to the United States: It is becoming the first universal nation in history. Wattenberg believes that the United States will be the first nation where large numbers of people from every region on earth live in freedom under one government. This diversity, he says, will give the nation great influence and appeal to the rest of the world during the twenty-first century.

39 Perhaps the United States will be described not as a "melting pot" or a "salad bowl," but as a "mosaic"—a picture made up of many tiny pieces of different colors. If one looks closely at the nation, the individuals of different colors and ethnic groups are still distinct and recognizable, but together they create a picture that is uniquely American. *E pluribus unum*—the motto of the United States from its beginning—means "one composed of many." Out of many, one.

---

[10] *trickle: a movement of people or things into a place in very small numbers or amounts*

AFTER YOU READ

Understand Main Ideas

Working with a partner, write the answer to each of the pre-reading questions on page 179. Then make up seven more questions about other main ideas, one question for each of the seven sections. Answer these questions, and then share them with another pair of students.

Understand Details

Write the letter of the best answer according to the information in the chapter.

_____ 1. Scholars who see the United States as a "salad bowl" emphasize
   a. the great extent of racial and ethnic assimilation in the United States.
   b. the many differences between different racial and ethnic groups in the United States.
   c. the rapid growth of the population of the United States.

_____ 2. In American society, there are some members of ethnic groups (such as some Jews and Hispanics) that are bicultural; they feel that
   a. they are fully assimilated into American society.
   b. they do not belong at all to American society.
   c. they belong to American society, but at the same time they also have another separate identity.

_____ 3. Which of the following was not a characteristic of the dominant American culture during the early decades of the nation's history?
   a. Catholic
   b. western European
   c. middle-class

_____ 4. Which of the following was true about the political bosses in northeastern cities during the late nineteenth and early twentieth centuries?
   a. They were more afraid of new immigrants than were other Americans.
   b. They were more cruel to new immigrants than were other Americans.
   c. They were more helpful to new immigrants than were other Americans.

_____ 5. Today ethnic groups in the United States
   a. have no feeling of belonging to an ethnic group (such as Irish, Italian, or Polish) whatsoever.
   b. consider themselves as part of the American culture in varying degrees, often depending on how similar their culture is to the majority.
   c. feel much more a part of their ethnic group than part of the American culture.

_____ 6. What was the <u>main</u> reason most northern whites disliked slavery?
   a. It went against their religious beliefs.
   b. It went against the U.S. Constitution.
   c. It threatened their own economic opportunities.

_____ 7. After the Civil War, African Americans in the South lived in a social system where
   a. many continued to be slaves.
   b. segregation was legal.
   c. there was racial discrimination, but no laws separated them from whites.

_____ 8. In 1954, the U.S. Supreme Court declared
   a. African Americans could not legally be denied their right to vote for racial reasons.
   b. racially segregated public schools are illegal.
   c. no one may be denied freedom of speech, press, or religion.

_____ 9. On which of the beliefs listed below did Malcolm X <u>disagree</u> with Martin Luther King?
   a. Black people should be assimilated into the larger American society.
   b. Black people were not treated fairly by the larger American society.
   c. Black people should have freedom and equality.

_____ 10. Which of these statements about race and ethnicity in America is <u>true</u>?
   a. Most young African Americans today have no interest in learning about the black culture and they identify fully with the white culture.
   b. Racial prejudice, segregation, and discrimination are at an all-time high in the United States today.
   c. Using the word mosaic to describe the American culture suggests a positive image.

Talk About It

Work in small groups and choose one or more of these questions to discuss.

1. What are the advantages and disadvantages to being a part of a multicultural society in the twenty-first century?

2. What is your country's policy on immigration? Would you want to be an immigrant in your country? Why or why not?

3. Should a country discourage people from segregating themselves by minorities? What are the advantages and disadvantages to people living in segregated communities?

4. This chapter describes the dominant American culture as being white, English-speaking, Protestant, and middle-class. How would you describe the dominant culture of your country, if there is one?

SKILL BUILDING

Improve Your Reading Skills: Scanning

Scan the chapter to find these dates. Write what happened next to the date to complete the time line about racial and ethnic diversity in the United States.

early 1600s: _____

1790: _____

1861–1865: _____

late 1800s and early 1900s: _____

1920s: _____

1950s and 1960s: _____

1965: _____

2008 and 2012: _____

Develop Your Critical Thinking Skills

This chapter has three definitions or descriptions of the diversity of the United States: *melting pot, salad bowl,* and *mosaic*. Reread the part of the chapter where each of these appears and write a brief definition for each. Evaluate these as definitions and explain how they are different. Would you rather live in a country that is described as a "melting pot," a "salad bowl," or a "mosaic"? Why? Share your answers with a partner.

Build Your Vocabulary

Definitions

Match the word with its definition. Then fill in the sentence blanks with the correct form of the word.

_____ 1. abolish   a. to meet and talk together

_____ 2. assassination   b. dishonest

_____ 3. civil rights   c. to officially end a law or system

_____ 4. corrupt   d. someone who suffers bad treatment

_____ 5. registration   e. to encourage someone to achieve something great

_____ 6. inspire   f. the murder of an important person

_____ 7. legacy   g. rights that every person should have

_____ 8. mingle   h. recording names on an official list

_____ 9. mosaic   i. to destroy something so that nothing remains

_____ 10. obliterate   j. a situation that exists as a result of things that happened at an earlier time

_____ 11. trickle   k. a picture made by fitting together small pieces of colored stones, glass, or paper

_____ 12. victim   l. a movement of people or things into a place in very small numbers or amounts

1. Although slavery had ended in the North by the late 1700s, it was not _____ in the rest of the country until the 1860s.

2. Black people in the 1950s and early 1960s did not have the same freedom and equality as whites in the South; they had to fight for their _____.

3. Martin Luther King, Jr., was able to _____ his followers to demonstrate against segregation.

4. King was the most important black leader in America from the late 1950s until his _____ by a white gunman in 1968.

5. Unfortunately, the _____ of slavery continues in the United States, and there are still problems between the races.

6. When John Lewis was organizing voter- _____ drives, he never dreamed that one day an African American would be elected president.

7. People who come to the United States from many different countries have _____, and many have married persons of a different national origin.

8. Often, it is the poor minorities who live in the inner cities who are the _____ of crime.

9. Perhaps the United States is really more of a _____ than a melting pot or a salad bowl.

10. Immigration by white Europeans has now slowed to a _____ ; the majority of the immigrants now come from Asia, Latin America, or the Caribbean.

11. Few people would really want to _____ the rich diversity of cultures living together in the United States.

12. Many of the big city political bosses of the late 1800s and early 1900s were _____ ; they stole money from the city governments.

More AWL Words

Test your knowledge of these AWL words Read the sentences below and notice the boldfaced AWL words. Then use context clues and write the correct AWL word next to its definition.

1. Some are **inclined** to see the United States as a salad bowl where the various groups have remained **somewhat** distinct and different from one another, creating a richly diverse country.
2. The **process** by which these many groups have been made a part of a common cultural life with commonly shared values is called *assimilation*.
3. Many Americans strongly disapproved of the political bosses. **Despite** these criticisms, many scholars believe that the political bosses performed an important **function**.
4. In 1948, President Harry Truman ordered that the military be fully **integrated**.
5. Some immigrants risk their lives to come to the United States without **documentation** to do agricultural or **construction** work.
6. In 1965, the United States made important changes in its immigration laws, allowing many more immigrants to come, and entirely **eliminating** the older laws' **bias** in favor of white European immigrants.
7. Segregation and **discrimination** are against the law, but **residential** patterns create largely segregated neighborhood schools, particularly in many urban areas.

_____ 1. have an opinion about whether something is good or bad that influences how you deal with it

_____ 2. working on new buildings

_____ 3. even though something else exists or is true

_____ 4. the practice of treating a person or group differently from another in an unfair way

_____ 5. official papers that are used to prove that something is true

_____ 6. getting rid of something completely

_____ 7. job

_____ 8. influenced toward a particular action or opinion

_____ 9. have all the races together, not segregated

_____ 10. a series of actions

_____ 11. relating to homes

_____ 12. more than a little, but not very

EXPAND YOUR KNOWLEDGE

Think, Pair, Share

Do you agree or disagree with these statements? Draw a circle around your response, and then share your answers with a partner and another pair of students.

1. I would emigrate to another country if I could have a better life there for myself and my family. — agree   disagree
2. Foreigners who come from any country in the world are welcomed in my country. — agree   disagree
3. My government should encourage refugees from other countries to settle in my country. — agree   disagree
4. My family would not object if I chose to marry someone of another nationality. — agree   disagree
5. My family would not object if I chose to marry someone of another race. — agree   disagree
6. It is important to maintain your own language and cultural traditions even if you have left your country. — agree   disagree
7. People are really basically the same all over the world. — agree   disagree
8. People who are very different from the dominant culture (race, religion, or ethnic background) have as high a status as anyone else in my country. — agree   disagree
9. Every person in the world should learn to speak at least one foreign language. — agree   disagree
10. I believe that my children will have a higher standard of living than I had growing up. — agree   disagree

Ask Americans

If possible, ask several Americans to tell you about their ethnic backgrounds. Or, ask immigrants in your own country about their backgrounds. Ask them the following questions. Then report your findings to the class.

1. What nationalities were your ancestors?
2. When did your ancestors immigrate to America?
3. Does anyone in your family still speak the language of the "old (original) country"?
4. Does your family maintain contact with any relatives in the old country?
5. What family customs or traditions from the old country do you observe?
6. Have you or any of your family members done any genealogy research to learn about your family history?

Observe the Media

Work in small groups to discuss these questions.

1. How are ethnic and racial minorities and women represented in the media?
2. If you are in the United States, watch national and local news broadcasts and count the number of women and minorities reporting the news. If you are not in the United States, observe the media in the country where you are. What percentages do you find?
3. Watch TV commercials and count the racial and ethnic minorities. How do the numbers compare with the news reporters? What conclusions can you draw from these observations?

Think, Pair, Share

Read the following information about choosing racial identity on the census form. Then answer the questions and share your answers with a partner.

The 2010 census had several choices for race including:
White
Black, African American, or Negro
American Indian or Alaska Native
(and other choices such as Chinese, Filipino, Japanese, etc.)

Americans could choose one race or more—as many as they wanted to—to describe their racial identity. (The census reported numbers of people of one race, or more than one race.) When asked to declare his race on the 2010 census, President Obama chose to check the box Black, African American, or Negro instead of checking multiple boxes. For Obama, the son of a white mother and an African father, the question of his racial identity has been a lifelong struggle. His choice on the census reveals his decision to identify with African Americans.

What do you feel defines your identity? Is it your race? Your ethnic background? The color of your skin? The language you speak? Your cultural heritage? What does identity mean to you?

Have a Debate

Unlike most countries, the United States does not have an official language. While English is widely understood to be the main language of government, commerce, and most education, the people who wrote the Constitution purposely did not declare any one language as the official language.

Look at the chart of languages below. What can you conclude about the number and variety of languages spoken in the United States?

LANGUAGES SPOKEN AT HOME: 1980, 1990, 2000, AND 2007

Characteristic	1980	1990	2000	2007	Percentage change 1980–2007
Population 5 years and older	210,247,455	230,445,777	262,375,152	280,950,438	33.6
Spoke only English at home	187,187,415	198,600,798	215,423,557	225,505,953	20.5
Spoke a language other than English at home[1]	23,060,040	31,844,979	46,951,595	55,444,485	140.4
Spoke a language other than English at home[2]	**23,060,040**	**31,844,979**	**46,951,595**	**55,444,485**	**140.4**
Spanish or Spanish Creole	11,116,194	17,345,064	28,101,052	34,547,077	210.8
French (incl. Patois, Cajun, Creole)	1,550,751	1,930,404	2,097,206	1,984,824	28.0
Italian	1,618,344	1,308,648	1,008,370	798,801	−50.6
Portuguese or Portuguese Creole	351,875	430,610	564,630	687,126	95.3
German	1,586,593	1,547,987	1,383,442	1,104,354	−30.4
Yiddish	315,953	213,064	178,945	158,991	−49.7
Greek	401,443	388,260	365,436	329,825	−107.1
Russian	173,226	241,798	706,242	851,174	391.4
Polish	820,647	723,483	667,414	638,059	−22.2
Serbo-Croatian	150,255	70,964	233,865	276,550	84.1
Armenian	100,634	149,694	202,708	221,865	120.5
Persian	106,992	201,865	312,085	349,686	226.8
Chinese	630,806	1,319,462	2,022,143	2,464,572	290.7
Japanese	336,318	427,657	477,997	458,717	36.4
Korean	266,280	626,478	894,063	1,062,337	299.0
Vietnamese	197,588	507,069	1,009,627	1,207,004	510.9
Tagalog	474,150	843,251	1,224,241	1,480,429	212.2

[1] The languages highlighted in this table are the languages for which data were available for the four time periods: 1980, 1990, 2000, and 2007.
[2] The total does not match the sum of the 17 languages listed in this table because the total includes all the other languages that are not highlighted here. Note: Margins of error for all estimates can be found in Appendix Table 2 at <www.census.gov/population/www/socdemo/ language/appendix.html>. For more information on the ACS, see <www.census.gov/acs/www/>. Source: U.S. Census Bureau, 1980 and 1990 Census, Census 2000, and 2007 American Community Survey.

Organize a debate on whether or not a country should have an official language, or languages. Have one team argue in favor of an official language and the other team argue against it. When planning your arguments, consider the following questions.

1. Why do you think the founding fathers omitted the designation of an official language?
2. What are the possible consequences of having one official language to speakers of other languages?
3. Do you think that most immigrants recognize the value of knowing the language of their new country?

New immigrants study English in community education classes.

Use the Internet

Choose one of these topics to research on the Internet.

1. Working in small groups, choose an ethnic group in the United States to research online. For example, you might choose Turkish Americans, Korean Americans, Ethiopian Americans, Nigerian Americans, Peruvian Americans—any group you wish. Decide what questions you want answered. These might include the following:

    Where do they live in the United States?

    How many of them live here?

    What festivals do they have?

    What are some typical foods?

    Are there native-language newspapers?

    Are there special schools?

    What kinds of websites are there for this group?

   When you have finished your research, make a report to the rest of the class on what you learned. Begin by giving your classmates clues and having them guess which group you have chosen. You could use the clues for a scavenger hunt and have the last clue direct them to the group's home country on a world map.

2. A Smithsonian museum in Washington, D.C., is dedicated to the cultures of the American Indian. Visit its website, www.nmai.si.edu, and write a report on what you learn about the museum.

3. In 2013, Rosa Parks made history for a second time when she became the first black woman to be honored with a full-length statue in the U.S. Capitol's Statuary Hall. President Obama and leaders of Congress were there for the presentation of the statue. Look online and learn about this interesting woman. Who was Rosa Parks? What was her important role in the civil rights movement?

WRITE ABOUT IT

Choose one of the following topics. Then write a short composition about it.

1. Describe a time when you or a friend or a family member experienced discrimination. Write it as a narrative, following chronological order, with an explanation. You could use either the past or the present tense. Include information such as the following:

    Where this occurred

    What happened

    Who was involved

    What the result was

    How each of the people involved felt

    What can be done to eliminate discrimination and prejudice

2. Write a letter to the president of the United States or to the leader of your country proposing a new immigration policy. Explain how many people should be admitted each year, from what countries, on what basis, and what should be done once they have arrived. Support your opinions carefully. Offer solutions to any problems that might be anticipated. (If you write about the United States, you may wish to do research about what is happening to the children of immigrants who came without legal documents and the "Dream Act.")

EXPLORE ON YOUR OWN

Books to Read

Julia Alvarez, *How the Garcia Girls Lost Their Accents*—Four sisters from the Dominican Republic adjust to life in the United States and try to integrate their old culture into their new one.

Langston Hughes, *Let America Be America Again*—The African-American poet examines the ideals of the American dream of freedom, the value of hard work, and the reality of the limitations that some Americans face.

Sonia Sotomayor, *My Beloved World*—In this memoir, the first Hispanic Supreme Court Justice tells about her journey from a Bronx housing project into the university world.

Rachel L. Swarns, *American Tapestry: The Story of the Black, White, and Multiracial Ancestors of Michelle Obama*—This book is based on extensive research on several generations of the First Lady's family.

Ronald Takaki, *Strangers from a Different Shore*—The author presents a history of Asian Americans using personal experiences mixed with historical facts.

Movies to See

America America—In this story of the early life of a Greek immigrant, positive first impressions of America are soon compromised by reality.

American History X—A former neo-nazi skinhead tries to prevent his younger brother from going down the same wrong path that he did.

Freedom Riders—This film tells the story of the Civil Rights movement interstate busing protest campaign.

The Help—During the Civil Rights movement of the 1960s, a young author writes a book about African-American maids' views about their white employers and their daily lives.

Lincoln—This movie focuses on the president's last months in office during the Civil War as he tries to hold the country together while abolishing slavery.

CHAPTER 9

EDUCATION IN THE UNITED STATES

Americans regard education as the means by which the inequalities among individuals are to be erased and by which every desirable end is to be achieved.

George S. Counts (1889–1974)

Who pays for education in the United States and how does that affect what is taught in American schools?

BEFORE YOU READ

Preview Vocabulary

A. Read the following sentences from the chapter and notice the words in italics. These key AWL words will help you understand the chapter reading. Use context clues to help you figure out the meanings. Then choose which definition is best for the italicized word.

_____ 1. Parents who live in large cities may send their children to Catholic or other religious schools because they believe that these schools are safer and have higher *academic* standards than the public schools.
   a. relating to education
   b. relating to danger

_____ 2. Although the amount of money spent per child is not always the best *indicator* of the quality of education the child receives, it certainly is an important factor.
   a. increase
   b. sign

_____ 3. Many of the new jobs in the United States either require a college education, even a graduate degree, or are low-paying jobs in the service *sector* of the economy—such as in fast-food restaurants, small stores, and hotels.
   a. information
   b. part, area, or segment

_____ 4. In a test case in 1896, the Supreme Court of the United States stated that racial segregation in public schools and other public facilities in the southern states did not *violate* the Constitution.
   a. protect
   b. disobey or do something against

_____ 5. The Supreme Court of the United States invented what is called the "separate but equal" doctrine to *justify* racial segregation in public schools and other public facilities in the southern states.
   a. to give a reason for something
   b. prevent something from happening

_____ 6. The public schools in the inner city were composed *predominantly* of African-American students and often shared the neighborhood problems of high crime rates and other forms of social disorder.
   a. mostly or mainly
   b. definitely or exactly

_____ 7. There are some bilingual programs in areas where there is a large *concentration* of one language group, particularly Spanish speakers.
   a. academic achievement
   b. large amount of something in one place

_____ 8. The goal of the American education system is to teach children how to learn and to help them reach their *maximum* potential.
   a. largest possible
   b. minimum

_____ 9. These standards are not only in line with college and career requirements, but they also ensure that students who move from one state to another during school will be taught and *assessed* with the same standards.
   a. given scholarship money after careful examination
   b. had a judgment made after careful examination

B. Read these two sentences from the chapter and notice the words in italics. Then use context clues and write the correct word next to its definition.

1. Americans *regard* education as the *means* by which the inequalities among individuals are to be *erased* and by which every desirable end is to be *achieved*.

2. Toqueville *eventually* decided that the tendency of public education to encourage people to *seek* a higher *status* in life was in *harmony*, not in *conflict*, with the customs of American society.

_____ 1. agreement, working together

_____ 2. got rid of something so that it did not exist anymore

_____ 3. social position

_____ 4. think about

_____ 5. finally

_____ 6. a method or system

_____ 7. gotten, reached

_____ 8. look for

_____ 9. disagreement or argument

Preview Content

A. Think about the George S. Counts quotation at the beginning of the chapter. In small groups, discuss how education can erase inequalities. Make a list of some examples.

B. Discuss these questions with your classmates.
1. What are the differences between public and private schools? Which are better? Why?
2. What qualities do you think American universities are looking for when they decide who will be admitted?

Education often takes place in an informal setting.

3. What do you know about the system of education in the United States? Work with a partner to fill in the K-W-L chart with what you *know* about education in the United States and what you *want* to know. Then, as you read the chapter, fill in what you have *learned*.

K	W	L
What We <u>Know</u> About Education in the United States	What We <u>Want</u> to Know About Education in the United States	What We Have <u>Learned</u> About Education in the United States

C. Read the headings in the chapter and look at the illustrations. Write five topics that you predict will be covered in this chapter.

1. _____
2. _____
3. _____
4. _____
5. _____

THE ESTABLISHMENT OF PUBLIC SCHOOLS IN AMERICA: TOCQUEVILLE'S OBSERVATIONS

1. As might be expected, educational institutions in the United States reflect the nation's basic values, especially the ideal of equality of opportunity. From elementary school through college, Americans believe that everyone deserves an equal opportunity to get a good education.

2. From the beginning, when Americans established their basic system of public schools in 1825, they reaffirmed[1] the principle of equality by making schools open to all classes of Americans and by financing the schools with tax money collected from all citizens. Those who favored public schools believed that these institutions would help reduce social-class distinctions in the United States by educating children of all social classes in the same "common schools," as they were known at the time.

3. When Alexis de Tocqueville arrived in the United States in 1831, he found a great deal of enthusiasm about the new and growing public elementary schools. The mayor of New York City gave a special dinner for Tocqueville during which a toast[2] was offered in honor of "Education—the extension of our public schools—a national blessing."

4. Because he was a French aristocrat, Tocqueville at first shared the fears of some wealthy Americans who believed that universal education would be a danger rather than a national blessing. He eventually decided, however, that the tendency of public education to encourage people to seek a higher status in life was in harmony, not in conflict, with the customs of American society. The ideal of equal opportunity for all regardless of family background was much stronger in the United States than in France.

5. Tocqueville also noted that American public education had a strong practical content that included the teaching of vocational[3] skills and the duties of citizenship. Thus, public education not only gave Americans the desire to better themselves, but it also gave them the practical tools to do so. Moreover, the material abundance of the United States provided material rewards for those who took full advantage of the opportunity for a public education.

6. During the next century and a half, public schools in the United States were expanded to include secondary or high schools (grades 9–12) and colleges and universities, with both undergraduate and graduate studies.

The Educational Ladder

7. Americans view their public school system as an educational ladder, rising from elementary school to high school and finally college undergraduate and graduate programs. Most children start school at age five by attending kindergarten, or even at age three or four by attending preschool programs. Then usually there are five to six years of elementary school, two to three years of middle school, and four years of high school. (School systems may divide the twelve years a bit differently, usually depending upon school-age population, but all do have twelve years of elementary, middle school, and senior

---

[1] *reaffirmed: formally stated an intention or belief again, especially as an answer to a question or doubt*

[2] *toast: the action of drinking wine or other drink in order to thank someone, wish someone luck, or celebrate something*

[3] *vocational: training or advice relating to the skills needed to do a particular job*

high school.) Most school systems have kindergarten as well.

8   After high school, the majority of students go on to college.* Undergraduate studies lead to a bachelor's degree, which is generally what Americans mean when they speak of a "college diploma." Students may also receive an associate degree for two years of study at a community college. Some of these associate degrees are in vocational or technical fields.

9   The bachelor's degree can be followed by professional studies, which lead to degrees in such professions as law and medicine, or graduate studies, which lead to master's and doctoral degrees. The American public schools are free and open to all at the elementary and secondary (high school) level, but the public colleges and universities charge tuition[4] and have competitive entrance requirements.

10 The educational ladder concept is an almost perfect reflection of the American ideal of individual success based on equality of opportunity and on "working your way to the top." In the United States, there are no separate public educational systems with a higher level of education for the wealthy and a lower level of education for the masses. Rather, there is one system that is open to all. Individuals may climb as high on the ladder as they can. The abilities of the individuals, rather than their social class, are expected to determine how high each person will go.

11 Although the great majority of children attend the free public elementary and high schools, about 10 percent choose to attend private schools. The majority of these are religious schools that are associated with particular churches and receive financial support from them, though parents must also pay tuition. A major purpose of these schools is to give religious instruction, which cannot be done in public schools, but that is not always the reason that parents send their children to these schools. Parents who live in large cities may send their children to Catholic or other religious schools because they believe that these schools are safer and have higher academic standards than the public schools. The public schools in many of these cities have encouraged

Harvard University in Cambridge, Massachusetts

---

* *The word* college *is used in several different ways. It is generally used instead of* university *to refer to the education after high school, as in the expressions "go to college" and "get a college education." It is also used to refer to the school, as in "Where do you go to college?" Often, people use the word college to refer to a small school that does not offer graduate degrees or to a two-year community college. University is used for large schools that offer both undergraduate and graduate degrees. Universities often call the divisions within them colleges, as in the College of Arts, Humanities, and Social Sciences of the University of Maryland, Baltimore County.*

[4] *tuition: the money you pay for being taught at a school or college*

parents and community members to establish charter schools[5] in an attempt to keep these children in the public schools.

12 There are also some elite[6] private schools that serve mainly upper-class children. For these private schools, students must pay such high tuition costs that only wealthier families can afford them, though scholarships are usually offered to some talented, less affluent children who cannot pay the tuition. Parents often send their children to these schools so that they will associate with other upper-class children and maintain the upper-class position held by their parents, in addition to getting a good education.

13 Unlike private religious schools, elitist private schools do conflict with the American ideal of equality of opportunity. These schools often give an extra educational and social advantage to the young people whose families have the money to allow them to attend. However, because these schools are relatively few in number, they do not displace the public school as the central educational institution in the United States. But attending a good private school does give students an advantage when competing with public school graduates for admission to the best universities in the nation. Thirty-five percent of the students admitted to Harvard, for example, graduated from a private school.

14 There is another area of inequality in the American education system. Because of the way that schools are funded, the quality of education that American students receive in public schools varies greatly. Traditionally, the largest percentage of the money for schools came from the local level (cities and counties), primarily from property taxes. School districts that had middle-class or wealthy families had more tax money to spend on education. Therefore, wealthier school districts had beautiful school buildings with the most up-to-date technology and the latest science equipment, and poorer school districts had older buildings with less modern equipment. Today, the states pay the largest amount for funding elementary and secondary schools, and the federal government pays an average of ten percent of the cost. However, the amount a local district spends on the schools still has a huge impact, and students living in low-income communities go to schools with the least resources and often the least experienced teachers.

15 Although the amount of money spent per child is not always the best indicator of the quality of education the child receives, it certainly is an important factor. Some believe that all schools, public or private, religious or not, should be eligible for public school funding. They would support a system of vouchers,[7] which parents could use to help pay tuition at any school of their choice. Some states are now experimenting with voucher systems.

Attending an American University

16 Money is also increasingly a factor in receiving a college education. All university students must pay tuition expenses in the United States, and the cost of an education is rising much more rapidly than is the average family income. Because tuition is much lower at public universities than at private ones, wealthy students have more choices. There are a number of financial aid programs in

---

[5] *charter schools: schools to which the state, local, or federal government (or private organization) has given money and special permission to operate but that are operated by parents, private companies, etc., rather than by the public school system*

[6] *elite: limited to wealthy people with a high social status*

[7] *vouchers: types of tickets that can be used instead of money for a particular purpose*

the form of loans and scholarships available at both public and private schools. About 80 percent of college students have some form of student aid. However, the expenses of buying books and living away from home make it increasingly difficult for many students to attend even the less expensive public universities. The majority of students must work during their college years to help meet costs, and sometimes their work schedule reduces the number of courses they can take and increases the time it takes them to complete a college degree. Most young people graduate from college with significant debt from student loans.

17 A growing number of students cannot afford to go away to college and pay the tuition and living expenses for a public or private university. They choose instead to attend community college programs for two years in their hometowns, paying much less in tuition. These two-year colleges offer a wide range of programs. Some offer two-year degrees called associate degrees. Students may also take their first two years of college at a community college and then transfer to a state university. Community colleges feed into the state university systems and offer educational opportunities to large numbers of students who ordinarily would not be able to attend a university. The popularity of community colleges continues to grow. Now a number of the community colleges offer four-year bachelor degree programs through state systems.

The differences in yearly cost among public two- and four-year colleges and private four-year colleges is significant:

	Public two-year (in-state)	Public four-year (in-state)	Private four-year
Tuition & fees	$ 3,131	$ 8,655	$29,056
Room, board, books, etc.	$12,453	$13,606	$14,233
Total cost	$15,584	$22,261	$43,289
Net price (after scholarships, grants, aid)	$ 4,350	$ 5,750	$15,680

Source: The College Board's Trends in College Pricing 2012 and Trends in Student Aid 2012 reports.

18 Despite its costs, the percentage of Americans seeking a college education continues to grow. In 1900, less than 10 percent of college-age Americans entered college. Today, over half of all Americans have taken some college courses, and many have attended for four years or more. There are more than 20 million students attending college now, and there are roughly 3,000 different colleges and universities to choose from. Today, many parents who were not able to attend college when they were young have the satisfaction of seeing their sons and daughters attend. About half of the students enrolled in college today are the first generation of their family to attend.

19 As we have seen in earlier chapters, the American definition of success has traditionally been one of acquiring wealth and a good standard of living. It is not surprising, therefore, that Americans value education for its monetary[8] value. The belief has been widespread in the United States that the more schooling people have, the more money they will earn when they leave school. The belief is strongest regarding the desirability of certain undergraduate university degrees, or a professional degree such as medicine or law following the undergraduate degree. Both undergraduate and graduate degrees in science, technology, engineering, and

[8] *monetary: relating to money*

math (STEM) fields offer high salaries. In the United States, there are not enough graduates with STEM degrees to fill the jobs now available, so employment prospects in these fields are excellent. The monetary value of graduate degrees in "nonprofessional" fields such as literature, art, music, history, or philosophy, however, is not as great.

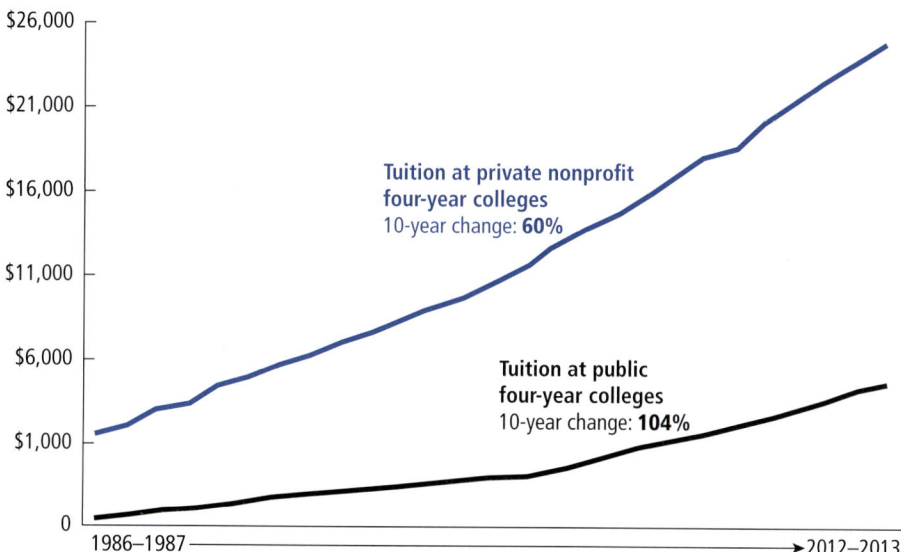

TRENDS IN COLLEGE TUITION PRICES

Tuition at private nonprofit four-year colleges
10-year change: **60%**

Tuition at public four-year colleges
10-year change: **104%**

Source: The College Board's *Trends in College Pricing 2012*.
Note: Tuition for public four-year colleges is for in-state students.

20 In recent years, there has been a change in the job market in the United States. In the past, it was possible to get a high-paying factory job without a college education. Workers with skills learned in vocational schools, training programs, or on the job could do work that did not require a college education. These were among the jobs that new immigrants were often able to obtain. Increasingly, however, the advent[9] of new technologies has meant that more and more education is required to do much of the work. Many of the new jobs in the United States either require a college education, even a graduate degree, or they are low-paying jobs in the service sector of the economy—such as in fast-food restaurants, stores, and hotels. New manufacturing jobs often require a knowledge of robotics, for example.

21 Because of the importance of higher education, many adults combine working with taking classes at a college. Many public and private colleges and universities are making it easier for students to take classes through *distance learning*, using the Internet to provide materials and lectures as well as to engage students in discussion. Some students who are living on campus or commuting to classes take at least part of their coursework by distance learning, but it is also possible for a student to obtain both undergraduate and graduate degrees without ever being on a college campus.

22 An exciting new trend is the growth of MOOCs—Massive Open Online Courses—where thousands of people can participate in courses taught by some of the most important scholars in the United States. It began with a few professors at elite American universities, but it is becoming much more frequent, and other universities around the world are joining in. The focus has been on the learning experience, not on earning college credits, though some are exploring ways of providing certificates for successfully passing the examinations that go with the courses.

[9] *advent: the time when something first begins to be widely used*

Educating the Individual

23 American schools tend to put more emphasis on developing critical-thinking skills than they do on acquiring quantities of facts. American students are encouraged to ask questions, think for themselves, and express their own opinions in class, a reflection of the American values of individual freedom and self-reliance. The goal of the American education system is to teach children how to learn and to help them reach their maximum potential.

24 The development of social and interpersonal skills may be considered as important as the development of intellectual skills. To help students develop these other important skills, schools have added a large number of extracurricular[10] activities to daily life at school. These activities are almost as important as the students' class work. For example, in making their decisions about which students to admit, colleges look for students who are "well-rounded." Grades in high school courses and scores on pre-college tests like the Scholastic Aptitude Test (SAT) are very important, but so are the students' extracurricular activities. It is by participating in these activities that students demonstrate their special talents, their level of maturity and responsibility, their leadership qualities, and their ability to get along with others.

25 Some Americans consider athletics, frequently called *competitive sports*, the most important of all extracurricular activities. This is because many people believe it is important for all young people, young men and young women, to learn how to compete successfully. Team sports such as American football, basketball, baseball, and soccer are important because they teach students the "winning spirit." At times, this athletic competition may be carried to such an extreme that some students and their parents may place more importance on the high school's sports program than its academic offerings.

26 Student government is another extracurricular activity designed to develop competitive, political, and social skills in students. The students choose a number of student government officers who compete for the votes of their fellow students in school elections. Although these officers have little power over the central decisions of the school, the process of running for office and then taking responsibility for a number of student activities if elected is seen as good experience in developing their leadership and competitive skills, and in helping them to be responsible citizens.

27 Athletics and student government are only two of a variety of extracurricular activities found in American schools. There are clubs and activities for almost every student interest—art, music, drama, debate, foreign languages, photography, volunteer work—all aimed at helping the student to become more successful in later life. A number of school districts now require all students to engage in community service—tutoring, meeting with the elderly in nursing homes, cleaning up community parks, etc.—as a requirement for high school graduation. Many parents watch their children's extracurricular activities with as much interest and concern as they do their children's intellectual achievements in the classroom.

The Standards Movement

28 In the late 1990s, international comparisons of education revealed that, in general, American students did not perform as well in math, science, and other subjects as students from many

---

[10] *extracurricular: sports or other activities that you do in addition to your usual classes*

other developed countries. Some believed this was because American standards for education might not be high enough. Unlike the situation in many other countries, traditionally, local community school districts have had responsibility for determining school curricula and selecting textbooks, with only limited state and national supervision. However, since the 1990s, both the state and the federal government have become more involved in determining school standards. The federal government has set national goals for education that include standards for early childhood, elementary, secondary, and adult education. Even teacher education programs have to meet federal and state standards. Most major educational associations, such as national associations of teachers of science, math, or language arts, have also evaluated the current curricula and criteria for certification and developed new standards.

29 To ensure that standards are met, the federal government now requires annual testing in reading and mathematics in most elementary and middle grades; states also may require students to pass a series of examinations in such subjects as reading, writing, mathematics, and civics before they can graduate from high school. While most states have already set standards, at least for mathematics and reading, for all students, more recently the governors of 45 states, the District of Columbia, and four U.S. territories, created a new set of standards for mathematics and English language arts. Only Alaska, Minnesota, Nebraska, Texas, and Virginia have remained outside. These Common Core Standards focus on concepts and procedures that are needed for entry into college or the workforce. These standards are not only in line with college and career requirements, but they also ensure that students who move from one state to another during school will be taught and assessed with the same standards.

30 Standardized tests are not without controversy, however. In the early 2000s, the federal government began a program called No Child Left Behind (NCLB), with the goal of holding schools and teachers accountable for student progress. Schools were given grades to measure the progress of their students on standardized tests. Parents were given the opportunity to remove their children from schools with low or failing grades and send them to schools with better grades. However, several problems have occurred. The emphasis on standardized testing takes a lot of classroom time. Estimates are that preparing for or taking these standardized tests can consume up to 20 percent of the school year. Some teachers are spending more time "teaching to the test" than making sure students understand important concepts. A number of educators fear that the American tradition of asking questions and thinking for oneself is being replaced by memorization of facts to be tested.

31 One of the strongest critics of emphasizing standardized testing is Diane Ravitch, who was originally a strong supporter of NCLB. In her book, *The Death and Life of the Great American School System: How Testing and Choice are Undermining Education,* Ravitch explains why she believes NCLB has failed. When local schools are given a failing grade (because the students have failed to improve enough on the tests), parents can choose to have their students transfer to a better school, but they do not. Parents want to have their children attend a school in their home neighborhood. Ravitch says that after 10 years of NCLB, we should be able to see dramatic improvement in our schools and

the progress of our students, but we do not:

> By now, we should be able to point to sharp reductions of the achievement gaps between children of different racial and ethnic groups and children from different income groups, but we cannot....Many children continue to be left behind...and they are the same children who were left behind 10 years ago.

32 Ravitch believes that it is the responsibility of our public schools to provide equality of educational opportunity to all students, regardless of race, ethnicity, or income, and if they are unable to reach equality of educational attainment, we must give them special help. We cannot afford to leave any of our children behind, without the education they need to compete for good jobs and a decent standard of living—without a chance to achieve the American Dream.

Inequalities in the American Education System

33 The most significant departure from the ideal of equality of opportunity in education occurred in the education of African Americans. As we saw in the previous chapter, after the Civil War in the 1860s, the southern states developed a social and legal system that segregated the former black slaves from the white population in all public facilities, including schools. Blacks had separate schools that were inferior to the white schools by almost any measure.

34 The *Brown versus the Board of Education* Supreme Court decision of 1954 ended legal segregation in the southern schools, but segregation continued until the *Civil Rights Acts* of the mid-1960s. During the late 1960s and the 1970s, a series of court decisions forced the nation to take measures to integrate all of its public schools, in both the South and

Before segregation ended, black students often attended schools with crowded, substandard classrooms and inadequate resources.

the North. Although there had been no legal segregation in the North, the neighborhood schools of both the North and the South reflected the makeup of the races who lived in the neighborhood. These residential patterns resulted in a number of segregated schools in the North, particularly in big cities. Many public schools in the inner city were composed predominantly of African-American students and often shared the neighborhood problems of poverty, high crime rates, and other forms of social disorder. These schools were clearly unequal to those in the predominantly white, middle-class neighborhoods in the suburbs.

35 For the next twenty years, the courts required Americans to try to achieve racial balance in the public schools. The most controversial method used to deal with unequal neighborhood schools was the busing of schoolchildren from their home neighborhoods to schools in more distant neighborhoods in order to achieve a greater mixture of black and white children in all schools. Black children from the inner city were bused to schools in predominantly white, middle-class neighborhoods, and students living in the middle-class neighborhoods were bused into the poorer black neighborhood schools. Most students did not like it, and neither did their parents, who wanted their children to attend neighborhood schools. Busing continued through the 1970s and the 1980s with mixed success, and it has been largely abandoned. Most school districts now allow children to attend school in their own neighborhood, even if it is predominantly black or white.

36 In addition to trying to end segregation, the federal government created assistance programs for the neediest children. These included special reading instruction, smaller classes, early childhood programs, and some economic assistance. As a result, according to Paul Barton of the Educational Testing Service, the racial achievement gap was cut in half in the 1970s and 1980s. However, since the 1980s, the gap has remained almost unchanged.

37 At the college level, during the 1970s there was a growth in affirmative action programs. Because African Americans and other minorities had experienced discrimination in the past, colleges and universities tried to actively recruit minority students. The goal was to have the student population reflect the percentages of minorities in the population of the state or country as a whole. All minority students were recruited, Hispanics as well as blacks. In the previous chapter, we mentioned that Supreme Court Justice Sonia Sotomayor experienced the benefits of affirmative action, with admission to and scholarship offers from many top universities.

38 Over the years, there have been challenges to the use of affirmative action in determining college admissions. In 2003, the Supreme Court ruled that the University of Michigan could consider a student's ethnic or racial heritage during its decision-making. As Justice Sandra Day O'Conner wrote in the Supreme Court decision, "Effective participation by members of all racial and ethnic groups in the civic life of our nation is essential if the dream of one Nation, indivisible, is to be realized."

39 In 2013, the Supreme Court considered another challenge to affirmative action brought by Abigail Fisher, a white honor roll student who had been denied admission to the University of Texas at Austin in 2008. The University guaranteed admission to the top ten percent of all graduating Texas high school students regardless of race, but it considered race

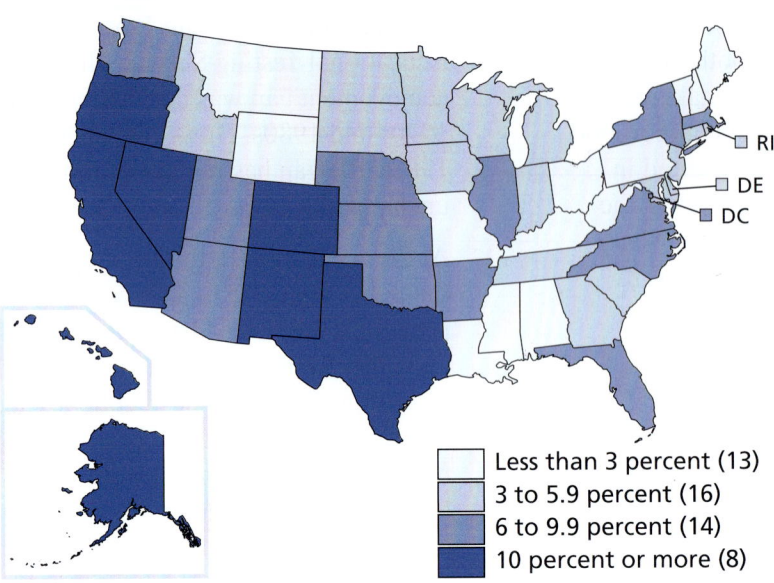

Source: U.S Department of English, National Center for Education Statistics

and ethnicity as factors for all other students. Fisher was in the top 12 percent of her class and claimed that minority students with lower qualifications were admitted instead of her, violating her constitutional rights. The Supreme Court ruled that universities should try to achieve diversity with "race-neutral policies." These complex legal issues cause Americans to ask themselves how to provide equality of educational opportunity to all students—white, black, Hispanic, Asian, and other minorities.

The Increasing Responsibilities of Public Schools

40 Americans place the weight of many of their ideals, hopes, and problems on the nation's public school system. Some observers believe they have placed more responsibilities on the public schools than the schools can possibly handle. For example, public schools are often expected to solve student problems that result from the weakening of family ties in the United States. Rising divorce rates and births to single mothers have resulted in an increasing number of children in the public schools who are raised by only one parent. Studies have shown that these children are more likely to have problems school than children raised in families with two parents.

41 The education of the new immigrant children provides the public school system with some of its greatest challenges. Many of the children come from countries where they have not had strong educational preparation, and their academic skills are below grade level. Others have come from school systems with standards similar to, or even more advanced than, the American schools, and their academic adjustment is much easier. However, all these children must learn English. This means that they are trying to learn new concepts at the same time that they are struggling to learn a new language. Studies show that it takes five to seven years in order for them to be able to compete with English-speaking American children on an equal basis in classes where English is the language of instruction. There are some bilingual programs in areas where there is a large concentration of one language group, particularly Spanish speakers. However,

there are more than 400 languages spoken in the United States, and some school districts report that 100 or more different languages are spoken by children in their schools. It is not uncommon for five or six different native languages to be spoken by the students in one classroom.

42   It is obvious that children who are not native speakers of English are going to be at a disadvantage when taking standardized tests. Many are not going to be able to compete with native speakers on these tests. Under the No Child Left Behind program, their lower scores may affect the rating of their school, and they affect the overall average test scores of American students. Thus, school districts with high concentrations of non-native speakers of English may have lower test scores than districts that do not. Unfortunately, many of these school districts are the ones that have limited financial resources and may not be able to provide students with all the extra support that they need. In general, during times of economic downturns, there is less money going to the public schools from the state and local governments that fund them. (As stated before, the national government only provides an average of 10 percent of the funding for American elementary and secondary schools.)

43   The limitations on school funding create fewer problems for wealthier Americans. In the last few years, the testing scores of high-income students have gone up while the scores of black students, Hispanic students, and low-income students have remained unchanged. Some reading scores have actually gone down. The lowest scores are in school districts—such as Detroit (Michigan) and Washington, D.C.—where poverty and racial segregation are most concentrated. The inner-city public school system in Washington, D.C. has the largest achievement gap of any city in the nation between white and black students. And yet, in the area surrounding the city are seven of the ten wealthiest counties in the country, with some of the best schools and highest concentrations of adults with advanced college degrees.

44   In a controversial book entitled *Coming Apart: The State of White America, 1960–2010*, Charles Murray describes the widening gap between what he sees as a new upper class and a new lower class. Murray says that members of the new upper class live in certain super zip codes in the United States, where the income and education levels are high, and the people are often the leaders and decision makers of the country. Four cities are the centers of power: "It is difficult to hold a nationally influential job in politics, public policy, finance, business, academia, information technology, or the media and not live in the areas surrounding New York, Washington, D.C., Los Angeles, or San Francisco."

45   Murray worries that these elite Americans are isolated from the rest of the country and do not understand the problems of the middle class. They are economically secure and often some of the wealthiest people in the country. During the economic recession, their incomes went up while the rest of Americans saw their incomes fall. They have their own subculture. Generally, they are married, religious, socially liberal, physically fit, and very concerned about their children's education. They want to send their children to the right preschool, so that they can go to the right elementary school and the right high school, so that they can get admitted to one of the most prestigious universities, particularly Harvard, Princeton, or Yale. Interestingly, all the present Supreme Court Justices have law degrees from either Harvard or Yale, and all the U.S. presidents from George H. W. Bush through President Obama (Presidents George H. W. Bush, Bill Clinton, George W. Bush, and Barack Obama) have

degrees from either Harvard or Yale.

Twenty-first Century Challenges to American Education

46   We began by observing that the public schools in the United States reflect the ideal of equality of opportunity. When they began in the early 1800s, there was a belief that if children from all classes attended the same schools, there would be fewer social class distinctions. From the beginning, of course, the reality was that the schools were not open to all. In many parts of the country, African Americans could not attend public schools. After the Civil War, the Supreme Court tried to justify segregated schools by saying that they could be "separate but equal." Justice John Marshall Harlan believed that the decision violated the nation's highest law and its basic values. "Our Constitution is color-blind," he said, "and neither knows nor tolerates classes among its citizens." Then, in 1954, the Supreme Court held that laws that forced black students to go to racially segregated schools violated the U.S. Constitution because such schools could never be equal. The opinion of the Court was that "to separate [black school children] from others...solely because of their race generates a feeling of inferiority...that may affect their hearts and minds in a way unlikely ever to be undone."

47   And now, in the 2000s, we find that American schools are once again largely segregated, this time not by law, but because of residential patterns and the love of local neighborhood schools. Now we find that the children of new immigrants may also be in schools where there are a majority of minority students. And we learn that the high school graduation rate for both African Americans and Hispanics is below that of white students. How will we address these critical problems? What does the future hold? On the one hand, local schools reflect residential patterns where there is significant segregation. On the other hand, however, neighborhoods are becoming increasingly integrated as minorities settle in the suburbs. Another factor is that young people are marrying other races and ethnic groups at an increasingly rapid rate. More and more children are born of mixed race/ethnicity.

48   The impact of the enormous number of new immigrants cannot be overstated. From 1980 to 2010, the percentage of foreign-born Americans more than doubled. One in four school children lives with a parent who was born outside the United States. Forty-five percent of the students in U.S. schools are a member of a racial or ethnic minority group. This has caused schools to examine the curricula and try to make it more inclusive. Many schools have adopted history or social studies textbooks that include more information about African Americans, Hispanic Americans, and other minorities, and literature texts that include poetry and fiction written by Americans of all ethnic backgrounds.

49   The challenge is to find ways to give all students, in whatever schools they are attending, the very best education possible. Most Americans would probably agree that there should be minimum core standards that all school districts meet, but there should also be flexibility to account for local diversity. There has always been an effort to find a balance between educational standards and the unique circumstances of local neighborhood schools. Americans of all races, ethnic groups, and levels of income care deeply about the education of their children. And the majority of parents want their children to attend their neighborhood school. If it is not a good school, they want to see it improved, not closed.

50   In contrast to many other countries, the

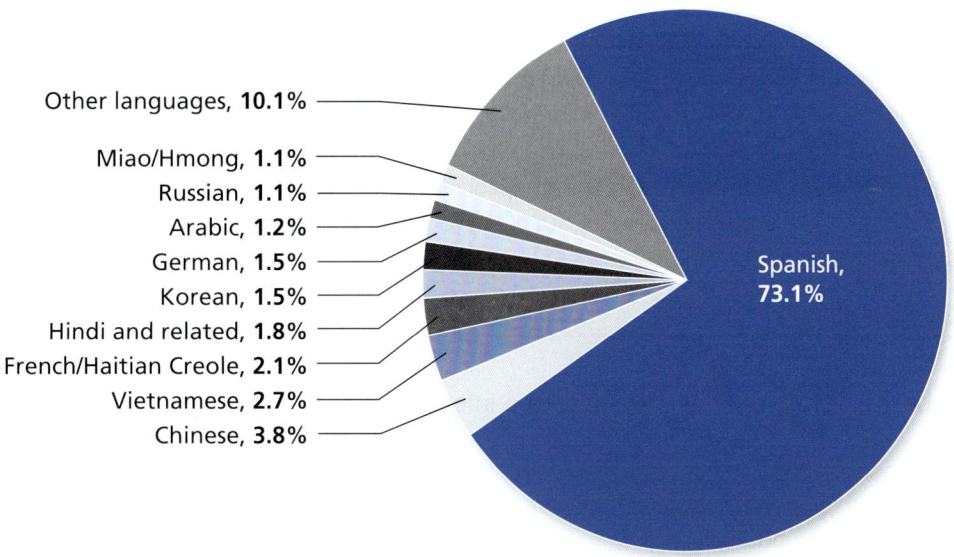

TOP TEN SPOKEN LANGUAGES IN LEP STUDENTS' HOMES

- Other languages, **10.1%**
- Miao/Hmong, **1.1%**
- Russian, **1.1%**
- Arabic, **1.2%**
- German, **1.5%**
- Korean, **1.5%**
- Hindi and related, **1.8%**
- French/Haitian Creole, **2.1%**
- Vietnamese, **2.7%**
- Chinese, **3.8%**
- Spanish, **73.1%**

Note: Refers to limited English proficient (LEP) students, ages 5 to 18, currently enrolled in school. LEP students are those who reported speaking English less than "very well."
Source: MPI analysis of the 2009 American Community Survey.

local school district has always had a great deal of control over neighborhood schools. Americans are often suspicious of the federal government telling them how to run their local schools. Many school districts are administered by local school boards elected by the people in the district. There are often public school board meetings where parents debate what is happening in the schools—sometimes about what is being taught or what books are being used.

51 American public schools have generally served the United States well by educating a diverse population and working to bring people together. Americans face increased challenges now as they struggle to find ways to provide all students equality of educational opportunity. And they are now debating how to bring equality of achievement to more young people. The future wellbeing of America depends on it.

AFTER YOU READ

Understand Main Ideas

Read the predictions you made on page 204 before reading the chapter. If you have not already done so, complete the L (What We Have Learned) part of the chart you started on page 204 before you read the chapter. With your partner, make up five questions about main points in the chapter and ask another pair of students to answer the questions. Then share your K-W-L chart with the other pair of students.

Understand Details

Write the letter of the best answer according to the information in the chapter.

_____ 1. In the beginning of the chapter, it is implied that some wealthier Americans opposed the first public schools in the United States because
   a. they cost too much money.
   b. they would weaken social-class barriers.
   c. people who did not pay for their education would not value it.

_____ 2. Tocqueville finally concluded that public education in the United States would
   a. give Americans not only the desire but also the means to better their position in life.
   b. not provide any practical training in vocational skills.
   c. not work because people would be prevented from rising to a higher class by the aristocracy.

_____ 3. Which of these statements is false?
   a. American high school students have the choice of going to a free public school or a private one where they must pay tuition.
   b. The American education system is based on strong principles of equality of opportunity—all students should have an equal opportunity to get a good education.
   c. After twelve years of school, American students receive a bachelor's degree diploma at graduation.

_____ 4. Which of these statements is true?
   a. Most of the money to pay for American public schools comes from state and local taxes.
   b. Religious schools that serve middle-class students receive money from the national government, but elite private schools do not.
   c. The national Department of Education determines the curriculum for all schools and sets the standards for high school graduation and college admission.

_____ 5. From 1900 to 2000, the percentage of young Americans who take at least some college courses
   a. increased enormously, from less than 10 percent to over 50 percent.
   b. increased slightly, from about 10 percent to about 20 percent.
   c. stayed about the same, at around 20 percent.

_____ 6. What the majority of Americans probably value most about higher education is
   a. its cultural value.
   b. its monetary value.
   c. its moral value.

_____ 7. Which of the following would not be considered an extracurricular activity?
   a. a school baseball team
   b. the student government of a school
   c. a classroom research project

_____ 8. In 1896, the U.S. Supreme Court said that racially segregated schools and other public facilities
   a. violated the principle of equality.
   b. violated the U.S. Constitution.
   c. did not violate the principle of equality or the U.S. Constitution.

_____ 9. Which of these statements about American schools is <u>false</u>?
   a. Public schools that are mainly black or mainly white today usually are the result of the racial makeup of neighborhoods.
   b. African Americans are the fastest growing minority in the schools today.
   c. In some school districts, 100 different languages may be spoken.

_____ 10. Which of these statements about multiculturalism in the United States is <u>true</u>?
   a. In the United States, all immigrant children attend bilingual programs until they learn English very well and are allowed to attend regular classes with native speakers.
   b. In the United States, there are almost no uniform standards for any schools.
   c. Multicultural education discusses history from the perspectives of all the ethnic groups involved, not just the Anglo-American.

Talk About It

Work in small groups, and choose one or more of these questions to discuss.

1. Should universities be free or have very low tuition? Why or why not?
2. Are most schools in your country coeducational? What are the advantages and disadvantages of having boys and girls in the same classroom?
3. Is it possible for college teachers and students to be friends? What do you think the role of a teacher should be?
4. What should the requirements for entering a university be? Should extracurricular activities in high school or personal characteristics be considered? Why, or why not?

SKILL BUILDING

Develop Your Critical Thinking Skills

In this chapter, there are references to two important goals of education: teaching students facts, and teaching them creative thinking skills. These two approaches to teaching can be summed up in the question, "Are students vessels to be filled or lamps to be lit?" Which do you think is more important—learning a large quantity of facts or learning to think creatively? Why?

Do some research to support your opinion. Reread the last three sections of the chapter, concentrating on paragraphs 23, 24, 28, 29, 30, 41, and 49. Think about your own experience and consider these questions.

- Which approach is used more in your country?
- How do the college admission standards in the United States compare to those in your country?
- Which approach prepares students better for the world of work?
- How do you teach a large quantity of facts to students?
- How do you teach creative thinking?

Think of three more questions raised by this contrasting approach and then share your opinions and your questions with other students in a small group.

Build Reading Skills: Types of Supporting Details

Usually, each paragraph has a topic sentence that states the main idea of the paragraph. Often, this is the first sentence. The rest of the paragraph contains supporting details that develop or explain the main idea. There are many types of supporting details:

- definitions
- facts or opinions
- statistics
- examples or illustrations
- descriptions
- quotations

Look back at the reading and find the paragraphs that begin with the following topic sentences. Then find the details that support the main ideas stated in the topic sentence. Write at least one detail for each sentence, and identify the type of detail that it is.

1. Despite its costs, the percentage of Americans seeking a college education continues to grow.

   _____

   _____

2. In the late 1900s, international comparisons of education revealed that, in general, American students did not perform as well in math, science, and other subjects as students from many other developed countries.

   _____

   _____

3. One of the strongest critics of emphasizing standardized testing is Diane Ravitch, who was originally a strong supporter of NCLB.

   _____

   _____

4. The impact of the enormous number of new immigrants cannot be overstated.

   _____

   _____

Build Your Vocabulary

Vocabulary Check

Use the words in the box to complete the sentences.

| attainment | elite | facilities | obvious | tuition | vocational |
| displace | extracurricular | isolated | remove | violated | zip codes |

1. In 1954, the Supreme Court ruled that segregation denied black children an equal opportunity to an education; segregation _____ the Constitution.

2. In the past, many students who went to competitive schools such as Harvard received their high school education at _____ private schools for the rich.

3. Sports, clubs, and other _____ activities held after school help students get a well-rounded education.

4. Ravitch believes that it is the responsibility of our public schools to provide equality of educational opportunity to all students, regardless of race, ethnicity, or income, and if they are unable to reach equality of educational _____, we must give them special help.

5. Murray says that members of the new upper class live in certain super _____ in the United States, where the income and education levels are high, and the people are often the leaders and decision makers of the country.

6. However, because these schools are relatively few in number, they do not _____ the public school as the central educational institution in the United States.

7. Murray worries that these elite Americans are _____ from the rest of the country and do not understand the problems of the middle class.

8. At the university level, there is no free system of public education; even universities supported by public funds charge students _____.

9. It is _____ that children who are not native speakers of English are going to be at a disadvantage when taking standardized tests.

10. Before the civil rights laws were passed, segregation of public _____ was legal in the South.

11. Parents were given the opportunity to _____ their children from schools with low or failing grades and send them to schools with better grades.

12. Some American high schools offer _____ education to prepare students for jobs right after school; these students do not attend college.

EXPAND YOUR KNOWLEDGE

Ask Americans

Find out how Americans feel about education. Ask several Americans the following questions and record their answers. If you cannot interview Americans, interview a classmate and share the responses with another student.

1. Where do you think your child would get the best education—public school, private school, or charter school? And why?
2. How do you feel about the American education system? What would you do to improve it, if anything?
3. How does the quality of American education compare to other countries? Is there a difference between the quality at the high school level compared to the university level?
4. Are drugs and/or violence problems in the schools in your neighborhood? How should we protect children in schools? Should there be armed guards?
5. How important is a college education? What is the value of a college education? What difference does it make in a person's life? Is it worth the cost?
6. What do you think about ebooks? Should they replace paper textbooks? Why or why not?

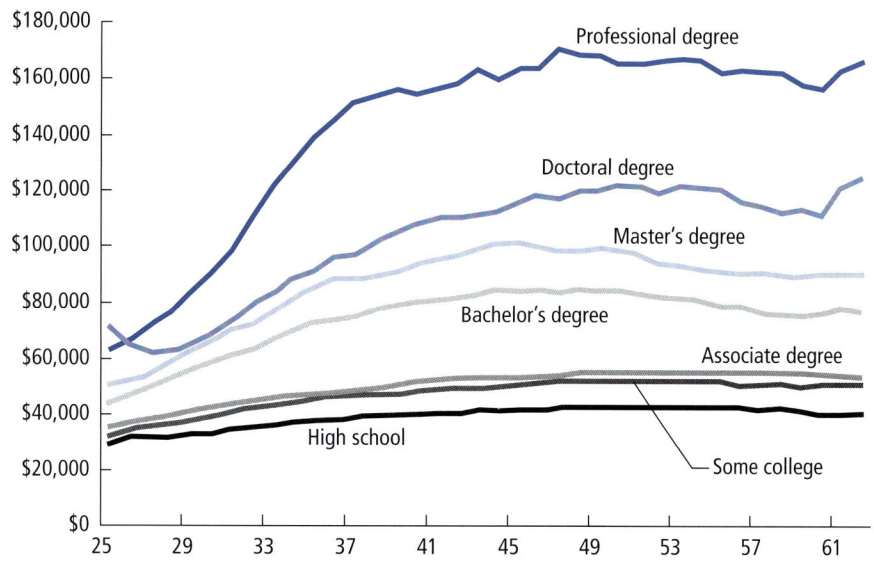

MEAN EARNINGS BY AGE, 2009

Source: 2009 American Community Survey (ACS) Integrated Public Use Micro Sample.
Notes: Estimated for full-time, full-year workers. Plots show a 3-year moving average.

Think, Pair, Share

What should be taught in public schools? What should be the priorities? Read the following list of areas that are covered in American schools, and decide which are the most important.

Arrange the items in order from most important to least important by renumbering the sentences. Then share your list with a partner and with another pair of students.

_____ 1. Developing students' moral and ethical character

_____ 2. Teaching students how to think

_____ 3. Preparing students who do not go to college for a job or career after graduation

_____ 4. Helping students to become informed citizens so that they will be adequately prepared to vote at age eighteen

_____ 5. Preparing students for college

_____ 6. Developing students' appreciation of art, music, and other cultural pursuits

_____ 7. Other (your opinion) _____

Small-Group Project

Some American parents are so dissatisfied with the public schools that they are educating their children at home. Homeschooling now provides education for an increasing number of American children, and the trend is growing. Some public school educators agree that the current model for public schools needs to be changed, and some have begun to create—or to work with a company or a private business—alternative or charter schools, experimenting with class size, grouping, schedules, and curriculum. Perhaps most dramatic, these alternatives to traditional public or private schools are sometimes transforming the roles of the teachers and the students, giving students much more power to decide what they want to learn.

Plan an ideal school. With your group, decide whether it would be homeschooling or an alternative school. Name your school, and then describe it in detail. Decide on school colors and a motto for your school. You may include these points in your description:

- Who would the students be (age, social class, ethnicity)?
- What kind of a building would you use?
- Would the school have a special emphasis (science, music)?
- What would the teachers be like (age, experience, roles)?

- How many students would be in a class?
- Who would determine the curriculum?
- What about tests and homework?
- How would discipline be maintained?
- What would be the role of the parents?
- What special activities would the students have?
- What would a typical day be like?
- What do you think others would say about this school?

When your description is complete, share your new school with the rest of the class.

People Watching

Find the answers to the following questions. Then compare your answers with those of your classmates.

1. When is the right time to ask a question in an American classroom? Watch others and notice the following. (If you have difficulty finding the answers to these questions, ask a fellow student, or ask the teacher to explain when it is the right time for questions.)
    a. Is the teacher talking when students ask questions?
    b. How do students indicate that they have a question to ask?
    c. How does the teacher indicate that he or she is ready for questions? Does the teacher ask, "Are there any questions?" Does the teacher pause and look up from notes or from the chalkboard?
    d. What other signals does a teacher send to indicate that questions are invited?

2. One of the most difficult things for students to understand is when an interview or an appointment with a teacher or professor is over. How do you know when you should leave? Watch a teacher and student in an interview or appointment, if possible, and see which of these are used to indicate the appointment is over. If you cannot observe a teacher and student, perhaps you can watch another similar situation, such as a job interview, a meeting with a counselor, or an appointment with a doctor. Look for the following:
    a. The teacher moves noticeably in the chair—maybe closer to the desk or toward the door.
    b. The teacher says, "Well... " or "It has been nice talking to you" or "I think you understand now... "
    c. The teacher turns his or her attention to other business such as papers on the desk or a schedule of appointments.
    d. The teacher moves the chair back from the desk.

Ask Yourself / Ask Americans

Schools around the world differ in their expectations of students. In some schools, students are expected only to listen and remember what their teachers say; in others, they are expected to ask questions. It's important to know these differences if you are going to be successful in a school in another country.

Respond to the following statements. Write **T** (True) or **F** (False) in the first column to indicate how you think students should behave in your country. Then ask an American (preferably a student) for his or her opinion, and record those answers in the second column.

	You	American Student
1. Students should not ask questions; they should only answer them.	_____	_____
2. Students should rise when the teacher enters the classroom.	_____	_____
3. Asking a teacher questions challenges his or her authority.	_____	_____
4. Students should never address teachers by their first names.	_____	_____
5. Students should memorize everything their teachers assign; education is primarily memorizing books and teachers' lectures.	_____	_____
6. Male and female students should attend the same classes.	_____	_____

What differences do you notice in the responses? Compare your answers with others in the class.

Use the Internet

Work with a partner and do one of these activities.

1. Some people predict that of the 6,000 languages currently spoken in the world, about half will not be spoken by the next century. Use the Internet to find information about languages in danger of becoming extinct. Then discuss these questions in small groups.

    a. Why should anyone care if a language is "dying"?

    b. What can be done to help maintain or revitalize a language that is in danger of being lost?

    c. How important do you think it is to preserve languages?

2. American Indian languages are among the most endangered in the world. Many of the 155 languages have not been written. Even those that have been written may have very few people who still speak the language. Use the Internet to find information about Native American languages spoken in the United States and the number of their speakers. Then work with a partner and answer these questions.

    a. How many speakers are there of the most widely spoken languages, Navajo and Ojibwa?

    b. In what states do most of these people live? (What are the five most common states?)

    c. How many languages have twenty speakers or fewer?

3. There are a lot of sources for instruction online. The chapter mentions MOOCs, massive online open courses. Do some research to find out more about MOOCs. Also, look at the free courses offered online by the Khan Academy at http://www.khanacademy.org/

WRITE ABOUT IT

Choose one of the following topics. Then write a short composition about it.

1. What are the advantages and disadvantages of working while attending college?

2. What do you think the real value of a college education is? Is it monetary? Is it intellectual? Is it social? Write an essay explaining your views.

3. The English language has always been friendly to *borrowing* from other languages. Given the closeness of so many Spanish-speaking countries to the United States, and the presence of Spanish-speaking peoples in the Southwest before the colonists moved there from the East Coast, it is not surprising that a number of Spanish words have entered English, especially the English spoken in the United States. Look at this list of words borrowed from Spanish.

    | alcove | broncos | chaps | patio | siesta | tango |
    | alfalfa | burrito | desperado | poncho | stampede | tornado |
    | alligator | cafeteria | lasso | rodeo | taco | vanilla |
    | avocado | canyon | macho | | | |

    What do you notice about these words? How many words relate to food? How many words relate to the life of the cowboy or to the West? (Note: The word for the fair that brings horseback riding, cow roping, and other cowboy feats to many western towns each year is *rodeo*.) Were there any words that surprised you?

Compare borrowings in English with those in other languages that you know. What similarities or differences do you see? Write a report about your findings.

EXPLORE ON YOUR OWN

Books to Read

Lawrence Blum, *High Schools, Race, and America's Future: What Students Can Teach Us About Morality, Diversity, and Community*—This book describes a high school course on race and racism taught in a racially, ethnically, and economically diverse high school, with insights about how the course relates to students' daily lives.

Jonathan Kozol, *Savage Inequalities: Children in America's Schools*—Kozol takes a disturbing look at the differences in public schools attended by rich children versus those attended by poor children and the consequences of the inequalities.

Arthur Levine and Diane Dean, *Generation on a Tightrope: A Portrait of Today's College Student*—Levine and Dean give an account of a generation that is sophisticated about technology but has limited preparation for the world of work.

Charles Murray, *Coming Apart: The State of White America, 1960–2010*—Murray describes the widening gap between what he sees as a new upper class and a new lower class.

Diane Ravitch, *The Death and Life of the Great American School System: How Testing and Choice are Undermining Education*—Ravitch explains why she believes the No Child Left Behind government education program has failed.

Movies to See

The Blindside—This movie is based on a true story of a homeless teen who is taken in by a wealthy family and becomes the star player on the high school football team.

The Interrupters—This is a documentary film that tells the story of three violence interrupters who try to protect their Chicago communities from the violence they once used themselves.

Lean on Me—This film is based on the true story of Joe Clark, a dedicated, but extremely tough, principal of a terrible inner-city school that he is determined to improve.

Stand and Deliver—A dedicated teacher inspires his disadvantaged Latino students to learn calculus to pass an advanced placement exam and build up their self-esteem.

Waiting for "Superman"—This documentary analyzes the failures of the American public education system by following several students trying to gain admission to a charter school.

CHAPTER 10

HOW AMERICANS SPEND THEIR LEISURE TIME

The form and type of play and sports life which evolve in any group or nation mirror the development in other segments of the culture.

American Academy of Physical Education

How do Americans' values affect how they spend their leisure time?

BEFORE YOU READ

Preview Vocabulary

A. Read these sentences from the chapter. Then use context clues to figure out the meanings of the AWL words in italics.

1. The form and type of play and sports life which *evolve* in any group or nation mirror the development in other segments of the culture.

2. The competitive ethic in organized sports contains *elements* of hard work and physical courage. Hard work is often called "hustle," "persistence," or "never quitting" in the sports world, while physical courage is referred to as "being tough" or "having guts."

3. "The Bible says leisure and lying around are morally dangerous...sports keep us busy....There are probably more really *committed* Christians in sports, both collegiate and professional, than in any other occupation in America."

4. Some people are particularly concerned about the injuries that high school players get in football games. The pressure to "hit hard" and win high school games is *intense*.

5. In the past, teams and most players stayed in one city and *bonded* with the fans. Now professional sports are more about money and less about team loyalty.

6. Many worry about the amount of sex and violence that children are *exposed* to as they watch TV, play games, and explore the Internet.

7. Mississippi officials *attribute* the drop in childhood obesity to a local focus on the issue, a 2007 law that mandated more physical education, and a decision by the state school board to put more fruits, vegetables, and whole grains on menus.

8. First Lady Michelle Obama started a campaign to fight childhood obesity by stressing children's health and fitness. She *advocated* for federal legislation requiring schools to offer healthier lunches, and she is encouraging kids to exercise more.

Now write the correct AWL word next to its definition.

_____ 1. willing to work very hard at something

_____ 2. parts or features of a whole system

_____ 3. develop by gradually changing

_____ 4. to say that an event is caused by something or someone

_____ 5. very strong

_____ 6. shown, faced with

_____ 7. acted and spoke out in support of

_____ 8. developed a special relationship

B. Classification: Recreational activities are usually not competitive and are done for fun, relaxation, and, sometimes, self-improvement. Sports are more organized and usually involve competition and rules of how to play.

Write **S** if the word or phrase concerns sports and **R** if it has to do with recreation.

_____ 1. team

_____ 2. hobby

_____ 3. handicrafts

_____ 4. hustle

_____ 5. gold medal

_____ 6. do-it-yourself projects

_____ 7. professional tennis

_____ 8. going to the theater

_____ 9. video games

_____ 10. skiing

Preview Content

A. Think about the quotation by the American Academy of Physical Education at the beginning of the chapter. Then discuss these questions with your classmates.
  1. How do you think Americans like to spend their leisure time?
  2. What are the advantages and disadvantages of playing competitive sports?
  3. What do you know about Americans' eating habits? What is "junk food"?
  4. What is the impact of television and video games on children?
  5. How has technology impacted leisure time?

B. Read the headings in the chapter and look at the illustrations. Write five topics that you predict will be covered in this chapter.

  1. _____
  2. _____
  3. _____
  4. _____
  5. _____

SPORTS AND AMERICAN VALUES

1. Most social scientists believe that the sports that are organized by a society generally reflect the basic values of that society and attempt to strengthen them in the minds and emotions of its people. Therefore, organized sports may have a more serious social purpose than spontaneous, unorganized play by individuals. This is certainly true in the United States, where the three most popular organized sports are American football,* basketball, and baseball, with soccer gaining in popularity.

2. Traditionally, Americans have seen organized sports as an example of equality of opportunity in action. In sports, people of different races and economic backgrounds get an equal chance to excel. For this reason, notes sociologist Harry Edwards, Americans have viewed organized sports as "a laboratory in which young men, regardless of social class, can learn the advantages and rewards of a competitive system." Although Edwards specifically mentions young men, young women also compete in organized sports without regard to their race or economic background. The majority of American football and basketball players, both college and professional, are African-American, and about one-third of professional baseball players are Hispanics or Latinos. Women's sports have grown in popularity in the United States, and they now have more funding and stronger support at the college level than in the past. The Olympics provide evidence of the increased interest in women's organized sports. American women have won gold medals for several team sports—softball, basketball, and soccer.

3. The American ideal of competition is also at the very heart of organized sports in the United States. Many Americans believe that learning how to win in sports helps develop the habits necessary to compete successfully in later life. This training, in turn, strengthens American society as a whole. "It is commonly held," says one sports writer, "that the competitive ethic taught in sports must be learned and ingrained[1] in youth for the future success of American business and military efforts." In fact, about two-thirds of American boys play organized sports outside of school, and more than half of the girls do, too.

4. Amateur athletics, associated with schools and colleges, are valued for teaching young people traditional American values. The competitive ethic in organized sports contains elements of hard work and physical courage. Hard work is often called "hustle," "persistence," or "never quitting" in the sports world, while physical courage is referred to as "being tough" or "having guts." Slogans are sometimes used to drive home the competitive virtues for the young participants:

    Hustle—you can't survive without it.

    A quitter never wins; a winner never quits.

    It's easy to be ordinary, but it takes guts to excel.

5. In the process of serving as an inspiration for traditional basic American values, organized sports may be considered as part of "the national religion," a mixture of patriotism and national pride on the one hand, with religious ideas and symbols on the other (see Chapter 3). Billy Graham, a

---

*Generally, in the United States, when the word "football" is used, it refers to the American game of football. What is known as football in other countries is called "soccer" in the United States.

[1] ingrained: attitudes or behavior that are firmly established and therefore difficult to change

famous American Protestant religious leader, once observed: "The Bible says leisure and lying around are morally dangerous... sports keep us busy... There are probably more really committed Christians in sports, both collegiate and professional, than in any other occupation in America." On the other hand, in recent years there have been a number of examples of professional sports stars behaving very badly, and there have been significant scandals in college sports as well.

Competition Carried to an Extreme?

6   Although sports in the United States are glorified by many, there are others who are especially critical of the corrupting power of sports when certain things are carried to excess. An excessive desire to win in sports, for example, can weaken rather than strengthen traditional American values.

7   Critics have pointed out that there is a long tradition of coaches and players who have done just this. Vince Lombardi, a famous professional football coach, was often criticized for stating that winning is the "only thing" that matters in sports. Woody Hayes, another famous football coach, once said: "Anyone who tells me, 'Don't worry that you lost; you played a good game anyway,' I just hate." Critics believe that such statements by coaches weaken the idea that other things, such as fair play, following the rules, and behaving with dignity when one is defeated, are also important. Unfortunately, many coaches still share the "winning is the only thing" philosophy.

8   There is, however, also a tradition of honorable defeat in American sports. Sociologist Harry Edwards, for example, has pointed out:

American football is a rough sport that sometimes causes injuries.

> *The all-important significance of winning is known, but likewise, there is the consoling[2] "reward" of the "honorable defeat." Indeed, the "sweetness" of winning is derived...from the knowledge of having defeated a courageous opponent who performed honorably.*

9. When the idea of winning in sports is carried to excess, however, honorable competition can turn into disorder and violence. In one baseball game, the players of two professional teams became so angry at each other that the game turned into a large-scale fight between the two teams. The coach of one of the teams was happy about the fight because, in the games that followed, his team consistently won. He thought that the fight had helped to bring the men on his team closer together. Similarly, a professional football coach stated, "If we didn't go out there and fight, I'd be worried. You go out there and protect your teammates. The guys who sit on the bench, they're the losers." Both coaches seemed to share the view that if occasional fights with opposing teams helped to increase the winning spirit of their players, so much the better. Hockey coaches would probably agree. Professional hockey teams are notorious[3] for the fights among players during games. Some hockey fans seem to expect this fighting as part of the entertainment.

10. There are some who criticize this violence in sports, particularly in football, which may be America's favorite spectator sport. From time to time articles appear in newspapers or magazines such as *Sports Illustrated,* one of the nation's leading sports magazines, criticizing the number of injuries that have resulted from the extreme roughness of the game, increased by a burning desire to defeat one's opponent. In recent years, there has been a lot of attention paid to head injuries—brain concussions that cause problems as athletes age. There is evidence that these injuries cause brain damage that can be severe, even resulting in dementia.[4] People are particularly concerned about the injuries that high school players get in football games. The pressure to "hit hard" and win high school games is intense. In some parts of the country, especially in the South, boys start playing tackle football in elementary school, bringing the risks of competitive pressure to nine- and ten-year-olds. Concussions are also a problem for soccer players, particularly for girls (when "heading") because their necks are not as strong as boys.

11. Most Americans would probably say that competition in organized sports does more to strengthen the national character than to corrupt it. They would probably say that eliminating competition in sports and in society as a whole would lead to laziness rather than hard work and accomplishment. One high school principal, for example, described the criticism of competitive sports as "the revolutionaries' attempt to break down the basic foundations upon which society is founded." Comments of this sort illustrate how strong the idea of competition is in the United States, and how important organized sports are as a means of maintaining this value in the larger society.

12. Another criticism of professional sports is that the players and the team owners get too much money, while fans have to pay more and more for tickets to the games. Basketball, baseball, and football stars get multi-million-dollar contracts similar to rock singers and movie stars. Some have

---

[2] *consoling:* making someone feel better when he or she is feeling sad or disappointed

[3] *notorious:* famous or well known for something bad

[4] *dementia:* loss of the ability to think normally

asked whether these players are really athletes or entertainers. Furthermore, players are often traded to other teams, or choose to go as free agents, and a whole team may move to another city because of money. In the past, teams and most players stayed in one city and bonded with the fans. Now professional sports are more about money and less about team loyalty.

13 College football and basketball programs are also affected by big money. The teams of large universities generate millions of dollars, and there is enormous pressure on these sports programs to recruit top athletes and have winning seasons. The pressure is on the young athletes as well. There are some high school students who would not be able to afford college if they did not get a sports scholarship. Once they are in college, it is often difficult to balance the demands of daily sports practice and the season game schedule with the need to study. Some colleges have a lower rate of athletes graduating than others. In addition to the danger of failing academically, there is another reason why some athletes do not finish college. The very best football and basketball players are often recruited by professional teams while they are still in school. Some students may choose to give up studying for a college degree for the chance to earn big money and early success as a pro.

14 Another problem facing organized sports is the use of performance-enhancing drugs.[5] With the pressure to win so strong, a number of athletes have turned to these drugs. Although the use of most performance-enhancing drugs is illegal, it has now spread from professional sports down to universities and even high schools and middle schools. The use of these drugs puts the health of the athletes in danger, and it is ethically wrong. It goes against the American values of equality of opportunity and fair competition. But by 2004, the problem had become so significant that President George W. Bush mentioned it in his State of the Union address:

> Athletics play such an important role in our society, but, unfortunately, some in professional sports are not setting much of an example. The use of performance-enhancing drugs like steroids in baseball, football, and other sports is dangerous, and it sends the wrong message—that there are shortcuts to accomplishment, and that performance is more important than character.

The use of these drugs has called into question the achievements of some baseball players and their records for homeruns, etc., and several players have been denied admission to the Baseball Hall of Fame.

15 The case of cyclist Lance Armstrong and his use of performance-enhancing drugs has received intense international attention. Armstrong was widely respected in the United States (although many overseas were suspicious) for his seven Tour de France wins and his charity work fighting cancer. The U.S. Post Office was even an official sponsor of his cycling races. It was a shock to many Americans when the evidence of his drug use was revealed, and he was stripped of his cycling victories.

Recreational Activities

16 Unlike organized sports, what is generally called recreation in the United States is not expected to encourage competition. For this reason, recreation is much more spontaneous and serves the individual's needs away from the competitive world of work. Nevertheless, much can be learned

---

[5] *performance-enhancing drugs: drugs such as steroids that some athletes use illegally to improve their strength or endurance*

about the values of Americans from an examination of the kinds of recreation in which they engage. Many recreational activities are organized at the local level and are paid for (in part) by local governments. Local Parks and Recreation organizations often offer a wide range of activities to community members. There is usually a Parks and Recreation department that operates a recreation center that has fitness equipment and offers classes, and it maintains outdoor facilities. These may include public parks, playgrounds, soccer and baseball fields, basketball and tennis courts, golf courses, walking and bike trails, and swimming pools. These facilities are open to all at little or no cost. During good weather, many communities sponsor outdoor activities and festivals that feature events such as food tasting, outdoor concerts, county fairs, contests, and races. Often, these are attended by whole families and groups of friends.

17 Some Americans prefer recreation that requires a high level of physical activity. This is true of the most popular adult recreational sports: jogging or running, tennis, and skiing. It would seem that these Americans carry over their belief in hard work into their world of play and recreation. The expression "We like to work hard and play hard" is an example of this philosophy.

18 Physical fitness is a way of life for these Americans. Some of them regularly work out at community gyms or private sports clubs—lifting weights, swimming, playing squash or racquetball; participating in aerobic exercise classes; or using exercise bikes, treadmills, rowing machines, or stair-steppers. Some choose to do long-distance running and may participate in a marathon race. In addition to the famous Boston and New York marathons, there are races in many other cities and even in small towns, drawing from several hundred to thousands of participants. Few of the runners expect to win—most just want to finish the race, and over a half a million people do finish a marathon each year. The number of people participating in marathon races has gone down dramatically, but the number finishing them has gone up.

19 Most races are open to all, young and old alike, even those in wheelchairs, and many encourage walkers as well as runners. Charity races are also very popular. Participants ask people to sponsor them by contributing to the charity if they finish the race. The distances vary from 5K to 10K to full marathons and often include social events. The Race for the Cure to raise money for breast cancer research draws women who are breast cancer survivors and their friends and family, and those who participate to honor a loved one who has (or had) the disease.

Serious runners train hard for their races.

20 The interest that Americans have in self-improvement, traceable in large measure to the nation's Protestant heritage (see Chapter 3), is also carried over into the recreation habits of some people. It is evident in the joggers who are determined to improve the distance they can run, or the people who spend their vacation time learning a new sport such as sailing or scuba diving. The self-improvement motive, however, can also be seen in many other popular forms of recreation that involve little or no physical activity.

Many Americans enjoy rock climbing, white-water rafting, and motorcycling.

21 Interest and participation in cultural activities, which improve people's minds or skills, are also popular. Millions of Americans go to symphony concerts, attend live theater performances, visit museums, hear lectures, and participate in artistic activities such as painting, performing music, or dancing. Many Americans also enjoy hobbies such as weaving, needlework, candle making, wood carving, quilting, and other handicrafts.[6] Community education and recreation programs offer a wide range of classes for those interested in anything from using computers to gourmet cooking, learning a foreign language, writing, art, self-defense, yoga, and bird-watching.

22 The recreational interests of Americans also show a continuing respect for the self-reliance, and, sometimes, the adventure and danger of frontier life. While some choose safe pastimes such as handicrafts, gardening, or DIY (Do It Yourself) projects like building bookcases in their den, others are ready to leave home and take some risks. Adventure travel has grown to be a multi-billion-dollar business. Millions of Americans have bought mountain bikes to explore the wilderness on their own. Many others are choosing to go white-water rafting, mountain climbing, rock climbing, skydiving, helicopter skiing, and bungee jumping. U.S. park officials complain about the number of people who take life-threatening risks in national parks and have to be rescued. "It is as if they are looking for hardship," one park official stated. "They seem to enjoy the danger and the physical challenge."

23 Not all Americans want to "rough it" while they are on their adventure holidays, however. There are a number of travelers who want "soft adventure." Judi Wineland, who operates Overseas Adventure Travel, says, "Frankly, it's amazing to us to see baby boomers seeking creature comforts." On her safari trips to Africa, she has to provide hot showers, real beds, and

---

[6] handicrafts: skills needing careful use of your hands, such as sewing or making baskets

night tables. The Americans' love of comfort, mentioned in Chapter 5, seems to be competing with their desire to feel self-reliant and adventurous. Others simply enjoy being outdoors in the United States fishing, birding, or observing other wildlife. More than 90 million Americans a year participate in these activities.

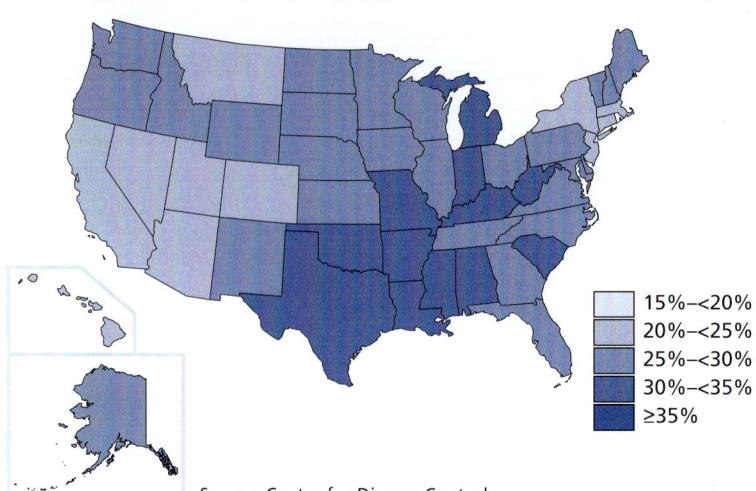

PREVALENCE OF SELF-REPORTED OBESITY AMONG U.S. ADULTS BEHAVIORAL RISK FACTOR SURVEILLANCE SYSTEM, 2011

15%–<20%
20%–<25%
25%–<30%
30%–<35%
≥35%

Source: Center for Disease Control.

Health and Fitness

24 In spite of all these opportunities to be physically active, however, many Americans are not physically fit, or even try to be. The overall population is becoming more overweight, due to poor eating habits and a sedentary[7] lifestyle. Government studies estimate that fewer than half of Americans exercise in their leisure time. Experts say that it is not because Americans "don't know what's good for them"—they just don't do it. By mid-2000, the Centers for Disease Control (CDC) sounded the alarm—almost two-thirds of Americans were overweight, and more than one in five were obese. The CDC reported that obesity had become a national epidemic. After smoking, obesity was the number two preventable cause of death in the United States. The government began a campaign to urge people to lose weight and get more exercise. But by 2011, the numbers were worse: More than one-third of American adults were obese. Incidentally, the obesity rate is higher in some states than others. The map above shows the percent of obese people in each state.

25 It's not that Americans lack information on eating well. Newspapers and magazines are full of advice on nutrition, and diet books are best-sellers. Indeed, part of the problem may be that there is too much information in the media, and much of it is contradictory. For thirty years, the government encouraged people to eat a diet high in carbohydrates and low in fat to avoid health risks such as heart disease and certain types of cancer. Many Americans ate low-fat, high-carbohydrate foods and gained weight. Then in the early 2000s, high-protein, low-carbohydrate diets became popular.

26 Many Americans have tried a number of diets, searching for the magic one right for them. Some overweight people say the diet advice is so confusing that they have just given up and eat whatever they want. Since 1994, the government has required uniform labeling so that consumers can compare the calories, fat, and carbohydrates in the food they buy. More than half of Americans say they pay attention to the nutritional content of the food they eat, but they also say they eat what they really want when they feel like it. For example, they may have switched to skim milk but still buy fancy, fat-rich ice cream. As one American put it, "Let's

---

[7] *sedentary: doing or requiring much sitting*

face it—if you're having chips and dip as a snack, fat-free potato chips and fat-free sour cream just don't taste as good as the real thing."

Nutrition label from a small bag of chips

27 Experts say that it is a combination of social, cultural, and psychological factors that determine how people eat. A *Newsweek* article on America's weight problems referred to "the culture of overindulgence"[8] seemingly ingrained in American life. "The land of plenty seems destined to include plenty of pounds as well," they concluded. Part of the problem is that Americans eat larger portions[9] and often go back for second helpings, in contrast to how much people eat in many other countries.

28 Another factor is Americans' love of fast food. Although the fast-food industry is offering salads on its menus, most Americans still prefer "junk food." They consume huge quantities of pizza, hamburgers, French fries, and soft drinks at restaurants, not only because they like them, but also because these foods are often the cheapest items on the menu. Another significant factor is Americans' busy lifestyle. Since so many women are working, families are eating a lot of fast food, frozen dinners, and restaurant takeout. Some experts believe that Americans have really lost control of their eating; it is not possible to limit calories when they eat so much restaurant and packaged food. It takes time to prepare fresh vegetables and fish; stopping at a fast-food chain for fried chicken on the way home from work is a much faster alternative. Often, American families eat "on the run" instead of sitting down at the table together.

29 First Lady Michelle Obama started a campaign to fight childhood obesity by stressing children's health and fitness. Her program is called "Let's Move," and it focuses on better nutrition as well as increased physical activity. She advocated for federal legislation requiring schools to offer healthier lunches, and she is encouraging kids to exercise more. At the White House, she planted a garden with the help of kids from D.C. inner city schools and called attention to the fact that many poor inner city neighborhoods do not have grocery stores that sell fresh fruits and vegetables. Many have only small neighborhood stores that sell chips and sodas and other "junk food" that is high in calories and low in nutritional value. Often, both children and adults who live in poverty have higher rates of obesity than the general population.

30 There is evidence of some improvement in the rates of childhood obesity. Mississippi is among the most obese states in the nation, according to the Centers for Disease Control and Prevention (CDCP), but its rate of childhood obesity has dropped in recent years. The state made important changes in the time for exercise and the type of food served in the public schools:

> *Mississippi officials attribute the drop to a local focus on the issue, a 2007 law that mandated more physical education and a decision by the state school board to put more fruits, vegetables, and whole grains on menus.*

---

[8] *overindulgence:* the habit of eating or drinking too much

[9] *portions:* the amount of food for one person, especially when served in a restaurant

31 Not everyone thinks that having the government mandate exercise programs or school lunch menus is a good idea, but it does seem to be helping. The problem of childhood obesity is truly alarming: Nearly one in three children in the United States is overweight or obese. The numbers are even higher in the African-American and Hispanic communities, where nearly 40 percent of the children are overweight or obese.

First Lady Michelle Obama has created a program to fight childhood obesity.

The Impact of Television, Video Games, and the Internet

32 Ironically, as Americans have gotten heavier as a population, the image of a beautiful woman has gotten much slimmer. Marilyn Monroe, a movie star of the 1950s and 1960s, would be overweight by today's media standards. Television shows, movies, and TV commercials feature actresses who are very slender.[10] Beer and soft drink commercials, for example, often feature very thin girls in bikinis. As a result, many teenage girls have become insecure about their bodies and so obsessed[11] with losing weight that some develop eating disorders such as anorexia or bulimia.

33 Another irony is that although television seems to promote images of slender, physically fit people, the more people watch TV, the less likely they are to exercise. Television has a strong effect on the activity level of many Americans. Some people spend much of their free time lying on the couch watching TV, channel surfing,* and eating junk food. They are called "couch potatoes," because they are nothing but "eyes." (The small marks on potatoes are called *eyes*.) Couch potatoes would rather watch a baseball game on TV than go play softball in the park with friends, or even go to a movie. Cable and satellite TV bring hundreds of stations into American homes, so there is an almost limitless choice of programs. Americans spend more of their leisure watching TV than doing any other activity.

34 Another challenge is the effect of all this technology on children. Some worry that American children and young people are spending too much time watching television, using the Internet, and playing video games. One effect is that channel surfing and surfing on the web shorten a child's attention span. Also, research shows that multitasking is really switching rapidly from one task to another, and it is not really doing several tasks at the same minute. There is evidence that the brains of children and young people are being rewired by these activities. There is an effect on both their minds and their bodies. Clearly, they are not getting enough exercise. The government estimates that eight to 18-year-olds spend an average of 7.5 hours a day using entertainment media, including TV, computers, video games, cell phones, and movies. Only one-third of high school students get the recommended levels of physical activity.

---

[10] *slender:* thin, graceful, and attractive

[11] *obsessed:* thinking about a person or a thing all the time and being unable to think of anything else

* Constantly clicking the remote control to change from channel to channel. (Note also the term "surf the web" that means to go from site to site, and surfing refers to the sport of riding the waves on a special board.)

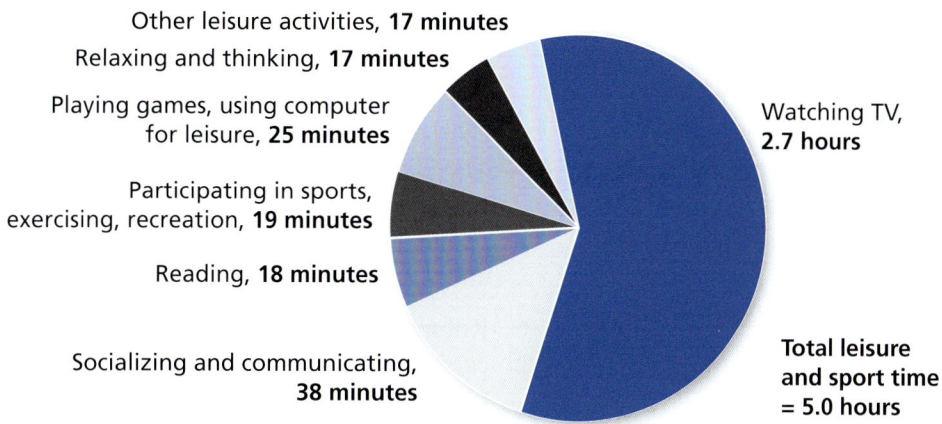

LEISURE TIME ON AN AVERAGE DAY

- Other leisure activities, **17 minutes**
- Relaxing and thinking, **17 minutes**
- Playing games, using computer for leisure, **25 minutes**
- Participating in sports, exercising, recreation, **19 minutes**
- Reading, **18 minutes**
- Socializing and communicating, **38 minutes**
- Watching TV, **2.7 hours**
- **Total leisure and sport time = 5.0 hours**

Note: Data include all persons age 15 and over. Data include all days of the week and are annual averages for 2010. Source: Bureau of Labor Statistics, American Time Use Survey.

35 Others worry more about the quality of what children are watching on TV, the content of video games, and what they are seeing on the Internet. Many worry about the amount of sex and violence that children are exposed to as they watch TV, play games, and explore the Internet. Americans face a constant dilemma[12]— how to balance the right to free speech with the need to protect children and maintain standards of decency.[13] Because Americans place such a high value on individual freedom, particularly freedom of speech, they have traditionally been very hesitant to censor,[14] or even restrict, the flow of information by any means of communication. True censorship occurs when the government sets the standards; most Americans would prefer that the entertainment industry regulate itself, and the movie industry does have a rating system for films. The Entertainment Software Rating Board (ESRB) "assigns the age and content ratings for video games and mobile apps, enforces advertising and marketing guidelines for the video game industry, and helps companies implement responsible online privacy practices."

"On the Internet, nobody knows you're a dog."

36 On the one hand, some people believe that the federal government should regulate the Internet to protect children. There have been instances where adults

---

[12] *dilemma: a situation in which you have to make a difficult choice between two or more actions*

[13] *decency: basic accepted behavior, especially moral and sexual behavior*

[14] *censor: to examine books, movies, or letters to remove anything that is offensive*

have met children or teenagers over the Internet and have persuaded them to meet in person. In several instances, teenagers have been kidnapped. Parents have great fear about their children meeting strangers on the Internet and about their possible exposure to pornography. It is against the law to send pornography through the U.S. mail, and some wish it were outlawed on the Internet as well. (Child pornography is already against the law.) But it is not just children who can get into trouble on the Internet. Many adults have been the victims of scams where they are tricked into giving personal information that allows criminals to steal money from their bank accounts, or even their whole identity. The anonymity of the Internet is valued by many, but it also has hurt a number of people. Most alarming is the cyberbullying of some teenagers that has been so hurtful that the victims have committed suicide.

37 On the other hand, many Internet users believe that government regulation could threaten the growth and vitality of the Internet. Some would argue that the lack of regulation has permitted the Internet's explosive growth and the development of new technologies to deliver it. Wireless technology now allows Americans to access the Internet just about anywhere, including, ironically, many fast-food restaurants. Many people are happy that technology has made it possible for them to communicate with just about anyone anywhere. However, this 24/7 access (24 hours a day, 7 days a week) has a huge impact on leisure time and Americans' ability to relax. Joe Robinson, in his book *Work to Live: Reclaim Your Life, Health, Family, and Sanity*, states, "The line between work and home has become so blurred that the only way you can tell them apart is that one has a bed." Robinson and others are trying to get American companies to offer more vacation time. The majority of Americans work more than forty hours a week, and many only get one or two weeks a year of paid vacation time. When the economy has a downturn, many are afraid to take the short amount of vacation time they have. The U.S. Travel Association reports that the average American vacation is now 3.8 days; people are taking more long-weekend trips, and fewer one- or two-week-long trips.

38 Robinson has organized the Work to Live campaign, with the goal of changing the national labor laws so that everyone would be entitled to at least three weeks of vacation per year. He says that our founding fathers Thomas Jefferson and John Adams "believed that democracy was at risk if all attention in society was focused only on making money. It's hard to be an engaged citizen, not to mention a parent or actual human, when the overwork culture abducts you from all other responsibilities in life." He argues that Americans would be even more productive if they could have a month of vacation like most Europeans do.

39 Vacation time renews the spirit and gives people the energy and vitality to lead productive lives. Leisure time in the United States offers something for everyone; the only complaint that most Americans have is that they do not have enough of it. Americans, like people everywhere, sometimes choose recreation that just provides rest and relaxation. Watching television, going out for dinner, and visiting friends are simply enjoyable ways to pass the time. However, as we have seen, millions of Americans seek new challenges involving new forms of effort even in their leisure time. "Their reward," states *U.S. News & World Report*, "is a renewed sense of vitality,"[15] a sense of a goal conquered and confidence regained in dealing with life's "ups and downs."

---

[15] *vitality: great energy and cheerfulness, and the ability to continue working effectively*

AFTER YOU READ

Understand Main Ideas

Review the predictions you made on page 231 before you read the chapter. Were your predictions correct? Write the number of the paragraph where you found the information next to each prediction.

Understand Details

Write the letter of the best answer according to the information in the chapter.

_____ 1. Organized sports in a society
   a. are a poor reflection of the values of that society.
   b. are a good reflection of the values of that society.
   c. are leisure activities and games which tell us very little about the social values of a country.

_____ 2. Which of the following ideals is at the very heart of organized sports in the United States and is, therefore, the most important ideal expressed in organized sports?
   a. self-reliance
   b. self-denial
   c. competition

_____ 3. Which of these statements is not true?
   a. Billy Graham, a Protestant religious leader, has criticized sports for having a negative effect on the morals of young Americans.
   b. Most Americans would probably agree that organized sports are an important way for young people to learn to compete.
   c. Organized sports are an example of the "national religion," the mixing of national pride and religious values.

_____ 4. Vince Lombardi, a famous professional football coach, expressed the view that
   a. sports help boys grow into men.
   b. a good football player makes a good soldier.
   c. winning is the only thing that matters.

_____ 5. Leading sports publications such as *Sports Illustrated* have stated that
   a. sports are good in general, but excessive violence in sports should be stopped.
   b. sports corrupt the American spirit and should be replaced with noncompetitive activities.
   c. many aspects of American culture, such as music and art, have been replaced by the love of sports.

_____ 6. Some of the most popular forms of recreation in the United States, such as jogging, reflect the attitude that
   a. Americans like the challenge of adventure sports.
   b. contact with nature is good for the soul of man.
   c. it is good to work hard and to play hard.

_____ 7. Which of these statements is not true?
   a. Many Americans like to spend their leisure time learning new skills in order to improve themselves.
   b. The American respect for self-reliance can be seen in the popularity of adventure travel, where people often have to rough it.
   c. Because of their active lifestyles, the number of people who weigh more than they should is decreasing.

_____ 8. According to the chapter, why do so many Americans have poor eating habits?
   a. They are unaware of the dangers of high-fat diets.
   b. The foods that they buy in the stores have no labels that give nutritional information.
   c. They are too busy to cook, and they eat a lot of fast food.

_____ 9. Which of these statements is not true?
   a. The majority of American homes have TV systems that can get fifty channels or more.
   b. Most Americans have such a busy lifestyle that they watch very little TV.
   c. American children watch a lot of television, and play a lot of video games.

_____ 10. Which of these statements is true?
   a. Most Americans are not concerned about the level of violence on television.
   b. The federal government censors programs on TV to maintain high standards of decency.
   c. Some children's television programs are educational and have much less violence than adult programs.

Talk About It

Work in small groups and choose one or more of the following questions to discuss.

1. What is your favorite sport, and why? Have you ever played on a team? Explain.
2. What are popular forms of recreation in your country? What do you like to do in your leisure time?
3. How would you compare the day-to-day level of physical activity of people in your country with that of Americans?
4. Do you think college sports teams are really like professional teams? Should the players be paid? Why or why not?
5. What is the most violent sport? Have you ever been at a sports event where there was fighting? Explain.

SKILL BUILDING

Improve Your Reading Skills: Scanning

Scan the chapter for these names and terms. Then identify each with a short phrase.

1. junk food: _____
2. couch potato: _____
3. Vince Lombardi: _____
4. channel surf: _____
5. Michelle Obama: _____
6. cyberbullying: _____
7. Lance Armstrong: _____
8. Judi Wineland: _____
9. CDC: _____
10. Joe Robinson: _____

Develop Your Critical Thinking Skills

Work with a partner and find examples of how Americans' traditional values affect organized sports and other ways Americans spend their leisure time. Put the examples into the correct categories. First match the examples with the values they illustrate, and then look for additional examples in the chapter. Answers may be used more than once.

__e,h__ 1. individual freedom   _____ 4. competition

_____ 2. self-reliance   _____ 5. material wealth/the American Dream

_____ 3. equality of opportunity   _____ 6. hard work

a. both boys and girls play organized sports
b. hustle and persistence, never quitting
c. great emphasis on winning in sports
d. many blacks on professional basketball teams
e. Americans free to pursue a great variety of individual interests in their leisure time
f. love of adventure travel in the wilderness, roughing it
g. many children have smartphones and other digital devices

h. professional sports team members free to change teams as free agents
i. emphasis on children playing competitive sports
j. popularity of do-it-yourself projects
k. buying teenagers cell phones and computers
l. having very little vacation time

Build Your Vocabulary

Opposites

Read the sentences below that contain pairs of opposites in parentheses. Choose the correct words and write them in the sentence blanks.

1. Baseball, football, basketball, and soccer are popular (individual/team) _____ sports.

2. Slogans are sometimes used to drive home the competitive (vices/virtues) _____ for the young participants: A quitter never wins; a (winner/loser) _____ never quits.

3. When the idea of winning in sports is carried to excess, honorable competition can turn into (order/disorder) _____ and violence.

4. There are some who (criticize/praise) _____ this violence in American sports, particularly in football, which is probably America's favorite (participant/spectator) _____ sport.

5. (Amateur/Professional) _____ athletics, associated with schools and colleges, are valued for teaching young people traditional American values.

6. Most Americans would probably say that competition in organized sports does more to (corrupt/strengthen) _____ the national character than to (corrupt/strengthen) _____ it.

7. Some Americans prefer recreation that requires a high level of (physical/mental) _____ activity such as jogging, tennis, and skiing.

8. The overall population is becoming overweight due to poor eating habits and a (sedentary/active) _____ lifestyle.

9. Another irony is that although television seems to promote images of (obese/slender) _____, physically fit people, the more people watch TV, the less likely they are to exercise.

10. Unfortunately, most experts would probably say that the 1990s brought few (positive/negative) _____ changes in children's programming.

More AWL Words

Test your knowledge of these AWL words by matching them with their definitions.

comment	guidelines	item	overseas	range
contract	illustrate	label	principal	relax
derive	image	lecture	project	symbol
equipment	injury	likewise	psychological	uniform

_____ 1. most important

_____ 2. a piece of paper with information about the thing attached to it

_____ 3. a carefully planned work

_____ 4. a single thing in a group

_____ 5. the way a person or product is presented to the public

_____ 6. different things of the same general type

_____ 7. in the same way

_____ 8. to make the meaning of something clearer by giving examples

_____ 9. a legal written agreement

_____ 10. a word, principle, or instruction about the best way to do something

_____ 11. in a foreign country across the ocean

_____ 12. something that represents an idea

_____ 13. a wound to your body caused by an accident or attack

_____ 14. being the same in all its parts

_____ 15. relating to the way that people's minds work

_____ 16. a long talk given to a group

_____ 17. special things needed for a sport

_____ 18. an opinion that you express

_____ 19. to have its source in (something)

_____ 20. to feel calm and comfortable

Play a Vocabulary Game

Work in small groups, and think of words and phrases that would fit into categories. Challenge another group to a competition—you tell them the words and phrases, and they guess the category. You can use information in this chapter or choose other vocabulary having to do with sports, recreation, health and fitness, diet, television, or computer technology. Here are some suggestions for categories:

    things that have to do with soccer
    (names of) basketball players
    (names of) popular diets
    things relating to culture or the arts
    things you can do on the Internet
    things teenagers like to do
    food that is good for you
    junk food
    things that might happen to a couch potato
    things a couch potato might use
    dangerous leisure activities
    equipment you need for football
    Olympic sports

Classify Words

Work with a partner. Circle the words or phrases that do not belong in each category.

EXAMPLE: **team sports:** football, baseball, hockey, (tennis)

Tennis does not belong because it is an individual sport, not a team sport.

1. **adventure sports:** helicopter skiing, African safaris, white-water rafting, gardening, rock climbing, bungee jumping, skydiving, mountain climbing
2. **things parents worry about:** pornography, explicit sex on TV, strangers on the Internet, gourmet cooking, childhood obesity, shortening of child's attention span, violence
3. **reasons why many Americans are overweight:** fast-food restaurants, larger portions, second helpings, sedentary lifestyle, overseas travel, poor eating habits, lack of exercise
4. **hobbies:** weaving, playing professional football, painting, performing music, bird-watching, making candles, Chinese cooking, learning a foreign language, traveling
5. **things made possible by technology:** wireless networks, handicrafts, laptop computers, accessing the Internet in a Starbucks, cell phones, email, instant messaging, paging, Internet games, walkie-talkies, exchanging digital photos

EXPAND YOUR KNOWLEDGE

Think, Pair, Share

How do you prefer to spend your leisure time? Read this list of leisure-time activities and decide which you enjoy most. Number them in order of importance, with number 1 as your favorite choice. Share your list with a partner and then with another pair of students.

_____ Go on a walk or hike   _____ Go swimming

_____ Read a good book   _____ Listen to music

_____ See a movie   _____ Attend a concert

_____ Play a sport   _____ Have a family picnic

_____ Work out at a gym   _____ See a play

_____ Have dinner at a restaurant _____ Visit a museum

_____ Watch TV   _____ Go shopping

_____ Go to a friend's house   _____ Watch a game

_____ Have a friend visit you   _____ Other: _____

Ask Yourself / Ask Americans

If possible, ask several Americans the following questions. Then do a poll among your friends or classmates. Compare their responses with the pie chart on page 241 from the Bureau of Labor Statistics, American Time Use Survey.

1. Think about your daily schedule. How much time each day do you spend doing each of these activities:

    Working and related activities

    Leisure and sports

    Household activities

    Eating and drinking

    Caring for others

    Sleeping

    Other activities _____

2. What are your two or three favorite leisure activities?

People Watching

In some countries, lunch is a leisurely meal that may take two or three hours. Some people eat at a nice restaurant with friends or co-workers, while others return home to eat with their families. For many, lunch is the main meal of the day. In contrast, many Americans eat lunch "on the run."

If possible, observe Americans eating lunch. Compare their lunch habits with those of your culture. Record your observations in the chart. Compare your observations with those of your classmates.

Observation Questions	Americans at Lunch	_____ at Lunch
1. Where are they eating?		
2. What are they eating?		
3. What size are the portions?		
4. How long do they stay?		
5. Do they take any food with them when they leave?		

Use the Internet

Choose one of these activities and do research on the Internet with a partner.

1. Work with a partner to learn about popular American diets. Use the Internet and find information on several diets. Decide which one you think is best and why. Then share your diet choice with your classmates. These are some popular diets:

Vegetarian, or vegan	The Zone
Dean Ornish, or low-fat	Weight Watchers
Atkins, or low-carbohydrate	Jenny Craig
South Beach	Mediterranean

2. Reality TV shows have become very popular in the United States and in other countries. Use the Internet to find out how to become a contestant on these shows. Choose one program and write a report about how to apply to appear on the show.

3. Americans have started to move back into cities from the suburbs to live in communities where they can walk to work, shopping, entertainment, etc. At the same time, there is a trend to urbanize the suburbs by building walking communities that are more like small towns, with houses, schools, shopping, and offices close together. Look on the Internet for more information about these walkable, convenient urban and suburban communities. Some examples are: Capital Hill in Seattle, WA; Short North in Columbus, OH;
and Ballston, VA (in the Washington, D.C. area). Check out the website www.walkscore.com

Small-Group Projects

Some people say that Americans don't have any culture. By that they probably mean that the United States has not been a country long enough to have developed its own art forms—music, dance, or theater—usually referred to as the fine arts. Work in small groups to test that theory or hypothesis. If you are living in the United States, find out about your local community. Are there libraries? Museums? Theaters where concerts and plays are performed? Check the entertainment section of your local newspaper (or a website) and see if any of the following are scheduled:

1. Ballets or other dance performances
2. Art or other exhibitions
3. Symphony concerts
4. Other concerts or musical performances
5. Poetry readings
6. Operas
7. Plays

Dancers from Morphoses perform in Christopher Wheeldon's "Commedia" at New York City Center.

Make a list of these performances or exhibitions, and indicate the nationality of both the artist who is performing the work and the artist who created it. Share your findings with your classmates. Work in small groups and design a cultural-adventure travel brochure. Decide all the details of the trip.

1. What kind of adventure is it?
2. Where will it take place?
3. What are the dates?
4. How much will it cost and what is included?
5. What experiences will the travelers have?

You may wish to include an itinerary and some pictures, if possible. When you have finished, share your brochure with your classmates.

WRITE ABOUT IT

Choose one of the following topics. Then write a short composition about it.

1. Some would say that American homeowners have an obsession with having a beautiful lawn. In the United States, lawns occupy more land than any single crop, including wheat and corn, and in western cities as much as 60 percent of water is used for lawns. Do you think green spaces are important? Write about the use of land for private lawns or public parks, and describe differences between the United States and your country.
2. Write about the problem of protecting children from sex and violence in television programs and movies, on the Internet, and in video games. Use a graphic organizer to plan your essay.
3. Two of the fastest growing sports are NASCAR racing and golf. Write a report about why you think they are so popular, or choose another sport to

write about.
4. Many American children are very impressed with sports stars. Do you think sports superstars have a responsibility to be positive role models for young people? Write an essay explaining why or why not, and give examples.

EXPLORE ON YOUR OWN

Books to Read

H. G. Bissinger, *Friday Night Lights: A Town, A Team, and a Dream*—A successful sportswriter, Bissinger spent a year in the Texas town of Odessa writing about their high school football program.

Pat Conroy, *My Losing Season*—In this memoir, fiction-writer Conroy tells about his personal experience as a high school basketball player at the Citadel, a military college.

Michael Mandelbaum, *The Meaning of Sports: Why Americans Watch Baseball, Football, and Basketball and What They See When They Do*—The author, a well-respected foreign policy analyst, explores Americans' fascination with team sports and how they satisfy deep human needs.

George Plimpton, *Paper Lion*—Plimpton recounts his story of being a 36-year-old rookie playing for the Detroit Lions.

Cheryl Strayed, *Wild: From Lost to Found on the Pacific Crest Trail*—A woman's life changes on a 1,100 mile hike alone on the trail from the Mojave Desert to Washington state.

Movies to See

42—This film is based on the true story of Jackie Robinson, the first African American to play in American major league baseball.

The Fighter—A docudrama explores the remarkable rise of a Massachusetts-born, junior welter-weight champion boxer named "Irish" Micky Ward.

Moneyball—Oakland A's general manager Billy Beane assembles a successful baseball team on a lean budget by employing computer-generated analysis to choose new players.

Rudy—A boy who has always been told that he is too small to play college football is determined to overcome the odds and fulfill his dream of playing for Notre Dame.

The Social Network—This film tells the story of how Mark Zuckerberg and a friend started Facebook when they were students at Harvard.

CHAPTER 11

THE AMERICAN FAMILY

The American has fashioned anew the features of his family institutions, as he does everything else about him.

Max Lerner (1902–1992)

Is the changing structure of American families affecting the American Dream?

BEFORE YOU READ

Preview Vocabulary

A. Read the following questions and notice the words in italics. These key AWL words will help you understand the reading. Use context clues to help you figure out the meanings. Then work with a partner and answer the questions.

1. If a *nuclear* family consists of a husband, wife, and their children, what is an extended family?
2. If you had a problem to solve, would you want your family to offer their *insight* into ways to solve it?
3. If you had children, would sending them to private schools be a *priority* for you, or would something else be more important?
4. How does the *location* of your house or apartment affect your lifestyle? Does it matter where you live?
5. Do you think husbands and wives should be equal *partners* in a marriage?
6. If we say that *approximately* one out of every two marriages now ends in divorce, what does that mean? Does it mean "more or less" or "exactly"?
7. Do you think that men and women should be *compensated* equally for doing the same work, or should they be paid different salaries?
8. What might happen if conscientious parents keep their eyes *exclusively focused* on their children, thinking about what the children need instead of what responsibilities and obligations they have?
9. If we say that by the end of the 1970s *considerably* less than half of the women in the United States still believed that they should put their husbands and children ahead of their own careers, does that mean "a little less than half" or "a lot less than half"?
10. Do you think American families are more *stable* or less stable than families in your country, or is divorce common in your country also?

B. Read the following paragraph from the chapter and notice the words in italics. Then use context clues and write the correct word next to its definition.

Juggling career and family responsibilities can be as difficult for men as it is for women, especially if there is truly an equal division of duties. American fathers are often seen dropping the kids off at the babysitter's *or* taking a sick child to the doctor. Some businesses are recognizing the need to *accommodate* families where both parents work. They may open a daycare center in the office building, offer fathers *paternity* leave to stay home with their new babies, or have *flexible* working hours. Unfortunately, these *benefits* are not yet available to all. While young *couples* strive to achieve equality in their careers, their marriages, and their parenting, society at large still lacks many of the *structures* that are needed to support them.

_____ 1. advantages that you get from your job

_____ 2. accept someone's needs and try to do what they want

_____ 3. trying to fit two or more jobs or activities into your life

_____ 4. things arranged in a definite pattern of organization

_____ 5. a period of time away from work that a father of a new baby is allowed

_____ 6. pairs of people who are together

_____ 7. can be changed easily to suit any new situation

Preview Content

A. Discuss these questions with your classmates.

1. Read the quotation by Max Lerner at the beginning of the chapter. What changes do you think Americans have made in the institution of marriage?
2. Look at the photo on page 255. Why do you think the authors chose this family photo to begin the chapter? How do you think this family relates to the basic traditional values presented in this book?
3. Who do you think lives in a typical American household?
4. Compare what you know about American families with typical families in your country. Use a Venn diagram to list how they are the same and how they are different.

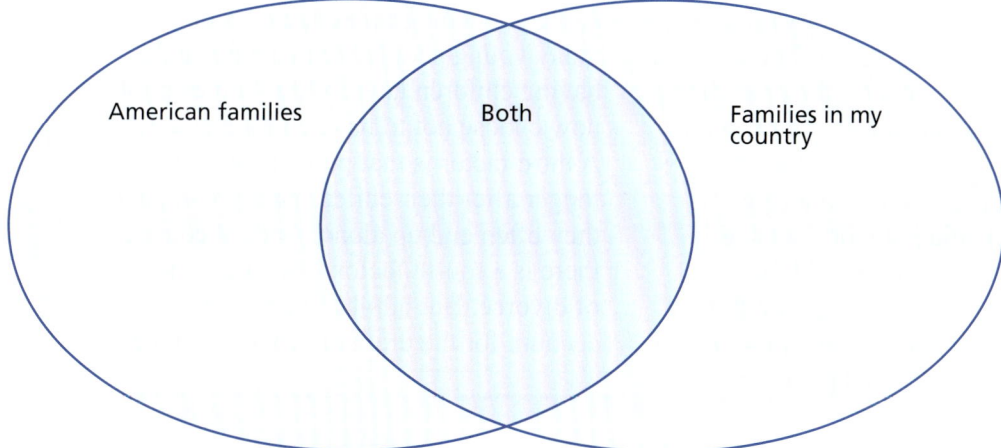

5. Americans often talk about "family values." What do you think they mean?

B. Read the headings in the chapter and look at the illustrations. Write five topics that you predict will be covered in this chapter.

1. _____

2. _____

3. _____

4. _____

5. _____

FAMILY STRUCTURES

1. What is the typical American family like? If Americans are asked to name the members of their families, family structure becomes clear. Married American adults will name their husband or wife and their children, if they have any, as their *immediate family*. If they mention their father, mother, sisters, or brothers, they will define them as separate units, usually living in separate households. Aunts, uncles, cousins, and grandparents are considered *extended family*.

2. Traditionally, the American family has been a nuclear family, consisting of a husband, wife, and their children, living in a house or apartment. Grandparents rarely live in the same home with their married sons and daughters, and uncles and aunts almost never do. In the 1950s, the majority of the American households were the classic traditional American family—a husband, wife, and two children. The father was the "breadwinner" (the one who earned the money to support the family), the mother was a "homemaker" (the one who took care of the children, managed the household, and did not work outside the home), and they had two children under the age of eighteen. If you said the word *family* to Americans a generation or two ago, this is the traditional picture that probably came to their minds.

3. Today, however, the reality is much different. A very small percentage of American households consist of a working father, a stay-at-home mother, and children under eighteen. Less than one-quarter of American households now consist of two parents and their children, and the majority of these mothers in these households hold jobs outside the home. The majority of American households today consist of married couples without children, single parents and their children, or unrelated people living together. Perhaps most surprising, 27 percent of Americans live alone. About one-third of those living alone are 65 years or older. Many of them live in small towns in the upper Midwest part of the country, where more people prefer to stay in their own homes as they age. Others who live alone are younger people who move to places such as Atlanta and northern Virginia (the Washington, D.C. area) in search of job opportunities.

4. What has happened to the traditional American family of the 1950s, and why? Some of the explanation is demographic.[1] In the 1950s, men who had fought in World War II had returned home, married, and were starting their families. There was a substantial increase (or boom) in the birthrate, producing the "baby boomers." A second demographic factor is that today young people are marrying and having children later in life. Some couples now choose not to have children at all. A third factor is that people are living longer after their children are grown, and they often end up alone. And, of course, there is a fourth factor—the high rate of divorce. But numbers alone cannot account for the dramatic changes in the

Less than 25 percent of American families are "traditional"—made up of two parents and their children.

[1] demographic: related to a part of the population that is considered as a group

family. Understanding the values at work in the family will provide some important insights.

The Emphasis on Individual Freedom

5 Americans view the family as a group whose primary purpose is to advance the happiness of individual members. The result is that the needs of each individual take priority in the life of the family. This means that in contrast to many other cultures, the primary responsibility of the American family member is not to advance the family as a group, either socially or economically. Nor is it to bring honor to the family name. This is partly because the United States is not an aristocratic society.

6 Family name and honor are less important than in aristocratic societies, since equality of opportunity is considered a basic traditional American value. Moreover, there is less emphasis on the family as an economic unit because relatively few families maintain self-supporting family farms or businesses for more than one generation. A farmer's son, for example, is very likely to go on to college, leave the family farm, and take an entirely different job in a different location.

7 The American desire for freedom from outside control clearly extends to the family. Americans do not like to have controls placed on them by other family members. They want to make independent decisions and not be told what to do by grandparents or uncles or aunts. For example, both American men and women expect to decide what job is best for them as individuals. Indeed, young Americans are encouraged by their families to make such independent career decisions. What would be best for the family is not usually considered to be as important as what would be best for the individual.

Marriage and Divorce

8 Very few marriages are "arranged" in the United States. Traditionally, young people are expected to find a husband or wife on their own; their parents do not usually help them. In fact, parents are frequently not told of marriage plans until the couple has decided to marry. This means that many parents have little control and, generally, not much influence over whom their children marry. Most Americans believe that young people should fall in love and then decide to marry someone they can live happily with, again evidence of the importance of an individual's happiness. Of course, in reality this does not always happen, but it remains the traditional ideal and it shapes the views of courtship[2] and marriage among young Americans.

9 Over the years, the value placed on marriage itself is determined largely by how happy the husband and wife make each other. Happiness is based primarily on companionship. The majority of American women value companionship as the most important part of marriage. Other values, such as having economic support and the opportunity to have children, although important, are seen by many as less important. If the couple is not happy, the individuals may choose to get a divorce. A divorce is relatively easy to obtain in most parts of the United States. Most states have "no-fault" divorce. To obtain a no-fault divorce, a couple states that they can no longer live happily together, that they have irreconcilable differences,[3] and that it is neither partner's fault.

---

[2] *courtship: the period of time during which a man and a woman have a romantic relationship before getting married*

[3] *irreconcilable differences: strong disagreements between two people who are married, given as a legal reason for getting a divorce*

10 The divorce rate rose rapidly in the United States from the 1960s through the 1980s and then leveled off. Overall, approximately one out of every two marriages now ends in divorce, but divorce rates vary according to the age of the couple and other factors. The younger people marry, the more likely that they will divorce. The new upper class described by Charles Murray in *Coming Apart: The State of White America* has a much lower divorce rate than the rest of the population (see Chapter 5). They are more likely to get married (usually after they have finished college), stay married, and raise their children in stable homes. These are the very well educated and often super rich, and include many of the nation's leaders. On the other hand, among the poor, there are more children born to single mothers. There are fewer marriages and there is more divorce. Often, children are involved.

11 The majority of adult middle-class Americans believe that unhappy couples should not stay married just because they have children at home, a significant change in attitude since the 1950s. Many people do not believe in sacrificing individual happiness for the sake of the children. They say that children actually may be better off living with one parent than with two who are constantly arguing. Divorce is now so common that it is no longer socially unacceptable, and children are not embarrassed to say that their parents are divorced. However, psychologists and sociologists are still studying the long-term consequences of divorce.

12 Judith Wallerstein has studied the effect of divorce on children as they grow up. In her book *The Unexpected Legacy of Divorce: A 25 Year Landmark Study,* she notes that by the year 2000, almost half of the American adults under the age of forty were children of divorced parents. For twenty-five years she followed a group of children whose parents were divorced and compared their experiences with others whose parents stayed together "for the sake of the children." She found that the key factor was whether or not the parents could set aside their differences enough to focus on the needs of their children, regardless of whether the parents divorced or stayed together. However, even in the best cases, divorce had a lasting effect on children as they grew into adulthood and formed their own relationships. In fact, over half of them said they did not want to have children of their own because they were afraid of causing their children the pain that they had experienced growing up.

The Role of the Child

13 The American emphasis on the individual, rather than the group, affects children in a contradictory way. On the one hand, it may cause them to get more attention and even have more power than they should. On the other hand, because most children have mothers who are working outside the home, they may not get enough attention from either parent. Worse yet, parents who feel guilty for not having enough time with their children may give them more material things to compensate for the lack of attention. Working parents constantly struggle to find enough time to spend with their children.

14 Some American families tend to place more emphasis on the needs and desires of the child than on the child's social and family responsibilities. In the years after World War II, much stress was placed on the psychological needs of children, and the number of experts in this field increased enormously. Child psychologists, counselors,[4] and social workers were employed to help children

---

[4] counselors: people whose job is to help and support people with personal problems

Ready to go trick-or-treating on Halloween

with problems at school or in the family. Many books on how to raise children became best-sellers. Sometimes these books offered conflicting advice, but almost all of them shared the American emphasis on the development of the individual as their primary goal.

15 Some Americans believe that the emphasis on the psychological needs of the individual child was carried too far by parents and experts alike. Dr. Benjamin Spock, one of the most famous of the child-rearing experts, eventually came to this conclusion. He said, "What is making the parent's job most difficult is today's child-centered viewpoint." Many conscientious[5] parents, said Spock, tend to "keep their eyes exclusively focused on their child, thinking about what he [or she] needs from them and from the community, instead of thinking about what the world, the neighborhood, the family will be needing from the child and then making sure that he [or she] will grow up to meet such obligations."

16 Today's parents seem more concerned about teaching their children responsibility. Although Americans may not agree on how best to nurture[6] and discipline their children, most still hold the basic belief that the major purpose of the family is the development and welfare of each of its members as individuals.

Equality in the Family

17 Along with the American emphasis on individual freedom, the belief in equality has had a strong effect on the family. Alexis de Tocqueville saw the connection clearly in the 1830s. He said that in aristocratic societies inequality extends into the family, particularly to the father's relationship to his children. The father is accepted as ruler and master. The children's relations with him are very formal, and love for him is always combined with fear. In the United States, however, the democratic idea of equality destroys much of the father's status as ruler of the family and lessens the emotional distance between father and children. There is less formal respect for, and fear of, the father. But there is more affection expressed toward him. "The master and constituted [legal] ruler have vanished,"[7] said Tocqueville; "the father remains."

18 What Tocqueville said of American fathers and children almost two centuries ago applies to relations between parents and children in the United States today.

---

[5] *conscientious: showing a lot of care and attention*

[6] *nurture: to feed and take care of a child or a plant while it is growing*

[7] *vanished: disappeared suddenly, especially in a way that cannot easily be explained; stopped existing suddenly*

There is much more social equality between parents and children than in most aristocratic societies or societies ruled by centuries of tradition. In fact, some Americans worry that there is too much democracy in the home. They would argue that there has been a significant decline in parental authority and children's respect for their parents. This is particularly true of teenagers. Some parents seem to have little control over the behavior of their teenage children, particularly after they turn sixteen and get their driver's licenses. Another problem parents have with teenagers is monitoring their activity online. It is very difficult for parents to know what sites their kids are visiting and even how much time they are spending online. Having a cell phone gives teenagers a special new kind of freedom, since they can talk to their friends and access the Internet almost everywhere.

19 On the other hand, many Americans give their young people a lot of freedom because they want to teach their children to be independent and self-reliant. Traditionally, American children have been expected to "leave the nest" at about age eighteen, after they graduate from high school. At that time they are expected to go on to college (many go to another city) or to get a job and support themselves. By their mid-twenties, if children are still living with their parents, some people will suspect that something is wrong. Traditionally, children have been given a lot of freedom and equality in the family, so that they will grow up to be independent, self-reliant adults. Today, however, a significant number of young people are living with their parents. Some are attending community colleges and living at home to save expenses. Others are unable to find jobs that support the lifestyle they have grown up with, and they continue to live at home or choose to move back in with their parents for a time. These young people are sometimes called the "boomerang generation," because they have left the nest once but are now back again. During bad economic times, multigenerational living may improve the standard of living for all. As different generations of the family share expenses, everyone may benefit. However, most people still have the expectation that this will not be a permanent living arrangement.

RISING SHARE OF YOUNG ADULTS LIVING IN MULTI-GENERATIONAL HOUSEHOLDS

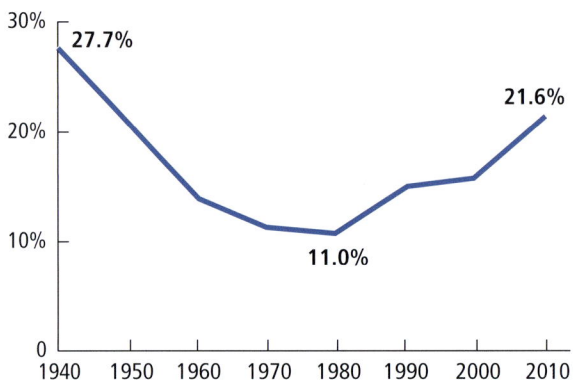

% of adults ages 25–34 living in a multi-generational household

Source: Pew Research Center analysis of U.S. Decennial Census data, 1940–2000 and 2010 American Community Survey (IPUMS).

Four Stages of Marriage Relationships

20 In addition to the relationship between parents and children, the idea of equality affects the family structure in other ways. It has a major impact on the relationships between husbands and wives. Women have witnessed steady progress toward equal status for themselves in the family and in society at large. According to Letha and John Scanzoni, two American sociologists, the institution of marriage in the United States has experienced four stages of development.* In each new stage, wives have increased the degree of equality with their husbands and have gained more power within the family.

---

*Scanzoni, Letha, and John Scanzoni, Men, Women, and Change. New York: McGraw-Hill, Inc., 1981.

21 **Stage I: Wife as Servant to Husband** During the nineteenth century, American wives were expected to be completely obedient[8] to their husbands. As late as 1850, wife-beating was legal in almost all the states of the United States. Although both husbands and wives had family duties, the wife had no power in family matters other than that which her husband allowed her. Her possessions and any of her earnings belonged to her husband. During the nineteenth century, women were not allowed to vote, a restriction that in part reflected women's status as servant to the family.

22 **Stage II: Husband-Head, Wife-Helper** During the late nineteenth and early twentieth centuries opportunities for women to work outside the household increased. More wives were now able to support themselves, if necessary, and therefore were less likely to accept the traditional idea that wives were servants who must obey their husbands. Even though the great majority of wives chose not to work outside the home, the fact that they might do so increased their power in the marriage. The husband could no longer make family decisions alone and demand that the wife follow them. The wife was freer to disagree with her husband and to insist that her views be taken into account in family decisions.

23 Even though the wife's power increased, the husband remained the head of the family. The wife became his full-time helper by taking care of his house and raising his children. She might argue with him and sometimes change his mind, but his decision on family matters was usually final.

24 This increase in equality of women in marriages reflected increased status for women in the society at large and led to women gaining the right to vote in the early twentieth century. Today, the husband-head, wife-helper marriage is still found in the United States. Economic conditions in the twentieth century, however, carried most marriages into different stages.

25 **Stage III: Husband-Senior Partner, Wife-Junior Partner** During the twentieth century, more and more wives took jobs outside the home. In 1940, for example, only 14 percent of married women in the United States held jobs outside the home. By the 2000s, more than 60 percent were employed. When married women take this step, according to the Scanzonis, their power relative to that of their husbands increases still further. The wife's income becomes important in maintaining the family's standard of living. Her power to affect the outcome of family decisions is greater than when her duties were entirely in the home.

26 Although she has become a partner, however, in this stage the wife is still not an equal partner with her husband, since in these marriages the husband's job or career still provides more of the family income. He sees himself as the senior partner, and she is the junior partner of the family enterprise. Even though she has a job, it has a lower priority than her husband's. If, for example, the husband is asked to move to advance his career, she will give up her job and seek another in a new location.

27 In the United States today, there are still a number of marriages that are the senior-partner/junior-partner type. However, the majority of women have jobs outside the home and some of them earn more money than their husbands do. More and more marriages are what the Scanzonis call Stage IV marriages.

---

[8] *obedient: always doing what you are told to do by your parents or by someone in authority*

28 **Stage IV: Husband-Wife Equal Partners** Beginning in the late 1960s, a growing number of women expressed a strong dissatisfaction with any marriage arrangement where the husband and his career were the primary considerations in the marriage. By the end of the 1970s, for example, considerably less than half of the women in the United States still believed that they should put their husbands and children ahead of their own careers. In the 2000s, most American women believe that they should be equal partners in their marriages and that their husbands should have equal responsibility for childcare and household chores.

29 In an equal-partnership marriage, the wife pursues a full-time job or career that has equal or greater importance to her husband's. The long-standing division of labor between husband and wife comes to an end. The husband is no longer the main provider of family income, and the wife no longer has the main responsibilities for household duties and raising children. Husband and wife share all these duties equally. Power over family decisions is also shared equally.

30 The reality of life in the United States is that although most American women now have an equal say in the decisions affecting the family, they sometimes earn less than men for the same work, an average of 77 cents for every dollar. Also, although women make up 49 percent of the workforce, most women still spend more time taking care of the children, cooking, and cleaning than their husbands do. Many women are resentful[9] because they feel like they have two full-time jobs—the one at work and the one at home. In the 1980s, women were told they could "have it all"—fast-track career, husband, children, and a clean house. Now, some women are finding that lifestyle exhausting[10] and unrewarding. Some young women are now choosing to stay at home until their children start school, but many others who would like to stay home cannot afford to do so.

In dual-income households with children, average number of hours spent each week on . . .

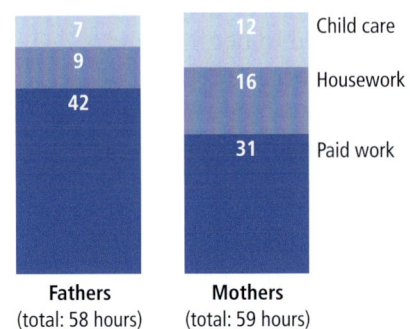

Fathers (total: 58 hours)   **Mothers** (total: 59 hours)

Source: Pew Research Center, 2013.

31 On the other hand, many women are still striving[11] for true equality in the workplace. Sheryl Sandberg, author of *Lean In: Women, Work, and the Will to Lead,* believes that women should actively seek more leadership roles. She notes that for the last 30 years more American women have graduated from college than men, but men still dominate politics and the corporate world. Today only 4.2 percent of the Fortune 500 companies have female Chief Operating Officers. Sandberg herself is the COO of Facebook, and she is offering advice to women to help them reach their potential. She says, "I believe women can lead more in the workplace. I believe men can contribute more in the home. And I believe that this will create a better world, one where half our institutions are run by women and half our homes are run by men."

32 Juggling two careers and family responsibilities can be as difficult for men as it is for women, especially if there is

---

[9] *resentful: feeling angry and upset about something that you think is unfair*

[10] *exhausting: making someone very tired*

[11] *striving: making a great effort to achieve something*

In an equal-partnership marriage, husbands share household duties such as cooking.

truly an equal division of duties. American fathers are often seen dropping the kids off at the babysitter's or taking a sick child to the doctor. Some businesses are recognizing the need to accommodate families where both parents work. They may open a daycare center in the office building, offer fathers paternity leave to stay home with their new babies, or have flexible working hours. Unfortunately, these benefits are not yet available to all. While young couples strive to achieve equality in their careers, their marriages, and their parenting, society at large still lacks many of the structures that are needed to support them.

The Role of the Family in Society

33 The American ideal of equality has affected not only marriage, but all forms of relationships between men and women. Americans gain a number of benefits by placing so much importance on achieving individual freedom and equality within the context of the family. The needs and desires of each member are given a great deal of attention and importance. However, a price is paid for these benefits. American families may be less stable and lasting than those of some other cultures. The high rate of divorce in American families is perhaps the most important indicator of this instability.

34 The American attitude toward the family contains many contradictions. On the one hand, Americans will tolerate a good deal of instability in their families, including divorce, in order to protect such values as freedom and equality. On the other hand, they are strongly attached to the idea of the family as the best of all lifestyles. In fact, the great majority of persons who get divorced find a new partner and remarry. Studies show consistently that the vast majority of Americans believe that family life is an important value.

35 What is family life? We have seen that fewer than one in four households consists of a traditional family—a father, mother, and their children. Many of these are actually *stepfamilies* or *blended families*. Since most divorced people remarry, many children are living with a stepmother or stepfather. In a blended family, the parents may each have children from a previous marriage, and then have one or more children together—producing "yours," "mine," and "ours." Such families often result in very complicated and often stressful relationships. A child may have four sets of grandparents instead of two, for example. Blending families is not easy, and, sadly, many second marriages fail.

36 In addition to traditional families and blended families, there are a number of single parents, both mothers and fathers (more mothers), raising their children alone. Many of the single mothers are divorced, but some have never married.

Three generations of a traditional family

Indeed, by 2012 almost one half of all new babies were born to single mothers, and this trend continues. Sometimes single parents and their children live with the children's grandparents for economic and emotional support. There are all sorts of living arrangements. In recent years, a number of gay and lesbian couples have created family units, sometimes adopting children and sometimes arranging to have their own biological children. Some states now recognize same-sex marriages, and others may recognize them as *civil unions*. The majority of Americans are now in favor of same-sex marriages and legal recognition is growing. There is no doubt that the definition of *family* has become much broader in the 2000s. The majority of Americans would now define a family as "people who live together and love and support each other."

Challenges to the American Family

37 Along with the problems of divorce, single parenting, and balancing family and career, there are other challenges that many Americans face. Because the general population is getting older and living longer, many middle-aged Americans are finding themselves in the *sandwich generation*. That is, they are "sandwiched" between taking care of their children, and taking care of their aging parents. The Pew Research Center reports that almost half of middle-aged Americans in their 40s and 50s have a parent age 65 or older, and they are either raising a young child or are giving significant support to a grown child (age 18 or over). For many, having to take care of adult children is a result of the last recession, which hit young people harder than other groups in the population. Members of the sandwich generation are pulled in many directions as they try to provide care, financial support, and emotional support to both their aging parents and their children.

38 Raising children in the digital age offers more challenges to sandwich generation parents. The use of digital devices that connect people to the Internet is having a profound effect on the family. Sociologists and psychologists tell us that the family is the best place for children to learn social skills, moral values, and a sense of responsibility. But in order to teach children, parents have to have face-to-face time with their kids. Increasingly, both parents and their children may be on separate digital devices visiting different Internet sites or sending email or text messages. It is not uncommon to see parents and their teenagers sitting at a restaurant using their smartphones and not talking to each other. In a *New York Times* article entitled "The Flight from Conversation" psychologist Sherry Turkle says that Americans have sacrificed conversation for connection:

> *We've become accustomed to a new way of being "alone together." Technology-enabled, we are able to be with one another, and also elsewhere, connected to wherever we want to be. We want to customize our lives. We want to move in and out of where we*

are because the thing we value most is control over where we focus our attention.

39 In reality, people cannot truly customize their lives. Successful adults must be able to respond to a variety of people in a variety of unpredictable situations that require good social skills. And developing good communication and social skills should start in the family. Unfortunately, children may find that their parents are unavailable to guide them, and parents may not understand what help kids need. For example, parents may not realize that their teenagers are not learning some important social skills while they are spending time in virtual reality. Increasingly, teenagers are using their smartphones for texting instead of talking. Consequently, kids are not learning the social skills that conversation teaches: understanding non-verbal cues, figuring out emotions, having the patience needed for a conversation to develop, and how to make "small talk." Surprisingly, New York University recently offered incoming students a class in how to make small talk. The students knew each other on Facebook but had no idea how to talk to start a conversation and get to know each other in person.

40 Today, the state of the American family is frequently discussed, not only by the experts, but also by the press, elected officials, and the general public. Some Americans believe that the institution of the family and family values are both in trouble. But if you ask Americans how their own families are, most will tell you they are generally happy with their family life. In *Values and Public Policy*, Daniel Yankelovich reports on surveys done on family values. There are eleven points that a majority of Americans agree are family values. Yankelovich classifies six of them as "clearly traditional":

- Respecting one's parents
- Being responsible for one's actions
- Having faith in God
- Respecting authority
- Remaining married to the same person for life
- Leaving the world in better shape

The other five are "a blend of traditional and newer, more expressive values":

- Giving emotional support to other members of the family
- Respecting people for themselves
- Developing greater skill in communicating one's feelings
- Respecting one's children
- Living up to one's potential as an individual

41 The ideal of the American family is group cooperation to help achieve the fulfillment of each individual member and shared affection to renew each member's emotional strength. Families can be viewed as similar to churches in this regard. Both are seen by Americans as places where the human spirit can find refuge from the highly competitive world outside and gain renewed resources to continue the effort. Although in a number of cases families do not succeed in the task of providing mutual support and renewing the spirit, for many Americans this remains the ideal of family life.

AFTER YOU READ

Understand Main Ideas

Working with a partner, discuss how the six traditional basic American values affect the American family. Fill in the chart with the value, the advantages and disadvantages to the individual, and the advantages and disadvantages to the family.

Value: _____

Advantage to the Individual	Disadvantage to the Individual
Advantage to the Family	Disadvantage to the Family

Value: _____

Advantage to the Individual	Disadvantage to the Individual
Advantage to the Family	Disadvantage to the Family

Understand Details

Write **T** if the statement is true and **F** if it is false according to information in the chapter.

_____ 1. One American household in four now consists of someone living alone.

_____ 2. "Baby boomers" are young people who are in their twenties.

_____ 3. Americans usually consider what is best for the whole family first and what is best for them as individuals second.

_____ 4. Americans believe that the family exists primarily to serve the needs of its individual family members.

_____ 5. Most Americans believe that marriages should make both individuals happy and that if they cannot live together happily, it is better for them to get a divorce.

_____ 6. American parents generally think more about the individual needs of their children than they do about what responsibilities the child will have to society as a whole.

_____ 7. Although Americans believe in democracy for society, they generally exercise strict control over their children, particularly teenagers.

_____ 8. The amount of equality between husbands and wives has remained pretty much the same since Tocqueville visited the United States in the 1830s.

_____ 9. If an American wife works outside the home, she is likely to have more power in the family than a married woman who does not work.

_____ 10. In the husband-senior partner, wife-junior partner type of marriage, the husband and wife both work, have equal power and influence in making family decisions, and divide the family duties equally.

_____ 11. In most American families, the father does just as much housework and child care as the mother.

_____ 12. Having faith in God and respecting authority are two of the traditional American family values.

_____ 13. Although one out of every two marriages ends in divorce, Americans still believe strongly in the importance of marriage and the family.

Talk About It

Work in small groups and choose one or more of these questions to discuss.

1. What do you think is the ideal number of children to have? Why? What responsibilities should children have in the family?
2. What type of parenting do you think is most effective? How would you discipline and parent your children? Would you give your teenagers the same amount of freedom as you had as a teenager? Why or why not?
3. Which type of marriage is most common in your country? Which of the four types do you think is ideal? Why?
4. How is divorce viewed in your country? If two people are unhappy, should they get a divorce? What if they have children? Under what circumstances would you get divorced?
5. Should husbands be able to choose to stay at home while their wives go to work? In the United States, these men are sometimes called "househusbands." Are there househusbands in your country?
6. In your country, who takes care of the children if both parents are working? Would you leave your child in a daycare center?

SKILL BUILDING

Develop Your Critical Thinking Skills

Analyzing Polls and Expressing Your Opinion

In most American families, both parents are employed. While they are at work, the children have to be cared for by another family member, a paid babysitter, or workers at a daycare center. Many American parents would say that it is the quality of time they spend with their children and not the quantity. About half of all working mothers and fathers say that it is difficult to balance the responsibilities of their job and their family.

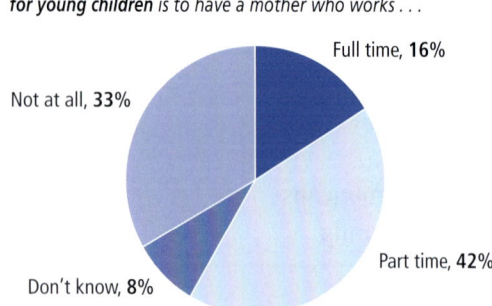

Percentage of **general public** who say the ideal situation **for young children** is to have a mother who works...
- Full time, **16%**
- Part time, **42%**
- Not at all, **33%**
- Don't know, **8%**

Percentage with children who say they spend... time with their children

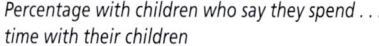
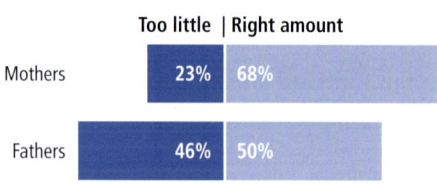

	Too little	Right amount
Mothers	23%	68%
Fathers	46%	50%

Source: Pew Research Center, 2013.

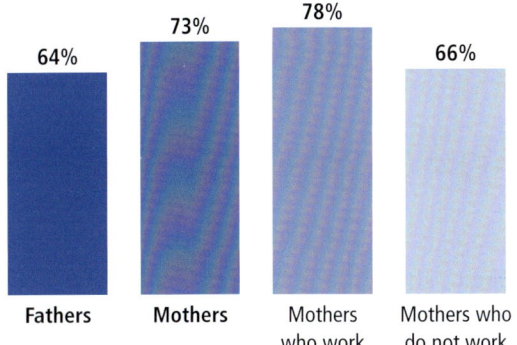

Source: Pew Research Center, 2013.

Analyze these polls and answer the questions that follow.

1. How do Americans feel about mothers who work? Do most people think the ideal would be for mothers to stay home with their children and not work at all? What percentages can you cite to support your conclusion?
2. Are there any differences in how American men and women feel about the time they have to spend with their children? Cite percentages.
3. Do mothers who work feel that they are not doing a good job parenting? Cite percentages. Why do you think they feel that way?
4. What generalizations can you make about how men and women view their jobs? Cite percentages.
5. Do you personally think it's important for one parent to stay home with the children? Why or why not? If these polls reflected the situation in your country, what would they reveal?

Improve Your Reading Skills: Highlighting and Summarizing

In the American education system, there is a great deal of emphasis on recognizing and remembering main ideas. Highlighting main ideas as you read helps you remember them. In previous chapters, we discussed identifying topic sentences and how they usually contain the main idea of a paragraph. Remember that most topic sentences are the first sentence of the paragraph. Therefore, if you just focus on the first sentence of the paragraph in an academic reading, you should have an understanding of many of the main ideas of the reading.

Work with a partner, and go back through the reading and highlight the main ideas. How many sentences did you highlight that were the first sentence of the paragraph? Compare your highlighting with another pair of students. Then work with your group to make an oral summary of the reading in your own words.

Build Your Vocabulary

Vocabulary Check

Use the words in the box to complete the sentences.

blended	courtship	juggling	refuge
compensate	demographic	nurture	stable
conscientious	exhausting	priority	vanish

1. Many _____ American mothers would like to stay at home with their young children, but they have to work to make ends meet.

2. _____ a career and family responsibilities is very stressful.

3. Many young mothers who work have an _____ lifestyle—they work all day at their jobs and then take care of their families and homes.

4. Most Americans would probably agree that fathers, as well as mothers, should be able to _____ their children.

5. Parents who do not have enough time for their children may feel guilty and then try to _____ by giving their children material gifts.

6. Sometimes a demanding career can be a _____ even though a parent would like to have more time to spend with the children.

7. _____ families may be a source of stress, as parents try to cope with raising each other's children, plus their own.

8. In the United States, _____ is the time that young people in love get to know each other and decide if they want to get married.

9. Although marriages are not very _____ in the United States, most Americans still believe that it is an important institution in society.

10. Families have traditionally provided an important _____ from the competitive stresses of American society.

11. _____ studies show that young Americans are now waiting longer to get married and have children.

12. In spite of all its problems, the institutions of marriage and the family will certainly never _____.

More AWL Words

Test your knowledge of these AWL words by matching the words and their definitions. Write the correct word in the blank next to its definition.

accommodate	emphasis	flexible	license	potential	restriction
consist	expert	generation	obtain	previous	role
contradictory	factor	institution	policy	primary	trend
dramatic	final	labor			

_____ 1. most important

_____ 2. an official document giving permission

_____ 3. exciting and impressive

_____ 4. in opposition or disagreement with something else

_____ 5. able to change or be changed easily

_____ 6. the possibility that something will develop in a certain way

_____ 7. to accept someone's needs and try to do what they want

_____ 8. to get something you want

_____ 9. all people of about the same age

_____ 10. principle, procedure, or way of doing something

_____ 11. a rule that limits or controls

_____ 12. someone who has special skill or knowledge

_____ 13. work using physical effort

_____ 14. the last in a series

_____ 15. the part someone plays

_____ 16. an established system in society

_____ 17. a general tendency

_____ 18. one of several things that influence a situation

_____ 19. to be made of

_____ 20. happening or existing before

_____ 21. special attention or importance

EXPAND YOUR KNOWLEDGE

Ask Americans

Interview several Americans of different ages and ask them about their families. Ask each one the following questions and record their answers. (You may want to interview friends or classmates about their families.)

1. Who are the members of your family? Name them and indicate their relationship to you (mother, sister, etc.).
2. Who lives in your household? Where do your other relatives live?
3. How often do you see your parents? Your grandparents? Your sisters and brothers? Your aunts, uncles, and cousins? Do you write, email, text, or telephone any of them regularly?
4. What occasions bring your relatives together (birthdays, holidays, weddings, births, deaths, trips)? Have you ever been to a family reunion?
5. Do you feel you have a close family? Why or why not?
6. Who would you ask for advice if you had a serious personal problem?
7. Who would take care of you if you became ill?
8. What obligations and responsibilities do you feel you have toward your family?
9. What duties and responsibilities do you believe children have toward their family?
10. On a scale of 1 to 10, with 10 as *most important,* how important are the opinions of the members of your immediate family concerning the following decisions?

    _____ Whom you marry

    _____ Where you live

    _____ Where you go to school

    _____ How you spend your money

    _____ What job you take

Ask Yourself / Ask Americans

Do you agree or disagree with each of the following statements? Put a check under the number that indicates how you feel.

+2 = Strongly agree
+1 = Agree
 0 = No opinion
−1 = Disagree
−2 = Strongly disagree

	+2	+1	0	−1	−2
1. Arranged marriages are better than marriages where the couple have met and dated on their own.	___	___	___	___	___
2. It is very important for my family to approve of the person I marry.	___	___	___	___	___
3. If my parents disapproved of my choice, I would still marry that person if we were very much in love.	___	___	___	___	___
4. A woman's place is in the home.	___	___	___	___	___
5. Married women with small children should not work.	___	___	___	___	___
6. Men should be able to stay home and take care of the children while their wives work.	___	___	___	___	___
7. Husbands and wives should share equally the work of taking care of the house and the children.	___	___	___	___	___
8. Unhappy couples should stay married for the sake of the children.	___	___	___	___	___
9. Married couples who choose not to have children are selfish.	___	___	___	___	___
10. Equality between a husband and wife causes divorce.	___	___	___	___	___

Read these statements to several Americans (or your friends) and ask them if they agree or disagree. Compare your answers with theirs.

People Watching

It has been said that in most societies children are often spectators watching adults interact. They are learning what it means to be an adult in their society. In American society, however, the adults are usually the spectators who are watching the children.

Observe American adults interacting with children in the following places:

- In restaurants
- On a playground or at a sports event
- At the movies
- On the street
- At home (If you are unable to visit an American home, watch American TV shows that have children as characters.)

Record your observations in your journal. You may wish to write up these observations as a report and present it to the class. What differences did you observe about how adults interact with children in other countries? (You may choose to observe adults and children in your own community in your country.)

Families often gather for celebrations.

Understand the Role of the Elderly in America

The role of the elderly is one that most foreigners cannot understand about American life. Some have heard that all the elderly are in nursing homes, but this is not true. Actually, only one in four Americans spends any time in a nursing home, and the average stay is two years. It is generally the sick and the disabled who require nursing home care at the end of their lives. Americans generally try to live on their own as long as possible, choosing to be independent and self-reliant. A few Americans (about 12 percent) purchase long-term care insurance that may provide nursing help in their own home. The vast majority of the care of the elderly is done by family members. Members of the "sandwich generation" strive to provide care and support to aging parents and their own children under the age of 18. However, as the baby boomers age, adult children who are taking care of their parents are themselves getting older and older.

A. To try to understand how Americans feel about being old and what they plan to do with their lives when they retire, ask several Americans who are not yet sixty-five the following questions:

1. What do you hope to do when you retire?
2. Where do you plan to live?
3. Would you move in with your children? Under what conditions?
4. What do you think life will be like when you are 65 or older?
5. Are you afraid of growing old? Are you looking forward to growing old?

B. Many retirement communities now have different kinds of living arrangements, from independent living in homes and apartments, to assisted living in buildings with private rooms and meals served in a common dining room, to nursing homes that offer full-time care by doctors and nurses. If you are able to, visit a retirement community for older Americans, or a nursing home. Answer the following questions.

1. Why do you think that many older people choose to live apart from their grown children?
2. Think about the description of the family presented in this chapter. What evidence do you see of the American values of equality in the family and the emphasis on individual freedom?

Proverbs and Sayings

Ask Americans to explain these proverbs and sayings to you. Then ask them for other examples of sayings about men, women, children, or the family. What sayings like these do you have in your language?

1. The hand that rocks the cradle rules the world.
2. As the twig is bent, so grows the tree.
3. That child is a chip off the old block.
4. A man may work from sun to sun, but a woman's work is never done.
5. Behind every successful man, there is a woman.
6. Blood is thicker than water.

Think, Pair, Share

Working mothers often feel that they have two full-time jobs—one outside the home, for which they get paid, and the other inside the home, for which they do not get paid. Most working American women still have the major responsibility for managing the household—cooking, cleaning, shopping, and seeing that the children are cared for—although American husbands are increasingly sharing more of these responsibilities. (See the illustration on page 264.) What do you think husbands with working wives should do around the house?

Write your answer, and then discuss it with your partner. Then share your answer with another pair of students.

Use the Internet

Many people have difficulty meeting others because of their busy lifestyles. Computer dating is becoming increasingly popular and more acceptable in the United States. People can find dates or even a potential husband or wife on the Internet. Men and women answer questions about themselves—their interests, hobbies, likes and dislikes—and they also indicate the qualities they are looking for in a date. Couples are then matched by the computer, and each person receives a list of names of people to contact.

Work with a partner and look at two popular websites, www.match.com and www.eharmony.com. Spend a few minutes learning about each website and how people meet others there. You may want to take the personality quiz on eharmony.

Read some of the profiles that people have written to introduce themselves. Imagine putting an ad on one of the websites. What would be your "catchphrase," and how would you introduce yourself? Write your ad without your name on it. Collect all the ads from the class and put them in a box. Have each person pick an ad, read it aloud, and guess who wrote it.

WRITE ABOUT IT

A. Choose one of the following topics. Then write a short composition about it.

1. Imagine that a foreign exchange student will be living with you for a year. Write a letter to him or her explaining how your family *is* or *is not* a typical family in your country.

2. Write about the person in your immediate or extended family whom you admire the most. Tell what makes the person special and what you admire.

B. Choose one of these Internet topics to write about.

1. Many Americans have pets that they consider to be part of the family. Some studies have shown that owning a pet lowers a person's blood pressure and helps to reduce stress. There are also dogs that are specially trained to comfort people or to help those who are sight or hearing impaired. Learn more about Americans and their pets. Find information on the Internet, and write a report about what you find. Or write about a pet you have or have had, or what would be your ideal pet.

2. What kind of companies are good places for working mothers? Search the Internet and write a report about how some American businesses accommodate working mothers.

Americans often have pets that are part of the family.

EXPLORE ON YOUR OWN

Books to Read

Andrew Cherlin, *The Marriage-Go-Round: The State of Marriage and the Family in America Today*—A sociologist discusses why Americans marry more and divorce more frequently than in other countries.

Dave Issay, *All There Is: Love Stories from StoryCorps*—Stories of love and marriage come from the national oral history project, StoryCorps, in which Americans across the country talk about their lives.

Sheryl Sandberg, *Lean In: Women, Work, and the Will to Lead*—A powerful business executive believes that women should actively seek more leadership roles.

Judith Wallerstein, *The Unexpected Legacy of Divorce: A 25 Year Landmark Study*—Wallerstein reports on a long-term study of the effect of divorce on children as they grow up.

Laura Ingalls Wilder, *Little House on the Prairie*—The author tells of growing up on the frontier in Kansas with her family.

Movies to See

Cheaper by the Dozen—While a wife is away publicizing her book, her husband must juggle his new job and take care of their twelve children.

Father of the Bride—In this comedy, a remake of the Spencer Tracy classic, a family plans the wedding of their daughter.

My Big Fat Greek Wedding—A young Greek-American woman falls in love with a non-Greek and struggles to get her family to accept him while she comes to terms with her heritage and cultural identity.

My Family, Mi Familia—This film traces the struggles, joys, and successes of an immigrant family over three generations.

Parental Guidance—A traditional grandfather and his eager-to-please wife agree to babysit their three grandchildren.

When Harry Met Sally—This romantic comedy tells about two friends who have known each other for years but are afraid that love would ruin their friendship.

CHAPTER 12

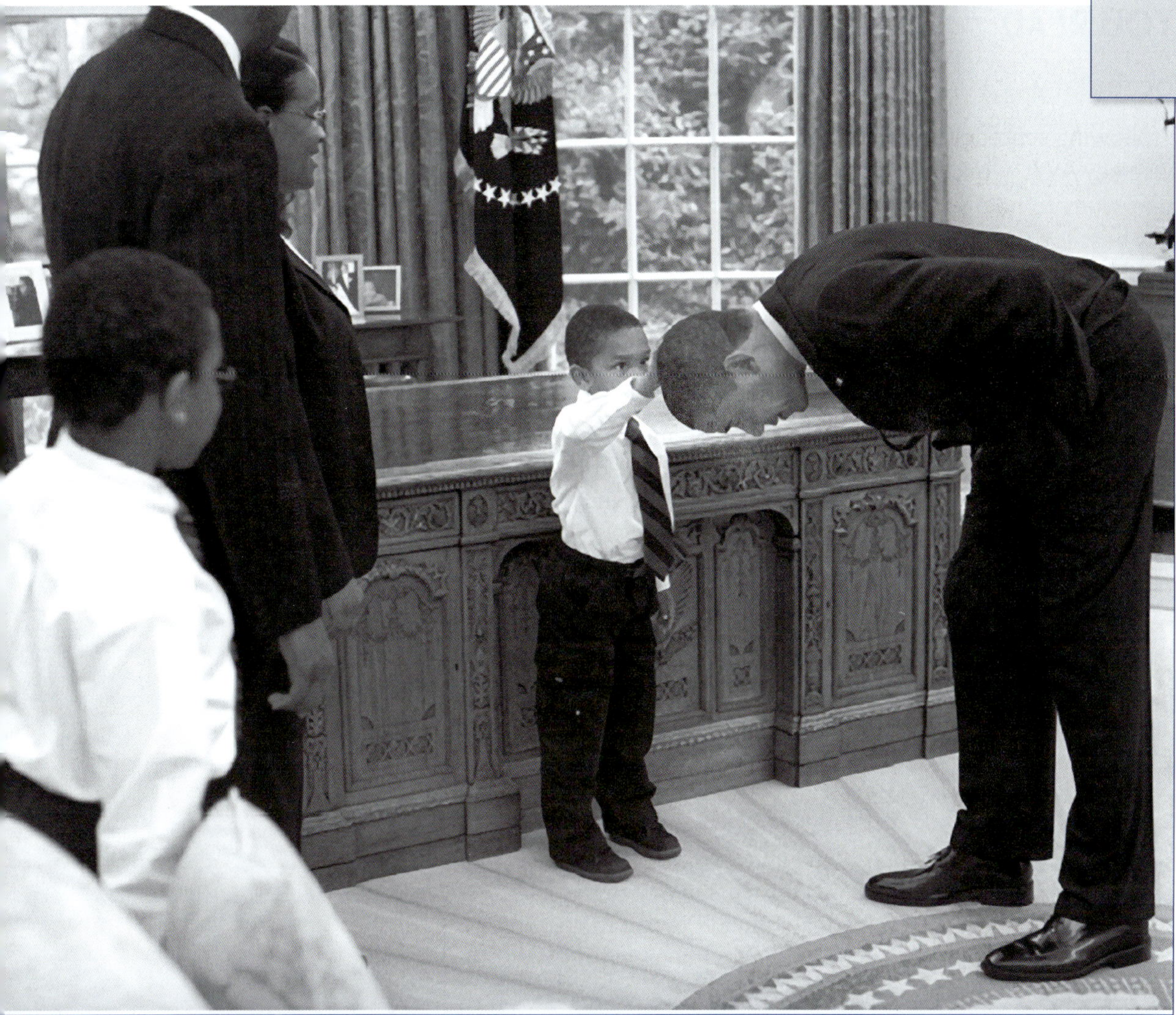

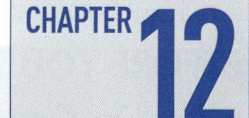

AMERICAN VALUES AT THE CROSSROADS

The sole certainty is that tomorrow will surprise us all.

Alvin Toffler (1928–)

Is there a change in the balance between the values representing benefits or rights and the values representing the prices to be paid or responsibilities for these rights?

BEFORE YOU READ

Preview Vocabulary

A. Read the following sentences from the chapter and notice the words in italics. These key AWL words will help you understand the chapter reading. Use context clues to help you figure out the meanings. Then choose which definition is best for the italicized word.

_____ 1. Throughout our history we have disagreed about the meaning of these rights and how far they should be extended. But at the same time we have all *internalized* these rights as our own.
   a. made a belief or attitude become part of your character
   b. rejected a belief or attitude as not important

_____ 2. Since the 1960s and the Great Society programs, the government has continued to *undertake* new responsibilities.
   a. start or agree to do something
   b. decide not to do something

_____ 3. In Chapter 6, we explored the ways that business has traditionally exemplified the ideal of competition and some of the problems that business has *encountered*.
   a. experienced for the first time
   b. succeeded in overcoming

_____ 4. "Our celebration of *initiative* and enterprise; our insistence on hard work and personal responsibility, are constants in our character."
   a. trying to finish something that you don't want to do
   b. making decisions and taking action without waiting for someone to tell you what to do

_____ 5. Hard America creates wealth; Soft America *reassigns* it.
   a. makes better products
   b. gives something to someone else

_____ 6. "Once they have paid the mortgage, payments on two cars, taxes, health insurance, and day care, these apparently prosperous two-income families have less *discretionary* income today and less money to save for a rainy day than a single-income family of a generation ago."
   a. money that you can spend in any way you want
   b. money that earns you a great profit

_____ 7. White says that those on either side of the values divide live in "two *parallel* universes. Each side seeks to reinforce its thinking by associating with like-minded people."
   a. unrelated
   b. similar

_____ 8. Many potential voters are not *registered* members of either party, and both parties must try to persuade them to vote for their party's candidate.
   a. recorded
   b. opposed

_____ 9. "*Oddly* enough for a nation that conducts, reads, argues over, and bashes polls, we still have difficulty understanding who we really are."
   a. obviously, or naturally
   b. strangely, or surprisingly

_____ 10. Democrats and Republicans seem to make decisions more on the basis of *ideology* and less on the best interests of the nation.
   a. a set of ideas on which a political system is based
   b. the rules for conducting an election

_____ 11. In spite of the current image of the United States and some of the actions the government has taken, there has been a long historical tradition of *isolationism*.
   a. belief that your country should not be involved in the affairs of other countries
   b. belief that your country should act as a "World Policeman"

_____ 12. Many Americans are very *reluctant* to see the United States become involved in international military actions unless they are convinced that there is some national interest to be protected.
   a. fast and enthusiastic
   b. slow and unwilling

B. Read this quotation from the chapter and notice the words in italics. Then use context clues and write the correct word next to its definition.

"Millions of middle-class Americans are living from *paycheck* to paycheck, struggling to pay their bills, having to borrow money and go into debt. Many families are just one *layoff* or one medical *emergency* away from going into *bankruptcy*."

_____ 1. a dangerous situation that you must deal with immediately

_____ 2. inability to pay your debts

_____ 3. check that pays someone's salary

_____ 4. stopping a worker's employment because there is not enough work

Preview Content

A. Read the quotation by Alvin Toffler at the beginning of the chapter. Do you agree with it? Why or why not? What surprising world events have taken place in recent years?

B. Discuss these questions with your classmates.
1. What impact do you think the traditional American values have on Americans today?
2. What are some of the problems Americans face now?
3. What status does the United States have in the world today?
4. What do you think will happen to American values in the twenty-first century?

C. Read the headings in the chapter and look at the illustrations. Write five topics that you predict will be covered in this chapter.

1. _____
2. _____
3. _____
4. _____
5. _____

THE ROLE OF VALUES IN THE NATIONAL IDENTITY

1 John J. Zogby, an American pollster, says that Americans really know very little about themselves. "Oddly enough for a nation that conducts, reads, argues over, and bashes[1] polls, we still have difficulty understanding who we really are." He notes that the same question is asked by every generation—What really makes us "American"? What is it that we all share? The nation has survived the American Revolution, the Civil War, the Great Depression, the civil rights struggle, assassinations, and several attempts to impeach[2] presidents. "The reason for this survival is simple—we all share a common set of values that make us Americans." Zogby agrees with Ben Wattenberg, an expert on American culture who believes that "values matter most." These values give Americans a unique identity, and whichever political candidate or party can best represent these values wins an election. The values are the basic rights first stated in the *Declaration of Independence*:

> *We hold these truths to be self-evident, that all men are created equal, that they are endowed by their Creator with certain unalienable rights, that among these are Life, Liberty and the pursuit of Happiness. That to secure these rights, Governments are instituted among Men, deriving their just powers from the consent of the governed.*

2 The rights were then described in the Constitution and in the first ten amendments to the Constitution, the *Bill of Rights*, written to protect the freedom and the rights of the American people. Zogby believes that "unlike any other nation or people, we are defined by the rights we have, not by geography, by the arts and letters, not by our cuisine[3] or sensibilities,[4] not religion or civilization, not by war.... Throughout our history we have disagreed about the meaning of these rights and how far they should be extended. But at the same time we have all internalized these rights as our own."

3 The six traditional basic values we have discussed in this book (individual freedom, self-reliance, equality of opportunity, competition, material wealth, and hard work) are still a major force in American society. In this chapter, we will review the six traditional basic values and what challenges they now face.

Individual Freedom and Self-Reliance

4 As has been noted earlier in this book, freedom (sometimes referred to as the "rights of the individual") is the most precious and the most popular of the six basic traditional values of the United States. The traditional ideas of freedom held by the founding fathers and written into the Constitution and the *Bill of Rights* were dominant until the 1930s. These freedoms included guarantees of the freedom of speech, freedom of the press, and freedom of religion. There were also freedoms guaranteeing a fair criminal trial—that is, the right to a speedy and public trial, the right to a trial by jury, and the right to a defense attorney. In the 1930s, during the Great Depression, the New Deal greatly increased the size and responsibilities of government. Since the 1960s and the Great Society programs, the government has continued to undertake

---

[1] *bashes: criticizes someone or something a lot*

[2] *impeach: to formally accuse a government official of a serious crime in a special government court*

[3] *cuisine: a particular style of cooking*

[4] *sensibilities: ways that people react to particular subjects or types of behavior*

new responsibilities. This has led to a new category of freedoms or rights that are economic in nature. For example, the Supreme Court ruled in 1963 that if a person on trial (for a crime) could not afford a defense attorney, the government must provide one for him or her.

5   Almost all Americans believe that their country should strive for a prosperity[5] shared by all. However, the idea of economic rights has a broader meaning. It means that government should (in one way or another) provide economic benefits for U.S. citizens. It is on this point that Americans differ. Indeed, this difference has been called the *values divide*. On the one hand, conservative, mostly Republican, Americans believe that the government has gone too far in creating and guaranteeing these economic benefits. They argue that the more the government makes itself responsible for providing economic benefits, the more it makes the American people dependent on the government for their standard of living. This, in turn, takes away the self-reliance of the people—a basic national value that has helped to make the country great.

6   On the other hand, liberal (or progressive), mostly Democratic, Americans believe that the guarantee of economic rights by the government broadens and improves the traditional idea of freedom. The process of expanding economic rights should, they believe, continue in the twenty-first century. The possible economic rights that are being proposed include the right to medical treatment and basic health insurance; the right to a college education; the right to have a job that provides a standard of living above the poverty level; and, when people are unemployed, the right to receive government assistance (especially for women and children). The debate about the proper balance between self-reliance on the one hand and government-provided economic security on the other will surely continue to be an important debate in the coming years.

Equality of Opportunity and Competition

7   As mentioned before, the American ideal of equality of opportunity can be simply stated—all Americans should have an equal opportunity to succeed in life, to gain prosperity, and to pursue happiness. The United States has sometimes failed to honor this value of equality of opportunity, particularly in the case of African Americans who were subjected to slavery and then to segregation and discrimination. But the nation eventually freed the slaves in the 1860s and then addressed segregation and discrimination with the *Civil Rights Acts* of the 1960s. Affirmative action programs were an important effort to deal with discrimination. Employers had to seek African-American workers, and colleges had to recruit African-American students, as well as other minorities. The philosophy of the affirmative action programs was that because of years of discrimination, many blacks did not have the skills they needed to successfully compete with members of the white majority. At first, standards of admission were

Courtroom trial in session

[5] prosperity: when people have money and everything needed for a good life

The U.S. Supreme Court building in Washington, D.C.

adjusted, in some cases, in order to allow black students to enter school.

8   Traditionally, equality of opportunity has not meant equality of results or attainment. If a number of people have the same opportunity to succeed, some may succeed more than others. It is not up to society or the government to make sure that every person ends up with the same amount of wealth or prestige. This traditional interpretation was challenged by affirmative action programs giving racial and ethnic preferences to blacks, Hispanics, and other minorities. Those who support affirmative action argue that it has helped make up for past discrimination against minorities and that it increases the racial and ethnic diversity on college campuses. Supreme Court Justice Sonia Sotomayor, the first Hispanic justice, is an example of someone who was helped by affirmative action. An excellent student from a poor background, she was offered scholarships from many top universities. She has written about the benefits she received from affirmative action in *My Beloved World.* On the other hand, there are those who argue against the policies of affirmative action. Those who oppose what they see as preferential treatment believe that everyone should have the same educational opportunities and that no one should get any special advantages. They defend the traditional idea of equality of opportunity and say that they believe in the natural diversity of the United States, not diversity mandated[6]

[6] *mandated: required by an official command*

by the government. There have also been claims of reverse discrimination, where qualified white students were denied admission to make room for a minority student.

9. The ultimate expression of equality of opportunity is the election of Barack Obama, the first African-American president. The columnist Ezra Klein writes, "The United States of America—a land where slaves were kept 150 years ago and bathrooms were segregated as recently as 50 years ago—elected and reelected its first black president." It is remarkable to see a black president in the White House, a man whose mother was white and whose father was from Kenya, a president who is married to a woman who is herself descended from slaves. But Barack and Michelle Obama are very mindful of what they represent—the evidence that a qualified individual from any minority background can potentially rise to the highest office in the land. In a very moving photograph, the president is leaning over to let a little black boy touch his hair, to see if Obama's hair feels like his. The message of this popular photo is that black children can now say, "Maybe one day I'll grow up to be president, too."

10. The nation often struggles for a balance between the values of equality of opportunity and competition. The value of competition is most clearly represented by the institution of American business. In Chapter 6, we explored the ways that business has traditionally exemplified the ideal of competition, as well as some of the problems that business has encountered. One of the biggest challenges facing the United States today is deciding what the role of government versus the role of the free enterprise system should be. How far should the government go to ensure the right of equality of opportunity for all? And should it be the right of "opportunity" or the right of "attainment"?

11. In his book *Hard America, Soft America: Competition vs. Coddling[7] and the Battle for the Nation's Future*, Michael Barone (a conservative) has written about this need for balance. He thinks that there should be a space in the middle, with a government "that saves people from undeserved social disaster, while preserving the will to achieve." This middle ground is between the conservative "hard" culture and the liberal "soft" culture. Noemie Emery, a conservative columnist, describes Barone's explanation of the division in the United States this way:

    Hard America values risk, innovation, effort, and enterprise. Soft America values security and equality. Hard America is ruled by the market, while Soft America is directed by government planning. Hard America creates wealth; Soft America reassigns it. Hard America causes undeserved suffering by making no distinction between poverty caused by sickness and poverty caused by laziness. Soft America causes its own suffering by making no distinctions between poverty caused by bad luck and poverty caused by bad habits....But the problem is really striking a balance that gets people to strive without making them desperate—that gives them support without sapping[8] their will.

12. President Obama (a liberal) would probably agree that the will to compete is healthy and important. In his second Inaugural Address, Obama said that throughout our more than 200-year history, we have always been suspicious of a strong federal government, and we have understood that not all of society's problems can be solved through government alone. Free enterprise has always played an important role. "Our

---

[7] coddle: to treat someone in a way that is too kind and gentle and that protects them from pain or difficulty

[8] sapping: gradually taking away something, such as strength or energy

celebration of initiative and enterprise; our insistence on hard work and personal responsibility, are constants in our character." Indeed, liberals and conservatives would probably agree that all of the six values explained in this book are important. However, liberals would probably argue that there are some Americans who are so poor and disadvantaged that they cannot be expected to be completely self-reliant or competitive. They need special help from the government and others to bring them up to the starting line of the race for success, so that they can compete on a more equal basis for the benefits of equality of opportunity and the American Dream.

Material Wealth and Hard Work

13 Material wealth has traditionally been seen as the reward for hard work. Although most people still believe in the ideal of the American Dream, many are now having a difficult time attaining or maintaining it. Middle-class families are under great financial stress. Mortimer Zuckerman wrote in *U.S. News & World Report*, "Millions of middle-class Americans are living from paycheck to paycheck, struggling to pay their bills, having to borrow money and go into debt. Many families are just one layoff or one medical emergency away from going into bankruptcy." Many young people believe that they will not have as good a financial future lifestyle as their parents, and one in four under age 30 feel that they are "downwardly mobile" rather than "upwardly mobile."

14 There are other signs that American families are falling behind: The middle class is smaller, making up only 51 percent of the population, down from 61 percent in the 1960s. Since 2000, their incomes have declined by 5 percent, and their net worth has shrunk by 28 percent. One-third of them are having trouble paying their bills. The distance between the middle class and the richest Americans is now enormous. As the recession was getting better, in 2011 the top 5 percent of the population (who earn more than $186,000 a year) saw their incomes rise by 5 percent. According to the Economic Policy Institute, households in the wealthiest 1 percent now have 288 times the amount of wealth as the average middle-class family. The Great Recession that began in 2008 hit middle-class families hardest, but it greatly increased the wealth of the richest 1 percent.

15 Several factors have caused this stress on the middle class. First, there has been a huge decline in the number of well-paying jobs that do not require a college degree. Back in the 1970s, there were still good jobs in the manufacturing sector, with about 25 percent of Americans (mostly men) employed in factories. Another significant percentage were employed in other sectors that required little formal education, like construction, mining, or utilities. These were jobs that men held until retirement, when they received a comfortable pension. Now these well-paying blue collar jobs are gone. Much of American manufacturing went overseas in the 1990s, and, although it is coming back, these new manufacturing jobs generally require education beyond the high school level.

16 The second factor affecting the middle class is the need for higher education, and, in fact, the numbers of students graduating from high school and taking some college courses has gone up. One reason is that the recession hit young people harder than other age groups, with unemployment rates as high as 24 percent. Many young people chose to stay in school because there weren't jobs available. Entry-level jobs usually taken by young people were often filled by older, more experienced workers who had lost their own jobs. A

Even two-income middle-class families may struggle to pay their bills.

significant problem that many Americans face is the incredibly high cost of a college education. The spread of community college programs has helped cut costs greatly. However, the United States really has a need for good vocational programs in fields such as informational technology and advanced manufacturing. Many believe that the United States should develop programs like some European countries have that would prepare students to take jobs that now go unfilled, even during the recession. This would require education and industry leaders to work together to develop the training programs and help put students on the pathway to these well-paying jobs.

17 In most middle-class families, both the husband and wife are working. Their combined family income is much larger than that of the single-income family a generation ago, but they are still struggling. Zuckerman says, "Once they have paid the mortgage, payments on two cars, taxes, health insurance, and day care, these apparently prosperous two-income families have less discretionary income today and less money to save for a rainy day than a single-income family of a generation ago....Many feel they are falling further and further behind, no matter how hard they work." Health care and health insurance have become more and more expensive, taking a larger percentage of a worker's paycheck. Many in the middle class bought homes when the prices were going up, and they lost much of the value of their homes when the housing bubble burst. Their net worth has fallen, and they are not saving enough for retirement. Only 25 percent of the baby boomers who are nearing retirement have enough saved to allow them to stop working. Their Social Security benefits will not be enough to support them in retirement. The plight of the middle class

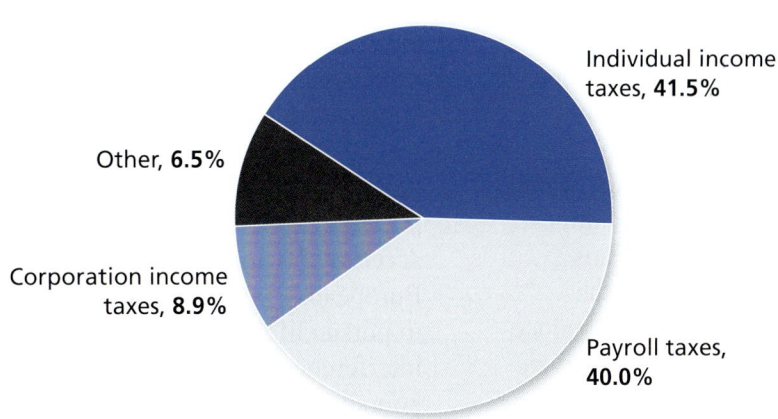

Source: Data from Office of Management and Budget

is one reason why some are now calling for the government to extend rights to include a right to health care, a right to a college education, and a right to a decent-paying job. It is also why there is so much concern over the mounting costs of Social Security and Medicare.

The Values Divide

18   The disagreement about what rights the government should guarantee has caused the "values divide" or the "culture wars" that began in the early 2000s. John Kenneth White has written about the split in *The Values Divide: American Politics and Culture in Transition,* with an introduction by John Zogby. White discusses the fact that Republican conservatives and Democratic liberals disagree strongly about the role of the government in solving the country's problems. He says that those on either side of the values divide live in "two parallel universes. Each side seeks to reinforce its thinking by associating with like-minded people." In a series of articles in *The Washington Post* titled "America in Red and Blue: A Nation Divided," David Von Drehle explored the political split. "This split is nurtured by the marketing efforts of the major parties, which increasingly aim pinpoint messages to certain demographic groups, rather than seeking broadly appealing new themes."

19   Why have the parties targeted certain groups for various political messages? First of all, the use of computers and demographic studies has made it possible to do so. Second, many Americans are only interested in one or two political issues. They respond well to targeted political messages about specific issues that concern them. Third, many potential voters are not registered members of either party, and both parties must try to persuade them to vote for their party's candidate. Neither party can win without securing some of the Independent votes. Increasingly, however, most Independents tend to lean toward one party or the other. Indeed, the country has become more and more polarized, to the point that the government seems to have difficulty functioning. Democrats and Republicans seem to make decisions more on the basis of ideology and less on the best interests of the nation. There is too often gridlock[9] and too seldom compromise, many would say.

[9] *gridlock: a situation in which nothing can happen, usually because people disagree strongly*

20 It is clear that the United States now faces many challenges. One of the most serious is the need to deal with the ongoing deficits and the growing national debt. Democrats believe it is an income problem—the government needs more money to run the programs that they want. Taxes should be raised, and the wealthiest should pay a higher rate. Republicans believe it is a spending problem—the government should lower taxes and reduce spending by cutting programs. The private sector—business—should take over programs now run by the government. Zogby says this split reveals more than a question about the role of government. "This is about how Americans define responsibility, citizenship and values they want their government to express."

21 CNN's chief political analyst Gloria Borger says that Americans have a love/hate relationship with their government:

> Americans want the government to fix our problems, but they don't trust the government to do it. We want health care to be fixed, Medicare and Social Security to stay intact, emergencies to be handled. We also want lower taxes along with a smaller—yet more responsive—government. All in all, we would like to spend less and get more....The public distrusts government because its leaders haven't been able to work together to produce much of anything....Ronald Reagan [a popular Republican president] understood the public's skepticism[10] about government. He often joked that the scariest sentence in America is "I'm from the government and I'm here to help."

22 This suspicion of government is not new. Tocqueville noted that Americans loved both freedom and equality. Throughout their history, Americans have lived with a tension between preserving freedom and promoting equality. Tocqueville believed that, in a democracy, Americans would eventually choose equality over freedom because of the material benefits that equality could bring. However, political scientists have disagreed, recognizing that Americans strongly value freedom, possibly more than any other country. A recent Pew poll asked Americans and Europeans to choose between "freedom to pursue life's goals without state interference" and the "state guarantees nobody is in need." In contrast to the Europeans, the majority of Americans chose freedom. (See page 158.)

The United States in the World

23 In spite of the current image of the United States and some of the actions the government has taken, there has been a long historical tradition of isolationism. President George Washington declared in 1796, "It is our true policy to steer clear of permanent alliances with any portion of the foreign world." The spirit of isolationism persists even today as Americans continue to debate their place in the world community. Many Americans are very reluctant to see the United States become involved in international military actions unless they are convinced that there is some national interest to be protected. Americans are also skeptical about international economic alliances and global agreements, wanting to be sure that their self-interests are protected before commitments are made to other countries. Many Americans are more interested in what is happening close to home than what is happening in the rest of the world. They want to know how events, national or international, will affect them personally.

24 Today, it would be impossible for the United States to isolate itself from the rest of the world even if it tried. While

---

[10] *skepticism: an attitude of doubt about whether something is true, right, or good*

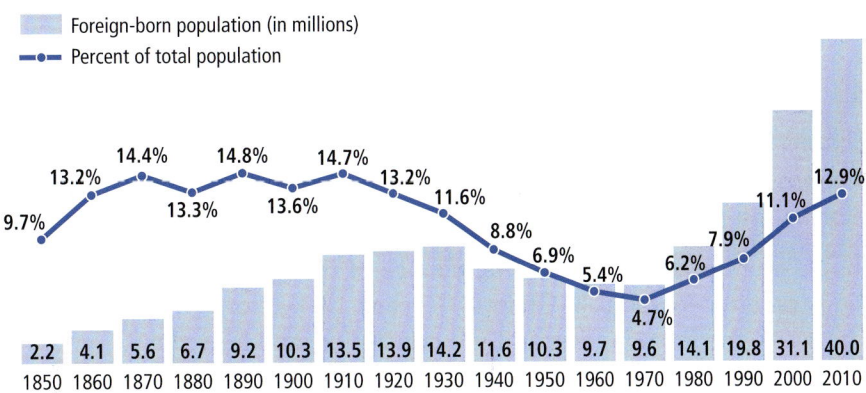

Source: U.S. Census Bureau, American Community Survey, 2010.

some scholars would say that the United States and its culture played a dominant role in the twentieth century, its role in the twenty-first is unclear. However, the rest of the world will certainly continue to have a great impact on the United States, particularly on its economy. A continuing concern for Americans will be protecting themselves from potential terrorist threats, both overseas and at home. There will be more consideration of how much power to give the government in exchange for this protection. In a free and open society, it is impossible to guarantee that terrorist attacks will never happen, and Americans must weigh how much freedom and privacy they will give up in order to be secure.

25 Finally, there is the question of immigration. The levels of legal and illegal immigration are high, and some Americans are worried about the assimilation of all these people from different countries. What will happen to the traditional American values as the population of the United States becomes increasingly diverse? On the other hand, many recognize that all these new immigrants bring new life and energy to the United States. They often come with a stronger belief in the six basic cultural values than many Americans have. As the baby boomers get older, immigrants are an important source of youth and vitality for the nation. A number of them are coming with the technical skills and STEM degrees (science, technology, engineering, mathematics) that the United States needs in industry.

26 Perhaps most importantly, the diversity of ideas and cultures in the United States is one of its greatest sources of strength in the twenty-first century. Ben Wattenberg, an expert in American culture, believes that the United States is becoming a microcosm of the world—it may be the first *universal* nation, where people from every race, religion, culture, and ethnic background live together in freedom, under one government.

27 The American people and their values have reached another historic crossroads. Will these traditional values endure through this century? One hundred years from now, will Americans still have a sense of national identity—of "being American"? What new challenges will this century bring? As Alvin Toffler said, "The sole certainty is that tomorrow will surprise us all."

AFTER YOU READ

Understand Main Ideas

A. Review the predictions that you made on page 284 before reading the chapter. Were your predictions correct? Write the number of the paragraph where you found the information next to your predictions.

B. Throughout the book we have discussed the importance of recognizing main ideas when reading academic material. In Chapter 1, (page 12) we looked at the relationship between the introduction and the conclusion, and how the headings signaled the main ideas. Chapter 2 (pages 38–39) explained how to do a simple outline of main ideas. Chapter 3 (pages 63–64) presented topic sentences and their relationship to main ideas. Chapters 5 (page 113) and 11 (page 271) had exercises on highlighting. Review these explanations. Then work with a partner and answer these questions:

1. What is the relationship between the opening quotation by Toffler, the introduction, and the conclusion of the chapter reading?
2. What is the purpose of the last paragraph in the first section, *The Role of Values in the National Identity,* paragraph 3, on page 285?
3. What is the main idea of the section *Individual Freedom and Self-Reliance*?
4. What is the main idea in the section *Equality of Opportunity and Competition*?
5. What words in the last sentence of paragraph 12 tie that section to the next one?
6. In the section *Material Wealth and Hard Work,* what is the relationship between these two values?
7. In the section *The Values Divide,* how would you describe the two groups on the opposite sides of the values divide?
8. What are the three reasons why the Republicans and Democrats try to target Independent voters with specific issues?
9. In the section *The United States in the World,* what positive contributions do immigrants bring to the United States?

Understand Details

Write *T* if the statement is true and *F* if it is false according to information in the chapter.

_____ 1. John J. Zogby believes that Americans have a clear understanding of their national identity.

_____ 2. Today, if you cannot afford a defense attorney, you will have to represent yourself in an American court of law.

_____ 3. In some ways Americans love their government, but in other ways they hate it.

_____ 4. Everyone agrees that economic rights should be expanded to include health care, a college education, and a good job.

_____ 5. One reason why Americans increasingly worry about their financial security is because there are not many jobs that pay well that do not require a college education.

_____ 6. In most American families today, only one spouse is working outside the home.

_____ 7. There is a split in the way liberals and conservatives view the role of government.

_____ 8. During the recession that started in 2008, the middle class and the upper class did not suffer—it was the low-income earners that were hit hardest.

_____ 9. The spirit of isolationism began when the United States first became a nation.

_____ 10. In contrast to some European countries, the United States does not have a problem with a large financial debt.

Talk About It

Work in small groups and choose one or more of the following questions to discuss.

1. What are the core values in your country? Are they similar to those of Americans?
2. How has your country changed in your lifetime? What changes do you think you will see in the future?
3. What do you think will happen to the balance of power in the world during the next ten years? What role do you think your country will have in this century?
4. How does your country view the United States?
5. Are you basically optimistic or pessimistic about the future? Why?

SKILL BUILDING

Improve Your Reading Skills: Scanning

Read the following quotations and scan the chapter to find who said each quote. Write the name next to each quotation. (Note: Several sources are quoted more than once.)

_____ 1. "Millions of middle-class Americans are living from paycheck to paycheck, struggling to pay their bills, having to borrow money and go into debt."

_____ 2. "The sole certainty is that tomorrow will surprise us all."

_____ 3. "The scariest sentence in America is 'I'm from the government and I'm here to help you.'"

_____ 4. "Unlike any other nation or people, we are defined by the rights we have, not by geography, by the arts and letters, not by our cuisine or sensibilities, not religion or civilization, not by war."

_____ 5. The people on either side of the values divide live in "two parallel universes. Each side seeks to reinforce its thinking by associating with like-minded people."

_____ 6. "Our celebration of initiative and enterprise; our insistence on hard work and personal responsibility, are constants in our character."

_____ 7. "This split is nurtured by the marketing efforts of the major parties, which increasingly aim pinpoint messages to certain demographic groups, rather than seeking broadly appealing new themes."

_____ 8. "It is our true policy to steer clear of permanent alliances with any portion of the foreign world."

_____ 9. "Hard America values risk, innovation, effort, and enterprise. Soft America values security and equality. Hard America is ruled by the market, while Soft America is directed by government planning. Hard America creates wealth; Soft America reassigns it."

_____ 10. "All in all, we would like to spend less and get more."

Develop Your Critical Thinking Skills

This chapter has information about two conflicting views of the role of government. Americans are divided about what role their government should have. Sometimes, it is difficult to know how a government should respond to social issues. For example, what should the government do to protect children from the effects of poverty?

Work with a partner to learn more about this important issue now facing Americans, and then come to your own conclusions. Gather information from several sources, and then answer the questions that follow. Read the information in the box about a major cause of childhood poverty. Reread paragraphs 5, 6, 10, 11 (and the quote), 12, 15, 16, and 17 in the reading.

More and more young Americans are separating marriage from child bearing—a personal decision that is having an impact on society at large. Recent studies show that 48 percent of all first births are now to single mothers, most of whom are high school graduates in their 20s and who may also have a year or two of college. College graduates tend to have their first child two years after marriage. However, the median age of all American women having their first baby is now lower than the median age of marriage. The median age for women to marry is 27 and for men it is 29. Many middle class women are living with their boyfriends and postponing marriage. By the time they are 25, almost half of them have a baby, and about half of those babies were "unplanned."

The problem is that many couples have not made a commitment to raise the child together, and almost 40 percent of them break up before their child is five years old. More than two-thirds of the fathers have little or no contact with their children and provide little or no financial assistance. Consequently, more than half of American single mothers are on some sort of government assistance. Nearly three out of four poor families with children are headed by single mothers. A family with two parents is 82 percent less likely to be poor. Children of single mothers are more likely to have health and emotional problems, do poorly in school, get into trouble with the law, live in poverty, be physically abused, and not graduate from college, which limits their future earning ability. They are also more likely to become single parents and repeat the cycle.

1. One of the reasons why middle-class women are postponing marriage is financial. Without a college degree, potential husbands are not earning enough money to pay for the married life that both want. Is having a baby before marriage a good financial decision? Why, or why not?

2. Another reason why unmarried women in their twenties are having babies is cultural. They do not believe that it is wrong to have a baby without getting married first. Where are they getting this message? What do you think?

3. The practice of single women having children began with low-income women. This started in the 1960s with the "Great Society" welfare programs. Aid to Families with Dependent Children gave government assistance to single mothers who were poor. Unmarried mothers needed more financial help, and they got more money from the government if they weren't married to, or receiving money from, the child's father. How do you think this affected the marriage rate?

4. Now that this practice has spread to the middle class, what do you think will happen? What are the consequences for a child born to parents who have no legal commitment to each other or to the child, particularly the father?

5. What is the responsibility of government to take care of children living in poverty? How is this best done? The federal and state governments now spend about $300 billion a year on payments to single parents with children, about $30,000 per household per year.

6. The government has campaigns against smoking, obesity, and teenage pregnancy. The teenage birth rate is now the lowest it's been since the 1940s, around seven percent. Should the government have a campaign to discourage single women in their twenties from having children? Why, or why not?

7. What role do the six American values play in this situation? What do you think liberals (or progressives) believe should be done? What do you think conservatives believe should be done? What is the basis for your conclusions?

8. How are these issues handled in your country? What are the similarities and differences? What do you think the answers are?

Build Your Vocabulary

Scrambled Words

Review words used frequently throughout the text. Read these definitions, and unscramble the vocabulary words that they define.

_____ 1. **ruectlu**—the ideas, beliefs, and customs that are shared and accepted by people in a society

_____ 2. **oefmred**—the right to do what you want without being controlled or restricted by the government, police, etc.

_____ 3. **drah kwro**—the price you pay for having a high standard of living

_____ 4. **auqytiel**—the state of having the same rights, opportunities, etc., as everyone else

_____ 5. **aaeilmtr thawel**—money and possessions

_____ 6. **lefs-lenaicre**—the state of being dependent on yourself

_____ 7. **pmctioetnio**—a situation in which people or organizations try to be more successful than others

Vocabulary Check

This chapter has several words that have to do with the criminal justice system. Circle the six words and phrases that are related to crime and punishment. Use them to complete the sentences.

court	justice
defense attorney	tension
jury	global
criminals	microcosm
discretionary spending	trial

1. There were also freedoms guaranteeing the right to a speedy and public

   _____.

2. Americans also have the right to a trial by _____ and the right to

   a _____ _____.

3. If someone cannot afford an attorney, one will be appointed by the

   _____.

4. The administration of _____ may be very difficult, but it must

   be fair.

5. People who are found guilty of breaking the law are _____.

More AWL Words

Test your knowledge of these AWL words by matching the words with their definitions. Write the word in the blank next to the correct definition.

category	define	identity	reveal	sole	survive
challenge	distinction	military	sector	stress	target
commitment	evidence	respond	security		

_____ 1. things done to keep a place, person, or thing safe

_____ 2. the qualities of a person or group that make them different from others

_____ 3. continuous feelings of worry about your work or personal life

_____ 4. a promise to do something or behave in a particular way

_____ 5. relating to or used by the army, navy, etc.

_____ 6. a clear difference between things

_____ 7. facts, objects, or signs that make you believe something is true

_____ 8. to continue to exist in spite of difficulties and dangers

_____ 9. to describe something correctly and thoroughly

_____ 10. a part of an area of activity, especially business or trade

_____ 11. to aim an idea or plan at a limited group of people

_____ 12. something that tests strength, skill, or ability

_____ 13. to react to something that has been said or done

_____ 14. a group of people or things that are all of the same type

_____ 15. the only one

_____ 16. to show something that was hidden

EXPAND YOUR KNOWLEDGE

Think, Pair, Share

Review paragraphs 5–8, 11, and the section The Values Divide. Look for the differences between liberal and conservative views mentioned there. Would you say that your own views are more liberal or conservative? Are you liberal on some issues and conservative on others?

Write a list of issues in the chart. You may wish to add social issues such as abortion, babies born outside of marriage, and same-sex marriage. Then write the liberal and conservative views in the chart, and your own view. (An example has been done for you.) Share your list with a partner, and then with another pair of students.

Issue	Liberal View	Conservative View	My View Liberal / Conservative (choose)
Government spending for the poor and middle class	Government should support needy people	People should be self-reliant and not have government support	

300 ★ Chapter 12

Ask Yourself / Ask Americans

Do you agree or disagree with these statements? Circle your answers. Then ask an American for his or her opinion. Compare your answers with the American's answers.

1.	Single women having children is not a problem.	agree	disagree
2.	Science and technology do more to improve the overall quality of life than do religion and philosophy.	agree	disagree
3.	Governments should pass laws to help stop global warming.	agree	disagree
4.	Governments should provide free health care for all the citizens of the country.	agree	disagree
5.	Governments should provide a free college education for all the citizens of the country.	agree	disagree
6.	I expect to have more material possessions than my parents do now.	agree	disagree
7.	I am confident that my children will have as good a life as mine, or better.	agree	disagree
8.	I am basically optimistic about the future.	agree	disagree

Small-Group Project

Work in small groups. Make three predictions about what you think will happen in the future, during your lifetime. Be specific.

Write your predictions on a piece of paper and give them to your teacher. As your teacher reads the predictions aloud, a classmate can write the predictions on a chart or on the chalkboard. Then the class can vote on which predictions they think are most likely to come true.

Use the Internet

Choose one of these and do research on the Internet with a partner. Then report your findings to your classmates.

1. The year 2000 caused many people to think about what life would be like in the future. How would life be different? A number of organizations prepared *time capsules* to be opened sometime in the future. A time capsule is a container filled with objects from a particular time, so that people in the future will know what life was like then. Do research on the Internet about time capsules. Then work in small groups to decide what you would put in a time capsule to be opened in 2100 or another year. Prepare a poster with a collage of photos, or bring in actual items for your time capsule. Present your ideas to the rest of the class and explain your reasons for your choices.

2. There is a summer festival in Chautauqua, NY, where people from all over the country come to discuss important issues; listen to lectures by experts on many topics; hear concerts; watch ballet, opera, and theater performances; participate in art activities; attend interfaith worship services and programs; take courses on a variety of topics; and enjoy outdoor recreation in a walking community by a lake. Chautauqua has had a summer program since 1874, and David McCullough, a noted historian and author, says that it is a treasure trove of Americana. Visit Chautauqua's website www.ciweb.org and learn more about this very special place. See what the theme weeks are for the coming summer. You can click on their YouTube link and watch short videos, and you can watch Chautauqua lectures at www.fora.tv

3. Some commentators think that the new generation of Americans coming of age now—the Millennials—will bring many positive qualities to the country.Do research on the Millennial generation. Who are they? What do they believe? What goals and plans do they have for the future?

WRITE ABOUT IT

Choose one of the final projects to write about.

1. Write about some aspect of American culture. Analyze an American movie, a TV show, commercials on TV, advertisements in newspapers or magazines, some current event in the news, the results of interviews or conversations you have had with Americans about their beliefs, or observations you have made about how Americans behave. Choose any aspect of life in the United States that you have observed. Be sure to mention at least two or three of the six values: individual freedom, self-reliance, equality of opportunity, competition, material wealth, and hard work.

2. Or approach the assignment from a different direction. Choose a value, and then give specific examples of how you have observed that value existing in American life. Contrast this value with your own culture and how things are done differently. When you have finished writing your analysis, prepare a short speech to report your findings to the rest of the class. Now that you have finished this text, what do you think the American Dream is? How can Americans protect it for future generations? How much can and should a nation do to ensure equality of opportunity for its people?

3. Read the following and write an essay in response.

Theodore H. White, a well-known political analyst, has said that the United States's problem is "trying to do everything for everybody." Ever since the early 1960s, he says, Americans have been making promises—

...promises to save the cities, promises to take care of the sick, the old, the universities....Many of our problems flow out of American goodwill, trying to do everything for everybody....In the 1960s we exploded with goodwill as blacks, who had been denied equality, rightfully demanded it. We could afford it, and we should have done what we did. But we have ended up pushing equality and other ideas to absurd limits as we sought perfect equality rather than realistic equality of opportunity....We have to choose what we can do; we have to discipline our goodwill.*

Contrast Theodore H. White's view with that expressed by Barack Obama in his second Inaugural Address on January 21, 2013, and the famous "I Have a Dream Speech" of Martin Luther King, Jr.

Martin Luther King, Jr., gave his famous "I Have a Dream" speech at the Lincoln Memorial, at the opposite end of the mall where Obama was inaugurated at the Capitol building. In 1963, on the 100th anniversary of the Emancipation Proclamation that freed the slaves in the southern states that had left the Union, there was a huge civil rights march in Washington, D.C. Martin Luther King, Jr., delivered his famous speech on the steps of the Lincoln Memorial to several hundred thousand marchers. In the speech, he spoke of the journey of African Americans from slavery into freedom, and the need to continue the journey so that they could one day have equality with whites and be truly free from prejudice and discrimination.

The "I Have a Dream" speech is one of the finest in the English language and one that you should hear. You can listen to the speech on the King website www.kinginstititute.info. During the speech, you can hear people speaking out agreeing with him, which is a custom in the African-American church. In the speech, King says that he has a dream "deeply rooted in the American dream

Dr. Martin Luther King, Jr., giving his famous "I Have a Dream" speech, August 28, 1963.

... that my four little children will one day live in a nation where they will not be judged by the color of their skin, but by the content of their character." The speech concludes with a quote from the *Declaration of Independence* and an old African-American spiritual (religious song), "Free at last! Free at last! Thank God Almighty. We are free at last."

America's Problem: "Trying to Do Everything for Everybody," U.S. News & World Report (July 5, 1982).

Obama's Second Inauguration, January 21, 2013, was held on the holiday honoring King's birthday, and many Americans thought about how Obama's presidency was in some ways a fulfillment of King's dreams. Here are some excerpts from Obama's speech:

> Each time we gather to inaugurate a president, we bear witness to the enduring strength of our Constitution. We affirm the promise of our democracy. We recall that what binds this nation together is not the colors of our skin or the tenets of our faith or the origins of our names. What makes us exceptional—what makes us American—is our allegiance to an idea, articulated in a declaration made more than two centuries ago:
>
> "We hold these truths to be self-evident, that all men are created equal, that they are endowed by their Creator with certain unalienable rights, that among these are Life, Liberty, and the pursuit of Happiness."
>
> Today we continue a never-ending journey to bridge the meaning of those words with the realities of our time. For history tells us that while these truths may be self-evident, they have never been self-executing; that while freedom is a gift from God, it must be secured by His people here on Earth. The patriots of 1776 did not fight to replace the tyranny of a king with the privileges of a few or the rule of a mob. They gave to us a Republic, a government of, and by, and for the people, entrusting each generation to keep safe our founding creed....
>
> That is our generation's task—to make these words, these rights, these values—of Life, and Liberty, and the pursuit of Happiness—real for every American. Being true to our founding documents does not require us to agree on every contour of life; it does not mean we will all define liberty in exactly the same way, or follow the same precise path to happiness. Progress does not compel us to settle centuries-long debates about the role of government for all time—but it does require us to act in our time....
>
> Let each of us now embrace, with solemn duty and awesome joy, what is our lasting birthright. With common effort and common purpose, with passion and dedication, let us answer the call of history, and carry into an uncertain future that precious light of freedom.
>
> Thank you, God Bless you, and may He forever bless these United States of America.

EXPLORE ON YOUR OWN

Books to Read

Margaret Hoover, *American Individualism: How a New Generation of Conservatives Can Save the Republican Party*—The great-granddaughter of President Hoover writes about how Republicans need to emphasize individual freedom in both economic and social policies to appeal to a new generation of voters.

Jeanne Marie Laskas, *Hidden America: From Coal Miners to Cowboys, an Extraordinary Exploration of the Unseen People Who Make This Country Work*—Laskas presents stories about the people who make our lives run every day, but whom we barely think of.

Thomas E. Mann and Norman J. Ornstein, *It's even Worse Than It Looks: How the American Constitutional System Collided with the New Politics of Extremism*—Congressional scholars from Washington "think tanks" representing both Republicans and Democrats discuss government gridlock.

Michelle Obama, American Grown: *The Story of the White House Kitchen Garden and Gardens Across America*—The First Lady shares her own experiences and encourages Americans to start planting their own gardens and eat healthy food.

Joseph E. Stiglitz, *The Price of Inequality: How Today's Divided Society Endangers Our Future*—A winner of the Nobel Prize for Economics examines the consequences of America's growing inequality and argues that there are ways to change it.

Movies to See

The Butler—Filmmaker Lee Daniels tells the story of the life of an African-American butler who served eight presidents through the civil rights era of the 1950s and 1960s and the decades of the 1970s and 1980s.

Hackers—A young boy is arrested by the Secret Service for writing a computer virus, and years later he and his friends try to stop a dangerous computer virus while being watched by the Secret Service.

The Namesake—American-born Gogol, the son of Indian immigrants, wants to fit in among his fellow New Yorkers, despite his family's unwillingness to let go of their traditional ways.

Chasing Ice—National Geographic photographer James Balog filmed this documentary about the melting of glaciers.

Supersize Me—In this documentary, a man eats nothing but fast food for a month.

ACADEMIC WORD LIST

The reading material in each chapter has been analyzed by comparing it to several vocabulary lists: the 2,000 Most Frequent Word Family List and the Academic Word List. Vocabulary words used in exercises (1) are from the Academic Word List or (2) are not from either of the two lists but are important to the context of the reading and are useful to know for academic reading in general.

The Academic Word List (AWL) was developed by Averil Coxhead. The list contains 570 word families that were selected by examining academic texts from a variety of subject areas. The list does not include words that are among the most frequent 2,000 words of English. Each word family has a headword (the stem form) and a list of other word forms (or parts of speech) for that headword.

AWL WORDS USED IN CHAPTER READINGS

The number after each AWL headword indicates all the chapters in which the words are used. (Note: Another form of the word may have been used, not the stem form.)

abandon 3, 5, 6, 7, 9
academy 5, 9, 10
access 4, 5, 6, 7, 10, 11
accommodate 8, 11
accompany 5
accumulate 2, 6
accuracy 5, 8
achieve 2, 3, 6, 7, 8, 9, 10, 11, 12
acquire 2, 4, 5, 6, 9
adapt 3, 6
adequate 4, 5, 6
adjust 5, 6, 7, 9, 12
administrate 6
adult 1, 2, 3, 4, 5, 8, 9, 10, 11
advocate 10
affect 2, 3, 5, 7, 9, 10, 11, 12
aid 6, 7, 9
alternative 6, 10
amendment 3, 4, 12
analyze 5, 8, 12
annual 6, 9
apparent 12
approach 1
approximate 11
area 3, 4, 5, 6, 7, 8, 9, 11
aspect 1, 2, 3, 4, 5, 6
assemble 5, 7
assess 9
assign 10, 12
assist 2, 9, 12
assume 5, 7
attach 2, 3, 11
attain 9, 12
attribute 10
attitude 3, 5, 7, 10, 11

author 11
authority 2, 3, 5, 6, 7, 11
automate 4, 5, 7
available 5, 9, 11, 12
aware 4, 5, 6, 7

benefit 2, 5, 6, 7, 8, 9, 11, 12
bias 8
bond 10

capable 4, 6
capacity 3
category 1, 12
challenge 2, 4, 5, 7, 9, 10, 11, 12
channel 5
chapter 1, 2, 3, 6, 7, 8, 9, 10, 11, 12
chart 1
circumstance 4, 7, 9
cite 3
civil 4, 7, 8, 11, 12
classic 1, 4, 11
codes 9
collapse 6
comment 3, 6, 10
commit 6, 7, 10, 12
communicate 5, 10, 11
community 1, 2, 3, 4, 6, 7, 8, 9, 10, 11, 12
compensate 11
complex 4, 6
compute 5, 10, 12
concentrate 9
concept 1, 2, 5, 9
conclude 5, 6, 7, 10, 11
conduct 3, 6, 8, 12

confine 4
conflict 5, 7, 9, 11
consent 7, 12
consequent 3, 5, 11
considerable 7, 11
consist 2, 4, 7, 10, 11
constant 2, 3, 4, 6, 10, 11, 12
constitute 1, 2, 3, 4, 7, 9, 11, 12
construct 4, 5, 8, 12
consume 5, 6, 7, 9, 10
contemporary 3
context 2, 3, 11
contract 10
contradict 3, 8, 10, 11
contrary 10
contrast 3, 6, 7, 9, 10, 11, 12
contribute 1, 3, 5, 6, 7, 10, 11
controversy 4, 5, 6, 7, 9
convene 7
convert 2
convince 1, 5, 7, 12
cooperate 4, 6, 7, 11
core 7, 9
corporate 6, 7, 11
couple 11
create 1, 2, 3, 4, 5, 6, 7, 8, 9, 11, 12
credit 3, 5, 6, 9
criteria 9
culture 1, 2, 3, 4, 5, 6, 7, 8, 9, 10, 11, 12
cycle 6, 7, 8, 10

data 1, 5, 6
debate 1, 3, 4, 5, 6, 9, 12
decade 1, 4, 6, 7

decline 1, 2, 3, 6, 11, 12
deduct 3
define 1, 2, 3, 5, 6, 8, 9, 11, 12
demonstrate 4, 6, 7, 8, 9
deny 4, 8, 9, 10, 12
depress 6, 7, 12
derive 2, 10, 12
design 3, 6, 7, 9
despite 8, 9
detect 4
device 5, 11
devote 3, 6
diminish 2
discretionary 12
discriminate 8, 9, 12
display 3
displace 9
distinct 1, 7, 8, 9, 12
distribute 6
diverse 1, 2, 3, 6, 8, 9, 12
document 8
dominate 1, 4, 5, 7, 8, 12
drama 2, 3, 4, 5, 6, 8, 9, 10, 11
dynamic 3

economy 1, 2, 6, 7, 8, 9, 10, 11, 12
edit 5, 6
element 10
eliminate 2, 5, 6, 7, 8, 10
emerge 1, 2, 6
emphasis 2, 3 4, 5, 7, 9, 11
enable 2, 4, 5, 6, 7, 11
encounter 12
energy 2, 5, 6, 10
enforce 5, 10
enhance 10
enormous 1, 2, 6, 7, 8, 9, 10, 11, 12
ensure 2, 6, 7, 9, 12
environment 5, 6, 7
equip 9, 10
establish 1, 2, 3, 4, 6, 7, 8, 9, 10
estimate 1, 3, 4, 10 5, 6
ethic 2, 3, 10
ethnic 1, 2, 3, 7, 8, 9, 12
evaluate 5, 9
eventual 1, 2, 4, 6, 8, 9, 11, 12
evident 1, 2, 4, 10, 11, 12
evolve 2, 3
exclude 1, 11
expand 5, 7, 8, 9, 12
expert 5, 7, 8, 10, 11, 12
export 5
expose 10

facilitate 8, 9, 10
factor 1, 2, 4, 5, 6, 9, 10, 11, 12
feature 4, 10
federal 7, 8, 9, 10, 12
fee 5
final 2, 4, 6, 8, 9, 11
finance 2, 6, 7, 8, 9, 12

flexible 6, 9, 11
focus 5, 7, 9, 10, 11
found 4, 6, 7, 8, 12
foundation 2, 3, 4, 5, 10
framework 2
function 3, 8, 12
fund 5, 6, 7, 9, 10
fundamental 2, 3
furthermore 6, 7, 10

gender 2, 5
generate 5, 10
generation 1, 2, 5, 6, 8, 9, 11, 12
globe 2, 12
goal 2, 3, 6, 7, 8, 9, 10, 11, 12
grade 7, 9
grant 3, 5, 9
guarantee 3, 4, 5, 6, 7, 9, 12
guideline 10

hypothesis 1

identify 1, 2, 5, 8, 10, 12
ideology 7, 12
illustrate 3, 7, 10
image 4, 5, 6, 10, 12
immigrate 1, 2, 3, 5, 6, 8, 9
impact 1, 4, 6 7, 9, 10, 11
implement 6, 7, 10
impose 3
income 9, 11, 12
incentive 5
incidence 1, 4, 8, 10
incline 8
income 5, 6, 7, 8, 9
index 6
indicate 9, 11
individual 2, 3, 4, 5, 6, 7, 8, 9, 10, 11, 12
infinite 5
infrastructure 7
injure 10
innovate 5, 6, 12
insight 11
initiative 12
instance 4, 7, 10
institute 1, 4, 5, 6, 7, 9, 11, 12
instruct 8, 9
interact 6, 7
integrate 8, 9
intelligence 2, 4
intense 6, 10
internal 12
interpret 5, 7, 12
invest 3, 5, 6
involve 2, 9, 10, 11, 12
isolate 9, 12
issue 1, 2, 4, 6, 9, 10, 12
item 4, 10

job 1, 2, 6 7, 8, 9, 11, 12
justify 9

label 10
labor 2, 5, 7, 8, 10, 11
lecture 9, 10
legal 1, 3, 7, 8, 9, 11
legislate 4, 7, 10
liberal 3, 7, 9, 12
license 1, 11
likewise 10
link 6
locate 5, 6, 11

maintain 1, 2, 5, 6, 8, 9, 10, 11, 12
major 1, 2, 3, 4, 5, 6, 7, 8, 9, 10, 11, 12
mature 9
maximum 9
measure 5
media 1, 5, 9, 10
medical 5, 6, 7, 8, 12
mental
method 6, 7, 9
migration 8
military 4, 6, 7, 8, 10, 12
minimum 9
minor 1, 7, 8, 9, 12
monitor 11
motive 1, 2, 3, 6, 10

negate 5
network 5, 6
neutral 1
nevertheless 2, 10
normal 4
nuclear 6, 11

obtain 9, 11
obvious 9
occupy 6, 10
occur 3, 4, 8, 9, 10
odd 12
ongoing 12
option 5
orient 3, 6
outcome 7, 11
output 6
overall 6, 10, 11
overseas 6, 7, 10, 12

parallel 12
participate 1, 6, 9, 10
partner 7, 11
perceive 2, 8
percent 1, 3, 4, 5, 6, 7, 8, 9, 10, 11, 12
period 1, 4, 5, 7, 11
persist 3, 6, 7, 10, 12
perspective 9
phase 4
phenomenon 8
philosophy 3, 9, 10, 12
physical 4, 9, 10
plus 6, 7
policy 6, 7, 9, 11, 12

portion 4, 10, 12
positive 5, 6
potential 2, 5, 6, 7, 9, 11, 12
predict 5, 7, 8, 11
predominant 9
previous 3, 7, 9, 11
primary 4, 7, 9, 11
principal 4, 10
principle 7, 9
priority 6, 11
proceed 7, 9
process 1, 5, 6, 7, 8, 9, 10, 12
professional 5, 9, 10
project 5, 7, 8, 10
promote 2, 7, 10, 12
prospective 5, 9
psychology 10, 11
publish 5, 6
purchase 5
pursue 2, 3, 7, 11, 12

range 4, 10
react 4
recover 6
refine 6
region 4, 8, 10
register 8, 12
regulate 4, 6, 7, 10
reinforce 3, 4, 5, 6, 8, 12
reject 2, 8
relax 10
reluctance 12
rely 2, 3, 4, 6, 7, 8, 9, 10, 11, 12
remove 9, 10
require 2, 3, 5, 6, 7, 8, 9, 10, 11, 12
research 3, 5, 6, 7, 10, 11
reside 1, 8, 9
resolve 7
resource 1, 2, 5, 8, 9, 11
respond 5, 6, 11, 12

restore 6
restrain 7
restrict 1, 7, 10, 11
retain 8
reveal 1, 4, 5, 6, 7, 9, 10, 12
revenue 5
reverse 7, 12
revolution 5, 6. 7, 8, 10, 12
role 1, 2, 3, 5, 6, 7, 10, 11, 12

schedule 9, 10
section 5, 8
sector 6, 9, 12
secure 4, 5, 6, 7, 9, 12
seek 2, 3, 4, 6, 8, 9, 10, 11, 12
select 1, 9
series 7, 9, 12
sex 3, 8, 10, 11
shift 2, 6, 7
significant 1, 3, 5, 6, 7, 8, 9, 10, 11, 12
similar 3, 7, 9, 10, 11
site 5, 6, 11
sole 3, 7
somewhat 8
source 2, 4, 5, 6
specific 1, 7, 10, 12
specify 1
stable 11
status 2, 5, 6, 8, 9, 11
strategy 7
stress 5, 10, 11, 12
structure 2, 5, 6, 11
style 6, 7
submit 6
subsidy 5
substitute 3
sum 2, 3, 6, 7
survey 2, 10, 11
survive 1, 4, 6, 10, 12
symbol 5, 7, 10

tape 3
target 4, 5, 7, 12
task 4, 5, 11
team 5, 6, 9, 10
technical 9
technique 5, 6
technology 5, 6, 8, 10, 11, 12
temporary 6, 7
tension 7, 12
text 1, 5, 9
theme 2, 6, 12
theory 6
trace 1, 8, 10
tradition 1, 2, 3, 4, 5, 6, 7, 8, 9, 10, 11, 12
transform 6, 9
transfer 9
transition 12
trend 1, 11

ultimate 6, 7, 8, 12
undergo 6, 7
undertake 12
uniform 2, 10
unique 1, 2, 6, 8, 9, 12
utility 12

vary 1, 7, 9, 10, 11
version 4
via 10
vision 6, 7
violate 9
virtual 1, 8, 11
visible 1
voluntary 3, 9

welfare 2, 7, 11
widespread 2, 7, 9

BIBLIOGRAPHY

PRINT SOURCES

"10 Ideas that are Changing Your Life." *Time,* 12 March 2012, 59–87.

"50 Years After Brown: Unequal Education." *U.S. News & World Report,* 22, 29 March 2004, 64–70.

"A Class of Their Own." *Time*, 31 October 1994, 52–61.

"A New Era of Segregation: Classrooms Still Aren't Colorblind." *Newsweek,* 27 December 1993, 44.

"A Rich Legacy of Preference: Alumni Kids Get a Big Break on Admissions." *Newsweek,* 24 June 1991, 59.

Aaron, Henry J., Thomas E. Mann, and Timothy Taylor, eds. "Introduction." *Values and Public Policy.* Washington, D.C.: The Brookings Institution, 1994.

Adelman, Larry. "Down the Road from the Michigan Rulings: Right Ruling, Wrong Reason." *Washington Post,* 29 June 2003, Outlook section B3.

Alger, Horatio. *Mark the Match Boy, or Richard Hunter's Ward.* Philadelphia: John C. Winston Company, 1897.

Alger, Horatio. *Tony the Tramp, or Right Is Might.* New York: The New York Book Company, 1909.

"America's Immigrant Challenge." *Time*, Special Issue, Fall 1993, 3–12.

Anthony, Ted. "America innovates, expands—digitally now." *Daily News,* 20 May 2012, A, 9.

Asnes, Marion. "The Affluent American: A Money Survey Delves into the Changing Definition of 'the Good Life.'" *Money.* December 2003, 40, 43.

Bacon, Perry, Jr. "How Much Diversity Do You Want from Me?" *Time,* 7 July 2003, 108.

Barlett, Donald L. and James B. Steele. *The Betrayal of the American Dream.* New York: PublicAffairs, 2012.

Barone, Michael. "A Tale of Two Nations: Why Coddled Kids Grow Up to Become Supercompetent Adults." *U.S. News & World Report,* 12 May 2003, 24.

Becker, Carl L. *The Declaration of Independence: A Study in the History of Political Ideas.* New York: Vantage Books, 1958.

"Been There, Done That" [Adventure Travel]. *Newsweek,* 19 July 1993, 42–49.

Begley, Sharon. "I Can't Think! The Twitterization of our culture has revolutionized our lives, but with an unintended consequence—our overloaded brains freeze when we have to make decisions." *Newsweek,* 7 March 2011, 28-33.

"Best Columns: The U.S.: American Culture: A Dwindling Export." *The Week,* 4 April 2003.

"Best Columns: The U.S.: Orange Alert: Why We're Laughing; Peace Protests: Giving Naivete a Chance; Bush: A Third Kind of President; Affirmative Action: What's Really at Stake. *The Week,* 7 March 2003, 12.

Bohr, Peter. "In the Age of Super-Sizing, Is There Room in America for the Small Car?" *AAA World,* January/February 2003, 30–36.

Bono. "The Resource Miracle: The rock star and activist explains why Africa could be this century's success story." *Time,* 28 May 2012, 28.

Boorstein, Michelle. "Delving into the study of secularism: Georgetown University course is part of a nascent field trying to define itself." *The Washington Post,* 17 December 2011, B 2.

Bowman, Karlyn, ed. "Men Today/Guy Talk." *The American Enterprise.* September 2003, 60–61.

Bradley, Bill. "Citizens United: Monied interests increasingly run the government. Only voters can reverse that." *Time,* 14 May 2012, 23.

Brascoupe, Jeremy. "My World: Young Native Americans Today." S*mithsonian National Museum of the American Indian.* Spring 2003, 9.

Bremmer, Ian. "5 Myths about America's Decline." *The Washington Post,* 6 May 2012, B, 2.

Brogan, D. W. *The American Character.* New York: Alfred A. Knopf, 1944.

Brogan, Hugh. *Tocqueville.* London: Fontana, 1973.

Brookheser, Richard. "We Can All Share American Culture." *Time*, 31 August 1992, 74.

Burns, James MacGregor. *Cobblestone Leadership: Majority Rule, Minority Power.* Norman: University of Oklahoma Press, 1990.

Burns, James MacGregor. *Deadlock of Democracy: Far-Party Politics in America.* Englewood Cliffs, N.J.: Prentice-Hall, 1963.

"Campaign Finance Reform: Opinions of People of Faith and the Clergy." A survey by the Gallup Organization for The Interfaith Alliance Foundation August 2001 in *Call for Reform,* published by The Interfaith Alliance Foundation.

Carlson, Margaret. "And Now, Obesity Rights." *Time*, 6 December 1993, 96.

Carnegie, Andrew. *Autobiography of Andrew Carnegie.* Boston: Houghton Mifflin, 1920.

Carnegie, Andrew. *The Gospel of Wealth and Other Timely Essays.* Cambridge: Harvard University, Belknap Press, 1962.

Cash, W. J. *The Mind of the South.* New York: Alfred A. Knopf, 1960.

Cater, Douglass, ed. *Television as a Social Force: New Approaches to TV Criticism.* New York: Praeger, 1975.

Chinni, Dante. "Inequality is bad for all of us. Even those at the top." *The Washington Post,* 26 August 2012, B1, 4.

Cloud, John. "Why the SUV Is All the Rage." *Time,* 24 February 2003, 35–42.

CNN/*USA Today*/Gallup Poll, 2–4 Sept. 2002. "How Important Would You Say Religion Is in Your Own Life: Very Important, Fairly Important, or Not Very Important?"

Cohen, Richard. "Intolerance Swaddled in Faith." *Washington Post,* 1 May 2003, A27.

Cohn, D'Vera, and Sarah Cohen. "Statistics Portray Settled, Affluent Mideast Community." *Washington Post,* 20 November 2001, A4.

Cohn, D'Vera. "Hispanics Declared Largest Minority: Blacks Overtaken in Census Update." *Washington Post,* 19 June 2003, A1, 46.

"Controversy of the week: The American Dream: What went wrong" *The Week,* 12 October 2012, 6.

Corliss, Richard, Jeffrey Ressner, and James Inverne. "Ladies' Night Out" [Movies]. *Time,* March 2003, 73–75.

Cose, Ellis. "The Black Gender Gap." *Newsweek,* 3 March 2003, 46–55

Counts, George S. *Education and American Civilization.* New York: Bureau of Publications, Teachers College, Columbia University, 1952.

Counts, George S. *Education and the Foundations of Human Freedom.* Pittsburgh: University of Pittsburgh Press, 1962.

Coy, Peter. "Right Place, Right Time." *Business Week,* 13 October 2003.

Cullen, Bob. "New Kids on the Block: As Affluent Schools in the Suburbs Grow More Diverse, They Face the Test That City Schools Failed: Can They Keep Everyone Happy?" *The Washingtonian.* April 2003, 29–34.

Cullen, Lisa Takeuchi. "Now Hiring!" *Time,* 24 November 2004.

"Daughters of Murphy Brown" [Single Motherhood]. *Newsweek,* 2 August 1993, 58–59.

Diamandis, Peter H., and Steven Kotler. *Abundance: The Future Is Better Than You Think.* New York: Free Press, 2012.

Dionne, E. J. Jr. *Our Divided Political Heart: The Battle for the American Idea in an Age of Discontent.* New York: Bloomsbury, 2012.

"Diversity or Division On Campus: Minority Graduation Galas Highlight a Timely Issue." *Washington Post,* 19 May 2003, A1, 8.

Dobbs, David. "Restless Genes: The compulsion to see what lies beyond that far ridge or that ocean—or this planet—is a defining part of human identity and success." *National Geographic,* January 2013, 44–57.

Dokoupil, Tony. "Tweets, Texts, Email, Posts: Is the Onslaught Making Us Crazy?" *Newsweek,* 16 July

2012, 24–30.

"Domesticated Bliss: New Laws Are Making It Official for Gay or Live-In Straight Couples." *Newsweek,* 23 March 1992, 62–63.

Douthat, Ross. "Divided by God: As the religious center erodes, it becomes tough to pull together as a nation." *The New York Times,* 8 April 2012, Sunday Review, 1, 6.

Duhigg, Charles. *The Power of Habit: Why We Do What We Do in Life and Business.* New York: Random House, 2012.

Elliott, Philip. "Schools shift from textbooks to tablets." *Daily News,* 10 March 2013, C, 11.

Ellison, Christopher G., and W. Allen Martin, eds. *Race and Ethnic Relations in the United States: Readings for the 21st Century.* University of Florida, 1998.

Ellwood, Robert S. "East Asian Religions in Today's America." *World Religions in America: An Introduction,* ed. Jacob Neusner. Louisville, Ky.: Westminster/John Knox Press, 1994.

Emery, Noemie. "America in the Middle: Michael Barone Seeks a Balance." *Weekly Standard.* 17 May 2004, 31–33.

Entine, John, Gary Salles, and Jay T. Kearney. *Taboo: Why Black Athletes Dominate Sports and Why We're Afraid to Talk About It.* New York: Public Affairs, 2001.

Esposito, John L. "Islam in the World and in America." *World Religions in America: An Introduction,* ed. Jacob Neusner. Louisville, Ky.: Westminster/John Knox Press, 1994.

Farrand, Max. *The Framing of the Constitution of the United States.* New Haven: Yale University Press, 1913.

Ferguson, Niall. "Rich America, Poor America." *Newsweek,* 23 January 2012, 42–47.

Fetto, John. "Reader Request: Your Questions Answered: Not Only Are Americans Going to School in Record Numbers, They're Also Staying in School Longer." *American Demographics.* April 2003, 8–9.

Fineman, Howard, and Tamara Lipper. "Do We Still Need Affirmative Action? Affirmative Action: Race in the Spin Cycle." *Newsweek,* 27 January 2003, 26–29.

Fineman, Howard. "Bush and God: A Higher Calling: How Faith Changed His Life and Shapes His Presidency." *Newsweek,* 10 March 2003, 22–30.

Finely, Bill. "Women's Game Is Looking Good, and Fans Notice." *New York Times,* 20 July 2003, Sports section: 5.

Florida, Richard. *The Rise of the Creative Class: and how it's transforming work, leisure, community, & everyday life.* New York: Basic Books, 2003.

Ford, Michael F. "5 Myths about the American Dream." *The Washington Post,* 8 January 2012, B, 2.

Fox-Genovese, Elizabeth. "Religion and Women in America." *World Religions in America: An Introduction,* ed. Jacob Neusner. Louisville, Ky: Westminster/John Knox Press, 1994.

"Fractured Family Ties: Television's New Theme Is Single Parenting." *Newsweek,* 30 August 1993, 50–52.

Friedan, Betty. *The Feminine Mystique.* New York: W.W. Norton, 1963.

Friedan, Betty. *The Second Stage.* New York: Summit Books, 1981.

Galbraith, John Kenneth. *American Capitalism: The Concept of Countervailing Power.* Classics in Economics Series. Boston: Houghton Mifflin, 1956.

Galbraith, John Kenneth. *The Affluent Society.* Boston: Houghton Mifflin, 1976.

Galbraith, John Kenneth. *The Culture of Contentment.* Boston: Houghton Mifflin, 1992.

Garreau, Joel. *The Nine Nations of North America.* New York: Houghton Mifflin, 1981.

Gibbs, Nancy. "The Vicious Cycle." *Time,* 20 June 1994, 24–33.

Gill, Sam. "Native Americans and Their Religions." *World Religions in America: An Introduction,* ed. Jacob Neusner. Louisville, Ky.: Westminster/John Knox Press, 1994.

Gladwell, Malcolm. "Big and Bad: How the S.U.V. Ran Over Automotive Safety." *The New Yorker,* 12 January 2004, 28–33.

Glazer, Nathan, and Daniel P. Moynihan. *Beyond the Melting Pot: The Negroes, Puerto Ricans, Jews, Italians, and Irish of NYC.* Publications of the Joint Center for Urban Studies. Cambridge: M.I.T.

Press, 1963.

Glazer, Nathan. "Multiculturalism and Public Policy." *Values and Public Policy,* ed. Henry J. Aaron, Thomas E. Mann, and Timothy Taylor. Washington, D.C.: The Brookings Institution, 1994.

Goldsborough, James O. "The American Political Landscape in 2004." *San Diego Union,* 1 January 2004.

Gonzalez, David. "What's the Problem with 'Hispanic'? Just Ask a 'Latino.'" *New York Times,* 15 November 1992.

Gonzalez, Justo L. "The Religious World of Hispanic Americans." *World Religions in America: An Introduction,* ed. Jacob Neusner. Louisville, Ky.: Westminster/John Knox Press, 1994.

Graham, Ruth. "Religion returns to New England: Evangelists focusing on area that has become nation's most secular." *Daily News,* 30 November 2012, B, 1, 3.

Greeley, Andrew M. "Religion and Politics in America." *World Religions in America: An Introduction,* ed. Jacob Neusner. Louisville, Ky. Westminster/John Knox Press, 1994.

Greeley, Andrew M. "The Catholics in the World and in America." *World Religions in America: An Introduction,* ed. Jacob Neusner. Louisville, Ky.: Westminster/John Knox Press, 1994.

Green, William Scott. "Religion and Society in America." *World Religions in America: An Introduction,* ed. Jacob Neusner. Louisville, Ky.: Westminster/John Knox Press, 1994.

Grossman, Lev. "Drone Home: They Fight and Spy for American Abroad. But What Happens When Drones Return Home?" *Time,* 11 February 2013, 26–33.

Grossman, Lev. "The Beast with a Billion Eyes: In just seven years, YouTube has become the most rapidly growing force in human history. Where does it go from here?" *Time,* 30 January 2012, 38–43.

Grunwald, Michael. "Immigrant Son: Marco Rubio wants to sell the GOP on a path to citizenship for undocumented Americans. So why is his mom calling?" *Time,* 18 February 2013, 24–30.

Hamilton, Anita. "Your Time: Find It on Craig's List." *Time,* 3 March 2003, 76.

Handlin, Oscar. *Race and Nationality in American Life.* Boston: Little, Brown, 1957.

"Happily Unmarried: How-to from a Guidebook for Couples Living Together Without Saying 'I Do.'" *Time*, Bonus Section, March 2003, A10.

Harris Interactive. *The Harris Poll ® #30,* 21 May 2003. "Americans Are Far More Optimistic and Have Much Higher Life Satisfaction Than Europeans" by Humphrey Taylor.

Henderson, Neil. "Greenspan Calls for Better-Educated Workforce." *Washington Post,* 21 February 2004, Business E3: 1, 3.

Henry, W. A. "Pride and Prejudice." *Time,* 28 February 1994.

Hertsguard, Mark. "The Pasta Crisis: Temperatures are rising. Rainfalls are shifting. Droughts are intensifying. What will we eat when wheat won't grow?" *Newsweek,* 17 December 2012, 30–35.

Hinson, Hal. "Life, Liberty and the Pursuit of Cows: How the Western Defines America's View of Itself." *Washington Post,* 3 July 1994, 1(G), 6(G).

Hofstadter, Richard. *Social Darwinism in American Thought.* New York: G. Braziller, 1969.

Hofstadter, Richard. *The American Political Tradition and the Men Who Made It.* New York: Vintage Books, 1954.

Huffington, Ariana. *Third World America: How Our Politicians Are Abandoning the Middle Class and Betraying the American Dream.* New York: Broadway, 2011.

Huffington, Arianna. *Pigs at the Trough: How Corporate Greed and Political Corruption are Undermining America.* New York: Crowne Publishing Group, 2003.

"In Search of the Sacred." *Newsweek.* 28 November 1994, 52–55.

"Income Report: The Near-Affluent, the Affluent, the Upper Echelon: Generosity and Income." *American Demographics.* December 2002/January 2003, 40–47.

Issenberg, Sasha. "A More Perfect Union: How President Obama's Campaign Used Big Data to Rally Individual Voters." *MIT Technology Review.* January/February 2013.

Jones, Malcolm. "The New Turf Wars: A Plague of Critics Bushwhacks the Venerable American Lawn." *Newsweek,* 21 June 1993, 62–63.

Joyce, Amy. "Balancing Their Personal Goals: Younger Employees Value Family Time as Highly as

Career Advancement." *Washington Post,* 24 October 2004, F5.

Kanag, Cecilia. "Survey finds e-reader devices fuel book consumption overall." *The Washington Post,* 4 April 2012, A, 11.

Kantrowitz, Barbara, and Pat Wingert. "Education: What's at Stake." *Newsweek,* 27 January 2003, 30–38.

Kegley, Charles, and Eugene Wittkopf. *World Politics: Trend and Transformations,* 3d ed. New York: St. Martin's, 1989.

Kennedy, John F. *A Nation of Immigrants.* New York: Harper & Row, 1958.

Kenworthy, Lane. "5 Myths about the Middle Class." *The Washington Post,* 5 August 2012, B, 2.

Kids Who Care: Everybody Wins When Students Volunteer to Help Out." *Better Homes and Gardens,* March 1992, 37–39.

Killian, Linda. "5 Myths about independent voters." *The Washington Post,* 30 May 2012, B, 2.

King, Martin Luther, Jr. *I Have a Dream.* Littleton, Mass.: Sundance Publications, 1991.

Klein, Ezra. "A remarkable, historic period of change." *The Washington Post,* 13 November 2012, A, 2.

Klein, Ezra. "America in decline? Not likely." *The Washington Post,* 18 May 2012, A, 2.

Klein, Joe. "The Education of Berenice Belizaire." *Time*, 9 August 1993, 26.

Klein, Joe. "Whose Family? Whose Values? Who Makes the Choices?" *Newsweek,* 8 June 1992, 18–22.

Konigsberg, Ruth Davis. "Chore Wars: Men are now pulling their weight—at work and at home. So why do women still think they're slacking off?" *Time,* 8 August 2011, 45–49.

Korte, Gregory. "Immigrants shine on U.S. civics lessons: But survey finds native citizens need to study up." *USA Today,* 27 April 2012.

Kristol, Irving. "The Rise of the Neocons." *The Week,* 23 May 2003, 13.

Langley, Alison. "It's a Fat World, After All: U.S. Food Companies Face Scrutiny Abroad." *New York Times,* 20 July 2003, Money & Business: section 3: 1, 11.

Lasch, Christopher. *The Culture of Narcissism: American Life in an Age of Diminishing Expectations.* New York: W. W. Norton, 1978.

Leinberger, Christopher B. "Now Coveted: A Walkable, Convenient Place." *The New York Times,* 27 May 2012, Sunday Review, 6–7.

Lemann, Nicholas. "Best columns: The U.S.: Viewpoint." *The Week,* 1 June 2012, 12.

Leo, John. "On Society: Pushing the Bias Button." *U.S. News & World Report,* 9 June 2003, 37.

Levy, Steven, and Pat Wingert. "The Next Frontiers [Series]: Spielberg Nation: With Digital Camcorders, PCs and Easy-to-use Software, Anyone Can Become a Film Auteur." *Newsweek,* 25 November 2003, 56–58.

Lewin, Tamar. "One Course, 150,000 Students." *The New York Times,* 22 July 2-12, Education Life, 33.

Lipset, Seymour Martin. *American Exceptionalism: A Double-Edged Sword.* New York: W. W. Norton, 1996.

Lipset, Seymour Martin. Continental Divide: *The Values and Institutions of the United States and Canada.* New York: Routledge, 1990.

Lowi, Theodore, and Benjamin Ginsberg. A*merican Government: Freedom and Power.* New York: W. W. Norton, 1994.

Lowi, Theodore. *The End of Liberalism: Republic of the United States.* New York: W. W. Norton, 1969.

Lowry, Rich. "The time-wasting network: Facebook might be fun for some people, but there is more to life." *Daily News,* 19 May 2012, A, 4.

Luscombe, Belinda. "Confidence Woman: Facebook's Sheryl Sandberg in on a mission to change the balance of power. Why she just might pull it off." *Time,* 18 March 2013, 34–42.

Macbay, Harvey. *Swim with the Sharks Without Being Eaten Alive.* New York: William Morrow Company, 1988.

Madrigal, Alexis. "The Last Word: My digital shadow: Who's following my every move on the web, asks Alexis Madrigal, and what do they want from me?" *The Week,* 20 April 2012, 40–41.

Malcolm X." *Newsweek,* 16 November 1992, 66–71.

Malcom X and Alex Haley. *The Autobiography of Malcolm X.* New York: Grove Publishers, 1966.

Mansbridge, Jane. "Public Spirit in Political Systems." *Values and Public Policy,* ed. Henry J. Aaron, Thomas E. Mann, and Timothy Taylor. Washington, D.C.: The Brookings Institution, 1994.

Marklein, Mary Beth. "Higher Education: Tribal Colleges Bridge Culture Gap to Future." *USA Today,* 13 April 1998, 4D.

Markon, Jerry. "Virginia Colleges May Bar Illegal Immigrants: Judge's Ruling Is Said to Be U.S. First." *Washington Post,* 26 February 2004, B1.

Marty, Martin E. "Protestant Christianity in the World and in America." *World Religions in America: An Introduction,* ed. Jacob Neusner. Louisville, Ky.: Westminster/John Knox Press, 1994.

Marty, Martin E. "The Sin of Pride: Vision Thing: Why His 'God Talk' Worries Friends and Foes." *Newsweek,* 10 March 2003, 32–33.

Mason, Alpheus T. *In Quest of Freedom: American Political Thought and Practice.* Englewood Cliffs, N.J.: Prentice-Hall, 1959.

Mason, Alpheus T., and Gordon E. Baker, eds. *Free Government in the Making: Readings in American Political Thought.* New York: Oxford University Press, 1949.

Meacham, Jon. "The American Dream: A Biography: It has seen better days, but it's an idea that has shaped the nation's destiny from the beginning—and can point the way to the future." *Time,* 2 July 2012, 26–39.

Michaud, Anne. "City Population Hits 8.1 Million, Keeps Growing: Reasons: Immigrants, New Housing." *Crain's New York Business.* 29 March–4 April 2004, 1, 24.

Morello, Carol. "Caroline County's Loving Revolution: Interracial couple fought Va. Law and pioneered a new sense of identity." *The Washington Post*, 12 February 2012, C, 1, 10.

Morello, Carol. "Interracial marriage rates soar as attitudes change: Virginia has highest percentage of unions between blacks, whites." *The Washington Post,* 16 February 2012, B 1, 5.

Morganthau, Tom. "America: Still a Melting Pot?" *Newsweek,* 9 August 1993, 16–23.

Morin, Richard. "Misperceptions Cloud Whites' View of Blacks." *Washington Post,* 11 July 2001, A1.

Morin, Richard. "Unconventional Wisdom: New Facts and Hot Stats from the Social Sciences: Church Givers vs. Church Goers." *Washington Post,* 4 April 2004, Outlook section: B5.

Morrow, Lance. "Family Values." *Time,* 31 August 1992, 22–27.

Murray, Charles. *Coming Apart: The State of White America 1960–2010.* New York: Crown Forum, 2012.

"National Endowment Campaign Launched to Spearhead Native Language Revitalization." *Native Language Network, Newsletter of the Indigenous Language Institute.* Winter/Spring 2002.

Naughton, Keith and Marc Peyser. "The World According to Trump." *Newsweek,* 1 March 2004, 48–57.

Nelan, Bruce W. "Not So Welcome Anymore." *Time,* Special Issue, Fall 1993, 10–12.

"Networks Under the Gun." *Newsweek,* 12 July 1993, 14–15.

Neusner, Jacob, ed. "Introduction." *World Religions in America: An Introduction.* Louisville, Ky.: Westminster/John Knox Press, 1994.

Nevins, Allan, and Henry Steele Commager. *America: The Story of a Free People.* Boston: Little, Brown, 1942.

Nielsen, Michael. *Reinventing Discovery: The New Era of Networked Science.* Princeton: Princeton University Press, 2012.

Noonan, Peggy. "The Working Spirit: Why We Work So Hard." *O* [Oprah]. May/June 2000, 90.

O'Keefe, Ed. "House freshmen thrown right in." *The Washington Post,* 13 November 2012, A, 6.

O'Neill, Helen. "Young illegal immigrants 'coming out:' States vary wildly on how to treat children of families who are living in country illegally." *Daily News,* 20 May 2012, C, 10.

Obama, Barack. *Dreams from My Father: A Story of Race and Inheritance.* New York: Three Rivers Press, 1995.

Obama, Barack. *The Audacity of Hope: Thoughts on Reclaiming the American Dream.* New York: Crown Publishing Group, 2006.

Obama, Michelle. *American Grown: The Story of the White House Kitchen Garden and Gardens Across*

America. New York: Crown, 2012.

Page, Clarence. "GOP needs to listen: Voters spoke their minds before and after election; Republicans' minds were elsewhere." *Daily News,* 13 November 2012, A, 4.

Paris, Peter J. "The Religious World of African Americans." *World Religions in America: An Introduction.* ed. Jacob Neusner. Louisville, Ky.: Westminster/John Knox Press, 1994.

Park, Alice. "Health & Science: The Reason for Recess. Children who are more physically active may do better in school." *Time,* 16 January 2012.

"Partnership or Peril? Faith-Based Initiatives and the First Amendment" by Oliver Thomas, First Reports, vol. 2. no. 1, May 2001, A First Amendment Center Publication, First Amendment Center, Funded by the Freedom Forum (an affiliate of the Newseum).

Pearlstein, Steven. "Washington is broken, just as intended." *The Washington Post,* 22 April 2012, B, 1, 7.

Peterson, Karen S. "Stay Close By, for the Sake of the Kids: Children of Divorce Suffer When a Parent Moves Away, Study Says." *USA Today,* 7 July 2003, Health & Behavior section: 7D.

Peterson, Peter. *Facing Up: How to Rescue the Economy from Crushing Debt and Restore the American Dream.* New York: Simon & Schuster, 1993.

Pink, Daniel H. *A Whole New Mind: Moving from the Information Age to the Conceptual Age.* New York: Riverhead Books, 2005.

Poniewozik, James, "Has the Mainstream Run Dry? What Does Mass Culture Without the Masses Look Like?" *Time*, 29 December 2003–5 January 2004, 148–152.

Popenoe, David. "The Family Condition of America: Cultural Change and Public Policy." *Values and Public Policy,* ed. Henry J. Aaron, Thomas E. Mann, and Timothy Taylor. Washington, D.C.: The Brookings Institution, 1994.

Potter, David M. *People of Plenty: Economic Abundance and the American Character.* Chicago: University of Chicago Press, 1969.

"Profile of General Demographic Characteristics for the United States: 2000 Census."

Putnam, Robert D., and David E. Campbell, with the assistance of Shaylyn Romney Garrett. *American Grace: How Religion Divides and Unites Us.* New York: Simon and Schuster, 2010.

Quinn, Jane Bryant. "Retire Early? Think Again." *Newsweek,* 21 July 2003, 43.

Rainie, Lee. "In the Know Opinion: Seniors' Moment in a Digital World: Fully 60 percent of Internet user 65-plus now get news online." *AARP Bulletin,* November 2012, 36.

Ravitch, Diane. *The Death and Life of the Great American School System: How Testing and Choice Are Undermining Education.* New York: Basic Books, 2010.

Reeves, Richard. *American Journey: Travelling with Tocqueville in Search of Democracy in America.* New York: Simon & Schuster, 1982.

Reich, Charles A. T*he Greening of America.* New York: Random House, 1970.

Reich, Robert. *The Work of Nations: Preparing Ourselves for 21st-Century Capitalism.* New York: Alfred A. Knopf, 1991.

Relin, David Oliver. "More Than 13 million Children in America Are Struggling to Survive: Won't You Help Feed Them?" *Parade,* 4 April 2004, 7–9.

Riesman, David. *Individualism Reconsidered and Other Essays.* Glencoe, Ill.: The Free Press, 1954.

Riesman, David. *The Lonely Crowd: A Study on the Changing American Character.* New Haven: Yale University Press, 1950.

Roberts, David. "Points of Interest: Whose Rock Is It Anyway?" *Smithsonian.* March 2003, pp. 26, 29.

Roberts, Johnnie L. "Rethinking Black Leadership: The Race to the Top." *Newsweek,* 28 January 2002, 42–45.

Roberts, Sam. *Who We Are: A Portrait of America Based on the Latest U.S. Census.* New York: Times Books, 1993.

Robinson, Joe. "Ahh, Free at la-Oops! Time's Up." *Washington Post,* 27 July 2003, Outlook section: B1–3.

Robinson, Joe. *Work to Live: Reclaim Your Life, Health, Family, and Sanity.* New York: Perigee Trade, 2003.

Rosenberg, Debra. "Justice: 25 Years After Bakke: Not Just Black and White." *Newsweek.* 30 June 2003, 37.

Sabato, Larry J., ed. *Barack Obama and the New America: The 2012 Election and the Changing Face of Politics.* Lanham: Rowman & Littlefield Publishers, Inc., 2013.

Samuel, Terrence. "Born-Again Agenda: The Peak of Political Power." *U.S. News & World Report,* 23 December 2002, 42–43.

Samuelson, Robert J. "Divided by our love of country." *The Washington Post,* 4 July 2012, A, 21.

Samuelson, Robert J. "Globalization Goes to War." *Newsweek.* 24 February 2003, 41.

Samuelson, Robert J. "We're not 'Coming Apart,'" *The Washington Post,* 26 February 2012, A, 15.

Sandberg, Sheryl, with Nell Scovell. *Lean In: Women, Work, and the Will to Lead.* New York: Alfred A. Knopf, 2013.

"Saving Youth from Violence." *Carnegie Quarterly.* Winter 1994, 1–15.

Scanzoni, John. *Opportunity and the Family.* New York: The Free Press, 1970.

Scanzoni, John. *Sex Roles, Lifestyles, and Childbearing: Changing Patterns in Marriage and the Family.* New York: The Free Press, 1975.

Schickel, Richard. "Ladies Who Lunge." *Time,* 7 July 2003, 96.

Schlesinger, Arthur M., Jr. *The Disuniting of America: Reflections on a Multicultural Society.* New York: W.W. Norton, 1992.

"Sexism in the Schoolhouse: A Report Charges That Schools Favor Boys Over Girls." *Newsweek,* 24 February 1992, 62.

Shapiro, Gary, Foreword by Mark Cuban. *The Comeback: How Innovation Will Restore The American Dream.* New York: Beaufort Books, 2011.

Sheler, Jeffery L. "All in the Family: As Billy Graham Steps Down, Will His Kids Shape the Future of American Evangelicalism?" *U.S. News & World Report,* 23 December 2002, 36–43.

Sides, Hampton. "Connecting the Dots: Shattered Faith: What the fall of Greg Mortenson tells us about America's irrepressible longing for heroes." *Newsweek,* 2 May 2011, 5–6.

Siegel, Lee. "The Kids Aren't Alright: The perils of parenting in the digital age." *Newsweek,* 15 October 2012, 18–20.

Singer, Audrey "At Home in the Nation's Capital: Immigrant Trends in Metropolitan Washington." A report by the Brookings Institution Center on Urban and Metropolitan Policy, June 2003.

Smolan, Rick, and Jennifer Erwitt, eds., *The Human Face of Big Data.* Sausalito: Against All Odds Productions, 2012.

Solomon, Andrew. "Meet My Real Modern Family: As a gay man, the author never expected to have children. Now he and his husband have four between them." *Newsweek,* 7 February 2011, 32–37.

Sotomayor, Sonia. *My Beloved World.* New York: Alfred A. Knopf, 2013.

Span, Paula. "Marriage at First Sight." *The Washington Post* Magazine, 23 February 2003, 16–23, 32–38.

Squires, Sally. "Food Labels Must List Trans Fats: Starting in 2006, Rule Targets Risk Factor for Heart Disease." *The Washington Post,* 10 July 2003. A3.

Stampp, Kenneth. *The Peculiar Institution: Slavery in the Ante-bellum South.* New York: Vintage Books, 1956.

Stein, Joel. "Your Data, Yourself: Every detail of your life—what you buy, where you go, whom you love—is being extracted from the Internet, bundled and traded by data-mining companies. What's in it for you?" *Time,* 21 March 2011, 40–46.

Stiglitz, Joseph E. *The Price of Inequality: How Today's Divided Society Endangers Our Future.* New York: W. W. Norton & Company, 2013.

Summers, Lawrence. "Our inequality of opportunity." *The Washington Post,* 16 July 2012, A 15.

Suro, Roberto. "Study of Immigrants Finds Asians at Top in Science and Medicine." *The Washington Post,* 18 April 1994, 6(A).

"Survey of the attitudes of the American people on highway and auto safety: Wave five of a periodic tracking survey." Louis Harris and Pete Harris Research Group, Inc., June 2004.

Takaki, Ronald. *A Different Mirror: A History of Multicultural America.* Boston: Little, Brown, 1993.

"Talking Points: Evangelicals: The Hidden Mainstream." *The Week,* 21 March 2003, 16.

"Talking Points: Retro-sexism: The Return of the Real Man." *The Week,* 21 March 2003, 17.

"The Dawn of Online Home Schooling." *Newsweek,* 10 October 1994, 67.

"The Fight to Bear Arms." *U.S. News & World Report,* 22 May 1995, 28–37.

"The Grid: Mapping Consumer Markets: Sweat Equity: Where Today's Do-it-yourselfers Are Most Likely to Stake a Claim." *American Demographics,* April 2003, 18–19

"The Simple Life." *Time,* 8 April 1991, 58–63.

"The War for the West." *Newsweek,* 30 September 1991, 18–32.

Tocqueville, Alexis de. *Democracy in America.* New York: J. & H. G. Langley, 1845.

Toffler, Alvin. *Power Shift: Knowledge, Wealth, and Violence at the Edge of the 21st Century.* New York: Bantam Books, 1991.

Treuer, David. "Warren says she's Native American. So she is. American Indian author David Treuer says self-identity is thicker than blood." *The Washington Post,* 6 May 2012, B, 6.

"Trouble at the Top: A U.S. Survey Says a 'Glass Ceiling' Blocks Women from Corporate Heights." *U.S. News & World Report,* 17 June 1991, 40–48.

Tumulty, Karen. "Female candidates make history, head for the Hill." *The Washington Post,* 8 November 2012, A, 42.

Turkle, Sherry. "The Flight From Conversation: We think that our sips of online connection add up to a gulp. They don't." *The New York Times,* 22 April 2012, Sunday Review, 1, 8.

Turner, Frederick Jackson. *The Rise of the New West.* New York: Harper & Brothers, 1906.

Tyrangiel, Josh. "The Center of Attention" [Yao Ming]. *Time,* 10 February 2003, 68–71.

Tyre, Peg and Daniel McGinn. "She Works, He Doesn't." *Newsweek,* 12 May 2003, 44–53.

Tyre, Peg. "Getting Physical: A New Fitness Philosophy Puts Gym Teachers on the Front Lines in the Battle Against Childhood Obesity." *Newsweek,* 3 February 2003, 46–47.

U.S. Department of Education, National Center for Education Statistics, *The Condition of Education 2003,* NCES 2003–067, Washington, D.C.: U.S. Government Printing Office, 2003.

Vargas, Jose Antonio. "The Last Word: My undocumented life: I came here illegally at 12, says Jose Antonio Vargas, but I've earned the right to be called an American." *The Week,* 19–26 August 2011, 44–45.

Von Drehle, David. "America in Red and Blue: A Nation Divided [Series]: Political Split Is Pervasive: Clash of Cultures Is Driven by Targeted Appeals and Reinforced Geography." *Washington Post,* A1, 10.

Waldman, Steven. "Benefits 'R' Us." *Newsweek,* 10 August 1992, 56–58.

Wallerstein, Judith. *The Unexpected Legacy of Divorce: A 25 Year Landmark Study.* New York: Hyperion, 2000.

"Washington Area School Superintendents Demand Changes in Testing Regulations Affecting LEP and Special Education Students." 2 February 2004, a press release by the Washington Area School Study Council.

Waters, Harry F. "On the Trail of Tears: Ted Turner's Massive, Compelling Chronicle of the Native American Order." *Newsweek*, 10 October 1994, 56–58.

Wattenberg, Ben J. *The First Universal Nation: Leading Indicators and Ideas about the Surge of America in the 1990s.* New York: The Free Press, 1991.

Wattenberg, Ben J. *The Good News Is the Bad News Is Wrong.* New York: Simon & Schuster, 1984.

Wattenberg, Ben J. *The Real America: A Surprising Examination of the State of the Union.* New York: Doubleday, 1974.

Wattenberg, Ben J. *Values Matter Most: How Republicans or Democrats or a Third Party Can Win and Renew the American Way of Life.* New York: The Free Press, 1995.

Weil, Andrew. "Don't Let Chaos get You Down: You aren't depressed; our brains just aren't equipped for

21st-century life." *Newsweek,* 7 & 14 November 2011, 9.

Weiss, Michael. *Latitudes & Attitudes: An Atlas of Tastes, Trends, Politics and Passions.* Boston: Little, Brown, 1994.

Whelan, David. "In a Fog about Blogs." *American Demographics,* July/August 2003, Media Channels: 22–23.

"When America Went to the Moon." *U.S. News & World Report,* 11 July 1994, 50–60.

White, John Kenneth. *The Values Divide: American Politics and Culture in Transition,* with forward by John Zogby. New York: Chatham House Publishers of Seven Bridges Press, LLC, 2003.

Will, George. "Land of entitlements: What once was a small portion of the U.S. budget now dominant spending category." *Daily News,* 28 October 2012, C, 2.

Wilson, James Q. "Culture, Incentives, and the Underclass." *Values and Public Policy,* ed. Henry J. Aaron, Thomas E. Mann, and Timothy Taylor. Washington, D.C.: The Brookings Institution, 1994.

Woodward, Kenneth L. "Gospel on the Potomac." *Newsweek,* 10 March 2003, 29.

Woodward, Kenneth. "Angels: Hark! America's Latest Search for Spiritual Meaning Has a Halo Effect." *Newsweek,* 27 December 1993, 52–57.

Woodward, Kenneth. "Dead End for the Mainline: The Mightiest Protestants Are Running Out of Money, Members and Meaning." *Newsweek,* 9 August 1993, 46–48.

Yankelovich, Daniel. "How Changes in the Economy Are Reshaping American Values." *Values and Public Policy,* ed. Henry J. Aaron, Thomas E. Mann, and Timothy Taylor. Washington, D.C.: The Brookings Institution, 1994.

Yankelovich, Daniel. *New Rules: Searching for Self-Fulfillment in a World Turned Upside Down.* New York: Random House, 1981.

Yen, Hope. "Census shows 1 in 3 U.S. counties are dying." *Daily News,* 17 March 2013, C, 9.

Zakaria, Fareed. "Bush, Rice and the 9-11 Shift." *Newsweek*, 16 December 2002, 35.

Zakaria, Fareed. "The Arrogant Empire: Part Three: America's Global Reach: Where Bush Went Wrong." *Newsweek,* 23 June 2004, 18–33.

Zoll, Rachel. "U.S. Protestants lose majority status, study finds: While the category of no religious affiliation as defined by Pew researchers includes atheists, it also encompasses majorities of people who say they believe in God, and a notable minority who pray daily or consider themselves 'spiritual' but not 'religious.'" *Daily News,* 12 October 2012, B, 1.

Zuckerman, Mortimer B. "A Truly Cruel College Squeeze." *U.S. News & World Report,* 8 March 2004, 80.

Zuckerman, Mortimer B. "America's High Anxiety." *U.S. News & World Report,* 15 March 2004, 83–84.

WEB SOURCES

"A history of mass shootings in the US since Columbine." *Telegraph Media Group Limited,* 24 August 2012. Telegraph website.

"A Third of Americans Now Say They are in the Lower Classes." *Pew Research Center: Pew Social & Demographic Trends,* 10 September 2012. Pew Social Trends website.

Alcorn, Shelly, and Mark Alcorn. "Benefit Corporations: A New Formula for Social Change." *ASAE [American Society of Association Executives] The Center for Association Leadership: Associations Now,* June 2012. ASAE Center website.

Alphonse, Lylah M. "Michelle Obama's White Heritage: New Book Explores Her Roots, Race." *Shine from Yahoo!* 18 June 2012. Shine Yahoo! website.

"American Schools Still Heavily Segregated By Race, Income: Civil Rights Project Report. *HuffPost Education,* 20 September 2012. Huffington Post website.

"American Time Use Survey." *Bureau of Labor Statistics,* 22 June 2012. Bureau of Labor Statistics website.

"Americans See Inequality as a Major Problem: Division as to who would be best to address it—Republicans or President Obama?" *Harris Interactive: The Harris Poll,* 5 April 2012. Harris Interactive website.

"Annual State of the American Dream Survey." *Center for the Study of the American Dream,* March 2011. Xavier University website.

Armarlo, Christine. "Average cost of four-year university up 15%." *USA Today: Money,* 13 June 2012. USA Today website.

Assessment, "The Globalization of Crime: A Transitional Crime Threat Assessment," Chapter 6 Firearms. *United Nations Office of Drugs and Crime,* 2010. UNODC (United Nations Office of Drugs and Crime) website.

"Back to school statistics: Fast Facts." *Institute of Education Sciences, National Center for Education Statistics.* National Center for Education Statistics website.

Begley, Sharon. "Fat and getting fatter: U.S. obesity rates to soar by 2030." *Reuters,* 18 September 2012. Reuters website.

Bennett, William J. "It's good news that government is stalled." *CNN.com,* 27 September 2012. CNN.com website.

Borger, Gloria. "America's love/hate affair with government." *CNN Opinion,* 29 September 2012. CNN.com website.

Brenner, Joanna. "Commentary: Social Networking." *Pew Internet: Social Networking*, 14 February 2013. Pew Internet website.

Brenner, Joanna. "Pew Internet: Mobile" *Pew Research Center: Pew Internet & American Life Project,* 31 January 2013. Pew Internet website.

Briggs, David. "Diversity Rising: Census Shows Mormons, Nondenominational Churches, Muslims Spreading Out Across U.S." *ARDA Blog,* 1 May 2012. ARDA website.

Burzynski, Andrea. "Hungry Americans get 'A Place at the Table' in new documentary." *Reuters,* 1 March 2013. Reuters website.

Castagnoli, Francesca. "The Giving Workout: Teach Your Kid the Value of Volunteering." *Parents,* November 2012. Parents website.

Chittum, Ryan. "Billionaires made from scratch? Hardly: Forbes spins a bogus Horatio Alger story about its 400 richest list." *Columbia Journalism Review,* 28 September 2012. Columbia journalism Review website.

"Civilian Firearms Ownership." United Nations Organized Crime Threat Assessment, "The Globalization of Crime: A Transitional Crime Threat Assessment," Chapter 6 Firearms. *United Nations Office of Drugs and Crime,* 2010. UNODC (United Nations Office of Drugs and Crime) website.

Cline, Seth. "Are Mass Shootings a Fact of Life in America?" *U.S. News & World Report,* 28 August 2012. U.S. News & World Report website.

CNN Political Unit. "Gun control opinions following shootings." *Political Ticker,* 8 September 2012. Political Ticker Blog CNN website.

Cohen, Aaron M. "The Emergence of a Global Generation: A review of *The Way We'll Be* by John Zogby. *The Futurist: The World Future Society,* January-February 2009. World Future Society website.

Cohn, D'Vera and Rich Morin. "Who Moves? Who Stays Put? Where's Home?" *Pew Research Social & Demographic Trends,* 29 December 2008. Pew social Trends website.

Cohn, D'Vera. "Second-Generation Americans, by the Numbers. *Pew Research Social & Demographic Trends*, 7 February 2013.

Confessore, Nicholas. "Tramps Like Them: Coming Apart: The State of White America, 1960–2012 by Charles Murray." *The New York Times,* 10 February 2012. The New York Times website.

"Daily Chart: Accounting for Time." *The Economist Online,* 25 June 2012. Economist website.

Davis, Jessica. "School Enrollment and Work Status: 2011." *American Community Survey Briefs: United States Census Bureau,* October 2012. U.S. Census Bureau website.

"Declining childhood obesity rates—where are we seeing the most progress?" *Robert Wood Johnson Foundation Health Policy Snapshot: Childhood Obesity Issue Brief,* 1 September 2012. Robert Wood Johnson Foundation website.

Emery, Noemie. "America in the Middle: Michael Barone seeks a balance: *Hard America/Soft America: Competition vs. Coddling.*" *The Weekly Standard*, 17 May 2004, The Weekly Standard website.

"Enrollment: Fast Facts." *Institute of Education Sciences, National Center for Education Statistics.* National Center for Education Statistics website.

"Environment." *Gallup Polls*, 2011–2012. Gallup website.

"Exercise Statistics." *Statistic Brain,* 7 March 2012. Statistic Brain website.

Florida, Richard. "Where to Find a Creative Class Job in 2020." *The Atlantic Cities,* 2 March 2012. The Atlantic Cities website.

"Focus on Prices and Spending: Consumer Expenditures: 2008." *U.S. Bureau of Labor Statistics: Office of Publications & Special Studies,* May 2010. U.S Bureau of Labor Statistics website.

Follman, Mark, Gavin Aronsen, and Deanna Pan. "A Guide to Mass Shootings in America." *Mother Jones,* 20 July 2012. Mother Jones website.

Ford, Michael. "Civic Illiteracy: A Threat to the American Dream." *Huff Post Politics,* 15 May 2012. Huffington Post website.

Francis, David. "Decline of the Middle Class: Behind the Numbers: An Inside Look at the Middle-Class Squeeze: From retirement to health how the struggle plays out in everyday life." *US News Money,* 16 October 2012. Money US News website.

"Frequently Asked Questions." *SBA [Small Business Administration] Office of Advocacy,* January 2011. SBA Office of Advocacy website.

Gabriel, Trip. "Despite Push, Success at Charter Schools Is Mixed." *The New York Times,* 1 May 2010. The New York Times website.

"Gallup Daily: U.S. Life Evaluation: Based on the Gallup-Healthways Well-Being Index." *Gallup Daily Poll,* February 2013. Gallup website.

Gelman, Andrew. "Charles Murray's *Coming Apart* and the measurement of social and political divisions." Written for *Statistics, Politics and Policy* Columbia University Journal, 20 September 2012. Columbia University website.

Gergen, David and Michael Zuckerman. "Is America becoming a house divided against itself?" *CNN Opinion,* 28 September 2011. CNN website.

"Higher Achievements: U.S. High School and College completion Rates Continue to Climb." *Pew Research Social & Demographic Trends,* 5 November 2012. Pew Social Trends website.

"Households and Families: 2010." *U.S. Census Bureau: 2010 Census Briefs,* April 2012. U.S. Census website.

Huffington, Arianna and Mary Matlin. "Author One-to-One." Editorial Reviews *Amazon.com Review.* Amazon.com website, 2011.

Huffington, Arianna. "Real Misery Index: highest level ever in April 2010." Quotation from *Third World*

America, p. 55, 2 September 2010. On The Issues website.

"If you had to choose, which of these groups are you in: the haves or the have-nots?" *Pew Research Center/Washington Post Poll,* 22–25 September 2011. Polling Report website.

"In Gun Control Debate, Several Options Draw Majority Support: Gun Rights Proponents More Politically Active." *Pew Research Center for the People & the Press,* 14 January 2013. People-press website.

"Is College Worth It?" *Pew Research Social & Demographic Trends,* 15 May 2011. Pew Social Trends website.

Jackson, Brooks. "Fiscal FactCheck: Does Washington have a spending problem or an income problem? We offer some key facts." *Fact Check,* 15 July 2011. Fact Check website.

Jamrisko, Michelle and Ilan Kolet. "Cost of College Degree in U.S. Soars 12 Fold: Chart of the Day." *Bloomberg,* 15 August 2012. Bloomberg website.

"John Lewis Georgia Congressman." *Time,* 15 January 2009. Time website.

Jones, Jeffrey M. "Nurses Top Honesty and Ethics List for 11th Year: Lobbyists, car salespeople, members of Congress get the lowest ratings." *Gallup Poll,* 3 December 2010. Gallup website.

Kadlec, Dan. "Social Security Now Takes More Than It Gives." *Times: Business and Money,* 7 August 2012. Time Business website.

Kaplan, Karen. "Knot Yet: Getting married later can have economic costs, benefits." *Los Angeles Times,* 15 March 2013. LA Times website.

Klein, Ezra. "Transcript: President Obama 2013 inaugural address." *The Washington Post,* 21 January 2013. Washington Post website.

"Knot Yet: The Benefits and Costs of Delayed Marriage in America." *The National Marriage Project: The University of Virginia,* March 2013. National Marriage Project website.

Kolata, Gina. "Well: Updating the Message to Get Americans Moving." *Personal Best blog The New York Times,* 19 November 2012. The New York Times website.

"Life." *PollingReport.com,* December 2012. PolingReport.com website.

Lindsay, Jay. "Religion And Giving: More Religious States Give More To Charity." *Huffpost,* 20 August 2012. Huffington Post website.

Livingston, Gretchen and D'Vera Cohn. "U.S. Birthrate Falls to a Record Low; Decline Is Greatest Among Immigrants." *Pew Research Social & Demographic Trends,* 29 November 2012. Pew Social Trends website.

Lopez, Mark Hugo. "Latinos and Education: Explaining the Attainment Gap." *Pew Research Center Publications,* 7 October 2009. Pew Research website.

Lowenstein, Roger. "Book Review: *Coming Apart* by Charles Murray. *Bloomberg Businessweek Magazine,* 19 January 2012. Business Week website.

Lynch, Matthew. "It's Tough to Trailblaze: Challenges of First-Generation College Students." *Diverse Education,* 23 January 2013. Diverse Education website.

"Majority of Americans See Connection Between Video Games and Violent Behavior in Teens: Harris Poll Finds One-Third of Those with Young Game Players Do Not Censor Games: Majority of U.S. Adults Admit to Understanding Little or Nothing About Video Game Rating System." *The Harris Poll,* 27 February 2013. Harris Interactive website.

May, Gary S. "Essay on what MOOCs are missing to truly transform higher education." *Inside Higher Education,* 11 September 2012. Inside Higher Ed website.

McColl, Lindsey. "Are Ads Really Following You Online?" *Lindsey McColl Blog,* 21 November 2012. Lindsey McColl website.

"Middle Class America: 5 Sad Charts About The Country's Favorite Demographic." *HuffPost Business,* 1 September 2012. The Huffington Post website.

Morales, Lymari. "U.S. Payroll to Population Rates Higher Among College Grads: Less educated Americans least likely to be employed full time for an employer." *Gallup Poll,* 18 September 2012. Gallup website.

Morello, Carol. "Study: Delaying marriage hurts middle-class most." *The Washington Post,* 15 March

2012. Washington Post website.

Morello, Carol. Census: Middle class shrinks to an all-time low." *The Washington Post Business,* 12 September 2012. Washington Post website.

Morin, Rich, Paul Taylor and Eileen Patten. "A Bipartisan Nation of Beneficiaries." *Pew Research Social & Demographic Trends,* 18 December 2012. Pew Social Trends website.

Morin, Rich. "The Public Renders a Split Verdict On Changes in Family Structure." *Pew Research Social & Demographic Trends,* 16 February 2011. Pew Social Trends website.

"Mother's Day: May 13, 2012." *Profile America Facts for Features: U.S. Census Bureau News,* 19 March 2012. U.S. Census website.

Msnbc.com staff. "Asians are fastest-growing race group in US, Census Bureau says." *US News: NBC News,* 21 March 2012. US News NBC News website.

"Municipal Solid Waste." *United States Environmental Protection Agency,* 15 November 2012. EPA website.

Nasser, Haya El. "Study: Some immigrants assimilate faster." *USA Today,* 13 May 2008.

Navarrette, Ruben Jr. "Are baby boomers to blame for broken government?" CNN Opinion, 29 September 2012. CNN.com website.

"New Immigrants Made Asians Fastest-Growing U.S. Group." *Los Angeles Times,* 19 June 2012. LA Times website.

"New TechNet Survey: Americans Support High-Skilled Immigration Reform." *TechNet,* 14 March 2013. *TechNet* website.

Newport, Frank. "Americans: Economy Takes Precedence Over Environment: First time majority has supported economy in 25 years of asking question." *Gallup Poll,* 19 March 2009. Gallup website.

Newport, Frank. "Mississippi Is Most Religious U.S. State: Vermont and New Hampshire are the least religious states." *Gallup Poll,* 27 March 2012. Gallup Poll website.

Newport, Frank. "Seven in 10 Americans Are Very or Moderately Religious: But Protestant population is shrinking as 'unbranded' religion grows." *Gallup Poll,* 4 December 2012. Gallup Poll website.

Nittle, Nadra Kareem. "Barack Obama's Irish Heritage." *Race Relations About.com,* 28 June 2012. Race Relations About.com website.

"'Nones' on the Rise: One-in-Five Adults Have No Religious Affiliation." *Pew Research Center: The Pew Forum on Religion & Public Life,* 9 October 2012. Pew Forum website.

"Overweight and Obesity: Adult Obesity Facts." *Centers for Disease Control and Prevention,* 13 August 2012. Centers for Disease Control website.

Parker, Kim and Eileen Patten. "The Sandwich Generation: Rising financial Burdens for Middle-Aged Americans." *Pew Research Social & Demographic Trends,* 30 January 2013. Pew Social Trends website.

Parker, Kim and Wendy Wang. "Modern Parenthood: Roles of Moms and Dads Converge as They Balance Work and Family." *Pew Research Social & Demographic Trends,* 14 March 2013. Pew Social Trends website.

Parker, Kim. "The Boomerang Generation: Feeling OK about Living with Mon and Dad." *Pew Research Social & Demographic Trends,* 15 March 2012. Pew Social Trends website.

Plumer, Brad. "Who receives government benefits, in six charts." *The Washington Post,* 18 September 2012. Washington Post website.

"Policy Basics: Top Ten Facts About Social Security." *Center on Budget and Policy Priorities,* 6 November 2012. Center on Budget and Policy Priorities website.

Preston, Jennifer. "Views on Gun Laws Unchanged After Colorado Shooting, Poll Finds." *The New York Times: The Lede, Blogging the News With Robert Mackey,* 30 July 2012. The New York Times website.

Ravitch, Diane. "We Must Out-Educate and Out-Innovate Other Nations." *Bill Moyers Group Think,* 8 February 2013. Bill Moyers website.

Rector, Robert. "Marriage: America's Greatest Weapon Against Child Poverty." *The Heritage Foundation,* 2 September 2012. Heritage Foundation website.

Rich, Motoko. "Segregation Prominent in Schools, Study Finds." *The New York Times,* 19 September

2012. The New York Times website.

Richmond, Emily. "Schools Are More Segregated Today Than During the Late 1960s." *The Atlantic,* 11 June 2012. The Atlantic website.

Roof, Wade Clark. "Religious Kaleidoscope: American Religion in the 1990s." *Temenos* 32, 1996, 183–193. Temenos website.

"School Finance: Federal, State, and Local K–12 School Finance Overview." *New America Foundation: Federal Education Budget Project,* 13 December 2012. New America Foundation website.

Schuessler, Jennifer. "A Lightning Rod in the Storm Over America's Class Divide." *The New York Times,* 5 February 2012. The New York Times website.

Skerry, Peter. "Do We Really Want Immigrants to Assimilate?" *Brookings: Society Article,* March/April 2000. Brookings website.

Smith, Mark S. "Obama Census Choice: African-American." *HuffPost,* 28 June 2012. Huffington Post website.

"Social Security Basic Facts." *Social Security Administration,* 7 February 2013. Social Security Administration website.

"STAND Lesson 1: Understanding your exposure to advertising." *University of Rhode Island, Harrington School of Communication and Media,* n.d. Media Education Lab website.

Story, Louise. "Anywhere the Eye Can See, It's Likely to See an Ad." *The New York Times,* 15 January 2007. The New York Times website.

Strauss, Valerie. "Report Reveals Trend of Segregation in Charter Schools." *CBS Local Detroit,* 10 March 2012. CBS Local website.

Strauss, Valerie. "Whose children have been left behind? Framing the 2012 ed debate." *Washington Post blog The Answer Sheet,* 3 January 2012. Washington Post website.

"Super PAC spending election 2012." *Los Angeles Times Data Desk.* LA Times website, 20 November 2012.

Taylor, Paul and D'Vera Cohn. "A Milestone En Route to a Majority Minority Nation." *Pew Research Social & Demographic Trends,* 7 November 2012. Pew Social Trends website.

Taylor, Paul. "The Growing Electoral Clout of Blacks Is Driven by Turnout, Not Demographics." *Pew Research Social & Demographic Trends,* 26 December 2012. Pew Social Trends website.

"The 2011 Metlife Study of the American Dream: The Do-It-Yourself Dream." *Metlife,* 29 November 2011. Metlife website.

"The American-Western European Values Gap: American Exceptionalism Subsides." *Pew Research Center: Pew Global Attitudes Project,* 29 February 2012. Pew Research Center website.

"The changing face of religious America: Census reveals how number of Muslims in U.S. has DOUBLED since 9/11—while Mormonism has spread to East Coast." *Mail Online,* 2 May 2012. Daily Mail website.

"The Foreign-Born Population in the United States: 2010." *American Community Service Reports,* May 2012. United States Census Bureau website.

"The Rise of Asian Americans." *Pew Research Center: Pew Social & Demographic Trends,* 19 June 2012. Pew Social Trends website.

"The Top 10 Outdoor Activities Based on Money Spent." *Adventure Lab: Outside Online,* 27 June 2012. Outside Online website.

Thompson, Derek. "Your Day in a Chart: 10 Cool Facts About How Americans Spend Our Time." *The Atlantic,* 25 June 2012. The Atlantic website.

Thompson, Krissah. "Michelle Obama to visit three states on 'Let's Move' tour, highlight successes." *The Washington Post,* 26 February 2013. Washington Post website.

"U.S. Religious Landscape Survey: Report 1 Religious Affiliation." *Pew Forum on Religion & Public Life,* 2007. Pew Forum website.

"U.S. Religious Landscape Survey: Report 2 Religious Beliefs & Practices/Social & Political." *Pew Forum on Religion & Public Life,* 2007. Pew Forum website.

"U.S. Travel Answer Sheet: Facts about a Leading American Industry That's More Than Just Fun." *U.S.*

Travel Association, January 2013. U.S. Travel website.

"Values." *PollingReport.com,* February 2012. PollingReport.com website.

"Views of Gun Control—A Detailed Demographic Breakdown." *Pew Research Center Publications,* 13 January 2011. Pew Research website.

Wang, Wendy. "The Rise of Intermarriage: Rates, Characteristics Vary by Race and Gender." *Pew Research Social & Demographic Trends,* 16 February 2012. Pew Social Trends website.

Washington, Jesse. "Obama's mixed background raises question of racial categories." *Columbia Missourian,* 13 December 2008. Columbia Missourian website.

Wesley, John. "John Wesley Quotes." *Good Reads.* Good Reads website.

"When Labels Don't Fit: Hispanics and Their Views of Identity." *Pew Research Publications,* 4 April 2012. Pew Research website.

Wike, Richard. "Anti-Americanism Down in Europe, but a Values Gap Persists." *Pew Research Global Attitudes Project,* 4 December 2012. Pew Global website.

Wilbert, Caroline, Reviewed by Louise Chang. "Are Americans Backing Off Exercise? Percentage of Americans Getting Regular Exercise Declines, Survey Finds." *WebMD,* 21 January 2010. WebMD website.

Wilcox, Bradford. "Values Inequality: 'Coming Apart' argues that a large swath of America—poor and working-class whites—is turning away from traditional values and losing ground." *Bookshelf: The Wall Street Journal,* 31 January 2012.

"Youth Sports Statistics." *Statistic Brain*, 26 January 2012. Statistic Brain website.

Zickuhr, Kathryn, and Aaron Smith. "Digital Differences: While increased internet adoption and the rise of mobile connectivity have reduced many gaps in technology access over the past decade, for some groups digital disparities still remain." *Pew Research Center's Internet & American Life Project,* 13 April 2012. Pew Internet website.

Zogby, John. "Drones and Dreams." *Forbes,* 10 February 2013. Forbes website.

Zogby, John. "It's Not Only the Economy, Stupid." *The National Interest,* 17 September 2012. The National Interest website.

Zogby, John. "Zogby: The Values Divide, 2012." *Forbes,* 7 September 2012. Forbes website.

CREDITS

PHOTOS

Page 1 Fuse/Thinkstock; p. 9 White House Photo/Alamy; p. 10 Reuters/Landov; p. 20 Jeff Greenberg/Alamy; p. 21 Goodshoot/Thinkstock; p. 27 DIZ Muenchen GmbH, Sueddeutsche Zeitung Photo/Alamy; p. 33 akg-images/Newscom; p. 35 Fuse/Thinkstock; p. 37 Barbara Helgason/Fotolia; p. 45 Lisa Sciascia/fStop/Getty Images; p. 51 (right) maksymowicz/Fotolia, (top left) ZUMA Press, Inc./Alamy, (middle left) GLOBAL LENS/Alamy, (bottom left) Jim Parkin/Fotolia; p. 55 James Steidl/Fotolia; p. 58 Jim West/Alamy; p. 59 RON ENNIS KRT/Newscom; p. 60 AP Images/CHARLES KRUPA; p. 61 Michael Ventura/Alamy; p. 77 imagebroker/Alamy; p. 81 AP Images; p. 85 TopFoto/The Image Works; p. 94 Silvy K./Fotolia; p. 97 James Southers/Alamy; p. 99 David R. Frazier Photolibrary, Inc./Alamy; p. 104 Yaacov Dagan/Alamy; p. 105 Ariel Skelley/Corbis; p. 107 Tom Merton/OJO Images/Getty Images; p. 117 Ronnie Kaufman/Larry Hirshowitz/Blend Images/Getty Images; p. 123 Andres Rodriguez/Fotolia; p. 128 Kevin Burke/Corbis; p. 130 Lebrecht Music and Arts Photo Library/Alamy; p. 132 AP Images/DAVID KARP; p. 149 Blend Images/Alamy; p. 153 GL Archive/Alamy; p. 160 William Thomas Cain/Getty Images; p. 177 The Washington Post/Getty Images; p. 179 The Protected Art Archive/Alamy; p. 182 The Protected Art Archive/Alamy; p. 184 Robert Abbott Sengstacke/Getty Images; p. 197 Jim West/Alamy; p. 201 Armadillo Stock/Shutterstock; p. 204 auremar/Fotolia; p. 206 col/

Shutterstock; p. 212 Time & Life Pictures/Getty Image; p. 229 PCN Photography/Alamy; p. 233 Nicholas Piccillo/Fotolia; p. 236 Peter Bernik/Shutterstock;

p. 237 Momentum/Fotolia; p. 239 BlueTulip/Alamy; p. 240 White House Photo/Alamy; p. 252 Julie Lemberger/Corbis; p. 255 CreaJHogan/Shutterstock; p. 258 Providgodfer/Fotolia; p. 261 Ethel Wolvovitz/Alamy; p. 265 Perry Gerenday/Getty Images; p. 266 Hill Street Studios/Blend Images/Getty Images; p. 276 Monkey Business Images/Shutterstock; p. 278 Bobby Earle/Fotolia; p. 281 White House Photo/Alamy; p. 286 Junial Enterprises/Fotolia; p. 287 Highsmith, Carol M/Library of Congress Prints and Photographs Division [LC-HS503-1651]; p. 290 WavebreakMediaMicro/Fotolia; p. 303 AP Images/ASSOCIATED PRESS.

ILLUSTRATIONS

Page 49, "The United States in A.D. 2000," *The Youth's Companion*, June 13, 1907; page 241 ©The New Yorker Collection 1993, Peter Steiner, from cartoonbank.com; all rights reserved.

TEXT

Page 15: Chart: Which Term Do You Use To Describe Yourself Most Often? © 2012 Pew Research Center. "When Labels Don't Fit: Hispanics and Their Views of Identity." http://www.pewhispanic.org/2012/04/04/when-labels-dont-fit-hispanics-and-their-views-of-identity. Reprinted by permission.; Page 31: Map: New World Colonies in 1750, © The McGraw-Hill Companies, Inc. Used by permission.; Page 47: Chart: Causes of Inequality: Based on Harris Poll, April 5, 2012.; Page 54: Chart: Religious Preferences in the United States. Reprinted from the Pew Research Center, "'Nones' on the Rise," © 2012, Pew Research Center. http://www.pewforum.org/unaffiliated/nones-on-the-rise.aspx; Page 67: Chart: Unaffiliated, But Not Uniformly Secular. Reprinted from the Pew Research Center, "'Nones' on the Rise," © 2012, Pew Research Center. http://www.pewforum.org/unaffiliated/nones-on-the-rise.aspx; Page 68: Chart: Religious Profile. Reprinted from the Pew Research Center, "'Nones' on the Rise," © 2012, Pew Research Center. http://www.pewforum.org/unaffiliated/nones-on-the-rise.aspx; Page 74: Map: Religiosity, 2011. t © 2011, Gallup Inc. All rights reserved. The content is used with permission; however, Gallup retains all rights of republication; Reprinted from the Pew Research Center, "'U.S. Religious Landscape Survey," © 2008, Pew Research Center. http://religions.pewforum.org/maps.; Page 75: Map: Majority Religion, by Country. Pew Research Center, "The Global Religious Landscape," © 2012, http://www.pewforum.org/global-religious-landscape-exec.aspx. Reprinted by permission.; Page 84: Chart: "Broad Public Support for Many Gun Policy Proposals," January 14, 2013. The Pew Research Center for the People & the Press, a project of the Pew Research Center.; Page 95: Map and Charts: Civilian Firearms Ownership. "The Globalization of Crime: A Transnational Crime Threat Assessment," published by the UN Office of Drugs and Crime in 2010. Reprinted by permission.; Page 118: Graph:"Public Continues to Support Broad Range of Energy Policies," March 19, 2012, The Pew Research Center for the People & the Press, a project of the Pew Research Center. http://www.people-press.org/2012/03/19/as-gas-prices-pinch-support-for-oil-and-gas-production-grows. Reprinted by permission.; Page 126: Graph: "Government regulation of business does more harm than good." From "Partisan Polarization Surges in Bush, Obama Years: Trends in American Values: 1987–2012,"June 4, 2012. The Pew Research Center for the People & the Press, a project of the Pew Research Center. http://www.people-press.org/values-questions/q30i/government-regulation-of-business-does-more-harm-than-good/#total.; Page 160: Chart: Gun Rights Proponents More Politically Active," January 14, 2013.The Pew Research Center for the People & the Press, a project of the Pew Research Center.; Page 163: Map: Percentage of Each State's Population That Affiliates with Evangelical Protestant Tradition. Reprinted from the Pew Research Center, "U.S. Religious Landscape Survey," © 2008, Pew Research Center, http://religions.pewforum.org/maps; Page 169: Chart: «Total Number of Benefits Received by Selected Demographic Groups.» Pew Research, Washington D.C. http://www.pewsocialtrends.org/files/2012/12/Benefits_FINAL_12-20.pdf.; Page 173: Graph: "Honesty/Ethics in Professions." http://www.gallup.com/poll/1654/honesty-ethics-professions.aspx. ©2013, Gallup, Inc. All rights reserved. The content is used with permission; however, Gallup retains all rights of republication.; Page 186: Graph: "Immigrant Gains in Income and Education from 1st to 2nd Generation."Data from "Second Generation Americans," Pew Research, Washington D.C. (February 7, 2013). http://www.pewsocialtrends.org/2013/02/07/second-generation-americans.; Pages 208–209: Chart and Graph of tuition rate changes at private and public 4-year colleges. Data are from Trends in College Pricing, 2012. © 2012. The College Board. www.collegeboard.org. Reproduced with permission.; Page 223: "Mean Earnings by Age 2009." From "Is College Worth It?" Pew Research Center, Washington D.C. (May 15, 2011).http://www.pewsocialtrends.org/2011/05/15/is-college-worth-it/6/#chapter-5-the-monetary-value-of-a-college-education?src=prc-number.; Page 241: Cartoon: Peter Steiner, "On the Internet, nobody knows you're a dog." PeterSteiner/The New Yorker Collection/www.cartoonbank.com.; Page 262: Graph: "Rising Share of Young Adults Living in Multi-Generational Households." From Kim Parker, "The Boomerang Generation," Pew Research Center (March 15, 2012). http://www.pewsocialtrends.org/2012/03/15/the-boomerang-generation.; Page 264: Chart: "In dual-income households with children, average number of hours spent each week on..." "Modern Parenthood Slideshow: How it adds up for spouses in dual-income families." Pew Research Center, Washington, D.C. (March 14, 2013). http://www.pewsocialtrends.org/2013/03/14/modern-parenthood-slideshow/modernparenthood-slideshow_003/; Page 270: Graph: "Percentage of general public who say the ideal situation for young children is to have a mother who works." "Modern Parenthood Slideshow: What's the ideal situation for kids?" Pew Research Center, Washington, D.C. (March 14, 2013). http://www.pewsocialtrends.org/2013/03/14/modern-parenthood-slideshow/modernparenthood-slideshow_006/.; Page 270: Graph: "Percentage with children who say they spend...time with their children. "Modern Parenthood Slideshow: Most parents give themselves an 'A'." Pew Research Center, Washington D.C. (March 14, 2013). http://www.pewsocialtrends.org/2013/03/14/modern-parenthood-slideshow/modernparenthood-slideshow_010.; Page 271: Graph: "Percentage with children saying they are doing an 'excellent' or 'very good' as parents." "Modern Parenthood Slideshow: What working moms and dads want in a job." Pew Research Center, Washington D.C. (March 14, 2013). http://www.pewsocialtrends.org/2013/03/14/modern-parenthood-slideshow/modernparenthood-slideshow_008.; Page 271: Graph: "Percentage with children who say...is extremely important to them."Modern Parenthood Slideshow: What working moms and dads want in a job." Pew Research Center, Washington D.C. (March 14, 2013).http://www.pewsocialtrends.org/2013/03/14/modern-parenthood-slideshow/modernparenthood-slideshow_008.; Page 291: Chart: 2010 Federal Revenues. Data from Office of Management and Budget. http://www.cbo.gov/publication/43153; Page 304: Excerpt from Barack Obama's Second Inaugural Address.

参考译文

第一章　引言：理解美国文化

> 文化中潜藏的内容远比显现的多。奇怪的是，文化所潜藏的内容更不易被其参与者觉察。多年的研究使我确信，真正应该做的不是去理解他国的文化，而是去理解我们自己的文化。
>
> 　　　　　　　　　　　　　　　　　　　　爱德华·T. 霍尔（1914—2009）

如何定义像美国这样的多元化国家的文化？作为一个美国人又意味着什么？

美国生活

人们与生俱来会对彼此感到好奇。当我们遇到来自不同国家的人时，总是有很多想去了解的，比如：

- 他们国家的生活是什么样子的？
- 他们住的房子是什么样子的？
- 他们吃些什么？
- 他们有什么习俗？

我们如果去到另一个国家，就可以观察那里的人，观察他们如何生活，并且可以回答以上一些问题。不过，最有趣的问题往往最难回答，比如：

- 那里的人们信仰什么？
- 他们最看重什么？
- 激励他们的动力是什么？
- 他们为何如此这般行为处事？

要回答这些关于美国人的问题，我们必须记住两点：一、美国幅员的辽阔；二、美国种族的多样性。不尝试一下城际旅行的话，你很难明白这个国家到底有多大。驱车从纽约前往洛杉矶，途中仅在加油、吃饭和睡觉时停车，全程需要四到五天。从纽约开车到佛罗里达，也需要整整两天。一个普通的冬日，也许华盛顿特区正阴雨绵绵，纽约和芝加哥雪花飘飘，而洛杉矶和迈阿密，天气却暖和得可以游泳。不难想象，如此不同的气候条件，日常生活会有多大差异；而相隔如此遥远的城镇，生活方式又会有多么不同。

另一个要素——种族多样性——可能对美国生活的影响更为重要。除了那些早在第一批欧洲定居者到来之前就已经生活在北美大陆的美洲原住民，所有美国人都来自其他国家——或者他们的祖先来自其他国家。（顺便提一下，某些原住民依然是各自独立的不同印第安部族的成员，每个部族有自己的语言、文化、传统，甚至政府。）16 世纪时，西班牙在佛罗里达、加利福尼亚和西南部地区建立了定居点，而法国则将美洲大陆中部广袤的土地据为己有。但自 17 世纪至 1776 年美国建国，移民大多数来自北部欧洲，主要来自英格兰，他们当时的殖民地成了日后美国的雏形。也正是这些人，塑造了美国主流与传统文化中的价值观和传统。

移民的国度

1815 年，美国人口为 840 万。在其后的一百年间，美国吸纳了约 3500 万移民，其中大部分是在 19 世纪末与 20 世纪初进入美国的。这些新的移民中很多人不再是来自北欧。1882 年，有 40000 名中国移民来到美国；1900 年至 1907 年间，30000 多日本移民涌入。但到目前为止，新移民中来自中欧、东欧和南欧的人数最多。这些新移民为美国带来了不同的语言和不同的文化，不过，渐渐地，大多数人都还是融入了当地的美国主流文化。

1908 年，100 万新移民来到美国，伊斯雷尔·赞格威尔在一部剧作中写道：

> 美国是上帝的坩埚，一个巨大的熔炉，将来自欧洲的所有种族熔化与重塑……德国人和法国人、爱尔兰人和英国人、犹太人和俄罗斯人，都一起到熔炉里来吧！上帝正在创造美国人！

自从赞格威尔第一次用"熔炉"形容美国之后，这一概念就一直颇具争议。第八章我们会更详细地探讨这个问题，并追溯非洲裔美国人的历史。有两点可以确定：美国的主流文化延续了下来，并在不同历史时期，或多或少成功地吸纳了大量移民。同时，它也随着时间的推移逐渐被定居在此的移民群体改变着。

观察 20 世纪的移民模式，我们就会发现世纪初和世纪末是移民人数最多的时期。20 世纪前 20 年里，每年都有多达 100 万的新移民，1910 年人口普查时，有近 15% 的美国人是出生于其他国家的。但自 1921 年起，美国开始限制移民，1924 年移民法的颁布几乎关闭了国门。每年接纳移民的总数从 100 万降至 15 万。这一时期美国还建立了一项配额制度，明确规定可接收来自每个国家的移民数量。该制度对来自北欧和西欧的移民格外倾斜，而对其他地区的移民则严格限制。这一制度一直实行到 1965 年，期间有少数例外，比如允许来自匈牙利、古巴、越南和柬埔寨等国的难民进入美国。

移民法自 1965 年起有所改变，每年的移民总数又再度增加——从 20 世纪 60 年代的每年 30 万上升至 90 年代的每年 100 多万。到 20 世纪末，美国接纳的移民数量超过了其他工业化国家的总和。除合法移民外，据估计每年还有超过 50 万非法移民。旨在帮助家庭团聚而对法律进行的调整使得大量非欧洲裔移民进入美国，并由此产生了另一个新的移民群体。20 世纪末，美国 90% 的移民都来自拉丁美洲、加勒比地区和亚洲。

进入 21 世纪，新移民的人数开始接近 20 世纪早期的比例。1990 年至 2010 年间，出生于外国的美国居民人数几乎翻了一番，从 2000 万增长到 4000 万，其中大约三分之一是在 2000 年之后来到美国的。这些新移民约占新增人口总数的三分之一，并对美国产生了巨大的影响。截至 2010 年，约有 13% 的美国人是出生于外国的。在 12 个州以及美国首都，海外出生的居民比例甚至更高：

- 加利福尼亚州，27%
- 纽约州和新泽西州，均超过 21%
- 佛罗里达州和内华达州，均超过 19%
- 夏威夷州和得克萨斯州，均超过 16%
- 亚利桑那州、伊利诺伊州、马萨诸塞州、康涅狄格州、马里兰州和哥伦比亚特区，均超过 13%

21 世纪的移民模式继续改变着美国人口的肤色和种族构成。首先，欧洲裔美国白人的比例持续下降。欧洲人现在很少移民到美国，而 20 世纪早期来到美国的欧洲人大多已去世。他们的后代与来自其他国家的移民的后裔通婚，而这些第二代和第三代移民，很多人已不再把自己视为爱尔兰人、德国人或英国人了。

其次，在 21 世纪初，新移民中有半数以上来自拉丁美洲，使得美国的西班牙语使用者更加密集，特别是在加利福尼亚州、佛罗里达州、得克萨斯州、亚利桑那州和其他西南各州。拉美裔如今是美国最大的少数族裔群体（16%），超过了非洲裔美国人（13%）。随着人口数量的增长，他们在政治、经济上的影响力也日渐增强。总统候选人如今需要考虑如何赢得拉美裔选民的选票，全国各地有 6000 多名当选的拉美裔领导人。拉美裔拥有的企业以及西班牙语的媒体也在增加。最大的影响大概是在学校，美国校园中超过 20% 的学生是拉美裔。

拉美裔美国人的数量可能还会继续增长，因为他们中有许多是年轻人和儿童。不过，新增拉美裔移民的人数已经下降。2000 年时，拉美裔占新移民总数的半数以上，而到了 2010 年，这一数字下降到约 30%。由于经济不景气，一些移民返回了他们在拉丁美洲的祖国。此外，更加严格的边境限制也减少了非法移民的数量，生活在美国的拉美裔人口总数实际上可能减少了。

来自亚洲国家的移民同样在为美国新的融合做出贡献。2010 年人口普查显示，亚裔移民数量首次超过了拉美裔。目前，第一代移民中有超过 35% 来自亚洲，占如今美国人口总数的 6%。如果这一趋势继续，亚裔移民对美国文化的影响将进一步增强。在美国非白人少数族裔人口持续增长的同时，占多数的白人群体人数却逐渐减少。2011 年，少数族裔新生儿数量首次超过白人新生儿。到 2040 至 2050 年间，白人人口比例很可能下降到 50% 以下。美国已经有几个州和许多大城市里，少数族裔成了"多数群体"，也就是说，半数以上的人口都是少数族裔。

美国的文化多元性

今天，美国所面临的一个重要问题，就是新移民在新的国度中将扮演什么样的角色。他们会在多大程度上选择接受美国的传统价值观和文化？他们又将保留多少自己的语言和文化传统？他们会在融合自身价值观与美国传统文化价值观的基础上创造出一种全新的文化吗？

历史上，尽管移民的子女长大会成为双语、双文化者，但出于一些原因，很多人并没有将自己的语言和文化再传承下去。因此，很多移民的孙辈并不会说祖国的语言，从文化上就已经只是美国人了。不过，在美国部分地区一些具有共同语言或文化的成熟社区中，双语和双文化现象仍继续存在，而在依然有新移民不断进入的社区尤其如此。例如，在加利福尼亚州，驾照考试有30多种不同的语言可选。总体而言，较之20世纪上半叶，文化多元性在当今的美国更被接受，一些学校还开设了双语课程和多元文化课程。

2010年的人口普查也考虑到了美国人口的更加多样化，因而提供了很多种族和民族类别可选择，并且可以多选。

2010年人口普查摘要：美国人口的多样性		
项目	数量	百分比
种族		
总人口	308,745,535	100.0
单一种族	299,736,465	97.1
白人	223,553,265	72.4
黑人或非洲裔美国人	38,929,319	12.6
美洲印第安人和阿拉斯加原住民	2,932,248	0.9
美洲印第安人（确指）	1,985,245	0.6
阿拉斯加原住民（确指）	100,522	0.0
美洲印第安人兼阿拉斯加原住民（确指）	869	0.0
美洲印第安人或阿拉斯加原住民（无确指）	845,612	0.3
亚裔	14,674,252	4.8
夏威夷原住民和其他太平洋岛民	540,013	0.2
其他种族	19,107,368	6.2
两种及以上种族	9,009,073	2.9
含其他种族的两种种族	2,464,690	0.8
不含其他种族的两种种族	5,800,628	1.9
含其他种族的三种及以上种族	176,026	0.1
不含其他种族的三种及以上种族	567,729	0.2
西班牙裔或拉美裔		
总人口	308,745,538	100.0
西班牙裔或拉美裔（任何种族）	50,477,594	16.3
墨西哥裔	31,798,258	10.3

续表

2010年人口普查摘要：美国人口的多样性		
波多黎各裔	4,623,716	1.5
古巴裔	1,785,547	0.6
其他西班牙裔或拉美裔	12,270,073	4.0
非西班牙裔或拉美裔	258,267,944	83.7
种族和西班牙裔或拉美裔		
总人口	308,745,538	100.0
单一种族	299,736,465	97.1
西班牙裔或拉美裔	47,435,002	15.4
非西班牙裔或拉美裔	252,301,463	81.7
两种及以上种族	9,009,073	2.9
西班牙裔或拉美裔	3,042,592	1.0
非西班牙裔或拉美裔	5,966,481	1.9

一方面，很多美国人在努力保持着自己的民族传承和文化传统；另一方面，跨种族婚姻的数量也在增加。大多数美国年轻人认为，与什么种族或民族的人结婚并不重要。2008年，巴拉克·奥巴马当选，成为美国历史上第一位黑人总统，也反映了这种种族接纳态度。奥巴马实际上是黑白混血，母亲是白人，父亲是土生土长的肯尼亚黑人。他还有一位1850年从爱尔兰移民到美国的天祖父。越来越多的孩子属于混合血统或混合族裔。到本世纪中叶，白人在美国很可能将不再占多数。有人说，由于跨种族和民族之间通婚，多数美国人的肤色将会是米黄色或浅棕色。

在美国，大多数人对描述种族和族裔群体的语言都很敏感，会尽量做到政治正确（P.C.）。比如，一些美国黑人表达自己的非洲血统认同，倾向于使用"非洲裔美国人"这种说法，而不使用"黑人"。对于北美大陆的原住民们来说，"美洲原住民"和"美洲印第安人"可以通用，但有些人会认同自己属于某个部落（纳瓦霍人、霍皮人之类）。有些讲西班牙语的人更愿意被称作拉美裔（表示来自拉丁美洲）而不是西班牙裔（表示来自西班牙），也有些人则倾向于用原籍来表示自己的身份（古巴裔美国人或古巴人、墨西哥裔美国人、奇卡诺人或墨西哥人，等等）。由于人口普查已使用了各种名称，我们也将采用如白人、美洲原住民或美洲印第安人、黑人或非洲裔美国人、西班牙裔或拉美裔这样的措辞。

尽管存在如此这般的多样性，美国人之间仍然有一条纽带将他们凝聚在一起，这就是国家认同感——认同自己是美国人。顺便提一句，当美国公民称自己为"Americans"（美国人，也指美洲人）时，并无意否定加拿大人和拉丁美洲人作为美洲大陆居民的身份。英语中没有类似"United Statesians"（合众国人）这样的词，所以大家才称自己为"Americans"。也因此，一个语言上的问题有时却会引起误会。虽然拉美国家的公民可能会称美国人为"North Americans"（北美人），但对很多美国人来说，这也并没有什么意义，因为除了美国公民，加拿大人和墨西哥人也是北美人。（例如，NAFTA，即"北美自由贸易协定"，是加拿大、美国和墨西哥三国之间的贸易协定）。因此，本文中还是用"American"这个词来表示生活在美国的人的国籍。

美国人的信仰概观

那么，我们该如何解读美国人呢？是什么把他们凝聚在一起并让他们拥有身为美国人的认同感呢？我们是否可以对美国人的信仰进行归纳概括呢？答案是肯定的。但在归纳概括时，我们需要慎重。当我们探讨美国的基本信仰时，必须记住，并非所有美国人都秉持这些信仰，而且人们信仰的程度也不尽相同。一些美国人践行信仰的方式也比较不同，从而形成了各种各样的生活方式。我们试图做的，就是去定义与解释那些多年来吸引移民来到美国的传统主流文化价值观。

应当了解的是，现在有很多关于美国价值观及其本质的讨论。争论大多围绕道德，或者说宗教价值观。在本书中我们不探讨道德价值观，而是要去描述作为国家文化引擎的文化价值观。正是这些文化价值观定义了美国，并让来自世界各地的人欣然接受了这里的生活方式，最终认同了自己是"美国人"。事实上，到了第三代，大多数移民已经丢掉了祖辈的语言和文化，他们认为自己就简单的是"美国人"。

本书中，我们将借鉴著名观察家阿历克西·德·托克维尔关于美国社会的智慧。1831年，年轻的法国人托克维尔来到美国，考察研究美国的民主制度及其对世界其他国家和地区可能产生的意义。仅仅游历了九个月之后，他就写成了著名的《论美国的民主》一书，该书是对美国生活方式的经典研究之作。托克维尔拥有超乎寻常的观察力。他不仅描述了美国政府的民主制度及其运作方式，还阐述了这种制度对美国人思想、情感和行为的影响。很多学者认为，托克维尔对美国传统信仰和价值观理解的深刻可谓前无古人。值得瞩目的是，将近两百年前他所观察到的美国人性格的许多特质，在今天依然显著而有意义。

托克维尔对美国人性格特质的观察结论有重要的价值，另一个原因在于他到访美国的时间。他于19世纪30年代美国尚未工业化之前来到美国。这是属于小农场主、小商人和西进拓荒的时代，也是这个新的国家传统价值观正逐渐形成的历史时期。仅仅用了一代人的时间，在美国宪法颁布大约四十年后，新的政府体制已经塑造出一个拥有独特价值观的社会。托克维尔所描述的，也正是今天许多美国人仍然引以为傲的性格特质。不过，他作为一名中立的观察者，既看到了这些特质的优点，也指出了其中的弊端。

这是一本关于美国传统基本信仰、价值观和性格特征的书，它并非是一些关于美国人行为或制度的事实的生硬堆砌，而是探讨在国民及其制度背后的原动力，阐述了传统价值观和信仰如何影响包括宗教、商业、工作和娱乐、政治、家庭以及教育在内的美国人生活的方方面面。

我们邀请你参与到本书中来。我们会描述多数美国人的想法和信念，但你也将有机会通过自己的观察来检验这些描述。读到这些传统基本价值观时，你不妨将它们当作一些工作假说，可以在美国人身上进行验证，并在其他国家的、你自己国家的人身上验证。将它们同你自己的价值观、信仰以及你生活中最看重的东西进行比较。在这一过程中，你不仅可以更好地了解美国人，也将对本民族的文化和你自身有更深刻的理解。我们正是通过研究他人来了解我们自己。

第二章　美国传统价值观与信仰

> 我们认为这些真理是不言自明的：人人生而平等，造物主赋予他们若干不可剥夺的权利，其中包括生命、自由和追求幸福的权利。
>
> 《独立宣言》（1776）

为什么有那么多人想要到美国生活？美国人的生活方式和社会价值观有什么样的吸引力？

美国传统价值观的背景：种族、民族、宗教及文化多样性

早在其历史的发端，美国就已颇具多样性——分布在整个北美大陆的美洲原住民、西南部和佛罗里达的西班牙定居者、密西西比河沿岸的法国传教士和毛皮商人、从非洲国家被贩运来的黑人奴隶、纽约的荷兰定居者、宾夕法尼亚的德国人，当然还有英国殖民者——英国殖民者的文化最终孕育了美国的语言，奠定了美国政治和经济体制发展的基础。

早期大多数美国人将这种多样性或多元性，视为生活的平常。各种各样不同的民族、文化和宗教群体意味着接纳多样性才是唯一务实的选择。尽管有些人并不看好这种多样性，甚或感到自己的生活受到其威胁。不过后来，许多美国人逐渐认识到了国家的多样性的优势。今天的美国人，特别是年轻人普遍都认同这种文化多样性的价值。

当我们分析形成于18世纪晚期的美国基本价值体系，并开始定义美国人的性格时，必须记住文化多元性这一背景。一个有着如此巨大多样性的国家是如何产生一种能被承认的国家认同感的呢？

美国民意调查员约翰·佐格比在谈到是什么将美国人凝聚在一起时说："共同的价值体系让我们成为美国人……我们所拥有的权利定义了我们自身……我们的权利就是我们的历史，也是最初欧洲的定居者及其后数百万人移民于此的原因。"

历史上,美国一直被视为"机遇的国度",吸引了来自世界各地的移民。大多数人到来之前对美国机遇的憧憬与他们到达美国之后的切身经历,共同形成了一套独特的价值体系。我们将研究这些成为美国传统价值观的六项基本价值观。其中有三项是吸引移民来到美国的传统理由:个人自由、机会均等以及物质财富。但要获得这些优势,就必须付出代价:自力更生、激烈竞争与勤奋工作。随着时间的推移,这些代价本身也成了传统价值体系的一部分。美国传统价值体系正是由三对优势以及为了取得这些优势人们所付出的代价组成:

· 个人自由与自力更生;
· 机会均等与参与竞争;
· 物质财富与勤奋工作。

上述三对价值观决定了美国的独特文化与它的人民。我们也可以从权利与责任的角度思考这些基本价值观。美国人认为,人们有权享有个人自由、机会均等以及物质成功的希望;但所有这些权利也要求与之相当的责任,也就是自力更生、竞争意愿以及勤奋工作。分析了上述每一对价值观的历史渊源之后,我们还将探讨这些价值观在美国的现状。

个人自由与自力更生

最早定居者来到北美大陆,是要建立摆脱了当时欧洲社会种种束缚的殖民地。他们想要逃离国王、政府、教士和教会以及贵族与统治阶层对他们生活各方面的控制。很大程度上,他们成功了。1776年,英国的殖民定居者宣布脱离英国,建立了一个新的国家——美利坚合众国。他们的做法,不仅公开挑战了英国国王的权威,也宣告了治理国家的权力应掌握在人民的手中。他们从此挣脱了王权的桎梏。1787年,他们为新的国家起草宪法,使政教分离,不再会有受政府支持的教会。这极大地限制了教会的权力。此外,起草的宪法中也明确取缔了贵族头衔,以确保不会形成贵族社会。这个新的国家中将不会有贵族统治阶级。

早期定居者做出的这些历史性决策对美国性格的形成产生了深远的影响。通过限制政府和教会的权力并消除正式的贵族,早期定居者们创造了一种重视个人自由的风气。在他们的心目中,美国已然与"个人自由"这一概念联系在了一起。个人自由大概也是所有美国价值观中最基本的一项。学者和外界的观察者经常把这一价值观称为"个人主义",但美国人大多倾向使用"自由"一词。这也是当今美国最受尊重与最受欢迎的词语之一。

自由,对美国人而言,意味着每个个体都有愿望和权利去掌握自己的命运,不受政府、贵族统治阶级、教会或其他权力机构等外界的干涉。自由掌控自己命运的渴望是1776年这个新国家的基本价值观,此后也一直吸引着移民不断前来。

不过,要获得个人自由也有代价——自力更生。个人必须要学会靠自己,否则就可能失去自由。个人必须为自己的行为负责。这意味着按照传统他们要尽早(通常是在18岁或21岁)实现经济上和情感上的独立,不再依赖父母。自力更生的价值观是指,美国人认为他们应该自己照顾自己,自主解决自己的问题,自食其力。托克维尔在19世纪30年代对美国人的自立信念有如下观察:

他们不亏欠任何人，也不指望任何人。他们习惯于把自己视作独立的个体，乐于相信命运完全掌握在自己手中。

这种强烈的独立自主的信念作为美国的传统价值观，延续至今。这或许是美国性格中最难理解的一个方面，但意义却极为重要。大部分美国人都认为，要保持自由就必须自力更生。如果过多依赖家庭、政府或任何组织，就可能会失去一部分随心所欲的自由。即便无法完全做到自食其力，大多数美国人认为，至少也要表现出自力更生的精神。一个人若想跻身美国生活的主流（掌握权力，赢得尊重），就必须成为别人眼中自力更生的人。

例如，有些成年子女因经济状况或婚姻失败回来与父母同住，多数家庭成员都会认为这只是暂时的安排，直到这些子女找到工作，可以自力更生为止。虽然可以从慈善机构、家庭或政府获得经济支持，但这通常都是暂时的，而且人们也普遍不赞赏这种做法。归根结底，大多数美国人还是会说，每个人都有照顾自己的责任。

机会均等与参与竞争

美国一直吸引着移民前来的另一个重要原因，是人们相信，人人都有机会在这里获得成功。怀揣这样的憧憬，一代又一代的移民来到了美国。他们认为，由于个体摆脱了宗教、政府和社会的过度控制，因而更有可能获得个人成功。尤为重要的是，美国没有世袭的贵族阶层。

由于宪法禁止贵族头衔，美国没有形成任何正式的阶级制度。在美国历史的早期，许多移民选择离开古老的欧洲社会，是因为他们相信在美国会有更多成功的机会。在他们所来自的"古老国家"，他们生活上的地位很大程度上取决于所出身的社会阶层，贵族家庭掌握巨大的权力，继承积累了数百年的财富。但人们知道，在美国他们不必在这样的贵族家庭之间挣扎。

这些早期移民有很多都在新的国家实现了希望和梦想。许多人出身于较低的社会阶层，但这并没有阻止他们努力取得更高的社会地位。很多人发现，比起故国，他们在美国的确更有机会成功。正是由于数百万的移民获得了成功，美国人开始相信"机会均等"。19世纪30年代托克维尔游访美国时，对这个新国家里生活条件的统一印象深刻。他写道：

> 我对美国社会研究得越深入，就越发现……条件均等是根本事实，其他一切由此而生。

当美国人说相信机会均等，他们究竟是要表达什么意思，理解这一点很重要。他们并不是指每一个人都是——或应该是——平等的。他们真正要表达的，是每个个体都应该有平等的机会去争取成功。美国人把生活看作是一场追逐胜利的赛跑。对他们而言，平等意味着每个人都应有均等的参与比赛并赢取胜利的机会。换言之，机会均等可以看作是一条道德准则，帮助确保这场追逐胜利的比赛是公平的竞争；一个人不会只因为出身富裕就获胜，也不会因种族或宗教背景而遭受失败。美国的这种"公平竞争"观念是机会均等信念的一个重要方面。

亚伯拉罕·林肯总统在19世纪60年代时就表达过这一信念，他说：

> 我们……希望让最卑微的人也和其他人一样，拥有均等的致富机会。当一个人起点不好，正如大多数人在生活的赛道上的境地，而一个自由的社会就是，他知道他可以改善自己的处境；他知道，他的工作条件不会一生一成不变。

但是，获得机会均等的代价是参与竞争。如果将生活看作一场比赛，那么一个人要成功，就必须参与其中。一个人有责任参与到与他人的竞争中来，虽然我们也知道并不是每个人都能成功。在美国，如果说成功的机会面前人人平等，那么努力去尝试也是每个人的责任。

美国人生活中的竞争压力从童年就开始了，并一直伴随他们直到退休。在美国，学习成功参与竞争也是成长的一部分，美国的公立学校和社区团体都会提供强有力的竞技体育活动项目，鼓励参与竞争。竞技体育目前无论是在男性还是女性当中，都颇受欢迎。

竞争的压力使美国人保持活力充沛，但也给他们带来持续的情绪紧张。只有到退休，他们才终于摆脱了竞争的压力。但到了那时，又会出现新的问题。在一个崇尚竞争的社会里，有些人会感到自己一无是处，甚至多余。老年人在美国不如在其他竞争较少的社会中受尊敬和尊重，这可能也是原因之一。事实上，总的来说，任何群体中未能成功参与竞争的人——无论出于什么原因——都不会如参与竞争并取得成功的人那样符合美国生活的主流。

物质财富与勤奋工作

移民纷纷来到美国的第三个原因，是为了追求更好的生活，或者说，为了提高生活水平。对于绝大多数美国移民来说，这或许是让他们选择背井离乡的最重要的理由。由于其极为丰富的自然资源，美国成为数百万来此寻求财富之人心目中的丰饶之地。当然，大多数移民并没有能"一夜暴富"，有些甚至还饱受疾苦；但大部分人最终都还是能够改善先前的生活条件。即便无法达到所期望的经济成功，他们也能相当肯定，他们的孩子会有机会拥有更好的生活。"从一无所有到发家致富"，这句话成为"美国梦"的口号。北美大陆所蕴藏的巨大财富，让许多移民梦想成真。他们取得了物质上的成功，许多人也变得非常依恋物质生活。物质财富成为美国人的一种价值取向。

对物质财富的重视与推崇，被称为"物质主义"。但大多数美国人却比较反感这个词。说一个人物质主义，无异于一种侮辱。因为对一个美国人来说，这表示此人把物质财富看得比什么都重要。美国人不喜欢被称为物质主义者，因为他们觉得这样指责他们只喜好物质享受，没有宗教价值观是不公正的。事实上，大部分美国人都是有信念有理想的。但对于大多数美国人而言，获取并保有可观的物质财富依然非常重要。为什么会这样呢？

其中一个原因是，物质财富在美国作为衡量社会地位的通行标准由来已久。由于美国人摒弃了欧洲的世袭贵族制度和贵族头衔，因此他们必须找到一种替代标准用以评判社会地位。个人拥有的物质财富的质量和数量从而成了衡量成功和社会地位的普遍依据。此外，正如我们将在宗教一章看到的，在清教徒的工作伦理中，物质成功和信仰虔诚是相关联的。

美国人当然也为获得物质财富付出了相应的代价：勤奋工作。当第一批定居者到达北美大陆时，这里有着丰富的自然资源，但尚未被开发。只有通过努力工作才能将这些资源转化为物质财富，进而获得更加舒适的生活。纵观美国历史，勤奋工作对于大部分美国人而言，都是必不可少且有回报的。正因如此，他们将物质财富看作是勤奋工作的顺理成章的回报。在某种程度上，物质财富不仅被视为工作努力的切实证据，更是能力的体现。18世纪末，美国宪法之父詹姆斯·麦迪逊就曾表示，物质财富的差距反映了个人能力的差异。

多数美国人依然相信勤奋工作的价值。人们大多认为，一个人应该有一份工作，而不能靠政府福利金过活。福利制度几经改革，以使人们不会依赖福利而放弃找工作维持生计。然而，更大的问题在于，要多努力地工作才能真正改善一个人的生活和物质财富水平。当今美国，是否还可能通过勤劳工作致富呢？

由于美国从工业经济转向服务和信息经济，工厂工人的高薪岗位减少。现在的美国，普通工人从一无所有到发家致富要困难得多；很多人也感到疑惑，传统的美国梦究竟怎么了。随着美国参与全球经济的竞争，很多工人正失去原来的工作，他们发现自己和家人需要工作更长时间，却只获得比原来更少的工资和福利。经济疲软，每个人都会受到影响。贫困劳动者的数量增加，他们努力工作，但低报酬的工作却难以让他们维持像样的生活水平，也负担不起健康和养老保险；很多人不得不依靠政府或其他来源的一些外部援助。

美国价值观和美国梦现状

近年来，由于经济低迷，许多观察家都提出了疑问，美国梦是否真的破灭了？大多数时候，美国梦并不表示普通美国人真的可以从一无所有到发家致富。传统上，它意味着通过努力工作，父母可以让孩子在长大后有更好的生活。每一代人都可以比他们的父辈更加富裕和成功。尽管最富有的1%的人口与普通美国大众之间的差距近年来急剧增大，但绝大多数美国人仍然坚信美国梦的理想，相信只要努力工作，他们和他们的孩子就会拥有更好的生活。向更高社会层次上进的理想在美国依然存在。但是，我们在理解美国人的信念和他们的生活状况之间的关系时，必须要分清理想主义与现实。有些人发现了自己工作时间更长却挣得更少，却仍然希冀着美国梦再次出现，就算不为他们自己，也要为了他们的孩子。

机会均等和自力更生等美国价值观是一种理想，也许并不足以描述美国生活的现实。例如，机会均等这一理想就常常无法付诸实现。现实中，总有些人比其他人更有机会成功。出身豪门的人比出身寒门的人拥有更多的机会。继承遗产无疑会带来决定性的优势。尽管有法律旨在促进所有个体的机会平等，但种族和性别可能依然是影响一个人成功的因素。当然，新移民也一直要面对其自身独特的处境所决定的各种挑战。

美国理想在实际生活中只有部分得到了实现，但这并没有削弱它们的重要性。大多数美国人依然坚信这些理想，并在日常生活中深受其影响。如果我们能够理解这些传统美国文化价值观的含义，以及它们如何影响了美国生活的方方面面，那么就不难理解美国人的思想和情感了。

关于这些价值观，有两点需要记住。其一，它们是文化价值观，是推动美国发展的文化引擎，持续提供着动力吸引世界各地的人们来到这个国度，成为"美国人"。其二，这六种价值观融合成一个体系，产生出了新的东西。正如亚里士多德所说，整体大于部分之和。这些价值观之间的关系——权利与责任——形成了美国社会的结构。正是这个结构定义了美国梦——相信如果人们对自己的生活负责，努力工作，就能拥有追求个人目标的自由，就有机会争取成功。这些价值观紧密交织在一起，其中任何一个被抽离或破坏，都将使整个结构受到影响甚至可能崩溃。

最后，个人自由、自力更生、机会均等、参与竞争、物质财富及勤奋工作这六种价值观并不能代表美国性格的全部。确切地说，它们组成了美国文化的基本结构或框架，使美国这样一个极具多样性的国家形成并保持一种国家认同。

在接下来的三章中，我们将分析三种强化和参与塑造这些价值观的历史因素——宗教传统、边疆传统和富足传统。其余章节则将探讨这些价值观在商业、政府、民族与种族多样性、教育、休闲以及家庭等美国文化各方面的体现。最后一章中，我们还将讨论美国所面临的挑战以及这些挑战对美国的未来及其价值观的潜在影响。

第三章　美国的宗教传统

每个人的灵魂都由自己来照料。

托马斯·杰斐逊（1743—1826）

宗教如何塑造了美国人的价值观？宗教在今天美国人的生活中起到了什么样的作用？

美国的宗教传统：强化美国文化价值观

从多方面来看，美国一直都是一个宗教国家。尽管信仰和习俗多种多样，但90%的美国人都表示自己信仰上帝，或一个无上/无所不在的神明。大多数美国人是基督徒，不过，世界上所有主要宗教在美国都有人信奉。在美国的有些地区，教会成员数量庞大，很多人每周参加不止一次礼拜仪式；而在其他较为世俗化的地区，人们参加教会活动就没那么活跃。越来越多的年轻人不属于任何教会或宗教团体，但大多数仍表示相信上帝。很多人会说自己是"有精神信仰"而不是"有宗教信仰"。

美国的宗教格局很复杂，并且不断在变化，但它一直是美国文化中十分重要的一个方面。在第二章我们介绍了六项基本的文化价值观——个人自由、自力更生、机会均等、参与竞争、物质财富及勤奋工作。这些价值观形成并发展于美国的宗教传统，也因之得到加强。其中，尤以对个人自由、自力更生、物质财富和勤奋工作的影响为甚。本章中，我们将首先分析历史环境是如何塑造美国的宗教传统，并催生与强化这些文化价值观的。之后，我们将考察这些价值观对当今宗教环境的影响。

在美国历史上，宗教从一开始就一直扮演着重要角色。16世纪时，西班牙人首次将天主教信仰带到了北美大陆。其后的三百年间，先后有来自西班牙和拉丁美洲的传教士和定居者到达现在的佛罗里达、加利福尼亚以及西南部地区。很多城市都以这些传教士和定居者的名字命名，例如圣奥古斯丁、圣弗朗西斯科（旧金山）、圣菲和圣安东尼奥等。法裔加拿大天主教传教士也跟随探险家和商人从魁北克沿密西西比河南下来到了新奥尔良。17世纪时，欧洲定居者开始在北美的东海岸建立殖民地。其中虽然也有天主教徒，但绝大多数欧洲定居者都是新教徒，大部分来自英国。新国家形成时，对美国宗教氛围的发展影响最大的就是基督教信仰的新教分支。

新教的发展

因为在宗教信仰上存在重大差异，16世纪时，基督教信仰的新教分支脱离欧洲的罗马天主教会。（东正教早在1054年就已经与罗马天主教会分离。）在新教改革的时代，罗马天主教会是西欧国家宗教生活的中心；天主教教皇和神父在人们的精神事务中扮演着家长的角色。他们告诉人们是非善恶，并宽恕人们的违背上帝和基督教信仰的罪过。

另一方面，新教徒们坚持认为，所有人都必须独自面对上帝。如果人们犯下过错，他们应该直接向上帝，而不是向那些以上帝的名义说话的神父们寻求宽恕。新教徒们以"信徒皆祭司"取代了神父的权力和权威。这一教义意味着，每个个体都对自己与上帝的关系全权负责。

脱离天主教会之后，新教徒们发现他们自己在很多信仰问题上也无法达成共识。于是，新教徒们开始建立各自的教会，称为教派（美国传统的新教教派有浸礼会、卫理公会、路德会、长老会、圣公会以及基督教联合会等）。17世纪时，一些宗教团体经历了不少苦难，许多新教教派也遭受了宗教迫害，有很多人甚至因为信仰而被杀害。这些迫害使得许多新教徒为了能够自由地实践他们特定的宗教信仰，毅然离开了自己的祖国。因此，17世纪来到美国的早期定居者中，有很多都是寻求宗教自由的新教徒。

上一章中我们提到，这种对于宗教自由的渴望是许多殖民定居者来到美国最重要的原因之一。总的来说，美国没有任何官定的国家宗教，这一点强烈地吸引着欧洲的新教徒，不论他们是否受到迫害。众多新教教派在美国纷纷建立了起来。起初，也有些教派希望将自己的观点和信念强加给他人，但殖民地实在太大了，任何一个教派都不可能掌控其他教派。政教分离的观念逐渐为人们所接受。

1789年通过的美国宪法禁止政府建立国家教会；任何教派都不得比其他教派更受优待。政府和教会必须保持相互独立，宗教自由受宪法第一修正案的保护。在这种情况下，各种不同的教派得以发展壮大，每个教派也都以"和平共存"的态度与其他教派相处。多样性被接受并得到了加强。今天，各种新教教派都有完全独立的教会组织；它们在教义和信条上虽有诸多相似之处，但差异同样也很显著。

自力更生和自我完善的新教传统

新教是塑造美国人价值观和信仰的一股强大的力量。与美国新教相关的最重要的价值观之一就是自我完善，它是自力更生的发展延伸。基督教经常强调人性的生而有罪。但与天主教徒不同，新教徒不会去向神父寻求宽恕；个体都要独自面对上帝以完善自己，并寻求上帝的指引、宽恕和恩典。因此，新教向来鼓励人们努力不懈地追求自我完善。

自我完善理念最引人注目的例子或许就是"再生"体验。有过这样体验的人表示，对上帝和耶稣敞开心扉，彻底改变了他们的生活，让他们如获重生。许多福音派信徒，或宗教保守派，都认为这是一种重要的体验。

自我完善的需要早已超越了单纯的道德或宗教层面。今天，自我完善在无数指导人们如何戒烟、减肥、发展人际关系等的书籍中均有体现。这类书经常向人们提供关于如何生活得更幸福、更成功的建议，被称为"自助"书籍，而且很多都是畅销书。它们正是这种相信"天助自助者"的文化自然而然的产物。

物质成功、勤奋工作和自律

在美国，实现物质成功可能是自我完善最广受尊重的体现方式。很多学者认为，在很大程度上，美国的新教传统与此有关。将物质主义和宗教混在一起的想法看似矛盾；宗教被认为关乎精神事务，而非物质财产。那这两者又是如何结合的呢？

早期的一些欧洲新教领袖认为，那些受到上帝庇佑的人会因其物质成就而得到世人的认可。另一些教会领袖，特别是在美国，将物质成功和受到上帝庇佑更加紧密地联系在一起。例如，1900年，威廉·劳伦斯主教曾宣称："虔诚与财富结盟……物质的繁荣使国民性格更加和善、快乐与无私，更接近基督"。

不过，美国的宗教领袖从不鼓励不经过勤奋工作和自律而获得财富的想法。许多学者认为，对于这两种价值观的重视为美国的工业发展发挥了重要作用。新教领袖们认为，不仅仅是神父的工作，所有人的劳动都是神圣的。他们还认为，自律能力是受上帝祝福的一种神圣的品格。自律通常被定义为自发将钱财储蓄与投资，而非用于即时的享乐。卫理公会信仰的领袖约翰·卫斯理曾告诉他的信众："尽你所能去获取，尽你所能去给予，尽你所能去积攒。"鼓励人们积攒财富也为美国的工业发展创造了勤奋工作、愿意储蓄与投资的良好环境。

通过勤奋工作和自律追求物质财富和其他目标，这一理念通常被称为"新教工作伦理"，或"清教工作伦理"。要了解的是，这种工作伦理的影响远远超出了新教教会。美国的许多宗教团体都奉行这样的工作伦理，甚至那些不属于任何特定教会的美国人在其日常生活中也都受到这种工作伦理的影响。有趣的是，美国是唯一没有法律规定工人享有一定的带薪假期的工业化国家。美国人每年平均仅有两周的假期，而其他国家的劳动者则有四五周，甚至更多的假期。此外，很多65岁或66岁可以退休的美国人还会继续再工作若干年。许多美国人对被称为"工作狂"颇为自豪，"工作狂"是指工作时间长，常常一周工作七天的人。

志愿精神和人道主义

自我完善不仅仅是指通过勤劳和自律获得物质财富，也包括通过帮助他人来完善自身的理念。换言之，个人可以通过为旨在帮助他人的慈善、教育或宗教事业贡献一些时间或金钱，使自己成为更好的人。这一理念有时被称为志愿精神或人道主义。

历史上曾有一些超级富豪慷慨解囊，帮助他人。例如，20世纪初，美国著名实业家安德鲁·卡内基就曾斥资三亿美元捐助各类学校，并在美国数千个社区建造公共图书馆。另一位著名实业家约翰·D. 洛克菲勒曾从其私人财产中掏出一大笔钱兴办大学，解释这样做的原因时他说："上帝赐予我这些财富，我又怎能把它们留着不用于芝加哥大学呢？"西尔斯罗巴克公司合伙人朱利叶斯·罗森沃尔德曾出资帮助在南部乡村建立了五千多所黑人学校。21世纪，比尔·盖茨、沃伦·巴菲特和其他很多富有的美国人创立了众多慈善基金会并捐献了巨额财富。传统上，许多普通美国人也认为自己应该为宗教和人道主义事业奉献部分时间和财富。他们这样做的动机一部分源于理想主义，另一部分则是为了自我完善，想要成为上帝眼中和其他美国人眼中合格的人。

慈善捐助和志愿服务的精神在今天的美国依然延续着。有些宗教信仰认为，其成员有责任将自己收入的10%捐赠给教会及其他慈善机构。顺便提一句，个人的慈善捐款可以得到税收减免。这种奉献精神在宗教之外也并不鲜见。许多企业都鼓励员工参与志愿者工作，例如在业余时间清扫公园，帮助学习有困难的孩子，或者到动物收容所帮忙。父母也会经常教育孩子，他们有责任帮助他人。《父母》杂志最近有一期的封面故事就在告诉父母如何"培养懂得回馈的孩子"。文章指出，应该教给孩子志愿服务的价值观，包括向慈善事业捐款。文章中还承诺，"志愿服务可以增强孩子的自尊心，并让他们学会感恩"，很好地说明了在美国理想主义和自我完善的结合。

2001年9月11日和国家宗教

所有美国人和世界其他地区的很多人都清楚地记得2001年9月11日，当得知恐怖分子袭击了世界贸易中心和五角大楼时，他们正在做什么。纽约市和华盛顿特区的人们更是极度悲痛，几乎每个人都有什么认识的人遭遇了不幸。一时间，举国上下爱心、慈善与爱国热情涌动。参与志愿服务的人太多，以至官方不得不限制人数。人们为遇难者家庭募集了数百万美元善款，美国人的胸中也激荡起对国家的无比自豪与热爱。80%的民众都在窗户上、车上，甚至在衣服上悬挂或佩戴国旗。人群自发歌唱《天佑美国》，这是一首比国歌更流行（也更容易唱）的爱国曲，还有《美丽的阿美利加》和《我的祖国》等。

宗教和爱国主义的这种结合是一些学者所称之为美国"国家宗教"的一种体现。国家宗教的起源可以追溯到殖民地时期。在美国殖民者的原籍国，国家的主导价值观往往受有组织的国家教会的支持。在这个年轻的国家，虽然美国人已明确不会存在有组织的国家教会，但多年来，他们也发展出一些将爱国主义和宗教结合起来的非正式的实践活动。这种国家宗教的主要功用是为主流价值观提供支持，并在需要的时候抚慰伤痛。因此，它是以一种非正式、非组织的方式发挥着早期欧洲国家中有组织的国家教会的作用。

但一些美国社会观察家认为，被称为国家宗教的各种实践活动可能会带来不利的影响。有时，这些做法可能会导致不宽松的社会氛围，不鼓励甚至不能包容对现行国家政策的不同意见。例如，当有公民反对政府发动战争的决定时，其他美国人就会指责他们不爱国。这种情况在越战期间曾发生过，当时的反战示威者被警告："美国，你要么爱它，要么离开它。"2003年，美国决定入侵伊拉克时，也发生过类似的分歧。

当今的宗教格局：两极化与多元化

美国的宗教格局复杂多变。《美国恩典：宗教如何分裂和团结我们》一书中，罗伯特·D. 普特南和戴维·E. 坎贝尔探讨了当今美国在起作用的两股力量——宗教两极化与多元化。福音派，或称宗教保守派，与世俗自由派之间的两极分化不断加剧。美国人逐渐发现，他们处于非此即彼的其中一端，而中间的温和派人数则不断减少。福音派坚信要严格遵循《圣经》的教义（他们与教会领袖对于《圣经》的解读），并应定期参加礼拜活动。他们的社会态度（通常在政治上）相较于宗教温和派或自由派，要更为保守。比如，他们或许会反对堕胎和同性婚姻，相信神创论而非进化论。宗教保守派与自由派之间的争论可能会变得相当激烈。一些评论家甚至将这一分歧描述为"文化大战"。不过，普特南和坎贝尔指出，还有一种力量也在发挥作用：

> 高度的宗教虔诚和巨大的宗教多样性——包括越来越多的非宗教信仰——在美国和平共处。……宗教多元化是如何与宗教两极化共存的呢？答案就在于，在美国，宗教有相当大的流动性……各宗教之间竞争、适应与发展，而个人可以自由地从一个会众转入另一个会众，甚至从一种宗教转向另一种宗教。

是什么样的美国价值观使得宗教两极化与宗教多元化能够和平共存呢？对个人自由及个人信奉宗教权利的基本信念是美国宗教经验的核心。种族背景的巨大多样性产生了宗教多元化的环境，世界上大多数的宗教在这里都有人信奉。虽然绝大多数美国人都是基督徒，但其他宗教信仰和来自其他文化的人们也为美国的宗教格局做出了重要贡献。目前，生活在美国的穆斯林和犹太教徒人数相当。天主教徒中有近一半为拉美裔。除佛教和印度教外，亚裔移民还带来了道教、儒家思想和神道教等其他东亚传统宗教。美洲原住民的宗教今天仍然在被实践和研究，尤其是其中关于与自然和谐相处的教义。

从阿尔巴尼亚东正教到拜火教，美国宗教会众人口普查每十年跟踪调查一次美国236种不同的宗教。最近的一次普查显示，穆斯林（伊斯兰教）和摩门教徒（后期圣徒教会）是全国增长最快的两个宗教群体。2000年至2010年间，穆斯林人数增长了66%，摩门教徒人数增长了44%，而新教徒人数则下降了5%，占总人口的比例首次低于50%。（另据估计，美国有约一百万佛教徒和印度教徒。）美国当前总人口数超过3.1亿，美国的十大宗教如下：

1. 天主教	5890万
2. 浸礼会	2720万
3. 卫理公会	1220万
4. 非教派福音派新教	1220万
5. 路德会	720万
6. 后期圣徒（摩门教）	640万
7. 五旬节派教会	580万
8. 长老会改革宗	500万
9. 伊斯兰教（穆斯林）	260万
10. 犹太教（犹太教徒）	230万

来源：宗教数据档案协会

近年来最为显著的发展之一，就是自称无宗教信仰的人数量迅速增加。近20%的成年人认为自己不归属于任何教会或信仰，对30岁以下成年人而言，这一比例则为1/3。这些人被称为无教派人士，或"无宗教归属"（因为他们在被问及宗教归属时选择"无"），目前人数已达4900万。有趣的是，他们之中有68%的人表示自己信仰上帝，但并不想加入任何有组织的宗教团体。通常他们会自称"有精神信仰，但无宗教信仰"。他们比那些属于特定宗教团体的美国人更为自由和世俗化。

另一个重要发展是传统的主流新教教会成员的减少。上面列出的十大宗教中，仅有四个是传统的新教教派（浸礼会、卫理公会、路德会和长老会）。除了浸礼会之外，主流教会一般比较温和，往往比福音派和宗教保守派更为开明。大部分浸礼会教友都是福音派。（五旬节派教会也是福音派，但一般不被视为传统主流新教教派。）

非教派福音派新教徒的人数也在增长。这类教会不属于传统的新教教派，通常是一些由活跃的宗教领袖组织的社区教会，其中有些已成为"超级教会"。在加利福尼亚奥兰治县，里克·沃伦的马鞍峰教会成立于1980年，现在已有十万名教友，周末参加教会活动的人数平均超过两万人。超级教会有现代化的礼拜活动，通常主要帮助人们实现"快乐与满足的基督生活"，而这正是关于自我完善的当代诠释。同时它们也体现出美国一些教会是如何发展与适应不断变化的需求，特别是年轻人的需求的。

美国的宗教多样性：精神的万花筒

在本章的开始，我们曾断言，美国一直以来都是，并依然是一个宗教国家，但其宗教格局复杂多变。历史上早期新教信仰所倡导的"和平共存"的宽容精神使得现代大多数美国人能够接纳各种各样的宗教。尽管也有一些人不能包容，持不同意见，但绝大多数美国人都认为，通往上帝的道路有很多，自己所信奉的宗教并非唯一有效的信仰。不同宗教成员间传统的界限已经打破，因而不同信仰的美国人之间通婚也很常见，在年轻一代美国人中尤其如此。越来越多不同文化和信仰的人一起工作、比邻而居、结为朋友。多姿多彩的信仰文化构建起了精神的万花筒，人们在各种信仰之间游走，有时汲取不同的宗教传统，创造出自己的信仰体系。

宗教生活的中心应当是个人，而非有组织的教会，这一信念鼓励了大多数美国人包容与接纳所有的信仰。大多数人还认为，必须保护宗教自由，每个人都有权利信奉自己的宗教，不受政府或其他任何人的干涉。美国的宗教传统似乎催生了一些让不同信仰者都易于接受的基本价值观。这使得许多不同的宗教团体可以团结起来，而不需要放弃各自的信仰。文化与宗教的多元性也创造了一种宽容的社会环境，而这种环境又会进一步强化美国不同宗教在一国之内和平共处的现实。

第四章　边疆传统

> 不断开拓自由疆土是美国发展之关键。
>
> 弗雷德里克·杰克逊·特纳（1861—1932）

为什么美国人对旧时西部边疆的生活仍然如此着迷？边疆如何塑造了美国人的价值观？

美国边疆的影响

尽管早在一个多世纪前美国文明就已经渗透并重新定义了边疆，但边疆传统在当今的美国依然清晰可见。由于边疆对美国价值观的形成起到了尤为重要的作用，许多人至今仍对边疆非常着迷。20世纪80年代罗纳德·里根任总统时喜欢追忆边疆生活。他经常被拍到在自己的西部牧场里——劈柴或骑马，还戴着牛仔帽。再近一些，21世纪初，乔治·W.布什总统也曾脚蹬牛仔靴，头戴牛仔帽，邀请媒体成员拍摄他在得克萨斯牧场的照片，强化他的牛仔形象。

多年来，边疆拓荒经历被那些渲染牛仔英雄勇斗印第安恶棍的影视作品赋予了一层浪漫的色彩。很少有人关注到发生在美洲原住民——印第安人——身上真实的悲剧。今天，大多数美国人对于美洲大陆定居历史的黑暗面也有了更多的了解，知道在这个过程中，成千上万的印第安人被杀戮，土地被侵占。北美野牛被白人定居者猎杀灭绝，使印第安人失去了食物和衣物的主要来源，印第安文化也被破坏殆尽。今天，人们对印第安文化又重新产生了兴趣，史密森学会在华盛顿特区就建有一座专门的印第安文化博物馆。

17世纪初，第一批殖民者在美洲大陆东海岸定居，开启了边疆拓荒的征程。开疆经历约于1890年结束，最后一片西部土地也成为了定居地。美国的边疆是指美国的相对未开发地区，多集中在西部。相比已经开发的东部地区，这里的生活和环境都更为艰苦和原始。一片土地被开发后，人们又继续向西，推进到下一片未被开发的区域，所到之处，印第安人被驱赶、屠杀。随着一片又一片疆域被开拓，美国人跨越并占领了2700英里宽的整个美洲大陆。他们开始相信，他们注定要掌控这所有的土地，并且最终他们也做到了。美洲原住民只得到一小部分可以处置的土地，称为保留地，但美国政府背弃了许多承诺，给印第安人造成了太多的不幸与苦痛。

虽然大多数美国人对西进历史都持较客观中立的态度，但仍有不少人认为，边疆、边疆人民，以及他们的信仰，乃是美国传统价值观以其原始和最纯粹的形式鼓舞人心的范例。这一持续两个多世纪的西进运动是如何塑造了这些美国基本价值观的呢？

可以肯定的是，在将森林变为小镇，进而又将小镇变为城市的过程中，拓荒者无疑提供了许多令人鼓舞的勤奋工作的范例。在西部边陲，追逐成功的激烈竞争无疑比其他地方更为多彩，也更富冒险精神。不论是加利福尼亚的淘金热，蒙大拿的淘银热，还是在西部所有地区对肥沃土地的争夺，都诞生了无数精彩刺激的冒险故事。1889年4月，当俄克拉荷马州两百万英亩良田将向定居者开放的消息公布时，数以千计的定居者云集边境，等待确切的公开时间。公开之后，他们真的是驾着马车、骑着马冲进了俄克拉荷马地界，去宣示对最好的土地的所有权。

尽管边疆的日常生活并不似边境冒险故事描绘的那般戏剧化，但即使边疆人民平凡的日常生活，也是美国国家价值观的体现，因为对许多美国人来说，这样的生活形式比东部较发达文明地区美国人的生活要更为纯粹。

个人自由、自力更生、机会均等或许是与美国边疆传统最密不可分的价值观。美国人历来倾向于将边疆拓荒者视为自由个体的榜样。这可能是因为边疆地区对于个体的管束比其他地区都要少。很少有法律和既定的社会或政治制度来限制边疆地区生活的人们。美国人向来崇尚不受外界社会束缚的自由，因此边疆被理想化，成为人们怀旧追忆的早期美国的蓝本。那是一个淳朴的时代，随着国家的城市化和日趋复杂而一去不返。今天，仍有许多生活在西部的人依然坚持着个体不应受政府控制的自由信念。

自力更生与顽强的个人主义者

与个体自由的边疆理想密切相关的是自力更生的理想。如果说生活在边疆的人们摆脱了社会的很多规则的束缚，那同时他们也失去了社会带来的许多舒适和便利。他们必须自力更生。人们通常自己动手建造房屋、狩猎、打理花园，还要自己制作衣物和家居用品。

自力更生的边疆拓荒者已被美国人理想化，并塑造成经典的美国男性英雄形象：顽强的个人主义者。边疆的生活条件将这个英雄磨砺得强壮而坚毅。他枪法精湛，能熟练使用各种武器。在故事中，他总是独来独往，没有家室，不需要任何人的帮助。他孑然一身，独自应对边疆生活中的一切危险；他也足够强大，不仅能保护自己，还能保护他人。

根据边疆生活不同的阶段，人们概括出两类英雄个人主义者。边疆拓荒的早期，也就是19世纪60年代的南北战争之前，主要是人与蛮荒自然的斗争。丹尼尔·布恩应该算是这个时期最著名的英雄。18世纪60年代和70年代，布恩在肯塔基的荒芜旷野冒险探索。他在荒野生活了两年，与狂野的自然和充满敌意的原住民斗智斗勇。1778 年，布恩被原住民抓住，但他们为其强大的体魄与技能所折服，让他加入了自己的部族。后来布恩成功大胆地逃了出来。布恩的英雄力量主要体现于他对抗荒野残酷挑战的能力。虽然他不时也得与印第安人斗争，但人们钦佩他主要因为他是残酷荒野环境的幸存者与征服者，而不是因为他是一名斗士。

第二类粗犷顽强的个人主义英雄形象出自西部拓荒的最后一个阶段，即从 19 世纪 60 年代一直到 90 年代。那时，荒原大多已被征服，斗争已不再是人与自然的抗争，而是人与人之间的争斗。牧场主和牛仔为了控制西部剩余的土地，与农场主、歹徒和原住民争斗，他们彼此之间也相互争斗。那时法制传统尚未完全确立，暴力冲突频繁发生。边疆被人们称为"狂野西部"。

因此，这一时期的英雄基本上就是一名斗士也就不足为奇了。他因能在格斗中打败对手，或在枪战中赢得胜利而受到人们的赞赏。他的英雄气概主要来源于强健的体魄，他强壮到可以一次打败两三个普通人。这种顽强的个人主义者通常是对抗邪恶的正义捍卫者形象。

狂野西部的英雄多以当时的枪手和治安官为原型，比如杰西·詹姆斯和怀亚特·厄普等。狂野西部的英雄对美国英雄主义观的影响超过了丹尼尔·布恩这样的早期荒野边疆英雄。这些狂野西部的英雄激发了无数西部电影的创作灵感；一直到 20 世纪 60 年代，所有美国电影中有 25% 都是西部片。

美国的硬汉英雄

通过各种影视作品，狂野西部的英雄形象塑造了美国人关于"硬汉"或男性力量的概念。很大程度上，影视作品中几乎所有的美国的男性英雄通常都有用身体暴力展示自身力量的能力。西部硬汉的英雄形象树立起来之后，这种英雄范型也被运用于其他场景中——战场上的士兵、硬汉侦探、打击犯罪的警察。从牛仔英雄到终结者、美国队长和警官延科，这些英雄会使拳头，会用枪，精通十八般武器。虽然也有一些影视剧中的英雄更多是因为智慧和敏锐而非体魄受人尊敬，但主宰美国娱乐及电子游戏的依然是这些经典的硬汉英雄形象。现在这类硬汉形象也有了女性版本，比如《饥饿游戏》中仅持一副弓箭参与竞争的凯特尼斯·伊夫狄恩。

这种顽强的个人主义者形象也受到了批评，被认为忽视了许多对边疆发展至关重要的因素。首先，彻底的个人主义者形象夸大了完全自食其力的作用，而淡化了合作对于从荒野中建设一个新国家来说的重要性。其次，由于这一形象通常都是男性，因而它也忽视了女性拓荒者的重要性，还有她们的力量、勤劳、智慧以及教化未开发的边远地区的重要作用。

最后，顽强的个人主义者形象也因其强调通过暴力和枪支来解决问题而受到诟病。在边疆地区，人们的确使用枪支狩猎、保护自己和家人，但西部片美化了旧时西部的枪战，将其浪漫化了。在《正午》等经典西部片中，好人和坏人通过"开枪决斗"来解决争端。顺便提一句，经典老西部片中，"好人"总是戴白帽子，而"坏人"戴黑帽子。不过渐渐地，电影中西部英雄逐渐被战士或打击罪恶的斗士所取代——但枪声依旧——暴力在电影以及后来的电视、电子游戏中有增无减。

一些美国人担忧这些娱乐英雄形象对年轻人的生活和想象力的影响。很多年轻人对暴力和杀戮的场景变得冷漠麻木。21世纪，多个公立学校和大学中发生校园枪击案，枪支已成为一项关键议题。青少年要获得枪支太容易了，而同时，他们丧生枪口的风险远高于成年人。在一些常有年轻帮派成员携带枪支的内城区，问题尤为严重。然而，几起最令人震惊的枪击事件却是发生在向来平静的郊区社区，现在许多学校都要求学生必须通过金属探测仪检查后才能进入教学楼。近些年发生在公共场所的其他大规模枪击事件包括，2011年国会议员加布丽埃勒·吉福兹女士遭枪击受伤、2012年一家电影院内观众被枪杀，以及一所小学的学生被杀害。

美国人拥有枪支由来已久，很多人坚信家中有枪是一项重要的权利。事实上，配备武器的权利甚至受到宪法第二修正案的保障，尽管人们对于开国元勋们下面这段话的含义有不同理解：

> 一个管理严密的民兵组织，对于一个自由国家的安全非常必要，人们持有和配备武器的权利不得被侵犯。

目前，美国私人拥有的枪支数远远超过两亿，足够每个成年人人手一把枪，估计的数量大多在2.7亿到3亿多支之间。这些还仅是公民私人持有的枪支，并不包括军队和警察的枪支。大多数枪械（步枪、散弹枪和手枪）都是由那些喜欢打猎、射击练习或收藏枪支的人所拥有，而且这些人通常有不止一支枪。还有一些人持有枪支是为了保护自己的住宅和家人。比如在2001年"9·11"恐怖袭击事件之后，美国枪支销量就有上升。据估计，目前美国有25%到45%的家庭至少拥有一把枪。

美国人对于2001年"9·11"恐怖袭击事件的反应也体现了边疆的另一个传统，即美国人将法律掌握在自己手中以保护自己和家人的意愿。通常在美国人认为警方无法充分保护他们时，会出现这种倾向。例如，"9·11"事件中，在那架最终坠毁于宾夕法尼亚州的航班上，当乘客同恐怖分子展开搏斗时，他们被赞誉为英雄。

在美国，枪支管制问题颇具争议，赞同者和反对者各执己见。有不少美国人都支持政府对枪支销售进行更严格的管控，而且他们也没有自己家中持有枪支的打算。反对者同样态度坚决，他们甚至成立了强大的政治压力集团，全美步枪协会（NRA）就是其中之一。这个组织不遗余力地阻挠了大部分枪支管制法案的通过。反对枪支管制者认为，限制枪支销售只会让守法的公民买不到枪，而不会影响罪犯拥有枪支。另一方面，美国社会也活跃着一些枪支管制组织，比如以吉姆·布雷迪名字命名的布雷迪防止枪支暴力组织，吉姆·布雷迪曾在一次有人试图刺杀里根总统时中枪并因此瘫痪；还有由加布丽埃勒·吉福兹女士与丈夫马克·凯利创立的新组织"美国人负责任解决方案"。这些团体尤其关注手枪和自动步枪销售。他们认为，没有枪支，美国的家庭，特别是有孩子的家庭，会更安全。有趣的是，公众关于枪支管制的态度十多年来几乎没有什么变化，依然是支持和反对各半。每当有大规模枪击事件发生，枪支销售量就会上升，而同时，反对枪械（特别是自动武器）的人就会呼吁更严格的枪支管制。

创造力和进取精神

边疆赋予粗犷顽强的个体以理想化色彩，使其成为美国英雄的形象；同时，边疆也尊重富有创造力的个体。边疆生活对自力更生的要求鼓励了人们的创造精神。拓荒者们不仅需要生活必需品自给，还要不断面对新的问题和状况，需要新的解决方法。在这种情况下，他们很快学会了尝试用新的方式做事。

来自其他国家的观察家们对男性拓荒者发明新农具的能力印象深刻，而女性拓荒者制作衣物、蜡烛、肥皂等家庭日常生活用品的能力也同样给他们留下了深刻印象。英国著名的美国生活观察家布莱斯勋爵认为，美国的拓荒者们出色的创造力使他们可以胜任其他国家的大多数普通人无法胜任的工作。虽然在这个新国家中，大多数重要发明都是由美国东部较发达地区的人们创造的，但是西部边疆让创造精神在整个国家弘扬开来，并使其成为一种民族性格特质。

乐于尝试与创造进而发展形成了另一种美国特质，那就是进取精神，即一种相信凡事皆有解决方法的乐观态度。美国人乐于相信，再困难的问题都是可以很快解决的，而所谓的无法解决的难题也只是需要多花一点时间而已。他们以直面挑战和克服困难为荣。这种进取精神一直以来让美国人对自己和国家都抱有乐观的态度。很多人说，既然美国可以把人送上月球，那么地球上就没有什么事情是不可能的。19世纪30年代，阿历克西·德·托克维尔曾说过，世界上没有哪个国家比美国"更自信地把握未来"。一直以来，每当时世艰难，政治领袖都会以边疆传统和先辈们的坚定决心感召美国人；这种进取精神至今依然是令美国人自豪、催人奋进的原动力。

机会均等

边疆以最纯粹（也最极端）的形式体现了个人自由和自力更生的精神，同时也是机会均等理想的一种纯粹表达。在西部边疆，人们比东部地区的人更倾向于彼此平等相待。在边疆地区，最重要的是人在自己的一生中能够做些什么，几乎没有人会在意你祖先的功业。边疆的人们喜欢说："地上生活着的比地下埋葬着的更重要。"

由于人们极少在意他人的家庭背景，边疆为许多寻求自我发展的美国人提供了一个新的开始。曾有一位在19世纪初来到美国的英国人发现，当美国人遭遇了生意失败、仕途受挫甚至情场失意，他们通常会前往西部寻求新的开始。边疆成为数百万美国人的希望所在，是他们重整旗鼓，追求成功和更加美好生活的崭新起点。边疆也一直需要新的务农者、熟练工人、商人、律师和政治领袖。

边疆的贫富差异也比其他较发达地区要小。这里的人们生活、穿着和行为方式更为相似。在这里，雇工不愿被称作"仆人"，或被如此对待，他们普遍认为个体之间是彼此平等的。一位欧洲游客观察到："在这里很少看到像我们的农民那样弯腰驼背、拙手笨脚……每个人都昂首挺胸、从容自信。"前往边疆旅行的有钱人会被警告，若想得到礼貌的对待，就不要炫耀自己的财富或显出高人一等的态度。

正如弗雷德里克·杰克逊·特纳指出的，边疆也许不是美国发展的关键，但它绝对是主要因素之一。边疆为强化个人自由、自力更生和机会均等这些美国理想提供了空间和条件。在边疆的土地上，这些理想被放大，并变得可行。在持续了两个多世纪的西进运动中，随着新的疆域不断被开拓，边疆的理想和习俗也不断传入美国其他较发达地区。就这样，许多边疆价值观逐渐成为美国的国家价值观。

第五章　富足传统

对世界各地许多人而言，过去的三个世纪里，美国一直象征着丰饶、富足与物资充裕。

戴维·波特（1910—1971）

自然资源的丰富对美国价值观的发展有怎样的影响？富足在今天又是被如何定义的？

富足的历史

虽然美国人口仅占世界总人口的约5%，但美国人每年却消耗了全世界20%以上的能源；人均每天产生约4.5磅垃圾。只有物产极为丰富的国家才禁得起这样扔东西。人们有时批评美国是一个"抛弃型"国家，丰饶富足，以至于国民有时会被认为是在浪费。包括美国历史学家戴维·波特在内的很多学者都认为，美国丰富的物质财富是美国人性格形成的一个主要因素。

这种丰饶是自然的恩赐。现在美国大陆的土地面积超过300万平方英里。17世纪和18世纪，欧洲移民最初到来时，这里多是良田沃土，有着大片的树木和成群的动物。生活在这里的美洲原住民相对较少，而且也从不曾拥有阻挡欧洲移民所必需的武器和组织。人类再也不可能找到这样一片广袤富饶，人口稀少而自然资源又极为丰富的未经开发的土地了。

但如果说北美丰富的自然资源是美国成为一个富强国家的唯一原因，却并不妥。因为早期移民的信念、决心和努力也同样重要。

在早期定居者所离开的那些欧洲贵族社会国家，统治阶层生来就享有财富和安逸。因此，正如托克维尔所说，有钱人把这一切看作是理所当然，并且认定他们会永远拥有这样的财富和地位。在这些贵族制的国家，穷人也不认为自己和财富有什么关系，因为他们知道自己发财致富或出人头地的机会相当渺茫。

但是在早期的美国，财富与地位并非与生俱来，永远注定的。在美国，机会均等的理念使得穷人和富人的物质财富水平都更加不确定。富人随时可能会失去一些财富，而穷人也可能增加自己的财富。因此，美国社会各个阶层的人都会想方设法保护自己的物质财产，并试图获取更多的财富。托克维尔认为，与其说这是出于贪婪，不如说是因为人们缺乏安全感。如果人们的物质财富，包括其子孙的财富，在短短一生，甚至一代人的时间里，都有可能迅速地增加或失去，那他们自然会没有安全感。托克维尔得出结论，增加个人财富和物质享受对于富有的和贫穷的美国人都是极其重要的。因此，全民都参与到了尽快提升国家物质财富水平的任务中来。

在美国脱离英国独立五十年之后，托克维尔到访了美国。这个国家在这么短时间内取得的巨大进步令他印象深刻。尽管当时美国尚处于发展的早期阶段，并没有多少钱可用于投资，却已在贸易和制造业方面取得了巨大的进步。那时，美国已成为世界第二大海上强国，修建的铁路里程数居世界首位。不过，托克维尔对这种物质成功的影响也有担忧。在这样的社会里，物质主义本身可能成为一种道德观，而不是达到目的的一种手段。

托克维尔的担忧在很大程度上变成了现实。在建设一个富饶国度的过程中，美国人开始用物质主义的标准来衡量自己。在很多国家，对物质财富的热爱被视为一种恶行或道德薄弱的体现；但在美国它却被视作一种美德，是激励人们勤奋工作的积极动力和对成功努力的回报。

一直以来，美国人对自己国家创造物质财富并使国民能够维持较高生活水平的能力引以为傲。这也说明了为什么美国人会用物质主义的标准来衡量作为个体以及作为国家的自己。同时，分享美好生活的机会也吸引了一代又一代的移民来到美国。

从生产者到消费者

美国人对于创造财富和维持高水平生活的重视观念经历了一段时间的发展。在 18 世纪和 19 世纪，大多数美国人认为自己主要是生产者，而不是消费者。作为农民，他们生产食物和自己家中的很多日用品；后来，作为工厂的工人，他们生产制成品。直到 20 世纪，美国人才开始更多地把自己看作消费者，而不是生产者。这一形象的转变很可能是由于大众广告的出现，20 世纪 20 年代广播的兴起和 50 年代电视节目的普及使其成为可能。20 年代时，企业同意付钱或赞助广播节目，并在其中插播一小段他们的产品广告。通过这种方式，企业可以一次接触到大量的美国民众，说服他们购买自己的产品；美国人的重点此时已转向了消费。

大众广告伴随着电视继续发展。到 20 世纪 60 年代末，学者们已经开始研究大众广告对美国社会的影响。历史学家戴维·波特发现，大众广告在美国从规模和影响上已相当重要，应被视为像学校或教会那样的一种组织机构。大众广告的一个影响是赞助商对电视节目内容有了一定的控制能力。如果企业不喜欢某些内容，他们就可以撤销赞助。第二个影响是，由于广告技术非常成功，逐渐被用来改变美国人的态度、行为和信仰。例如，政府发布广告要求年轻人远离毒品；慈善机构用广告来呼吁人们捐款；政治家们为自己的竞选活动花钱做广告。2012 年的总统竞选中，竞选者们仅在电视广告上就花费超过 9 亿美元，其中大部分钱都花在竞争激烈的那些州。

广告投入不仅是为了争取选民，也是为了吸引消费者。现在，几乎所有美国家庭都拥有至少一台电视（平均每户有两台以上），而且家庭电视机每天的使用时间达到8小时左右。有人估算过，美国人平均每年要看大约50000个商业广告。遇到超级碗这样的热门活动时，一个节目就可以让广告覆盖5000万甚至更多的电视观众。除了广播和电视，报纸杂志上也有广告，商家们试图让人们在家以外的地方都能接触到无处不在的广告。到2007年，许多美国人都感到大众广告已经失控。《纽约时报》上一篇题为《目之所及，皆为广告》的文章就谈到了当时新出现在纽约出租车和公共电梯上的显示屏，还有不断变化的新的数字广告牌。纽约市的时代广场是美国最著名也是最引人注目的户外广告范例，巨大的电子广告牌每天24小时播放着广告。

随后便是互联网的到来。2008年，美国已有超过75%的家庭拥有电脑，随后的几年中，美国人又逐渐抛弃了台式电脑，取而代之以笔记本电脑、平板电脑和智能手机。目前，超过80%的18岁以上的成年人在使用互联网，而且这一数字还在持续上升。数字媒体的使用对于广告有深远的影响，使其从大众广告转向目标营销。也就是说，广告商现在利用用户数字媒体使用情况的数据，针对网络上的个人用户定制广告。也许大众广告已经发展到了一定程度，如今消费者对大部分广告大多熟视无睹，而企业也认识到，通过迎合消费者个人的购买习惯和生活的其他各方面，可以更好地吸引消费者。目标营销商家考虑的方面包括地理位置和气候、性别、年龄、收入和教育水平，以及人们的价值观、生活态度和生活方式等。

美国消费者喜欢什么

从事广告业和其他研究美国社会的人都对这个问题感兴趣：美国消费者喜欢什么？研究美国社会的著名学者马克斯·勒纳曾说过，美国消费者对三样东西特别喜好——舒适、洁净和新奇。

勒纳认为，美国人对于舒适的热爱或许可以追溯到边疆拓荒的经历。那时生活艰苦，很少有舒适安逸。这种经历可能使拓荒者和他们的孩子对能让生活更舒适的商品产生强烈的渴望。今天，美国人对舒适的热爱体现在他们对自己房子的装修、汽车和旅行方式的设计上。从美国人如何为自己选一张新床垫上就能看出他们对于舒适的偏爱。很多美国人会到设有床铺以体验床品的商店，在每一种床垫上躺下试试，看哪一种最舒服。

美国人也很注重洁净。或许清教传统也在一定程度上影响了美国人对于洁净的渴望。清教是一个严格的新教教会团体，第一批来到美国的定居者中就有其成员。清教徒强调需要清除身体的污秽和一切邪恶的倾向，他们认为也包括性欲。"洁净近乎虔诚"这句格言就体现了多数美国人的信念：不仅要保持自己身体的洁净，还要保持衣物、居所、车辆的清洁，甚至宠物也要干干净净，没有异味。事实上，对许多美国人来说，如果谁不遵守公认的洁净标准，就是对他人的一种冒犯。

对美国消费者进行营销需要充分认识到他们对于洁净的渴望。查尔斯·杜希格在他的《习惯的力量：生活和工作中我们为何如此这般》这本书中，讲述了宝洁（P&G）空气清新喷剂Febreze的营销经验。实际上，Febreze能够破坏异味气体分子，所以宝洁公司相当确信这款产品会很畅销。他们的广告重点是这款产品如何能够消除，而不仅仅是遮盖异味——甚至包括宠物的气味。但令他们吃惊的是，产品竟然卖不出去。在分析了潜在顾客的行为后，他们认识到，消费者并不想时时被提醒自己的家中有异味而需要用到 Febreze。宝洁公司于是彻底更改了广告方案，不再把 Febreze 作为一种清洁产品进行销售，而是将其介绍为对人们做完清洁的一种回报："谁会愿意承认自己的家里有异味呢？……另一方面，很多人花了 30 分钟的时间打扫完卫生后，会期望家里气味清新。……一年之内，消费者购买这一产品的花费就超过了 2.3 亿美元。"一段时间之后，宝洁才又开始提醒消费者，Febreze 其实还能消除异味。

除了舒适和清洁，美国人还喜欢新奇和与众不同的事物。或许对于自己创造力的自豪也强化了这种对新奇事物的热爱。美国人一直对发明新产品、改进旧产品乐此不疲。广告则鼓励大家不管旧东西还能不能用，要扔掉它们，要不断尝试新产品。而如果人们现在买不起新产品，广告商就会鼓励消费者用信用卡支付——"先消费，后付款"。

除了勒纳提到的这三种，美国消费者热衷的第四种品质是便利。20 世纪后期，自动洗衣机、干衣机、洗碗机、食品加工机、微波炉、垃圾处理机、电动割草机等节省劳力的设备迅速发展。今天，所有这些以及更多其他设施，在普通的郊区家庭中都很常见。美国人对于便利的要求也催生了麦当劳和肯德基这样的快餐店概念。如今，它们已遍布美国的大大小小的城镇，并且出口到了世界各地。而那些喜欢自己在家做饭的人，也可以在美国的食品杂货店里找到各种包装好的方便食品，拿回家可直接烹煮，有些甚至是已预煮过的。

和微波炉、洗碗机一样，快餐店和方便食品也为美国消费者节省了大量原本花在做饭和清扫上的时间。然而，这些便利却并没有减少美国人的忙碌。女性目前占美国劳动力人口一半以上，大多数有未成年孩子的母亲也同样在外工作。由于父母都外出工作，孩子吃了很多外卖食品，而这也是导致儿童肥胖的重要原因。这种便利并没有反映出一种悠闲的生活方式，反而是一种连一分钟都舍不得浪费的忙碌生活。阿历克西·德·托克维尔是最早由此发现美国民族性格中这一奇怪悖论的学者之一。他认为，美国人为了获得舒适便利而拼命忙碌工作，以至于当他们拥有了舒适便利时，却不知该如何放松、享受闲暇了。今天，如同托克维尔的时代一样，很多美国人都患上了一种被医生称为"匆忙症"的病症。

技术的丰富

终日伴随我们的各种技术设备加快了在美国的生活节奏，也改变了人们接受和交流信息的方式。比如，电脑和其他数字设备改变了我们收看电视的习惯。到 2003 年，大部分美国家庭都有了有线电视或卫星电视。因此，除了传统的广播电视网——美国广播公司（ABC）、哥伦比亚广播公司（CBS）、全国广播公司（NBC）和福克斯——大多数美国人都还有数百个电视频道可以选择。从 24 小时新闻到电影、儿童节目、真人秀、体育和赛事，还有很多专业频道，关于烹饪、家装、音乐、旅游、历史、戏剧、喜剧、公众事务、娱乐新闻和时尚生活等，包罗万象。还有一些公共电视网络提供教育和文化节目，由观众捐款、私人企业和基金会捐资，以及政府的拨款支持。

如此众多的选择使电视观众群体变得更加分散，收看任何一种节目的观众比例都在减少。这意味着大众广告商也必须通过其他途径去接近大众。一些公司花钱将产品植入电视节目和电影中，比如主人公喝着可口可乐，还有许多公司则着手进行目标营销。大部分公司都会做一番广泛的市场调查，找出最有可能购买产品的个人。然后，重点把广告投放给这些个人，通常是利用互联网以及其他直销技术。

广告费用也正在流向互联网，因为越来越多的美国人都在上网，而根本不看电视了。美国人越来越多地使用电脑、智能手机、平板电脑及其他数字设备——而不是通过电视来获取资讯和娱乐。尤其是千禧一代。千禧一代是指在跨入新千年后长大，即2000年后成年的那一代年轻人。他们是最理想的市场群体，互联网上大量的广告费投入都是专门针对这个群体。电视、报纸、新闻杂志等传统新闻媒体失去广告收入，结果是，许多大的城市报纸因为没有足够的读者吸引广告商，从而无法负担出版成本，最终倒闭。一些新闻杂志也变成只在网上发行。问题在于，一直以来，报纸和杂志的大部分广告收入是用于支持报道新闻事件的。新闻记者为了新闻报道会花费几个月的时间搜集和分析复杂的重要新闻事件的详情。由于广告收入的减少，新闻机构不得不缩减规模，减少聘用的记者人数。这导致美国媒体有时很难对美国和世界新闻进行深入的报道和分析。

互联网和24小时有线新闻网络激发了人们对新闻事件进行即时报道和分析的欲望，而这种报道方式有时会导致对事实的错误报道或对真相的错误解读。有时新闻还有可能非常肤浅，甚至是愚蠢。例如，人们将大量的时间和关注都集中在名人的生活上，使得新闻与娱乐混淆，形成所谓的"新闻娱乐化"或"信息娱乐化"。不过，互联网也可以成为有价值的新闻报道的来源，世界各地事件目击者都可以通过互联网渠道发布新闻，虽然要鉴别那些用苹果手机拍摄的视频的准确性会很困难。互联网的另一个特点是人们可以定制或个性化设置自己接收的时事资讯，人们还可以创建自己的新闻网站或博客。随着越来越多的美国人将越来越多的时间用来上网，脸书、推特、汤博乐、品趣志等社交媒体正日益重要地传播并塑造着用户的看法。

知识的丰富：大数据

很多美国人大概是在2012年总统大选期间第一次听说"大数据"这个词的。奥巴马总统的竞选团队购买了海量关于潜在选民的数字信息，然后又对从不同渠道搜集来的大数据仔细分析，这使奥巴马团队能以一种全新的方式展开竞选活动，对选民有着相当深入的了解，从而能够一票一票地赢得这些选民的支持。这种做法使得这次竞选活动"颠覆了电视广告在美国政治生活中长期的统治地位，并在世界范围内开了先河——一场全国性的竞选活动竟然可以像地方选举一样，让个人选民的利益也能得到了解和关切"，《麻省理工技术学报》如是评论。

里克·斯莫兰与珍妮弗·埃维特曾合著了一本大型"茶几"书《大数据的人类面孔》。斯莫兰和埃维特说，有些人将大数据定义为超越个人电脑所能容纳的更为海量的信息；也有些人认为，大数据并不仅仅在于信息的数量，它还是帮助人们发现规律和运用知识的工具。"大数据是一场非凡的知识革命，几乎于无形之中，正在悄然席卷商业、学术界、政府、医疗卫生及日常生活"，两位作者这样指出。他们揭示了关于这场革命的一些惊人的事实：

> 今天一个普通人一天处理的数据比 16 世纪时一个人一生所能获得的数据还要多。
>
> 根据网站 BabyCenter.com 的数据，美国出生的孩子中，有三分之一出生前就已出现在了网络上（通常是以超声波扫描图的形式）。到他们 2 岁时，这一比例进一步增加到 92%……三分之一的孩子的照片及信息在出生后几周内会被发布到网上。
>
> 如今，我们每个人都在留下尾气般的数字痕迹，电话记录、短信、浏览历史、GPS 数据以及其他众多信息，将成为永不会消失的无限数据流。

这种有关我们个人信息的大数据引发了重要的个人隐私问题。这些信息会如何被使用？掌握我们一生从出生前直到死亡的所有数字记录又将意味着什么？这些与我们有关的个人信息将如何储存？谁会拥有我们的个人信息，又是谁来决定如何使用它们？其中一些问题已经引起了讨论。比如，谁会掌握我们发布或存储在网络上的照片？此外，还有一些问题涉及政府和执法机构可以如何使用我们的个人信息。政府可以用它做什么？警方呢？当然，也有对犯罪分子和恐怖分子获取我们个人信息的担忧。互联网上的身份盗用也是一个大问题，人们担心恐怖分子可以控制国家重要基础设施，如国防网络和电力系统等。

大数据引发的另一个更大的问题是人类如何使用所有这些新信息。在电脑诞生之前，人类总是苦于知识的匮乏；而现在很多人会觉得我们的知识太多了。计算机的处理能力每 18 个月就会提升一倍，而我们所拥有的知识量也在以指数方式增长。（1 + 1 = 2 + 2 = 4 + 4 = 8 + 8 = 16，依此类推。）这种令人难以置信的无限的信息量是一把双刃剑。也就是说，它既有积极的作用也有消极的影响。从积极的方面来讲，它使我们能够解决很多重要的问题，并可以造福人类；而从消极的方面来讲，海量的信息会将我们淹没，令我们不知所措，甚至做出错误的决定。大脑研究表明，当我们试图处理过多信息时，大脑中负责决策的部分实际上是关停的。这样的话，我们就会只关注最后摄入的信息，而忘记之前的重要事实。研究显示，此时我们会受到情绪的明显影响而做出糟糕的决定。在这种情况下，应该停下来，做些别的事情，让潜意识来为我们梳理信息。我们的潜意识可以评估数据、发现其中的联系，并创造性地运用知识。当我们再次回到任务上时，大脑就能够分清事情的轻重，使我们能够做出正确的决定。

要使大数据有价值、有用处，就必须对其进行管理。一种方法就是依靠专家来对大量的数据进行分析，然后告诉我们哪些是重要的。但问题是，如此海量的数据，就连专家有时也会无所适从。现在，我们不再只是简单地将信息载入电脑，告诉它该怎么做。如今，电脑可以相互交流，并且生成它们自己的新信息。由此产生了被一些人称为"大众科学"或"公众科学"的新的处理数据的方法。在《发现的革新：网络化科学的新时代》一书中，迈克尔·尼尔森解释了科学家是如何通过在线协作来解决复杂问题的。他们通过让公众参与对大量信息进行分类的工作，能取得事半功倍的效果。例如，"星系动物园"计划让人们在自己的智能手机上就能够对星

第五章　富足传统　357

系数据进行分类，从而扩大了尼尔森所说的集体智慧。实际上，正是一位民间科学家发现了一种全新的星系分类。

重新定义美国的富足

美国从来都是来自一种富足，而非匮乏的文化。摇滚明星、活动家博诺指出，美国人避开了一些发展中国家如今所面临的"自然资源诅咒"。美国人学会了开发他们大陆上巨大的自然资源；他们利用这些资源，"不仅是要建成一个现代化的社会，还要养活世界，供给世界的需求"。现在，美国人正在重新定义他们的富足，以使其成为能够帮助解决全球问题的一个强大的思想源泉。在《富足：未来比你想象的更美好》一书中，彼得·H. 迪亚曼迪斯和史蒂文·科特勒指出，资源短缺不过是视角和可获取性的问题。假如你有一棵橘子树，长满了果实，当你摘完了所有能伸手够到的橘子，那么你的橘子资源就枯竭了。但是如果有人发明了梯子，你就又能获得新的橘子供给了。

关于这一点有一个很好的例子，即"水力压裂法"这项颇具争议的技术。该技术使钻井公司从美国地下开采出原先无法获取的石油和天然气。由于石油和天然气资源丰富，2012年国际能源组织曾预测，到2020年，美国将成为世界最大的石油生产国。但是，环保组织却担心，这项技术将会对当地的水供给和生态环境造成什么影响。

迪亚曼迪斯、科特勒等人详细阐述了美国人与世界各地的人们合作，一起寻找创新的解决方案，以保障人们获得干净的水、充足的食物和足够的居所的各种方式。迪亚曼迪斯和科特勒将世界上缺乏基本必需品的人口群体称为"正在崛起的十亿人"。随着手机在全球的普及，任何地方的任何人都将有机会参与创造一个共享富足的世界。他们是这样定义富足的：

> 富足并不是要为地球上每个人提供奢侈的生活，而是要为所有人提供一种可能的生活。这样的生活需要先要满足基本需求，然后……如今，大多数美国贫困人口都有电视、电话、电力、自来水以及室内冲水卫生设施。

诚如迪亚曼迪斯和科特勒所提出的，贫穷和富足的定义可以是相对的。但是对于什么是基本需求，人们是有普遍共识的，那就是干净的水、充足的食物和足够的居所。大数据与网络技术的共享为我们提供了满足这些基本需求，并为所有人创造"一种具有丰富可能的生活"的工具。这种生活不会自动发生。需要克服的障碍有很多——环境污染、食品及清洁水源的短缺、政府领导人的错误决策，甚至还有人类的贪婪——但好消息是，全世界有很多人都在致力于实现这样的生活。

在本章的开始，我们就解释了美国人富足理想的历史缘起，以及其对美国发展的影响。与大多数国家不同，美国人一直相信，他们国家的财富就像一个越做越大的馅饼。随着馅饼不断扩大，并不是富人得到的就更大，穷人得到的更小，而是每人都可以分得一大块。最重要的是，他们相信，所有人都总会有足够的馅饼。对富足传统的坚定信念使美国人充满乐观与自信，他们相信人类的各种问题都是可以解决的。这也极大地减少了美国贫富之间的冲突，而这种冲突曾导致了其他许多国家的分裂。也许，最为重要的是，人们对于生活始终会更加富足的确信，也给予自由、自力更生、机会平等、竞争以及勤奋工作等基本民族价值观以有力的支撑。对美国人来说，高水平的生活正是他们实践这些价值观的回报。

今天，也有一些美国人担心，他们的经济馅饼也许无法再继续做大了。不过，迪亚曼迪斯和科特勒等人认为，大数据等利用与分享知识的新工具的变革会是美国的富足的新面貌。人们会做出更多的馅饼。

第六章　美国商业世界

美国的主业就是商业。

卡尔文·柯立芝 总统（1872—1933）

商业对美国价值观有何影响？美国人将企业主和商业领袖视为英雄还是恶棍？

美国商业的特点

要理解商业对于美国人的意义，必须要熟悉两个词——私营和利润。企业直接或间接由私人个体（或个人团体）所有与经营，并取得利润。与这些私有的、营利性企业相对，还有一些是（1）公众和政府所有和运营的机构，以及（2）非营利组织，如教堂、慈善组织和教育机构等。这些组织和机构不应与企业相混淆。不过，近年来出现了一种称为"大众目的"或"大众利益"的新型企业，实际上是营利性慈善组织的一种形式。本章后面我们会讨论这些新的公益企业。

商业竞争如何强化其他价值观

柯立芝总统在 20 世纪 20 年代时说过，"美国的主业就是商业"，时至今日仍然指出一个重要的事实——商业机构是美国生活方式的核心。其中一个原因是，美国人认为，商业比大多数其他社会机构更坚定地基于竞争的理念。由于多数美国人都将竞争视为进步和繁荣的主要来源，有竞争力的商业机构向来受到尊重。竞争不仅本身被视作一种价值观，同时它也是捍卫个人自由、自力更生、机会均等和勤奋工作等其他美国基本价值观的手段。

通过确保权力不被垄断，竞争保护了个体的自由。不同于一个全能的强大政府，许多企业会为了利润相互竞争。理论上，如果一家企业以不正当方式对待客户占了便宜，它就会输给对待客户更为公平的竞争对手。在有许多企业相互竞争争夺客户的情况下，没有企业能够承担提供劣质产品或服务的后果。

竞争激烈的商业和垄断权力的政府，两者常常会被拿来进行比较。由于商业的高度竞争性，很多美国人都认为，即便政府领导是由人民选出的，而商界领袖不是，商业也比政府更加支持自由。很多美国人认为，竞争对保护自由至关重要。在多数美国人心目中，竞争性的商业与自由的联系是如此紧密，以至于人们会用自由企业而不是资本主义来形容美国的商业制度。

人们认为商业竞争同样强化了机会均等的理念。美国人把商业竞争比作一场人人皆可参与的赛跑，不论出身，成功和地位将属于跑得最快的人。美国人选择通过竞争获得成功和地位，取代以出身决定地位的社会制度。因此，商业也被认为传达了机会均等的理念，而不是世袭特权的观念。

在很多美国人看来，商业竞争也强化了勤奋工作的价值观。两个生意人相互竞争时，工作更努力的那个人更有可能胜出，而投入时间和精力较少的那个人则有可能失败。由于生意人之间必须不断地相互竞争，要想不失败，他们就必须养成勤奋的习惯。

美国人也知道，商业机构其实常常无法贯彻竞争的理念，也并没有能支持自由、自力更生、机会均等、勤奋工作等价值观。美国人有时会怀疑商人们的动机，认为他们可能会以利为先，而忽视了产品安全和环境清洁。因此，多数美国人认为，企业需要一些政府监管，尽管对于监管的程度，大家莫衷一是。不过，瑕不掩瑜，人们大多还是相信，在日常实践中，商业比其他机构更鼓励竞争以及其他基本价值观。

致富梦想

商业机构在美国受到尊重还有另一个原因。伟大的美国梦其中一个方面就是从贫穷或小康到荣华富贵。在美国，这样的梦想通常是通过在商界打拼来实现。这个国家大部分私人财富都是通过商业成功创造的，其中有很多人都是白手起家。事实上，目前福布斯400（最富有的400名美国人）中约有35%的富豪都出身贫困或中产阶层。尽管有很多最富有的美国人都继承了家庭的财富，从商依然为雄心勃勃的人创造财富提供了最好的机会。

早在19世纪30年代，阿历克西·德·托克维尔就观察到了经商对美国人的巨大吸引力。他写道，比起务农，美国人更喜欢经商，因为经商更有机会快速致富。不过，即便是农业生产者也同样极具商业精神。他们经常会经营一些小生意来增加务农的收入。托克维尔还注意到，美国的农民对买卖土地来营利远比对耕作土地更感兴趣。因此，甚至是在托克维尔的时代，当大多数美国人仍是农业人口时，商业文明的种子就已经生根了。

商业不仅被视为个人致富的捷径，还被认为能造福于整个国家。通过竞争，更多的人获得财富，国家也因此而繁荣。相比之下，由政府主导的商品生产与分配体制则遭到诟病。人们不信任这种体制，因为政府对权力的垄断消除了竞争。多数美国人可能更倾向于限制政府对企业的管控，让自由企业制度或自由市场机制按自身的规律发展。但是，关于政府和企业在提供医疗保健和退休福利等服务方面各自应承担什么样的角色存在着很大的争论。美国是世界上少数几个没有由政府保障和管理的全民医疗保险的工业化国家之一。美国的医疗保险自20世纪40年代以来就一直是与就业挂钩的，不过，进入21世纪以来，政府的作用也在不断增强。《平价医疗法案》（2009年通过并于2010年—2015年实施）的目的就是使所有美国人都能够获得平价医疗保险。然而，这一计划（也被称为"奥巴马医改计划"）从一开始就争议不断，遭到许多商界领袖和保守派政客们的反对。

而关于退休保障，从20世纪80年代起，大多数企业已从向退休职工发放养老金转变为为他们设立401K账户，用于储蓄或投资。这使得员工在在职期间就可以动用退休基金，导致许多职工提前花掉了这笔钱而没有足够的储蓄养老。这在美国成为一个日益严重的问题。将来，当这些职工面临退休却没有足够的积蓄时，政府的退休金很可能也会减少。虽然目前企业和个人都要向政府的社会保障系统（以及医疗、政府的退休医疗保障系统）投入资金，但人们深切担忧，随着老龄化人口的增长，将没有足够的资金以负担这些福利。对这个问题我们还将在下一章关于政府的介绍中再进一步讨论。

作为商业英雄的企业家

由于有很多信念是将商业和财富与传统美国价值观联系在一起的，因此商业上的成功人士时常会成为美国人心目中的英雄。企业家以最纯粹的方式，为诠释传统美国价值观提供了范例，原因有几点。其一，他们自力更生，从无到有地创建了一些伟大的事业。一百多年前建立起钢铁、铁路、炼油等伟大民族工业的人大多都是企业家。他们在创业之初并没有什么钱或权力，却最终成为创造巨大财富的大企业的领袖。

这些早期的企业家白手起家，建立起了巨大的产业，这使他们在数百万美国人心目中如同拓荒时代的边疆英雄。边疆英雄进入了美国广袤的荒野，把森林变成了农场、村庄和小城市。而企业家们，就像早期边疆的英雄一样，被视为粗犷顽强的个人主义者，强化了自由、自立和勤劳等价值观。19世纪的企业家们往往出身普通，没有继承的社会地位或财富可倚仗，靠自己的奋斗成了百万富翁。他们也因此用行动为机会均等的美国理念提供了最佳例证。

19世纪末至20世纪初出版的一系列霍拉肖·阿尔杰的小说在美国广受欢迎，也体现了早期企业家的成功故事在美国的巨大影响力。这些书在美国民众中总共卖出了约1700万本。阿尔杰小说的中心主题是，农村或城市的穷小子如果勤奋工作，自力更生，就可以成为富有而成功的商人。因为美国是机会均等的国度，在这里人人都有机会成功。

在阿尔杰出版的第一部小说《衣衫褴褛的迪克》中，一个以给人擦鞋为生的贫穷年轻人变成了理查德·亨特，一名成功富有的商人。主人公白手起家，从贫穷到富有，实现了美国梦。迪克的成功仅有部分是由于他所处的是机会均等之国度。此外，就要归功于他践行了美国人自力更生和勤奋工作的美德。在阿尔杰的描述中，迪克"深知他只能依靠自己，他决心发挥自己最大的能量……成功十有八九都是因为这一秘诀"。迪克也是一个努力的擦鞋小子,"精力充沛,有着敏锐的商业头脑"。这一品质决定了他的成功,阿尔杰解释道,因为不论从事什么职业,"干劲和勤劳都会得到回报"。

尽管今天已经很少有美国人读霍拉肖·阿尔杰的小说了,但那些企业家们白手起家,创造财富与成功的理念依然鼓舞着他们。企业家们最吸引美国人的一个特点,就是他们不屈从于权威。历史上,美国人一向钦佩那些不听命于任何权威,经营自己的事业和生活的企业家。美国人非常尊重那些能够说"我是自己的老板"的人。美国有许多员工也依然梦想着有朝一日可以拥有自己的事业,做自己的老板。

企业 CEO/CFO

与创办新企业的创业企业家不同,还有一些现有大型企业领导人负责管理企业,比如 CEO(首席执行官)和 CFO(首席财务官)等。19 世纪后期,许多伟大的企业家建立了庞大的商业组织,在 20 世纪需要新一代的商业领袖去经营它们。这些商业领袖,有时被称为"组织人",如今经营着美国的大型企业。他们权力很大,通常积累了巨大的个人财富,但他们通常都没有创业企业家的英雄形象,因为他们只是管理别人创建的企业。美国人大多会钦佩创业企业家们创造财富的能力,觉得他们赚得再多也不为过;但他们对 CEO 的看法却没有这么大度。事实上,有很多高薪的 CEO 都因为数百万的年薪和利己的管理决策而受到严厉的抨击。

阿里安娜·赫芬顿在她的《食槽旁的猪:企业贪婪和政治腐败如何蛀蚀美国》一书中,详述了有些 CEO 如何从其管理的企业获取大量金钱并挪为私用。她描述了大型有线电视企业阿德菲亚公司的 CEO 约翰·里加斯是如何在公司陷入财政危机时从公司借走 31 亿美元并肆意挥霍的:

> 他花了 1300 万美元在自家后院建了个高尔夫球场,花 1.5 亿美元买下了水牛城军刀冰球队,花 6500 万美元资助自己女婿经营的一个风险投资集团,他的三架私人飞机仅维护就要耗费数千美元,他还花 70 万美元成为一个乡村俱乐部的会员。

受到抨击的不仅是一些企业领导者的贪婪,还有他们的决策对企业员工、股东以及整个社会所造成的影响。21 世纪初还发生过其他一些公司丑闻,公司 CEO 和其他高管从濒临破产的企业中获取巨额资金。其中最臭名昭著的例子就是安然公司,不仅造成了数千名员工失业,还使他们的养老积蓄也血本无归。激怒美国人民的不只是企业高管的贪得无厌,还有他们对股东的欺骗、对企业的违法经营管理,以及他们对待员工的残酷无情。

20 世纪的大部分时间里,美国都有很多报酬优厚的制造业工作。许多这些工厂工作并不需要大学学历,大量的普通美国人都可以赚到足够的钱,维持舒适的中产阶级生活。然而,全球经济的现实导致一些美国企业发生了重大变化。为了生产出在全球市场上价格具有竞争力的商品,许多公司将工厂迁往了海外。公司再也支付不起美国人高额的工资。其次,一些公司通过裁员来提升竞争力。IBM这样的老牌大公司裁减了数千名员工，缩减规模，以提高效率和竞争力。第三，一些公司减少了全职员工的人数，而代之以兼职员工，这样就不用缴纳医疗保险或退休金。最后，还有一些企业开始将工作外包到其他国家。一个很好的例子就是电话客服支持。今天，当一名美国消费者打电话投诉产品问题或询问订单状态时，接电话的人很可能是在印度或菲律宾，而并不是在美国。

21世纪，美国人不但眼睁睁看着CEO们把高薪的工作转移到海外，还遭受到经济衰退的打击。中产阶层最主要的财产就是他们所拥有的房屋。他们的房产价值在20世纪90年代末和21世纪初时曾大幅上涨，形成了"房地产泡沫"。当泡沫破裂时，中产阶层的房主遭受重创。突然之间，他们房屋的价值缩水了一半，同时很多人还失去了工作。雪上加霜的是，美国金融机构也陷入了危机。银行体系濒临崩溃，政府不得不借钱给银行以使其免于破产。政府还贷款给克莱斯勒和通用这两家美国汽车企业，防止他们倒闭。做出这样的决策，理由也很简单，有些企业"太大而不能倒"。

中产阶级与百分之一

到了2010年，许多美国中产家庭已经非常愤怒。他们的收入25年都不曾变化（考虑了通货膨胀后）。对于找到一份好工作并偿还房屋抵押贷款，他们已丧失了信心。为了生存，很多人不得不拿出退休账户里的钱。而且他们还得知，随着2008年股市的下跌，他们所剩的投资退休账户里的资产也已缩水。据《赫芬顿邮报》报道，中产阶层的真实民生痛苦指数达到了历史最高值。民生痛苦指数综合了失业率、信用卡负债以及汽油、食品、医疗费用和住房等必需品的通胀率等多种数据。在一些地区，大量房屋因房主无力偿还抵押贷款而丧失赎回权，被银行收回。

但也不是所有美国人都生活在水深火热之中。20世纪80年代末以来，最富有的人和其他人群之间的差距一直在扩大。现在，很清楚的是，最富有的1%的人在经济危机中变得更加富有。一些公司的CEO通过裁员和收购其他陷入财务困境的公司牟取了财富。银行和其他金融机构出售各种几乎没人理解的金融产品。对有些人来说，那些曾经为美国带来了就业、新产品和服务的商业机构，现在只是以钱生钱的工具。人们突然意识到，由于税收结构的问题，对投资收入征收的税率甚至要低于工资收入的税率。沃伦·巴菲特是最富有的美国人之一，他曾说过，他的秘书所缴的税率比他还高。这也成为2012年总统大选的一个议题，因为共和党候选人米特·罗姆尼就曾从他的企业对美国本土公司的裁员中获取了大量财富。同时，他的大部分收入都来自税率较低的投资收入，而且他的钱大多存在美国以外的离岸银行账户中。

此后，经济开始好转。随着股市复苏并不断上涨，美国劳动阶层的怒火也与日俱增。2011年秋，一些人发起了一场名为"占领华尔街"的运动，要求富人缴纳他们"理应缴纳"的税额。他们在纽约华尔街证券交易所附近的公园扎营，示威活动随后也蔓延到其他城市。虽然最终多数示威活动因天气寒冷和其他一些因素而停止，但愤怒却仍在延续。

不安的不只是美国的劳动阶层。时事评论家们开始质疑，美国梦是否已经破灭，各种关于拯救和重建美国梦的书籍纷纷问世。赫芬顿在她的《第三世界的美国：我们的政客如何抛弃中产阶级与背叛美国梦》一书中给美国人敲响了警钟。赫芬顿本人是希腊移民，她说自己写这本书是为了对于可能发生的情况提出警告。1980年，她来到美国寻找"更好的生活"，那时每个人都会把"更好的生活"一词与美国联系在一起。"社会的向上流动性一直都是美国梦的核心——它给了大家一种信心，只要你勤奋努力、遵守规则，你就会做得出色，而你的孩子就有机会做得更出色。"但赫芬顿也说，最近几年，她发现中产阶级"处境非常不利"。政府急于拯救华尔街，却忘记了"主要大街"（普通民众与小企业主）。她认为，美国的政治体系出了问题，而美国的经济体系则"沦落为反复发作的企业失控"。

美国人对商业机构的尊重是周期性起伏的。追溯到19世纪工业革命的时候，商业领袖时而被视作贪婪腐败的恶棍，时而又被赞颂为英雄。这并不是美国人第一次质疑商业领袖的动机。比如19世纪后期，就有一些商业领袖因其腐败行径和对他人的漠视而被称为"强盗贵族"。这也促使政府通过立法来规范商业行为。现在，当有商业丑闻发生时，政府会有更多的规章制度来作出反应。传统上，共和党人一直主张自由放任或不干涉的政策，民主党人则倾向于加强监管和保障措施。不变的一点是对于美国梦的价值与重要性的坚定信念。

重新定义美国梦

为什么追求更好生活的美国梦在经济不景气时或其他困境中依然顽强地延续呢？为什么它更多的是能激励和鼓舞着美国人，而不是让他们灰心沮丧呢？赫芬顿说，在写作《第三世界的美国》一书时，她一次又一次被美国各地展现出的韧性、创造性和善举所打动。

首先，许多美国人的确非常坚韧。也许这一品质部分源于美国人的边疆传统，人们相信他们可以依靠自己的力量渡过难关。对于自力更生和个人自由的坚定信念使许多美国人为自己重新定义了美国梦。美国大都会人寿保险公司是一家提供保险、年金及员工福利的大型美国公司，五年多来一直在进行关于美国梦的年度研究。他们最近的一份研究显示，美国梦的重心已有了重大转移。研究揭示了他们称之为"自己动手"（DIY）的美国梦的兴起，并描述了美国人所表现出的"韧性与适应力"。面对经济困境，现在美国人认为，与家人和朋友享有亲密的关系要比获得更多的物质财富更重要。他们更满足于现有的一切，并试图在工作和个人生活之间找到更好的平衡。研究得出的结论是，对于现在的大多数美国人而言，"获得自我实现感对实现美国梦比积累物质财富更为重要"。

其次，美国社会非常看重创造力。美国消费电子协会（该协会主办全球最大的年度技术贸易展）主席兼首席执行官加里·夏皮罗认为，企业创新至关重要。在《回归：创新将如何重塑美国梦》一书中，夏皮罗指出，纵观历史，伟大的创新者才是美国经济成功的真正驱动者。正是美国的创新创造了新的就业机会乃至前所未有的全新产业。"更重要的是，"夏皮罗总结道，"创新引领了我们民族的前进，推动我们取得成功并为更美好的明天而奋斗。简而言之，创新就是美国梦。"

《创意阶层的崛起》一书的作者，理查德·佛罗里达认为，创新和创造力在当今的美国作用正日益突出，而且并不仅限于在科技领域。佛罗里达对人口普查数据进行了分析并据此估计，目前美国有近三分之一的劳动力属于"创意阶层"。他们或在科学、教育、设计、艺术和娱乐等领域创造新的想法、技术或内容，或是解决商业、法律、金融和医疗等领域的复杂问题。这些创意工作者多聚集在东西海岸、高科技中心以及主要研究型大学和机构附近。他们对这些地区未来的经济发展有着巨大的积极影响。

第三，美国人富于同情心的天性以及他们对于意义的追寻也是美国梦重新定义的一部分。在《富足：未来比你想象的更美好》一书中，彼得·迪亚曼迪斯和史蒂文·科特勒谈到了DIY（自己动手）创新者。他们指出，自力更生和技术的结合，有利于将DIY创新者塑造成传播富足与创造美好的一支力量。DIY创新者如今掌握了技术工具，可以把他们对美好世界的构想变为实实在在的企业，解决实际的问题。比如，《连线》杂志主编克里斯·安德森领导了一个名为"DIY无人机"的非营利网络社区。利用大众科学技术，他的DIY创新团队学会了以每台300美元的成本生产无人机，而军方无人机的价格通常为35 000美元到250 000美元之间。现在，他们正在尝试用无人机运送物资到被季风雨水冲坏道路的地方或根本没有道路的地区。还有一家公司，作为被迪亚曼迪斯和科特勒称为"创客运动"的一部分，拥有一套无人机和装置在集装箱内的充电站网络，遍布整个非洲。在偏远地区的村庄里人们用智能手机下单，然后由无人机配送订单。像四轴飞行器这样的无人机可以携带包括药品到农机配件等在内的各种物品，而每千克每公里的运送成本不到6美分。

易贝首任总裁杰夫·斯科尔、脸书创始人马克·扎克伯格以及贝宝创始人埃隆·马斯克等都属于被迪亚曼迪斯和科特勒称为科技慈善家的新亿万富翁群体。他们在新的科技领域创造了自己的财富，如今他们正改变着美国慈善事业的面貌。传统上，慈善家多在生命行将结束时才开始把钱捐给慈善机构。可是，现在的科技慈善家很多人是在30岁之前就成了亿万富翁，致富之后便投身慈善事业。斯科尔说，他们精力充沛，意气风发，"自信源于他们如此年轻就建立起全球企业。他们想要去实现一些大胆而艰巨的目标，比如防止核扩散、流行病和保障水资源等"。他们敢想敢为，相信自己能够为"不可能解决"的问题找到解决办法，比如为全世界每一个人提供清洁安全的饮用水。因为年轻，他们相信自己有生之年能够真正有所作为，解决众多的社会问题。

这些科技慈善家中有相当一部分是自我创造的DIY社会企业家。迪亚曼迪斯和科特勒认为，他们是"将企业家务实和注重结果的方法与社会改革者的目标结合了起来"。一些社会企业家创立公益企业，将利润用于推动社会变革。这些公益企业的建立的目的是要解决特定的社会问题；他们也营利，但把钱用于通常由非营利组织进行的项目。协会领导力中心指出，新兴的公益企业正在淡化营利企业和非营利组织之间的传统界限。公益企业必须致力于创造社会或环境效益，"同时保证健康的底线"。他们"努力维护企业界所熟知的三条底线——人、地球和利润"，他们必须公开自己的社会与环保业绩。他们同时也是非营利组织潜在的经费来源。公益企业的利润结构使其不必过多寻找外部资金就能够继续运作下去。

易贝首任总裁杰夫·斯科尔说，社会企业家们有着高度的热情，热切渴望实现自己的目标。为了带来改变，他们会比慈善机构通常所做的要更多。斯科尔是这样描述社会企业家的：

在真正改变世界之前，社会企业家是不会满足的，他们会冲破一切阻碍，这是他们的天性。慈善机构也许会给人们提供食物，但社会企业家们却不会满足于只是教人们种植粮食——他们想教会农夫如何种庄稼、如何赚钱、如何把利润投入商业、如何再雇佣十名员工，并在这一过程中，改造整个行业，只有这样，他们才能感到欣慰。

美国商业的未来

不论经济状况是好是坏，总会有一些美国人试着开创自己的事业。这些满怀希望的创业者大多有固定的工作，他们利用业余时间，作为副业经营着自己的创业企业。政府通过小型企业管理局（SBA）鼓励扶持新创小企业，因为这些企业为美国创造了大部分的新就业机会，雇用了美国超过一半以上的劳动人口。SBA对小企业的定义是雇员少于500人的企业，但事实上大部分（四分之三以上）小企业根本没有雇员——只有个体经营业主自己。半数左右的小企业是居家办公的，互联网在其中起到了重要作用。令人惊讶的是，所有拥有雇员的美国企业中99%以上也都是小企业，其中有一半的雇员为10—99人。美国有超过2300万家小企业，而雇员超过500人的大企业仅有约18 500家。

互联网给个人提供了在几乎任何事情上进行合作的工具，许多有商业构想的美国人在互联网上找到了支持。像www.quirky.com这样的网站甚至帮助用户开发新的发明构想。你提交一个想法，网站会请网民投票决定这个发明是否有实现的价值。如果你的想法被选中，你就可以参与产品设计、工程、融资、制造和分销的众包过程。quirky网站在线记录每个人的贡献，所有参与者都可以从销售利润中分得相应的份额，虽然有人分到的还不到1%。这样的网站提供了最充分的合作形式。

互联网使全球联系在一起，大小企业都可以随时随地与潜在客户进行互动。美国仍然是世界上最大的市场之一，无疑也将继续作为全球经济的主要参与者。在世界银行的经商便利程度排名中，美国列第四位，仅次于新加坡、中国香港和新西兰。在未来几年中，美国多元文化背景的劳动力也将继续发挥重要价值。

一些将业务转移到了海外的美国企业现在也开始回归，制造业又回来了。不过，大多数新的制造业都使用机器人技术，并不需要多少工人，而工人也必须具备更高水平的技能。美国的教育系统和企业界正在尝试合作，为工人们提供未来就业所需的新技能。重大改变将是必然的。

尽管近几十年来美国商业制度确实经历了翻天覆地的变化，但它依然是美国最重要的制度之一。从很多方面来说，美国的主业仍然是商业。

第七章 美国的政府和政治

> 一个明智而节俭的政府应当制止人们相互伤害，并让他们自由地管理自己对事业和进步的追求。
>
> 托马斯·杰斐逊（1743—1826）

美国人认为政府在他们的生活中应该扮演怎样的角色？美国价值观对政府职能又有何影响？

强力政府的疑虑

自由个体的理想对美国人看待政府的眼光产生了深远的影响。传统上，人们对政府怀有深深的疑虑，认为政府是自由的天敌，即便它是由人民选举产生的。许多美国人觉得，政府越庞大和强势，对个人自由而言，也就越危险。

这种对于强力政府的怀疑可以追溯到1776年美国独立战争的领导者们。这些人认为，英国政府用苛捐杂税和其他手段打压美洲殖民者的自由及经济发展，最终目的是要让英国的权贵和君主受益。著名革命作家托马斯·潘恩曾说，"……政府，即使在其最好的状态，也不过是一种无可避免的灾祸；若处于最糟糕的状态，那便忍无可忍了……"这也代表了许多其他美国革命者的看法。

美国政府的组织形式

美国宪法中关于国家政府组织方式的规定很好地反映了美国人对于政府权力的疑虑。宪法的规定更注重防止政府作恶，而不是让其行善。比如，国家政府分为三个独立的部门。这种对政府权力的分割乃是基于这样一种信念，即如果政府的任何一个部分或部门掌握全部或者大部分的权力，就会威胁到公民个人的自由。

政府的立法部门被称为国会。国会有两院——参议院由各州每州出两名参议员组成，无论州人口多少；以及众议院，众议院由各州按人口比例选出，共435名众议员。（在众议院中，人口多的州比人口少的州有更多代表名额；而在参议院，各州的代表名额相同。）总统，或最高行政首长，是行政部门的首脑，负责法律的执行。司法部门由最高法院及下级国家法院组成。司法部门通过司法案例解决有关法律确切含义的争议。它既解释法律，也负责裁定法律是否符合宪法——法律是否在宪法允许的范围内。

三大部门中若有任何一方滥用权力，其他两方即可通过制约与平衡机制联合起来阻止。宪法在平衡立法和行政部门的权力方面慎之又慎，因为这两个机关（国会与总统）在三个部门中权力最大。在政府活动的几乎所有重要领域，如制定法律、宣战或与外国缔结条约的权力方面，宪法赋予这两个部门各自以足够的权力，以防止另一方自行行事。

美国的制度常常使其他国家的观察者困惑。国家政府似乎有两个声音在相互唱反调，一个来自总统，一个来自国会。例如，如果参议院拒绝批准，即参议院没有投票表决通过，总统签署的与外国政府的条约就无法生效。参议院在对外条约上有一定的权力，与众议院共同拥有军事行动方面的权力。总统在国际事务上采取某些行动前必须取得"参议院的意见和同意"。总统任命内阁的一切成员，如国务卿和国防部长，都必须得到参议院的批准。

另一方面，总统也可以阻止国会通过的法案成为法律。经众议院和参议院通过的立法或决议，须呈送总统。总统须在接到法案后十日之内（星期日除外）采取行动。对此，会有四种可能性：

1. 总统同意这项法案，签署，该法案即成为法律。

2. 总统不同意该法案，否决，并将该议案连同其反对意见退回国会。如国会两院三分之二议员投票推翻总统的否决，则该法案成为法律。

3. 如总统接到法案后十日之内（星期日除外）不采取任何行动，则该法案无总统签署即成为法律。

4. 如果十日期限结束前国会休会，而总统既未签署也未否决该法案，则该法案无法生效。这被称为搁置否决。有时，当总统既不赞同某些法案，又不想公开否决时，就会这样做。

虽然美国的政府分权制度在很多观察者看来是低效，甚至混乱的，但多数美国人仍然坚定地信任这一制度，原因有二：一、这个制度经受住了历史的考验；二、它有力地保护了个人自由。

除了政府权力三分，宪法还包括旨在保护具体个人权利和自由不受政府干涉的《权利法案》。《权利法案》中的一些保障涉及言论自由。政府不得干预个人的言论自由、宗教信仰自由以及集会（聚集）的权利。《权利法案》还保障被指控违法者接受公正的刑事诉讼的权利。这些权利有时被称为"正当程序"，包括如下规定，如某人被指控犯罪，就必须以该罪行被起诉，在被证实有罪之前被推定为无罪。被告人有取得律师的权利，在施加处罚之前必须经过审判宣判有罪。因此，《权利法案》是美国人相信个人自由的重要性的另一种表达。

总统及国会的选举

总统与国会两院之间政治上几乎完全相互独立，因为它们都是各自独立选举产生的。国会选举不会决定谁将当选总统，总统选举也无法决定谁能入选国会两院。这一制度和政府议会制选择总理的方式有很大不同。另一点不同是，美国只有两个主要政党：传统上较为自由进步的民主党与较为保守的共和党。在议会制中，组建政府必须取得一些主要政党的同意；而在美国却不是这样。总统、众议员和参议员都是由美国公民选举产生的。

由于总统选举和国会两院议员的选举是各自独立的，在美国的制度下就很可能出现一个政党的领袖赢得总统选举，而另一个政党则赢得了国会多数席位的情况。还有可能共和党控制了两院中的一个，而民主党则控制了另一个。20世纪后期，总统基本都是共和党人，但民主党经常控制国会中的一院或两院。1994年，情况发生了逆转：民主党人比尔·克林顿当选总统，而共和党则赢得了参众两院的控制权。然后在21世纪初，共和党人一度同时掌控总统职位（乔治·W. 布什）和国会两院。奥巴马（民主党人）总统任内又再次出现了分裂的政府；除了最初两年，他的两届任期内，都是由共和党控制众议院，而民主党控制参议院。

要想理解华盛顿发生的事情，不仅要了解总统的党派，还要知道控制众议院和参议院的是什么党派。由于所有立法在呈送总统之前必须经参众两院一致通过，立法很可能在国会一院通过而在另一院受阻。此外，众议院或参议院的控制权每两年就有可能发生变更。众议院议员任期两年，参议员任期六年。由于参议员任期是交错的，当众议院每两年举行一次选举，参议员只改选其中三分之一。

总统选举每四年举行一次，定在11月的第一个星期二。拟定宪法时，美国的开国元勋们就如何选举总统产生了分歧。一些人不希望总统由国会议员们选出，而另一些人则不愿意把选择权完全交给选民。最后的结果是一个折衷的方案——选举人团，一种间接选举总统的制度。这一制度延续至今。在总统选举中，选民实际上投票选举的是代表，称为选举人，再由这些选举人正式选出总统。根据选举人团制度，在本州获得多数选民票的候选人在大多数情况下（也有一些例外）将获得该州的所有选举人票。每个州的选举人票数与该州在参众两院的代表总人数相等。尽管选举人票数根据各州人口而有不同，仍然有可能出现没有获得多数选民票的候选人当选总统的情形。

虽然美国人都知道选举人团制度，但直到2000年大选之前，普通选民对此并没有太多关注。在此之前，只有过三次普选失利却因赢得了更多选举人票而当选总统的先例，因此大家都觉得可能性似乎很小。上一次发生这样的情况是在1888年，本杰明·哈里森赢得了总统大选，尽管对手格罗弗·克利夫兰在普选中赢得了多数选民票。整个20世纪，当选的总统除了赢得选举人票，都至少获得了多数选民票。然而在2000年的大选中，民主党候选人阿尔·戈尔比共和党候选人乔治·W. 布什赢得了更多的选民票，但布什却获得了多数选举人票，成为总统。（2004年乔治·W. 布什与约翰·克里之间的总统竞选不存在这个问题，因为布什同时赢得了选民票和选举人票。）

2000年选举的结果使美国的政治制度产生了震动。其中一个原因是，投票结果十分接近，令人难以置信，有几个州甚至不得不重新计票。结果最具争议的州是佛罗里达州，州长是乔治·W.

布什的弟弟杰布·布什。虽然戈尔的全国普选票数领先，但谁能赢得佛罗里达州的二十五张选举人票，谁就能赢得选举。佛罗里达州的重新计票结果显示，在近600万张投票中，布什以不到1000张选票的优势获胜。经过一系列的法律挑战，美国最高法院在大选一个月过后决定，佛罗里达州议会有权停止重新计票，并有权核实选举人票。最高法院裁定，各州对如何选择本州选举人有最终决定权。

自由个体的理想

18世纪末，大部分美国人都期待这个根据宪法创建的新的国家政府能够不干涉他们对个人目标的追求。他们认为，政府的中心任务是为自由个体的发展创造最有利的条件。

在19世纪60年代的南北战争之前，美国人对自由个体的理想是边疆拓荒者和小农场主。托马斯·杰斐逊总统曾表达过这一理想，他说："如果真有上帝拣选的子民，那么在土地上劳作的人们就是上帝的选民……"杰斐逊赞美农民，因为他们是自由的个体，他们的日常需要能够自给自足。他认为，农民不依赖于任何人，是最诚实的公民。杰斐逊一生都推崇小而弱的政府形式，他认为这样的政府能够促进一个由自由、自力更生的农民公民组成的国家的发展。

从南北战争结束，直至20世纪30年代的大萧条，成功的商人取代了农民和拓疆者，成为自由个体的理想代表。美国人普遍认为政府不应该干预商业。如果政府这样做的话，就会威胁到自由个体的发展，而正是这些自由个体的竞争精神、自力更生和努力工作，使美国发展成为一个物质文明日益繁荣的国度。

因此，相较于国家的广袤和商业企业所掌握的巨大权利，政府依然是小而无为的。在此期间政府出台了一些规定，但这些规定对商业活动影响不大。从19世纪70年代到20世纪30年代，商业组织和观念主宰了美国的政府和政治。这一时期大部分是共和党执政，而他们坚定地支持这些政策。

大政府的发展

传统上，共和党人倾向于让企业在很少或根本没有政府监管的情况下相互竞争：让自由企业制度在市场上自我调节。另一方面，民主党人却一直倾向于让政府来监管企业，保护消费者和工人，同时解决社会问题。因此，正是一位民主党总统主持创建了"大政府"也不算意外。

20世纪30年代的大萧条极大地削弱了商人作为美国自由个体理想的地位，大企业失去了人们的尊重。大萧条也造成美国的贫困人口达到此前和平时期所未见的规模，对政府采取紧急行动进行救助产生了需求。因此，政府应该小而无为的想法基本被摒弃了。此外，自由个体的理想也经历了一些非常重要的变化。

大萧条时期的普遍失业和其他经济困难引发了一种新的假设，即不能指望个人单单依靠自己来获得他们的经济安全。这种新假设转而又促使国家政府在帮助个人满足日常需求方面发挥了巨大而积极的作用。富兰克林·罗斯福总统带领的民主党在20世纪30年代进行了一些变革，他将其称为美国人的"新政"。

大萧条和"二战"之后，虽然美国恢复了经济繁荣，但政府在帮助个人提供经济安全方面作用的增强并没有结束。战后繁荣时期，政府的作用仍在继续加强，并且在20世纪60年代，另一位民主党总统，林登·约翰逊的任内，有了极大的扩展。罗斯福的新政发展出了一些人眼中的永久"福利国家"：为退休者提供养老金，给失业者发放政府支票，为抚养孩子却无收入来源的家庭提供支持，为穷人和老年人提供医疗保障，还有其他政府福利措施。约翰逊将新的福利计划称为"伟大的社会"。

福利的争议

大政府的发展和政府社会项目的建立并非没有争议。一方面，一些美国人担心政府提供的经济保障会削弱自力更生的精神，而这一精神在美国人心目中是与个人自由紧密相关的。最糟糕的情况是，政府的经济保障会使越来越多的美国人依靠政府而不再自立，从而危害个体自由。因此，强大的个人主义和自力更生的传统使美国人并不像其他民主国家，如西欧国家，的公民那样能够接受社会福利计划，在这些国家社会事业的覆盖要比美国更为广泛。

皮尤研究中心的一份调查显示了欧洲人和美国人态度的对比：

> 在对个人主义和政府角色的看法上，美国人与西欧人的观点也迥然不同。近六成（58%）的美国人认为，人人不受国家干预，追求自己的生活目标更为重要；而仅有36%的美国人认为，国家应该在社会中发挥更为积极的作用，保证没有贫困人口，这点更为重要。

美国人普遍不赞成欧洲式的社会主义，即保证所有贫困人口都能获得福利。事实上，有些美国人认为社会主义是一种有着潜在危险的外来经济制度。一些保守人士曾因奥巴马总统的一些自由主义立场而指责他是社会主义者。另一方面，大多数美国人认为，国家政府应该提供某种"安全网"帮助人们摆脱某些困境，比如暂时失业，遭受飓风等自然灾害，当然还有退休，等等。有趣的是，很多福利的名称也发生了变化。人们曾经明确区分社会救济和福利（权利）。诸如失业救济金、食品券和医疗补助计划（为穷人提供的医疗保障）等曾被认为是"社会救济"。社会保障和医疗保险（退休人员的医疗保障）被视为"福利（权利）"，因为美国人工作时和他们的雇主向这些制度缴纳了费用。因此，退休时，他们认为自己已经支付了，有权得到这些福利。现在，"救济"这个词几乎不再使用了，所有的政府福利都被称为福利。

虽然大部分美国人都认同，国家政府应该在他们需要时给予一些支持，但对于支持多少和支持多久，他们却无法达成共识。相比于共和党人，民主党人通常赞成政府应该提供更慷慨的支持。共和党人则认为政府的作用有限，更强调个人的责任。在2012年大选期间，共和党总统候选人米特·罗姆尼曾被人听到过相关言论，他说，47%的美国人都依靠政府过活，把自己当作无法照顾自己的受害者：

> 无论如何，有47%的人还是会把票投给总统的……这些人依靠政府过活，自以为是受害者……都是些不缴所得税的人……所以我要做的不是去理会这些人。我永远不会说服他们承担个人责任，照顾自己的生活。

事实上，大约半数的美国家庭都有成员接受联邦政府一定的援助。当然，这一数目包括了领取社会保障和医疗保险的退休人员，目前占总人口的14%；另外还有2%的人领取其他的社会保障福利。大多数美国人认为退休时享受的社会保障和医疗保险是自己应得的权利，但问题是，这些福利现在占到了联邦预算的三分之一左右。

随着人口的老龄化，缴纳社会保障税的年轻劳动者和他们的雇主也越来越少，而领取福利的退休人员却越来越多。美国人退休后的寿命也在延长，他们的医疗费用随之上涨。由于美国的老年人比年轻人更有可能会投票，因而政客们会特别关注他们的需求。政客们需要老年人的选票。然而，随着预算赤字的不断增长，现实情况却是，很有可能需要对包括社会保障和医疗保险在内的所有福利进行一些调整。

特殊利益集团的作用

长期以来，美国的几乎所有社会和经济阶层都认为，对于政府，特别是国家政府的行为，有必要充分加以利用，或者想办法保护自己免受其影响。为此，有着相似利益的美国人组成了特殊利益集团，以更有效地对政府行为施加影响。这些特殊利益集团常被称为"游说团体"或"施压集团"。虽然游说团体在美国历史上一直存在，但自20世纪后期起，他们的规模和影响力都有了显著的增强。

全美步枪协会（第四章中曾提及）就是一个很强大且有影响力的游说团体。其成员大多拥有自己的枪支，用于打猎、射击练习或个人保护。不过，全美步枪协会从枪支制造企业那里收了大笔的钱。由于其成员的态度和利益，全美步枪协会坚决反对政府对于各种枪支的几乎任何限制措施，包括手枪、步枪、猎枪甚至是半自动或攻击性武器。尽管普通民众大多支持采取一些枪支管制措施，但全美步枪协会却总能阻止大部分枪支管制立法的通过。（请参看167页的民意调查）

关注持枪权利的人在政治上更为活跃。在公众看来，美国的两党关于枪支管制和持枪权利也各自有支持的观点——保守派的共和党人更关心他们拥有枪支的权利，而自由派的民主党人则更倾向于支持更严格的枪支管制法律。

虽然很少有利益集团能像全美步枪协会那样成功，但大多数组织到位的利益群体还是取得了很大的成功。通过组成集团向政府官员施压，可以比个人行动获得更多的成果，也能更好地规避政府的限制。

基于这样的原则，近几十年，商业利益群体成倍增长，大部分主要行业、企业甚至职业在华盛顿都有自己的说客。有一些有影响力的游说团体，代表了工会、农业团体、教师、医生、律师以及石油天然气、制药和生物技术等特定行业。一些代表非洲裔美国人、美洲原住民、墨西哥裔美国人和犹太美国人等各种民族群体的利益集团也在扩大。还有一些利益集团代表各种寻求政府支持的理想或事业。这其中包括呼吁保护环境的团体和促进消费者保护的团体。正如一位国会议员所感叹的："在美国人人都有个游说团体！"

近几十年来的政治趋势是，政府规模的扩大导致利益集团的数量和规模在增加；而为了满足利益团体对政府越来越多的要求，政府的规模也在扩大。美国退休人士协会（AARP）等团体不仅要求政府为其成员提供新的政府项目、法规和福利，而且对于他们认为保障其权益的现行项目，如社会保障和医疗保险，政府若试图削减，一定会遭到他们强烈抵制。这样一种循环的结果就是所谓的"利益集团政府"。没有哪个单独的利益方可以像大萧条前的商业集团那样主宰政府和政治。相反，政府和政治的基础是与众多群体达成妥协并尽可能地满足更多群体的利益。

新个人主义：利益集团政府

利益集团政府可以被看作是美国个人主义的新的表达形式。不同于早期边疆或商业的个人主义，现在的个人并不主张依靠自己获得成功，而是通过组成集团去影响政府。但他们关注的焦点依然是个人及其权利、利益和野心，而不是整个国家的利益。利益集团不过是通过影响政府以实现个人目标的工具。

尽管许多美国人都或多或少从政府资助项目中受益，但有一些专家仍然认为，利益集团政府对美国是有害的。它对政府的影响是巨大的。首先，利益集团通常只关注个别对其成员而非对其他人来说重要的问题。例如，有些人坚决认为，堕胎在美国不应该是合法的。他们很可能就因为堕胎问题上的立场而把票投给某位候选人。一般说来，由于成员们的态度坚决，游说团体可以向候选人承诺，如果候选人承诺当选后会支持他们的立场，成员们就会投票给该候选人。全美步枪协会对国会议员关于枪支管制问题的投票记录进行评分，而这对参众议员的是否能连任，或击败其他议员，有着尤其重要的影响。

其次，特殊利益集团成员为竞选活动提供大量的资金支持。由于候选人主要依靠私人出资而非公共资金，他们往往不得不依靠利益集团来获取竞选经费。各级政府的候选人——国家、州以及地方——都必须为连任花费大量的时间筹集资金。比如，众议院议员每两年改选一次，他们因此不得不持续不断地筹款。参议员和总统候选人压力同样也很大。这一情形愈演愈烈，以至于人们开始赞同这样的说法，"我们有钱就可以买到最好的政府"。尽管人们也有过一些努力来改革这个制度，但是最高法院2010年联合公民诉讼案的裁决却认定，企业、个人及工会通过超级政治行动委员会为政治活动提供资助不受限制。根据联邦选举委员会的统计，在2012年的总统竞选中，超级政治行动委员会花费了超过5.24亿美元。

21世纪的政治版图：红州与蓝州

在报道总统选举结果时，电视新闻报道显示的美国地图通常用红色（选举人票投给共和党的州）和蓝色（选举人票投给民主党的州）标注。这两种颜色也已经成为美国的深刻分歧的象征。2004年，奥巴马在民主党大会上发表的第一次全国性演说中提出了他对于国家的愿景：我们不再有红州与蓝州之分——我们同属于一个国家——美利坚合众国。然而，分歧依旧。

阿兰·阿布拉莫维茨在《奥巴马与新美国：2012年选举及政治面貌的变化》一书中指出，美国选民的党派分歧巨大。在一场不同寻常的壁垒分明的选举中，90%以上的民主党人投票给奥巴马，而90%以上共和党人则把投票给罗姆尼。即使是占选民人数三分之一的无党派选民中，奥巴马和罗姆尼的支持者也是各占一半。此外，在选参议员和众议员时，90%以上的选民也会把票投给自己党派的候选人。阿布拉莫维茨指出，这种不寻常的党派忠诚程度反映了美国社会深刻的分歧。

> 仔细研究2012年的投票模式后不难发现，民主党和共和党之间存在着三大主要分歧——种族分歧，民主党越来越依靠非白人选民，而共和党则主要受到白人选民的支持；关于政府角色和规模的意识形态分歧，以及涉及价值观、道德观和生活方式的文化分歧。

首先，是种族分歧。2008年奥巴马赢得总统大选，无疑是一个创造历史的事件。美国有史以来第一次有一位非洲裔的总统。虽然民主党传统上就比共和党拥有更多的非白人支持者，但是这次选举使所有种族的人们团结起来，支持一位承诺"希望与改变"的候选人——承诺一个终极美国梦得以实现的美国。有些人认为他的当选只是侥幸，是一次偶然与意外的幸运。但奥巴马却激起了数百万美国人的想象。自20世纪60年代和70年代初的反战运动以来，年轻选民的激情第一次被点燃，社交媒体也首次在大选中发挥了重要作用。奥巴马建立了一个草根组织，这使他的竞选团队可以去当面认识潜在选民，让很多美国人都感觉自己参与创造了历史。2009年1月，超过100万人不畏寒冷，伫立在华盛顿国家广场，从巨型电视屏幕上观看奥巴马的就职典礼。

奥巴马在2012年成功连任，证明他在2008年的胜选并非侥幸。奥巴马失去了一部分白人选民的支持，而他的非白人选民联盟坚持了自己的选择。截至2012年，美国选民中非白人占到了28%，包括非洲裔美国人、拉美裔美国人、亚裔美国人和其他非白种人。共和党人对奥巴马的胜选感到非常意外，他们意识到这反映出美国的一个新的现实：在精神层面上，美国已经进入人口学家所预测的将在2050年达到的多种族、多文化国家的阶段。少数族裔占多数的国家的政治影响不必再等三四十年才能显现——人口组成的变化已经开始左右选举。共和党正在寻求新的方向。共和党希望争取新的选民，因此必须吸引拉美裔、非洲裔、亚裔和其他非白人美国选民。选举地图的颜色分布同样也在发生变化，新墨西哥州、科罗拉多州和内华达州等州的民主党拉美裔正在逐渐将这些红州变为蓝州。

其次，是关于政府角色和规模的意识形态上的分歧。共和党人传统上一直认为，大政府不仅效率低下，而且危害个人权利和自由。2012年，茶党推动共和党进一步向更加保守的右翼发展，坚持认为政府开支是所有经济问题的根源，要求政府大幅削减预算。罗姆尼曾计划通过大幅削减社会计划来减少巨额预算赤字；取消许多医疗、安全与环境法规；并废除奥巴马医保法，同时减少高收入家庭和企业的税收。奥巴马和民主党人则主张对金融机构和污染企业进行更多的政府监管，提高对高收入者的税收以资助社会项目，以及全面实施新的医疗保障法案。

第三，价值观、道德观和生活方式上的文化分歧。共和党越来越多地与各种信仰的宗教保守派，特别是福音派基督徒建立联盟。共和党已逐渐与传统的价值观及生活方式联系在了一起，比如限制堕胎、反对同性婚姻和同性恋者的其他相关权利。他们也反对一些避孕措施，包括服用紧急避孕药。与此同时，民主党在这些问题上的立场则进一步"左倾"。奥巴马允许同性恋者公开服兵役，并在其第二次就职演说中主张同性恋者结婚的权利和其他一些少数群体的权利。

整个国家在这些社会问题上的态度变得更加开明，现在大多数人都赞成同性恋婚姻和怀孕初期的堕胎权。大多数年轻人比父母更自由开放，更少信仰宗教，因而人口形势上，未来对民主党更为有利。其他一些生活方式上的差异包括在一些州大麻合法化，以及承认同性恋婚姻的法律的通过。看一看红州/蓝州分布地图，不难发现，在较自由开放的东北部和西海岸地区，民主党占优势；而共和党的支持者则多分布在相对保守的南部和乡村地区。

找寻前行之路

共和、民主两党都认为自己掌握着引领国家走向安全、繁荣未来的路线图。共和党认为，美国的经济困难是支出的问题，而民主党则认为这是收入的问题。共和党认为，对福利的依赖严重削弱了个人的自由与责任。他们认为美国人是在寅吃卯粮，靠借钱来维持不断扩大的政府，而这会给子孙后代造成可怕的财政负担。

民主党人关注的是最富有和最贫困人群之间不断扩大的差距。他们认为，政府可以通过制定法律，保障所有美国人享有平等的医疗保健和就业机会；通过政府项目引导发展方向，促使私营企业参与合作项目，重建所需的基础设施、道路和桥梁等；并建立校企合作伙伴关系，为未来培养高素质的劳动力。

在《我们分裂的政治心灵：不满年代的美国理念之战》一书中，小E.J.迪翁敦促美国人回顾自己的历史，了解自己是怎样的一个民族。美国人必须认识到，从一开始，他们就生活在两种核心价值观的紧张角力之中：对个人主义的热爱与对团体精神的尊重。这两种价值观共同作用，使国家达到一种平衡，并且两种价值观都与平等这一种重要价值观相互影响。

奥巴马曾谈到在私人企业的个人主义和公众政府的团体精神之间取得平衡的必要性。

> 从我们成为一个国家的那天起，我们就将自由市场和自由企业的信念视为美国财富和繁荣的引擎。相比其他任何国家的公民，我们都是更为坚定的个人主义者，自力更生，对过于

强大政府存在着合理的怀疑。

但还有另一条主线同样贯穿于我们的历史中——对于我们彼此紧密相连的信念；有些事情我们必须一起合作才能完成，作为一个国家……我所了解的美国是慷慨而富有同情心的，是一片充满了机会和乐观主义的土地。为了我们所期望的国家以及我们共同的未来，我们要为自己负责，也对彼此负责。

奥巴马所表达的是对美国传统价值观在国家及政府中作用的信念。在 21 世纪，美国公民及其政府领导人还会面对更多的挑战。我们希望，个人自由、自力更生、机会均等、参与竞争、物质财富和勤奋工作，这六种基本的文化价值观在未来将继续指导与引领美国及其人民一路前行。

第八章　美国的民族与种族多样性

> 因此，在这片大陆上，爱尔兰人、德意志人、瑞典人、波兰人等所有欧洲的民族，和非洲人、波利尼西亚人一同释放的能量，将创造一个新的民族、新的宗教、新的国家。
>
> 拉尔夫·沃尔多·爱默生（1803—1882）

在美国，来自不同国家、不同民族的移民是如何相处的？

熔炉还是沙拉碗

美国人口中包含了许多来自不同种族、民族和宗教的族群。这些众多的群体融入一种有着共同价值观的共同的文化生活中的过程被称为同化。关于美国的同化程度，学者们持不同意见。正如我们在第一章里提到的，有些学者将美国比作"熔炉"，各种族和民族在这里融合成了一种文化。另一些学者则把美国看作一个"沙拉碗"，各个族群彼此之间保持了一定的特点和差异，形成了一个极具多样性的国家。

现实的状况可能介于上述两种观点之间。自1776年以来，美国经历了大量种族与民族同化，但也有一些群体对整体文化仍有着相当的疏离感。这些群体中有许多是真正的双语和（或）双文化。也就是说，他们认为自己是美国人，但可能也希望保留自己原来文化的语言，有时甚至是文化传统。

17世纪早期，西班牙裔最先在其他欧洲国家移民到来之前定居北美大陆。早在十三个殖民地于18世纪后期联合起来建立美利坚合众国之前几个世纪，西班牙人和拉美人就已在佛罗里达州和西南部地区建立了定居点。由于他们在此的悠久历史，以及不断有新的移民涌入他们已有的社区，许多西班牙裔或拉美裔美国人对于保持自己的文化传统和使用西班牙语引以为傲。

总体而言，多年来，不同民族和宗教背景的白人群体已逐渐融入了美国的大文化中。当然，也有个别的例外。例如，美国犹太人在这种大文化中就一直保持着强烈的群体认同意识。这可能是因为历史上欧洲基督教国家曾长期迫害犹太人，而在美国有时也存在着一些不太明显的歧视和反犹主义情绪，另一方面，犹太人也有着强烈的民族自豪感。不过，大多数犹太人在保持自己的群体认同的同时，还是非常愿意融入美国大文化的。

主流文化的确立

美国建国之后的第一次人口普查是在 1790 年。统计出来的人口大约有 400 万，其中大多数是白人。在这些白人公民中，有 80% 的人祖辈来自英格兰。而非洲裔美国人也意外地占到了总人口的 20%，达到历史最高。当时有近 70 万名奴隶和大约 6 万名"自由黑人"。只有少数纳税的美洲原住民被计入了此次人口普查数字中，因此对于美洲原住民的总人口，并没有确切的统计数字。

在这个新的国家里，白人人口最多，掌握的财富和政治权力也最多，因此很快这个多数群体就决定了美国主流文化的内容。美国独立战争时期，白人人口绝大多数都是来自英国的中产阶级新教徒。这样的美国人有时被称为"WASPs"（白人盎格鲁－撒克逊新教徒）；不过，现在有不少人认为这个称呼带有侮辱性。他们的特征成了评判其他群体的标准。宗教信仰不同的人（如爱尔兰天主教徒），或说不同语言的人（如德国人、荷兰人和瑞典人）是少数，除非被同化，否则他们就会处于弱势。18 世纪末，对大多数移民来说，这种同化并不是很困难。历史学家艾伦·内文斯和亨利·斯蒂尔·康马杰曾写道："英国人、爱尔兰人、德国人……荷兰人、瑞典人——融合、通婚，并不介意彼此间的差异。"

因此，就其特点而言，形成于美国历史早期的主流文化是讲英语的、来自西欧的、新教信仰的中产阶层文化。正是这样的主流文化确立起了托克维尔 19 世纪 30 年代所描述的那些传统美国价值观。具有这些特点的移民大受欢迎，这一定程度上是因为美国人认为这样的新移民可以有力地支持主流文化中的核心价值观，如自由、机会均等、为获得更高水平的物质生活而勤奋工作等。

非新教徒和非西欧裔的同化

与许多文化中一样，一个少数群体与主流文化的差异程度决定了这个群体的被接受度。尽管许多与早期定居者相似的移民被接纳了，那些具有明显不同特征的移民却往往被视作对美国传统价值观和生活方式的威胁。

在 19 世纪末和 20 世纪初数百万涌入的移民中，情况尤其如此。这些人大多来自南欧和东欧的贫困国家，他们不讲英语，其中多数是天主教徒或犹太人。

当时的美国人对大量涌入的这些新移民非常恐惧。他们害怕这些人习惯了贫困与依赖他人的生活，无法理解美国传统的自由、自力更生和竞争的价值观。而且新移民人数众多，他们甚至可能会以负面的方式改变美国的基本价值观。

美国人向这些新移民提供英语教学以及入籍课程，教给他们基本的美国价值观，试图以此来应对他们所认为的对美国价值观的威胁。然而，这些移民却常常感觉到美国老师并不认同他们家乡的传统。而且，了解美国的价值观并不能满足他们最重要的需求，例如就业、食物和住房。

对新移民更有帮助的是美国东北部大城市的一些"党魁"，多数移民最先到达的就是这些城市。这些政客看到了移民的许多实际需要，对不同的家乡传统也更为接纳。他们帮助这些移民，以此拉拢选民，争取选票，维持其权势。

很多美国人强烈反对这种党魁政治。部分是由于这些党魁经常贪污腐败，他们常常从自己操纵的市政府中偷挪资金，从事各种非法勾当。但更重要的原因是，美国人认为这些党魁是在破坏自力更生和竞争等美国基本价值观。

他们觉得党魁们在引导移民去依附于他们，而不是让移民自力更生。更有甚者，许多大城市党魁为了掌握垄断的政治权力，会去收买移民的选票。这种做法破坏了政治活动的公平竞争，而美国人将竞争视为政治以及美国生活其他方面的重要传统。

虽然有诸多批评，仍有许多学者认为，党魁在19世纪末和20世纪初发挥了重要作用。他们帮助大量新移民找到工作和住房，融入了美国大文化，以换取移民的政治支持。后来，这些党魁也帮助了这些移民的子女找到工作，不过，第二代移民因为自小说英语，通常也已有了更多优势。

世纪之交的美国，经济快速扩张，在政客们的帮助下，这些新移民在美国的生活条件得以改善。也由于有了更多的机遇和更好的薪酬，移民们逐渐接受了美国大文化中大部分的价值观，从而也因此又被绝大多数美国人所接纳。故而，对于白人民族群体而言，他们对大文化的归属感——作为美国人的认同感——一般强于他们对单独某个民族群体的归属感，如作为爱尔兰人、意大利人、波兰人等等的认同感。

非洲裔美国人的经历

在美国，白人族裔群体的同化过程远比非白人族裔群体顺利得多。在非白人族裔群体中，尤以非洲裔在融入大文化过程中遇到的困难最大。非洲裔美国人当初是作为奴隶被贩卖被迫来此的。而除了第一批白人定居者到达之前就已居住在美洲的原住民以外，其他民族群体都是自愿来到美国的——大多都是想要改善生活条件的移民。

在美国，对黑人的奴役完全有悖于自由和机会均等这样的美国传统基本价值观。它将美国割裂为分歧不断加深的两部分：黑人奴隶制成为南方各州的经济基础，而北方各州则主张禁止奴隶制度。

在北方，有少数白人坚持认为，奴隶制和自由不能在一个自由的国家中共存，主张废除奴隶制，哪怕是要与南方开战。更多的北方白人则认为只需要保护白人的自由和机会平等，但他们也害怕黑人奴隶制最终会剥夺他们的经济自由。比如，如果允许南方的奴隶制扩大到西部边疆地区，那么对于贫穷和中等收入的白人而言，就不能再把西部边疆看作可以改善生活地位，平等与机遇的土壤了。相反，白人将不得不与没有报酬的奴隶劳动力竞争，他们认为这是对白人的工作的贬低，会降低他们的社会地位。

亚伯拉罕·林肯能够成为美国总统，不仅是因为吸引了那些不满于奴隶制对非洲裔美国人不公的白人理想主义者，更是受到了大量认为奴隶制威胁到自身的北方白人的支持。林肯的观点是，如果奴隶制继续向西扩展，白人的自由和平等就会受到威胁。林肯还认为，自由和机会均等这些权利适用于所有人，不分黑人、白人，否则它们就无法继续作为美国的基本价值观传承下去。

1860年，林肯当选总统，南方各州退出联邦，试图建立一个奴隶制的新国家。这导致了南北方之间内战（1861—1865）的爆发，这是美国历史上最血腥、最具破坏性的一场战争。战争最后以北方的胜利告终，黑人奴隶制在美国被废除。

早在19世纪30年代时，托克维尔就曾预测美国黑人和白人之间会有冲突：

> 这两个种族彼此紧密相连，却并没有相互融合；他们既无法完全分离也不能结合。法律也许可以废除奴隶制，但只有上帝才能抹去其存在的痕迹。

虽然奴隶制在19世纪60年代被废除了，但其余孽犹存，非洲裔美国人融入美国大文化并不容易。大多数人留在了南方，在那里，他们被禁止投票，法律上也被与白人隔离。例如，黑人儿童不得进入白人的公立学校，很多黑人只能接受劣质的教育，这使得他们无法获得平等的机会在白人统治的社会中参与竞争。许多曾经的奴隶以及他们的家庭陷入了代代贫困的恶性循环。虽然黑人的处境在实施种族隔离的南方更为糟糕，但在北方，黑人也同样无法免于受到强烈的种族歧视。

20世纪50年代和60年代的民权运动

这种状况一直持续，直到"二战"后才有所改变。"二战"期间，有超过100万非洲裔美国人曾在种族隔离的部队中服役。战争结束后，黑人领袖们开始领导争取与白人平等权利的民权运动。1948年哈里·杜鲁门总统下令全面废除军队体系的种族隔离制度。之后，在1954年，美国最高法院判定，实施种族隔离的公立学校，没有为黑人提供平等的教育机会，因此是违法的。值得一提的是，全国有色人种协进会（NAACP）首席顾问瑟古德·马歇尔曾为此案辩护，他在1967年成为美国历史上第一位非洲裔最高法院大法官。

1954年废除学校种族隔离制度的决定极大地鼓舞了美国各地的黑人领袖。他们决意要努力结束美国生活各个领域的种族隔离。这些领导人中最重要的一位是黑人新教牧师马丁·路德·金，他非常善于鼓舞人心，启发民众。从20世纪50年代后期，直至1968年被一名白人持枪者暗杀，金领导了成千上万的民众，进行各种反对种族隔离和其他形式的种族歧视的非暴力游行和示威活动。金的目标是让更多的黑人融入美国大文化中。他的理想很大程度上是由美国基本价值观发展而来的。他想要他的同胞们获得更多平等的机会和"现在的自由"。他并不希望将黑人从美国社会中分离出来，相反，他们是要争取更多地参与其中。

一些黑人领袖，如马尔科姆·X，则极力主张摒弃美国的基本价值观，要求黑人与白人文化彻底分离。马尔科姆·X认为，美国价值观只不过是使黑人处于劣势的"白人的价值观"。他认为黑人需要与白人分开，根据自己创造的价值观建立自己的社会，必要时可以使用武力。由于马尔科姆将基督教视为"白人"的宗教，因此他转向了基于伊斯兰教的信仰，并成为"黑人穆斯林"信仰（创立于1930年）的领袖。不过，绝大多数美国黑人与马丁·路德·金一样，信仰新教，目标是同化而非分离。大多数非洲裔美国人一直将金视为他们的领袖。

很大程度上要归功于金的活动，20世纪60年代通过了两部重要的民权法律，给南方带来了巨大的改变。其中一项法律规定了公共设施方面的种族隔离违法；而另一项法律则规定限制黑人的选举权为非法。

20世纪60年代的民权法对黑人融入美国大文化起到了重要的推动作用。最重要的是，这些法律最终有助于减少全国各地对于黑人的种族歧视。一项名为"平权法案"的联邦计划要求企业积极招募黑人员工，大学积极招收黑人学生。得益于民权法和平权法案，20世纪60年代后期和70年代，进入国内的大学和高校、担任公职以及获得较高收入的非洲裔美国人人数大幅度增加。如今，非洲裔美国人成为体育和娱乐明星，成为大学教授、医生、律师、企业家和记者。现在的美国黑人中产阶级规模相当可观，富有的非洲裔美国人也不在少数。

非洲裔美国人在政治上非常活跃，在2008年和2012年的选举中投票率都很高。如今，他们担任着大城市的市长、国会议员；他们任职于各级政府部门——地方、州以及联邦政府。2008年，奥巴马成为美国第一位黑人总统，对于许多民权运动参与者来说，这是梦想终于成真的时刻。国会议员约翰·路易斯本人也是一位黑人民权运动领袖，他是这样描述奥巴马当选对于他个人的意义的：

> 当我们组织选民登记运动、自由乘车运动、静坐时，当我们第一次来到华盛顿时，被捕、入狱、被殴打时——我做梦也没有想过——非洲裔美国人有一天会被选为美国总统。我的母亲活着看到了我当选国会议员，但我希望我的双亲都能在身边。他们会无比高兴与自豪，他们将感到欣慰。他们会说，所有的斗争，我们所做的、努力过的一切都是值得的。

21世纪的多样性

民权运动不仅帮助了非洲裔美国人，也使美国的所有少数族裔——美洲印第安人、拉美裔、亚裔及其他族裔——都从中受益。法律禁止在就业和住房方面的种族歧视。民权法律也提高了妇女的权利，强化了所有美国人机会平等的理想。最近，性取向又成为争取平等的新阵地。奥巴马总统在其第二次就职演说中就呼吁同性恋者的平等权利，支持法律规定同性婚姻合法。民意调查显示，大多数美国人都同意他的观点。尽管还没有达到国家整体多样化的程度，但那一年上任的国会已是有史以来最多样化的一届。在全部535名议员中，有98名女性，43名非洲裔美国人，31名拉美裔，12名亚裔和太平洋岛民美国人，7名公开同性恋或双性恋者，2名穆斯林，1名佛教徒和1名印度教徒。

虽然非洲裔美国人占总人口的13%，但他们在国会的代表席位仍严重不足，拉美裔美国人的情况也是如此。已婚黑人或拉美裔全职工作者的收入中位数仍明显低于已婚白人。虽然种族隔离和种族歧视是违法的，但有时却是居住格局造成了社区学校的严重隔离，特别是在许多城市地区。相比于黑人和拉美裔，白人更有可能居住在郊区，那里的社区学校通常条件更好、教育质量更高。而许多生活在内城贫民区的黑人和其他少数族裔陷入了贫困、失业、暴力与绝望的恶性循环之中。黑人是暴力犯罪最常见的受害者，而同时五分之一的黑人年轻男性都有犯罪记录。黑人和拉美裔儿童生活在贫困和单亲家庭的比例也远高于白人儿童。

另一方面，美国人依然对机会均等的理想坚信不疑，并不断寻求途径，让每个人都有平等的机会去获取成功。美国梦仍然吸引着移民，并激励着所有种族和民族背景的人们。现实中，一些移民群体较之另一些更为成功。历史正如人们所预期的那样，有一定财力、良好教育背景和必要工作技能的移民通常更有优势。比如，来自中东的移民往往比一般的美国白人有更高的社会经济水平。亚裔作为一个群体，也是如此。那些没有财力和良好教育背景的人处境则没有那么好。不过，研究表明，第二代移民比第一代情况要好得多。移民的成年子女有着更高的生活水准：

> 一项对2000万在美国出生的移民成年子女的新的分析显示，他们的总体境况比移民自己好很多；他们有更高的收入，更多人拥有大学教育背景和住房，贫困人口也较少。在拉美裔和亚裔美国人中，第二代移民通常比第一代更有可能讲英语，结识自己种族和民族群体之外的朋友，并把自己视为"典型的美国人"。

索尼娅·索托马约尔，美国最高法院第一位拉美裔大法官，就是一些拉美裔美国人取得成功的一个鼓舞人心的榜样。在自传《我深爱的世界》一书中，她描述自己出生与成长的世界，是"拉美裔纽约城的一个小小缩影"。她的祖父母、叔叔阿姨和堂兄弟姐妹们都生活在南布朗克斯区的几个街区里：

> 我的玩伴就是我的堂亲。我们在家都说西班牙语，家里很多人几乎都不会说英语。我的父母都是1944年从波多黎各来到纽约的。我的母亲在陆军妇女团，而我父亲则是同他的家人一起来找工作的，当时，由于经济困难，大批波多黎各人移民离开了岛。

索托马约尔的父亲在她小时候就去世了，她的家庭经济拮据。他们住在低收入住房里，她和弟弟都在课余做兼职工作，并在暑期全职工作，以贴补家用。孩提时代，她对自己社区之外的世界知之甚少，是电视剧《佩里·梅森律师》激励了她想要成为一名律师。索托马约尔学业出色，不过，对于有那么多知名大学想要录取她，甚至还提供全额奖学金，她还是感到十分惊讶。她说，接下来的几年中，她过上了"平权法案想要实现的每一天的生活"。当时因为平权法案，大学刚刚开始招收少数族裔学生，作为一位拉美裔的少数族裔女性，她也受益于此。在众多录取她的学校中，她最终选择了普林斯顿大学，后来她又赴耶鲁大学修读了法律学位。

今天，具有不同背景和技术水平的移民都想方设法来到了美国。他们中有一些人受过高等教育，可能会从事技术、医学和科学等领域的工作。有一些可能来自贫困的农村或城区，受教育程度有限。他们之中有很多年轻人是冒着生命危险非法移民的，从事一些农业或建筑工作。还有一些人找的是照顾孩子、打扫房间或清洗建筑物之类的工作。他们通常比合法的工人薪资要低。不过，他们把赚取的美元收入寄回国，就可以养活那里的家人。他们中许多人并不想成为美国公民，他们唯一的愿望就是可以在这里工作。美国人正努力寻找办法，既安置好这些工人，同时也保护好美国公民的利益。

世界性的美国

要记住的一点是，早期定居者确立的美国的主流文化和价值体系，源于白人、新教和西欧。19世纪末和20世纪初，数以百万计的东欧和南欧移民来到美国，带来了被认为与主流文化截然不同的异类文化传统。到了20世纪20年代，美国人决定对大规模移民关闭大门，于是新移民数量大为减少。尽管主流文化的人们有着种种担忧，但这些新移民还是融入了美国的生活。他们极大地丰富了美国的文化多样性，而且最终也并没有动摇美国的政府体制、自由企业制度或传统价值观。

1965年，美国的移民法发生重大变化，允许更多的移民进入美国，并彻底废除了旧法律中偏向欧洲白人的内容。新的移民法律使美国接纳了更多非白人、非欧洲裔的移民，其中有大量是来自亚洲和拉丁美洲。除了大量合法移民之外，美国也首次出现了大批的非法移民。许多人担心这对美国社会产生的影响。美国经济能够为这些新移民提供与他人同等的机会吗？美国200多年来的传统价值体系又会受到什么样的影响呢？

也有不少美国人看到了对国家的益处。本·瓦滕伯格是一位受人尊敬的美国文化专家，他认为，新移民将对国家有很大的帮助。瓦滕伯格表示，美国正在经历着重大的变化：它正成为有史以来第一个世界性的国家。他认为美国将是第一个让来自世界各地的人们在一个政府领导下自由生活的国家。这种多样性将使美国在21世纪对世界其他国家和地区产生强大的影响力和吸引力。

或许不应再把美国称为"熔炉"或"沙拉碗"，倒不如将其比作一幅"马赛克"——一幅由无数不同颜色的小碎片拼就的画作。仔细观察这个国家，你会发现，不同肤色和民族的人们特点仍然鲜明可辨，而他们在一起，又共同创造了独一无二的美国画卷。"合众为一"，这是美国建国至今的国家箴言，意为团结统一。众多不同的元素结合在一起，成就了一个整体。

第九章　美国的教育

美国人将教育视为消除个体间不平等以及实现所有理想目标的途径。

乔治·S. 康茨（1889—1974）

在美国谁在为教育花钱？这对学校的教学内容又有何影响？

美国公立学校的建立：托克维尔的观察

正如人们预料的那样，美国的教育体制也反映了国家的基本价值观，特别是机会均等的理想。美国人认为，从小学到大学，每个人都应该享有接受良好教育的平等机会。

自1825年美国公立学校基本体制建立之初，他们就在重申平等的原则，向所有社会阶层敞开学校的大门，并用向公民征收的税收资助学校。那些支持公立学校的人认为，这样的制度让所有社会阶层的孩子在同样的"平民学校"接受教育，有助于减少美国社会的阶层差异。

1831年，阿历克西·德·托克维尔到达美国之后，发现人们对新兴发展起来的公立小学具有极大的热情。纽约市长为托克维尔举办了特别宴会，其间曾祝酒纪念"教育——公立学校的扩展——乃是国家的福祉"。

由于托克维尔本身是法国贵族，起初他也与许多富有的美国人一样担忧，认为全民教育对国家是威胁，而非福音。不过，最后他还是转变了看法，认为公共教育鼓励人们追求更高的生活地位，这与美国社会的习惯是一致的，并不冲突。让所有人不论家庭背景都拥有平等机会的理想在美国要远比在法国强烈得多。

托克维尔还发现，美国的公共教育有实用性很强的内容，包含职业技能和公民义务教育。因此，公共教育不仅能激励美国人自我完善的上进心，也为他们提供了实现这一目标的实用工具。

此外，美国物质的富裕也有能力为那些充分把握公共教育机会的人提供物质奖励。

在其后的一个半世纪里，美国的公立学校继续发展，扩大到中学或高中（9 至 12 年级）以及高等院校，包括大学本科与研究生阶段。

教育阶梯

美国人将其公立学校体系看作是一条教育的阶梯，从小学到中学，最后到大学、研究生课程，一级级往上。大多数孩子 5 岁进入幼儿园开始上学，有的甚至三四岁就读学前班。接着，小学阶段通常是五六年，中学二到三年，高中四年。（不同的学制体系对这 12 年的划分方式可能有所不同，一般取决于学龄人口数量，但都包括小学、中学和高中共 12 年的学习。）大多数学校体系都包含幼儿园阶段。

高中毕业后，大部分学生会继续上大学。完成本科学位课程可以获得学士学位，也就是美国人通常所说的"大学文凭"。完成社区大学两年学习的学生可以获得副学士学位。副学士学位中有一些是职业与技术领域的。

获得学士学位后，可以进入专业领域学习，取得法律和医学等专业的学位，或者攻读硕士和博士学位。美国的公立学校在小学和中学阶段都是免费并向所有学生开放的。但公立高校是收取学费的，并且需要通过竞争性的入学选拔。

教育阶梯的概念几乎完美地体现了美国人以机会均等和"一步一个脚印走向顶峰"为基础的个人成功的理想。在美国，并没有什么区别对待的独立公共教育体系，没有为富人专设高水平的教育而只给大众提供低层次的教育。相反，只有一个对所有人开放的体系。每个人都可以尽其所能地沿着阶梯向上攀登。每个人可以达到的高度不是由他们的社会地位决定的，而是由个人能力决定的。

大多数美国孩子都上免费的公立小学和中学，不过也有约 10% 的孩子选择上私立学校。这些私立学校大部分是与特定教会有关并受其资助的宗教学校，但学生家长也必须交纳学费。这些学校的一个主要目的是进行宗教教育，而在公立学校是不能这样做的，但这并非家长送孩子就读这些学校的全部原因。生活在大城市的家长会把孩子送到天主教或其他宗教学校，是因为他们相信这些学校比公立学校更安全，学术水平更高。为了将这些孩子留在公立学校，许多这些城市的公立学校鼓励家长和社区成员建立特许公立学校。

也有一些主要服务于上层社会孩子的精英私立学校。这些学校学费昂贵，只有富裕的家庭才能负担得起，不过，学校通常也会给一些有天赋却不那么富裕、付不起学费的孩子提供奖学金。常有父母将孩子送到这些学校去，除了让孩子接受良好的教育之外，也是希望孩子可以与其他上层社会的孩子结交，保持父母的上层社会地位。

与私立的教会学校不同，私立精英学校是有悖于美国的机会均等的理想的。这些学校往往给予了富裕家庭的年轻一代更多的教育和社会优势。但这类学校由于数量相对较少，并不能取代公立学校成为主要的教育机构。不过，在与公立学校毕业生竞争进入美国最好的大学时，这些学校的学生的确有一定的优势。以哈佛大学为例，其录取的学生中有 35% 毕业于私立学校。

美国教育体制还有另一个不平等的方面。由于学校资金来源的不同，美国学生在不同公立学校所接受的教育质量参差不齐。传统上，学校资金中最大的部分来自地方（县市），主要来自财产税。中产阶层和富裕阶层家庭所在的学区有更多的税收可以用于教育。因此，较富裕的学区通常有漂亮的校舍以及最先进的技术和最新的科学设备，而较贫穷的学区则校舍陈旧、设备落后。现在，各州承担了中小学的绝大部分经费，联邦政府也平均负担10%的费用。然而，地方政府对公立学校的投入依然发挥着巨大的影响，生活在低收入社区的学生就读的学校通常资源最少，教师也是最缺乏经验的。

尽管每个孩子花了多少钱并不一定是衡量孩子所接受教育质量的最佳指标，但绝对是一个重要因素。一些人认为，所有的学校，不论公立还是私立，是否是宗教学校，都应该有资格获得公立学校经费。他们主张实施教育券制度，父母可以使用教育券交纳他们选中的任何学校的学费。一些州现在正在试行这项制度。

在美国读大学

钱的因素对于接受大学教育也越来越重要。在美国，所有大学生都必须支付学费，而且大学教育费用上涨的速度远高于平均家庭收入的增长速度。由于公立大学学费比私立大学低得多，富裕的学生就有更多的选择。在公立和私立大学都有一些贷款和奖学金形式的资助项目。80%左右的大学生都有某种形式的学生补助。不过，购买书籍和离家生活的各种费用使得很多学生连就读学费较低的公立大学都越来越吃力。大部分学生大学期间都必须打工来平衡支出，而有时打工占用了他们上课的时间，他们只好减少修课数量，延长大学毕业的时间。大多数年轻人从大学毕业的时候都背负着相当数额的学生贷款。

越来越多的学生无法负担离家上大学所需的学费和生活费，不管是公立大学还是私立大学。因此，他们选择在家乡读两年社区大学课程，学费要少得多。这些两年制大学讲授的课程范围十分广泛。一些学校还提供两年制学位，称为副学士学位。学生也可以先上两年社区大学，然后转入州立大学。将社区大学纳入州立大学体系，为大量原本上不起大学的学生提供了教育机会。社区大学越来越受到欢迎。现在也有些社区大学通过州立体系开设四年制本科学位课程。

公立两年制、四年制及私立四年制大学的年均费用的差异非常显著：

费用 \ 学制	公立两年制（本州学生）	公立四年制（本州学生）	私立四年制
学杂费	$3 131	$8 655	$29 056
食宿、书籍等	$12 453	$13 606	$14 233
总费用	$15 584	$22 261	$43 289
净价格（减去奖学金、助学金、补助之后）	$4 350	$5 750	$15 680

数据来源：美国大学理事会《2012年大学费用趋势》及《2012年学生资助趋势》报告

尽管费用高昂，寻求大学教育的美国人比例仍然一直在增长。1900年时，大学适龄人口中只有不到10%上了大学。而现在，半数以上的美国人都接受过大学教育，其中有很多读了四年甚至更长的时间。美国目前大学在读的学生人数超过2000万，有大约3000多所不同的高校。许多自己年轻时没能上大学的家长现在都满意地看到子女进入了大学。今天，大约有一半的大学生都是自己家庭中第一代上大学的人。

正如我们在前面的章节中所看到的，美国人对于成功的传统定义是获得财富和良好的生活水平。因此，美国人对教育的经济价值的重视也就不足为奇了。美国人普遍认为，受教育程度越高的人，离开学校时能赚到的钱也越多。特别是关于对某些大学本科学位，或医学和法律等专业学位的期许，这种信念最为强烈。科学、技术、工程和数学（STEM）领域的本科和研究生学历都能获得高薪。在美国，STEM学位的毕业生不足，无法填补职位的空缺，所以这些领域的就业前景非常好。而在文学、艺术、音乐、历史、哲学等一些"非职业"领域，学位则没有那么大的经济价值。

近年来，美国就业市场出现了一些变化。过去，没上过大学的人也可能在工厂里找到一份报酬优厚的工作。工人在职业学校、培训课程或岗位中学习的技能就足以使他们胜任工作，并不需要接受大学教育。新移民们能找到的通常是这一类工作。然而，随着越来越多新技术的出现，大量的工作需要有更高的教育程度才能完成。在美国，许多新工作要么要求有大学学历，甚至研究生学历，要么就是服务行业（如快餐店、商店和酒店）的低薪工作。例如，新型制造业的工作往往就要求工人具备机器人科学方面的知识。

由于高等教育的重要性，许多成年人都边工作边读大学。许多公立及私立院校正在通过远程教学、利用互联网提供材料和课程，以及让学生参与讨论，让学生们学习课程更加方便。一些住校或走读的学生也都至少有部分课程是通过远程学习完成的，甚至一个从未到过大学校园的学生也有可能获得本科和研究生学位。

一个振奋人心的新趋势是大型开放在线课程（MOOC）的发展，成千上万的人可以参加由美国一些最重要的学者讲授的课程。它最初是由美国精英大学的几位教授发起的，但现在已经越来越普遍，世界各地的其他大学也纷纷加入。课程的重点在于拥有学习经历，而不是为了获得大学学分。不过现在也有一些课程正在探索一些方式，为通过课程相关考试的学生颁发证书。

个体教育

比起获取大量的知识，美国学校往往更注重培养批判性思维能力。他们鼓励学生在课堂上提出问题、独立思考，以及表达自己的观点，这体现了个人自由和自力更生的美国价值观。美国教育体系的目标是教给孩子如何学习，并帮助他们发挥自己最大的潜力。

美国人认为，社会和人际交往能力的培养与智力水平的培养同等重要。为了帮助学生发展这些重要的技能，学校除了日常的学习活动，还增设了大量的课外活动。这些课外活动几乎与学生的课业一样重要。比如，美国大学录取时就很看重"全面发展"的学生。高中学业成绩和学习能力倾向测验（SAT）等大学入学考试成绩固然非常重要，但学生在课外活动中的表现也同样关键。通过参加这些活动，学生展示出他们的独特天赋、成熟度和责任感、领导才能和与他人相处的能力。

一些美国人认为竞技体育在所有课外活动中是最重要的。这是因为很多人相信，对所有年轻人来说，不论是男孩还是女孩，学会如何成功地参与竞争都非常重要。美式橄榄球、篮球、棒球、足球等团体运动的意义就在于它们教给学生"求胜精神"。有时，对体育竞技的推崇甚至可能更为极端，一些学生和他们的父母可能对学校的体育项目比对其学术资源更为重视。

学生自治会是另一类课外活动，旨在培养学生的竞争能力、政治能力和社交能力。学生们选出一些学生会干部，他们在学校选举中争取同学的支持和选票。虽然这些学生会干部并不能左右学校的核心决策，但参与选举的过程，以及当选后负责大大小小学生活动的经历也被认为是很好的培养领导能力和竞争能力的体验，能够帮助他们成为负责任的公民。

体育运动和学生自治会仅仅是美国学校丰富多彩的课外活动的两项。除此之外，还有几乎可以满足每个学生兴趣的各类俱乐部和活动——艺术、音乐、戏剧、辩论、外语、摄影、志愿活动——都是旨在帮助学生在以后的生活中可以取得更大的成功。有些学区现在要求所有学生都必须参与社区服务——家教、去养老院看望老人、打扫社区公园等等——作为高中毕业的一项要求。许多家长对待孩子的课外活动，表现出了与对孩子的学业成就同样多的兴趣与关注。

标准化运动

20世纪90年代，关于教育的国际对比数据显示，美国学生在数学、科学和其他一些学科上表现总体不如其他许多发达国家。有人认为这是因为美国教育的标准可能不够高。与其他很多国家不同，美国传统上是由当地社区学区负责决定学校课程和选择教材，州和国家只有有限的监督。不过，自20世纪90年代以来，州和联邦政府都越来越多地参与学校标准的制定。联邦政府制定了教育的全国目标，包括幼儿、小学、中学和成人教育标准。甚至师范教育课程也必须符合联邦和州的标准。大多数主要的教育协会，如全国科学、数学或语文教师协会，也对现行的教学大纲和认证标准进行了评估，并制定了新的标准。

为了确保达到这些标准，联邦政府现在要求大多数小学和初中必须每年进行阅读和数学测试；各州也可能要求学生通过阅读、写作、数学和公民教育等科目的一系列考试才能从高中毕业。虽然多数州都已经至少是在数学和阅读方面针对所有学生制定了标准，但在最近，美国45个州、哥伦比亚特区以及四个海外属地的州长和总督又制定了一套数学及英语语言艺术的新标准。只有阿拉斯加、明尼苏达、内布拉斯加、得克萨斯和弗吉尼亚这几个州没有参与。这套共同核心标准重点是大学入学和工作所需的概念和程序，不仅符合大学和职业的要求，也确保学生从一个州转学至另一个州可以按照相同的标准接受教学和评估。

不过，标准化测试也并非没有争议。21世纪初，联邦政府启动了一项名为"不让一个孩子掉队"（NCLB）的计划，目的是让学校和老师为学生的进步负责。学校会因学生在标准化测试中的进步表现而被评分；家长则有机会把孩子从得分低或不及格的学校转到得分更高的学校去。然而，这些政策也引发了一些问题。对标准化测试的重视占用了大量的课堂时间。据估计，准备或参加标准化测试花费的时间占学年的 20%。一些老师把更多的时间花在"应试教学"上，而不是确保学生真正理解这些重要概念。一些教育家担忧，美国人提出问题与独立思考的传统正在被死记硬背的考试内容所取代。

戴安·拉维奇是对强调标准化测试最激烈的批评者之一。而她原来曾是 NCLB 计划坚定的支持者。在她的《伟大的美国学校制度的生与死：考试和选择如何破坏教育》一书中，拉维奇解释了为何她认为 NCLB 计划失败了。如果当地学校评分不及格（因为学生的考试成绩不够好），家长可以选择把孩子转入更好的学校，可他们并没有这样做。父母希望让自己的孩子在家附近的学校上学。拉维奇说，NCLB 计划实施 10 年了，按理我们应该能够看到学校的显著改善和学生的进步，但是我们却什么也没看到：

> 到现在，我们本应该能够看到不同种族和民族群体、不同收入群体的孩子们成绩上的差距显著缩小，可我们并没有看到……很多孩子依然还是掉队了……而他们正是十年前掉队的那些孩子。

拉维奇认为，公立学校有责任为所有学生提供平等的教育机会，无论种族、民族或收入如何，而如果他们无法实现受教育程度的平等，我们就应该给予他们特殊的帮助。我们不能让任何一个孩子掉队，没有争取好工作与体面的生活所需的教育的话，也就没有机会去实现美国梦。

美国教育体制中的不平等

美国教育中对机会均等理念最重大的背离体现在非洲裔美国人的教育上。我们在前一章中介绍过，19 世纪 60 年代的南北战争结束后，南方各州建立了一套社会和法律制度，在包括学校在内的所有公共设施中，把原来的黑人奴隶与白人隔离开来。黑人有单独的学校，而这些学校几乎从哪方面来看都比白人的学校差。

1954 年布朗诉教育委员会案最高法院的判决结束了南方学校在法律上的种族隔离，但事实上种族隔离仍一直在延续，直到 20 世纪 60 年代中期的民权法案。20 世纪 60 年代末到 70 年代，一系列的法院判决迫使国家采取措施整合南方和北方的所有公立学校。虽然北方不曾有过法律上的种族隔离，但不论在北方还是在南方，社区学校都反映了附近居民的种族构成情况。这种居住格局导致北方，特别是在大城市中，也有不少种族隔离的学校。内城贫民区的许多公立学校主要由非洲裔美国学生组成，与贫民区有着共同的一些问题，比如贫困、高犯罪率和其他各种社会乱象。很明显，这些学校与郊区那些白人中产阶层为主的社区的学校相比，绝对是不平等的。

在接下来的 20 年里，法院要求美国人努力实现公立学校的种族平衡。解决社区学校间不平等问题时，最有争议的做法是跨区校车接送学童到离家更远的学区的学校上学，以使得所有学校都能更多融合黑白不同种族的学生。来自内城的黑人孩子被送到以白人中产阶层为主的社区的学校，而居住在中产阶层社区的孩子们则被送到贫穷的黑人社区的学校。大多数学生都不喜欢这种做法，学生的父母也不喜欢，父母希望孩子能就近入学。跨区校车接送在20世纪70年代和80年代一直持续，得失参半，如今基本上已经被废弃了。现在，大多数学区都允许孩子就近入读本社区的学校，即便这所学校的学生基本都是同一肤色的。

除了努力结束种族隔离，联邦政府还为最需要帮助的孩子制定了援助方案，包括特殊阅读指导、小班教学、幼儿教育课程和一些经济援助。根据美国教育考试服务中心的保罗·巴顿的说法，由于这些努力，20世纪70年代和80年代，不同种族学生成绩上的差距缩小了一半。然而，自那以后，这种差距几乎再没有变过。

在大学层面，20世纪70年代时，平权法案的项目有所发展。由于非洲裔和其他少数族裔美国人过去曾遭受歧视，因而高校努力积极招收少数族裔学生。目标是要让学生群体的人口构成能够与整个州或整个国家人口中少数族裔成比例。大学招收所有少数族裔的学生，包括拉美裔与非洲裔。在上一章中我们介绍过，最高法院大法官索尼娅·索托马约尔就曾受益于平权法案，被多所名校录取，还获得了奖学金。

多年来，在决定大学招生方面采用平权法案的做法也遇到过挑战。2003年，最高法院裁定，密歇根大学在招生时可以考虑学生的族裔或种族背景。大法官桑德拉·戴·奥康纳在最高法院的裁决中写道："如果要实现一个不可分割的国家的梦想，那么所有种族和民族的成员都必须有效地参与国家的公民生活。"

2013年，最高法院审议了另一项由2008年被得克萨斯大学奥斯汀分校拒绝录取的白人优秀学生阿比盖尔·费希尔发起的对平权法案的挑战。该大学保证对得克萨斯州所有排名前10%的高中毕业生优先录取，不论种族，但对除此之外的所有其他学生，种族和族裔背景会被作为录取的考虑因素。费希尔在班级排名前12%，她诉称，学业成绩比她差的少数族裔学生被录取，而她却被拒，这侵犯了宪法赋予她的权利。最高法院裁定，大学应该努力通过"种族中立政策"来实现多样性。这些复杂的法律问题使得许多美国人开始自问，如何才能为所有的学生——白人、黑人、拉美裔、亚裔和其他少数族裔——提供平等的教育机会。

公立学校任重道远

公立学校体系承载了美国人的许多理想、希望和问题。一些观察家认为，他们让公立学校承担了太多超出学校所能承担的责任。比如，人们常常期望公立学校能够解决由于美国家庭关系弱化而导致的学生问题。离婚率和单身母亲数量的上升，导致公立学校中单亲家庭孩子的人数也在不断增加。研究显示，在学校中，这些孩子会比双亲家庭孩子更容易出现问题。

新移民子女的教育是公立学校面临的最大的挑战。很多孩子来自的国家未能让他们建立坚实的教育基础，他们的学业能力低于平均水平。还有一些孩子来自教育标准与美国相似，甚至高于美国的国家，他们在学业上的适应就容易得多。但是，所有这些孩子都必须学习英语。这就意味着他们在努力学习新的概念的同时，还必须努力学习一门新的语言。研究显示，他们需要五到七年的时间才能在用英语授课的课堂中与以英语为母语的美国孩子平等竞争。在一种语言群体较为集中的地区，尤其是讲西班牙语的地区，也会有一些双语的课程。不过，美国有400多种语言，有些学区的学校里的儿童说着100种以上的不同语言。在一个教室里学生们讲五六种不同的母语的情形也并不罕见。

很明显，英语非母语的孩子在标准化考试中会处于劣势。很多人无法在这些考试中与英语母语的学生竞争。在"不让一个孩子掉队"计划中，这些学生的成绩会影响所在学校的评分，也影响美国学生整体的平均成绩。因此，非英语母语者较为集中的学区考试分数可能会低于其他学区。不幸的是，这些学区大多资金有限，无法为学生提供他们所需的额外帮助。一般来说，经济不景气时，州和地方政府投入公立学校的资金也较少。（如前所述，国家政府平均只为美国中小学提供10%的经费。）

学校经费有限对富有的美国人而言并不是大问题。在过去几年中，高收入家庭的学生考试成绩普遍有所提高，而黑人学生、拉美裔学生和低收入家庭的学生成绩则保持不变，一些学生的阅读成绩甚至有所下降。成绩最低的学区是在底特律（密歇根州）和华盛顿特区等贫困人口和种族隔离最为集中的地区。华盛顿特区内城的公立学校系统在全国所有城市中是白人和黑人学生学业成绩差距最大的。但在城市周围却是全国最富有的十个县里的七个，拥有一些最好的学校，也是有高等教育学历的成年人最为集中的地区。

在一本名为《分崩离析：美国白人状况，1960—2010》的颇具争议的书中，查尔斯·默里描述了他眼中的新上层阶级与新下层阶级之间日益拉大的差距。默里说，新上层阶级的成员居住在美国的某些"超级邮编"地区，收入和教育水平都很高，而且这些人常常是国家的领导和决策阶层。有四座城市是权力的中心："不住在纽约、华盛顿特区、洛杉矶和旧金山附近地区，就很难在政治、公共政策、金融、商业、学术界、信息技术或媒体方面拥有一份具有全国影响力的工作。"

默里担心，这些美国精英阶层脱离大众，无法理解中产阶层面临的问题。他们经济有保障，通常是美国最富有的人。经济衰退期间，其他美国人收入都减少了，而他们的收入却增加了。他们有自己的亚文化。一般来说，他们已婚、信仰宗教、社会观点比较开明、身体健康，并且非常关心孩子的教育。他们想把孩子送到合适的学前教育机构，以便将来可以上好的小学和好的中学，然后进入一所最具声望的大学，特别是哈佛、普林斯顿或耶鲁大学。有趣的是，所有现任最高法院法官都拥有哈佛或耶鲁大学的法律学位，历任美国总统从老布什到奥巴马（乔治·H. W. 布什、比尔·克林顿、乔治·W. 布什和奥巴马总统）也都毕业于哈佛或耶鲁。

21世纪对美国教育提出的挑战

开始时我们便提到，美国的公立学校反映了机会均等的理想。19世纪早期，在公立学校体系建立之初，人们就相信，如果不同阶层的孩子们都上同样的学校，那么社会阶层差异就会变小。当然，现实是从一开始学校就并不是对所有人开放的。在美国很多地方，非洲裔美国人是不能上公立学校的。南北战争之后，最高法院曾试图为实行种族隔离的学校辩护，表示他们可以"分隔但平等"。大法官约翰·马歇尔·哈兰认为，这一决定违反了国家的最高法律和基本价值观。他说："我们的宪法是不分肤色的，它既不知道也不容忍公民中不同阶级的存在"。随后在1954年，最高法院认定，强迫黑人学生去上种族隔离学校的法律违反了美国宪法，因为这样的学校永远不可能是平等的。法院的意见是："将黑人学生与其他学生分隔开……单纯是因为他们的种族会使他们产生低人一等的自卑感……这可能会对他们心灵和精神造成无法弥合的伤害。"

而现在，进入21世纪，我们发现美国的学校种族隔离又再一次盛行，这次不是因为法律，而是由于居住格局以及就近入读本地社区学校的习惯。我们发现，目前新移民的孩子就读的学校大多也是以少数族裔学生为主的。我们还了解到，非洲裔和拉美裔美国学生高中毕业率低于白人学生。我们将如何去解决这些严峻的问题？未来该何去何从？一方面，地方学校反映出居住格局上种族隔离严重；但另一方面，随着少数族裔在郊区定居，社区正日益融合。还有一个因素是不同种族和族裔的年轻人相互之间通婚的数量正快速增加，跨种族/族裔的混血孩子越来越多。

大量新移民涌入所产生的影响也是不可低估的。从1980年到2010年，外国出生的美国人比例增加了一倍多。学校中有四分之一的孩子父母中有一方是在美国以外出生的。美国的学校中有45%的学生是少数种族和族裔的成员。这也让学校重新审视课程内容，试图使其更具包容性。很多学校现在采用包括更多有关非洲裔美国人、拉美裔美国人和其他少数族裔知识的历史或社会研究教材，以及包含由各种民族背景的美国人创作的诗歌和小说的文学作品。

现在的挑战是要找到办法让所有的学生，不管他们读的是什么学校，都尽可能地接受最好的教育。大多数美国人可能都会赞同，所有学区都应该达到最低的核心标准，但也应该根据地方的多样性具有一定的灵活性。美国人一直努力在教育标准化与地方社区学校的特殊情况之间找到平衡点。所有种族、民族和收入水平的美国人都非常关心子女的教育。而且大多数家长都希望孩子能够就近在本社区的学校就读。如果学校不够好，他们更愿意看到的是对其进行改善，而不是关闭。

与其他许多国家不同，美国各地方学区很大程度上控制着社区学校。对于联邦政府提出的当地学校的办学方法，美国人总是充满怀疑。很多学区都是由该地区居民选举的当地学校理事会管理。常常会有家长在公立学校理事会上讨论学校发生的事情——有时是关于目前的教学内容和教材。

美国的公立学校总体而言发挥了良好的作用，教育了美国多样化的人口，致力于将人们凝聚在一起。美国人正努力找到办法为所有学生提供平等的教育机会，同时他们也面临着越来越多的挑战。此外他们还在讨论该如何让更多年轻人获得成就上的平等。这关乎美国未来的福祉。

第十章 美国人如何休闲

> 任何一个群体或民族的游戏和运动生活的形式与类型都反映了该文化其他方面的发展。
>
> 美国体育学会

美国人的价值观对他们的休闲方式有何影响？

体育与美国价值观

大多数社会科学家都认为，社会所组织的体育活动通常反映该社会的基本价值观，并试图在人们的思想和情感上强化这些价值观。因此，有组织的体育运动可能比个人自发的、无组织的运动有着更为严肃的社会目的。在美国当然也是如此。美国最受欢迎的三项有组织的体育运动是美式橄榄球、篮球和棒球，此外，足球也正越来越受欢迎。

传统上，美国人认为有组织的体育活动是机会均等在行动中的体现。在体育运动中，不同种族和经济背景的人都有平等的机会取得出色的表现。因此，社会学家哈里·爱德华兹指出，美国人将有组织的运动看作是"让任何社会阶层的青年都可以了解竞技体系的优势和回报的实验室"。尽管爱德华兹特别提到了年轻男性，但是年轻女性们同样也在有组织的体育比赛中不分种族和经济背景，平等竞争。大多数美国橄榄球和篮球球员，包括大学的和职业的，都是非洲裔美国人，职业棒球选手中有三分之一是西班牙裔或拉美裔。女子运动在美国也越来越受欢迎，目前大学级别的女子运动项目较以往得到了更多的资金和支持。从奥运会中也反映出人们对有组织的女子运动项目有越来越多的兴趣。美国女子运动员在垒球、篮球和足球等多项团体运动上都获得了金牌。

美国的竞争理念也是美国有组织体育运动的核心。许多美国人认为，学习如何在体育比赛中取胜有助于人们培养在以后的生活中成功竞争所必需的一些习惯。这样的训练反过来又使美国社会作为一个整体得到强化。一位体育作家说："人们普遍认同，为了美国未来商业和军事行动的成功，必须从青少年时期就开始通过体育运动了解竞争伦理，并将其深深印入脑海中。"事实上，美国大约三分之二的男孩和半数以上的女孩都会在校外参加有组织的体育活动。

在学校和大学开展的业余体育运动向年轻人传达传统的美国价值观，因而非常受重视。有组织的体育运动中的竞争伦理包括勤奋努力和体魄的勇气等。在体育世界里，努力往往被称为"拼命""坚持"或"永不放弃"，而身体的勇气则有"硬汉"和"有胆量"这样的表述。有时会用一些标语来让年轻的参与者们更好地理解竞争的美德：

> 拼搏——生存之道。
> 放弃永远无法成功，成功者永不言弃。
> 平庸容易，出类拔萃则需要勇气。

在激发传统美国基本价值观的过程中，有组织的体育活动也会被视为"国家信仰"的一部分，一方面融合了爱国主义和民族自豪感，另一方面又带有宗教的观念和象征（参见第三章）。美国新教著名宗教领袖比利·格雷厄姆曾经说过："《圣经》上说，闲暇和无所事事在道德上是危险的……体育运动让我们忙碌……大学和职业体育运动选手中真正虔诚的基督徒可能比其他职业中都要多。"但另一方面，近些年来发生了不少职业体育明星恶劣行为被曝光的事件，大学体育比赛中也丑闻迭出。

竞争走向了极端？

虽然体育运动在美国受到了许多的推崇，但当这种推崇走向极端时，也引起了一些人对体育运动负面影响的强烈不满。比如，在体育比赛中对胜利的过度渴望非但不能强化，反而还会削弱美国的传统价值观。

批评者指出，教练和运动员一直以来都沿袭着这样的传统。著名职业橄榄球教练文斯·隆巴迪就常常因发出胜利是体育运动中"唯一"重要的事这样的言论而受到批评。另一位著名橄榄球教练伍迪·海耶斯曾说过："我讨厌谁对我说'输了不要紧，不管怎样，你表现得很好了'这样的话。"批评者们认为教练们这样的言论削弱了人们对除比赛之外的其他一些东西重要性的信念，比如公平比赛、遵守规则以及失败时也要保持尊严，等等。然而不幸的是，许多教练依然信奉着"胜利就是一切"的理念。

不过，在美国体育运动中也有虽败犹荣的传统。比如，社会学家哈里·爱德华兹曾指出：

> 胜利的至关重要性人所共知，但对于"光荣的失败"同样也有可以慰藉的"回报"。事实上，胜利的"甜蜜"就源于此……因为知道自己击败的是一位勇敢的、值得尊敬的对手。

但是，当体育比赛中求胜心过分强烈时，荣誉的竞争就可能变成混乱和暴力。曾经在一场棒球比赛中，两支职业球队选手彼此之间的愤怒，最终使比赛演变为两支球队的大规模斗殴。其中一队的教练对这场架感到很高兴，因为在随后的比赛中，他的球队一路取胜。他觉得正是打了那场架，让他的球员们更加团结了。同样，一位职业橄榄球教练也说："如果当时我们没有冲出去打架，那我会感到担心。你们要冲出去，保护自己的队友。那些坐在板凳上无动于衷的家伙都是输家。"两位教练似乎都认为，如果偶尔和对手队打一架能激发队员的求胜精神，那打架再好不过了。冰球教练可能会很赞同。职业冰球队球员在场上打架斗殴是臭名昭著的。一些冰球迷甚至把这些打斗看成是娱乐的一部分。

有人严厉批评体育运动中的这种暴力行为，特别是橄榄球运动中，这可能是美国人最喜欢的观赏性运动。不时会有文章出现在报纸或杂志上，比如全美最主要的体育杂志之一，《体育画报》，抨击比赛极度粗暴，选手因此受伤，过于强烈的胜利欲望导致了伤病数量的增加。近些年来，头部伤害——脑震荡引起了很多重视，随着运动员年龄增大，还带来很多问题。有证据表明，这些伤害会造成严重的脑损伤，甚至导致痴呆。人们尤其担忧高中选手在橄榄球比赛中受伤。"痛击对手"与赢得高中比赛的压力非常巨大。在美国的一些地区，特别是南部地区，男孩们从小学开始玩橄榄球，9到10岁的孩子们就要承受竞争压力的风险。脑震荡对于足球运动员也是一个问题，特别是对女孩（头球时），因为她们的脖颈不如男孩强壮。

大多数美国人还是会认为，有组织的体育活动中的竞争更多还是加强，而不是败坏国民性格。他们可能会说，消除体育运动乃至整个社会中的竞争会导致懒惰、不思进取。例如，一位高中校长曾把对竞技体育的批评形容为"革命者试图摧毁社会建立的根本基础"。这种评论说明了竞争的理念在美国根深蒂固，而有组织的体育运动作为在更广泛的社会中维护这种价值观的手段又是何其重要。

另一种针对职业体育运动的批评是，球队老板和球员赚得太多，而球迷们却不得不花更多的钱买票。篮球、棒球和橄榄球明星们签下数百万美元的合同，赚得跟摇滚歌手和电影明星一样多。这使一些人质疑，这些球员究竟是运动员还是艺人。此外，为了钱，球员经常被卖到别的球队，或成为自由球员，甚至整个球队会搬到另一座城市。过去，球队和大部分球员待在一个城市，与球迷联系紧密。而现在，职业体育多以赚钱为目的，团队忠诚已不那么重要了。

大学橄榄球和篮球项目也同样受到赚大钱的影响。大型高校的球队能创造数百万美元的收入，但这些体育项目承受着招募顶级运动员和取得赛季胜利的巨大压力。年轻的运动员也有着同样的压力。还有一些高中生，如果拿不到体育奖学金，就上不起大学。但上了大学之后，他们却往往难以在日常训练及赛季日程需求与学习的需要之间取得平衡。有些大学的运动员毕业率要低于其他人。除了学业上不合格的危险外，还有另一个原因也使得一些运动员学生无法完成学业。顶尖的篮球和美式橄榄球选手通常在上学期间就被职业球队招募。一些学生可能会为了有机会成为职业选手，早日成功赚大钱，而选择放弃攻读大学学位。

有组织的体育运动所面临的另一个问题是兴奋剂的使用。由于获胜的压力太大，一些运动员选择求助于此类药物。虽然大多数兴奋剂的使用都是违法的，但它们却还是从职业运动扩散到了大学，甚至高中和初中。服用这类药物会危害运动员的健康，而且是不道德的。它与美国的机会均等与公平竞争的价值观相违背。然而，这种现象持续到2004年，问题已非常突出，乔治·W. 布什总统甚至在他的国情咨文中提到：

> 竞技体育在我们的社会中扮演着十分重要的角色，但不幸的是，一些职业运动选手却并没有树立好的榜样。在棒球、橄榄球和其他运动中使用类固醇等兴奋剂是非常危险的。它传达了一个错误的信息——成功有捷径，成绩比品格更重要。

这类药物的使用引起了人们对一些棒球运动员的成绩和他们的本垒打纪录的质疑，有几名球员也因此没能进入棒球名人堂。

自行车运动员兰斯·阿姆斯特朗及其服用兴奋剂事件引起了国际上的高度关注。阿姆斯特朗在美国非常受尊敬（尽管许多海外人士非常怀疑），他曾七次在环法自行车赛中获胜并积极参与抗癌慈善活动。美国邮政甚至还曾是他的自行车比赛官方赞助商。他使用兴奋剂的证据被披露，并被剥夺了所有自行车比赛胜利荣誉，令许多美国人都感到非常震惊。

娱乐活动

与有组织的体育活动不同，在美国，人们通常所说的娱乐并不鼓励竞争。因此，娱乐活动更多是自发的，为了满足个人远离工作中的竞争的需求。尽管如此，从美国人所进行的娱乐活动的种类中，也能够了解很多关于美国人的价值观。很多娱乐活动都是由地方组织的，并由地方政府提供（部分）经费支持。当地的公园及娱乐组织经常向本社区居民提供各种各样的活动。通常会有一个公园或娱乐部门，运营一个娱乐中心，里面有健身器材，并开设课程，同时还有户外设施，如公园、游乐场、足球场、棒球场、篮球场、网球场、高尔夫球场、步道、自行车道以及游泳池等。这些设施对所有人开放，且费用低廉，甚至是免费的。天气好的时候，许多社区都会举行各种户外活动和节庆活动，如美食品尝、户外音乐会、乡村集市、比赛和赛会等。通常都是全家出动，或是呼朋唤友一起参加。

一些美国人喜欢对体能要求较高的娱乐活动。比如，慢跑、网球和滑雪等成为美国成年人最喜爱的娱乐运动。这些美国人似乎把工作中努力拼搏的信念也带进了游戏和娱乐中。"努力工作、尽情玩耍"这样的表达就是这种理念的体现。

健身对这些美国人而言是一种生活方式。他们中有些人会定期去社区健身中心或私人俱乐部锻炼——举重、游泳、打壁球，参加有氧运动课程，或者练习健身自行车、跑步机、划船器或台阶练习器械。还有些人喜欢长跑，可能还会参加马拉松比赛。除了著名的波士顿及纽约马拉松赛外，许多其他城市甚至小镇，都有马拉松赛，吸引了成百上千的参赛者。很少有参赛者是为了获胜而来，大多数人只想完成整场比赛，每年都有超过五十万人完成马拉松比赛。虽然参与马拉松比赛的人数大幅下降，但是跑完全程的人数却在增加。

大多数比赛都是对所有人开放的，不管是年轻人还是老年人，甚至坐轮椅的人都可以参加，很多比赛会鼓励人们可以跑完全程，同样也可以走完全程。慈善赛跑也很受欢迎。参赛者会请大家通过向慈善机构捐款来赞助他们跑完比赛。赛跑全程长度不一，从5公里到10公里到马拉松全程不等，通常会包括社会活动。防治乳腺癌慈善竞跑"为治愈而奔跑"就吸引了乳腺癌存活者及其亲人朋友的参与，还有一些参与者是为了纪念罹患（或曾患过）这一疾病的挚爱之人。

美国人对自我完善的追求，很大程度上可追溯到国家的新教传统（参见第三章），同样也体现在一些人的娱乐习惯中。比如，慢跑者决心不断挑战更长的距离，还有些人利用假期学习帆船或潜水等新的运动项目。在一些对体能要求不高的流行娱乐活动中也可以看到这种自我完善的倾向。

提高思维与技能的文化活动在美国也很受欢迎，人们非常关注并积极参与。数百万的美国人会经常去听交响音乐会、看现场戏剧表演、参观博物馆、听讲座，或参加绘画、音乐演奏、舞蹈等艺术活动。很多美国人也喜欢编织、针线活、做蜡烛、木雕、缝被子等手工艺活动。社区的教育和娱乐项目也为感兴趣的居民提供电脑、烹饪、外语学习、写作、艺术、防身术、瑜伽乃至观鸟等各式各样的培训课程。

美国人的娱乐兴趣也体现了他们对自力更生精神的一贯推崇，有时还反映出他们对边疆生活与冒险的某种向往。一些人喜欢安全的消遣，比如手工、园艺，或像是在书房里组装书柜这样的DIY（自己动手）项目等；而有一些人则喜欢离开家去冒险。探险旅游已经发展成为数十亿美元的产业。数百万的美国人购置了山地自行车去探索荒野。还有很多人选择去漂流、登山、攀岩、跳伞、直升机滑雪和蹦极等。美国一些公园管理者抱怨，有很多人在国家公园内进行一些有生命危险的活动，而我们又不得不对他们进行救援。"他们就像是在找罪受，"一名公园负责人说，"他们似乎很享受危险和体能挑战。"

不过，并非所有的美国人都想在探险假期"吃苦"。有相当多的游客更喜欢"舒适探险"。朱迪·瓦恩兰经营着海外探险之旅公司，她说："坦率地讲，看到婴儿潮一代如此追求物质享受，我们也觉得不可思议。"在非洲观兽之旅中，她就必须为游客们提供热水淋浴、舒适的床和床头柜。我们在第五章中提到过美国人对舒适生活的热爱，而这种热爱似乎又与他们对自立和冒险的渴望相矛盾。另外一些人只是喜欢待在美国国内，去户外钓鱼、观鸟或观察其他野生动物。每年有9000多万美国人会参与这些活动。

健康与健身

尽管有这么多体育锻炼的机会，但很多美国人的体型却不怎么样，甚至根本不在意要保持体型。由于不健康的饮食习惯和久坐不动的生活方式，美国人整体上超重愈发严重。据政府研究估计，只有不到半数的美国人会在闲暇时锻炼身体。专家表示，这并非是因为美国人"不知道什么对自身有益"——他们只是不去做。美国疾病控制中心（CDC）曾发出警告，到2000年中期，会有近三分之二美国人超重，超过五分之一的人肥胖。疾病控制中心的报告指出，肥胖已经成为全国性的流行病。在美国，肥胖已经成为仅次于吸烟的第二大可预防的死亡原因。政府发起了活动，敦促人们减肥和锻炼。但到了2011年，情况却更糟糕了：三分之一以上的美国成年人肥胖。另外，有些州的肥胖率要高于其他州。

美国人并不缺乏健康饮食方面的信息。报纸杂志上有很多的营养建议，饮食类书籍也是畅销书。事实上，问题一部分可能是媒体上此类信息太多，而且很多是相互矛盾的。曾有30年的时间，政府一直在鼓励高碳水化合物和低脂肪的饮食，以预防心脏病和某些癌症的健康风险。很多美国人吃着低脂肪、高碳水化合物的食物，然后就长胖了。此后在21世纪初，高蛋白质、低碳水化合物的饮食开始流行起来。

许多美国人尝试了各种饮食，希望能找到一种适合自己的神奇食谱。一些超重人士说，那些膳食建议太让人困惑，他们就索性什么也不听了，想吃什么就吃什么。自1994年起，政府要求所有饮食都统一标注营养成分，以便消费者比较所购买食物的热量、脂肪和碳水化合物。半数以上美国人表示，自己会注意所吃食物的营养成分，但他们同时也表示，想吃东西时还是会吃自己真正喜欢的。比如，他们可能会把牛奶换成脱脂的，但却还是会买花哨的、脂肪含量很高的冰激淋。就像一个美国人所说的："还是面对现实吧——如果你喜欢把薯片和蘸酱当零食，不含脂肪的薯片和不含脂肪的酱料就是没有原汁原味的好吃。"

专家说，人们的饮食习惯是由社会、文化和心理等多种因素共同决定的。《新闻周刊》上一篇有关美国人体重问题的文章提到了美国人生活中似乎根深蒂固的"暴饮暴食文化"。"这片富饶之地似乎注定了要承载大量超重人口。"专家们如是说。问题的部分原因是，比起其他很多国家的人，美国人每餐都吃得很多，而且常常还要加餐。

另一个原因是美国人喜爱快餐。虽然快餐店也提供沙拉，但大多数美国人还是更喜欢"垃圾食品"。他们在餐馆里消费大量的比萨饼、汉堡包、薯条和软饮料，不仅因为他们喜欢，还因为这些食物便宜。另一个重要原因是美国人忙碌的生活方式。由于越来越多的妇女外出工作，人们在家也会经常吃快餐、速冻食品或餐厅外卖。一些专家认为，美国人已经完全无法控制自己的饮食了；频繁去餐馆，吃那么多包装食品，他们根本不可能限制热量的摄入。烹饪新鲜蔬菜和鱼需要花费时间，而下班回家的路上到快餐连锁店吃炸鸡却省事得多。通常，美国家庭都是"边跑边吃"，而不是围坐在餐桌边共享美食。

美国第一夫人米歇尔·奥巴马发起过一项强调儿童健康和健身，对抗儿童肥胖的活动。该项目名为"让我们动起来"，关注改善儿童营养以及增加体育锻炼。她倡议联邦立法要求学校提供健康午餐，她还鼓励孩子们多运动。她和华盛顿内城学校的孩子们一起在白宫开辟了一个菜园，并以此呼吁人们关注，许多贫穷的内城社区没有出售新鲜蔬菜和水果的食品店。很多社区只有卖薯片、汽水等热量高而营养价值低的"垃圾食品"的小店。通常，贫困人口中儿童及成人的肥胖率都高于一般人群。

有证据表明，儿童肥胖率已有所改善。据美国疾病控制与预防中心（CDCP）统计，密西西比州是美国最肥胖的州之一，但近年来儿童肥胖率有所下降。该州在公立学校的体育锻炼时间和供应食物种类上都做出了重要的调整：

密西西比州有关部门将儿童肥胖率的下降归功于当地对这一问题的重视：2007年出台的一项法律规定学校增加体育课程，州教育委员会也做出决议，要求学校提供更多水果、蔬菜和全麦食品。

虽然并非所有人都赞同政府强制规定体育锻炼和午餐食谱，但这种做法看起来确实有帮助。儿童肥胖问题的确让人忧心：美国有近三分之一的儿童超重或肥胖。在非洲裔和拉美裔社区中这一比例更高，达到了近40%。

电视、电子游戏及互联网的影响

讽刺的是，随着美国人口越来越重，美丽女人的形象却越来越苗条了。按照今天媒体的标准，20世纪五六十年代的电影明星玛丽莲·梦露也算超重了。电视节目、电影及电视广告中的女演员都非常苗条。比如在啤酒和软饮料的广告中，常会出现身着比基尼身材纤细的美女。这也导致很多少女对自己的体型变得不自信，痴迷于减肥，一些人因此患上厌食症或暴食症等饮食失调症。

另一点讽刺的是，尽管电视上似乎都是在宣传身材苗条、健康的形象，但实际上，人们看电视越多，就越不可能去锻炼。电视严重影响了许多美国人的活动量。有些人大部分的空闲时间基本都是躺在沙发上看电视，拿着遥控器不停地换频道，吃着垃圾食品。这些人被称为"沙发土豆"，因为他们除了眼睛，哪里都不动（土豆上的小点也被称作"眼"）。沙发土豆们宁愿在电视上看棒球，也不愿和朋友一起去公园玩垒球，甚至去电影院看电影也不愿意。有线电视和卫星电视让美国人不出家门就可以收看数百个频道，几乎有无限的节目可以选择。美国人花在看电视上的空闲时间比花在其他任何活动上的都多。

随之出现的另一个问题是这些技术对于儿童的影响。有人担心，孩子们和年轻人花在看电视、上网和打游戏上的时间太多了。其中一个后果就是不停换台浏览电视频道和浏览网页缩短了孩子注意力集中的时间。研究还显示，多任务情境中人并不能真的一心多用，同时操作多项任务，只不过是在多个任务间快速切换而已。有证据表明，这些活动会改变青少年和年轻人的大脑，对他们的身心都会有影响。很显然，他们也缺乏运动。政府估计，8到18岁的孩子平均每天花在电视、电脑、电子游戏、手机和电影等娱乐媒体上的时间为7.5小时。只有三分之一中学生的体育运动量达到了建议标准。

还有一些人更担心孩子们在电视、电子游戏和互联网上所看到的内容。许多人对孩子们看电视、玩游戏和上网时会接触到大量有关性和暴力的内容深感担忧。美国人一直面临两难的困境——如何平衡言论自由的权利与保护儿童及维护道德标准。由于美国人高度重视个人自由，特别是言论自由，因而对于审查，甚至限制用任何通信手段进行的信息流通，他们一直非常犹豫。只有当政府制定了标准，才会实施真正的审查制度；多数美国人还是希望娱乐业能够自我规范，美国电影业确实有电影分级制度。娱乐软件评级委员会（ESRB）"根据年龄和内容对电子游戏、移动应用软件进行分级，为电子游戏业制定广告和营销指导方针，并帮助企业执行网络隐私责任规范"。

一方面，有人认为联邦政府应该规范互联网以保护儿童。因为确曾发生过一些事件，有些成年人在网上结识儿童或青少年，并诱劝他们线下会面。在一些案例中，未成年人因此而被绑架。家长们非常害怕孩子们在网上结识陌生人或接触色情内容。在美国，通过邮件传播色情内容是违法的，一些人希望法律能够禁止互联网上的色情内容（儿童色情本来就是违法的）。然而不只是儿童会在网络遇到麻烦，很多成年人也成了网络诈骗的受害者，他们被犯罪分子骗取了个人信息，造成银行账户内资金被盗，甚至有人整个身份都被盗用了。互联网的匿名性受到了很多人的看重，但它也伤害了许多人。最令人震惊的是一些青少年网络霸凌，造成的伤害非常严重，有些受害者甚至因此自杀。

但另一方面，也有许多互联网用户认为，政府监管会威胁到互联网的发展与活力。有些人会说，正是因为没有监管，互联网才得以爆发式增长，新技术的发展才成为可能。如今，无线技术让美国人可以在任何地方上网，甚至包括许多快餐店。许多人都很高兴，科技使得人们可以随时随地与他人沟通。然而这种24/7（每天24小时，每周7天）的全天候在线却严重影响了美国人的休闲时间和放松能力。乔·罗宾逊在他的著作《工作是为了生活：找回你的生活、健康、家庭和理智》中指出："工作与家庭的界限变得模糊不清，唯一的分别就是家里有张床。"罗宾逊与其他一些人正争取让美国企业给员工更多的休假。大多数美国人每周工作超过四十小时，而且许多人每年只有一到两周带薪休假。经济不景气的时候，很多人连短暂的休假也不敢享受。美国旅游协会的报告显示，目前美国人平均假期仅为3.8天；人们更多会选择长周末旅行，一两周的旅行已经越来越少了。

罗宾逊组织了"为了生活而工作"活动，目的就是要改变美国的劳动法规，让每个美国人每年有至少三周的假期。他说，美国开国元勋托马斯·杰斐逊和约翰·亚当斯"都认为，如果全社会都把注意力集中在赚钱上，那民主就濒临险境了。当你被过度工作的文化绑架，无暇顾及生活中所有其他责任时，你连做一个合格的公民都很困难，更遑论做父母或成为真正的人了"。罗宾逊认为，如果美国人能像欧洲人那样有一个月的悠长假期，那他们的工作效率会更高。

休假可以让人们养精蓄锐，恢复能量与活力，更加充实高效地生活。在美国，人人都能从休闲时间里得到收获，唯一让大多数美国人抱怨的是休闲时间还不够多。美国人和世界各地的人一样，有时也会选择纯粹为了休息和放松的娱乐活动。看看电视、出去吃饭、走亲访友都是愉快的休闲方式。不过，正如我们所看到的，还有数百万美国人即便休闲时也要不断尝试新的花样、寻求新的挑战。《美国新闻与世界报道》指出："他们所获得的是一种重新焕发的生命力"，是一种在应对人生的"浮沉跌宕"中征服目标的感受与重拾的自信。

第十一章　美国家庭

美国人重塑了其家庭结构的特点，正如其重塑了有关自己的一切那样。

马克斯·勒纳（1902—1992）

美国家庭结构的变化是否正在影响着美国梦？

家庭结构

典型的美国家庭是什么样的？如果让美国人说出自己的家庭成员，那么家庭的结构就很清晰了。已婚的美国成年人会把自己的丈夫或妻子还有孩子（如果有的话）称为直系亲属。提到父母、姐妹或兄弟时，会将他们视为各自独立的家庭，通常他们也不住在一起。叔舅姑姨、堂表亲和祖父母则属于大家庭。

传统上，美国家庭一直是核心家庭，由一对夫妻及其子女组成，居住在一套房子或公寓里。祖父母很少会和他们的已婚子女居住在一起；叔舅姑姨等更不会一起住。20世纪50年代，大多数美国家庭都是这种典型的传统美国家庭——一对夫妻和两个孩子。父亲是养家者（挣钱养家），母亲是持家者（照顾孩子，操持家务，不在外工作），膝下一对未成年的子女。一两代人之前，如果你对美国人提起"家庭"这个词，那他们脑海中浮现的应该就是这样一个传统的画面。

然而今天，情况已大不相同。只有很小一部分美国家庭仍然是由外出工作养家的父亲、居家操持的母亲和未成年的孩子组成。现在父母双全、儿女绕膝的美国家庭不到四分之一，而即使在这样的家庭中，母亲也大多在外工作。现在多数的美国家庭或是只有无子女的夫妻二人，或是单亲父母和孩子，又甚或是无亲属关系的人合住在一起。也许最令人惊讶的是，27%的美国人孑然独居。其中约有三分之一的独居者年龄在65岁以上。他们中的许多人生活在中西部北方地区的小城镇，这里的人们更愿意在自己家里养老。还有一些独居者则多是为了寻找工作机会而来到亚特兰大和北弗吉尼亚（华盛顿地区）等地的年轻人。

20世纪50年代时传统美国家庭究竟发生了什么？又为何会出现这样的变化呢？这其中有一些人口方面的解释。20世纪50年代，参加过"二战"的男人们回到了家乡，结婚成家。这一时期婴儿出生率大幅度提高，产生了"婴儿潮一代"。第二个人口因素是，现在的年轻人普遍晚婚晚育，还有些夫妻选择不生孩子。第三个因素是人们的寿命更长了，在子女成年后，人们常常独自终老。当然，还有第四个因素——高离婚率。但是，仅凭数字并不足以解释家庭的巨大变化。了解家庭生活中的价值观将为我们提供一些重要的见解。

强调个人自由

美国人把家庭视为一个团体，它的根本目的是增进每个成员的幸福。因而，在家庭生活中，每个个体的需求占据了首要位置。这就意味着，与其他很多文化形成了对比，美国家庭成员的首要职责不是提升家庭的社会或经济地位，也不是为家族增添荣光。这也许是因为美国并不是贵族社会。

由于机会均等被认为是美国的基本传统价值观，因而家族的声望和荣耀并没有像在贵族社会里那样重要。而且，美国人也不太会把家庭看作一个经济单位，因为相对来说很少有家庭能连续两代经营自给自足的家庭农场或家族企业。比如，农场主的儿子很可能要上大学，就会离开家庭农场，到另一个地方从事一份完全不同的工作。

美国人渴望自由，不愿意受到外部控制，这种渴望也延伸到了家庭中。他们不喜欢被其他家庭成员掌控。他们要独立做决定，而不是由祖父母或叔叔阿姨们告诉自己该怎么做。例如，美国的男性和女性都期望能自己决定什么样的工作最适合自己。事实上，在美国，家人会鼓励年轻人独立做职业决定。美国人认为更重要的不是怎样做对家庭最有利，而是怎样做对个体更有利。

结婚与离婚

在美国很少有"包办"婚姻。年轻人一般都希望自己在不受父母干涉的情况下找到另一半。事实上，很多父母在孩子决定结婚前对此并不知情。这就意味着很多父母在孩子的择偶问题上几乎没有什么控制权，也不会有多少影响力。大多数美国人认为，年轻人应该先相爱，然后再决定是否与能让自己幸福生活的人结婚，这也再次证明了个人幸福的重要性。现实当然并不总是这样，但它仍然是传统的理想，并塑造着年轻美国人的婚恋观。

一直以来，婚姻本身的价值很大程度上取决于夫妻能够给对方带来多少幸福。幸福的基础主要是陪伴。大多数美国妇女会将陪伴作为婚姻中最重要的部分。经济支持、生养孩子的机会等其他一些婚姻的价值虽然重要，但很多人认为它们并不是那么重要。夫妻若不幸福，他们很可能就会选择离婚。在美国绝大多数地区，离婚都是比较容易的。多数州都适用"无过错"离婚。无过错离婚是指夫妻只要说明双方无法继续幸福地共同生活，双方之间存在不可调和的分歧，就可以获得法庭的离婚判决，而这并不是任何一方的过错。

美国的离婚率从 20 世纪 60 年代到 80 年代快速上升，之后又趋于稳定。总的来说，现在美国有一半的婚姻都是以离婚收场，不过离婚率也会因夫妻的年龄和其他因素而有所不同。结婚越早通常离婚的可能性就越大。查尔斯·默里在《分崩离析：美国白人状况》一书中所描述的新上层阶级离婚率远低于其他阶层（参见第五章）。他们更有可能结婚（通常是大学毕业后）、维持婚姻，并在稳定的双亲家庭中养育孩子。这些人受过良好的教育，通常相当富有，其中还包括许多国家领导者。而另一方面，穷人中则有更多的单身母亲。结婚率更低而离婚率更高。孩子们常常也会被牵涉其中。

大多数美国中产阶层成年人认为，夫妻如果不幸福，就不应该因为有孩子而勉强维系婚姻，这是 20 世纪 50 年代以来人们对于婚姻态度的一个重大转变。很多人不再认为应该为了孩子而牺牲自己的个人幸福。他们觉得，与其让孩子和不断争吵的父母生活在一起，跟着其中一个生活实际上可能对孩子更好。离婚现在非常普遍，已为社会所接受，孩子们也不会因为父母离异而觉得难堪。不过，心理学家和社会学家仍然在研究离婚对孩子的长期影响。

朱迪思·沃勒斯坦研究了父母离异对孩子成长的影响。她在《离婚之后：25 年孩子的心路研究》一书中指出，到 2000 年，40 岁以下的美国成年人中有近一半成长于离异家庭。她在 25 年中跟踪研究了一些父母离异的孩子，并将他们的经历与那些父母"为了孩子"而未离异家庭的子女进行了比较。她发现，无论父母离婚与否，最重要的是父母能否搁置分歧，更多地关注孩子的需求。但是，情况再好，父母离异也会对孩子成年后的婚恋产生长久的影响。事实上，有超过一半的人表示不想要孩子了，因为他们害怕让孩子经历自己成长过程中的痛苦。

孩子的角色

美国人强调个体，而不是群体，这对孩子的影响是非常矛盾的。一方面，这可能会让孩子得到过多的关注，甚至过多不应有的权力；另一方面，由于大多数孩子的母亲都要外出工作，他们很可能得不到父母任何一方足够的关心。更糟糕的是，父母因为没有足够时间陪伴孩子而感到内疚，可能会以更多的物质来补偿。上班族父母总是要努力挤出足够的时间和孩子在一起。

一些美国家庭更重视孩子的需求和愿望，而不是孩子对社会与家庭的责任。"二战"后的几年，人们非常注重儿童的心理需求，这个领域的专家数量也大量地增加。众多儿童心理学家、咨询师和社会工作者受聘帮助那些在学校或家庭中遇到问题的孩子。许多育儿类书籍成了畅销书。尽管有时这些书提供的建议是彼此矛盾的，但几乎所有这些书籍都认同美国人对个体发展的重视，并将其作为首要目标。

一些美国人认为，家长和专家对儿童个体心理需求的重视有些过头了。本杰明·斯波克是美国最著名的育儿专家之一，他就曾总结道："今天这种以孩子为中心的观点让做父母成了最难的工作。"斯波克说，很多认真尽责的父母往往"只关注自己的孩子，只考虑孩子对父母和社会的需求，而不考虑这个世界、社区和家庭对孩子有什么要求，孩子长大后该如何去履行这些责任"。

现在的父母似乎更关注培养孩子的责任感了。尽管美国人对教养孩子的最佳方式也许莫衷一是，但大多数人仍然坚信，家庭的主要目标是实现每个成员作为个体的发展和幸福。

家庭中的平等

与美国人对个人自由的重视一样，平等的信念也对家庭产生了重要的影响。阿历克西·德·托克维尔早在19世纪30年代就洞察到了这种联系。他说，在贵族社会，不平等延伸到了家庭，特别是在父亲与子女的关系上。父亲被认为是统治者与主人。孩子与父亲的关系非常拘谨正式，孩子对父亲的爱也往往夹杂着畏惧。但在美国，平等的民主思想很大程度上打破了父亲作为家庭统治者的地位，也拉近了父亲与孩子的情感距离。孩子对父亲没有那么拘谨与敬畏，会更多地对父亲表达自己的感情。"主人和被建构的（合法）统治者形象不见了，"托克维尔说，"而留下了父亲的身份。"

近两个世纪以前托克维尔对美国父子关系的描述依然适用于今天美国父母与子女之间的关系。父母与子女之间的关系比起大多数贵族社会或历史传统悠久的社会要平等得多。实际上，有些美国人也担心家庭中太过民主了。他们认为，父母的权威和孩子对父母的尊重被严重地削弱了，尤其是在青少年中。有些父母似乎已经无法管教他们的青春期孩子的行为，特别是孩子16岁拿到驾照后。父母与青少年之间的另一个问题是关于监控孩子的网上活动。家长们很难知道自己的孩子都在访问些什么网站，甚至无从知晓他们有多少时间是在上网。手机给青少年们带来了一种不一样的新自由，让他们可以随时随地与朋友聊天、上网。

另一方面，很多美国人给年轻人相当大的自由，以培养孩子独立自主的能力。习惯上，美国孩子在18岁左右高中毕业后就要"离巢"了，或者去上大学（很多人会去外地），或者找份工作养活自己。如果20多岁的年轻人还和父母住在一起，人们会觉得这是有问题的。传统上，孩子在家庭中拥有充分的自由和平等，成人后通常会比较独立自主。但现在也有相当数量的年轻人与父母生活在一起。有些是在就读社区大学，为了节省开支住在家里；还有一些是因为找不到一份工作能维持其从小习惯的生活方式，所以就一直住在家里，或是又搬回去暂时与父母同住。这些年轻人被称为"回巢族"，因为他们曾经离开了巢穴，现在又回来了。经济不景气的时候，多代同堂的生活可以提高所有人的生活水平，因为几代人可以分摊开支，对每个人都有利。不过，大多数人不会指望以此作为长久之计。

婚姻关系的四个阶段

除了父母与子女之间的关系之外，平等的观念还影响了家庭结构的其他方面。它对夫妻之间的关系有着重要的影响。妇女在家庭与社会中整体的地位稳步提升。根据两位美国社会学家，莱莎·斯坎佐尼与约翰·斯坎佐尼的研究，美国的婚姻制度经历了四个发展阶段。每一个新阶段，妻子与丈夫平等的程度都有提高，她们在家庭中也掌握了更多的权力。

第一阶段：妻子是丈夫的仆人。 19世纪时的美国，妻子要完全顺从丈夫。一直到1850年，殴打妻子在美国几乎各州都是合法的。尽管夫妻双方都承担家庭责任，但妻子除了丈夫允许的事之外，对家庭事务没有任何权力。妻子所有的财产和收入都属于她的丈夫。19世纪，妇女没有选举权，这样的限制也在一定程度上反映了妇女作为仆人的地位。

第二阶段：丈夫是领导，妻子是助手。 19世纪末到20世纪初，女性外出就业的机会增加了。越来越多的妻子必要的话都能够自食其力，因此她们也不再接受妻子是丈夫的仆人，必须服从丈夫的这种传统观念。虽然大多数妇女并没有选择外出工作，但她们有能力这样做的事实增加了她们在婚姻中的权力。丈夫再也不能对家中事务独断专行并要求妻子服从。在家庭决策中，妻子有了更多表达异议与坚持己见的自由。

虽然妻子有了更多的权力，但丈夫依然是家中的领导。妻子打理房屋、养育孩子，成为丈夫的专职助手。她也许会和他争论，有时也能说服他，但通常还是他掌握对家庭事务的最终决定权。

女性在婚姻中平等地位的提升反映了她们整体社会地位的提升，妇女终于在20世纪初获得了选举权。在今天的美国，这种丈夫领导、妻子助手的婚姻依然存在，但20世纪的经济状况使大部分婚姻都进入了不同的阶段。

第三阶段：丈夫是高级合伙人，妻子是初级合伙人。 20世纪时，越来越多的妻子外出就业。例如，1940年，美国只有14%的已婚妇女在外工作，而到了2000年代，这一比例上升到了超过60%。在莱莎和约翰看来，当已婚妇女迈出这一步，她们相对于丈夫的权力就进一步地提高了。妻子的收入对于维持家庭生活水平变得更加重要。比起在家做全职妻子时，她们影响家庭决策的权力也更大了。

尽管她已成为一个合伙人，但在这一阶段妻子仍然不是与丈夫完全平等的合作伙伴，因为在这些婚姻中，丈夫的收入高于妻子。如果把家庭看作是企业，丈夫自视为高级合伙人，而妻子则是初级合伙人。虽然她也有工作，但远不如丈夫的重要。比如，假使丈夫得到异地升迁的机会，妻子通常会放弃自己的工作，追随丈夫到新的地方另谋一份工作。

今天的美国仍有一些高级合伙人/初级合伙人的婚姻。不过，如今大多数女性都外出就业，有些比自己的丈夫挣得要多。越来越多的婚姻进入了莱莎和约翰所定义的第四阶段。

第四阶段：夫妻是平等合作伙伴。 从20世纪60年代后期开始，越来越多的女性对以丈夫及他的事业作为首要考虑的婚姻安排表示强烈不满。到20世纪70年代末，只有不到一半的女性依然认为丈夫和孩子比自己的事业更重要。21世纪，大多数美国妇女都认为她们在婚姻中应该是平等的合作伙伴，丈夫在育儿和家务方面应承担同等的责任。

在平等的合伙婚姻中，妻子从事着一份与丈夫的事业同等重要甚至更加重要的职业或事业。长久以来的夫妻分工方式走向了终结。丈夫不再是家庭收入的主要来源，妻子也不再负担家务和养育孩子的主要责任。夫妻平等分担所有这些责任，也平等分享家庭决策的权力。

目前，在美国的实际生活中，尽管大多数女性在家庭事务的决策中有了平等的发言权，但女性从事同样的工作薪资有时会低于男性，其平均工酬仅为男性的77%。而且，尽管女性占劳动力人口的49%，但大多数女性在照顾孩子、做饭和清扫等方面花的时间仍然比丈夫要多。不少女性对此颇为愤慨，她们觉得自己就像是同时在做两份全职工作——一份在职场、一份在家。20世纪80年代时，女性们被告知她们可以"拥有一切"——成功的事业、丈夫、孩子，还有整洁的家。现在，一些女性渐渐发觉，这样的生活方式让人疲惫不堪，却又劳而无功。有些年轻女性现在会选择留在家里不出去工作，直到孩子上学，可还有很多想留在家里做全职妈妈的女性，因为经济负担又不得不外出工作。

另一方面，许多女性仍在努力争取职场上真正的男女平等。《向前一步：女性、工作与领导意愿》一书的作者谢丽尔·桑德伯格认为，女性应该积极寻求更多的领导角色。她指出，过去30年里，美国女性大学毕业的人数已经超过了男性，但政坛和商界却依然由男性主宰着。目前，只有4.2%的财富500强企业由女性担任首席运营官。桑德伯格本人担任脸书的首席运营官，她向女性提供各种建议，帮助她们发挥自己的潜能。她说："我认为女性可以在职场担当更多领导职务，同样我认为男性在家中也可以承担更多家务。我相信这会创造一个更美好的世界，各种机构一半由女性在管理，而家庭生活一半也有男性在操持。"

对于男性来说，兼顾职业和家庭两份责任与对于女性来说一样都非易事，特别是如果做到真正平等分工的话。在美国经常可以看到父亲送孩子去保姆那里或带生病的孩子去看医生。一些企业也认识到需要为双职工家庭提供一些服务，或在办公楼内开设日托中心，或让父亲休陪产假，在家陪伴新生的宝宝，或实行弹性工作时间。遗憾的是，这些福利还未能惠及所有人。尽管年轻的夫妻在事业、婚姻和养育子女方面努力追求实现平等，但整个社会仍然缺乏很多他们所需要的制度结构支持。

家庭在社会中的角色

美国的平等理念不仅影响婚姻，对男女之间各种形式的关系都有影响。美国人非常重视在家庭范围内实现个人自由与平等，并因此获益匪浅。每个家庭成员的需求和愿望都得到了很大的关注与重视。但美国人也为此付出了代价。相比于其他一些文化中的家庭，美国的家庭可能不够稳定与长久。美国的高离婚率或许就是这种不稳定最重要的体现。

美国人对家庭的态度相当矛盾。一方面，为了保护自由和平等的价值观，他们要忍受家庭中包括离婚在内的诸多不稳定。另一方面，他们又坚定地认为家庭生活是所有生活方式中最好的选择。实际上，大多数离异的人都会找到一个新的伴侣，再次步入婚姻。各种研究都一致显示，绝大多数美国人都相信家庭生活非常重要。

什么是家庭生活呢？前文已介绍了，如今只有不到四分之一的美国家庭还是传统的家庭，即由父亲、母亲和孩子组成。而这之中其实有很多都是再婚家庭或混合家庭。由于多数人离婚后会再婚，因而很多孩子是与继父或继母生活在一起的。在一个混合家庭中，父母可能各自带着与前妻或前夫生的孩子，然后他们之间又有一个或几个孩子——于是有了"你的""我的"和"我们的"孩子。这样的家庭往往会引起相当复杂且时常会很紧张的关系。比如，一个孩子可能会有四对祖父母。混合家庭有很多困难，而且遗憾的是，许多二次婚姻都是以失败而告终。

除了传统家庭和混合家庭之外，还有一些单身母亲或单身父亲（以母亲居多）独自抚养孩子。许多单亲妈妈是离婚的，但也有些没有结过婚。事实上，到2012年，新生婴儿中有一半为单身母亲所生，而这一趋势还在继续。有时，为了寻求经济和情感的支持，单亲父母会带着孩子与祖父母同住。除此之外，还有很多不同的居住方式。近些年来，一些同性恋伴侣也组建了家庭，他们有的会领养孩子，有的也会通过安排使自己的生物学子女降生并养育。现在有一些州已经认可同性婚姻，还有一些州认可其为"民事结合"。如今，同性婚姻得到大多数美国人的支持，也获得了越来越多的法律承认。毫无疑问，到了2000年代，"家庭"的定义已经变得更加宽泛。现在多数美国人会将家庭定义为"一起生活、彼此相爱并相互扶持的人"。

美国家庭面临的挑战

除了离婚、单亲、平衡家庭与事业等问题，许多美国人还面临着其他的挑战。由于人口老龄化，并且人的寿命普遍越来越长，许多美国中年人发现自己成了"三明治一代"，他们处在夹层中，上有年迈的父母需要照顾，下有子女需要抚养。皮尤研究中心的报告称，美国几乎一半四五十岁的中年人有一位65岁以上的父母，同时他们还在抚养年幼的孩子或为成年子女提供重要支持。许多人不得不照顾成年子女是因为上一次的经济衰退，年轻人在其中受到的打击最为沉重。三明治一代要努力同时为年老的父母和子女提供生活上的照料，还要给予他们经济上与情感上的支持，承受着多方面的压力。

处在数字时代，养育孩子又对三明治一代提出了更多的挑战。可以将人们接入互联网的数字设备对家庭产生了深刻的影响。社会学家和心理学家指出，家庭是孩子们学习社交技能、道德观和责任感的最佳场所。但要教育孩子，父母必须要有和孩子面对面的时间。而现在，越来越多的父母和孩子都是各自用着自己的数字设备浏览网页或收发邮件和信息。经常可以看到这样的场景，父母与青少年子女一起坐在餐厅里，却各自玩着手机，互不交谈。在《纽约时报》一篇名为《逃离交谈》的文章中，心理学家雪莉·特克尔指出，美国人为了联络却放弃了交谈：

> 我们已经习惯了一种新的"群体性孤独"的生活方式。技术使我们可以随时随地与任何地方的人彼此联络。我们想要定制自己的生活，想要自由进出于我们所处之处，因为我们最重视的是掌控自己所关注的领域。

现实中，人们无法真正定制自己的生活。成功的成年人必须能够在各种难以预料的情况下应对各种各样的人，这需要良好的社交能力。而良好的沟通和社交能力的培养始于家庭。但不幸的是，孩子们可能会发现父母无暇指导自己，而父母也可能不知道孩子需要什么样的帮助。例如，父母们也许没有意识到，他们的孩子沉迷在虚拟现实中时，并没有学会什么重要的社交技巧。青少年越来越多地用智能手机收发信息，而不是交谈。这使得他们无法学会那些通过交谈掌握的社交技巧：理解肢体语言，分辨他人情绪，培养进行对话所需的耐心，以及学会如何"闲聊"等。纽约大学最近就出人意料地为新生开设了一门有关如何闲聊的课程。学生们在脸书上互相认识，但却不知道当面该如何寒暄、如何开始交谈以了解彼此。

今天，不仅专家、媒体、当选官员和普通大众也都在讨论美国家庭的状况。一些美国人认为，无论是家庭制度还是家庭观念，都陷入了困境。但如果你问美国人他们自己的家庭如何，多数人还是会告诉你他们对自己的家庭生活总体很满意。在《价值观与公共政策》一书中，丹尼尔·扬克洛维奇报告了一些关于家庭价值观的调查，有十一点被大多数美国人认同为家庭价值观。扬克洛维奇将其中六点归类为"明显传统的价值观"：

·尊敬父母
·对自己的行为负责
·信仰上帝
·尊重权威
·坚守同一个人一辈子的婚姻
·体面地离开人世

另外五点被归类为"兼具传统与现代、更重表达的价值观"：

·给予其他家庭成员情感上的支持
·尊重他人
·提升交流情感的技巧
·尊重孩子
·充分发挥个人的潜能

美国家庭的理想是通过团队合作，帮助实现每个成员的自我价值，相亲相爱，为每个成员注入情感的力量。在这方面，家庭和教堂颇为相似。两者都被美国人认为是可以让人类心灵远离外部世界激烈竞争的庇护之所，人们在此养精蓄锐，汲取继续前行的力量。尽管很多时候，家庭并未能使人们做到相互扶持，也没能让人重振精神，但在许多美国人心中，这依然是家庭生活的理想状态。

第十二章　十字路口的美国价值观

唯一确定的是，明天会令所有人大吃一惊。

阿尔文·托夫勒（1928—　）

代表利益和权利的价值观与代表代价或责任的价值观之间的平衡是否发生了变化？

价值观在国家认同中的作用

美国民意测验专家约翰·佐格比说，美国人其实对自身了解甚少。"在这样一个热衷于实施、解读、争论乃至抨击民意调查的国家，奇怪的是，我们却仍然难以理解我们自身究竟是谁。"他指出，每一代人都追问同样一个问题——到底是什么使我们成为"美国人"？我们的共同点是什么？美国经历过独立战争、南北战争、大萧条、民权斗争、暗杀、几次试图弹劾总统等种种危机。"能渡过危机，原因很简单——我们拥有塑造我们成为美国人的共同价值观。"佐格比赞同美国文化专家本·瓦滕伯格的观点，那就是"价值观最重要"。这些价值观赋予美国人独特的身份认同，而最能代表这些价值观的候选人或政党就会赢得选举。这些价值观是最初《独立宣言》中所阐明的基本权利：

> 我们认为这些真理是不言自明的：人人生而平等，造物主赋予他们若干不可剥夺的权利，其中包括生命、自由和追求幸福的权利。为了保障这些权利，人们才在他们中间建立政府，而政府的正当权力，则是经被治理者同意而获得的。

之后，这些权利又被写入宪法及第一至第十条宪法修正案（即《权利法案》）中，以书面的形式保护美国人民的自由和权利。佐格比认为,"不同于其他任何国家和人民,我们是由我们拥有的权利所决定的,而不是地理、艺术和文字,或是美食与情感,也不是宗教或文明,更不是战争……纵观历史,我们对这些权利及其适用范围有过争议,但同时,我们都已将这些权利内化为了自己的一部分"。

我们在本书中论述的六项基本价值观(个人自由、自力更生、机会均等、参与竞争、物质财富和勤奋工作)依然是影响美国社会的主要力量。在本章中,我们将回顾这六项传统的基本价值观,并探讨它们现在所面临的挑战。

个人自由与自力更生

正如前面提到过的,自由(有时被称为"个人权利")是美国六项传统基础价值观中最被珍视,也最受欢迎的。在20世纪30年代之前,一直居于主导地位的是开国元勋们所坚持的传统的自由观,被写入了宪法和《权利法案》。这些自由权利包括言论自由、新闻自由和宗教自由,还包括保障公正刑事审判的自由,即接受迅速和公开审判的权利,由陪审团审判的权利和有辩护律师的权利。20世纪30年代,大萧条时期的新政极大地扩大了政府的规模和责任。自20世纪60年代和"大社会"计划以来,政府不断承担了更多新的责任。这催生了一个本质上是经济性的新的自由或权利范畴。例如,最高法院在1963年规定,如果刑事被告受审时无钱聘请辩护律师,则政府必须为其提供一个辩护律师。

几乎所有美国人都认为,国家应该努力创造一个所有人共享繁荣的社会。但是,经济权利的概念还有更广泛的含义。它意味着政府应该(以某种方式)为美国公民提供经济利益,而正是在这一点上美国人产生了分歧。这种分歧事实上被称为价值差异。一方面,保守派,大多是共和党人,认为政府在创造和保护这些经济利益方面做得太多了,过犹不及。他们认为,政府越多承担提供经济利益的责任,美国人民就越是依赖于政府来改善其生活水平。这反过来会使美国人丧失自力更生的精神——这正是这个国家之所以伟大的一项基本价值观。

另一方面,开明的(或进步的)美国人,主要是民主党人,认为政府对经济权利的保障拓展与改进了传统的自由观念。他们认为,扩大经济权利的进程在21世纪还应当继续下去。他们提出的可能的经济权利包括获得医疗和基本健康保险的权利;接受大学教育的权利;拥有能维持生活水平在贫困线以上的工作的权利;以及,失业时获得政府援助(特别是妇女和儿童)的权利。如何在自力更生与政府提供的经济保障之间取得平衡,必将继续成为今后几年重要的争论议题。

机会均等和参与竞争

如前所述,美国人的机会均等理念可以简单表述为,所有美国人都应有平等的机会争取成功、获得富足和追求幸福。美国有时并未能履行这项机会均等的价值观,特别是对那些遭受奴役、隔离和歧视的非洲裔美国人。不过这个国家最终在19世纪60年代解放了奴隶,并通过20世纪60

年代颁布的《民权法案》解决种族隔离和种族歧视问题。平权法案是针对种族歧视问题的一次重要努力。雇主们不得不聘用非洲裔美国人，大学也必须招收非洲裔和其他少数族裔的美国学生。平权法案的理念是，由于多年来的种族歧视，许多黑人并不具备和白人竞争所需的技能。因此，一开始，调整某些情况下的入学标准，是为了让黑人学生能够进入学校。

传统上，机会均等并不意味着结果或成就的平等。一些人如果有着同等的成功的机会，其中就有些人可能会比其他人更为成功。确保人人都拥有相同的财富或声望，这不是社会或政府能够做到的。这种传统的说法受到了对黑人、拉美裔及其他少数种族和族裔给予优先权的平权法案的挑战。平权法案的支持者认为，平权法案有助于弥补过去种族歧视带给少数族裔群体的伤害，并且增加了大学校园的种族和民族多样性。美国第一位拉美裔最高法院大法官，索尼亚·索托马约尔就是从平权法案中受益的一个例子。她学业优秀而家境贫寒，许多顶尖大学都向她提供奖学金。她在《我深爱的世界》一书中记述了自己从平权法案中所受的益处。另一方面，也有一些人反对平权法案的政策。他们反对那些优待的做法，认为每个人都应享有平等的受教育机会，没有任何人应该得到任何特殊优势。他们捍卫传统的机会均等理念，并表示他们相信美国自身天然的多样性，而不是由政府人为规定的多样性。还有人称平权法案为逆向歧视，合格的白人学生因为要将名额留给少数族裔学生而不能被大学录取。

机会均等理念的最佳体现就是巴拉克·奥巴马当选成为第一位非洲裔美国人总统。专栏作家埃兹拉·克莱因写道："美利坚合众国——一个150年前还保留着奴隶制，50年前连厕所都种族隔离的国家——选择并再次选择了它的第一位黑人总统"。奥巴马的母亲是白人，父亲是肯尼亚人，妻子的祖辈曾是奴隶。这样一位黑人总统入主白宫，意义非凡。但巴拉克·奥巴马和米歇尔·奥巴马也时刻谨记着自己代表了什么——证明在这片土地上，任何少数族裔背景出身的个体，只要资质足够，都有可能成为这个国家的最高长官。在一张非常感人的照片中，总统俯身，让一个黑人小男孩摸自己的头发。这张非常受欢迎的照片所传达的信息是，黑人孩子现在可以说，"也许我长大之后，有一天也能成为总统"。

美国一直在机会均等和竞争这两种价值观之间努力寻求平衡。竞争的价值观在美国商业机构中得到了最明显的体现。在第六章中，我们探讨了商业上传统的竞争理念，以及商业所遇到的一些问题。美国当前面临的最大挑战就是政府和自由企业制度之间各自的角色定位。为了保障所有人机会均等的权利，政府干预究竟应该到什么程度？要保障的究竟是享有"机会"的权利，还是享受"成果"的权利呢？

在《强硬的美国，温和的美国：竞争与娇养以及为国家未来而战》一书中，迈克尔·巴龙（保守派）论述了这种对平衡的需求。他认为应当在中间留有空间，政府"救助遭受社会灾害的无辜民众，同时也要保护人们进取的意愿"。这个中间地带介于保守派"强硬"文化和自由派"温和"文化之间。保守派专栏作家，诺埃米·埃默里这样描述巴龙对美国的分化的解释：

> 强硬的美国推崇冒险、创新、努力和创业精神，温和的美国则重视安全与平等。强硬的美国由市场主宰，温和的美国则由政府规划指导。强硬的美国创造财富，温和的美国则重新

分配它。强硬的美国不会区别对待疾病导致的贫困与懒惰导致的贫困，让无辜者痛苦；而温和的美国则不问是坏运气还是坏习惯导致的贫困，使自己苦恼……但真正的问题在于需要达成一种平衡，鼓励人们努力奋斗，但让他们不至于孤注一掷——支持他们，但不能消磨他们的意志。

奥巴马总统（自由派）大概会赞同这种观点，即竞争的意愿是健康且重要的。他在第二次就职演说中表示，在两百多年的历史中，我们一直对一个强大的联邦政府怀有疑虑，同时我们也都明白，政府解决不了所有的社会问题。自由企业一直发挥着重要的作用。"对创新和创业的颂扬，对勤奋工作和个人责任的坚持，这些是我们民族性格中不变的特质。"的确，自由派和保守派应该都会认同本书中所阐述的六项价值观的重要性。但自由派可能会认为，有一些美国人处于极度贫穷与弱势，不可能指望他们也完全自力更生或参与竞争。他们需要政府和其他人特别的帮助，才能站到追逐成功的起跑线上，才能在更加平等的基础上去争取机会均等的益处，去实现美国梦。

物质财富和勤奋工作

传统上，物质财富被看作是勤奋工作的回报。虽然大多数人依然相信美国梦，但如今对很多人而言，实现或维持美国梦是很困难的。中产阶层家庭承受着巨大的经济压力。莫蒂默·朱克曼在《美国新闻与世界报道》上写道："数百万中产阶层的美国人靠领薪水过着月光族的生活，为生计奔波发愁，还不得不借钱负债。很多家庭都是勉强维持着，一次失业或一次急诊就会让它们陷入破产的境地。"许多年轻人认为他们未来的经济生活状况会不如他们的父母，四分之一的30岁以下的年轻人认为自己"社会地位趋向下降"，而不是在"向社会更高层次流动"。

还有其他迹象也显示，美国家庭每况愈下：中产阶层在萎缩，占总人口的比例从20世纪60年代的61%下降到了51%。自2000年以来，他们的收入下降了5%，资产净值缩水了28%。其中三分之一的人陷入付不起账单的困境。中产阶层与最富有的美国人之间现在的差距巨大。随着经济逐渐复苏，2011年美国最富有的5%人口（年收入超过18.6万美元）的收入增长了5%。根据经济政策研究所的数据，最富有的1%的家庭现在的财富是普通中产阶层家庭的288倍。2008年开始的经济衰退对中产阶层家庭打击最为严重，但却极大地增加了最富有的1%家庭的财富。

造成了中产阶层的这种压力的有几个因素。首先，不需要大学文凭的高薪工作大幅度减少。20世纪70年代时，制造业仍有不少好工作，约有25%的美国人（主要是男性）在工厂工作。还有相当一部分人在其他不需要太多正规教育背景的行业就业，如建筑业、采矿业和公用事业等。从事这些工作的人通常会一直干到退休，然后拿一笔不错的退休金。现在这种薪资优厚的蓝领工作已经没有了。20世纪90年代，美国制造业大量迁往海外；尽管现在制造业在回流，但这些新的制造业岗位一般都要求高中以上的学历。

影响中产阶层的第二个因素是对高等教育的需求，事实上，高中毕业以及上大学课程的学生人数已经在上升。其中一个原因是，经济衰退对于年轻人比对其他年龄段的人的打击更甚，失业率高达 24%。很多年轻人因为找不到工作而选择留在学校。原来通常由年轻人来做的入门级工作大多被那些丢掉了自己的工作的、更年长有经验的人担任了。许多美国人面临的一个重要问题是大学教育难以置信的高昂费用。社区大学课程的推广，帮助节省了不少花费。但美国在信息技术和先进制造等领域确实需要良好的职业教育课程。很多人认为，美国应该像一些欧洲国家那样开发一些课程，培养学生在那些经济衰退期间依然人手不足的领域找到工作。这就要求教育界和行业领导者共同合作，开发培训课程，帮助学生迈上通向这些高薪工作的通途。

大多数中产阶级家庭中，夫妻双方都在工作。他们合起来的家庭收入远高于一代前的单收入的家庭，但他们仍然是在艰难维持。朱克曼说："在支付了房贷、两辆汽车的贷款、税款、医疗保险、孩子的日托费后，这些看起来殷实的双收入家庭的可自由支配收入和以备不时之用的积蓄比原来的单收入家庭还要少……很多人觉得，不管他们多么努力，日子还是一天天在走下坡路。"医疗保健和健康保险变得越来越昂贵，占去了职工工资相当大一部分的比例。许多中产阶级在房价上涨的时候都买了房，而房地产泡沫破灭后，房屋的价值大幅缩水。他们的资产净值下降了，而且还没有攒够退休的钱。临近退休的婴儿潮一代中，只有 25% 的人已有了足够的储蓄，可以不用再工作了。他们的社会保障福利并不足以支持他们的退休生活。中产阶级的困境使一些人现在呼吁政府扩大权利范围，包括享有医疗保障、大学教育和体面工作的权利。同时也使人们倍加关注不断上涨的社会保险和医疗保险费用。

价值观分化

关于政府应该保障什么样的权利而产生的意见分歧导致了 21 世纪初开始的"价值观分化"，或称"文化战争"。约翰·肯尼思·怀特在《价值观分化：转型中的美国政治与文化》一书中写到了这一分裂；约翰·佐格比为该书作序。怀特讨论了共和党保守派和民主党自由派对于政府在解决国家问题上应承担的角色而产生的强烈分歧。他写道，价值观分化的双方生活在"两个平行世界中。双方都试图通过结交志同道合的人来为自己的想法增援"。在《华盛顿邮报》的一组题为《红与蓝的美国：一个分裂的国家》的系列文章中，戴维·冯·德雷勒探讨了这种政治分裂。"这种分裂的滋长是由于主要政党的宣传努力，这些宣传越来越以向特定人群传达特定信息为目的，而不是去寻找受到广泛关注的新问题"。

为什么政党会针对特定群体发出各种政治信息呢？首先，计算机的使用与人口统计学的研究使得这一做法成为可能。其次，许多美国人只对一两个政治问题感兴趣。他们对针对跟自己有关的具体问题的政治信息反应比较好。最后，许多潜在选民并非任何一方的注册党员，两党都必须设法说服这些人支持自己的候选人。不锁定一些独立选票，任何一党都无法取胜。不过，越来越多的独立选民往往会倾向于其中一方。事实上，美国已经变得越来越两极化，以至于政府的运作似乎都出现了困难。民主党和共和党在决策时似乎更多基于意识形态，而不是为了国家的最大利益。因此许多人会说，两党之间太多僵局，太少妥协。

很显然，美国现在面临着许多挑战。其中最严峻的挑战是要处理持续的赤字和不断增长的国家债务。民主党认为这是收入的问题——政府需要更多的资金来运作他们想要的项目。应该提高税收，最富有的人应该支付更高的税率。共和党则认为这是开支的问题——政府应该通过削减项目来降低税收和减少支出。应该由私营部门——企业——接管目前由政府运作的项目。佐格比指出，这种分裂反映的不只是政府角色的问题。"这关乎美国人如何界定责任、公民权利，以及他们希望政府传达怎样的价值观。"

CNN（美国有线电视新闻网）首席政治分析家，格洛丽亚·博格表示，美国人对政府又爱又恨：

> 美国人既希望政府解决他们的问题，又不相信政府能做到。我们希望能有固定的医疗，医疗保障和社会保障能不受影响，紧急情况能得到处理。同时我们又希望少交税，想要一个更小，但更负责的政府。一言以蔽之，我们想花更少的钱，得到更多……公众不信任政府，是因为政府的领导一直不能合作共事，许多事情都做不了……罗纳德·里根（一位受欢迎的共和党总统）理解公众对政府的怀疑。他常常开玩笑说，在美国最可怕的一句话就是"我是政府的人，我是来帮助你的"。

对于政府的这种怀疑并不新鲜。托克维尔曾指出，美国人热爱自由和平等。纵观他们的历史，美国人一直生活在一种维护自由与促进平等的矛盾之中。托克维尔认为，在民主制度下，美国人最终会宁可优先选择平等而不是自由，因为平等可以带来物质利益。不过，政治学家们对此并不认同，他们认为，美国人高度重视自由，可能比任何其他国家都更为强烈。皮尤研究中心最近的一项民意调查，让美国人和欧洲人在"没有国家干预地追求人生目标的自由"和"国家保障所有人的基本需求"之间进行选择。与欧洲人相反，绝大多数美国人选择了自由。（参见第158页）

世界上的美国

不管目前美国的国际形象如何，也不管政府采取过一些什么样的行动，美国长期以来一直有着孤立主义的传统。乔治·华盛顿总统1796年时曾宣布："我们真正的政策是避免与任何外国订立永久的同盟。"直到今天，在美国人对他们在国际社会中的地位的持续争论中，这种孤立主义精神依然存在。许多美国人非常不愿意看到美国卷入国际军事行动，除非他们相信，此种行动是为保护国家利益。美国人对国际经济联盟和全球协议也同样持怀疑态度，在向其他国家做出承诺之前，他们希望首先确保自己的利益不受损害。许多美国人更关心发生在自己周围的事，而对世界其他地区的事情则没多少兴趣。他们想知道的是事件，无论是国内或国际的，对他们个人会有什么影响。

今天，就算美国努力尝试与世界其他国家和地区隔绝开来，也是不可能了。虽然有学者会说，美国及其文化在20世纪占据了主导地位，但它在21世纪会发挥怎样的作用，目前尚不明确。不过可以肯定的是，世界其他国家和地区对美国，尤其是对美国的经济会继续有着很大的影响。美国人将持续关注保护自己免受国内外的潜在的恐怖主义的威胁。人们会更多地思考，应该赋予政府多少权力以换取这种保护。在一个自由开放的社会中，无法保证恐怖主义袭击永远不会发生，美国人必须权衡，为了安全，他们愿意放弃多少自由和隐私。

最后，还有移民问题。美国的合法及非法移民数量很多，一些人对这么多来自不同国家的人的同化问题感到担心。美国人口日益多样化，这将会对美国的传统价值观产生什么影响？另一方面，也有很多人承认，这些新移民为美国注入了新的生机与活力。对于六种基本的文化价值观，这些移民经常会比许多美国人有着更强的信念。随着婴儿潮一代逐渐老去，移民成为美国年轻和活力的重要来源。他们中的一些人拥有专业技能和STEM（科学、技术、工程、数学）学位，这些都是美国产业方面所需要的。

也许最为重要的是，美国思想与文化的多样性将是其在21世纪最主要的力量来源之一。美国文化专家本·瓦滕伯格认为，美国正成为世界的一个缩影——它可能会是第一个"世界性"的国家，来自不同种族、宗教、文化和民族背景的人们在同一个政府的领导下自由生活。

美国人及其价值观又走到了另一个历史性的十字路口。这些传统价值观是否能持续到下个世纪？一百年后，美国人还会有"作为美国人"的国家认同感吗？这个世纪还将带来什么样新的挑战？正如阿尔文·托夫勒所说："唯一确定的是，明天会令所有人大吃一惊。"

Teacher's Manual and Answer Keys

指导手册及参考答案

Contents

PART 1: HOW TO USE THIS MANUAL — 421

    Teaching American Culture in the Language Classroom — 421
    How to Use the Activities in the Text — 423
        Before You Read — 424
        After You Read — 426
        Skill Building — 427
        Expand Your Knowledge — 428
        Write About It — 434
        Explore On Your Own — 435

PART 2: ANSWER KEY FOR STUDENT TEXT — 437

    Chapter 1 — 437
    Chapter 2 — 438
    Chapter 3 — 441
    Chapter 4 — 443
    Chapter 5 — 445
    Chapter 6 — 447
    Chapter 7 — 449
    Chapter 8 — 451
    Chapter 9 — 453
    Chapter 10 — 454
    Chapter 11 — 455
    Chapter 12 — 457

PART 3: REPRODUCIBLE ACTIVITY MASTERS — 459

PART 1 HOW TO USE THIS MANUAL

Teaching American Culture in the Language Classroom

Why Include Culture in Language Classes?
There are a number of reasons for including culture in your language classes:

- Culture provides interesting content for language learning, leading to engaging discussions, writing assignments, or group projects, and also can be used to develop both informal social language and more formal academic language.
- Culture can also be used to increase the cognitive component of the language class, helping students to develop higher order thinking skills as they analyze, compare, and discuss the cultural content.
- Reading about and discussing other cultures can serve as a valuable backdrop for analyzing students' own cultures. It is often said that we do not really understand our own culture until we have lived outside it, or seen it through another person's eyes. In the words of a famous proverb, "A fish that never leaves the water does not discover water."
- Studying culture can lead to a better understanding of people's behavior and help students move from ethnocentric pronouncements of what is "right" or "wrong" to more thoughtful tolerance of cultural diversity.

Culture, then, can be interesting content, even for those students whose primary motivation for learning English is academic, for it promotes complex linguistic and cognitive interaction and encourages students to use the kinds of skills and language that are required for both academic and professional contexts.

What Culture Should Be Taught?
Traditional definitions of culture—or what has been called "culture with a capital C"—focus on the literature, music, dance, drama, and other arts of a group or a country. That is often the focus of cultural studies in traditional language classrooms, especially the study of literature as a window to that culture.

Although this "Culture" is important, what may be of more interest to students and potentially more useful to them, if they are going to interact with people from a new culture, is to understand culture as it is more commonly understood by anthropologists: that is, the set of beliefs, attitudes, and behaviors or customs that define or distinguish a group of people. Or as Edward T. Hall defines it, "a set of ideals, values, and standards of behavior . . . that make the actions of individuals intelligible to the group." In this book, culture represents the ways of perceiving, thinking, communicating, behaving, and evaluating that characterize Americans.

Culture is shared, but in a country as large and diverse as the United States, there is also a great deal of cultural diversity based on ethnicity, race, gender, and/or social class, all of which create a number of different societies in the country. But even with these differences, there is still a kind of overarching culture that people grow up with that distinguishes them from those who live in other countries. Moreover, culture is dynamic: cultures change as their populations change. Nowhere is this more obvious than in the United States where immigration, refugee resettlement, and a number of other demographic patterns have created a rapidly changing population and country. That overarching culture, the traditional mainstream core, the changes it is undergoing, and its many variations form the substance of this book.

What Should Be the Goals of a Culture Class or a Cultural Component?
There are a number of goals that you and your students might set for studying culture.

- At the most basic level, that goal may be to make students more aware of American cultural patterns and how they differ with or are similar to their own.

- At a deeper level, that goal may be to help students learn the reasons for those practices; that is, to understand why people do what they do. This requires some knowledge of a people's history and traditions, and the geography, and climate in which they live.
- For those students who may be going to live, work, or study with Americans, the goal may be to also develop the skills to interact appropriately with Americans in a variety of contexts. This involves much more detailed attention to social roles, nonverbal communication, and speech acts. Observing the media, interviewing Americans, or other activities such as these are intended to help students move from awareness and understanding to being able to predict or avoid problems and to resolve them effectively. The language classroom is often the only "safe" place where students can express their frustration or ask cross-cultural questions without fear of ridicule or hostility.

The goal of the cultural component is not to explain away problematic features of the United States or to promote cultural imperialism; rather, it is to promote cross-cultural awareness, tolerance, or even acceptance, and greater global understanding.

Students come to the language classroom with different goals. They are also likely to have different perspectives regarding the cultural component. Taking the time to ask them their goals will lead to better discussions and a more fruitful class.

Is It Possible to Teach American Culture?

Even with a small country or culture with few members, it may be difficult to make cultural generalizations, especially when one considers the relevance of gender, age, social status, or other factors. In a country as large as the United States, with people who have come from so many different countries, bringing with them so many different languages, religions, and customs, it may seem impossible to talk about "American culture" or even "American cultures."

As you and your students read *American Ways*, discuss this issue and return to it several times. Does the set of core values that has served as a basis for definition for generations of Americans continue to help define American people? Do even those who disagree with some or all of these values also acknowledge their existence? Answering this may be a central focus of your class.

Getting Started

A number of games can be used to get your class started. One of our favorites is a game of "shapes" that we learned many years ago from a cross-cultural trainer, Sandra Mumford, but we do not really know its origin. In this game, tags are made out of different colors in a variety of odd shapes, with some common features among them (a rounded corner, a triangle, a square corner, a serrated edge, and so on). (See **Activity Masters 1** and **2 Shapes**, on pp. 460–461 of this Teacher's Manual, for ideas.) You can use the Activity Masters as patterns to cut out shapes in different colors, or you can use your imagination and create your own. Just be sure that every shape has at least one feature in common with one other piece of a different color. You will also need an envelope and some straight pins or paper clips so that students can wear the shapes like tags.

Here are the rules of the game:

1. Tell students that beginning now, they are not to talk.
2. Have students choose one tag from the envelope and one of the pins or paper clips to put the tag on. Remind them not to talk.
3. After everyone is wearing a tag, tell the students to walk around the room and look at each other's tags, without talking.
4. When they have walked quite a bit and have looked at all the tags, ask them to form groups without talking.
5. Give students enough time to form groups. Some students may find that no one "matches" them or invites them to join the group. Others may find that several groups invite them in. Remind them to look at the tags and find their group, and not to talk.

6. Then ask them to look around their group and notice why they all belong to the group. Have them notice what they have in common, but remind them not to talk.
7. After some time, ask them to walk around again, look at each other's tags, and again to form new groups, and then to look around their group, noticing the tags, but not to talk.
8. After several rounds (at least three, but four or more is better), when students have formed the more typical groups based on color, or shape, or size, you will notice that they have to look much more carefully to find things that they have in common. Some students will find that no one thinks their tag is like any others, and they may find themselves standing alone, outside a group. Other times students will form one large group.
9. Now it's time to discuss the activity with them. You might ask these questions:

   What did you notice?

   Did anyone feel left out? Ignored?

   Did anyone invite you to form a group? How did you feel?

   Did anyone exclude you? How did that make you feel?

   Did you notice any changes in the size of the groups over time? Why do you think that happened?

This game can lead to an interesting opening discussion for the culture class or component and suggest ways in which we may differ, but also have a lot in common. It can lead to discussions about the importance of belonging to a group and how we exclude or include people, as well as discussion about tolerance or acceptance, or even prejudice and discrimination. It can also serve as a place to begin setting ground rules for your class. This is important, especially in multicultural classes, where there is likely to be misunderstanding. You may want to remind students that in this class you will expect all of them to be respectful of each other as individuals and as members of different cultures. They may have questions; they may be surprised or even shocked at what they read or hear; but they should refrain from judging each other, other customs, or cultural differences before they have tried to understand how a custom or practice fits in with the entire system of the culture.

It can often be difficult to discuss values, beliefs, attitudes, or cultures. Not only may the content be sensitive, but the words may not be readily available. For that reason, we have provided a number of activities to be used in pairs or small groups where students may feel freer to speak up, and have suggested a number of ways in which you can organize these activities (**Think, Pair, Share; Small-Group Projects; Talk About It**; etc.).

The culture class is a community of individuals working together to understand each other. It is a microcosm of the global community, and the efforts of you and your students represent one small but important step toward greater global understanding.

How to Use the Activities in the Text

This section reviews the types of activities that are included in the text and provides some ideas of how they might be used in the class.

All chapters have the same six major sections, though the activities within each section may vary:

Before You Read

   Preview Vocabulary

   Preview Content

   (Chapter Reading)

    After You Read

        Understand Main Ideas

        Understand Details

        Talk About It

    Skill Building

        Improve Your Reading Skills: Scanning, Skimming, Highlighting, or Note Taking

        Develop Your Critical Thinking Skills

        Build Your Vocabulary

    Expand Your Knowledge

        Think, Pair, Share; Small-Group Discussion; Have a Debate; Small-Group Project

        Ask Americans; Ask Yourself; People Watching; Observe the Media; Proverbs and Sayings

        Understand or Compare Polls

        Use the Internet

    Write About It

    Explore On Your Own

        Books to Read

        Movies to See

Each of these sections (except for the chapter reading) is discussed below.

BEFORE YOU READ

All chapters include pictures, quotations, and two sets of activities preceding the reading text: **Preview Vocabulary** and **Preview Content**. The purpose of this prereading section is to:

- Activate students' prior knowledge;
- Identify key vocabulary that will be needed to understand and discuss the text;
- Develop common background knowledge from various students in the class to facilitate discussion;
- Focus attention for the reading of the chapter;
- Identify or predict themes that will be discussed in the chapter.

There are many ways of using the **Preview Vocabulary** and **Preview Content** activities and most of the other activities in this text:

- Students can try to answer or do the activities individually, in pairs, or in small groups.
- The activity can be assigned as homework. Then students can compare and discuss their answers in class. Let students be the "teacher" here.
- Students can be asked to locate the place in the text where they found the answer.
- The activity can be used to teach test-taking strategies. Ask students to read questions before they read the chapter and then read to find the answer.

Preview Vocabulary

Because this is a reading text designed to prepare students to read and write academic English, great thought has been given to the vocabulary used in the chapter readings and then selected for the vocabulary exercises. The emphasis is on academic vocabulary from the Academic Word List (AWL) developed by Averil Coxhead: a set of some 500 key words that are frequent and important in academic texts used in university or professional education. (For more information on the AWL, see www.victoria.ac.nz/lals/resources/academicwordlist.)

The AWL contains 570 word families that were selected by examining academic texts from a variety of subject areas. The list does not include words that are among the most frequent 2,000 words of English. Each word family has a headword (the stem form) and a list of other word forms (or parts of speech) for that headword. On page 306, of *American Ways,* there is a list of the AWL headwords used in the readings. (Another form of the word may have been used, not the stem form.) After each word are the numbers of all the chapters in which these words appear.

The reading material in each chapter has been analyzed by comparing it to both the AWL and the 2,000 Most Frequent Word Family List. The language analyzer shows the reading in different colors for the 2,000 most common words, the AWL words, and the off-list words that do not appear on the other lists. It also gives the number and percentages for each type of vocabulary item. Vocabulary words used in exercises (1) are from the AWL or (2) are not from either of the two lists but are important to the context of the reading and are useful to know for academic reading in general. Words from the 2,000 most common words are not used in vocabulary exercises.

The language analysis allows us to tightly control the vocabulary and carefully construct vocabulary exercises. Our analysis of the readings in *American Ways* shows that 90–96% of all the vocabulary is either from the most frequent 2,000 words or the AWL. The AWL words make up between 5% and 7%, and the off-list words (words that are neither among the most frequent 2,000 words nor on the AWL) average 6.6% per chapter. Interestingly, Chapter 4 has the highest percentage of off-list words because words such as *frontier* are not used so often, although it is probably one of the easier chapters because much of the content is concrete. *American* is another off-list word appearing frequently in the text. The percentages of 2,000 AWL, and off-list words are remarkably constant throughout the readings, so the reading level is very consistent. The grammar used in *American Ways* has not been controlled, but there is an attempt to avoid overly long and complicated sentences.

A number of different activities activate the key vocabulary for the chapter and help students learn it. In this edition, many of the words that are highlighted in vocabulary activities in this section are drawn from the AWL. (See pp. 306–308 of the text for more discussion.) They are important because they are:

- Key words;
- Likely to be new or unfamiliar words;
- Words that students will need to understand to make sense of the text and be able to discuss the text or write about the ideas in the chapter;
- Words that are often used in many related forms; for example, *economy, economic, economics, economize, economical, economically, uneconomical, economist.*

In some cases, the words are presented in questions that are intended to get students thinking about the chapter. Other activities include matching, classifying, identifying connotations or opposites, and completing sentences.

Preview Content

For every chapter, students are asked to predict what the chapter will be about by looking at chapter headings, pictures, charts, and polls and by analyzing the quotation that precedes the text. They are also asked to think about their own experiences related to the themes in the text. You might ask students to:

- Read this section and quickly look through the text as homework, writing brief answers to the questions and noting anything they find confusing or surprising;
- Share their written answers with a partner;
- Discuss this as a large group, writing students' ideas on the board;
- After they read the text, go back and compare what they now think with what they predicted or thought before reading the text.

AFTER YOU READ

This section provides a number of activities that can be done immediately after reading the chapter. The exercises ask students to: **Understand Main Ideas**; **Understand Details**; **Talk About It**.

Understand Main Ideas

These activities help students understand the ways academic texts in English are constructed: from main ideas, to supporting details in a kind of "T." This T shape (or "I," if the main idea is repeated at the end) also is the format that whole sections or chapters take, and the same organizational format that students should use in their academic writing. As they progress through the chapters, they will begin to look for the main ideas and supporting ideas and notice that the main ideas are usually at the beginning of paragraphs and also in the beginning of sections and chapters, followed by supporting details. The goal is to enhance their reading (and listening) comprehension and also their academic writing in English, since they will be expected to follow this same kind of T format in their paragraphs. In writing an essay, they may use an I format to return to the main ideas and summarize them in the conclusion. (See p. 63 of the Student Book.)

Often, in these activities, students will be asked to go back to the predictions they made before beginning the chapter. Discuss in class how they arrived at their predictions and what has led them to confirm or change their ideas.

Spend some time helping students to see how a paragraph, a section, and the chapter are constructed. You can:

- Ask students to work together in pairs, highlighting introductions, conclusions, and topic sentences.
- Discuss how they arrived at their choices. Note the repetition of main ideas in the chapter title, the headings, and the sections in the chapter.
- Ask them to read a paragraph and then look away and try to write a one-sentence summary of the paragraph or to tell their partner what the main idea is. Together they can construct a sentence that summarizes the paragraph. Do this for an entire section of the chapter, then for the entire chapter.
- Ask them to make up questions for various sections.
- Assign some of these activities for homework, giving students more time to think about the main ideas of the chapter.

This section also uses a progressive sequence of activities to help students understand and better visualize the ways in which academic texts are organized in American textbooks (and the ways in which they should organize their academic writing in English). Students are asked to identify main ideas or supporting details, to highlight topic sentences, to develop questions related to the main idea, to complete an outline, or to fill in a graphic organizer drawn from those in the text or in the **Reproducible Activity Masters** (on pp. 459–471 of this Teacher's Manual). When they have completed these activities in Chapter 12, they should have a very good sense of the structure of American academic reading (and writing and lecturing) and should be able to apply what they have learned to improve both their reading and writing of American English texts.

Understand Details

These activities help students to understand and remember some of the important details in the chapter. The activities include **True/False**, **Matching**, and **Selecting the Best Answer to Complete a Sentence**. You can use any of the suggestions for activities suggested in **Before You Read** (on pp. 424–426 of this Teacher's Manual). Frequently a graphic organizer is suggested to help students identify and organize main ideas and details. Graphic organizers provide excellent support for students when they are trying to organize their thoughts and remember key details for discussion or writing. If there is no graphic organizer suggested, look through those provided in the **Reproducible Activity Masters** (on pp. 459–471) section for ones that might fit with the activities.

Talk About It

This section asks students to get into small groups and to choose one or more questions to discuss, based on the readings and their own experiences. You can let students form their own groups, have students count off to form small groups of three to five, or assign students to specific groups on the basis of similarities or differences in background, experience, or personalities of the students. Remind students that this is an opportunity for free discussion and that they should be respectful of one another's opinions. See the discussion on **Think, Pair, Share; Small-Group Discussion; Have a Debate;** etc. (on pp. 429–431 of this Teacher's Manual) for ideas on ways to organize and manage the discussion.

SKILL BUILDING

This section helps students improve their reading skills: scan, skim, highlight, or take notes; develop critical thinking skills: analyze, evaluate, use, and create polls; evaluate and compare definitions, pros and cons; express opinions; and build vocabulary.

Improve Your Reading Skills: Scanning, Skimming, Highlighting, or Note Taking
Each chapter also has an activity that requires students to go back through the chapter to locate information by a variety of means.

Scanning activities ask the students to look quickly down the page to find specific information or details such as a date, a location, a name, or an event in history so that they can answer questions, fill in blanks, or complete a timeline or other graphic organizer.

Skimming activities ask students to read a paragraph or a section of the chapter quickly to find main ideas.

Highlighting activities ask students to underscore or use a highlighter to identify specific portions of the text. This helps students identify and remember main ideas.

Note-Taking activities ask students to take notes about important information as they read.

For these reading skills activities, you can:

- Write items on the board or on a transparency, and have the students find the information individually, or in pairs.
- Read the items aloud one at a time. Limit the time you allow for students to find the answers. Make this into a competition.
- Divide the class into teams and see which team can correctly find all the answers first.
- Have students work in pairs. Give one student the questions and the other the answers from the **Answer Key**.
- Give each student a scanning/skimming/highlighting/note-taking handout to be completed as a homework assignment.

Develop Your Critical Thinking Skills

New to the 4th edition of *American Ways* are the activities labeled **Develop Your Critical Thinking Skills**. These activities focus on the development of skills that are key to mastering academic English, including understanding, evaluating, analyzing, and using data from polls, charts, and short readings. For example, exercise questions may not only check comprehension, but also ask students to interpret meaning, synthesize several sources, make inferences, evaluate definitions, express opinions, draw logical conclusions, decide what data supports various conclusions, and/or conduct their own research including creating polls of their own. (See also the suggestions for using polls on pp. 433–434 of this Teacher's Manual.)

In several cases, students are asked to reflect on complicated ideas such as: What should the goals of education be? Are students vessels to be filled or lamps to be lighted? How important is creativity? How do you teach someone to be creative?

Be sure to allow students adequate time to do the critical thinking called for in the exercises.

- Assign the activity as homework, or set aside class time for them to work on their own.
- Have them share their answers and conclusions in pairs, or small groups, and then report to the class.
- Ask them to write a paragraph about how they arrived at their decisions, describing the process they used.
- Discuss the critical thinking skills used in the activity and write strategies students used on the board or on a transparency.

It should be noted that many of the other exercises and activities in *American Ways* also support the development of critical thinking skills: identifying main ideas, identifying and using different types of supporting details, summarizing and paraphrasing, organizing and ordering information, comparing and contrasting, deciding on pros and cons, classifying and categorizing, conducting interviews, expressing and defending opinions, and participating in values clarification activities. Many of these skills are reinforced in pair and small group activities, and they often lead to oral reports and writing assignments. Additionally, the very activity of participating in small group discussions and projects often fosters critical thinking skills. (See suggestions for small-group activities on p. 430–431 of this Teacher's Manual.)

Build Your Vocabulary

This edition of *American Ways* provides students with a great deal of focus on developing their academic English vocabulary, drawing upon research on corpora (corpus linguistics), collocations, and their role in vocabulary learning and use. In this section, students are asked to use a number of different strategies to learn key vocabulary from the chapter. They are asked to:

- Use context clues (looking at the words around an unfamiliar word to see if they can figure out the meaning);
- Recognize and use word partners (collocations or combinations of words in English that recur frequently) such as "cultural pluralism," "working hypotheses," or "industrialized countries" from Chapter 1);
- Understand prefixes and the ways that these change the meanings of words;
- Match words with definitions;
- Identify synonyms or antonyms;
- Categorize words in relation to topics (for example, sports or recreation);
- Fill in words to complete sentences.

EXPAND YOUR KNOWLDEGE

This section asks students to synthesize and integrate what they have learned from the chapter and to extend that knowledge by thinking about and discussing their own culture and lives; engaging in small-group discussions, debates, or group projects; interviewing others or reflecting upon their own values and behaviors; observing others or looking at ways in which people or their behaviors are presented in the media; thinking about proverbs that are popular in the United States and comparing them with those of their own countries; and using the Internet for research on related topics.

The following activities in this section are discussed individually below:

- **Think, Pair, Share; Small-Group Discussion; Have a Debate; Small-Group Project**
- **Ask Americans; Ask Yourself; People Watching; Observe the Media; Proverbs and Sayings**
- **Conduct or Create Polls**
- **Use the Internet**

Think, Pair, Share; Small-Group Discussion; Have a Debate; Small-Group Project

The text contains a number of activities that can be used with pairs or small groups of students. One of these activities (**Think, Pair, Share**) is often referred to as a "cooperative learning activity" because it promotes student interaction and cooperation in completing an assignment, and it is intended to encourage students to share their ideas and opinions in a small, safe group, before they are asked to share their ideas or opinions with the whole class. Two other cooperative activities discussed below (**Round Robin and Round Table**) are not included in the text, but they provide interesting ways in which you can get students engaged in small-group discussion.

In addition to **Think, Pair, Share,** the text includes a number of activities that encourage students to share their ideas and then discuss them in a small group, use them to debate two sides of an issue, or to develop a group project. They offer some interesting ways of engaging your students in academic speaking activities.

Think, Pair, Share This is a cooperative learning activity that provides students with extensive time to think about and rehearse what they want to say before they share their ideas with a larger group. This activity is especially appropriate for new students and/or new classes, students who are shy or uncomfortable speaking in large groups, or class discussion of personal or sensitive issues. In a **Think, Pair, Share,** students:

1. Think about a question or group of questions, taking notes as they think;
2. Share their ideas with one other student, using their notes to help them;
3. Share their ideas with another pair of students, a small group, or the entire class.

The opportunity to think, take notes, and then explain their ideas to one student helps students to develop their ideas more clearly and also offers them a chance to rehearse their answers and receive feedback (through requests for clarification and corrections of their pronunciation, grammar, or vocabulary) before they are asked to answer publicly. Students can use a graphic organizer as they do the activity.

Round Robin / Round Table Although neither **Round Robin** nor **Round Table** is a specific activity in the text, both can be used as a means of eliciting ideas from students, reviewing ideas from the text, generating key vocabulary, or fostering other preview or review activities that can accompany small-group discussion. These activities provide a structured way to elicit responses (spoken or written) from each member of a small group. In this activity, students are invited to provide one answer or comment either orally or in writing each time that their turn comes around. They are also permitted to pass (skip their turn) if they cannot think of anything new to contribute and also to join in again on the next round if they have something to add. Quiet students are encouraged to share their ideas; more extroverted students are encouraged to reduce their output and to listen to their peers.

To do these activities:

1. Divide the class into small groups of three to six.
2. Identify the student who will provide the first response. (This student—who can be closest to the door, closest to the windows, or whatever you decide on that day—is assigned the number 1).

3. Either read a question or series of questions aloud, or ask someone in the group to read the question(s).
4. Then have the first student provide the first response.
5. Going clockwise around the group, have the second student provide a new response. He or she should not repeat what another student has said.
6. At any time, a student who does not have a contribution to make can pass for that round. That student can enter the discussion on the next round. (Explain that there is nothing wrong with deciding not to take a turn.)
7. Continue around the group until all students have exhausted all of their responses or time has run out.

Students can pass a pencil or pen and one piece of paper around the group and record all their responses on that paper, or they can simply discuss their views in sequence. In that case, one student may want to serve as a Recorder, providing a written list of ideas that can be reviewed before presentation to the larger group. You may want to ask each group to select three or four of their best ideas to present to the class, taking care not to repeat ideas that another group has already presented. You may also want to ask groups to indicate whether they had similar ideas after a group has completed its report, to identify the most common responses.

These two activities work best when you know that students have a number of things to share. They can be used to:

- Summarize what has been discussed or learned;
- Quickly develop the combined knowledge of a number of students before reading or discussing the content further;
- Encourage all students to participate, even those who are least likely to take part in group discussions;
- Allow students with lots of ideas the opportunity to present a number of these without overly dominating the class;
- Serve as an opportunity for small-group rehearsal before the idea is presented to the whole class.

Small-Group Discussion There are a number of ways to encourage small-group discussion. **Think, Pair, Share** and **Round Robin** or **Round Table** can help. Another way is to assign roles to everyone in a small group, so that no student is able to dominate and all students have an important role to play in the completion of the task.

Sample roles include:

- **Recorder**—who writes down the group's ideas. This is a good role for someone who is comfortable or confident in writing in English.
- **Facilitator**—who makes sure that the discussion is on track and that all in the small group are participating. This is a good role for someone who is comfortable with social language and speaking.
- **Reporter**—who reports the group's discussion to the entire class. This is a good role for someone who is confident in making oral presentations.
- **Timekeeper**—who makes sure that the group keeps to the time constraints and reminds the group to move on when they have spent too long a time on one question or item. This is a good role for a student whose English proficiency is lower than the other students or is new to the class.
- **Artist/Graphics Expert**—who develops a poster or illustrates a report or presentation that can be used by the Reporter in presenting the group's ideas to the class. This is also a good role for someone whose English proficiency is lower and/or someone who communicates best visually.
- **Praiser**—who compliments students on their participation and supports their ideas. This is a difficult role and may seem unnatural for many students, but it can be a way to encourage positive feedback and encouragement in discussion. This is a good role for someone who is comfortable with social language and social roles.

Have a Debate Almost every chapter has the kinds of controversial topics that can lead to a debate. Ideas for these can come from the **Ask Americans** or **Ask Yourself** activities, or from **Small-Group Discussion**. In some chapters, debate topics are suggested.

Debates can get students to discuss and develop arguments and to organize them in logical and persuasive ways—skills they will need when they answer essay questions or write papers and reports. To prepare students for debate, have them do the following:

- Consider alternative viewpoints for any issue, writing down reasons why they or someone else might have a particular perspective.
- Organize these into "Pro" and "Con," perhaps using **Activity Master 10, Decision Making**, (on p. 469 of this Teacher's Manual). for that purpose.
- For each Pro argument, have them reflect on and identify at least one counterargument.
- For each Con argument, have them identify at least one counterargument.
- Then have each side practice its position, with members of the team serving to ask questions or to offer contrasting points of view.
- Finally, get the two sides to debate the issue, using the following format:

    1. The Pro side has five or ten minutes to present its case.
    2. The Con side has five or ten minutes to present its case.
    3. Then each side has five minutes to refute what the other has said.
    4. Finally, each side has a few minutes to make a closing argument, restating key points.

You may want to select a couple of students to serve as judges to decide who has made the stronger argument, or you can serve in this capacity.

Debates help students to sharpen their analytical skills and also provide practice in arguing a point of view, something that is critically important in academic contexts, where students often have to engage in reasoned, persuasive discussion or writing.

Small-Group Project Some of the chapters have activities in which students work together on a project. For example, in Chapter 6, they create their own small business, name it, develop a slogan for it, advertise it, etc. When assigning these projects, make sure you do the following:

1. Set a timeline for each stage of the project.
2. Have students give brief progress reports after each important date on the timeline.
3. Check in frequently with the project teams to make sure that they are on track and not having difficulty in finding the information they need or in making progress on their project.
4. Include some kind of final presentation of the project in any project assigned. The presentation could be:
    - A poster presentation to the class;
    - An oral briefing to the class;
    - A PowerPoint presentation to the class;

Projects are excellent ways to involve students in talking and doing research. They also provide practice in giving academic presentations, including the poster presentations that are often expected of undergraduate or graduate university students.

Ask Americans; Ask Yourself; People Watching; Observe the Media; Proverbs and Sayings

All of these activities encourage students to reflect personally on what they are reading. They also encourage students to observe and interact with people—and to analyze traditional sayings or proverbs—in order to gain additional information while using oral and written English.

Ask Americans These activities consist of questions that students can ask of Americans. If they are unable to interview Americans, they can be encouraged to write to Americans using email (key-pal) or pen pal letters, or other forms of communication. Many ESL classes in the United States want to partner with English classes overseas to exchange information. You may want to investigate ways to create email partnerships to facilitate this kind of exchange of information.

Some students feel shy about approaching Americans. You might want to encourage students to do these activities in pairs. Explain to students that they should tell the person that they are interviewing that this is part of a class assignment. In general, Americans are remarkably willing to answer questions and to take time for an interview if they know that it is for a class assignment. If someone appears reluctant to be interviewed, the student should find someone else to talk with. To facilitate this activity, some teachers provide a brief written explanation of the assignment that students can hand to strangers. Note, however, that you should not put the questions in writing, or students may simply hand the form to people to fill out, missing out on some aspect of oral communication, which is part of the value of the assignment.

Sometimes students are asked to complete a chart or form as they interview a person. If there is no chart provided, you may want to look at the **Reproducible Activity Masters** (on pp. 459–471) for ideas. After students interview Americans, they can:

- Discuss their findings in pairs;
- Present their findings to the class as an oral or written report;
- Make a chart or graph to represent their findings;
- Write a brief summary of their findings;
- Compare their findings with what the chapter said, explaining why there might be differences;
- Develop a class summary of the individual findings.

Note that summarizing, comparing, synthesizing, and presenting findings orally or in writing are all academic tasks that are common assignments for students at American universities.

Ask Yourself There are a number of different types of activities under this heading. However, all of them require the student to think about his or her position on an issue and then to record some kind of opinion or answer.

Sometimes students are asked to complete a Likert scale, where they indicate whether they agree or disagree with a statement, using a scale of +2 to –2. After each student has completed this, you can assign a part of the room for each of the five possible answers (+2, +1, 0, –1, –2) and ask students to go to the part of the room that best represents their answer to each question. When they are grouped next to the different numbers, ask them to discuss why they answered the way they did. They can answer individually or the group can choose someone to represent them and explain their position to the class. Make sure the groups report to the whole class after each question and that a different person reports for the groups each time.

You should also encourage students to look at how the composition of the groups changes as the questions change. This will help them understand the principle that there is more diversity within a culture than between cultures: that is, people who seem to be alike in their opinions on one aspect of a topic have quite different opinions on another. There are a number of options with these activities:

- Ask students to complete the activity as homework.
- Ask students to do the activity in class and then share their responses with another student, a small group, or the class.
- Ask students to work in pairs. Have them record their answers. Then they can ask each other the question, but before letting the other student answer, they should predict how the student will answer. Reverse the roles. Then have the students discuss why there were differences in their answers.

People Watching; Observe the Media In these activities, students are asked to observe Americans in different settings, such as at work or as a family. They are also asked to look at advertisements in magazines or on television, at products displayed in a store or featured on television or in magazine advertisements, at book displays, or at Internet sites in response to questions related to the theme of the chapter. Although it is easier to watch people in the same community, it is also possible to do this activity using television or movies. If you are using this text outside the United States, you may want to look through videotapes or movies to see if there are sequences that relate to the **People Watching** assignments. For example, you might look for an interview situation for Chapter 9, or segments showing adults and children interacting for Chapter 11. If American domestic comedy shows are available on television or DVD, they are often good sources of information to complete **People Watching** activities. A list of **Movies to See** is provided at the end of each chapter. They may have some scenes that you can use after careful previewing.

Students should be instructed to take notes immediately after doing the activity, or they are likely to forget what happened. These notes can be used to:

- Write a brief summary of the findings;
- Share with other students and develop a Venn Diagram of similarities and differences (see **Activity Master 7, Venn Diagram**, on p. 466 at the end of this Teacher's Manual);
- Share with the entire class to develop a composite portrait of the class's findings.

Proverbs and Sayings Proverbs and traditional sayings are rich sources of cultural values and beliefs. All students know these in their own languages, and they are usually eager to discuss them with other students. Students will also be fascinated by the similarities in proverbs across cultures and countries. Ask them to discuss what proverbs reveal about their own cultures and those of other cultures.

The easiest way for students to discover American proverbs or sayings is to ask Americans to share them with them. They may want to make a list of proverbs from their own country related to the chapter topic and then ask Americans if they know of any similar proverbs.

If the students do not have access to Americans, you may want to bring collections of proverbs to class. You can also suggest that students look for proverbs on the Internet. There are a number of websites that provide lists of proverbs or sayings.

To report their findings, students can:

- Create a chart that compares proverbs in their country with American proverbs;
- Make a poster of American proverbs;
- Chart proverbs with similar meanings;
- Create a collage of the proverbs;
- Narrate an incident that illustrates the proverbs;
- Develop a role play that illustrates the proverbs.

Understand or Compare Polls (and Understand Graphs, Maps, and Charts)

The book includes a number of graphs and charts that summarize polls or opinion surveys that have been conducted in the last few years on a number of different topics. It also includes maps that relate the chapters to particular geographic regions of the United States. Students may need to be taught how to read and interpret these various forms of "document literacy," which are an important part of academic work in American universities. Students are also asked to give their opinions on the same events or issues that are illustrated in the polls. When doing so, they need to explain the basis for them.

The polls or opinion surveys, graphs, charts, and maps are included to:

- Illustrate or expand the discussion in the text;
- Provide more detail about particular issues that are introduced in the chapter;
- Indicate the range of opinions on several issues.

You can use these polls, surveys, graphs, charts, or maps to ask students to:

- Answer the questions themselves, and then compare their responses with those of the people surveyed.
- Chart their responses or those of their classmates.
- Interview Americans or others on these questions and see what kinds of similarities or differences exist.
- Compare the poll results with information provided in the chapter.
- Write a brief summary of what the poll or graph or map presents.
- Predict what the answers are likely to be in ten or twenty years. Give reasons for the predictions.
- Select one fact from the poll, graph, chart, or map that they find most interesting or surprising and then discuss or write about why that is.
- Compare the answers provided by Americans with what they think would be answers to similar questions in their own countries.

Use the Internet

An important feature of this edition of *American Ways* is the extensive use of the Internet as a tool for research. Each chapter has at least one activity that requires the students to find information about people, events, or facts about their own country or the United States, or other topics related to the chapter's theme. The activities were selected to provide interesting and enjoyable reasons to search the Internet. For example, in some of the chapters they are asked to learn about endangered animal species or to find out about ghost towns in the American West. There is always some written or oral reporting that they are expected to do after locating the information. Please remind students that not all websites are legitimate sources of information. Just as all printed texts are not equally valid, not all online sources are credible.

The Internet activities can be done in several ways:

- Ask the students to search the Internet as homework and then share their findings with a partner or the class.
- Take the class to a computer lab to do the assignments. If possible, ask them to work in pairs, talking about what they are finding. One person should record the results to share with the class.
- Ask students to do the work at home and to write a brief description of what they have found and the website URL. If possible, for the next class, meet in a networked computer lab or one in which there is a computer projection system. Ask the students to demonstrate the website and talk about what they have learned, while other students are also looking at the website.

WRITE ABOUT IT

Every chapter has activities designed to stimulate students' curiosity and to encourage them to think about issues, to formulate questions, to do library or Internet research to find answers, and then to write up their findings. Of course, there are many suggestions for writing included in the directions for other activities, but you may want to focus on the writing activities in **Write About It** for longer, and perhaps more formal writing assignments. You may choose to assign a particular topic or give students a chance to choose their topics from the ones suggested in the text.

If your students are preparing to attend classes in an American university, they will need to know how to write essays or research papers and other forms of academic writing, as well as answer essay exam questions, using the format expected in academic English writing. The suggestions for writing in these activities may act as a springboard for students to develop their academic writing skills. For example, some of the suggestions of topics for these writing activities ask students to compare/contrast, to analyze a cause/effect relationship, or to hypothesize solutions for problems.

Remind the students to think about what they have learned about how paragraphs and sections in this text are organized through the activities in **Preview Content**, **Understand Main Ideas**, and **Understand Details** and to follow that format in their own writing.

If you are teaching both reading and writing, you can do the following to incorporate research and writing:

- Review rhetorical patterns, such as comparison/contrast or cause/effect.
- Review the language structures needed for each pattern.
- Have pairs or small groups of students brainstorm ideas for essays or reports.
- Write ideas on transparencies or on the board.
- Use an appropriate graphic organizer (see the **Reproducible Activity Masters** on pp. 459–471) to organize information that they may use in their essays or reports.
- Have students formulate a thesis statement and topic sentences for their essays or reports.
- Have students complete an informal outline with supporting details such as facts, statistics, examples, and illustrations.
- Discuss purpose, audience, and tone for their writing.
- Have students focus on writing a good introduction or good conclusion.

EXPLORE ON YOUR OWN

The final section of each chapter lists books and movies that relate to the topic of the chapter, as well as brief descriptions of each. Obviously there were hundreds of titles we could have recommended for each chapter, but we have selected only five of each that we think are either classics or would potentially be of interest to your students. The following are suggested ways to use both of these sections: **Books to Read** and **Movies to See**.

Books to Read
At the end of each chapter, there is a list of five books, with brief descriptions of each. You can use these books in a number of ways:

- Assign a Book Talk (see **Activity Master 3 Book Talk**, on page 462 of this Teacher's Manual). The students can make brief presentations about their books, focusing on something they found especially interesting or intriguing.
- If two or more students read the same book, have them discuss the book in a small group and then do a composite presentation.
- Ask students to locate reviews or to read the book covers or other summaries of their book to compare their reaction to the book or to summarize how the book is related to the ideas in the chapter. Online booksellers such as Amazon or Barnes and Noble often provide extensive information and reviews of books.
- Have students interview others about the books to see which ones they have read and what they have learned from it. Students can use **Activity Master 4, Critic's Corner** (on p. 463 of this Teacher's Manual), to get ideas.
- Encourage students to read at least one book during the course. Explain the important role that extensive (informal, extended) reading plays in helping them to develop their English vocabulary, their reading fluency, and their general language proficiency.
- Allow brief periods in the class during which all students can read. In American classrooms this is referred to as SSR (Sustained Silent Reading) or DEAR (Drop Everything And Read). Tell students that they are to read one of the books listed at the back of the chapters or any other book that is approved by you.

Movies to See
The movies listed at the end of each chapter can be used to augment discussion of the ideas in the chapter. These movies are either classics or more recent films; they were chosen because they are more

likely to be available on videotape or DVD. These movies not only extend the discussion and activities in the chapter, they also offer an opportunity to augment the listening component of the culture course.

We recommend that you review each movie very carefully before deciding to use even a part of it with a class. Look especially for language, depiction of male-female relationships, violence, or any other content that might be objectionable to your students. Since you will likely be able to use only a very small portion of any movie in class, it should be possible to find an appropriate sequence that is both relevant to the discussion and not culturally offensive.

Some general suggestions for activities for students when using a movie:

- Watch a segment with the sound off and ask students to note the setting, the characters, and the mood. Students may also be asked to predict what the characters are saying or to write a dialogue for the characters based just on what they have seen.
- Listen to a segment without the picture and discuss what the video might show. Then have students look at the movie and compare their imagined scene with the actual video.
- Watch and listen to a segment and predict what follows or precedes it.
- Predict an ending or develop a new ending.
- Focus on only one character and then write a brief character description.
- Focus on the physical and emotional setting of the movie. Describe the ways that the setting is conveyed.
- Develop dialogue for the characters.
- Role-play some scenes.
- Have students watch different movies and do reviews of them. Have a **Critic's Corner** (see **Activity Master 4** on p. 463 of this Teacher's Manual) for reviews, which could be oral or written. Reviews should include a summary of the plot, a scene that students particularly remember, and a statement of whether they would recommend the movie to others.

In addition to the movies listed at the end of the chapters, we would suggest you watch for new movies and those out on DVD. Keep in mind that all movies are not appropriate for use in the classroom and be sure to preview them before using them. Also, the Internet, and especially YouTube, is an excellent source for speeches, short video clips, and other useful material. Pew Research is an excellent source of up-to-date polls and research studies on many aspects of American life. Pew's websites are easy to use and some have interactive pages. Finally, we invite you to visit our website www.theamericanways.net and the Pearson website, www.pearsoneltusa.com/americanways, for more resources, teacher tips, and suggestions for activities that will complement the 4th edition of *American Ways*.

PART 2 ANSWER KEY FOR STUDENT TEXT

CHAPTER 1

BEFORE YOU READ

Preview Vocabulary (p. 2)

A.
1. yes
2. yes
3. answers will vary
4. Internet
5. English
6. yes; answers will vary

B.
1. convinced
2. reveals
3. culture
4. job
5. participants

Understand Main Ideas (p. 12)

1. size, ethnic diversity
2. A Nation of Immigrants
3. different cultures living together peacefully
4. it's difficult, but possible (Tocqueville)
5. They provide the main ideas or focus of this book—American culture, American values, and the way in which studying another culture helps you to understand your own.

Understand Details (p. 12)

1. T
2. F
3. F
4. T
5. T
6. T
7. F
8. T
9. F
10. T

SKILL BUILDING

Improve your Reading Skills: Scanning (p. 13)

1. p.5—CA, NY, NJ
2. p.11—1831
3. p. 6, chart—14.8%
4. p.8, chart—308,745,538
5. p.4—1908
6. p.9—great, great, great grandfather came from Ireland

Develop Your Critical Thinking Skills
Analyzing Polls (p. 14)
1. country where they came from, 51%, Mexico, Cuba
2. all the people who are about the same age; first generation—immigrant, second—born in the U.S., third—grandchild of immigrant; experience of generations is different
3. new immigrants

4. 21%, those born in the U.S.
5. stop identifying with country of grandparent, identify with American friends and think of themselves as American

Build Your Vocabulary
Use Context Clues (p. 16)
A.

1. quota
2. minority
3. neutral observer
4. identity
5. distinct

1. identity 2. distinct 3. minority

B.

| 1. (d) | 3. i | 5. b | 7. j | 9. a | 11. h |
| 2. f | 4. k | 6. g | 8. l | 10. e | 12. c |

Understand Prefixes (p. 17)

1. il — not
2. bi — two
   multi — many
3. im — in
   em — out
4. inter — between

Word Partners (p. 18)

| 1. (c) | 3. h | 5. a | 7. d |
| 2. g | 4. f | 6. b | 8. e |

1. (established communities)
2. neutral observer
3. significant factor
4. working hypotheses
5. legal immigrants, industrialized countries
6. cultural pluralism
7. dominant culture

CHAPTER 2

BEFORE YOU READ

Preview Vocabulary (p. 28)

B.

Answers to the second part of each question will vary.

1. constitution
2. status
3. individual
4. achieve
5. resources—land, water, forests, etc.
6. benefit, reliant
7. ethical
8. foundation—England
9. welfare

C.

1. pursuit
2. self-evident
3. inalienable
4. endowed

AFTER YOU READ

Understand Main Ideas (p. 38)

A.

2. values

B.

2. self-reliance

C. Equality of Opportunity and Competition

1. succeed
2. The price for equality of opportunity is competition.

D. Material Wealth and Hard Work

1. living
2. The price for material wealth is hard work.

E. American Values and the State of the American Dream

1. happen/come true
2. almost every facet of American life

Understand Details (p. 39)

1. a	3. a	5. c	7. b	9. a
2. c	4. c	6. a	8. b	10. c

SKILL BUILDING

Improve Your Reading Skills: Scanning (p. 40)

1. p. 32—freedom from the power of kings and governments, priests and churches, noblemen and aristocrats
2. p. 32—Declaration of Independence
3. p. 32—1787
4. p. 32—desire and right of all individuals to control their own destiny without government interference
5. p. 34—forbidden by the Constitution
6. p. 36— father of the American Constitution; differences in material possessions reflect differences in personal abilities
7. p. 34—Abraham Lincoln

Develop Your Critical Thinking Skills
Using poll data to support research conclusions (p. 41)

1. e
2. d
3. a
4. c
5. b

Build Your Vocabulary
More AWL Words (p. 42)

1. d	5. g	9. b
2. f	6. c	10. j
3. h	7. i	11. l
4. a	8. k	12. e

Use Context Clues (p. 42)

1. b   2. a   3. a   4. a   5. a

Word Partners (p. 43)

1. surveys public opinion
2. control their own destiny
3. seek their fortunes
4. provide a decent standard of living
5. face challenges

Word Forms (p. 44)

1. reliance
2. emphasize
3. concept
4. achieve
5. reject

CHAPTER 3

BEFORE YOU READ

Preview Vocabulary (p. 52)

A.

1. a
2. a
3. a
4. a
5. b
6. a

B.

1. R
2. R
3. R
4. W
5. R
6. W
7. R
8. R
9. W
10. R
11. W
12. W
13. R
14. R
15. R
16. R

Preview Content (p. 53)

B.

1. p. 54—The Religious Heritage of the United States: Strengthening American Cultural Values
2. p. 54—The Religious Heritage of the United States: Strengthening American Cultural Values, chart, and The Religious Landscape Today: Polarization Vs. Pluralism
3. p. 59—September 11, 2001, and the National Religion
4. p. 62—Religious Diversity in the United States: A Spiritual Kaleidoscope; all sections have information

AFTER YOU READ (p. 63)

1. 90%
2. Christian (Catholic, Protestant: Baptist, Methodist, Evangelical, Lutheran; Mormon)
3. No, but they have a mixture of patriotism and religion
4. Strengthened self-reliance, hard work, self-discipline, volunteerism, humanitarianism, individual religious freedom, religious and cultural pluralism

Understand Main Ideas (p. 63)

1. "Godliness is in league with riches."
2. Self-discipline was often defined as the willingness to save and invest one's money rather than spend it on immediate pleasures.
3. John D. Rockefeller gave money to establish a university and said, "The good Lord gave me my money, so how could I withhold it from the University of Chicago?"
4. There was an outpouring of love, charity, and patriotism: volunteering to help, donating money, displaying the American flag, and singing patriotic songs.
5. Rick Warren's Saddleback Church, founded in 1980, 100,000 members, weekly attendance of 20,000.

Understand Details (p. 65)

1. F
2. F
3. T
4. F
5. T
6. T
7. T
8. F
9. F
10. T

SKILL BUILDING

Improve Your Reading Skills: Compare and Contrast Information (p. 66)

Information from the text: paragraph 10—born again, 22—strict following of Bible, socially and politically conservative (against abortion and gay marriage, may believe in creationism, not evolution), 26—more conservative than most mainline Protestant churches, except Baptists. The National Association of Evangelicals website and Wikipedia both mention being born again and the authority of the Bible. They both also mention action—social reform (but no specifics) and missionary work (sharing the gospel). And they both mention an emphasis on the death and saving power of Jesus Christ.

Build Your Vocabulary

Use Prefixes (p. 69)

1. in- 2. un- 3. dis-
4. un- 5. dis- 6. un-

1. improving yourself
2. disciplining yourself
3. relying on yourself

Use Suffixes (p. 69)

1. belief in/engaging in volunteering
2. acting to bring about social or political change
3. belief in/practicing the Hindu faith
4. belief in/practicing the Catholic faith
5. belief that God does not exist
6. not knowing whether God exists or not
7. belief that religion should not influence government
8. belief in/practicing the Mormon faith
9. belief in/practicing the Jewish faith
10. belief in/practicing the Protestant faith

Recognize Word Forms (p. 70)

1. solely   4. spontaneously   7. traditionally
2. Consequently   5. particularly
3. Historically   6. Immediately

Collocations (p. 71)

1. banks   2. grief   3. examples

More AWL Words (p. 71)

1. d   3. f   5. i   7. j   9. a
2. g   4. b   6. e   8. h   10. c

CHAPTER 4

BEFORE YOU READ

Preview Vocabulary (p. 78)

A.

1. body
2. disagreement
3. some influence
4. cowboy boots, hat
5. optimist
6. yes—an issue; no, all Americans do not think everyone should have access to guns; answers will vary

B.

1. adequately
2. hailed
3. reveals
4. reacted
5. legacy

Preview Content (p. 79)

A.

1. a relatively unsettled region
2. answers will vary
3. all can be a frontier

AFTER YOU READ

Understand Main Ideas (p. 87)

A.

1. individual freedom, self-reliance, and equality of opportunity
2. inventiveness and the can-do spirit
3. one who struggled against the wilderness and nature (like Daniel Boone); one who struggled against man (the Wild West hero like Wyatt Earp)
4. someone who believes every problem has a solution
5. belief in individual freedom, self-reliance, equality of opportunity, a new beginning for everyone, inventiveness, and the can-do spirit

Understand Details (p. 87)

1. F	3. F	5. F	7. T	9. F
2. T	4. T	6. F	8. F	10. F

SKILL BUILDING

Improve Your Reading Skills: Scanning (p. 88)

1760s and 1770s: p. 82—Daniel Boone explored the wilderness country of Kentucky.
1860s: p. 82—the beginning of the last phase of the western frontier, when man fought against man.
April 1889: p. 80—2 million acres of good land in Oklahoma were opened for settlement and thousands gathered on the border waiting for the exact time to be announced.
1890: p. 80—the last western lands were settled and the frontier experience ended.
1980s: p. 80—Ronald Reagan was President—cowboy image.
2001: p. 84—on September 11, terrorist attacks on New York City and Washington, D.C., led many more people in the United States to purchase more guns.

Develop Critical Thinking Skills (p. 89)

Answers will vary.

Build Your Vocabulary

Use Context Clues (p. 89)

1. fists
2. romanticize
3. fascinated
4. exemplified
5. obstacles
6. nostalgic
7. desensitized

More AWL Words (p. 90)

1. q	6. b	11. d	16. j
2. i	7. l	12. e	17. a
3. g	8. h	13. p	
4. c	9. f	14. k	
5. n	10. m	15. o	

Word Partners (p. 91)

1. e
2. d
3. b
4. a
5. f
6. c

1. founding fathers
2. law-abiding citizens
3. unsettled region
4. rugged individualism/physical prowess
5. physical prowess/rugged individualism
6. can-do spirit

CHAPTER 5

BEFORE YOU READ

Preview Vocabulary (p. 100)

A.

1. a	3. a	5. a	7. a	9. a
2. a	4. b	6. a	8. b	

B.

1. centuries
2. symbolized
3. goods
4. plenty
5. abundance

Preview Content (p. 101)

A.

Answers will vary.

AFTER YOU READ

Understand Main Ideas (p. 111)

1. hard work, equality of opportunity, material wealth
2. mass advertising
3. comfort, cleanliness, novelty, convenience
4. multiple TV channels lead to fragmented viewing or smaller numbers of people viewing any one program; computers and Internet are sources of information and entertainment
5. a very large amount of information (some say more than can fit on a personal computer) and some say it is also the tools that allow us to see patterns and make use of the knowledge; who owns our personal data and how can it be used?
6. Americans are redefining their abundance as a powerful supply of ideas that can help bring solutions to the problems of the world.

Understand Details (p. 111)

1. c	3. b	5. b	7. b	9. b
2. b	4. a	6. c	8. a	10. c

Build Your Vocabulary

Opposites (p. 114)

1. e	3. a	5. j	7. f	9. c
2. h	4. i	6. b	8. g	10. d

1. vice, virtue
2. upward, downward
3. consumer
4. scarcity
5. Public
6. poverty
7. downsize

Technology Words (p. 115)

Advertisements—B

Blog—I

Cable—B

Channel—TV

Commercials—B

Data—B

Digital—B

Entertainment—B

Facebook—I

Mass marketing—B

Movies—B

Network—B

News—B

Online—I

Pinterest—I

Satellite—B

Sponsor—B

Targeted marketing—I

Twitter—I

Video—B

Viewer—B

Website—I

World Wide Web—I

More AWL Words (p. 116)

1. insecure
2. generation
3. concluded
4. task
5. emphasis
6. maintaining
7. period
8. consumers
9. image
10. technique
11. institution

EXPAND YOUR KNOWLEDGE

Think, Pair, Share (p. 117)

endangered species—P

trash and garbage—P

recycling—S

wastefulness—P

conserving energy—S

protecting wildlife—S

air pollution—P

global warming—P

CHAPTER 6

BEFORE YOU READ

Preview Vocabulary (p. 124)

B.

1. Theoretically
2. alternative
3. aid
4. submitting
5. ultimate
6. overseas
7. cycles
8. policy
9. priorities

AFTER YOU READ

Understand Main Ideas (p. 137)

B.

1. (freedom)
2. the ideal of equality of opportunity
3. the value of hard work

C.

1. the best opportunity for becoming wealthy
2. a government-run system of production and distribution of goods

D.

1. they succeed in building something great out of nothing
2. the heroes of the frontier who were rugged individualists
3. novels about poor boys who become successful businessmen
4. submitting to higher authority

E.

    1. run businesses someone else started
    2. so many take huge sums of money from their corporations and spend it on themselves

F.

    1. finding a good job and paying the mortgage
    2. the rich had gotten richer and the middle class had stayed the same or gone down
    3. how to save or restore the American Dream

G.

    1. resilient and self-reliant
    2. creativity and innovation
    3. meaning in their personal lives and a way to help others
    4. billionaires who are social engineers trying to solve the world's problems

H. The Future of American Business

    1. start their own business
    2. provides global connections for businesses to interact with customers around the world

Understand Details (p. 138)

1. F	**3.** F	**5.** T	**7.** T	**9.** F
2. T	**4.** F	**6.** F	**8.** F	**10.** T

SKILL BUILDING

Improve Your Reading Skills: Scanning (p. 139)

    1. p. 126—said "The business of America is business."
    2. p. 130—wrote *Pigs at the Trough* about the greed of American businessmen
    3. p. 134—founded Facebook
    4. p. 132—one of the richest Americans who said his secretary paid a higher tax rate than he did
    5. p. 134—head of the Consumer Electronics Association and author of *The Comeback*
    6. p. 134—eBay's first president
    7. p. 134—editor of *Wired* magazine and leader of DIY Drones, an online community
    8. p. 129—the author of novels, such as *Ragged Dick*, about poor boys who become rich businessmen
    9. p. 134—author of *The Rise of the Creative Class*; believes one-third of Americans have jobs that create
    10. p. 132—ran for President in 2012 and had a company that made money downsizing other companies

Develop Your Critical Thinking Skills
Analyze a Reading (p. 139)

1. The intended readers are small business owners because it begins, "As a small business owner you are not alone!"

2. There are 23 million small businesses accounting for 54% of all sales; they provide 55% of all jobs and 40% of new jobs; they account for 40% of all retail sales and provide jobs for 8 million; they occupy 30%-50% of all commercial space.
3. Answers will vary.

Build Your Vocabulary

Same or Different (p. 140)

1. d
2. b
3. c
4. c
5. a

More AWL Words (p. 141)

1. l
2. d
3. i
4. f
5. b
6. n
7. r
8. k
9. p
10. j
11. q
12. o
13. c
14. a
15. g
16. h
17. m
18. e

Idiom and Popular Phrases (p. 142)

1. (a)
2. d
3. b
4. c
5. e
6. f
7. g
8. h

CHAPTER 7

BEFORE YOU READ

Preview Vocabulary (p. 150)

A.

1. a
2. a
3. b
4. a
5. b
6. a
7. a
8. b
9. a
10. a

B.

1. pursuits
2. restrain
3. regulate
4. injuring

AFTER YOU READ

Understand Main Ideas (p. 165)

1. government might take away individual freedom
2. president signs it into law, vetoes it (but two-thirds of House and Senate may vote to overturn the veto and it becomes law), takes no action (then bill becomes law after ten days), or does a pocket veto (the bill is defeated if Congress adjourns within a ten-day period)

3. electors are the representatives who officially choose the president; winner of plurality of votes in a state gets all electoral votes; the number of electoral votes is equal to the number of representatives the state has in the House and Senate
4. ideals of the free farmer and small businessman kept government small because if it were large it would interfere with individuals, competition, and self-reliance
5. need for economic programs resulted in big government
6. entitlements are government benefits such as unemployment benefits, food stamps, Medicaid, Social Security, and Medicare; controversial because some people worry that relying on the government could endanger the value of self-reliance
7. special interest groups represent about every issue and every group (trades, industries, unions, ethnic groups, etc.); goal is to influence government to pass laws they want
8. help elect or support candidates who will vote in favor of their issues
9. Republicans are pro-business, laissez-faire, or anti-government (conservative); Democrats see government as solution to social problems (liberal); Independents vote for candidates who reflect their wishes, regardless of party; three differences: racial divide—Democratic Party have more support from non-white Americans; ideological divide over the role and size of government—Republicans are against big active government; cultural divide—Republicans tend to be more socially conservative than Democrats
10. Republicans believe government spending should be reduced and that entitlements weaken American values; Democrats worry about the widening gap between the very rich and the very poor; need to have individual responsibility for ourselves and each other—self-reliance but also a safety net for those who need it

Understand Details (p. 165)

1. b
2. c
3. b
4. b
5. a
6. b
7. b
8. b
9. a
10. c

SKILL BUILDING

Improve Your Reading Skills: Note Taking (p. 168)

Branch	People	Responsibilities
(Executive)	President	Sign or veto bills
		Carry out laws
	(Cabinet)	Administer government programs
Legislative	(Congress)	(Enact laws)
		Make laws
	(Senate and) House of Representatives	Ratify treaties
	(100) Senators	
	(435) Representatives	

Judicial   (Supreme Court)   Interpret laws

             (9 Justices)   Settle disputes

Develop Your Critical Thinking Skills (p. 169)

Women—black, Democrat, income less than $30,000 (3 or more benefits)
Someone in a rural area
Older people receive Social Security and Medicaid
The lower the income the more benefits
Republicans say they are against entitlements, and 48% of them receive no benefits (but more of them receive 2 benefits than Democrats or Independents

Build Your Vocabulary
More AWL Words (p. 170)
1. b
2. f
3. m
4. h
5. a
6. l
7. k
8. d
9. e
10. i
11. j
12. g
13. c

1. specific
2. grades
3. infrastructure
4. impact
5. area, conclude

Which Word Doesn't Belong? (p. 171)

1. Congress
2. Supreme Court
3. vice president
4. veto
5. Bill of Rights

Collocations (p. 172)

1. law
2. bill
3. treaty
4. ballots
5. term
6. disputes

CHAPTER 8

BEFORE YOU READ

Preview Vocabulary (p. 178)
A.

1. help them succeed
2. be treated worse
3. national
4. likely
5. teacher
6. yes
7. residential
8. continue speaking native language at home
9. no
10. Answers will vary.

B.

Positive connotation:
accommodation   inspire
civil rights   integrated
enrich   resources

AFTER YOU READ

Understand Details (p. 189)

1. b   3. a   5. b   7. b   9. a
2. c   4. c   6. c   8. b   10. c

SKILL BUILDING

Improve Your Reading Skills: Scanning (p. 191)

early 1600s   p. 180—people of Hispanic origin lived in North America
1790   p. 180—first census; 80% population white; 20% African-American
1861–1865   p. 183—Civil War
late 1800s and early 1900s   p. 188—millions of immigrants from eastern and southern Europe came to the United States
1920s   p. 188—borders closed to immigrants
1950s and 1960s   p. 184—civil rights movement
1965   p. 188—immigration law changed to allow more immigrants
2008 and 2012   p. 185—Barack Obama elected president

Build Your Vocabulary

Definitions (p. 191)

1. c   4. b   7. j   10. i
2. f   5. h   8. a   11. l
3. g   6. e   9. k   12. d

1. abolished
2. civil rights
3. inspire
4. assassination
5. legacy
6. registration
7. mingled
8. victims
9. mosaic
10. trickle
11. obliterate
12. corrupt

More AWL Words (p. 193)

1. bias
2. construction
3. despite
4. discrimination
5. documentation
6. eliminating
7. function
8. inclined
9. integrated
10. process
11. residential
12. somewhat

CHAPTER 9

BEFORE YOU READ

Preview Vocabulary (p. 202)

A.

1. a	3. b	5. a	7. b	9. b
2. b	4. b	6. a	8. a	

B.

1. harmony
2. erased
3. status
4. regard
5. eventually
6. means
7. achieved
8. seek
9. conflict

AFTER YOU READ

Understand Details (p. 218)

1. b	3. c	5. a	7. c	9. b
2. a	4. a	6. b	8. c	10. c

SKILL BUILDING

Build Reading Skills: Types of Supporting Details (p. 220)

1. Paragraph 18—statistics: today over half of all Americans have taken some college courses, more than 20 million college students now, half of college students are first generation of their family to attend
2. Paragraph 28—fact: standards used to be set by local school districts but since the 1990s states and the federal government are setting them; examples: teacher education programs must meet federal standards, and national education professional associations are supporting and developing new standards
3. Paragraph 31—quotation: "By now, we should be able to point to sharp reductions of the achievements gaps between children of different racial and ethnic groups and children from different income groups, but we cannot."
4. Paragraph 48—statistics: one in four children lives with immigrant parent, 45% of students are members of ethnic or racial minorities; fact: more inclusive curricula; example: textbooks with information about minorities

Build Your Vocabulary

Vocabulary Check (p. 221)

1. violated
2. elite
3. extracurricular
4. attainment
5. zip codes
6. displace
7. isolated
8. tuition
9. obvious
10. facilities
11. remove
12. vocational

CHAPTER 10

BEFORE YOU READ

Preview Vocabulary (p. 230)

A.

1. committed
2. elements
3. evolve
4. attribute
5. intense
6. exposed
7. advocated
8. bonded

B.

R—hobby, handicrafts, do-it-yourself projects, going to the theater, video games

S—team, hustle, gold medal, professional tennis, skiing

AFTER YOU READ

Understand Details (p. 243)

1. b
2. c
3. a
4. c
5. a
6. c
7. c
8. c
9. b
10. c

SKILL BUILDING

Improve Your Reading Skills: Scanning (p. 245)

1. p. 239—fast food such as french fries
2. p. 240—people who watch a lot of TV: they are nothing but "eyes"
3. p. 233—professional football coach who said winning is the "only thing" that matters in sports
4. p. 240—changing channels on TV frequently
5. p. 239—First Lady who started "Let's Move" program to encourage good nutrition and healthy exercise
6. p. 242—teenagers bullying others on the Internet sometimes pushing victims to commit suicide
7. p. 235—popular American cyclist who used performance-enhancing drugs
8. p. 237—operator of Overseas Adventure Travel company
9. p. 238—Centers for Disease Control
10. p. 242—author of *Work to Live: Reclaim Your Life, Health, Family, and Sanity*

Develop Your Critical Thinking Skills (p. 245)

1. (e, h)
2. f, j
3. a, d, e, g, h, k
4. a, b, c, i
5. e, g, k, h
6. b, f, i, j, l

Build Your Vocabulary

Opposites (p. 246)

1. team
2. virtues, winner
3. disorder
4. criticize, spectator
5. Amateur
6. strengthen, corrupt
7. physical
8. sedentary
9. slender
10. positive

More AWL Words (p. 247)

1. principal
2. label
3. project
4. item
5. image
6. range
7. likewise
8. illustrate
9. contract
10. guidelines
11. overseas
12. symbol
13. injury
14. uniform
15. psychological
16. lecture
17. equipment
18. comment
19. derive
20. relax

Classify Words (p. 248)

1. gardening
2. gourmet cooking
3. overseas travel
4. playing professional football
5. handicrafts

CHAPTER 11

BEFORE YOU READ

Preview Vocabulary (p. 256)

B.

1. benefits
2. accommodate
3. juggling
4. structures
5. paternity leave
6. couples
7. flexible

AFTER YOU READ

Understand Main Ideas (p. 268)

Note: Use **Activity Master 12, Values**, on p. 471 of this Teacher's Manual. Make extra copies if students are to do all 6 values.

Answers will vary.

Understand Details (p. 269)

1. T
2. F
3. F
4. T
5. T
6. T
7. F
8. F
9. T
10. F
11. F
12. T
13. T

SKILL BUILDING

Develop Your Critical Thinking Skills
Analyzing Polls and Expressing Your Opinion (p. 270)

1. These polls reflect the reality that most couples depend on two incomes and they are not against mothers with small children working. The largest percentage (42%) believe that it would be better for a mother to work part time as opposed to full time (16%), and only 33% believe it would be better for the mother not to work outside the home at all.
2. Yes, 68% of woman and only 50% of men feel the amount of time they spend with their children is "the right amount."
3. No, 78% of mothers who work say they are doing an "excellent" or "very good" job parenting, compared with only 66% of mothers who do not work outside the home. Answers will vary as to why this is so.
4. For both working mothers and working fathers job security is most important (78% for women and 80% for men). For both, having a job they enjoy (74% of women and 69% of men) is more important than having a high paying job (30% of women and 40% of men). The biggest difference is the importance they put on having a flexible work schedule—more then two-thirds of women and less than half of men (70% of women and 48% of men) say this is extremely important to them. This is probably because mothers are more likely than fathers to deal with sick children and other problems.
5. Answers will vary.

Build Your Vocabulary
Vocabulary Check (p. 272)

1. conscientious
2. Juggling
3. exhausting
4. nurture
5. compensate
6. priority
7. Blended
8. courtship
9. stable
10. refuge
11. Demographic
12. vanish

More AWL Words (p. 273)

1. primary
2. license
3. dramatic
4. contradictory
5. flexible
6. potential
7. accommodate
8. obtain
9. generation
10. policy
11. restriction
12. expert
13. labor
14. final
15. role
16. institution
17. trend
18. factor
19. consist
20. previous
21. emphasis

CHAPTER 12

BEFORE YOU READ

Preview Vocabulary (p. 282)

A.

1. a	3. a	5. b	7. b	9. b	11. a
2. a	4. b	6. a	8. a	10. a	12. b

B.

1. emergency
2. bankruptcy
3. paycheck
4. layoff

AFTER YOU READ

Understand Main Ideas (p. 294)

B.

1. not sure what future challenges will do to traditional American values
2. states thesis for the chapter and organizational plan; reviews six values and challenges
3. Should rights to individual freedom be expanded to include economic freedom? Would this damage the value of self-reliance? Values divide between conservatives and liberals
4. the struggle for a balance between giving everyone an equal chance to succeed without destroying fair competition. Should minorities be given special opportunities to help create "a level playing field"?
5. the American Dream
6. Even though many Americans are working harder than ever, they are struggling to maintain a comfortable lifestyle.
7. left, liberal Democrats believe it is an income problem; right, conservative Republicans believe it is a spending problem
8. (1) they can, thanks to computers and demographic studies; (2) many Americans are interested in only one or two political issues; and (3) about one third of Americans are independents and both parties need their votes to win
9. Immigrants bring new life and energy and youth to an aging country; they have a strong belief in American values; many have technical skills needed in the United States; they may help create the first universal nation

Understand Details (p. 294)

1. F	3. T	5. T	7. T	9. T
2. F	4. F	6. F	8. F	10. F

SKILL BUILDING

Improve Your Reading Skills: Scanning (p. 296)

1. p. 289—Mortimer Zuckerman
2. p. 293 —Alvin Toffler
3. p. 292 —President Ronald Reagan quoted by Gloria Borger
4. p. 285 —John J. Zogby
5. p. 291 —John Kenneth White
6. p. 285—John J. Zogby
7. p. 291—David Von Drehle
8. p. 292—George Washington
9. p. 288—Noemie Emery
10. p. 292—Gloria Borger

Build Your Vocabulary

Scrambled Words (p. 298)

1. culture
2. freedom
3. hard work
4. equality
5. material wealth
6. self-reliance
7. competition

Vocabulary Check (p. 298)

Words that have to do with the criminal justice system: court, defense attorney, jury, criminals, justice, trial

1. trial
2. jury, defense attorney
3. court
4. justice
5. criminals

More AWL Words (p. 299)

1. security
2. identity
3. stress
4. commitment
5. military
6. distinction
7. evidence
8. survive
9. define
10. sector
11. target
12. challenge
13. respond
14. category
15. sole
16. reveal

PART 3 REPRODUCIBLE ACTIVITY MASTERS

1.	Shapes	460
2.	Shapes	461
3.	Book Talk	462
4.	Critic's Corner	463
5.	K-W-L	464
6.	Semantic Web	465
7.	Venn Diagram	466
8.	Plus-Minus	467
9.	Compare and Contrast	468
10.	Decision-Making	469
11.	Decision-Making	470
12.	Values	471

Shapes 1

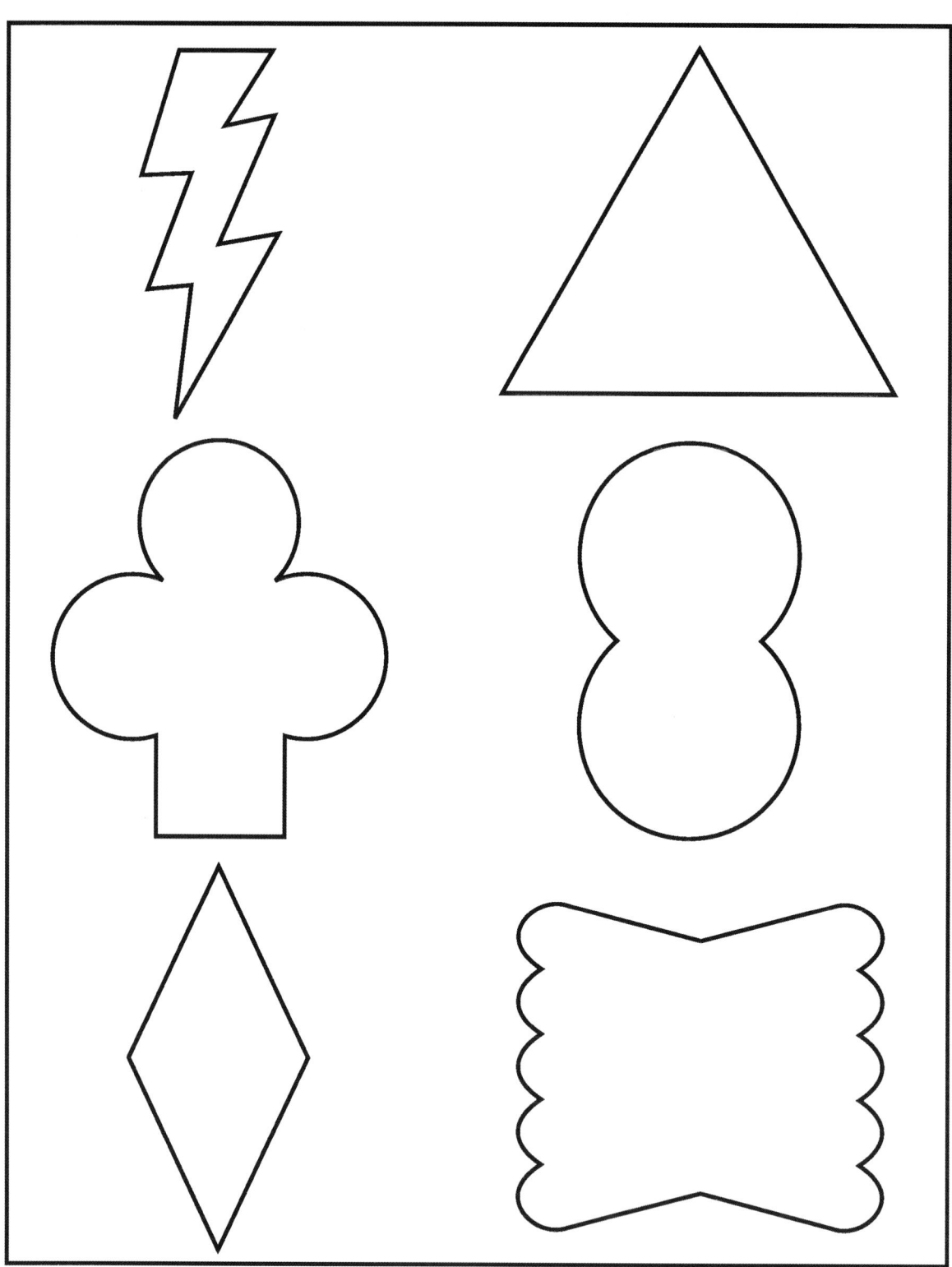

© 2014 Pearson Education
Duplication for classroom use is permitted.

Shapes 2

Book Talk   3

Title

Author

Publisher, and Publication **Date**

Brief **Summary** of the Book (setting, major characters, major events)

Personal Reaction/Response to the Book (most interesting aspect, a particularly interesting sequence or scene, a fascinating character, etc., with some discussion of the reasons for that view)

Critic's Corner

4

Title

Setting

Characters _____   _____

_____   _____

_____   _____

_____   _____

Memorable Scene

Did you like this movie? Why or why not? Would you recommend it to others?

K-W-L

TOPIC:		
K What we KNOW	**W** What we WANT to know	**L** What we have LEARNED

Semantic Web

6

Venn Diagram   7

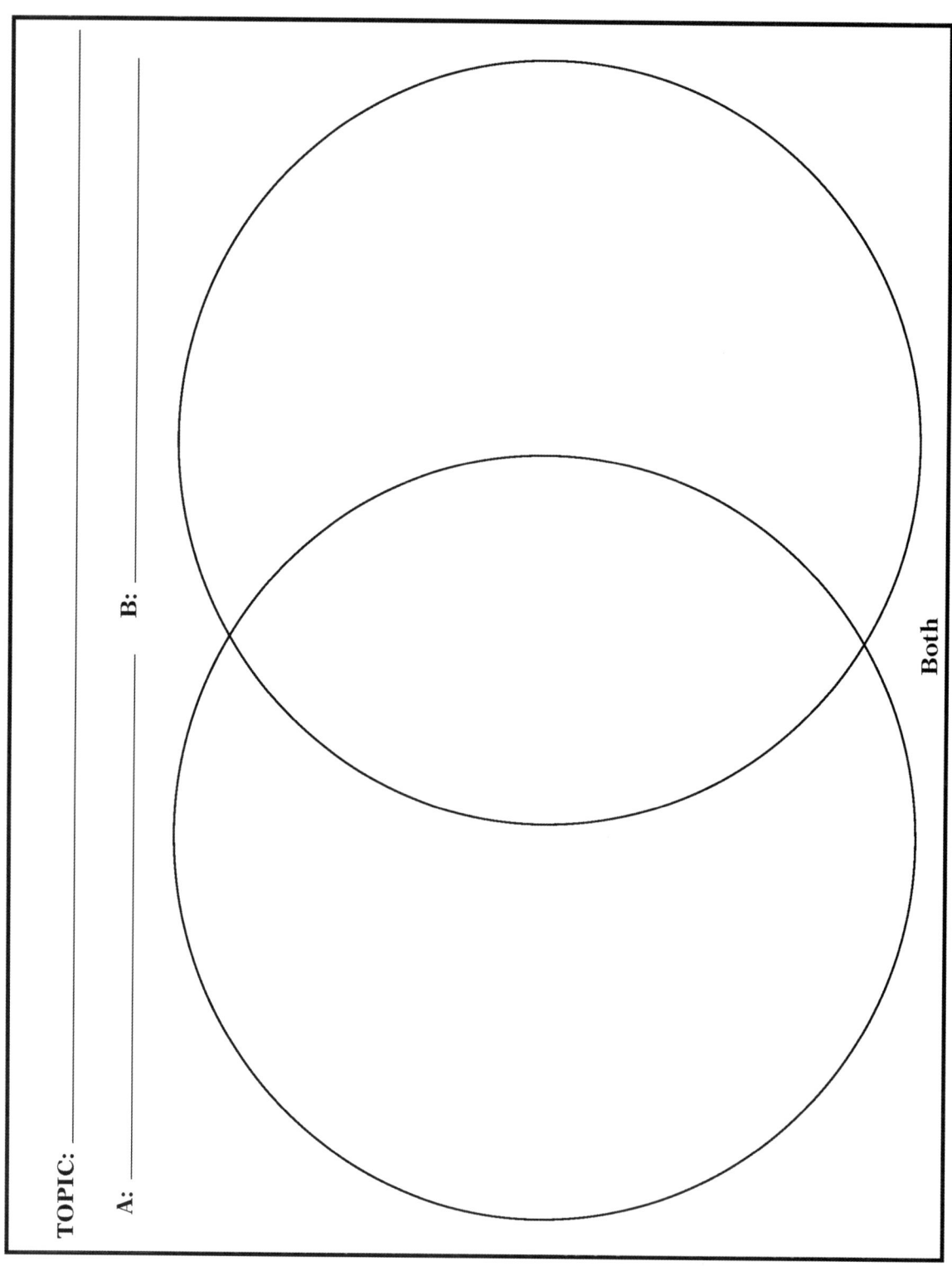

Plus—Minus
(pros and cons)

8

TOPIC: _____

PLUS + (pros)	**MINUS −** (cons)

© 2014 Pearson Education
Duplication for classroom use is permitted.

Compare and Contrast

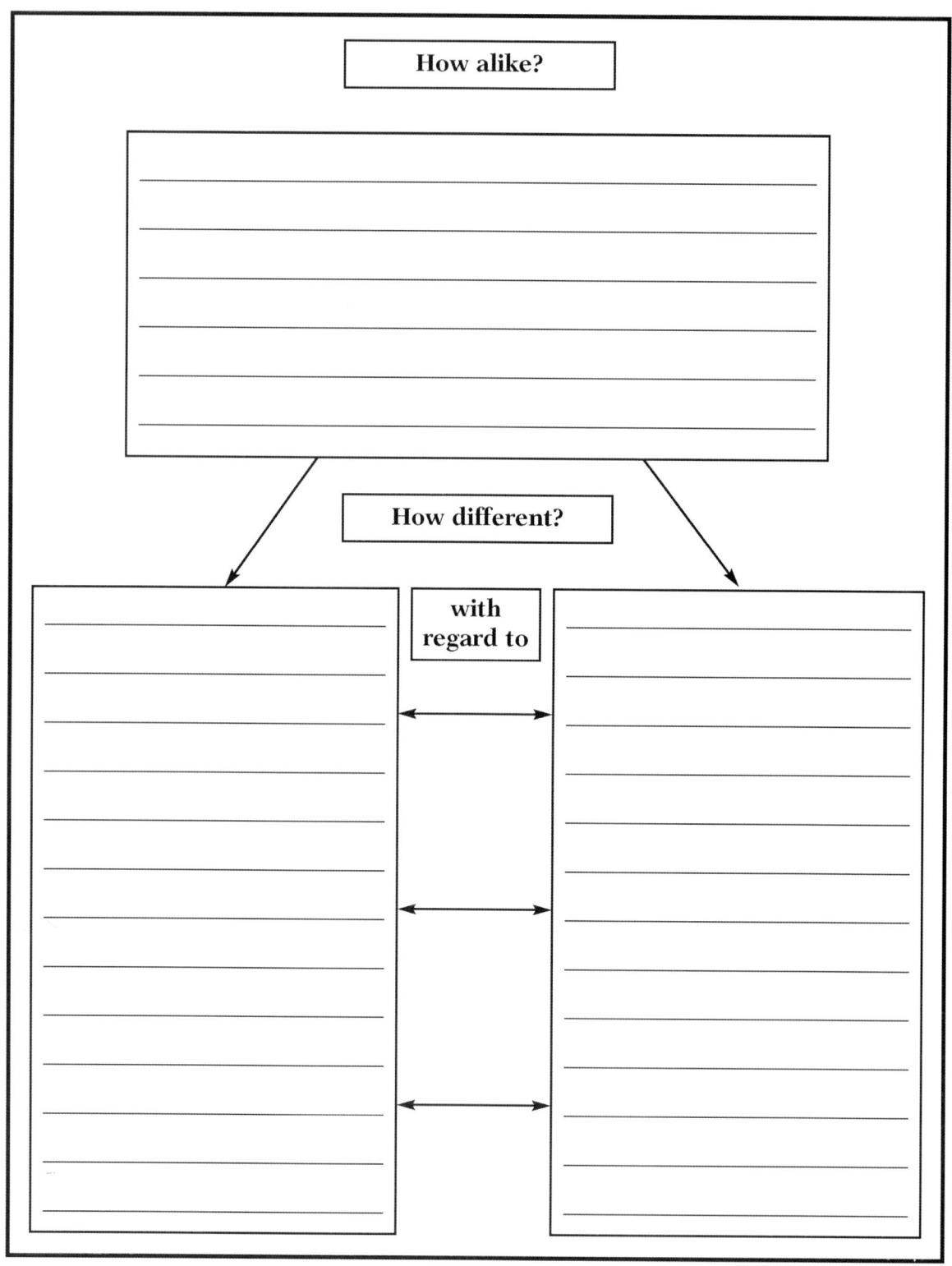

Decision-Making: Debate/Lobby

10

Topic/Cause

Pros	Cons

Related topics

1. _____
2. _____
3. _____

Research sources (where to find information)

1. _____
2. _____
3. _____

Decision-Making   11

Problem	Goal(s)

Alternatives	Pros + and Cons −
	+
	−
	+
	−
	+
	−
	+
	−

Decision(s)	Reason(s)

© 2014 Pearson Education
Duplication for classroom use is permitted.

Values   12

Value: _____

Advantage to the Individual	**Disadvantage to the Individual**
_____	_____
_____	_____
_____	_____

Advantage to the Family	**Disadvantage to the Family**
_____	_____
_____	_____
_____	_____

Value: _____

Advantage to the Individual	**Disadvantage to the Individual**
_____	_____
_____	_____
_____	_____

Advantage to the Family	**Disadvantage to the Family**
_____	_____
_____	_____
_____	_____

© 2014 Pearson Education
Duplication for classroom use is permitted.